In Harm's Way

In Harm's Way

A History of Christian Peacemaker Teams

KATHLEEN KERN

CASCADE *Books* · Eugene, Oregon

IN HARM'S WAY
A History of Christian Peacemaker Teams

Cascade Books
A Division of Wipf and Stock Publishers
199 W. 8th Ave., Suite 3
Eugene, OR 97401

www.wipfandstock.com

ISBN 13: 978-1-55635-134-1

Cataloging-in-Publication data:

Kern, Kathleen, 1962-

In harm's way : a history of Christian Peacemaker Teams / Kathleen Kern.

xvi + 604 p. ; 23 cm. — Includes bibliographical references.

ISBN 13: 978-1-55635-134-1

1. Christian Peacemaker Teams. 2. Peace — Religious aspects — Mennonites. 3. War — Religious aspects — Mennonites. I. Title.

BX8128.P4 K43 2009

Manufactured in the U.S.A.

Dedicated to the memory of CPTers George Weber and Tom Fox,
who lost their lives in Iraq because they took risks for peace,
and to all peacemakers everywhere who put their lives on the line
and never know how their unsung efforts change history.

Contents

An index can be found online at www.CPT.org/harmsway

Acknowledgments

ALTHOUGH WRITING THIS BOOK has been in some ways a solitary endeavor, I had dozens of eager helpers from all over the world who offered comments on chapter drafts, answered questions I had about incidents that did not appear on CPTnet or in other CPT reports, and sent me files and other useful written resources. I want to thank these CPT support staff, full-timers, reservists, and office interns who contributed to the accuracy of this text—especially Gene Stoltzfus, Sara Reschly and Doug Pritchard, who probably read more of the manuscript at its various stages than anyone else. Particular thanks goes to my former Hebron teammate, Dr. Jane Adas, who volunteered to format the chapters according to Wipf and Stock guidelines, a task that, because of an eye condition, would have been painful for me to do. I would also like to thank my copyeditor at Wipf and Stock, Camille Stallings, and my editor, Charlie Collier, for their patience in accommodating other work I was doing for CPT during the revisions of this manuscript, the idiosyncratic and inconsistent methods that CPT has employed for attributing and preserving written records over the years, and my fit of temper when I found out I had to redo all the footnotes.

My first year of marriage and stepmotherhood coincided with my last year of writing this manuscript. Thus, I want to thank Beth Melissa, David Mark and my husband Michael for the adaptations they have made to my CPT History lifestyle, including navigating around the boxes that have remained unpacked since we moved in June 2006 and the many piles of paper in the office. I would also like to thank the members of my faith community, Rochester Area Mennonite Fellowship, whose support and prayers have made it possible for me both to continue working with Christian Peacemaker Teams and to finish this manuscript.

Preface

SOON AFTER I BEGAN writing this history in 2003, I realized that I was operating under certain limitations. Each Christian Peacemaker Team (CPT) project has generated enough material to merit its own book; I had to leave out so many valuable, wise and funny insights that CPTers and their coworkers have shared in writing and in person. Additionally, as someone who has worked with Christian Peacemaker Teams since 1993, I know that my analysis of and reaction to its work are subjective. I have tried to represent the views of other CPTers, but know I have not always succeeded, so I encourage the reader to view me more as an organizer of information rather than "the authority" on CPT.

When I describe incidents in which I played a part, I refer to myself as "Kathleen Kern." When I am describing the process of writing or researching this book, I refer to myself as "the author." If no footnote appears for an incident in which I took part, the reader may assume I am writing from my memory of the event.

Most CPTers are not professional writers, and spelling and grammar errors have cropped up in CPTnet releases over the years. I have chosen to correct these errors without using *sic*, unless I think preserving the original is important. This face-saving measure benefits me as well as my colleagues, since I have edited most of the releases coming out over CPTnet since 1998.

Between 1992 and 1993, I had written two books in the space of about a year. I blithely assumed I could write this history in about the same amount of time. Instead, the writing has taken four years. During those four years, I worked in the field very little and had to put other writing projects on hold. I did not anticipate how the history would change my identity both as a CPTer and a writer.

I also did not anticipate how much the writing would engage my emotions. I cringed all over again at the mistakes I made in Haiti as a dilettante peace activist. I grieved as I relived the downward spiral in Hebron that wiped out almost all the progress that our team there been a part of before the al-Aqsa Intifada. I was charmed and inspired once more by the Abejas' living out of the Gospel in Chiapas. I felt a growing dread as I read through the Iraq team's 2005 releases, knowing that they were leading to a crisis that resulted in the kidnappings of two CPT delegation members and two of my colleagues, one of whom, Tom Fox, was murdered.

I suspect that once I let go of this history, once I've sent the boxes of files to the CPT archives and cleared up space on my hard drive, I will be left with an underlying sense of wonder (perhaps over-reiterated in the pages that follow) at how Christian Peacemaker Teams has succeeded when other peace and justice groups have failed or lapsed into a state of institutional self-preservation. The history has made me aware of the stumbles that CPT made as it was finding its feet, of less-than-successful initiatives, like CPT Europe, which Dutch Mennonite Marten VanderWerf tried to organize around the issue of NATO's low level flights over Innu lands (see chapter 8) or the "Pledge by Christians to our Jewish Neighbors" (see chapter 6). But usually, the right people with the right talents came along at the right time and put in grueling hours of work to give the organization what it needed to grow and confront violence on its various project locations. I feel a sense of wonder at my continuing participation in CPT, because I had not anticipated making it my career at the age of twenty-nine when I filled out the application for training.

I thank God for that wonder. It helps me see—at times when I lapse into a glum ennui over the state of the world, mistakes I have made, or mistakes that CPT as an organization has made—that God works through sinful, stumbling people. I thank God for sending us Jesus, who has armed ordinary people with the weapons of nonviolence to battle Systems of Domination that kill and exploit our brothers and sisters.

I am forty-five as I write this Preface, and I still have not found anything better to do with my life.

—Kathleen Kern
October 2007

Prologue

O N JANUARY 10, 1999, a group of Palestinian men belonging to the Fatah party organized a nonviolent demonstration protesting the closure of the Ibrahimi Mosque and the curfew placed on the thirty thousand Palestinians living in the part of Hebron under Israeli control. The Israeli military had imposed the curfew a week earlier after two Israeli settler women were injured, one seriously, when Palestinian militants shot at their van near the Mosque. The Christian Peacemaker Team in Hebron heard about the demonstration and went to observe.

Holding long banners reading, "No For Closure of Ibrahimi Mosque," and "No For Collective Punishment," a group of seventy to one hundred Palestinians marched from the Hebron municipal offices to the border that separates the Palestinian and Israeli-controlled areas. As the marchers approached, the Israeli soldiers and border police—armed with rubber-coated metal bullets, tear gas, and sound grenades—took positions behind large cement barriers, ready to fire.

CPTers Pierre Shantz, Sara Reschly and Joanne "Jake" Kaufman jumped in front of the soldiers and their guns, crying, "This is a nonviolent demonstration! They are not throwing rocks!" The soldiers, not knowing how to respond, tried to push the CPTers away. Some lowered their M-16 rifles, but other soldiers threw sound grenades that sent the crowd scurrying. After the demonstration's leadership calmed the Palestinians observing and participating in the demonstration, the crowd returned, standing face to face with the soldiers.

Older Palestinians leading the procession circulated among the youth, telling them not to throw rocks. After about thirty minutes of this standoff, soldiers began pushing the Palestinians. The marchers started to run away and some threatened to stone the troops. Soldiers quickly moved into firing positions; CPTers again got in the way, standing in front of the rifles and saying, "This is a nonviolent demonstration!" Only a couple of rocks were thrown before the Palestinian leaders restrained the youth. No one was injured.

One of the military officers, furious with the CPTers for interfering, began shouting in the faces of CPTers Mark Frey and Shantz, telling them to leave the area. Shantz retorted that the demonstration was nonviolent, and the officer slapped him twice. At another point, a soldier physically restrained Kaufman as she tried to stand in front of soldiers taking aim. When the Israeli civilian police arrived, the enraged officer demanded that they arrest Shantz and Reschly. The police also detained Sydney Stigge-Kaufman for a short time on location, and then released her.

The remaining CPTers circulated among the crowd or positioned themselves between soldiers and Palestinians. About an hour and a half after the demonstration began, the Palestinian leadership called for everyone to pray in the street to defuse mounting tension. The older men lined up on rugs to pray, calling for the younger ones to join them. An Israeli Druze officer circulated among soldiers, telling them to stay calm; in Arabic, he encouraged Palestinian youth to join the prayers. After praying, the leaders declared the demonstration finished and called for everyone to return to the Palestinian area. No clashes developed after the demonstration ended.

A Palestinian leader formally thanked CPTers after the march, saying, "Thank you. You have done your work."

"The success of the intervention was due to three things," Shantz reported later. "The discipline of the men on their way to pray, the efforts of the Druze Border Police officer, and our standing between the soldiers and the demonstrators. If any one of those three things had been missing, someone would have gotten shot. There was one officer there who obviously wanted to shoot someone."[1]

The authorities charged Shantz with "pushing two border police and hitting one on the helmet" and "interfering with police doing their duty." They charged Reschly with "yelling 'don't shoot' at soldiers," and "assaulting a soldier," i.e., pushing him. Reschly and Shantz told the court their commitment to nonviolence would prohibit them pushing or hitting anyone. A third charge by a Russian-speaking soldier that Reschly called him a Nazi was dropped after the court discovered that he did not speak English. Video footage of the event later shown on Israeli TV proved that

---

1. The soldier, known to the team as "Avi" was to have several negative interactions with the team in the next few years. See chapter 6.

Reschly and Shantz had intervened nonviolently. The court told Shantz and Reschly to hand in their passports and 2,000 shekels bail each while the police investigated the incident for two weeks. After that time, the police returned the passports and money (which had been raised on the spot at their hearing by Israeli and international supporters), and dropped all charges.

The January 1999, CPT intervention in Hebron is the sort of experience that most members of Christian Peacemaker Teams dream of having. They were accompanying a Palestinian group that had, on its own, organized a solid, nonviolent demonstration. At the crucial time, CPTers were able to intervene to prevent violence against unarmed demonstrators. The Palestinian organizers, the Israeli Druze officer, and the CPTers all had a role in stopping soldiers from shooting. An Associated Press photo of Reschly and a Palestinian man[2] standing in front of soldiers with arms outspread went all over the world, testifying to the effectiveness of unarmed peace activists. Finally, video footage of the event, as well as Reschly and Shantz's arrest for "Getting in the Way" mustered the support and enthusiasm of Israelis, Palestinians, and internationals for CPT's work in Hebron.

But "dream" is the operative word of the last paragraph. For every encounter in which CPT volunteers have been at the right place at the right time to prevent violence, they have spent hundreds of hours drinking tea on routine visits to families more interested in talking about the small details of their lives than theory and practice of nonviolence. They have spent hundreds of hours documenting violence that happened before CPT could prevent it, hundreds of hours planning nonviolent strategies and public witnesses that in the end bore little fruit.

In this book, I hope to cover both the dream moments and the mundane realities of Christian Peacemaker Team's work since 1986. For adding to the pool of knowledge about Nonviolent Direct Action strategies, the dream moments are probably most useful. A cloud of nonviolent witnesses since the time of Jesus Christ has gifted CPT with examples of courageous, effective resistance to evil. CPTers have learned from them, modified their strategies, and in turn inspired other organizations to confront violence without using violence. However, writing about the mistakes CPT has made, its floundering as the organization found its voice,

2. The man was a Hebron municipal observer who, sadly—since he was more at risk than Reschly—went unnamed.

and the negative consequences of certain CPT actions, also adds to the pool.

The poet Adrienne Rich writes about casting her lot with those "who age after age, perversely / with no extraordinary power / reconstitute the world."[3] While many CPTers do have extraordinary abilities, most accomplish what they do simply by following the extraordinary example of Jesus Christ, who nonviolently got in the way of systems that dealt in death and exploitation. As ordinary people, they have changed CPT from a small initiative of the historic peace churches to an expanding, ecumenical, nonviolent movement–a movement that has called other ordinary people to put their bodies and faith on the line to accompany the oppressed, and create space for dialogue and reconciliation.

Writing a history at this time may seem premature. The full power of organized, faith-based Nonviolent Direct Action probably has not manifested itself yet. However, the institutional memory of the early days of CPT has already begun to slip, as this author has found during her research. Knowing how a small, struggling initiative grew into a bigger, widely respected organization in twenty years may prove useful to other small struggling nonviolent initiatives in the years to come.

3. Rich, "Natural Resources," in *Dream of a Common Language.*

1

Before the Corps

IN 1984, RON SIDER challenged the Mennonite World Conference in Strasbourg, France with these words:

> Over the past 450 years of martyrdom, immigration and missionary proclamation, the God of shalom has been preparing us Anabaptists for a late twentieth-century rendezvous with history. The next twenty years will be the most dangerous—and perhaps the most vicious and violent—in human history. If we are ready to embrace the cross, God's reconciling people will profoundly impact the course of world history . . .
>
> This could be our finest hour. Never has the world needed our message more. Never has it been more open. Now is the time to risk everything for our belief that Jesus is the way to peace. If we still believe it, now is the time to live what we have spoken. . . .
>
> Even small groups of people practicing what they preach, laying down their lives for what they believe, influence society all out of proportion to their numbers. I believe the Lord of history wants to use the small family of Anabaptists scattered across the globe to help shape history in the next two decades.
>
> But to do that, we must not only abandon mistaken ideas and embrace the full biblical conception of shalom. One more thing is needed. We must take up our cross and follow Jesus to Golgotha. We must be prepared to die by the thousands. Those who believed in peace through the sword have not hesitated to die. Proudly, courageously, they gave their lives. Again and again, they sacrificed bright futures to the tragic illusion that one more righteous crusade would bring peace in their time, and they laid down their lives by the millions.
>
> Unless comfortable North American and European Mennonites and Brethren in Christ are prepared to risk injury and death in non-violent opposition to the injustice our societies foster and assist in Central America, the Philippines, and South Africa, we dare never

whisper another word about pacifism to our sisters and brothers in those desperate lands. Unless we are ready to die developing new nonviolent attempts to reduce international conflict, we should confess that we never really meant the cross was an alternative to the sword. Unless the majority of our people in nuclear nations are ready as congregations to risk social disapproval and government harassment in a clear ringing call to live without nuclear weapons, we should sadly acknowledge that we have betrayed our peacemaking heritage. Making peace is as costly as waging war. Unless we are prepared to pay the cost of peacemaking, we have no right to claim the label or preach the message.

Unless we . . . are ready to start to die by the thousands in dramatic vigorous new exploits for peace and justice, we should sadly confess that we never really meant what we said, and we dare never whisper another word about pacifism to our sisters and brothers in those desperate lands filled with injustice. Unless we are ready to die developing new nonviolent attempts to reduce conflict, we should confess that we never really meant that the cross was an alternative to the sword.[1]

Although many point to Sider's speech as the "beginning" of Christian Peacemaker Teams, in reality, certain members of the historic peace churches[2] had for years discussed developing groups of trained Christian volunteers who would intervene nonviolently in violent situations.

According to Gene Stoltzfus, CPT director (1987–2004), "There were those of us in the seventies who were pushing the church to take a more activist position in the areas of peace and social justice. We wanted members of the church to move from focusing on what Jesus could do for them to thinking about what it means to follow Jesus. Sider's speech legitimized this position in the wider church."[3]

Among the activists involved in these discussions were former Mennonite Central Committee (MCC)[4] volunteers like Edgar Metzler,

1. Sider, "God's People Reconciling." Sider expanded on this address in his book, *Nonviolence: The Invincible Weapon?*

2. The historic peace churches generally include the many branches of the Mennonite and Amish churches, Church of the Brethren and Friends (Quakers.) Certain other related groups, such as the Mennonite Brethren and Brethren in Christ, have historically had pacifism as a part of their theology, but currently emphasize evangelism more.

3. Gene Stoltzfus, interview, May 1, 2003.

4. MCC is a relief and development organization sponsored by different branches of the Mennonite and Amish churches. Founded in the 1920s to help Mennonites fleeing persecution and starvation in Russia, it has since expanded to aid sustainable development on every inhabited continent.

who under the leadership of Vincent and Rosemary Harding, were arrested for participation in Civil Rights marches. Many volunteers with Mennonite agencies had also participated in nonviolent demonstrations against the Vietnam War and nuclear testing.[5] Other MCC alumni exploring the possibility nonviolent Christian peace teams had worked in international settings with people systematically oppressed by their governments. Because criticizing these governments and their U.S. sponsors would endanger years of development work, MCC volunteers often could not speak out publicly about the oppression they witnessed. These alumni were thus seeking a venue in which they could speak out against, and even intervene in, systemic violence. They also had an appreciation for the damage that hundreds of naive North Americans without international experience could do if they were suddenly dumped into a violent conflict. The MCCers' participation, and later the participation of those who had worked with Brethren agencies, helped bring a reality check to Sider's vision.

Outside of the Mennonite Church, other religious and secular organizations were also exploring active, organized, and risky nonviolent direct action as an alternative to military or police actions. Several factors influenced these organizations. Gandhi's movement in India and the American Civil Rights movement demonstrated the power of Nonviolent Direct Action. Human rights organizations such as Amnesty International had involved ordinary citizens in advocating on the behalf of unknown political prisoners in remote nations. Such successful advocacy naturally led grassroots networks into exploring ways that international activists could intervene to prevent the torture and massacres committed by totalitarian governments.

Then, in the 1980s, the Central American Solidarity movement gave birth to two organizations committed to accompanying civilians targeted by their governments.

In April 1983, a delegation of American Christians, including the future director of CPT, Gene Stoltzfus, went to Nicaragua on a fact-finding tour. During a visit to a small village that U.S.-backed paramilitaries (called "Contras") had just attacked, the U.S. activists asked the people of the village why the Contras were no longer shooting. "Because you're here," the villagers told them. After hearing about the effect of their pres-

---

5. Metzler, letter, Aug 5, 2004.

ence, some considered staying, but instead went home to organize a long-term presence of U.S. citizens in Nicaragua. Those efforts turned into the organization Witness for Peace.

Three years earlier, at an international conference on nonviolence held at Grindstone Island in Ontario, Canada, participants from Europe, Asia, and the Americas met to discuss ways that active nonviolence could become a practical tool for confronting violent conflicts. This meeting led to the founding of Peace Brigades International. A second meeting in the Netherlands in 1982 approved committees to investigate project possibilities in Central America, Sri Lanka, Namibia, Pakistan, and the Middle East. In March 1983, PBI set up its first team in Guatemala, where the government was pursuing a vicious, genocidal campaign against indigenous people, as well as killing and torturing political dissidents.[6]

Thus, Sider's proposal for a nonviolent army did not cover completely new ground. He even cited Witness for Peace as a model Christians should duplicate and expand.[7] Nevertheless, he brought the principles of Nonviolent Direct Action to the notice of all Mennonite and Brethren in Christ churches—not just the ones inclined toward social action.[8] He also advocated the use of spiritual interventions more associated with apolitical or conservative Christianity. In addition to the necessity of "sophisticated expertise in diplomacy, history, international politics, and logistics" for the nonviolent peace army, he advocated " a radical dependence on the Holy Spirit. Such a peacekeeping task force of committed Christians," he said, "would immerse every action in intercessory prayer. There would be prayer chains in all our congregations as a few thousand of our best youth walked into the face of death, inviting all parties to end the violence and work together for justice."[9]

---

6. Mahoney and Eguren, *Unarmed Bodyguards*, 4–5.

7. Sider, "God's People Reconciling."

8. In his book *Rich Christians*, Sider accomplished a similar feat by urging Evangelicals to take an unflinching look both at Jesus' excoriations of the wealthy and at the crushing grip of poverty under which most people in the world live.

9. Sider, "God's People Reconciling."

BRINGING THE MESSAGE TO THE CHURCHES:
THE 1986 STUDY DOCUMENT

Sider's call sparked discussion in the historic peace churches across North America. The Council of Moderators and Secretaries (CMS) of the Mennonite, General Conference Mennonite, Mennonite Brethren, and Brethren in Christ churches discussed Sider's proposal in late 1984 and asked MCC Peace Section to study the issue and bring back a proposal to the council. After the proposal had gone through many drafts, the CMS, in an October 1985 meeting, approved the concept of Christian Peacemaker Teams in principle. The council then appointed a committee[10] to oversee a yearlong process of "prayerful discussion and dialogue" in the churches.

The language in a flier put out to advertise the study guide reflected the theological emphases in Sider's presentation. The Council of Moderators and Secretaries said that the "starting point for CPT is biblical obedience to Jesus Christ our Savior and Lord . . . Christians give themselves for others in obedience to their Redeemer who gave himself for the sins of the world."[11]

Such language carried over to the study guide. Under the "Proposal and Goal" section the authors wrote, "The goal of CPT would be to witness to Jesus Christ as we seek to identify with the suffering, promote peace, reduce violence, identify with those caught in violence and oppression and foster justice by using the techniques of non-violent direct action."[12] Of the nine Guiding Principles of CPT, the one listed first reads, "The Central purpose of CPT is *to glorify the Prince of Peace.*"[13]

Looking at the study document twenty years after it circulated among the Mennonite churches, one of course notes the disparities between vision and reality. The authors confidently proposed an initial training group of one hundred to two hundred volunteers. The first Corps training began with eight people—four full-timers and four reservists. In January 2006, the numbers of volunteers had increased to thirty full-timers and about 159 reservists. In the "Assumptions" section, the authors assert

---

10. Don Shafer, Lois Kenagy, Helmut Harder, Harold Jantz, Kathy Royer, and Ron Sider.

11. Sent from MCC headquarters in Akron, PA, and Winnipeg, MB on January 30, 1986.

12. MCC, "Christian Peacemaker Teams: A Study Document," 2.

13. Ibid., 7.

that at least some CPTers would practice forms of structured mediation and reconciliation work. In practice, CPTers have sometimes performed these functions informally, but the organization as a whole has carefully made distinctions between the work of Nonviolent Direct Action and mediation—viewing them as complementary disciplines.[14] If warring parties were to ask CPTers to take on a mediation role, the CPTers would probably swiftly contact mediators who had formal conflict resolution training.

In the area of qualifications and training, the authors envisioned a corps of volunteers with much better facility in languages than has been the case. They also imagined that training would take five months. Currently CPT volunteers receive less than a month's worth of training in Nonviolent Direct Action techniques, spirituality, technology (e.g., digital photography and computer skills), conflict resolution skills, and spiritual disciplines.[15]

None of the proposed settings for CPT projects in the 1986 Study Document ever resulted in having a project set up. They included

- *Nicaragua*, where the Contra war was still ongoing.

- *Laos*, where the authors envisioned CPT helping with MCC efforts to clear landmines.

- *Guatemala*, where CPTers would aid Peace Brigades' accompaniment of activists protesting the government-supported death squads "disappearing," torturing and murdering their loved ones.

- *Chile*, where CPTers would aid the Catholic anti-torture organizations.

- *South Africa, Ireland, and the Philippines*, where, the authors noted vaguely that some groups "may be receptive to some modified CPT approaches."

- *North American interventions* designed to reduce police harassment. The authors cited a 1969 conference in Philadelphia, during

14. Most CPTers would sheepishly admit that most of the conflict-resolution skills they learn in training are practiced largely within the teams. However, managing conflict well within a team is not a small thing.

15. The first training in 1993 lasted a little over a month, but since then CPT has realized that most training actually happens on the project site. CPTers in Colombia, for example, need to learn a set of skills that CPTers in Palestine do not need to learn.

which Quakers trained in Nonviolent Direct Action positioned themselves between black activists and a racist police department.

- *Nuclear Weapons Alternative Teams,* perhaps the most romantic part of the proposal, the authors imagined teams addressing "the illusion of nuclear security" through educating the wider church and having a prayerful witness at nuclear weapons installations and plants.

Finally, just before proposing an initial $800,000 budget for the support and training of one hundred volunteers, the booklet called for the development of Faithful Witness Groups. These groups, based on the models of Christian Base Communities in Latin America, Koinonia Farms and Catholic Worker (among other communities) would commit themselves to a life of prayer, study, discernment, witness, service, and resistance. Presumably, these groups were to provide volunteers or some sort of support for CPT, but the document did not make that connection explicit. [16]

Despite the fact that much of the current CPT structure and activity does not match the vision of the 1986 booklet, many of the theological underpinnings of current CPT work do echo that of the authors. The acknowledgement that the example of Jesus Christ forbids the killing other human beings, the call for an active peacemaking that goes beyond traditional peace church relief and development efforts, the vision to expand CPT beyond the historic peace churches into a more ecumenical movement have all taken a firm hold in CPT culture today. Likewise, the booklet's nine "Guiding Principles" and four "Criteria for Intervention" are not far different from those used by current CPT workers,[17] although

16. MCC, *Christian Peacemaker Teams: A Study Document,* 13–19.

17. Guiding Principles

   A. The central purpose of CPT is to glorify the Prince of Peace.

   B. In all its activity, CPT will use only nonviolent methods grounded in an Anabaptist theology of the cross.

   C. CPT is international in outlook and does not seek to promote or undermine any nation or group, although in specific situations a particular aspect of the policy of one nation or group will be challenged.

   D. To the highest degree possible, CPT is non-partisan. There fore, it always, at every phase of its activity, seeks to establish and maintain dialogue with all parties to the conflict.

some of the less religious volunteers might not put the same priorities on worship and prayers that other volunteers do.

More than four hundred congregations and seven hundred individuals submitted responses to the Study guide before the December 1986 meeting of the CMS at a retreat center in Techny, Illinois, a suburb of Chicago. The approximately one hundred people attending included rep-

---

E. CPT is a peacemaking body, not a political party. Therefore, it never attempts to impose a specific political, constitutional, or economic proposal, but rather seeks to create a context where the warring parties themselves can peacefully negotiate a solution appropriate for their unique setting.

F. CPT is not neutral on questions of injustice, poverty, hunger or oppression. Although it never seeks to impose a particular solution, CPT is not indifferent to the biblical call for justice and freedom for all people. Therefore, CPT always seeks to act in ways that promote religious and political freedom, including freedom of worship, speech, democratic elections and equality before the law. It also seeks to foster economic justice where all are genuinely free to enjoy adequate food, housing, clothing, education, health care and meaningful work to earn their living.

G. Study, analysis and research are important aspects of CPT's program.

H. CPT will work sensitively and cooperatively with North American Mennonite agencies and departments (mission boards, MCC, etc.) and with national church leaders and others in planning and implementing the peacemaking activities.

I. It is important to remember, however, that behind these basic guidelines lies the most important factor—a clear recognition of our dependency on God's spirit for security and leading. This suggests that in all planning CPT wait, listen, share and earnestly seek God's direction. This, above all, must remain the determinative factor in all CPT planning.

VII. Criteria for Intervention

A. CPT would intervene only after a careful attempt to dialogue with, understand, and affirm the legitimate concerns of all parties to a conflict.

B. CPT would intervene only after at least one major part in the conflict had issued an invitation and agreed to give CPT the freedom to operate in their area.

C. CPT would always seek to operate in the territory of both sides to a conflict and would decide to operate exclusively in the territory of one side only after CPT's offer to operate on both sides had been rejected.

D. CPT would intervene only when it believes that it can operate according to Jesus' nonviolent example in a way that will likely promote peace, justice and freedom. (Ibid.)

resentatives of the General Conference Mennonite Church, Mennonite Church, Brethren in Christ Church, and Mennonite Brethren Church. Church of the Brethren staff members participated as observers.

The conference issued a "Techny Call" to congregations, church agencies, and conferences:

> 1. We believe the mandate to proclaim the Gospel of repentance, salvation and reconciliation includes a strengthened biblical peace witness.

> 2. We believe that faithfulness to what Jesus taught and modeled calls us to more active peacemaking.
>
> We believe a renewed commitment to the gospel of peace calls us to new forms of public witness which may include nonviolent direct action.
>
> We believe the establishment of Christian Peacemaker Teams is an important new dimension for our ongoing peace and justice ministries.
>
> We ask our conferences and congregations to envision Christian Peacemaker Teams as a witness to Jesus Christ by identifying with suffering people, reducing violence, mediating conflicts and fostering justice through peaceful, caring direct challenge of evil. This may include biblical study and reflection, documenting and reporting on injustice and violation of human rights, Nonviolent Direct Action, education, mediation and advocacy. To be authentic, such peacemaking should be rooted in and supported by congregations and church-wide agencies. We will begin in North America, but will be open to invitations to support initiatives in other places.
>
> It is understood that in a growing emphasis on peacemaking, the Christian Peacemaker Teams vision is only one means of providing an opportunity for God's people to express a faithful witness to Jesus Christ, the Prince of Peace.
>
> We want to acknowledge our complicity in violence and oppression. Peacemaking is most of all the work of God. The Spirit of God will nurture this work within us.[18]

The CMS also agreed to sponsor a "Christian Peacemaker Teams"[19] steering committee comprising representatives from the Brethren in

18. MCC, "Techny Call," 1. The Mennonite Brethren came to Techny with this call already written and the participants largely adopted it as it was, with minor modifications.

19. The working title of the organization eventually became permanent. In the 1986 study booklet the authors wrote,

Christ, Church of the Brethren, General Conference Mennonite Church, Mennonite Brethren and Mennonite Church along with "individuals who have participated in various forms of public witness."[20]

In June 1987 the CPT Steering Committee met for the first time. Members included Chuck Boyer, Eber Dourte, Dorothy Friesen, Harry Huebner, Frances Jackson, Harold Jantz, Ruth Stoltzfus Jost, Edgar Metzler, and Hedy Sawadsky. After that meeting, the Church of the Brethren became an official sponsor and the Mennonite Brethren pulled out.[21] The Brethren in Christ pulled out in 1990. Two years later, in July 1988, the Conference of Mennonites in Canada adopted a resolution endorsing CPT.

This Steering Committee met twice in 1987 and hired Gene Stoltzfus as a half-time coordinator in 1988.[22] Stoltzfus had worked with the International Voluntary Service in Vietnam and with MCC in the Philippines. These international experiences gave him an understanding of how the United States dominated countries by supporting totalitarian regimes and of the limitations of relief and development work. Upon his return to the United States, he had developed skills as a political organizer

---

The name, 'Christian Peacemaker Teams,' signifies the basic characteristics of the group; it is Christian and emphasizes active peacemaking rather than only peace keeping. The name suggests a number of units, rather than a single body. Modifications of this general idea could include the names Christian Nonviolent Peace Teams or Mennonite Peace Teams.

Other names that have been suggested are Anabaptist Peace Guard, The Lamb's Reconcilers, The King's Reconcilers, Reconcilers of the Kingdom, Jesus' Conciliation Movement, Anabaptist Peace Teams, Christians for Non-Violent Reconciliation, Love Guard, and the Cross of Christ Guard. (MCC, "Christian Peacekeeper Teams: A Study Document," 6)

20. MCC, *MCC Peace Section Newsletter*.

21. Some of the ambivalence the MB's felt toward the CPT enterprise is reflected in the address that John Toews, Academic Dean of Mennonite Brethren Biblical Seminary gave at the Techny conference. "I am uncertain if the nonviolent resistance or direct action strategies undergirding the Christian Peace Teams [sic] proposal represents a faithful interpretation of New Testament kingdom-peace theology. I am inclined to believe that the concrete shape that such theology should take in the life of the Mennonite church is still to be fashioned." *MCC Peace Section Newsletter,* 10.

22. Stoltzfus was not invited to the Techny meeting, but came anyway. Carol Rose, who, along with Doug Pritchard succeeded Stoltzfus as CPT co-director in 2004 also crashed the Techny conference. She was spending a year at Associated Mennonite Biblical Seminaries after completing her MCC assignment in Honduras.

in social justice movements, and had committed himself to living on a sub-poverty income so that he would not have to pay war taxes. In many ways he was the ideal candidate for the job, and Stoltzfus himself said he felt the job was made for him. "I was able to bring my faith perspective, my experience with organizing and how I understood the way the world worked," he said. He bristles, however, when people refer to him as the "founder" of CPT. "CPT," he said, was a "natural outgrowth of the Anabaptist tradition."[23]

At the time he was hired, the Steering Committee was no longer talking about one hundred full-time volunteers, but twelve—a goal that the organization did not achieve until 1998. Reality had begun to temper the vision.

Small Initiatives

According to Gene Stoltzfus, the period between 1987 and 1993 indirectly addressed the question, "Why do we need another peace organization?" The work of CPT during this period mostly involved sponsoring individual initiatives, delegations, and conferences. Perhaps the most important of these initiatives was Oil-Free Sunday in 1990, on the eve of the Gulf War, which called Mennonite and Brethren church-goers to walk to worship (or find a means of transportation not fueled by oil) as a way to draw attention to the role that control of oil plays in Middle Eastern violence. During this period, CPT also began working on the issue of violent toys, i.e., toys that taught violence was an acceptable way of settling disputes, encouraged children to create enemies, glamorized the military, or promoted racism and sexism.

A variety of other small initiatives—some coming from CPT staff and Steering Committee and some from various individuals supportive of CPT—illustrate the organization's search for identity. CPT sponsored individuals traveling to Central America, Haiti and the Israeli-occupied Palestinian territories who documented the violence happening there. Between July 26 and September 27, 1990, CPT chairperson Robert Hull made three trips Montreal to intervene in a confrontation between members of the Mohawk nation and the Quebec Provincial police at Oka.[24] Phil Stoltzfus (a nephew of Gene Stoltzfus) traveled through the U.S., Canada,

23. Gene Stoltzfus, interview, May 23, 2003.
24. More information on the incident appears in chap. 8.

and Central America on a CPT stipend collecting stories of Brethren and Mennonites involved in "nonviolent prophetic witness." These stories were eventually collected into a book, entitled, *The Anabaptists Are Back* (1991.)

CPT also organized eight conferences between 1988 and 1992 that included training in Nonviolent Direct Action, and political advocacy. Two that were to have a special impact on the organization occurred in Ottawa, Canada, and at the Mennonite World Conference in Winnipeg. In February 1990, CPT sponsored an Innu solidarity conference to listen to Innu leaders describing the damage done to their Labrador homelands by NATO low-level flying. Afterward, a regional CPT organization formed in Ontario to plan the conference and continue the witness against the government. Doug Pritchard—who would later become coordinator of CPT Canada and then co-director of CPT with Carol Rose in 2004—first became involved with CPT at this meeting.

In July 1990, CPT led nonviolence-training seminars at Mennonite World Conference in Winnipeg, Manitoba and organized a vigil with 350 participants at a Minuteman II nuclear missile silo in North Dakota. Stoltzfus, who worked for nearly a year organizing the vigil, remembers feeling at this time that CPT might actually succeed in becoming the broadly supported grassroots initiative envisioned by its founders. Once the witness hit the front-page news in Canada, he recalls thinking, "Now we're in business."[25]

Delegations

Delegations to regions of conflict continue to be an important part of the CPT witness. They are, perhaps, the most significant source of education for congregations, since participants go back to their churches and provide eyewitness reports that people do not receive from the mainstream media. Delegations also serve as a method for recruiting CPT full-timers

25. Gene Stoltzfus, interview, May 23, 2003. Stoltzfus went on to say that Hans Ulrich Gerber, a staff person of Mennonite World Conference did CPT an "enormous favor" when he told him, "Gene, we want CPT to be visible."

At the Winnipeg conference, news of a standoff between the Mohawks and the Quebec provincial police arrived and Bob Hull and John Paul Lederach left early to mediate (see chapter 9). For descriptions of other conferences during this period, see CPT, "Christian Peacemaker Teams Activities."

and help to screen out "loose cannons," i.e., people who are interested in CPT but not temperamentally suited to work on projects.

Before 1990, CPT had commissioned people to participate in delegations organized by other groups, but the 1990 delegation to Iraq was the first one that CPT had sponsored on its own. The delegation included thirteen Mennonites, Brethren, and Friends, most of whom had spent time in the Middle East. Delegation members hoped to negotiate the release of international hostages Saddam Hussein was holding and end the blockade of food and medicine imposed by the U.S.-led coalition. (More information on the delegation will appear in chapter 11.)

In June 1991, Stoltzfus and Sawadsky led a delegation to Israel, the West Bank, and Jordan, visiting groups involved with Nonviolent Direct Action. They participated with hundreds of international, Israeli, and Palestinian peace activists in a walk from Jerusalem to Ramallah that crossed the border between Israel and the West Bank. A year later, Stoltzfus and Sawadsky led another eleven-member delegation to the West Bank, where they joined other Israeli, Palestinian, and International activists in the "Walk for a Peaceful Future" through the Valley of Megiddo on Pentecost Sunday. (Megiddo is the place where Christians who follow pre-millennialist eschatology believe the battle of Armageddon will take place.) The Israeli authorities arrested six members of the delegation and 113 Israeli and international activists who tried to cross the green line. Among the activists participating were John Reuwer, Dianne Roe, Anne Montgomery, and Duane Ediger who would later go through CPT trainings in 1993, 1994 and 1995."[26] Prior to the first trained full-timers setting up the project in Haiti, CPT sent a delegation to Miami to work with local churches and the Haitian Refugee Center to draw public attention to the fact that the US was not granting asylum to Haitians fleeing the political violence in their country. In May 1993, CPT, working with Witness for Peace, sent eight people to Haiti to document the increasing human rights abuses in the country.[27]

Signs of the Times

A final important initiative of Christian Peacemaker Teams that began before the development of the Christian Peacemaker Corps was its news-

26. Gene Stoltzfus, interview, May 23, 2003.
27. CPT, "Christian Peacemaker Teams Activities."

letter, *Signs of the Times,* which continues as the official publication of
CPT today. Before 1993, the newsletters appeared irregularly and each issue was devoted to a theme. The first one, which appeared in March 1991,
focused largely on the upcoming Capitol Sabbath in Spring 1991 and reflections from people who had participated in the "Emergency Sabbath"
on January 21, 1991. During this "Sabbath," CPT called its constituents
to take a day away from work to engage in peacemaking activities on the
Monday following the beginning of the hostilities in the Persian Gulf.[28]
The second issue in July 1991 largely covered the Israeli-Palestinian conflict, and the third was dedicated to the work of Cathy Stoner and Andre
Gingerich Stoner, who counseled American soldiers in Germany during
the first Gulf war. As time passed, *Signs of the Times* became more of a
clearinghouse for information on social justice movements around the
world. The newsletter now focuses mostly on the work of the teams in
various CPT project locations.

1993—THE FIRST TRAINING OF THE CHRISTIAN PEACEMAKER CORPS

Since Ron Sider's address to Mennonite World Conference in 1984,
many working with CPT held on to the vision of a full-time peace army
comprising hundreds of well-trained, highly- disciplined volunteers who
could walk into a crisis situation and use Nonviolent Direct Action to
deter and/or transform the violence in these locations. When the necessary funds and multi-lingual volunteers with years of service in peace and
social justice movements failed to materialize, those working with CPT
explored other models. "We were probing for our voice," Gene Stoltzfus
said of this period.[29]

Since CPT delegations to the Middle East and Haiti had already had
positive impacts, some thought that CPT could follow in the tradition
of Witness for Peace and primarily send delegations as a way of deterring violence. However, Stoltzfus and others within the organization

28. On the final page of this newsletter, in the box giving permission to reprint articles
and listing the Steering Committee members, someone inserted, "We apologize for the
disproportionately large focus of this issue on U.S. concerns at the expense of Canada.
Perhaps this is a reflection of the New World Order." Dealing with how to integrate both
Canadian and US constituents into projects CPT set up because of harmful US foreign
policies would be a struggle in the future of the organization.

29. Gene Stoltzfus, interview, May 23, 2003.

also believed that CPT could not continue growing until it had a core group of full-time volunteers who would establish a track record of active peacemaking.

The 1992 Los Angeles riots/insurrection provided the catalyst for CPT's decision to plunge ahead with the Corps, despite the organization's lack of funding or trained volunteers. In March 1991, someone had taken a video of fifteen Los Angeles police officers beating Rodney King, an African American, with clubs as he lay on the ground. When the police officers involved went to trial, the African American community watched the trial carefully, wondering if this time, given the video evidence, white police officers would finally be held accountable for their violence against African American residents of Los Angeles. In April 1992, as the sentencing approached, Mennonite Church leaders in Los Angeles told CPT's Chicago office that the situation there was about to "explode" and that they would welcome a CPT presence.

CPT, however, did not have the financial or personnel resources to send a delegation at that point. Several weeks later on April 29, after the court acquitted King's attackers, the streets of Los Angeles did indeed explode in an insurrection that left thirty-eight dead, more than a thousand injured, and hundreds of shops, residences, and vehicles looted and burned.

Accordingly, at the 1992 CPT steering committee meeting in Richmond, Virginia, members of the CPT Steering Committee decided to proceed with a training of full-time volunteers, despite the fact that funding was not in place.[30] The November 1992 issue of *Signs of the Times* thus called for the establishment of a "Peace Reserve," trained in public witness, nonviolent action, and mediation. The article read, "The Peace Reserve will consist of persons with experience in Nonviolent Direct Action, a commitment to peacemaking, a firmly grounded faith and adequate freedom from family responsibilities to move into life-threatening situations on short notice." The article described an additional "on-call" group of CPT supporters with experience in Nonviolent Direct Action and cross-cultural relationships. The members of the Peace Reserve would undergo a four to eight week period of training in Bible study, role-plays, personal spirituality, Nonviolent Direct Action, and mediation.

30. "We limped along with budget of about $20,000 for years and had trouble making that," recalls Steering Committee member Hedy Sawadsky. Interview, June 24, 2003.

CPT staff and Steering Committee estimated that each Peace Reservist would cost about $12,000 a year for room, board, travel, program costs and administrative support. Recruitment would happen in collaboration with denominational service and mission programs. Reservists would live in groups of two to four people throughout North America and spend approximately two-thirds of their time on assignment and one-third of their time "speaking, training, story-telling or [doing] other volunteer peace work within their local community."

"Emergency response peacemaking will receive priority," the article concluded, "but team members may be called to travel within North America in order to teach and train others in mediation and Nonviolent Direct Action. The goal is to train the first Peace Reserve during the summer of 1993."[31]

By December 1992, CPT staff, which now included personnel director Jane Miller, had drawn up a nine-page *Christian Peacemaker Corps Proposal,* a slightly revised version of which was reprinted in March 1993. The proposal defined the need for a twelve-person Christian Peacemaker Corps (CPC), listing the following objectives

- To advance the cause of lasting peace by giving skilled, courageous support to peacemakers working locally in situations of conflict
- To provide congregations with first-hand information and resources for responding to worldwide situations of conflict, and to urge their active involvement
- To interpret a nonviolent perspective to the media

The proposal went on to list case studies in Los Angeles, the Persian Gulf, and Oka, Quebec where having a trained team might have helped prevent or diminish violence. It then described the philosophical, biblical, and theological bases for the Corps and how recruitment and training would take place. The projected budget for the support of a twelve-member team for three years came to $421,500, of which $53,843 had been raised at the time the Proposal had been written.

The February 1993 *Signs of the Times* announced that "for reasons of clarity" the CPT Steering Committee had changed the name of the Peace

---

31. "Peace Reserve."

Reserves to the Christian Peacemaker Corps or CPC.[32] "But what will a 12-person peacemaker corps be when it begins?" The article asked. "If we had our Christian Peacemaker Corps in place today we would:

- Station two persons in Miami for three months to develop a continuing presence and help churches and the Haitian Refugee Center focus on the critical matter of Haitian refugees

- Send a team to Croatia in response to a call from German Mennonite Peace Committee members and their connections in Croatia

- Work with leaders in Los Angeles where tensions are still high due to the Rodney King affair

- Send two or more people to travel with Russian student aid and peace workers to Georgia in response to repeated requests from Moscow-based contacts

- Develop a peacemaker team manual that will include songs, worship materials, basics in nonviolent action, guidelines for working with the public media, skills for observer missions, mediation basics, suggestions for organizing vigils and symbolic public actions and more

- Develop a fact-finding team that will investigate how the North American church can support people in Burma who now live under brutal military rule despite a massive nonviolent movement which began some years ago[33]

By June 1993, applicants for the first Christian Peacemaker Corps received a letter from Jane Miller that nine applicants were currently in the interview process, but that funding for only six had been raised. By July 1993 funding for eight became available.

32. According to Gene Stoltzfus, the main reason for the change had to do with the fact that they had already decided that CPTers would be divided into full-time volunteers and reservists, who would donate whatever time they had available in the course of a year. They thought people would get "Peace Reserves" and "reservists" confused. Using military terminology, like "Corps," was somewhat controversial, but in the end, Stoltzfus said, "We decided that since the Bible was militant we could use military language." Interview, June 11, 2003.

33. *Signs of the Times,* November 1992, 5–6.

Kryss Chupp came on part-time as a training coordinator in the late summer. Chupp had met Stoltzfus and his wife Dorothy Friesen when she came to Chicago as a Bethel College undergraduate to participate in Chicago's Urban Life center. After serving for four years in Nicaragua with Mennonite Central Committee doing popular education, she had returned to Chicago and worked with Synapses, an organization that connected North Americans with progressive movements around the world. Both jobs combined to make her particularly suitable for training North Americans to work in cross-cultural situations.

On September 25, 1993, Cole Arendt, Miriam Maik, Kathleen Kern, and Lena Siegers arrived for training in Chicago intending to become CPT full-timers; John Reuwer, Phoenix Hocking, Mary Wells, and Pete Begly came intending to become CPT reservists.[34] Ranging in ages from mid-twenties to early sixties, the trainees came from a variety of backgrounds. Some had extensive experience in peace activism; others had only had brushes with it. Most had done volunteer work of one sort or another and had worked in the "helping" professions.

From the beginning, the first training was beset by difficulties that one might expect to happen when part-time staff people are working more than full-time hours. For example, the staff that sent the "runners up" the letter saying that CPT had funding only for six trainees, never sent a follow-up letter saying that the money had been found. Thus, several of the trainees did not know they had been invited to training until about a month before they were due in Chicago. The reservists at the training did not know until they were in Chicago that CPT would expect reservists to raise their own funds.

The first training group was also invited to help draft the CPT slogan,[35] a mandate for the Christian Peacemaker Corps, and a logo. While involving the training group in these decisions helped make the trainees feel included and develop consensus decision-making skills, these activities also left the trainees with an unclear sense of how decision-making actually happened among CPT staff and steering committee, especially when the trainees' suggestions were discarded. Additionally, the trainees had different ideas of what the Corps should do. Should they be a nonviolent swat team entering crisis situations as a sheriff would enter a town controlled

34. Hocking chose to leave before completing the training.

35. "Discovering Christ in Crisis," which was quickly replaced with "Getting in the Way" by the 1995 training group.

by outlaws in a cowboy movie? Should they be community organizers? Should they simply plug into projects already working to deter violence? Why, some wondered, were they being trained to work as a team, when it appeared that the Chicago office intended to disperse them among several projects?

The personalities of the trainees also factored into the stresses of that training. Several had take-charge working styles and often clashed with each other. Some stressed the importance of physical fitness as part of the work. ("What if you were hanging from a cliff and had to pull yourself up?" one of the athletes told the non-athletes.) Introverted and extroverted personalities also collided.

Six of the eight people in the group had had catastrophic life experiences involving domestic abuse or medical crises, which may have led them consciously or subconsciously to CPT work. While having suffered made them eager to help the suffering, tensions arose several times as the trainees' emotional wounds bumped against each other. According to Chupp, most of the subsequent trainings would also contain people who had survived great life tragedies, but in none of these trainings were the psychological scars as marked as those of the first trainees.[36]

Chupp would go on to lead every subsequent CPT training—which by 2007 were held at least twice a year. She was hired as a full-time training coordinator in 1997. Although she has experimented with different style and content, she says all of the trainings have covered basically the same material. All of the trainings have included Bible study and spiritual disciplines, analysis of working styles, organizing campaigns and public witnesses, conflict transformation skills, working with technology, facilitating group decision-making, racism awareness, and role-playing how to intervene in crisis situations.[37]

Case studies of CPT work in the field have constituted the biggest change in trainings since 1995. CPT full-timers who are in North America when trainings are happening at the Chicago office often participate as trainers, sharing from their experiences.

According to Chupp, the quality and abilities of people coming to training has steadily increased since 1995, as CPT has developed a success-

36. Chupp, e-mail, June 5, 2003.

37. These have included regional trainings in Boulder, Ontario, Cleveland, Washington, DC, Manitoba, and Northern Indiana.

ful track record on various projects.[38] However, although the first trainees had significant deficits, one should bear in mind that CPT continued to grow and expand based on the successful projects that people from this group established in Haiti, Washington, DC, and Hebron. Three of the eight, including the author, continued to work with CPT as full-timers or reservists for the next fourteen years. Noting the shortcomings of the first training group does not dishonor the trainees, but rather testifies to the grace of God and to the working of the Holy Spirit in their efforts and the efforts of the hundreds of CPTers who followed them.

38. Chupp, interview, May 23, 2003.

2

Haiti

Let the people come
Let the people of the world
charter flights, rent boats
and create a civilian invasion.
Let them come by the hundreds
to stand beside the Haitian people and say
"This situation is finished."
Let the people come from all over the world.
Let the boats bring people to,
not carry refugees from, Haiti.
If two or three thousand
come to stand with us and say
"There must be an end to this injustice."
Then the United Nations
or the Organization of American States
would not need their weapons.
This is the greatest philosophy on earth,
to come and stand in solidarity with
sisters and brothers.
People like you can do this, and in doing so,
you are fulfilling the mission of Jesus
to set at liberty those who are bound.

—Ari Nicola[1]

IN A CLOSELY MONITORED 1990 election, an overwhelming majority of the Haitian people chose Jean Bertrand Aristide to be their president. After serving in office for seven months, he was overthrown in a coup

1. Nicola, "Let the People Come," 1. This call was a spontaneous spoken invitation to a CPT delegation from Nicola, one of the Haiti team's most trusted advisors. Nicola was in hiding during the coup years, so his name was withheld in the article for reasons of security.

d'état led by the man he appointed to head the Haitian military, Raoul Cedras. Thousands of Haitians began fleeing the political persecution in vessels not made for travel on the high seas. The U.S. State Department, under the George Herbert Walker Bush administration, refused to grant them asylum, insisting they were economic refugees, despite its knowledge of the human rights abuses committed by the military junta running the country. Given that the U.S. treated refugees from another Caribbean island—Cuba—quite differently, human rights groups and African American leaders charged that U.S. policies toward Haiti smacked of racism.

In July 1993, the U.S.-brokered Governor's Island agreement signed by both Aristide and Cedras specified that Cedras would step down at the end of October 1993. In return, Aristide agreed to refrain from criticizing U.S. policy and to encourage Haitians not to flee the country.

As the end of October approached, U.S. President Bill Clinton sent the warship Harlan County to Port-au-Prince to set the stage for Aristide's return. On October 25, hundreds of armed paramilitary thugs greeted the Harlan County at the dock, and Clinton ordered the ship to pull away. Conventional wisdom attributed this withdrawal to Clinton's recent embarrassment in Somalia where eighteen U.S. soldiers had died in intense street fighting on October 3, 1993. Later revelations by Emmanuel Constant, leader of paramilitary group FRAPH (Revolutionary Front for Haitian Advancement and Progress[2]) indicated that the CIA may have supplied Clinton with false information that led him to believe the armed paramilitaries were more dangerous than they actually were.[3]

During the period between July and October, CPT joined with a coalition of organizations that operated under the title of Cry for Justice (CFJ).[4] The stated purpose of CFJ was to send teams to different areas

2. Pronounced, not coincidentally, like *frappe*—French for "to hit." In French, the title is *Front Révolutionnaire pour l'Avancement et le Progrés Haïtiens.*

3. See Weiner, "Haitian Ex-Paramilitary Leader."

4. The other groups who participated in the Steering Committee were Pax Christi/U.S.A., Peace Brigades International, Washington Office on Haiti, Fellowship of Reconciliation Task Force on Latin America and the Caribbean, Global Exchange, Haiti Communication Project, Sojourners, and World Peacemakers, Inc. Co-sponsoring were American Friends Service Committee, Baptist Peace Fellowship, Clergy and Laity Concerned, Conference of Major Superiors of Men, Fellowship of Reconciliation, Maryknoll Fathers and Brothers, Quixote Center/Haiti Reborn, War Resisters League and Witness for Peace. Kinane, "Cry for Justice in Haiti." 210–11. Kinane's chapter provides a good overview of the basic structure and purpose of Cry for Justice.

of Haiti in order to provide a violence-deterring/human- rights-monitoring presence. In September 1993, when Dante Caputo pulled out the Organization of American States (OAS) human rights monitors from Haiti because he deemed the situation too dangerous for them, the need for international observers became even more desperate.

October 31, 1993, came and Aristide did not. The U.S. appeared to have lost interest (if it had ever had any) in restoring Aristide to power. Cry for Justice disbanded. At the invitation of St. Helene's parish and its priest in the western seaport town of Jérémie, CPT stayed on.

CPT's connection with Haiti had begun early in 1988 when CPT Steering Committee chairperson, Ruth Stoltzfus Jost, tried to organize a meeting of former aid and development workers in Haiti to strategize about possible CPT responses to the ongoing violence and instability that began after the fall of the Duvalier regime.[5] In November 1992, CPT sponsored the participation of Elaine Stoltzfus and Gordon Hunsberger in a fact-finding mission to Haiti with a Chicago Religious Task Force

---

5. In an August 28, 2003 e-mail to the author, Stoltzfus Jost wrote the following (brackets and ellipses represent later clarifications):

> The debate within the steering committee for some reason centered on the "triumphalism" some thought this idea represented, in that it would involve North Americans solving other people's problems when we should be working on our own problems here in the U.S. [or in international problems in which the U.S. was implicated.] It's hard to believe, but there was no international dimension to CPT at that point that I recall, and as you can see, considerable ideologically based opposition to it.
>
> Since I was not able to convince the group to do a Haiti CPT project I decided to just explore the idea on my own. I held a sort of conference at my home in Columbus, Ohio . . .
>
> It was a wonderful time which, at least in the short term, did not have a real impact on the direction of CPT. I think the meeting was the fortunate result of a certain stubbornness on my part when I think I have a good idea and naiveté about the need to work subject to group decisions. I remember that I gave a pretty brief [and, I'm afraid, verbal] report [to the steering committee], which the group graciously received.

Jost clarified her memories of the Steering Committee process in six e-mails sent to the author in September 2004, and in telephone interviews on September 29 and October 28 that year. She thinks financial considerations may have also been a factor in the decision not to proceed, given that CPT's budget was about $20,000 at the time.

Delegation and in the next year sent five of its own delegations to Haiti and Miami (where Haitian refugees were awaiting deportation).[6]

For all of the delegations to Haiti, Carla Bluntschli and Ari Nicola served as point persons. Bluntschli and her husband Ron had served in Haiti with Mennonite Central Committee for about ten years and then stayed on to work independently as hosts of delegations seeking contact with grassroots Haitian groups. Nicola, who wrote the call at the beginning of this chapter, was one of nearly a million Haitians in "hiding" because coup supporters had arrested him previously for his work as an animateur, i.e., someone who trained Haitian peasants in agriculture and community development.[7] (Coup supporters viewed most professions that bettered the lives of the poor as a threat to their hegemony.) Living hand-to-mouth, in faith that delegations and paying translation jobs would come, the Bluntschlis and Nicola would become the primary point people for CPT's Haiti teams until CPT ended its presence in Haiti in 1997.

Criteria for Intervention

CPT's extensive involvement with Haitian issues in 1992–1993 made it the obvious choice for a first project staffed by trained full-time CPT volunteers. Additionally, the project fit the Considerations for CPT Decision Making [sic] Entering into Crisis Situations approved by the CPT Steering Committee on October 10, 1993:

1. *Is the proposed action one our constituency can support? Is there a critical mass of supporters?*

Mennonite Central Committee had worked in Haiti since 1958. One of its most important development projects—building silos so that peasant farmers could store their grain until a better price came on the

6. The findings of the delegation appeared in "Report of Peacemaker Delegation to Haiti, May 5–15, 1993," in a special, undated *Signs for Our Times* [sic]: Haiti that CPT sent out to its constituency. Responding to a hunger strike called by 160 Haitian refugees in Miami's Krome Detention Center in January 1993, CPT sent a ten-person delegation to Miami. The participants held a vigil outside of Krome to call attention to the treatment of the refugees awaiting deportation there.

7. "In hiding" could refer to several different levels of concealment. Many Haitians threatened by coup supporters in their home regions simply took up residence a different part of the country where they could move about openly. Nicola had come from the Cape Haitien region originally. Others had to operate with more caution.

market—was sabotaged by supporters of the coup d'état. They destroyed all these silos and threatened the Haitian nationals working with MCC, which made the Mennonite Church constituency take notice of what the coup regime was doing. Additionally, many North Americans were moved by stories and video footage of Haitian refugees drowning or getting turned back by the U.S. Coast Guard as they tried to reach Florida.

2. Is there a trusted welcoming body in the crisis setting with whom we connect? Is the area one in which CPT or its supporting denominations have experience and relationships of trust established?

The previous delegations to Haiti had forged positive connections with many Haitian grassroots organizers and especially with Carla Bluntschli and Ari Nicola. In Jérémie, Father Joachim Samedi issued an invitation on behalf of St. Helene's parish for CPT to establish a violence-deterring presence there.

3. Is the action explainable as a Christian witness?

Given that the invitation had come from a priest and his parish, the Christian connection was clear, but also controversial. Bishop Willi Romélus from Jérémie was the only one of ten Haitian bishops who spoke out in favor of Aristide and his reforms.[8] The Vatican was the first "state" to recognize the coup leaders as the rightful governors of Haiti after the coup. Additionally, many evangelical missionaries and their followers had an anti-Aristide bias because he was Catholic. In fact, one of the most notorious and vicious FRAPH members in Jérémie was Pastor Bonhomme, a Pentecostal minister.[9]

4. Can we talk freely and with integrity in our constituency about what we do?[10]

8. For a profile of Romélus and the parish of St. Helene, see Puleo, "A Bishop Who Hears."

9. Kathleen Kern and Joel Klassen had a face-to-face encounter with Bonhomme in 1993 as he and a group of his followers were dragging a terrified, screaming woman into a house on the beach. When she and Klassen asked what he was doing, he told them, in good English and with gun in hand, that when he visited America, he did not interfere with what Americans were doing. Much to her regret, Kern did not get a chance to reply that if he came to America and saw people kidnapping a woman, she hoped he *would* intervene. The team found out later that the woman survived the attack.

10. CPT, "Considerations for CPT decision making [*sic*] entering into crisis situations."

The original guideline in May 1993 read, "Can we talk about what we do freely and with integrity? We do not do covert, clandestine witness." The change probably reflected a practical acknowledgment that people whom CPT supported were often involved in clandestine activities for reasons of personal security.

CPTers in Jérémie felt free to say they were there to deter violence. However, several of the Jérémie team's most trusted advisors were forced to live "clandestine" and "covert" lives, because supporters of the coup government killed those who criticized the regime. The political atmosphere was such that even ordinary schoolteachers with no particular interest in politics suffered attacks from coup sympathizers because their profession could be construed as inherently sympathetic to the poor. Any casual remark viewed as anti-government left Haitians vulnerable to attack. Similar remarks made by CPTers would not have put the CPTers in danger, but they might have left Haitians associated with CPT vulnerable. The team in Jérémie, and in most future CPT projects, thus had to balance their protection of people living clandestinely with remaining true to what CPT was and the principle of Satyagraha, or "truth-force."[11]

5. Is there enough stability in the area that sending people is not negligent? What is the likelihood people will get killed without making a witness? Is it a situation in which there is time for love and nonviolent engagement to work?

Gene Stoltzfus, to illustrate this point, often said, "If we get killed because they're bombing the airport in Sarajevo, we're not going to make

11. In a January 5, 1994, "Reflection on the Considerations for CPT/CPC Decision Making," Cole Arendt wrote the following regarding this point:

> We are continually reminded of the need for not only sensitivity to the political context, but the need for outright deceit in some situations. We are certainly not at liberty to speak freely and with integrity in local contexts, and measure the ability to do so in our constituency against the variable levels of security in available methods of communication and the likelihood of what we say "back home" getting back here to other local elements antagonistic to our presence. Much of what we do is therefore surreptitious and oblique. Further involvement with the self-help project [proposed by the team's friends in KOREGA—a pro-democracy group, to raise money as a cover for conveying intelligence] could include us in a great deal of subterfuge and conspiracy (and is somewhat difficult to reconcile with our desire to hold up the Lavalas principles, esp. "Transparency").

much of a witness." CPT has generally not put volunteers into situations where open warfare has broken out and peace workers might get killed in the crossfire. Instead CPT has responded to invitations from locations where "effective racism" is at work. "Effective racism" basically means using the fact that North American and European lives are considered more valuable than African, Asian, and Latino lives to protect threatened people. In Haiti, this principle operated almost as if it were part of the legal system. Whites, or "*blans*," (from "blanc," the French word for "white") were virtually untouchable by the army and paramilitaries.[12]

This principle became controversial among CPT volunteers in ensuing years. CPTers have prevented death and injuries to others because systems of domination considered the CPTers' lives more valuable. The principle, however, does damage to the soul who dreams of an egalitarian society. Additionally, as more people of color have joined CPT and Colombian nationals have gone through training in order to work on CPT's Colombia project, the organization has had to re-evaluate using "effective racism" as tacit principle of its work.

6. *Are our governments part of the problem?*[13]

Since the nineteenth century, the U.S. has supported policies that have kept the Haitian people downtrodden. In January 1804, after several years of slave revolt against French plantation owners, Jean-Jacques Dessaline declared that Haiti was a free and independent nation. To North American plantation owners, slaves claiming the same rights to life, liberty, and the pursuit of happiness that American colonists had claimed aroused horror. For several decades Europe and the United States shunned Haiti, which probably resulted in its happiest period of history. Possessing enough land to feed themselves after a land distribution program, and freed from the demands of export agriculture, Haitians developed a unique culture,

12. Haitians also refer to Africans and African Americans as "*blans*," which means the status does not just refer to one's color. After the U.S. Special Forces landed in Haiti in 1994, one of the African American servicemen asked Kathleen Kern in exasperation, "Why do they keep telling me I'm white?"

13. CPT has always had a large number of Canadian volunteers. Thus, an ongoing difficulty of this criterion is the fact that the Canadian government is usually not as culpable for abetting violent conflicts around the world as the United States is. For this reason, many Canadian CPTers choose to work in the area of indigenous issues, for which the Canadian government is culpable.

language, and religion that combined African and European influences. More powerful nations characterized this period of relative prosperity as "a return to barbarism."[14] The United States would not recognize the government of Haiti until 1862, after the southern states seceded from the Union.

In the late nineteenth century the U.S. began to make concerted efforts to gain military and commercial control of Haiti. By 1905, the U.S.-controlled Haitian customs. In 1915, the U.S. Marines began an occupation of Haiti that lasted for nineteen years.[15] The Marines supervised an election in 1918 and introduced a constitution that reversed a previous law stipulating that foreigners could not own land in Haiti. They prevented the Haitian legislature from meeting between 1917–1930, reinstalled the mulatto elite to govern the "inferior" black Haitians and began a program of forced labor that took peasants away from their land for U.S. building projects. They also armed, trained and centralized the military, laying the groundwork for future military control of the country.

Even after the U.S. formally withdrew its troops, it continued to control Haiti's economy, helping to install a tax system that collected revenue from the produce of Haitian peasants. At the same time, it freed the land-and-business-owning class, including North American conglomerates, from having to pay income or property taxes. Haitian farmers in the Artibonite region had, until the late 1980's, grown enough rice to feed the whole country. When the U.S. flooded the Haitian market with rice costing 30-50% less than locally grown rice, it put these small farmers out of business. In 1988, the U.S. insisted that Haitians kill all their pigs in order prevent an outbreak of Asian Swine Flu. The U.S. replaced the hardy little Creole pigs that lived on garbage with larger American varieties requiring feed that Haitians had to buy from the U.S. Ill-adapted to Haiti's tropical climate, most of these pigs died even when supplied with the expensive American feed.

---

14. Burns, *Latin America: A Concise Interpretive History,* 112.

15. The U.S. military also ventured into Cuba, Mexico, Nicaragua, the Dominican Republic, and Honduras during this period, opening these countries to the control of U.S. corporations. This egregious imperialism caused philosopher William James to say in the early twentieth century that his country had finally "vomited the Declaration of Independence." Galeano, *Open Veins of Latin America,* 122.

The U.S. generally supported the Duvalier family dictatorship from 1957 to 1986. In 1986, Baby Doc Duvalier fled to France on a U.S. Air Force jet with millions of dollars from the Haitian treasury.

During the 1990 election, which Aristide won by an overwhelming majority, former U.S. President Jimmy Carter adjured Aristide to concede defeat before any of the votes had been counted—an interference still bitterly resented by Haitians.[16]

After a military coup—led by Haitian officers trained in the U.S.—overthrew Aristide in 1991, the U.S. did little to enforce a U.N. embargo, leaving the Haitian military and aristocrats who had fomented the coup free to travel back and forth between Miami and Port Au Prince, stocking up on luxuries.

The U.S. State Department, the CIA and Presidents Bush and Clinton were often working at cross-purposes when it came to restoring Aristide. While the presidents nominally supported the return of Aristide to power, the CIA funded FRAPH—the paramilitary organization that committed most of the violence during the Coup years. Bill Clinton made granting Haitian refugees asylum a part of his platform during the election. Once in office, he reneged on that commitment.

So yes, "our governments," that is, the government of the United States, was part of the problem.

7. Is it a situation for which we have people available who can imagine new ways of thinking nonviolently? Do we have people who can think fresh thoughts, develop ideas for actions that move things along in a stuck situation and leave a residue of hope?

Part of the reason that CPT worked with Bluntschli and Nicola had to do with their analysis of what needed to happen in order to bring about a just, democratic society in Haiti. After the Duvaliers left power in 1986, a bloody dechoukaj ("uprooting") took place in which the Haitian people killed Ton Ton Macoutes and other minions of the Duvaliers who had terrorized them. The Haitian elite and their supporters in the U.S. pointed to the dechoukaj as proof that poor Haitians were primitive savages, inca-

---

16. Kern was surprised to hear the team's translator in Jeremie speak with such venom of Carter when she compared him to Ronald Reagan in 1993. Even though Carter has a reputation among Americans as "the human rights president," people in Nicaragua and Haiti view him as yet one more U.S. president who thought he had the right to tell them how they should be governed. Haitians thus looked at Carter's efforts to forestall a U.S. military invasion of the island in 1994 with a jaundiced eye.

pable of governing themselves. The U.S. press repeatedly referred to about twenty-six "necklacings"—filling a tire with gasoline, putting it around the condemned person's neck and setting it on fire—of Duvalierists that occurred during Aristide's first eight months in office. (The subsequent slaughter of three to five thousand people by coup supporters did not receive anywhere near the same coverage.) Nicola and Bluntschli saw how an international violence-deterring presence might both provide protection for ordinary Haitians and throw a wrench into the cycle of violence, most of it blamed on the disenfranchised.

Later, the team in Jérémie was to find introducing "fresh" thoughts problematic, because the local hosts wanted CPTers simply to be present. Thus, the merits of solidarity versus the merits of Nonviolent Direct Action arose, beginning a tension that continues within project sites to this day.

8. *Can provision be made for coping with language barriers?*

Language was to prove a difficulty for the Haiti team.[17] Despite the fact that members of the team spent hours studying Creole each day, only one member of the initial team sent there achieved a conversational level of the language in the first month. As time passed, however, CPTers fluent in French joined the teams working in Jérémie, the Artibonite, and Port-au-Prince. This fluency naturally led to a facility in Creole.

9. *In the context of these considerations, does a process of prayer, Bible reading, and discernment give a sense of leading to enter the situation?*

Prayer and devotions have been a part of CPT Steering Committee meetings since 1986, so one could say that these spiritual disciplines have undergirded all decisions to authorize projects in various locations. Cliff Kindy, who served on the Crisis Intervention/Program task force at the time the Steering Committee gave the Haiti project its blessing, said that the work of Christians like the Bluntschlis and Ari Nicola in Haiti probably provided the biggest impetus for going to Haiti. "Our leading came

---

17. It has been a weakness in subsequent teams as well. Unlike Peace Brigades International, which requires volunteers to have language facility prior to working on a project, CPT has placed mostly English-only speakers on assignments, believing that international presence without language facility is better than no international presence at all. The Colombia team, on which Colombian nationals began serving in 2002, was the first to conduct meetings in the language of the country in which team members worked.

from their encouragement for us to be there," he told the author in an August 28, 2003, phone interview.

CRY FOR JUSTICE IN JÉRÉMIE

Prior to placing trained full-timers in Jérémie, CPT placed Joel Klassen with the Cry for Justice team there in the unfinished rectory of St. Helene.[18] St. Helene had been the first parish to nominate Aristide for the presidency in 1990 and so was a particular target for right-wing paramilitary violence.

Jérémie, whose residents claimed it was third or fourth largest population center in Haiti, is a coastal city lying at the top of horizontal leg of Haiti's backward L-shape. It briefly made world news in February 1993 when a ferry overloaded with eight hundred people en route from Jérémie to Port-au-Prince capsized, drowning four hundred. Archbishop Willi Romélus, an outspoken critic of the coup, had his gated residence in Jérémie. At the time that Cry for Justice set up its two-month presence there, Father Samedi, the priest of St. Helene, was living in the manse because of threats on his life.

Three political murders in the neighborhood occurred in the fall of 1993. Jean-Claude Dimanche was a local Aristide supporter who played his radio loud enough for the surrounding houses to hear as a form of resistance to the coup's status quo (the radio at that time was the only source of news in Jérémie). FRAPH members had come to his house several times before, and he had jumped out of his window into the ocean to escape. But in October, around the time of the Harlan County fiasco (see above), he came to the door. The FRAPH gang dragged him into the street and shot him.

Bob Bartel, who had joined the CPT Steering Committee in 1993, and Klassen were in the rectory the night an elderly couple that lived below the rectory was murdered. According to the local people, Madame

---

18. Klassen, who was to become a linchpin for the Jérémie project, had been in Haiti visiting a friend in December 1992 and was staying at the guesthouse that Ron and Carla Bluntschli were running under the auspices of MCC. When he heard that a CPT delegation was coming to Haiti the same month, he called the Chicago office and asked if he could join. After Klassen returned to Canada, he was looking for a way to get back to Haiti, and thus jumped at the opportunity when Stoltzfus asked him to be part of the CFJ team in Jérémie. Klassen would go through CPT training in 1998 as a reservist. Interview, July 21, 2003.

and Monsieur Elwime had refused to sell their land to Pastor Bonhomme, a particularly vicious FRAPH leader, and he had them killed.

Because Cry for Justice and members of the St. Helene community strongly discouraged participants from going out at night, Klassen, Bartel and the other Cry for Justice participants remained inside.[19] The next day, Klassen and Bartel, went to investigate and found the body of Madame Elwime in the culvert below the rectory. Her killers had cut a hand off, carved a "Z" onto her belly and left the mutilated corpse in a place where community members would see it when they went to fill their water buckets. Neighbors later found Monsieur Elwime's body washed up on the beach. [20]

Klassen and Ed Kinane, from Peace Brigades International (PBI), became the longest serving Cry for Justice volunteers in Jérémie during the

---

19. This decision not to intervene clearly still troubled Klassen more than ten years later during a July 21, 2003 phone interview with Kern. In a follow-up e-mail on November 27, 2004, Klassen responded to her question about what he might have done differently, in hindsight, after having served with CPT for a number of years:

> ... after learning more about the situation, and having been with CPT, I/ we probably would have been much more willing a) to go out there that night b) to have already experimented with some kind of night routine that might have had an influence on events. What that influence would have been, is, of course, impossible to tell ...
>
> How do I feel? Kind of sick, wondering if M. and Mme. Elwime might have lived had we done something more, and even if, perhaps, their deaths were somehow related to our presence in the presbytery. This last is personal speculation. I don't recall thinking it at the time, nor do I recall anyone else bringing up the possibility. On the other hand, I think it's always very important to weigh the tendency that I and a lot of CPTers have to be "little Messiahs" going around and saving people. I think it's important to underline that in St. Elen in general, especially up on the hill, FRAPH was pretty loathe to come. Whenever they tried anything, the residents, mostly the young men, and some women, responded—often for example, throwing showers of rocks on roofs to make a thundering noise and alert everyone in the neighbourhood, which at least on two occasions (one being Avner Joseph's abduction) succeeded in inducing the FRAPH to flee.

20. In an August 27, 2003 e-mail to the author, Bartel wrote, "During the time we were there, the woman's husband was not found. People speculated then that he would not be found. The murders happened between the time the United Nations personnel were evacuated from Jérémie and Haiti and before FRAPH realized that CPT had not left the town." He also noted that Bonhomme's people had tried to drag the couple off their property several times before, but neighbors had always intervened to help them. He speculated that this time they were just too afraid to help.

autumn of 1993.[21] Their primary work involved hosting CFJ delegations. However, the two were able to intervene on November 27, 1993, when FRAPH members kidnapped Abner Joseph, a hearing- and visually-impaired adolescent who had not heard their command to leave the steps of the rectory (a favorite place for other disabled and indigent people to spend time). Klassen challenged them, asking where they were taking the young man. When they said they were going to a meeting, Klassen said, "It looks like someone doesn't want to go with you." The abductors then fled with their captive down the hill, brandishing pistols. Abner Joseph's mother ran after him. She told the Cry for Justice volunteers later that the FRAPH members beat her to the ground several times before they reached their headquarters in downtown Jérémie, about a mile away.

Kinane and the other CFJ volunteers joined Klassen in the street and proceeded quickly to the cazerne (a military base) to ask for the army's intervention. The officer in charge said he could not intervene unless the volunteers supplied him with a name. He then asked why they should be concerned with a mere Haitian.

While one volunteer ran back to find out the name of the young man whom FRAPH had kidnapped, the others gathered outside the FRAPH Headquarters near the cazerne with a gathering crowd of Haitians. A man approached them and introduced himself, in well-spoken English, as Wilner Guerrier, "a delegate of the Prime Minister," (former de facto minister Marc Bazin, to whose presidential campaign the U.S. had contributed large sums of money in the hope that he would beat Aristide). He offered to go to the FRAPH headquarters and seek Abner's release.

Klassen, Kinane, and Sister Anita von Wellsheim[22] accompanied the delegé to the FRAPH headquarters, where men inside screamed at them and Pastor Bonhomme menaced the three *blans* with a knife. As FRAPH members threatened the delegé, he repeatedly said, "We can't let the foreigners see us acting this way." Kinane said in his write-up of the event that the delegé seemed fearless.

When ordered to do so, Klassen, Kinane, and Sister Anita went outside, leaving the delegé alone with the FRAPH members. Ten to twenty men stood between them and the door to the office, trying to intimidate

21. Kinane would later serve with the Iraq Peace Team, under whose auspices CPT also worked prior to and during the U.S. invasion of Iraq in 2003.

22. Von Wellsheim, a Sister of the Sacred Heart, represented Pax Christi in the CFJ coalition.

the internationals and cursing Father Samedi. One man sidled up to them to make sure they saw the pistol protruding from his pocket.

Eventually the delegé came out of the office with Abner, who appeared to be in shock. He had a large lump on his jaw and his left arm was bruised and dangling. Later, he told team members that when the delegé came into the office, the FRAPH members had thrown a noose over a rafter and were preparing to hang him.[23] The CFJ participants demonstrated the violence-deterring power of international accompaniers working in coordination with local Haitians. The day after Abner was rescued, November 28, 1993, Father Samedi celebrated a 6:30 a.m. Mass in his parish for the first time in three months.[24]

In a report evaluating Cry for Justice's ten-week presence in Jérémie, Ed Kinane wrote that he, Klassen, and other volunteers who came for shorter periods had fulfilled CFJ's mandate by providing a sense of security for the people of St. Helene, especially after the OAS human rights observers had left.

Of the "weak points" that Kinane listed, "poor communications" would later be one of CPT's Jérémie team's most difficult hurdles as well. Because of the oil embargo, the electricity needed to run the phone system was not available, although it worked sporadically during the time that Klassen and Kinane were there. Thus, reports and press releases that Kinane and Klassen wrote never reached the CFJ coordinators in Port-au-Prince. Nor did the CFJ committee in Port-au-Prince choose to send messages explaining budget details, staff changes, or other items of important information with the delegates who were constantly cycling in and out of Jérémie. Finally, CFJ abruptly shut down because of dissension in the coordinating committee, even though the team in Jérémie sent a report stressing the importance of their presence shortly after Abner Joseph was almost killed.[25]

---

23. Kinane, "Cry for Justice in Haiti," 224–25.

24. Puleo's article, "A Bishop Who Hears the Cry of Haiti's Poor," describes the attack on Samedi's parishioners during a Mass that led to his taking up residence in Bishop Romélus' manse. See also ibid., 226.

25. Kinane, "Cry for Justice in Haiti," 226. More details on issues raised in Kinane's chapter can be found in his "Project Evaluation: Cry for Justice, Jérémie." See also CPT Haiti, "Jérémie Final Report."

JÉRÉMIE: THE FIRST CPT PROJECT

In November 1993, CPT sent Cole Arendt[26] and Miriam Maik, freshly
out of the first training, to provide press support for Cry for Justice. Lena
Siegers and Kathleen Kern joined Maik and Arendt at the beginning of
December 1993. Ten days later, the four of them traveled to Jérémie—
approximately two hundred miles and a thirteen-hour drive—from Port-
au-Prince.

According to Arendt, Bluntschli and Nicola, who lived in Port-au-
Prince, decided Jérémie was the best location for the Corps members,
because Klassen had already established a connection between St. Helene
and CPT there, and because of the direct invitation from Father Samedi.
When CPT ended its presence in St. Helene in February 1995, Nicola said
he would never forget the moment when he and Bluntschli arrived with
Maik, Arendt, Kern, and Siegers at the rectory in Jérémie. "Joel was in
Jérémie, but nobody knew when we would be coming and the neighborhood was waiting with baited breath, afraid that they might be left alone
before the others came," Bluntschli wrote for Nicola in a reflection paper
about the end of the CPT project. "As we drove into town in the dark,
the word passed from person to person that replacements had come and
people ran alongside the truck as we wound our way up to the Presbytery.
There was such a clamor when we arrived that we were almost thrown
into the air because of so much relief and happiness."[27]

The day after Siegers, Kern, Maik, and Arendt arrived, soldiers detained Jean-Role Jean Louis, a young man who had translated for CFJ in
Jérémie and whom Bluntschli arranged to serve as a translator for CPT
in Jérémie. Jean Louis was accompanying the newcomers on a tour of
Jérémie, when a corporal dressed in civilian clothing demanded to know
why he was hanging out with the *blans*. When Jean Louis told him it was
none of his business, the corporal pulled a gun on him and ordered him
to go to the cazerne. The CPTers and Kinane held on to the translator
physically as he told them under his breath, "Don't leave me alone." As it
happened, the delegé, who had intervened on behalf of Abner Joseph, was
in the commander's office when they got there. He assured them that Jean

26. When Arendt married in 1995, he changed his name to Hull. At his request, he
will be referred to as Arendt in this and the next chapter and as Hull for CPT work he
participated in after 1995.

27. CPT Haiti, "Closing Week."

Louis was perfectly safe. Noting their hesitation, the delegé, visibly annoyed, asked, "Don't you trust me?" Kinane and the CPTers, said they did, not quite truthfully, and Jean Louis went in alone. Ultimately, the delegé was able to negotiate Jean Louis's release, after adjuring him and the corporal who had arrested him for "insolence" to shake hands.

Kinane concluded his report of the incident with, "Freeing Jean-Role was the new team's baptism of fire, a fine orientation to Jérémie . . . and to the power and ambiguities of accompaniment."[28]

This fire quickly spluttered out as the team began a more mundane daily routine. Initially, the team in St. Helene began every morning with devotions and a meeting, although at times this morning meeting was more or less abandoned (depending on the theological predispositions of the team). The team would then separate and go visiting throughout the community of St. Helene. They accumulated information about military and paramilitary activity during these visits and would make a point of visiting the areas in which this activity occurred.

When Haitians in Jérémie told the team about significant human rights abuses, team members wrote reports and sent them to Nicola and Bluntschli via various people traveling to Port-au Prince.[29] Bluntschli in turn distributed them to various human rights agencies. Eventually people began coming to the team with stories of human rights abuses they wanted documented.

Generally, the pace of life in Jérémie was slow. Probably the most dramatic event to happen in the first six months of the project was the "bat teneb."

At noon on February 7, 1994, the bells of the downtown cathedral in Jérémie began to chime as usual, but were soon drowned out by the noise of dozens of people banging on pots, pans, and the tin roofs of their houses.

That morning, Jean Louis had told the team that people would be participating in a "bat teneb"—or "beating away the shadows"—all across Haiti that day. Bat teneb has a long tradition as a form of social protest in Haiti. February 7, 1994, marked the third anniversary of Aristide's inau-

---

28. Kinane, "Cry for Justice in Haiti," 231–32.

29. Sometimes these couriers delivered the information to Bluntschli and Nicola and sometimes they did not. The trip to Port-au-Prince required a thirteen-hour ride in a bus over the mountains or about the same amount of time in the ferry.

guration and the people of St. Helene chose to perform a bat teneb as a call for Aristide's return.

The CPTers walked through the neighborhood to see how many people would pick up their pots. They were disappointed that the pot banging, with a few people shouting, "Viva Aristide" and "Down with the coup d'état" lasted for a minute or less.

But they understood why when two hours later, ten heavily armed Haitian soldiers gathered outside the rectory compound. Siegers, Maik, Kern, and Joel Klassen (who had rejoined the team in January) approached the heavy metal gate. As they did so, a soldier with grenades hanging from his belt dashed to the side—SWAT-team style—and covered them with his automatic rifle. The officer in charge told the team that someone had reported that several Haitians had been standing on the roof of the rectory, banging drums and generally disturbing the peace.

"What is the purpose of the people who were making that noise?" the interrogating soldier asked in Creole, "Are you satisfied with what they did?"

"It is not for us to be satisfied or dissatisfied with what they did," replied Klassen. He then pointed out that no one in the neighborhood seemed disturbed by the noise. After further dialogue, the military person said, "Give a message to the people who made this noise. If they do this again, they will be arrested, and you will be arrested, too."

The military and CPT members concluded their conversation with both parties claiming to be working for peace. The soldiers departed, accompanied by two members of FRAPH.

Most of the releases written between February and September 1994 reflected the team's sense of helplessness as they watched the Haitians around them go hungry and die of diseases that a few dollars' worth of antibiotics could have cured. A litany read during Mass at St. Helene's church on August 18, 1994, the feast day of St. Helene, captures well the sense of despair felt by the residents and the CPTers living among them:

HAITIAN PRAYER FOR DELIVERANCE
ON THE FESTIVAL DAY OF ST. HELENE

RT: Lord God, we Haitians are worn out. We are exhausted. Reach out your hand to help us.

LT: Lord God, we are out of breath. See how we suffocate under the hand of these evil ones.

L: Great Master, we're worn out under "the big shots." Thirty-four months of coup d'état means thirty-four months of hell.

The country has become a slaughterhouse. Like water in a river, they make the people's blood flow. Dogs and pigs never stop singing the funerals of the poor. The nations around us never cease toying with us.

ALL: Have pity on us, O God, we are out of breath.

L: O God, we are worn out beneath all these lies and treachery.

Don't you see these assassins, these bandits, these smooth talking opportunists who are finishing off the country?

They kill your children!

They fill their pockets with the nation's money.

They profit from the embargo and stash away stacks of bills while employees and schoolteachers go unpaid.

ALL: Have mercy on us, O God, come deliver us.

L: O God, we are out of breath.

We're exhausted under two cups of sugar at 42 cents.[30]

We're exhausted under one cup of rice at 12 cents.

We're exhausted under two cups of flour at 15 cents.

We're exhausted under a half cup of oil at 21 cents.

To buy a half-cup of gas, you have to pay 48 cents.

ALL: O God, how far is this going to go? We are worn out.

L: O God, our old houses are falling apart.

If you don't have money, you can't buy a tin sheet for your roof.

Port-au-Prince has become a foreign country.

If you don't have money, you can't get on the boat or the bus.

ALL: O God, say something to us. Come quickly, deliver us.

L: O God, look in the faces of your young men and women.

This year 18,000 students wrote their graduating exams.

Is there any university to receive them?

30. 1 Haitian gourde = 6 cents U.S.

What work will they be able to do, O God?

Please answer us. Who is the future of our country?

ALL: O God, hurry, bring us help.

L: O God, de facto governments come and go.

They are skilled in stealing and killing for any reason. The leaders of the church are more at ease with these criminals than with a popular, honest government. They give permission to stealing, raping and killing. The chalice from which they drink their wine is full of the people's blood.

ALL: O God, we are worn out under their over-indulged hands.

RT: O God, you are not an overlord on the earth, a leader who crushes, a leader who commands without respecting the liberty of others.

LT: You are a servant, a pastor, a leader who gives life so that all may have life.

RT: Teach us how to love like your child, Jesus Christ, with a love that removes all evildoing, all vengeance all hypocrisy.

ALL: Please, dear God, pour out a flood of love on all of Haiti, on each Haitian.

LT: If we are tired of evil, it's because we are thirsty for love, justice, and harmony.

ALL: Please, God, restore these things again, and we will praise and adore you. Amen, Amen, Alleluia![31]

Fast for Life

As months passed, the team became increasingly distraught by the hunger and anxiety they saw taking hold of the people among whom they worked. Weeks went by without the ability to contact Bluntschli or Nicola via a ham radio supplied by a helpful religious order in Jérémie. Father Samedi likewise did not often make himself available to the team for con-

---

31. CPTnet, "Haitian Prayer for Deliverance on the Festival Day of St. Helen's," Aug 18, 1994. The CPT Chicago office sought to connect its constituency with conditions in Haiti by asking them to fast. In the Winter 1994 *Signs of the Times*, CPT encouraged people to join in the Haiti Hunger for Justice Fast sponsored by the Campaign to keep Haiti Alive. Organizers were looking for four thousand people to fast—one for every person murdered during the coup. According to a CPTnet posting on February 27, 1994, at least 150 CPT constituents joined the four team members working in Haiti in fasting for various lengths of time.

sultation. When Kathy Kelly, a veteran peace activist who had helped train the first CPT group, suggested the team do a fast and vigil in the public square in Jérémie and Samedi offered a tepid approval of the plan, the team decided to proceed.[32]

On July 29, 1994, the team began a weeklong fast in Jérémie's central plaza.[33] The four-member team, consisting of Kelly, Kern, Siegers, and Janet Shoemaker walked to the plaza across from the cathedral as early morning Mass was ending. They carried a large cross and a sign that said in Creole, "We are fasting for peace, for the defense of life and against violence." People coming from Mass, having heard about the fast from the priest, walked up to the team and expressed support.

In a statement distributed to government authorities and religious communities prior to the vigil and to those passing by during the vigil the team wrote, "Like you, we have watched with dismay the growing hunger in Haiti. We long for an end to the suffering. We look to our Christian tradition of fasting and prayer to help us identify with the suffering of our Haitian friends. We remember especially Jesus' love for children."

An hour and a half later, members of the Haitian military ordered the group to vacate the premises and to appear with their passports at military headquarters. On their way to the cazerne, CPT members held up their cross and their sign to give people a chance to see it. Chief of Police Rigaud kept them waiting for two hours before an underling ushered them into an office for interrogation.

In the presence of other military and paramilitary leaders, Rigaud sent the passports to an immigration official for inspection. The interrogators said that the words "Peace" and "Violence" on the sign were political and that under Article 56 of the Haitian constitution, foreigners were not allowed to participate in Haitian politics. Throughout the ensuing discussion, Rigaud kept calling out "Larús!" and team members thought he was

32. When Carla Bluntschli finally found out about the fast, she said she would have counseled against it, because it was the job of the team to wait and follow the lead of the people among whom they lived. However, the team had not been able to contact her for weeks at that point.

33. In an August 5, 1994 release about the fast (CPTnet "Peacemaker Team Challenged by Soldiers in Vigil") the team noted that they were participating in the fast as an alternative to "National Macoute Day." The Ton Ton Macoutes had been a paramilitary organization that violently enforced the commands of the Duvaliers' military dictatorship. By 1993–1994, FRAPH had more or less taken over that function, but Haitians referred to anyone who sympathized with the coup regime as a "macoute." For further information on Macoutes and Macoute Day, see Danner, "Beyond the Mountains II."

summoning some sort of aide, until a soldier appeared with the Larousse French-English dictionary. Noting that the dictionary said that "violence" was an undue use of force, the commander said that therefore "violence" was a political word.

Other men in the room told the women that there was no violence in Jérémie. When team members described hearing of rapes as a form of intimidation and seeing people getting beaten in St. Helene, the military and paramilitaries insisted that such affairs did not concern internationals. They threatened to deport CPT members if they held another public prayer vigil. Commander Rigaud kept interrupting Lena Siegers as she tried to explain the team's motives and purpose. Later, after the team thought it through, and after they discovered that Rigaud was not unsympathetic to the work of the team, they suspected he had interrupted Siegers to protect the team.[34]

The group continued the fast for a full week without their signs, maintaining a daily silent vigil in the town plaza. They told passersby who attempted to engage them in conversation that the military had said they could not speak about their witness, assuming that many of the people who asked were military informants.

The U.S. Invasion

A week after the fast, as talk of a U.S. invasion of Haiti gained momentum in Washington, the team sent a letter to President Bill Clinton, urging him to publicly express support for Aristide and questioning his plan to retrain the Haitian military and police. Rather than empower one group of Haitians to use threat and force against their own people, the team wrote,

> Why not instead invest in training people to rebuild and vastly improve Haiti's battered infrastructure? Why not rely on unarmed international peacekeepers to maintain order during a period of transition and concentrate massive aid to help create jobs for Haitians. There are innumerable needs to be met, rebuilding roads, homes, schools and clinics. Why not promote literacy, reforestation, building co-operatives and efforts to teach people their legal

---

34. An aide to Father Samedi reported that Rigaud had said he was "ashamed and embarrassed" that the *blans* in St. Helene had been doing the job of the police, i.e., providing security for the people of Jérémie in the previous months. For an approximate quotation, see Sidebar, *Signs of the Times*.

rights? (Haiti would not be the only country in Latin America and the Caribbean without a military. A successful precedent for disbanding an armed force has already been set in Costa Rica.)[35]

This letter to Clinton reflected the team's paradoxical feelings regarding an impending U.S. military invasion of Haiti. Because of the long history of U.S. intervention, most Haitians felt a sense of revulsion at the prospect of yet another invasion. But as the embargo tightened, starvation spread, and people were killed for merely mentioning Aristide's name many Haitians began to see an invasion as the lesser of two egregious evils. As one friend of the team told them, "It is better for my neck to be under the U.S. boot than under the boot of Cedras."

U.S. constituents of CPT also found themselves in a paradoxical position. The right-wing element in the congress was arguing against military intervention, using some of the same arguments that pacifists have made against military interventions in other countries, while members of the Congressional Black Caucus and other congress people who had a record of sensitivity to human rights were arguing in favor of the military invasion.[36]

Every night during that long summer of 1994, the team in Haiti listened to Voice of America (VOA) for indications of when the U.S. military would arrive. Several times they heard the invasion was imminent and then called off for one last round of diplomatic efforts. Sometimes

35. CPTnet, "Haiti: An Open Letter to President Bill Clinton," Aug 19, 1994. The actual letter was dated August 4, 1994.

36. The CPT Chicago office sought to shift the discussion from military and political solutions to spiritual solutions, as demonstrated in this CPTnet post:

NATIONAL DAY OF PRAYER FOR HAITI: AUGUST 30, 1994

Prayer for a just and non-violent return for Aristide is so urgently needed.

On Tuesday August 30th, we invite Christians across the nation to gather for intercessory prayer for Haiti. Many of us will be fasting as well.

Local Organizers Are Needed. Each organizer should arrange a place, set a time, and contact people through local churches and peacemaking organizations. As well, the local representative to Congress should be invited to attend.

Even if no one is able to organize such a gathering, invite a few friends to set aside time for prayer (and fasting?) with you on that day. Where two or three are gathered . . .

they would go for more than a week without hearing anything about Haiti on VOA although it provided a daily update on the O. J. Simpson trial.

Not surprisingly, given the dearth of information, rumors abounded and the team sometimes had difficulty telling the difference between rumors and actual news.

On July 18, a week before the team embarked on their public fast, the following release appeared on CPTnet:

URGENT ACTION

Peasants in St. Helene, a neighborhood in the province of Jérémie, Haiti, anticipate that the local Haitian military will immediately attack them, should the U.S. invade Haiti. CPT's network should ask political representatives and journalists to inquire about what precautions the U.S. military would take, in the event of an invasion, to safeguard Haitian civilians.

Residents of St. Helene, Jérémie, believe that local commandants have orders to attack the neighborhoods sympathetic to President Aristide as soon as there is evidence of an invasion.

A gatekeeper at a church in one neighborhood claims "total war will break out because peasants will use machetes, knives and other tools to defend themselves against the automatic rifles and grenades of the Haitian (& possibly U.S.) Military."

Many people are aware that at least 6,000 Panamanians were killed during the Dec. 1989 U.S. invasion of Panama and that active neighborhoods suffered the most severe bombardment and bloodshed.

The situation in St. Helene may be typical of perceptions and expectations throughout Haiti. Please inform legislative and executive branch representatives of these fears arising from millions of Haitians at the grass roots. Congregations are encouraged to initiate letter writing and fax campaigns. Please communicate the ways in which you carry this out to CPT so that your creativity can encourage others.

The U.S. Special Forces landed in Port-au-Prince on September 19, 1994. Several days later, enormous black helicopters flew over Jérémie, looking for a place to land. Thus began a new chapter in the work of CPT-Haiti: intervening with and monitoring the behavior of US soldiers. This work would cause dissension within the team as members discussed how they should or should not engage the military.[37]

37. See the section below, "Relationships with the US Military."

Demonstration, September 30

On September 30, 1994, Haitians organized nationwide demonstrations to commemorate the estimated five thousand people murdered for political reasons since the 1991 coup. September 30 marked the date of the coup d'état that had sent Aristide into exile. In the days before the demonstration, patrols of soldiers from the US Special Forces began to come up to the rectory several times a day, asking for Father Samedi (who was usually not there, and when he was, refused to speak to them). When the team finally learned that the soldiers wanted to talk to Samedi about the demonstration, they told them that he was not in charge of organizing it, but that the team could introduce them to the people who were.

Someone from the rectory ran to fetch the demonstration's organizers. Obviously expecting to meet resistance, the officer in charge began the conversation by explaining why it was important for everyone to work together. The St. Helene organizers assured the Americans that they had things under control.

Not satisfied, the commander began to explain the things that could happen if the St. Helene people were not more forthcoming about certain details, such as the route of the demonstration . . .

"Oh," said one of the leaders of the parish. "You want to know the route. We're going to start in the church, make a right go down the road until we reach . . ."

Everyone visibly relaxed. The organizers began describing how they were going to monitor the parade to ensure that no violence would occur.

The American officers, for their part, told the St. Helene organizers that the Haitian military had said that the people of St. Helene were going to go on a rampage of indiscriminate killing and looting during the demonstration.

Everyone laughed. Then the church choir director said, "Well, we wanted to dump the [cement slab upon which the army and paramilitary units had performed ritual sacrifices] into the ocean. Is that looting? And we wanted to do the same to the one in the FRAPH compound."

Therein followed a twenty-minute discussion over whether dumping the slab on the wharf into the sea and destroying the slab in the FRAPH compound constituted looting. The Americans were about evenly divided in their thinking. Finally, the organizers from St. Helene and the military agreed that the one on the wharf was fair game and the one in the FRAPH compound was not. As the soldiers left, one who had talked to Kathleen Kern earlier in the week told her, "Now we know who the good guys are."

At the request of demonstration's organizers, Father Joachim Samedi initiated the march with a memorial Mass for the thousands of people killed by the military and its allies during the coup d'état. Into the same church—where two years earlier the Haitian military had fired tear gas canisters into the congregation and beaten worshippers—Father Samedi invited both Haitian and American troops to participate in the Mass. Two American soldiers and the commander of the Haitian troops accepted the invitation.

As part of his sermon, Samedi planted a machete with its blade pointing up on a chair and offered $1000 to anyone present who would dare to sit on the blade. When no one took him up on his offer, he explained that he was illustrating the Chinese proverb, which said power cannot rest on weapons. He said that the coup regime had attempted to rely on its arms for three years and had ultimately failed.

He ended his sermon with a call for the marchers to maintain discipline and not to allow themselves to be provoked into violence during the march. He asked to cultivate a spirit of forgiveness rather than vengeance.

From the Mass, the marchers followed a route that led through the downtown and eventually back to the church. They sang, danced, and shouted joyfully to the beat of drums. Some carried signs calling for Aristide's prompt return and the disarming of paramilitary civilians.

As the gradually swelling numbers of demonstrators wound their way through the streets of Jérémie, the people watching applauded and broke into spontaneous choruses of song and dance.

CPTers accompanied the march and facilitated communication between the demonstration's organizers and American troops both before and during the march.

An estimated five thousand Haitians participated. As he watched the returning demonstrators from the roof of the church, one of the organizers turned to Kern and said with emotion, "It's a beautiful thing." Of all the major population centers in Haiti that were venues for demonstrations on September 30, Jérémie alone had a demonstration in which no one was hurt.

The amity between the U.S. soldiers, the team, and the people of Jérémie did not last. Increasingly, when Haitians and CPTers reported on coup supporters who had caches of weapons, soldiers gave detached, non-committal answers. At times, they appeared to be working closely with the Haitian military and at other times, they seemed to want a closer relationship with the pro-Democracy activists.[38] In October, the Special Forces began extending special protection to FRAPH members in the community, despite the fact that Father Samedi had specifically told his parishioners, the victims of these thugs, not to take revenge. Seeing men who brutally abused and murdered people receiving such protection cast a pall on relations between the Haitians and the military—which grew worse when U.S. soldiers began arresting pro-Democracy advocates, including friends of the team, at the behest of the Haitian military and FRAPH members.

On November 24, the Haitian police, accompanied by Australian international police monitors, arrested Father Samedi, charging him with attempted murder, looting, and other crimes based on a complaint made by a known murderer with connections to the Haitian military. Joel Klassen was in the rectory at the time of the arrest and accompanied Samedi to the cazerne. About three thousand citizens of Jérémie gathered outside the military compound to show support for the priest. When Klassen and CPT reservist Duane Ediger tried to photograph the event, U.S. troops pushed them aside. One soldier threatened Klassen with deportation if he did not get out of their way.[39]

Father Samedi was held for one hour and then given a provisional release, which left him subject to prosecution at any time by a district attorney who was the local president of FRAPH. CPT put out an Urgent

---

38. The team was not imagining this erratic behavior. In *The Immaculate Invasion*, Bob Shacochis tells the story of the U.S. Special Forces who invaded Haiti, and how they had to slog through "a foggy, swamp-bottomed no-man's land the military calls OTW—operations other than war: an empty space in the army's traditional reality, where there are no friends and no enemies, no front or rear, no victories and likewise, no defeats and no true endings" (xv). He documents the contradictory orders the soldiers kept receiving: one day, Aristide was the democratically elected president and FRAPH were right-wing paramilitary thugs, but the next day, Aristide became a crazed communist and FRAPH became the loyal opposition.

39. Joel Klassen, e-mail, Feb 7, 2000. Klassen was responding to a request for information for the author's February 14, 2000 column in *Mennonite Weekly Review*. He noted in this e-mail that the Australian troops had been in town for only three days and did not know what was happening.

Action encouraging people to contact the State Department and the U.S. Ambassador to Haiti on Samedi's behalf.[40]

A still darker side of the U.S. Special Forces in Haiti showed itself in the Winter 1995 issue of *The Resister: The Official Publication of the Special Forces Underground*—a newsletter that catered to current and retired Special Forces operatives with far-right sympathies.

In an article titled, "Field Report: The Truth about Haiti," Richard Crossman asserted that FRAPH, responsible for assassinating more than one thousand Haitians, was analogous to the American Legion or Veterans of Foreign Wars in the United States. With pride, he noted that the Special Forces underground had helped FRAPH and Haitian military officers escape to the Dominican Republic. He described Aristide's Lavalas movement as follows:

> If every street gang, vagrant, opportunistic criminal welfare moocher, labor union agitator and unemployed layabout, homosexual, drug addict, ethnic tribalist and other assorted street garbage formed a loose political coalition; [sic] whose cadre consisted of high school and college "students" putting into practice the collectivist lessons of their teachers and professors; the leader of this organization was an insane TV evangelist; and this "movement" was lent legitimacy by some foreign government and received sympathetic coverage from the media; this, then, would define Aristide's Lavalas movement.

His article also referred to Christian Peacemaking [sic] Teams as "an organization with close ties to the Communist Party United States of America (CPUSA) and the Socialist Workers Party (SWP)," whom "Special Forces detachments were ordered by joint Special Operations Task Force . . . to render every assistance and support" when team members gave them information about weapons caches.[41] (If true, then the soldiers to whom the Jérémie team gave information were not following orders.)

End of the Jérémie Project

As the weeks passed after Samedi's arrest and release, local people increasingly asked the team in Jérémie to help support economic ventures. The

40. CPTnet, "Major Religious Leader in Jérémie Arrested," Nov 24, 1994.

41. Crossman, "Field Report: The Truth about Haiti," 9–11. CPT's Chicago office received the article as a fax from the International Liaison Office for President Jean-Bertrand Aristide, which had received it in late December 1994.

team concluded that St. Helene needed aid and development workers more than it needed violence deterrence. Joel Klassen, Rebecca Logan,[42] and Pete Begly, in consultation with Father Samedi, Carla Bluntschli, Ari Nicola, and the CPT Chicago office, decided it was time to end the project.[43]

Nicola and Bluntschli arrived from Port-au-Prince in late January 1995 to help shut down the project. They also collected testimonies from various people in Jérémie and St. Helene, who uniformly expressed disappointment that the team would leave while the U.S. Special Forces were still there and before the elections.

At an afternoon Mass intended to express thanksgiving for the CPT's presence, Father Toni, who had moved into the rectory in the late summer of 1995 along with Father Samedi, said,

> God would have us all live as one family and that is what CPT did. When Jesus was preaching and they said his brother and mother were outside asking for him, he said, "My mother and brother are those who do the will of God." CPT's presence helps us understand that there really isn't a thing called nationalism.

Samedi offered the following reflections:

> We felt we were in security—as though we had our own lawyers. Anywhere we were, they were there. If we were in prison, they were there. If we were in the FRAPH, they were there. Every night and every day, they were one with us. . . .
>
> We want to say thank you to God for them and say thank you to God with them. Now the time has come for them to leave, but they have marked us much, and I don't believe they'll forget us. I was saying a little while ago that if Joel has ambition for power, he

42. Logan was a friend of Klassen, and fluent in French, Spanish, and Creole.

43. In his "Memo to Program Committee and interested persons" on January 6, 1995 Stoltzfus noted the closing also had to do with Bluntschli and Nicola believing that the "overt repression" was almost over, at least for the time being. In his eighth point discussing the "new realities," Stoltzfus wrote:

> Finally, of course there is the possibility that we should jump in a van and go to Plains, Georgia to sit under the teaching of Gen. Raoul Cedras who according to reports is slated to come visit President Carter and teach his Sunday School class. [This comment referred to Carter's notorious praise of Cedras after he negotiated with him to relinquish his hold on power.] This is partly said with tongue in cheek and partly to help readers of this to remember the tenuous commitment to real justice in Haiti that so much of this international cheerleading brings to that situation.

could naturalize and become a Haitian and run as candidate for deputy or mayor and he would win....

We give this mission, this departure this family, this team and our lives, to God. We believe God is together with us. We give this to the mother Mary, into her hands to protect these traveler ... so that we may become even more in solidarity one with another.... As you leave, know that there are people that will never stop loving you, or thinking of you or praying for you.[44]

After Jérémie

Haitian friends and advisors encouraged CPT to continue its work in Haiti after learning of the decision to close down the Jérémie project. The ongoing military occupation by the U.S., the enormous number of firearms possessed by opponents of Aristide, and resistance to the prospect of genuine land reform all had the potential to foment violence. CPT therefore sponsored three short projects between 1995 and 1997:

- A full-time team in the Artibonite Valley from May 1995 to March 1996

- A mobile team that moved around the country in response to specific requests for justice-making and violence-reduction from various locales

- A four-month project related to the government's implementation of land reform in the Artibonite Valley and issues surrounding Haitian sweatshops

Monitoring the Justice System

Lena Siegers and CPT reservist Duane Ediger were the first two CPTers to set up in the Artibonite Valley, near the town of Ti Rivye where a corrupt judicial system had added to the systemic oppression of the peasants. In a letter to his supporters, Ediger mentioned in particular an eighteen-year-old woman who told them how a group of men involved in a land dispute had come into her house at midnight, made her and her nine brothers and sisters leave, and decapitated her father. Two of the men went to jail until they paid Judge Gerard Richard $200 to let them go.[45]

44. CPT Haiti, "Closing Week of CPT's long term presence," 3–4.
45. Duane Ediger, "Letter," 7.

Men called zenglendos perpetrated these sorts of attacks and were a central concern for all the remote mountain communities that Ediger and Siegers visited in the Artibonite region and the Northwest Department (province) of Haiti. In a letter to her supporters, Siegers related the story of one remote community begging the CPTers to come live with them, because if they did, "the zenglendos would run away." When Siegers asked who the zenglendos were, people told her, "The zenglendos live with us. They go to church with us. They wear masks at night. We cannot identify them." [46]

In a letter dated July 23, 1995, Siegers wrote that violent thefts by zenglendos were happening almost every night in Ti Rivye and the surrounding communities. One incident that Siegers found particularly distressing concerned a group of townspeople who caught three young zenglendos in the act of stealing and hacked them to death, leaving their bodies to rot in the street.

Siegers wrote,

> As I walked the streets this morning, I talked to many people about those three men who died. Many were happy they were dead. They said if they kept them alive, and put them in prison, the judge would release them after a few days and they would rob and kill again ... I pointed out that Jesus forgave his perpetrators [sic] while he was dying. One man said, "We can never be Jesus." ... I have no chance now to show charity. If we could have convinced the Judge to keep them in prison. [sic] If people could have brought them food and shown a forgiving spirit, maybe they could have changed and become better citizens and not rob any more.[47]

The team in the Artibonite, which Joel Klassen later joined, made a point of monitoring the judge whom the Haitians accused of going easy on zenglendos. The judge, Mereus Dorlisme, seemed to favor criminals who shared his political sympathies. Ediger, Klassen, and Siegers attended his court once a week and visited prisons. In an August 27, 1995, letter to her supporters, Siegers wrote,

> Three prisoners in one cell told me an interesting story. They said 3 [sic] prisoners from their cell had escaped mystically. They really

---

46. Siegers, letter, June 19, 1995. She added in the letter that she did not know if the people really were unaware of the identities of these violent thieves or just afraid to name them.

47. Siegers, letter, July 23, 1995.

believed that 3 men had miraculously escaped while they & the guards slept. Later, I questioned the 21 year old guard who holds the keys for all the prison cells. He repeated the Mystical story and when I suggested maybe someone used a key to open the door when everyone else was sleeping, he became agitated and insisted it was mystics that caused the escape.

Childeric is very young. He is a friend of judge Merius [*sic*]. He had been watching us ... Now he has keys given to him by the judge Merius. I will watch Childeric and Merius both. Maybe more prisoners will escape ... Maybe only those with money can escape mystically?

CPT has repeatedly passed on to U.S. and U.N. officials what it has heard: If the U.N. won't disarm criminals, the people will do it themselves. The U.N. has always expressed fear of disorder and abuses at the prospect of Haitian citizens carrying out their own disarmament, and some of these fears have been borne out. If they were more honest, though, the U.N. would admit their greater fear has been for their own safety. The U.S. has shown in word and deed that it does not want to break ties with traditional allies who have always ruled by force.[48]

Lena Siegers, Joanne Kaufman, and Beulah Shisler closed the Artibonite project in March 1996.

Mobile Teams

Before the Artibonite team disbanded, Siegers, Kaufman, and Carla Bluntschli wrote a proposal for a new mobile team project, to begin in April 1996. According to the proposal, a four- to five-person team would split in half, with one half traveling the countryside monitoring the justice system, documenting human rights abuses, and conducting informal nonviolence education seminars. The other half would live in Cite Soleil, Port-au-Prince's notorious slum, and provide a violence-deterring presence. Ari Nicola believed an additional benefit of these teams would be "demystifying *blans* [whites]" for the Haitians who hosted them, given that many believed they could not survive without aid donated by countries whose citizens were mostly of European heritage.[49]

A January 22, 1997, evaluation of the project noted that the team's work changed significantly from the tasks in the original proposal. The

48. Siegers, letter, Aug 27, 1995.
49. Kaufman, Comments on a draft of chap. 2; Kaufman, e-mail, Oct 4, 2004.

team scrapped the Cite Soleil project after people in the slum attacked a North American delegation that Bluntschli and Ari Nicola had brought there. Because of this incident, their chief contact said he would no longer accompany foreigners into Cite Soleil.

Siegers, Kaufman, Pierre Shantz, and Joshua Yoder continued to monitor courtrooms, prisons, and police in seven towns lying within the northern and western parts of Haiti. Some leaders of newly formed police riot squads/SWAT teams were former Haitian military officers, so the team's monitoring of the police gave people a greater sense of security.

The team also met with many "popular" groups, (the term used for grassroots organizations in Haiti), that talked to the team about changes needed in the education and health care systems. These groups were also concerned with international structures imposing painful economic regimens on Haiti. Haitians educating the team on these issues asked team members, in turn, to give input during human rights and nonviolence trainings.

Another function of these meetings was the collection of testimonies from people who had suffered under the coup regime. CPTers then visited the Justice Ministry, diplomats, and representatives of international organizations in Port-au-Prince to report what the peasants had told them. Joanne Kaufman describes listening to these testimonies as a "searing part of the work." Some of these testimonies included the following:

> "Big boots men killed my uncle. They shot him with a gun, in the river. He had a child overseas who sent money to us. The child died of grief."
>
> "No one here slept in their homes. When we left our houses, we put blankets under our arms. We took to the mountains—three and four of us at a time. We couldn't light matches. We had meetings out there. We each took a child and a mat under our arms. Ants ate our feet . . . The women became dry and thin. We didn't have time to make supper. We didn't talk out loud. Each person, in order not to die, paid money [to the authorities]."
>
> "When I was caught, I took beatings for three hours. My hands were tied behind my back. I was nearly senseless when they finished. The chief told me to stand. I could not, so he kicked me until I defecated and urinated on myself. I had a cow, a pig and a goat. Nothing remains. The cow was sold to free me."[50]

50. Kaufman, "From the 'Violence of the Stick,' to the 'Violence of the Stomach,'" 109–10.

In a November 13, 1996, meeting, team members realized that their focus had shifted significantly from violence reduction to education and addressing economic violence. The shift made certain team members uneasy. However, Haitians told them that their visits to peasants were "revolutionary" and "unique." Nicola expressed embarrassment when the team returned from a trip to Dondon in the north. "You did work we as Haitian leaders should be doing—educating and talking with our people," he said.[51]

Government Land Reform in the Artibonite and Factory Issues in Port-Au-Prince

Because Haitian contacts had expressed fears that violence would erupt as the government continued its land reform process, CPT sent another team to Haiti in 1997. From February 26 to June 27, Shantz and Yoder monitored the government's land reform program, observed parliamentary and local elections, and encouraged international support for assembly factory workers in Port-au-Prince. The project's original emphasis on violence reduction "quickly proved to be inappropriate to a situation evolving quite peacefully," wrote Shantz and Yoder in a June 24, 1997 report. Although the team listened to Haitians expressing fears of violence during their visit to Artibonite villages, no incidents of violence around the issue of land reform occurred during the four months that Yoder and Shantz were there.

This lack of violence also led the two-man team to take on other projects, such as monitoring elections in Jérémie and supporting sweat-shop workers in Port-au-Prince.

The election in Jérémie was an uncomfortable experience for Yoder, Shantz, and the delegation they led. They went to Port-au-Prince to become certified as observers, but received no training in how to monitor the election. They received no further training in Jeremie, as they had hoped they would. When they arrived in Jérémie, the delegation was divided between polling stations, with Yoder and Shantz remaining in the main office of the electoral council.

The people running the election office belonged to KOREGA—an organization of the pro-Democracy activists who had been primary contacts for the Jérémie team in 1993–1994. The votes that one of their

---

51. CPT Haiti, "Evaluation of Mobile Teams in Haiti Project."

candidates received exceeded the number of people living in the candidate's district, but even with those ballots thrown out, KOREGA won that election. In an August 30, 2003, phone interview, Yoder reflected that perhaps their team and delegation should have monitored an election in a community with which CPT had less emotional connection.

CPT's final Haiti-related campaign developed as a result of the mobile teams' work on the issue of sweatshops in Port-au-Prince. The team focused particularly on the Classic Apparel factory, which assembled clothing bearing trademarked Disney characters such as Pocahontas. In spite of intimidation by factory guards, Classic Apparel workers were asking for a raise from $2.25 a day to $4.68 a day. (At the time, a gallon of rice was selling for $1.87 and transportation to and meals at the factory cost $1.85.) CPT put out a pamphlet/church bulletin insert entitled "Disney: Pass the Bread! Let's Share with the Global Family," that encouraged its constituents to send a post card to Michael Eisner, Disney's CEO and hold public witnesses at Disney stores. The pamphlet included worship resources for people to use at these public witnesses. During the 1997 Mennonite Church Conference and the 1998 Church of the Brethren Conference in Orlando, Florida, CPT conducted daily prayer vigils at the convention center and outside Disney World.

Connections they made with Haitian sweatshop workers led Shantz and Yoder to broaden the focus of the project to include economic injustice arising from World Bank and IMF-imposed restructuring programs. Shantz and Yoder noted at the end of the June 1997 report that the broadening of the team's focus caused a loss of direction. "The team concluded that it is better to start from a clear focus on specific issues such as land reform or assembly factories and then show how larger issues of economic injustice tie in to the team's work."

On a positive note, the report records that Yoder and Shantz were able to connect Peace Brigades International and the National Coalition for Haitian Rights with people working for land reform in the town of Desdunes. The report recommended a follow-up presence of two CPTers to start in August or September 1997 to monitor land reform progress during harvest time, report on the struggle of factory workers, and "illuminate connections" between the challenges faced by rice farmers of the

Artibonite, factory workers in Port-au-Prince, and economic policies of international banking concerns. [52]

With projects in Hebron, Ontario, and Washington DC working on more immediate responses to violence, no personnel were available for Haiti. CPT's presence in Haiti came to an end when Shantz and Yoder left the country.

Delegations

Throughout the 1994–1997 period, CPT continued to send delegations to Haiti so that participants could report on the evolving political situation under the coup and the subsequent U.S. and U.N. occupation. Ironically, delegates spending ten to twelve days in Haiti on the tours organized by Bluntschli and Nicola sometimes returned to the states with a broader view of what was happening in the country than people working on the projects in Jérémie and the Artibonite. Team members generally were living in isolated communities that had few means of communication with Port-au-Prince and news was passed about in the form of rumors.

The report from the June 8–19, 1996, delegation covered the main issues facing post-coup Haiti—economic privatization, disarmament, justice for victims of the coup, and coerced forgiveness—and tied them in with the biblical witness for CPT's church constituency. Regarding the last issue, John Sherman and Pierre Gingerich wrote,

> Under the guise of pardon and reconciliation, poor Haitians are being asked to forget the injustices done them during the 1991–1994 era of Army-FRAPH terror. As Christians, we believe that this is wrong. The United States government, in particular, continues to stand in the way of prosecuting torturers like Emmanuel Constant (who, fortunately, still faces the civil lawsuit of a woman whose limbs were sawed off in a FRAPH torture chamber). Impunity for murderers, many of them apparently hired by the United States is a foundation for future abuses in Haiti and is unworthy of the sheep's clothing of "reconciliation." True reconciliation means healed relationships in which the abusive behavior of the few will not occur again. This is our prayer for Haiti and the purpose of our work."[53]

52. CPT Haiti, "Report on Activities February 26–June 27 [1997]."

53. "Report of the CPT Delegation to Haiti, June 8–19, 1996." CPT also sent a delegation to Washington, DC in May 1994 to lobby congress members and the State Department about the need for the US to support people working for justice in Haiti

ISSUES ARISING FROM HAITI PROJECT

Working in Coalition with Cry for Justice

Much about the Cry for Justice coalition was dysfunctional, although it did offer some measure of protection for Haitians in various parts of the country during its three-month existence. The fact that Bluntschli and Nicola (among others in the coalition) were in conflict with Nadja Papillon, who appointed herself leader of the CFJ, meant that CPTers Maik and Arendt were drawn into the conflict as well.[54] Additionally, CFJ left unpaid bills when it disbanded. Father Samedi had bought a refrigerator for the rectory, in anticipation that income generated by Cry for Justice delegations would cover the cost.[55] When CFJ disbanded he was not reimbursed for the appliance and may have had other expenses left unpaid as well. After he moved back into the rectory in the late summer of 1994, he began charging CPT $15 per person per day for room and board, and some on the team speculated that he hoped to recoup the expenses that CFJ had failed to reimburse.

The Cry for Justice experience made CPT more cautious about entering into future coalitions.

Incorporating Non-CPTers into the Team

A related issue involved working with people not connected with CPT who wanted to be part of the Jérémie team. At the time the project in Jérémie began, only seven people had completed training, and three of them were reservists, so CPT needed other people to keep the project going. Joel Klassen would not go through training until 1998, but had strong grounding in nonviolent theory and practice, connections to Mennonite churches, and a general willingness to abide by CPT policies. Kathy Kelly, an activist friend of the Gene Stoltzfus and Kryss Chupp, had led a significant chunk of the first training and trainings to follow. Janet Shoemaker, who went through training in 1997, also had an affinity for CPT work when she joined the team in the summer of 1994.

---

rather than FRAPH and the Haitian military. CPTnet, Kern, "CPT Delegation Finishes 3-Day Lobbying Effort in Washington," May 28, 1994.

54. Arendt, interview, June 20, 2003.

55. He thought that North Americans might need a refrigerator for their comfort. However, since the electricity did not function for most of the time the team was in Jérémie, team members used it mostly for storage.

However, others who joined the team in Jérémie did not feel bound by CPT policies on issues such as providing economic aid, nonviolence, or living a Christian lifestyle.[56] One of these coworkers disparaged the principle underlying violence-deterring presence, i.e., "effective racism"— a principle that the organization itself rejected a decade later. In future years, others who had not gone through CPT training would join teams on various project locations—sometimes because they had language facility the team lacked or a strong background in working with grassroots organizations—but the Chicago office and others on the team screened people wanting to join teams more carefully.

Perception of the Jérémie Team being "Owned" by Father Samedi

CPT Reservist Rey Lopez, who had actively worked in Filipino social justice movements, identified the phenomenon of being "Samedi's *blans*" as one of the Jérémie team's chief difficulties. Because Father Samedi had invited the team to Jérémie, members felt that they needed to consult with him before taking any significant action. However, he often did not show up for appointments the team made with him, which left the team unsure how to proceed. Lopez felt that if the team had not been so clearly identified with Samedi, team members would have had more freedom to talk with members of the Haitian military and FRAPH, which would have enabled them to do more active strategizing and direct interventions.[57]

56. Of course, as will be noted later, almost everyone eventually broke this rule, but CPTers understood why the policy was important and usually regretted offering handouts later.

57. In an October 29, 2003 e-mail to the author, Lopez wrote:

"I befriended a sergeant with the military who always beat people with his stick for no reason at all; who had limited facilities with English. I was made aware of the fears of the Haitian military, that is when the people got organized they will be killed in a dejouke or uprooting so they have always to beat them up so that they will not have time to organize a dejoukaj. When I shared this friendship with the team, the team consulted a certain woman who was the confidant of Fr. Samedi . . . who advised us not to develop any kind of relationship with the other side since this may give the wrong signal to the people who were being oppressed by the Haitian military. The team made a decision that out of respect to our host Fr. Samedi who was providing us with a place to stay, we should not develop any kind of contacts other than provided by Fr. Samedi's group . . . In retrospect, I think it was a mistake to be solely dependent on one contact or group of contacts of the same

In later projects, the teams would have a more diverse group of people and organizations to which they felt accountable at their locations. They would also intentionally make contacts with people working within oppressive power structures.

Relationships with Other Church Organizations

CPT's mandate sets it apart from most Christian missionary, relief, and development enterprises. In Haiti, CPT's mandate actually brought them into conflict with more traditional church organizations. Most of the Catholic religious orders in Jérémie were avowedly apolitical and clearly did not want to discuss the political situation with the team, although team members sensed a general sympathy among the nuns for the violence-deterring work they were doing. (The team had an especially warm relationship with the Missionaries of Charity who appreciated their coming to rock abandoned babies in the afternoons.) The American evangelical missionary in town, like many other evangelical missionaries in Haiti, had strong reservations about Aristide because he was a Catholic priest. Rightly or wrongly, most of the Jérémie team's Haitian acquaintances believed that the missionary worked with the CIA, so the team had to be cautious about interactions with him.[58]

Of more concern were the disagreements the team had with Mennonite Central Committee's country coordinators in Port-au-Prince,

---

political leanings since it limited our ability to do broader networking for peace and result in incestuous political relationship. I admit that we must be clear on whose side we are with, that is with the small guys, but dialogue is basic tool in peacemaking and to a large extent our complete dependence on Fr. Samedi for our living arrangement caused us to lose our independence and missed some doors of opportunity with the dominant side which I maintain is also needed to promote peace."

58. The almost default Haitian assumption that most Americans in Haiti were working for the CIA was not entirely groundless. Gene Stoltzfus, who had significant experience with CIA operatives in Vietnam, once told the author that missionaries and other international workers often unwittingly supply intelligence to "spooks" residing in various embassies throughout the world. When U.S. Ambassador to Haiti William Swing came out to Jérémie to visit the Americans living there, Kern had a pleasant conversation with one of the Embassy employees who strongly urged her to go out to lunch with her next time Kern was in Port-au-Prince. After Stoltzfus told Kern that this employee was probably the spook, she reflected on the conversation and realized that the employee had indeed asked her many pointed questions. Kern had assumed she was simply friendly and maybe a little lonely—which of course, might also have been the case.

who shared a distrust of Aristide with other evangelical churches.⁵⁹ MCC came out officially against the U.N. embargo on Haiti, because they said it was hurting the poor and not Haiti's elite. Since grassroots Haitian organizations were calling for a tighter embargo, CPT felt it had to be in solidarity with them. The MCC country coordinator was also a "warden" of the U.S. Embassy, which CPT felt was too close of a relationship with the U.S. government.⁶⁰ After the Jeremie project closed down, the CPT Artibonite and mobile teams related to new MCC country coordinators who were more supportive of their work, and even sent an MCCer with Kaufman and a Haitian employee to visit Northwest Haiti in 1996. Later, teams in the Palestine and Chiapas, Mexico would develop good working relationships (though not always without tensions) with MCC representatives in those regions.

Relationships with the U.S. Military

The four members of the Jérémie team that were present when the U.S. Special Forces landed in September 1994 had four very different opinions regarding how to relate to the troops. One person felt strongly that the team should have nothing to do with American soldiers and treated them coldly. One felt that the team should have nothing to do with them, but had a naturally gregarious personality that caused her to respond warmly when she had to interact with them. One felt that since Haitians were asking the team to interact with the military and serve as mediators, the team was obligated to do so. Finally, one member of the team felt team members should seek out opportunities to relate to the military for the purpose of information-gathering and to be examples of nonviolent witness to the soldiers. These differing opinions caused considerable dissension within the team.

59. In hindsight, perhaps some of this distrust was warranted, although not because of Aristide's Catholicism. CPT reservist John Engle had lived in Haiti for many years when the Aristide government fell again in February 2004. By that time, he and many progressive Haitians felt that the Aristide government had become hopelessly corrupt. Although he believes that economic pressures imposed by the United States may have compromised Aristide, he also believes that progressive internationals were too quick to absolve him of anti-democratic actions. See Engle's entries from his time in Haiti (especially Feb 28–Mar 16, 2004) on his blog, *Circles of Change*.

60. Wardens keep an eye on American citizens living within a particular area and then report to the Ambassador as issues arise. The evangelical missionary mentioned earlier was the warden for the Jérémie area.

Nonetheless, as the portion of this chapter dealing with the September 30 demonstration shows, interactions with these soldiers at times had positive results, and after months of soul-crushing oppression and starvation, the arrival of the troops was at least a change. Regardless of how they felt about the U.S. military presence, team members became more convinced of the power of nonviolence when they saw the fear on the faces of heavily armed, highly trained officers as crowds of Haitians followed them on their patrols, dancing, singing, and waving branches in joyful celebration.

In future years, similar disagreements would crop up among members of the Hebron and Iraq teams regarding their relationship to Israeli and U.S. soldiers. In Mexico and Colombia, relationships with militaries and paramilitaries offered greater opportunities for witness. Two Mexican soldiers and one Colombian paramilitary attributed their departures from armed life to conversations with team members. However, interactions with armed groups in Colombia and team denunciations of their human rights abuses also affected team members' ability to obtain visas.[61]

61. On October 8, 2004, the author posted this analysis of "right" relationships with soldiers on CPT's discussion list, GITW (Getting in the Way), and asked for feedback from CPTers who had worked on different projects. William Payne, who served in Chiapas, Colombia and Hebron responded:

> My experience was limited in Hebron, but I felt we operated with a similar experience to how we operate in Colombia and did in Chiapas, i.e. with a goal to engage any and all armed actors as human beings capable of leaving armed methods behind, so worth talking about those issues with.
>
> The issue I remember from Chiapas was that we generally didn't want to be 'chummy' with soldiers, and in that sense follow the lead of the Abejas, but we DID want to engage them in human conversation that was hopefully real, non-judgmental, but at the same time an invitation to consider nonviolence. . . . In Colombia for me it was much the same, though I don't recall any discussions.

Sara Reschly, who worked on the same three teams, responded in an October 12 e-mail:

> In Mexico, we did agree to have meetings with the Mexican military. However, when we were staying in the Abejas communities, our relations to the Mexican military was much more unclear. The Abejas were clear that they did not want to "dialogue" with the military—so that put us in a tough position. On the one hand, we believed it was through relationships with the military that transformation could take place, on the other hand, we did not want to be used by the military as a bridge

Relationships with Haitian Co-Workers Not Committed to
or Interested in Nonviolence

Nicola, Bluntschli, and Father Samedi all had a deep understanding and appreciation of the power of nonviolent movements. However, most of the people in St. Helene's parish were not committed in principle to nonviolence. They chose to resist nonviolently because of the horrific consequences of violent resistance under the coup. The Artibonite team had to deal with the fact that Haitians terrorized by zenglendos generally supported vigilante violence against zenglendos.

Likewise, the principle of Satyagraha—Gandhi's "truth force"—was a foreign concept to most Haitians. The team's Haitian contacts in the democratic underground operated in extreme secrecy and viewed lying as a necessary part of remaining safe. Given the extreme brutality of the coup regime against those who supported or were suspected of supporting Aristide, the team in Jérémie did not fault Haitians for operating covertly. However, their training had been based on the presupposition that they would be working with movements that operated in the open. They found themselves at a loss much of the time for how to support Haitians in the underground.[62]

After the U.S. Special Forces landed in Jérémie, the hope expressed by some of their primary contacts that the Special Forces might set up an outpost in St. Helene took the team aback. Likewise, when U.S. soldiers asked the Jérémie team if they thought Father Samedi would approve of their attending the first Mass after the invasion, team members said they thought it would be all right if the soldiers did not bring their guns into the church. When they checked with Samedi, he told them the soldiers were welcome to bring their weapons into the church if they used them to protect the people.

---

to the Abejas—who wanted very little contact with them. The way we related to the military while out in the communities was, at times, a contentious issue for the team.

Perhaps the "contentiousness" also had to do with the personalities involved on the teams during different periods of time.

62. Lying is one way that oppressed and disenfranchised people all over the world maintain some control over and protection of their lives. Accordingly, most powerless people assume that those standing in solidarity with them will also lie for them. On several projects, CPTers have found it hard to explain to these nationals why it is important to think of ways that it is possible *not* to lie without endangering others.

Poor Communication

In none of CPT's subsequent projects did CPTers have so little access to advice from CPT's Chicago office or national "point persons," i.e., advisors within the country but outside the immediate locality where the team worked. Most of this poor communication could not be helped. Phone connections were rare and during most of the time the team was in Jérémie, the city had no electricity, which rendered existing phone lines nonfunctional. Although Bluntschli arranged with a religious order that had convents in both Port-au-Prince and Jérémie to use their ham radios to communicate with the team, on most of the appointed days and times for communication, Bluntschli was unable to get to the convent in Port-au-Prince. Traveling to Port-au-Prince from Jérémie involved a thirteen-hour bus or ferry ride under extremely overcrowded and unhygienic conditions.

When Stoltzfus and Bluntschli made their first trip out to Jérémie in the spring of 1994, they had been dealing with the big picture of U.S. policy toward Haiti and wanted to strategize with the team about some sort of massive nonviolent witness. The Jérémie team was operating on a "micro" level. Their concerns included whom to trust among the people seeking to relate to them, what to do when some trusted associates told them to do one thing and other trusted associates told them to do another, why Father Samedi seemed reluctant to speak with them, how they should respond to servants asking for increasing sums of money, how to deal emotionally with the constant requests for material aid from friends and strangers, when team members would go home, and difficult intra-team dynamics around decision-making issues. When Bluntschli and Stoltzfus left, the team had not received answers to most of these questions, although Stoltzfus saw clearly that the team was not able to organize the march that he and Bluntschli were envisioning.

Dealing with Extreme Poverty

"A list of people's unmet needs in this neighborhood would rival the length of the Bible," Joel Klassen wrote in October 1993.[63] From the beginning of Cry for Justice to the mobile team's attempt to educate the North American constituency about sweatshops in Haiti, poverty was the most serious and most difficult issue that CPTers in Haiti had to face. In

63. CPTnet, "Haiti as viewed from Sent Elen."

releases, reports, and letters to their constituents, CPTers expressed grief and anger over the extreme physical needs of the people they worked among and their weariness at being asked, without exaggeration, up to fifty times a day for handouts. Dealing with this poverty infiltrated every aspect of team life.

CPT had, and continues to have, a policy against giving handouts, based on the experiences of its organizers who had lived in the Two-Thirds world. Nearly every team member violated this policy at some point, and nearly every team member regretted doing so. The policy was at odds with Haitian culture, in which generosity is a highly prized character trait. Haitians generally feel free to ask each other for material aid when necessary. However, years of living on handouts from US mission agencies had also created a culture of dependency in Haiti that pro-Democracy activists wished to change.[64] Ari Nicola told Siegers and Kern before they headed out to Jeremie that he never gave money to children because he did not want to help raise another generation of beggars. However, he encouraged people to give money to the indigent elderly who had no one to take care of them.

Haitian culture also expected that people with the means to do so would have servants to do washing and cooking as a way of spreading wealth. Thus, Bluntschli engaged a cook and a laundress for the Jérémie team shortly after their arrival in December 1993. In the months that followed, the cook kept asking for increasing amounts of money and working less. The team at first was inclined to give her the money, given that they were eating so cheaply anyway, and given that food prices were indeed increasing, but other Haitians told them doing so would set a bad precedent. Jean-Role Jean Louis, the team translator, tried to mediate but soon found himself absorbing hostilities because local people viewed him

64. "Haiti: Oh Lord, We Are Just by Ourselves," appears as an unattributed paragraph in *Signs of the Times* 6:4 (1996):

> "Next door to where we are staying, people were gathered for an in-house prayer service. As we returned from the market, we could see arms raised in loud prayer and signing. Our Haitian co-worker Ari came running over to us exclaiming, "You won't believe what I just heard." He went on to explain that they were praying to God, "O Lord, we have no whites. We're just by ourselves and have only You. Help us work together because we have no whites."

Joanne Kaufman later told the author she had written it during a visit to Boulder, CO.

as getting in the way of their making money from the *blans*.[65] The team was willing to eat vegetarian, but the twelve or so other people that the cook fed with the team's money were not. Thus, the relationship became increasingly tense until Father Samedi moved back into the rectory, installed his own cook, and charged the team for the meals. After the projects in Haiti closed down, CPT projects would never again have servants on a payroll.

The poverty poisoned other relationships as well. Friends in St. Helene who had welcomed the team with great hospitality begged the team for desperately needed food and medicine at times. Team members usually turned them down, although sometimes they did not. Klassen, the team member most fluent in Creole, was the one most aware of the reality of their need and several times reported feeling "sickened" when he turned them down.[66] After Klassen told members of the St. Helene community that he had raised $1500 of support to return to Haiti in the summer of 1994, someone misunderstood and assumed that Klassen had raised the money to give to the people of St. Helene. Rumors then spread that he had embezzled the money.

When a team member did give out money or gifts, word spread, and that team member became a target for dozens of people with varying degrees of need in the community. Team members who considered themselves generous in North America learned to live with the stigma of stinginess. As the embargo dragged on in 1994, team members watched men, women, and children around them suffer and die of malnutrition and easily treatable diseases.

When the mobile teams traveled around rural areas in the Dondon and Grand Anse regions of Haiti, their guide—who had been clearly briefed about CPT's policy forbidding the distribution of aid—still implied that maybe the CPTers could find monies for the community. Joanne Kaufman wrote,

---

65. Stresses such as these led to depression for Jean-Louis, who came from a middle-class background. After he received some death threats from coup supporters in Jérémie he felt almost relieved, because it gave him a way to return to his home in St. Mark without feeling he was letting down the Jérémie team, whose work he supported. By that time, several members spoke enough Creole to get by in any case.

66. See also Joel Klassen, "Grief and Hope in Haiti"; Kinane, "Cry for Justice in Haiti," 229.

I introduced CPT's human rights work and stressed the fact that we could not give aid. I ended with the thought that children should learn to read and write so they can hold officials accountable to do their jobs. "Learn well so no one takes advantage of you," I said, hoping that the kids would someday have a chance to make their voices heard or to vote on the "debt restructuration plan" which the U.S. Canadian and French Banks had imposed on Haiti. . . . Despite my intent to educate, the teacher, the children and the parents looking from the sides of the open pole structure continued to look at me as though they were waiting for something. Knowing they would inevitably ask if we could offer aid, I gave up. "What concerns you-what kinds of questions do you have for me?"

"We would like a place to sit and write."

"My parents can't buy notebooks or books for me."

"The Professors cannot buy chalk."

"We come to school barefoot—it's embarrassing."

"I'm hungry—my parents can't give me food."

"We want a ball to play soccer."

Children from a neighboring school trudged up the hill and formed a circle in the muddy yard, and the litany of need began again.

At another meeting, Kaufman, who was coming down with flu at the time, refused to give a woman her CPT hat. Later, she wrote,

My shoulders heaved with tears I couldn't shed. Even if I gave that woman my hat, what would it do? I would just be one more foreigner giving away a manufactured object that would enhance dependency. Part of our purpose in Haiti was to try to instill a sense of pride and confidence in what was Haitian-made—not only in a physical sense, but in an emotional, psychological sense. I almost vomited from the weariness of it all.[67]

In many ways, Haiti may not have been an ideal location for the very first CPT project. Because the Jérémie team was inexperienced, one might assume that they should have begun in a place where they had access to more guidance from advisors in Port-au-Prince and Chicago. On the other hand, Haiti taught those who worked there not to take for granted the privileges of easy access to communication and transportation on future projects. Haiti exposed them to the naked consequences of

67. Kaufman, "From the 'Violence of the Stick.'" Her words were altered in the published chapter.

economic control exerted on poor nations by the world's elite. Haiti made Matthew 25:32–46 assume gigantic proportions for some on the team, as they turned away from the hungry and sick who asked for help.

More significantly, Haitians taught the first CPTers how to work in a culture significantly different from their own and the vital importance of small talk in building trust. They also showed team members how disenfranchised people could organize and hold on to a dream of dignity and equality in spite of crushing political and economic conditions. After centuries of people in power telling Haitian peasants that their lives were worth little, these peasants still spoke up and asserted their right to control their own destiny.

When the author asked Joel Klassen to tell her the most important thing he learned from his experience in Haiti, he said,

> There was a tremendous amount of unity between the vast majority of the Haitian people. That's what brought Aristide back. It didn't come from anything that anyone told people to do. It happened because of a mysterious process where people came together. There was no parliament. Just a refusal to accept what people were deciding outside the country.[68]

68. Joel Klassen, interview, July 21, 2003.

3

Urban Projects: DC, Richmond, and Cleveland

An alcoholic in complete denial counseling on the virtues of sobriety comes to mind when I see so many good-willed organizations flying off to developing nations to help fight social ills. How many ravaged blocks do these people have to pass to get to the airport?

Homelessness in a country filled with houses, hunger on a continent stocked with mega food marts, abuse neglect and violence in a nation that engraves "In God We Trust" on its currency have not encouraged any vigor for efforts to reduce these horrors.

In come the PEACEMAKERS. I was surprised and delighted to learn that Christian Peacemaker Teams would like to help us rid the community of a house that was the source of many, many problems. In a few weeks, the group helped us to obtain the best of Christmas gifts: a victorious battle and peace of mind

—Letter written by Barbara Cameron, a resident of Columbia Heights after the crack house on Girard Street closed.[1]

CITIZENS OF THE UNITED States who are uncomfortable with CPT's overseas work often pose the question, "With so much violence happening in this country, why aren't you doing anything about that?" Most often (although not always) people asking the question are uncomfortable with CPT's activist mandate in general. However, many people involved with CPT in its early years envisioned CPT developing domestic projects that addressed North American urban violence. Gene Stoltzfus, Kryss Chupp, and CPT's first Personnel Director, Jane Ramseyer Miller, all lived in low-income neighborhoods in Chicago and Minneapolis and participated in neighborhood solidarity efforts.

1. Cameron, "Letter by Barbara Cameron, Community Resident," 2.

When Cole Arendt[2] went through CPT's first training in 1993, he had worked with Mennonite Board of Missions (MBM) Voluntary Service for eight years and had extensive contacts with organizations addressing urban violence throughout the greater DC area. Although he had not come to CPT training in 1993 with the plan of setting up a project in Washington, he told the author, "I always thought we needed to work in our own backyards," in a September 8, 2003 phone interview. He also wanted to participate in smaller, community-based initiatives, which possibly reflected the influence that eight years working in Church of the Brethren and Mennonite voluntary service had on him.

Washington DC was an appropriate place for an urban project to start for several reasons besides Arendt knowing the area well. Mennonite Central Committee, the Church of the Brethren, and other denominations had offices there that lobbied for peace and social justice issues. U.S. policy that resulted in violence and human rights abuses in the rest of the world issued from Washington. Residents of DC had no voting representation in congress despite the fact they paid Federal taxes.[3] Given the fact that the residents consistently voted Democratic in local and presidential elections, Republicans consistently squelched any movements toward DC statehood. Thus, the residents of Washington DC had little control over legislative decisions affecting their lives—a situation they shared with Haitians, Palestinians, and other people among whom CPT has worked.

Getting mugged two weeks after he returned from Haiti in February 1994 galvanized Arendt's determination to set up a project addressing urban violence.[4] Accordingly, Arendt and CPT reservist John Reuwer made a proposal for an exploratory project in April 1994, which the CPT Steering Committee approved during its April meetings.

2. When Arendt married in 1995 he changed his name to Hull. At his request, he will be referred to as Arendt in the first and second chapters and as Hull for CPT work he participated in after 1995.

3. The population of Wyoming is smaller than that of DC, and yet, Wyoming residents have two senators and one congressperson representing them. See U.S. Census Bureau, "Statistical Abstract."

4. CPT reservist Tom Malthaner was also mugged while working with the DC project on September 22, 1995. See his *Signs of the Times* article, "The night I was mugged." Maxine Kaufman-Lacusta, an Israeli-Canadian friend of CPT, was also mugged while on her way to visit the DC team. Ironically, for several years these assaults made that project more dangerous than either Haiti or Hebron, if one graded danger by the sort of injuries sustained.

The Proposal

In May and June 1994, Arendt, Reuwer, and Kathleen Kern contacted dozens of organizations in the DC area that worked to address urban violence. At the end of June, the team wrote up a proposal for the project in response to a set of questions that Gene Stoltzfus had sent them. The initial "proto"-proposal listed three partners who had issued invitations for CPT to work with them.

1. The first partner was the Sojourners Neighbor Center, a ministry of the intentional Christian community in the Columbia Heights neighborhood. (The community also published *Sojourners*, a magazine internationally known for its radical Christian theology.) The neighborhood center provided tutoring services, classes in conflict resolution skills, and a soup kitchen. The year before, a seventeen-year-old boy had died from a machine gun attack across the street from the community and Jim Wallis, the charismatic founder of *Sojourners* had been mugged.

2. Beverly Wheeler, the president of the Advisory Neighborhood Commission (ANC) in Columbia Heights, also extended an invitation for CPT to set up a "violence-free zone" in her neighborhood. At the time that CPT was investigating project locations, children in Wheeler's neighborhood congregated in the middle of the street, because parents were afraid to let them out of their sight. Parents also did not want their children walking two blocks to the local recreation center. CPT thus proposed a goal of making the neighborhood safe enough for both parents and children to feel secure enough to walk to the recreation center.

3. Ayuda (Spanish for "help") provided legal services to immigrant women, mostly from Latin American backgrounds, often helping them get restraining orders against abusive partners. When the abused women would come to retrieve clothing and personal belongings or transferred custody of children, violence often occurred. A lawyer at Ayuda thus suggested that calling on CPT to provide a violence-deterring presence during these times might prove useful.

Although Wheeler and staff at Ayuda continued to serve as consultants during the DC project, the focus of the DC project for the next year became the area around Sojourners Neighborhood Center.

PROJECT IN URBAN PEACEMAKING, PHASE 1: FALL 1994

In an October 10, 1994, report charting the progress of the Project in Urban Peacemaking—called "PUP" by the CPTers running the project— Arendt noted that the project had gotten off to a slow start:

> We have established two specific neighborhood foci and have be-gun attempting to assist in the creation of a "violence-free" zone. In many ways we have met with some disappointment in our neighborhood partners who seem not to be utilizing our willing-ness to work as effectively as we would like. But it would be unfair to lay all the fault at the feet of our neighborhood partners. We have waited for Americorps funding[5]; we waited for applicants, for bodies; and we busied ourselves with administrative details. This project is often more about community organizing than it is about peacemaking. Not that the two are incompatible by any means. It may sometimes be our own impatience as much as anything else that trips us up, as we must always keep in mind that if it becomes a program we DO for the community, it is the long term mainte-nance of the project that will suffer.

In his "Areas of Success" portion, Arendt noted that Americorps agreed to fund the project, even though in the end PUP could not accept the money because of Mennonite Board of Mission's scruples. Several area conferences and events had invited the PUP team to speak. Tammy Krause and Jeff Heie filled out their staffing roster and the team had be-come known in the Columbia Heights neighborhoods where they were working.

As disappointments, Arendt listed the fact that none of the team spoke Spanish (and were thus of limited usefulness to Ayuda), the great deal of work that went into filling out the Americorps grants with nothing at the end to show for it, dealing with fear and apathy in the neighborhoods

---

5. Initially, Arendt sought funding from Americorps, a voluntary service program set up by the Clinton administration, because Americorps funding had already underwritten ten volunteers of Mennonite Board of Mission's voluntary service unit in DC. MBM had agreed to send six people to the PUP project. Unfortunately, MBM decided in the sum-mer of 1994 that Americorp's requirement that agencies not discriminate on the basis of religion would compromise their work, so they chose not to avail themselves of the fund-ing after all. However, the Church of the Brethren agreed to support two volunteers—Jeff Heie and Tammy Krause—and MBM continued to support Cole Arendt. John Reuwer was able to provide his own support working as an Emergency Room physician while he lived with the Assisi community in a low-income neighborhood of DC. The first phase of the PUP project was thus self supporting.

where the team was working, and lack of enthusiasm from local churches. Regarding the last point, Arendt noted that the churches seemed at best inactive and at worst detrimental to neighborhood cohesion/organizing. And as partial fulfillment of goals, Arendt listed substantive conversations with two neighborhood organizations, the development of a non-violence training curriculum, nightly patrols of the area with Orange Hats, the first attempts to track violent crime statistics in the area, and conducting a "Listening Project."[6]

It was this last item, the "Listening Project," that would prove to be their greatest success—although members of the PUP team did not know it at the time Arendt was writing the report. They had begun the project, with the help of a Sojourners intern, which involved visiting homes in the two neighborhoods where they focused their efforts. Thirty-six families and individuals responded to twenty-four questions, including the following list:

1. What is the biggest problem facing the city?

2. Given the increase in violent crimes, do you think anything can be done to turn things around (be specific)?

3. What are your feelings about people who deal drugs in the city?

4. What is your opinion of the police?

5. How do you think police respond to calls from this neighborhood?

6. Do you know ten other people on your block?

7. What do you like most about living in this neighborhood? Why?

8. Does your neighborhood feel safe to you?

9. What makes it that way?

10. What ideas do you have for how to help improve things and move toward a more peaceful and secure neighborhood?

11. Do your children use the recreation center? Why or why not?

12. Have you ever heard of Orange Hat patrols? What do you think of them?

---

6. CPT PUP, "Listening Project in Urban Peacemaking, Washington, DC."

13. In your opinion, how many violent crimes (shootings, rapes, physical attacks) occur in this neighborhood each month?

14. Have you yourself been involved in a violent incident?

15. Do you personally feel like you have the power to make a difference in this neighborhood?

16. Do you think owning a gun would make you feel safer?

17. Do you know of any households in this neighborhood that suffer from in-home violence or abuse?

18. What specific neighborhood programs would you like to see?

19. About half of every federal income tax dollar goes to the military. Many people say that this has drained our economy and added to our domestic problems like housing, education, and healthcare. What do you think about this?[7]

20. Can you tell us about any experience in your life when you or someone used nonviolence as a way of solving a problem?

In a report summarizing the findings of the Listening Project, the team noted that while most of those interviewed identified drugs as the greatest problem facing the city, the most common response to how they felt about people who deal drugs was, "there's a living to be made from it." Thirteen had some connection to the drug trade themselves or through family and friends. most of the people underestimated the number of violent crimes occurring in their neighborhood, even though 50 percent had been involved with some sort of violent attack.[8]

As a result of the Listening Project, the PUP Team learned that the neighbors in Columbia Heights clearly identified a crack house as the locus of violence in the neighborhood. (They had begun the project, which involved visiting homes in the two neighborhoods where they focused their efforts, with the help of a Sojourners intern.) They also learned from the residents what the neighborhoods were like before drugs flooded into

---

7. Most of the people responding to this question asserted the need to support the efforts of the US military. The issue of working for peace with non-pacifists has been a recurring tension for CPTers on most project locations.

8. CPT PUP, "CPT Listening Project." In keeping with the self-critical attitude of the first PUP worker reports, team members noted that they ought to have taken a larger survey sample.

them in the 1980s.[9] One of them wistfully told team members, "I miss having my children be able to do the things that I used to do." The person interviewed specifically mentioned trick-or-treating as an activity that children in the neighborhood could no longer do because of the high level of violence in the area.

Thus, the first collaborative effort CPT-PUP undertook was working with local organizations to set up a several-block area where children could trick-or-treat. The team and neighborhood parents distributed fliers with safety information and invitation to participate. More than forty residents displayed fluorescent green signs that said, "Trick-or-Treaters Welcome."

On Halloween night 1994, more than two hundred children in costumes participated in trick-or-treating under the watchful eyes of parents and Orange Hat patrols, who helped children cross dangerous intersections. A police officer in the area said he had never seen so many people out in the neighborhood. Not only children considered the evening a roaring success. Other residents caught a glimpse of what their neighborhood once was. "Even though my children are grown, I still like to celebrate with the neighborhood," one older woman told the PUP team. "I miss seeing children come to my door."[10]

The success of Halloween in south Columbia Heights gave CPT and its partners credibility with the neighborhood and inspired them to focus on the crack house at 1304 Girard Street, owned by Mr. Kingsley Anyanwutaku. Mr. Kingsley, as the neighbors called him, owned more than forty properties in the DC area—most, if not all, of which were connected to drugs, prostitution, and other illegal activities. In the course of the Listening Project, the PUP team had learned that for the previous ten years, several neighbors had appealed to the DC government to close the house, with no significant results. Neighbors who had made efforts to intervene by and large had no idea that other residents were doing the same thing.

9. In the summer of 1994, a member of an Orange Hat patrol told Kathleen Kern that his neighborhood had never had problems with drugs and crime until Reagan took office. Other people speaking with the PUP team at various times also connected the beginnings of the drug problems in their neighborhood with Reagan's ascent to power.

10. "CPT Rallies neighborhood for Halloween," 3. Not all of the CPT constituency approved of these activities, believing that CPTers should not be helping people celebrate a holiday they viewed as satanic.

Thus, CPT and Sojourners Neighborhood Center invited neighbors tired of the drug dealing, prostitution, noise, and violence associated with 1304 Girard Street to meet and strategize a campaign to pressure the city into enforcing housing and safety codes.

The DC bureaucracy presented a significant obstacle to the neighbors who had made individual efforts to close the house. Since many of them worked two jobs or had small children at home, they did not have the time to jump through all the hoops that the city government put in front of people trying to make changes. A significant contribution the PUP team made to the neighbors' campaign was doing the legwork of going from office to office. Sometimes they went full circle: the fifth or sixth person to whom they had been referred, referred them back to the original office from which they had sought help. In the course of their research, they collected information on the numerous building code violations for which Mr. Kingsley had been cited. CPTers then shared the results of their research at the neighborhood meetings.

At one of these meetings, as the neighbors grumbled about the people living in the crack house, Tammy Krause suggested that they talk to the residents of the crack house—mostly prostitutes and drug addicts. So a delegation of them went to the crack house, knocked on the door, and invited the residents over to Sojourners Neighborhood Center for pizza. To their surprise, they found out that the tenants of the crack house were just as upset with Mr. Kingsley as the neighbors were. They paid $95 a week and often received no heat or hot water. Their ceilings leaked and Kingsley never made repairs to plumbing, stoves, refrigerators, or anything else in the house that broke down. For a time, the house had had no front door and most of the doors inside the house had no locks and no knobs. Kingsley had divided the house, which was zoned for three bedrooms, into eleven bedrooms with three bathrooms.[11]

The tenants were thus open to moving out of the building, which would aid the neighbors' efforts to close it down. The neighbors began looking for alternative housing for tenants and storing the belongings of those who wished to look for their own housing. In one case, they helped a woman return to her home community in rural Georgia, because she

11. Melillo, "D.C. Landlord Given Nearly 6 Years." See also Melillo, "D.C. Landlord Pleads Guilty"; Lacharite, "City eliminates problem house." An account of a fourteen-year-old girl who lived in the crack house appeared in CPT, "CPT Sunday," worship materials for Oct 27, 1996.

said she thought she could kick drugs more easily there. As Krause and Heie drove her to the bus station, she threw her crack pipe out the window, saying she would not need it anymore.

Once the tenants left, the neighbors planned a candlelight vigil in front of the crack house to call attention to the city's refusal to take action against the house. When informed of the vigil, DC Council and enforcement agencies urged the neighbors and CPT to "cool your jets," according to Arendt, assuring them that the authorities would take action. The neighbors and CPTers politely informed them that the demonstration would take place, regardless.[12]

Signs prepared for the vigil read, "Just Say 'Neighborhood,'" "We Are All Victims of Drugs," "Up With Neighbors," "This Street is Ours," and "Taking Back our Block, Taking Back Our City." The event turned into a celebration when the Department of Public Works personnel finally did their job and bricked up the house before the scheduled time of vigil on December 7, 1994.[13]

Although the first phase of PUP ended with the closure of the crack house, the story of the crack house did not. On June 10, 1995, the District of Columbia brought charges against Kingsley for operating slum houses in violation of building codes, tax codes, and permit regulations. At that time, Kingsley owed more than $150,000 in fines assessed in 1989, 1990, and April 1995. On August 8, 1995, Kingsley pled guilty to operating rooming houses illegally and failing to pay taxes from 1986–1993. A *Washington Post* reporter quoted Tammy Krause as saying after the verdict: "He has preyed on people for so long. He can't get away with gross negligence."[14]

David Rosenthal, the prosecuting attorney, had contacted people involved with closing the crack house and collected video evidence of the conditions of his properties. Rosenthal said that the Columbia Heights crack house was the "tip of the iceberg" in a larger picture of slumlords'

12. Arendt, interview, Oct 21, 2003.

13. See Arendt, "Urban Peacemaking: Neighbors work together." Prior to the vigil, on November 25, 1994, five city agencies and three utility companies inspected the house and condemned the building.

14. Melillo, "D.C. Landlord Pleads Guilty." See also CPTnet, "Kingsley's Kingdom Falling Down," June 27, 1995 (incorrectly dated 1996). Krause said that the judge took the unusual step of putting Kingsley in jail between the August 8 verdict and the September sentencing, even though Kingsley offered to surrender his passport. Krause, interview, Nov 15, 2004.

blatant disregard for the law in DC. The fact that the DC government pulled Rosenthal away from his duties with the Juvenile Division indicated to the neighbors that DC was finally taking the damage that Kingsley's properties did to the community seriously. (Kingsley's case getting handed off to one overworked lawyer to another had allowed his flagrant legal violations to continue.)

Kingsley and his lawyer did not appear for the June hearing—which typified his response to the justice system in previous years, i.e., simply ignoring legal actions brought against him. This time, however, the judge issued twenty-eight bench warrants for his arrest and a $200 fine for each property with cited violations. In total, the judge noted that Kingsley's properties had received citations for twenty-four hundred building code violations. Kingsley and his lawyer showed up in the afternoon—after the prosecution had retired and the judge had moved along to other pending cases—claiming a scheduling mix-up and the judge rescinded the warrants. The judge then moved Kingsley's case to July 14.[15]

Kingsley told a *Washington Post* reporter in August 1995 that city officials had singled him out unfairly while allowing other landlords to commit the same abuses. "Never did I ever know about [anyone] going to jail for housing and business code violations," he said. Everybody knew that I did not have business licenses or occupancy permits." He said the city should commend him for providing inexpensive housing for tenants. "I am a single-man welfare organization for the District of Columbia," he said.[16]

In September 1995, a DC court sentenced Mr. Kingsley Anyanwutaku to six years in prison. CPT-PUP had encouraged Columbia Heights neighbors to send letters to the judge prior to sentencing describing the effect Kingsley's properties had in their neighborhoods. The judge allowed these letters to be used as evidence of the "will of the people." Originally charged for violations in twenty-eight of his properties, Kingsley could have faced thirteen years in prison and roughly $239,000 in fines. Kingsley and his lawyer, a former DC legal counsel, entered a plea bargain that resulted in

15. The author could find nothing about a legal proceeding against Kingsley in July 1995. Also, Cole Arendt and Tammy Krause did not remember a legal proceeding in July, so the author assumes the judge extended the trial date to August 8, 1995, when Kingsley pled guilty.

16. Melillo, "D.C. Landlord Given Nearly 6 Years"; CPTnet, "District of Columbia Slum Lord Goes to Jail," Oct 23, 1995.

charges for violations in eleven of his houses. As part of the plea bargain, Kingsley would have spent twenty-one days in jail, to be served on weekends and paid $100,000 in fines.

However, because of the letters he received, Chief Judge Hamilton set aside the plea bargain and sentenced Kingsley to a six-year jail term. Twenty-two days into his sentence, Kingsley reappeared before the judge to appeal his sentence and possibly have the judge reinstate the plea bargain. The judge noted that while his sentence was pending, Kingsley continued to advertise his properties, transfer deeds, and try to collect rents on units the court had seized. Thus, the judge said he was unwilling to hear any further pleas until Kingsley had dispossessed himself of all his properties and paid approximately $110,000 in fines.[17]

"The sentence is a lot better than the plea agreement," Columbia Heights resident Lynn French told *The Washington Post*, "I think it reflects justice."[18]

17. Kern, "Christian Peacemaker Teams," 186–87. Interestingly, the *Washington Post* attributed the Anyanwutaku's incarceration to maverick building inspector James Delgado:

> As he drives past vacant buildings and littered alleys, he points out landmarks of lengthy past struggles. In Columbia Heights are the boarded-up rooming houses once owned by Kingsley Anyanwutaku, a slum landlord whom Delgado ferociously pursued for two years after learning that children took sick in his vermin-infested properties. In 1995, Anyanwutaku pleaded guilty to 1,318 building and housing code violations and, thanks in large part to Delgado's agitation, was sentenced to nearly six years in prison, the first District landlord prosecuted criminally in more than a decade. (Perle, "Building inspector")

See also Mencimer, e-mail to themail@DCWatch.com, Feb 25, 1998. In a November 15, 2004 phone interview with the author, Tammy Krause affirmed that Delgado deserved credit for the tenacity with which he set about closing the house, but said that he did so because he saw the neighbors already engaged in the struggle to close the house and followed their lead. She noted that Teresa Lewis of the DC Department of Consumer and Regulatory Affairs only grudgingly agreed to help after the neighbors and CPT became a real nuisance to her. Krause recalls that after many contacts and pleas for help, she finally brought out of her office two foot-high stacks of papers detailing Kingsley's building code violations.

18. Melillo, "D.C. Landlord given Nearly 6 Years." Following French's comment, Melillo recorded that Tammy Krause, of "Christian Peacemaker Corps," said, "Amen." Krause told the author in a November 16, 2004 interview that after Judge Hamilton set aside the plea agreement, the CPTers organized the neighbors to send him letters of gratitude. "Never in my career as a judge have I had such an outpouring of concern," he reportedly said in open court.

Cole Arendt's media savvy also contributed to the successful first phase of the DC-PUP. Besides getting local coverage from the *Washington Post*, the *Washington Times*, and DC radio and television stations, he got stories of the DC project in most Mennonite, Church of the Brethren and Quaker publications as well as *Christianity Today* and *Sojourners*. Future phases of PUP in DC and Richmond were not able to garner the same coverage. Hull (Arendt) attributes this failure to the lack of continuity in DC after the first phase closed. It is difficult, he told the author, to publicize the ongoing work of a project when most of the people in the project are there for only two to three week terms.[19]

Project in Urban Peacemaking, Phase 2: The Warner

In the program report for the March 1995 Steering Committee meeting, Stoltzfus noted that the Washington Team had "dispersed." Arendt was busy doing follow-up and networking, among other activities, and Tammy Krause had joined the Sojourners Neighborhood Center staff as a community organizer. "We need to do several more domestic urban projects before making generalizations and models," Stoltzfus noted, "The genius of the past project was to help with everything that was already going on—civilian patrols, police activity and initiatives in community organizing."

The Warner Apartments—a 45-unit, Section 8 public housing building that was the site of drug dealing and violent crime—thus became the test case for whether PUP was replicable. As with the previous project, individuals living in the neighborhood of the Warner Apartments had made attempts to get the police more involved and consulted with *pro bono* lawyers to get the situation under control. Police response to their concerns often involved telling them to move out of the neighborhood. Additionally, the FBI, National Park Police, and the Municipal Police Department all had roles in neighborhood law enforcement, because of DC's unique nature as a Federal district. The effect of having so many different policing agencies—fourteen with jurisdiction in all—was the tendency of law enforcement officials to assume that another agency would deal with persistent problems.

---

19. Arendt, interview, Oct 21, 2003. He attributes his media savvy to what he learned in the 1993 CPT training.

As had happened with the first phase of the PUP project, CPT involvement with the Warner Apartments and surrounding Columbia Heights neighborhood began with a Listening Project. In conjunction with the American Friends Service Committee, Mid-Atlantic District, and local community groups,[20] CPT interviewed more than 120 residents of the Warner Apartments and the surrounding neighborhood, beginning on July 22, 2003. Twelve two-member teams, composed of a member of the immediate community and a volunteer from outside the community, visited home and apartments within a two-block radius of the Warner.

On the whole, residents of the area liked living there because of its ethnic diversity and its proximity to public transportation and shopping. However, almost 25 percent had strong negative feelings about the community and wished to move if they could.

Problems that the community cited included:

1. Lack of jobs, which the neighbors said led to drug dealing and prostitution

2. Drugs, which the neighbors said were the source of most violent crime in their neighborhood. Neighbors complained that many of the people coming to purchase drugs in their neighborhood had Virginia and Maryland license plates, and thus believed "outsiders" contributed as much to the problem as local residents.

3. Availability of guns. "Even my five year old could get a gun," one man said. The fear of stray bullets kept many residents inside at night.

4. Community apathy. As the neighborhood had become more diverse, people did not know their neighbors as well anymore. Fear for personal safety and young people also kept some residents from getting involved.

5. Lack of role models for young people and parents not taking responsibility for their children.

Once the interviewers had collected and analyzed the data in fall 1995, they noticed some interesting correlations. People who had positive

20. These groups included the Washington Area Council on Drugs and Alcohol Abuse, the Catholic University Advocacy for Victims of Gun Violence Clinic, Mennonite Board of Missions Voluntary Service and Sojourners Neighborhood Center.

feelings about the Orange Hat patrols tended to feel far more positively about the police. Those who had negative things to say about police response time were five times more likely to say that Orange Hat patrols were not visible enough. Those who had not known anyone injured by a gun believed by a two to one ratio that if guns were difficult to obtain, there would be less violence in their neighborhood. Residents who knew someone injured by a gun believed twelve to one in more restrictive gun control. Most people believed that owning a gun would make them less safe. However, even people who owned a gun for protection felt that guns should be less easy to obtain.

Residents who felt safe in their neighborhood were more likely to say there was a strong sense of community in their neighborhood, while those who said they felt unsafe regarded their neighbors as unsupportive. Women were twice as likely to identify getting rid of drugs as the most pressing need of their community. Men tended to want to change structural things such as roads, housing, and the availability of recreational programs. Men were also twice as likely to identify "lack of morality" or "social breakdown" as the cause of their neighborhood's problem. Those who attended religious services regularly were twice as likely to identify drugs as the most pressing crisis in their neighborhood. Those who did not belong to a house of worship tended to identify the need to get certain people off the street, such as prostitutes and kids, as the best way to solve problems.[21]

The Warner Apartments team continued to supplement Orange Hat patrols in the neighborhood, noting that when these patrols took down license numbers or attempted to talk to drug dealers and prostitutes, they would hurry away. CPTer Matt Sears, organized a vigil on the evening of September 12, 1995, in reaction to the slaying of twenty-four-year-old Darnell "Diamond" Williams on the previous day. Fifty people from the community gathered at the corner where the murder took place to demand an end to killings in the neighborhood.[22]

The team's follow-up efforts after the vigil brought in additional community members for the Orange Hats. These Orange Hat patrollers received credit for deterring a potentially violent situation in Columbia

21. CPT PUP, "Christian Peacemaker Teams." See also CPTnet, "Neighbors Listen for a Change," July 26, 1995.

22. Arendt, "D.C. Project moves in." Regarding the Williams killing, see Thompson, "D.C. Police Often Close Cases."

Heights five weeks later. A man from the community known as O. J. approached the patrol and told them that earlier in the evening, the police had raided the house where he lived for the second time in two weeks and confiscated about $400 worth of drugs. Around 8:00 p.m. the man that owned the drugs returned. Believing that the other residents in the building had "snitched" on him, he gathered them into one room and held them at gunpoint. O. J. told them that the man with the gun decided not to shoot them because they heard the Orange Hats and a police motorcycle pass by.[23]

On October 31, 1995, CPT helped neighbors organize another safe trick-or-treating in the neighborhood around the Warner Apartments, doubling the territory in which children could safely go door to door. More than twenty-five Orange Hat patrollers in four squads kept watch on every block and helped the 350 children who participated to cross dangerous intersections. A northeast Columbia Heights neighborhood also organized a safe trick-or-treating on its own initiative. Bernice Taylor, a worker at Sojourner's Neighborhood Center, helped with the organization and told CPTers later, "We stole your idea and we are glad we did."[24] Another somewhat smaller trick-or-treating occurred a year later in October 1996.

On March 5, 1996, Columbia Heights celebrated the closure of another "nuisance property" in the neighborhood, two blocks away from the Mr. Kingsley's property. The house had been a source of violence and crime for the past decade. Neighbors also viewed the house as a hygiene risk. Residents of the house threw garbage and waste in the alley between the house and those of other neighbors. After repeated complaints by residents and members of Christian Peacemaker Teams, city authorities inspected the house and discovered numerous violations, leading to the closure.

Wes Hare and Tammy had gone inside after James Delgado inspected the house (See footnote 18). "I worked as a social worker for years," he said in a phone interview. "I'm not a greenhorn in human squalor, but I never saw anything that bad." The water having been cut off for weeks, residents of the house had used tubs, sinks and nearly every other receptacle in the house to defecate and vomit in. Additionally, maggots covered a refrigera-

23. CPTnet, "Orange Hat Patrol stops violence," Oct 25, 1995.
24. CPTnet, "D.C. Children Take Back Halloween," Nov 8, 1995.

tor containing spoiled food. Drug paraphernalia such as needles, razor blades, pills, and related refuse was strewn throughout the rooms. Used condoms and condom wrappers littered the floor.[25] Tammy Krause found looking through the house so traumatizing that she blocked many of the visual images out for years, including the five-gallon pails of human excrement lining the walls of the basement. She recalls going home after the inspection, stripping off all her clothes, and standing naked by the washing machine, unaware that one of her housemates was in the room with her. She also remembers how ashamed two prostitutes she had befriended were when she saw how they had been living in the house..[26]

After the closure, a group of thirty stood in front of the condemned building with candles and signs to celebrate the neighborhood's effort in March. Rush-hour traffic came to a halt as motorists stopped to watch the festivities. Neighbors continued to join the group as the news spread that the house had indeed been closed. They continued to socialize long after the vigil was over, turning the event into an impromptu block party.

Francine McGill, a mother who lived across the street from the house, told the group, "I would never allow my children to play outside because of the danger this house created. Women committed demeaning acts in my alley, and that was difficult to explain to my children. Now, because of the work of the neighborhood, I am able to relax on my own street again."

The owner of the house, Russell Hughes, voluntarily closed the house rather than correct all of the housing violations cited a week earlier.[27]

According to Hare, the Orange Hat patrols began to peter out in the spring of 1996. The closure of the crack house and another crime-plagued apartment building had reduced crime significantly. Cole Arendt and his wife Amy Hull had moved to Washington state, and Jeff Heie and Tammy Krause went back to school. Wes Hare had been undergoing treatments for prostate cancer in Richmond and felt he no longer could make the commute between Richmond (where his wife coordinated a Mennonite

25. Hare, interview, Sept 16, 2003; CPTnet, Krause, "Neighborhood Celebrates," Feb 28, 1996.
26. Krause, interview, Nov 16, 1993.
27. CPTnet, "Washington, D.C.: Neighborhood Gathers," Mar 6, 1996.

Voluntary service unit) and DC. Lacking personnel, the Washington PUP closed down in June of 1996.[28]

Those who had actively developed and promoted the CPT-PUP felt some sadness at leaving, given the continuing needs of the community. In a 1996 reflection piece noting these needs, Tammy Krause wrote,

> The walk to work this Monday morning was different. I think it was the awareness that someone had been shot twice in the head two nights ago, just yards from where I walked. The night before that, another man was shot and killed in the same alley. Neighbors talked about the killings with a distant, matter of fact tone, and I wondered if this was to hide the pain.
>
> Between January 1 and June 27 1996, there have been 196 murders in Washington, D.C., up from 169 killings for the same period last year. The number of victims between 14 and 18 years old has doubled.
>
> On my way to work this morning, a neighbor called out to me, "We need to do something, Tammy, What do you think we should do?" I called one of the neighbors today to ask about organizing a candlelight vigil for the murder victims. I haven't heard back from him yet. I think I will make the arrangements myself. [29]

Val Liveoak, a CPT reservist who went through training in 1994, conducted an evaluation of the project at the end with local residents who had worked with CPT. Most people could not separate the second phase of the project at the Warner Apartments from the first phase, so their positive comments included the first trick-or-treating and the closing of Kingsley Anyanwutaku's crack house. Those surveyed praised the energy that CPT-PUP volunteers brought to the neighborhood, their work with DC officials, their Listening Projects, and their willingness to live in the neighborhoods where they worked.

Criticisms of the work focused on the PUP team's lack of racial diversity, the lack of continuity, and the short-term nature of the project. Respondents felt CPTers had lost opportunities to network and outreach. On these topics, Liveoak wrote,

> A failure to effectively pass on leadership of the Orange Hat patrols and the skills to undertake a campaign to close crack houses was noted, not so much as criticisms, but as things that respondents

28. Hare, interview, Sept 16, 2003.
29. Krause, "Murders up in D.C."

would have liked to have seen accomplished. The long-term nature of the problems to be addressed and the complexity of engaging residents in this work was acknowledged. 'Not having achieved your goals yet is not a criticism,' said one resident.[30]

Everyone to whom Liveoak spoke wanted PUP to stay. The team recommended that PUP enter a third phase and that staff in the CPT's Chicago office find team members for it, since the PUP team had not been able to find team members themselves, although they had been making enquiries since the previous fall.[31] They wrote that if PUP was phased out, it should be done over a two-month period and that CPT should then seek another urban area in which to work. The phase-out plan should include "holding one or more meetings to motivate neighbors to revitalize the Orange Hats" and finding a way to pass on the PUP archives for the use of the neighbors. They also recommended that an Urban/Domestic Peacemaking taskforce be formed within CPT to plan and oversee domestic projects. As noted above, however, the CPT presence in DC had effectively ended by the time Liveoak wrote the evaluation.[32]

---

30. CPT PUP, "Evaluation and Reflection on CPT Washington Work."

31. At the time the DC project closed other projects were also strapped for personnel. Four months after Liveoak's report, Gene Stoltzfus sent the following e-mail on October 7, 1996 to the CPT Steering Committee and other persons within the organization, calling for the fulfillment of the plan to have twelve full-time Corps members in place:

> We are at the point of being in over our head. We cannot continue in this way. We need able trained people for Hebron. Hebron is in crisis. As I write, we have three persons there. In a few days, this number will drop to two. *We receive consistent and timely calls for more domestic projects. I hear frustration that we are not doing better. We don't have people in place to do the projects* (emphasis added). Bosnia is urgently calling for more help and deserves it as soon as possible. The Haiti project is fully staffed for now, but we are pushing the limits there as well.
>
> If we continue in this mode, our staff will be depleted, our peacemaker corps will be burned out. Is CPT a vision that is deeply rooted in the peace church tradition? Are our congregations and members prepared to make the sacrifices? Is God calling or are we pushing something out of our own ego energy? "Report to Steering Committee," October 6, 1996.

32. CPT PUP, "Evaluation and Reflection on CPT Washington Work." Members of PUP expressed some bitterness about what they perceived as lack of support from the Chicago office for the Washington project. This perception will be discussed below under, "Issues Arising from the Urban Projects."

At the 1996 Christian Peacemaker Congress in Washington DC, CPT corps members and reservists gathered to discuss their work with each other, and those who worked on the DC project shared the following reflections:

1. The initial project was the most effective in involving community members—the real value of the Halloween events and closing the crack house was in the empowerment of the neighborhood people. The value of the candlelight vigil following a neighborhood killing was in providing space for frightened people to gather.

2. When the team had a diversity of skills, personalities and abilities, it did its most effective work.

3. A Corps member who had worked in Hebron and Haiti noted that the DC project lent credibility to other CPT projects (because it answered the question of why CPT sent people to address violence in other countries, but not their own).

4. Urban projects need a very clear focus.

5. How CPTers can address structural/systemic violence. This question would ultimately apply to most CPT projects. [33]

Richmond

After the Washington project closed, Wes Hare wrote a proposal for a new CPT Project in Urban Peacemaking to be located in the neighborhood around First Mennonite Church in Richmond.[34] The Park Realty Apartments, consisting of seven hundred units, surrounded the church on three sides and had been the location of numerous acts of violence, including a Cambodian mother killing her young sons and then herself in March 1997. Richmond and the surrounding Henrico County had experienced a sharp increase in violent crime, and the sensational nature of some of the killings resulted in the formation of the Coalition for a Safer Richmond. Hare would attend most of its meetings.[35]

33. Christian Peacemaker Teams, "Notes from December 1996 CPC/Reserves Gathering Washington DC."

34. Hare's wife, Jane, was the coordinator of a Mennonite Voluntary Service unit associated with the church.

35. CPT Richmond PUP, "Proposal: A Richmond VA Project." Hare said that CSR was a "quasi-political ploy" intended to confront the police department about its ineffec-

Hare helped establish twice-weekly citizen patrols of the area, conducted a Listening Project, and began networking with various groups in the area seeking to deal with urban violence. In an October 1997 proposal to extend RichPUP for a year, Hare noted that while his efforts were based on his experiences working in DC, significant differences also existed between the two locations. The violence was less pervasive in the Park Realty Apartments than it was in Washington, DC, and was located outside Richmond's city limits. The church and the Park Realty Apartments also had no community center or history of community programs as the neighborhoods in Columbia Heights had.

Approximately a year after the RichPUP began on April 18, 1998, it sponsored a community carnival with games, food, and live music. Local peace groups, food banks, and civic organizations set up booths. About two hundred people from the neighborhood and nearby churches attended. Another carnival in June, sponsored by CPT and First Mennonite Church in Richmond, kicked off the church's summer program.

On January 30, 1999, RichPUP sponsored a candlelight service of healing following the shooting of a young mother in the Highland Park neighborhood. Seventeen family members, neighbors, and clergy joined in prayer and sharing to reclaim the area as "holyground."

The CPT project in Richmond closed in December 1999 when Wes and Jane Hare completed their terms of service with CPT and MVS and moved to Chapel Hill, North Carolina.

Cleveland

In November 2000, CPT responded to an invitation from the Lee Heights Community Church in Cleveland to begin a regional training there. CPT had previously conducted trainings for regional groups in Boulder, Columbia, Kitchener, Ontario, and Winnipeg, Manitoba. The Cleveland group, however, was the first to go through training specifically to address the issues of violence in the members' own neighborhood. The trainings continued on the first weekend of every month for the next six months.

A large part of the group's focus during its first year was gun violence and drug dealing in the area around the Lee Heights Community Church.

---

tive work. After a time CSR "just kind of dissolved," but it was instrumental in working out a deal with federal law enforcement that anyone carrying out a crime with a gun in Richmond would automatically receive five years in prison. This move resulted in a significant decrease in gun violence. Hare, interview, Oct 22, 2003.

The group organized public vigils at places like the Mirage nightclub, the site of frequent killings. They engaged the young men who were hanging out on the steps of the church, buying and selling drugs—which turned out to be a surprisingly effective way of ending these activities. "I didn't know you cared," one young man told the Cleveland CPTers after they told him their concerns. The Lee Heights group was so successful at reducing violence in their own neighborhood that other groups in the Cleveland area began to consult with them about ways of dealing with violence in their own neighborhoods.

The Cleveland group provided most of the leadership for the September 2003 Peacemaker Congress held in Youngstown, Ohio. When Congress participants held a public witness at the Youngstown courthouse against the USA Patriot Act—which had resulted in massive violations of civil rights—they were approached by people from Warren, Ohio. Police brutality in Warren, including summary executions, had hit an all-time high. Congress participants went with people organizing against the brutality to pray outside of the courthouse in Warren. The Cleveland group then provided ongoing support for the organizers in Warren, including participating in an October 18 prayer vigil in the Warren town square.[36]

However, CPT-Cleveland did not devote itself strictly to local issues. After the September 11, 2001, hijacker catastrophes, the group organized a prayer vigil in Cleveland and Columbus. They also joined with other national and state groups to protest the death penalty and the impending US invasion of Iraq in 2003.

ISSUES ARISING FROM URBAN PROJECTS

Statistics

On most CPT projects workers have difficulty proving they caused something *not* to happen. Jeff Heie spent hours tracking statistics of the Columbia Heights neighborhood in the first phase of the DC project, but the DC CPTers found that they could not empirically prove that the CPT project reduced crime rates. (Although they did establish that most crimes happened in the vicinity of certain buildings.) The "success" of the Columbia Heights project rested more on the feelings of the community that they had the power to make Columbia Heights a safer place.

36. CPTnet, "Youngstown, Ohio: Peacemaker Congress," Oct 3, 2003. See also CPT, "Cleveland."

Lack of Continuity

According to (Arendt) Hull, the lack of continuity was the "bane" of the Washington Project.[37] After John Reuwer left, the project in the Warner was mostly run by people who came in for two to three week stints. This lack of continuity made it difficult to effectively promote the project with the media, as noted above. It also negatively affected organizing and relationship-building efforts with neighbors. Short-term people generally have less emotional investment in a project, so the drive to make a project successful is also less.

Community Organizing vs. NVDA

In a July 1996 sermon at the Seattle Mennonite Church (which referenced Matthew 13:24–30), Cole Hull wrote,

> The causes and faces of violence are many. So too must be our methods and techniques in confronting and diffusing it. This looks like accompaniment in Haiti, this looks like community organizing in Washington, D.C. In Hebron, it was human rights documentation and often nonviolent direct action ... Restless persuasion and relentless persistence is what I have begun to call it.[38]

The CPT training that Urban Project personnel received focused mostly on the fundamentals of Nonviolent Direct Action. Although participants received training in how to organize campaigns and public witnesses, community organizing was not really a part of the cur-

37. Arendt, interview, Oct 21, 2003.
38. Hull, "Weed and Seed."

riculum.[39] Yet, community organizing constituted the bulk of the work in Washington, Richmond, and Cleveland.[40]

Ironically, many CPTers who would not hesitate to stand in between soldiers pointing guns at unarmed civilians find the thought of going door to door and asking strangers to talk about their neighborhood daunting. To some extent, the Washington and Richmond projects closed because CPTers who had gone through training did not want to work in DC or Richmond. Perhaps some of them thought working overseas was more exciting, but some also said that they had come into CPT to do the work of unarmed soldiers, not community organizers.

Outsider Status

The fact that CPTers on the urban projects came from outside the communities they served also constituted a challenge. The best community organizing happens when people within a community take responsibility for the organizing. Outsiders cannot continue the work indefinitely. Significantly, the "phase out" plan in Liveoak's report specifically mentioned having to motivate neighbors to continue the Orange Hat patrols.

Wes Hare wrote in a 1998 report,

39. A reservist who spent time in Warner Apartments wrote in his largely negative evaluation of his experience:

> On the CPC application it lists worship leading, photography, public speaking, First Aid, political campaigns, organizing, visual arts, fundraising, CPR, writing, video, music, teaching, group facilitation computers, organizing volunteers, mediation. I was excited, because many of these were things I had done. On this project, I have done little but organizing, which I simply don't enjoy . . . I did not enjoy my stay with CPC. I did not enjoy the work, nor did I get the sense that anyone else did. Perhaps "service" means to some doing what they do not enjoy; if that is the case, I am not cut out for "service." (e-mail to CPT Chicago, Nov 6, 1995)

In an April 7, 2007 e-mail to the author, the former reservist told her that when he realized CPTers in DC had been "unwitting agents of gentrification," he "decided that spiritual growth starts from within one's community rather than imposing a solution from the outside" and so decided to work within his own ethnic religious community.

40. Kryss Chupp noted that conflict-resolution trainer Mark Chupp presented a model related to community organizing to the Cleveland training group, but not in depth. Chupp said he would serve as a resource if the Cleveland group wanted more in-depth training. E-mail, Oct 26, 2003.

> As I review my past two years of time and energy with primary effort on urban violence reduction, there seems no doubt that this is a long struggle of foundation building. My primary criticism of the Columbia Heights PUP . . . Is that there is no apparent active remaining life there to sustain and maintain that very visible and "successful" effort. The impact of the D.C. PUP was made and expressed in active "Orange Hat patrols, crack house closings, and the jailing of a notorious slumlord," etc. However in spite of significant press and visibility, there remains no organized and active energy within CPT, MVS, Sojourners Neighborhood Center, AFSC-D.C. or any other organization to my knowledge. The D.C. PUP did not build a foundation and beyond learnings and reflections of individuals, some still in D.C., does not exist. Equally, in spite of major recruiting efforts to involve "persons of color" in that PUP team . . . [sic] that goal was not realized. With this awareness, I've tried to build the base, seeking to maintain it and to reach outward to other cultural groups as well as reaching outward to other neighborhoods . . . [41]

Related to the problem of being "outsiders" was the lack of racial diversity amongst CPTers working on the project. With the exception of Rey Lopez, a Filipino CPTer, all of the volunteers in DC and Richmond were white.

Nimby—Not In My Backyard

Although the Columbia Heights project helped neighbors change the atmosphere for the better in their own neighborhoods, it did not take other parts of the city suffering from drug-related violence into consideration. When crack houses move out of one neighborhood, crack houses in other neighborhoods generally open up. The DC project did not have the resources to go after the problem on a macro level.

41. CPT Richmond PUP, "Extending the RichPUP through 1998." Tammy Krause has a different analysis of what happened in the D.C. neighborhoods after CPT PUP left. The neighborhood was already in transition before the Washington project ended. Incidents of violent crime reduced significantly, so neighbors stopped feeling the need to do regular Orange Hat patrols. Many people involved in the struggle to reclaim the neighborhood from drugs and crime are still there as of 2004. "That's what gives me strength," Krause told the author in a November 15, 2004 phone interview. "There are good people still there. This is their community."

On the other hand, CPT Cleveland has served as a resource for other neighborhoods in the Cleveland area that want to duplicate their success-ful efforts to remove drug dealers from their neighborhood.

Perceived Lack of Support from Chicago Office

One of the people who worked longest with CPT's urban projects once told the author that DC was the "bastard stepchild" of CPT projects. People who worked in DC and Richmond saw the attention paid to international projects within CPT, especially to Hebron, and perceived that the Chicago office did not support their efforts with the same enthusiasm. Other proj-ects, they said, did not have to recruit their own people or raise their own funds. One corps member told the author that they never had a worker who could write releases well. He said that the urban projects thus had a lower profile than Hebron, which was started by two CPTers, Kathleen Kern and Wendy Lehman, who had extensive writing experience.

From the perspective of staff in the Chicago office, they always had an understanding of the need for domestic projects. In a December 25, 1996 memo to CPT staff, steering committee and workers, Stoltzfus wrote,

> There is much concern that we have not initiated another project in Washington, D.C. and failed to open one or more additional domestic projects. We receive occasional feelers from Wichita, KS and other places. In addition we have ongoing conversations with Reservist [sic] Jeff Heie and Tammy Krause who continue to live in the Columbia road [sic] area about another project. We should have one or more new urban projects.[42]

Constituent Support

While people who worked on the urban project perceived a lack of support from other CPTers and staff in the organization, the DC project received overwhelmingly positive responses from CPT's church constituency.[43] For many people, reducing drug-related crime in a neighborhood was cause for unreserved celebration. The first phase of the DC project was largely self-supporting because of the donations and the participation of Brethren Voluntary Service and Mennonite Board of Missions.

42. Gene Stoltzfus, "Memo to CPT co-workers."

43. An exception to this general approval came from those who believed CPT should not have enabled the observance of a satanic holiday like Halloween.

Sometimes the approval of CPT's urban projects was backhanded. People who disapproved of CPT's work in Palestine/Israel and Haiti would urge CPTers to put more resources into urban violence.[44] Most people, however, asked the question legitimately and honestly, "Why do we have to fly halfway around the world to address violence in other countries, when we have so much violence going on here at home?"

In August 2000, all full-time CPTers, staff and certain trusted advisors participated in a retreat at Cliff and Arlene Kindy's Joyfield Farm. At the end of the retreat, the participants affirmed that CPT should continue to grow. In five years time, they set a goal of fifty full-timers and 250 reservists keeping six to ten projects running. At least one project, they decided, would always be in a North American urban center. So far, that project has not materialized, even though the organization has grown significantly since 2000. Nevertheless, CPT now has trained regional groups in DC and Cleveland, and has two offices located in Toronto and Chicago. While the organization as a whole has not committed itself to urban projects, among its personnel are many workers who have made a commitment to "seek the welfare" of the cities they have chosen to call home.[45]

44. One prominent Mennonite theologian made a point of coming up to Kathleen Kern after she had given a presentation on CPT's work in Hebron and Haiti to express his disapproval of those projects. When she told him about the work in DC, he said, "Well, *that* seems like a worthwhile project."

45. See Jeremiah 29:7.

4

Hebron, West Bank 1995–2000

"We have everything here: land, water; it could be very beautiful. What we are missing is love between people. There is enough for everyone if everyone is willing to share. Engineers should be studying how to grow bread in the desert, not inventing new weapons. Palestine needs factories to make medicines to heal diseases, not to manufacture weapons."

—'Atta Jaber—whose home was destroyed twice, on August 19, 1998 and September 16, 1998, by the Israeli military authorities. The second time, he was arrested and charged with "assault by infant," because he thrust his baby son Rajah into the arms of a soldier and said, "Here, you take him; I can no longer take care of him."[1]

CPT's work in Hebron and the surrounding district is a study in "mosts": It is the longest running CPT project. It has generated the most releases.[2] More CPTers have been arrested and assaulted in the Hebron District than on any other project location. The deep relationships CPTers have formed with Israelis in various peace and human rights organizations make Hebron the project in which CPTers have had the warmest relationships with people in the dominant or "oppressing" culture (with the exception of those CPTers who have worked with indigenous communities in North America). CPT's West Bank work probably has drawn the most criticism of any project due to Israel's mythical, or

1. Quotation from Campaign for Secure Dwelling materials in Atta Jaber's file at CPT Hebron's office. CPT Hebron, "Chronology, 1995–2003."

2. Until 2003, when CPT's Iraq project began sending out numerous releases as war approached, 40–49 percent of all releases from project locations came from Hebron.

symbolic, status.[3] It has also probably brought the most praise for CPT's efforts from its constituency and human rights organizations.

But when CPTers Wendy Lehman and Kathleen Kern wrote the proposal for the Hebron project in spring 1995, they had no idea the project would still be running ten years later, nor did they know how much the project would shape the functioning of teams on other project locations. They suggested that CPT have a team there for five months only to provide a violence-deterring presence until the Israeli military re-deployed from Hebron as part of the Oslo Peace process.

BACKGROUND[4]

About 120,000 Palestinians and 450 Israeli settlers lived in Hebron when CPT set up its project in 1995.[5] The city is also home to the Al-Ibrahimi Mosque/Cave of Machpelah, where legend has it that Abraham, Sarah, Rebekah, Isaac, Jacob, and Leah are buried. In 1929 an Arab mob attacked the Jewish Quarter established in the sixteenth century by Jews fleeing the Inquisition in Spain.[6] At least sixty-seven Jewish men, women, and children were hacked to death and many more wounded. The Arab neighbors of those living in the Jewish Quarters saved more than four hundred Jewish residents. But the slaughtered Jews, rather than the rescued, loom

3. To many Jews, Israel represents safety and pride in Jewish culture. To Christian Zionists it represents a tool in an eschatological drama, wherein all Jews around the world must emigrate to Israel in order to precipitate Jesus' second coming. To Palestinians, Arabs, and Muslims around the world, Israel embodies ruthless colonialism.

4. The following are good sources for an overview of the Israeli-Palestinian conflict: Abu-Sharif and Mahnaimi, *The Best of Enemies*; Avnery, *My Friend, the Enemy*; Benvenisti, *Conflicts and Contradictions*; Benvenisti, *Intimate Enemies*; Benvenisti, *Sacred Landscape*; Chacour, *Blood Brothers*; Chomsky, *The Fateful Triangle*; Cohen, *Israel and the Arab World*; Elon, *A Blood-Dimmed Tide*; Finkelstein, *Image and Reality of the Israel-Palestine Conflict*; Flapan, *The Birth of Israel*; Khalidi, *Palestinian Identity*; Morris, *1948 and After*; Morris, *The Birth of the Palestinian Refugee Problem*; Reuther and Reuther, *The Wrath of Jonah*; Rokach, *Israel's Sacred Terrorism*; Said, *The Politics of Dispossession*; Said, *The Question of Palestine*; Said and Hitchens, *Blaming the Victims*; Segev, *1949: One Palestine*; Segev, *The First Israelis*; Segev, *The Seventh Million*; Shlaim, *The Iron Wall*; Turki, *The Disinherited*.

5. Exact numbers are difficult to obtain, since interested parties tend to maximize their own numbers and minimize the numbers of their opponents—unless they are describing people attacking them, in which case they maximize the number of opponents.

6. Muslims fleeing the Inquisition also settled in Hebron during the same period. Their influence can be seen in the name of Qurtuba (Cordoba) girls' school and the Andalus mall.

large in Israeli history and the memories of the Jews in Hebron. (Muslims descended from families who rescued Jews are still proud, of their families' efforts, however. "We considered them Arabs, like us," one descendant of these families told the team.) The massacre still affects current interactions between the two groups.[7]

When Israel's settlement policy began to take root after the 1967 war, the Hebron area became a special target for the rightwing religious adherents of Gush Emunim (Bloc of the Faithful), because the Patriarchs and Matriarchs are purportedly buried there.[8] Rabbi Moshe Levinger and a band of armed supporters took over the only hotel in Hebron in 1968 and refused to leave. To appease them, the army gave them a Jordanian army camp on the outskirts of Hebron that later became the settlement of Kiryat Arba. In 1979, Levinger's wife, Miriam, and a group of women and children moved into Hebron under the protection of the Israeli military and over the protests of the local Palestinian inhabitants. A militant wing of the Palestinian Liberation Organization (PLO) killed six yeshiva students in Hebron in 1980.[9] Israeli military response was swift: It authorized Miriam Levinger's settlement of Beit Hadassah, next to the pre-1929 Jewish synagogue, as well as two new settlements in the center city.

7. Oded Avissar wrote a history of the Hebron Jewish community, *Sefer Hevron*, which included the names of both those slaughtered and those rescued, as well as the names of the rescuers. Yona Rochlin, a descendant of the pre-1929 Jewish community who opposes the presence of the settlers in Hebron, told the team that the settlers had bought all available copies of *Sefer Hevron*, now out of print, and burned them. (Other descendants of the pre-1929 community do support the Hebron settlers). Segev, *One Palestine, Complete*. "Jewish History records very few cases of a mass rescue of this dimension," notes Segev (326). The grandfather of team friend Hisham Sharabati had worked as a "shabbos goy" for the Jewish community (i.e., he turned out their lights for them on the Sabbath). He told Lehman and Kern that on the day of the massacre he witnessed the British officers opening the gate leading into the Jewish Quarter and telling the Arab mob to "get the Jews." The author has not been able to verify this claim in any other written source, but many Palestinians in Hebron also blame the British.

8. Founded in 1974, Gush Emunim was an organization for people who believed that settling the West Bank and Gaza would help hasten the coming of the Messiah. Not all who belonged to the organization were violent. Some thought that the coming of the Messiah would benefit the Palestinians living in the Occupied Territories as well.

9. The attack was launched from Dubboya Street (see below), which may have factored into settlers targeting the people living there at the time that CPTers began their presence on the street in the summer of 1995.

Relations between the settlers and Palestinians continued to deteriorate throughout the period of the first Intifada[10] and culminated in the
February 1994 massacre in the Al-Ibrahimi mosque.[11]

Reports of the massacre stated that the settler Baruch Goldstein,
a medical doctor born in Brooklyn, New York, began spraying Muslim
men and boys with bullets at 5:30 a.m. Twenty-nine worshippers died
in the mosque before two Palestinians (subsequently shot by Israeli soldiers) beat him to death with a fire extinguisher.[12] The Israel Defence
Force (IDF) killed another twenty-nine Palestinians in the demonstrations that followed—including one notorious incident when soldiers shot
Palestinians standing in line to donate blood to the massacre victims. The
army put all Palestinians in Hebron under curfew for approximately six
weeks,[13] while allowing the settlers to roam the streets freely. By the time
Wendy Lehman and Kathleen Kern arrived a year later, people expressed

10. "Intifada" means "shaking off" in Arabic, and refers to Palestinian attempts to
"shake off" the Israeli military occupation of the West Bank and Gaza. The Intifada that
began at the end of September 2000 is called the "Al-Aqsa Intifada" because it began
after Ariel Sharon, surrounded by hundreds of riot police, visited the Haram al-Sharif
compound, which includes the Al Aqsa mosque, the third holiest site of Islam.

11. In March 1994 CPT put out a paper, developed in consultation with Mercy Corps
International, entitled "Discussion Points for Middle East Peacemaking Hebron Ibrahimi
Mosque Massacre." It included the following positions: (1) the tragedy in Hebron suggested that the Occupation must end in "specific phased withdrawal strategies" based
upon U.N. resolutions; (2) US aid to Israel needed to be reviewed; (3) the Palestinian
population must be protected and settlers disarmed; (4) an independent international inquiry should investigate the Hebron massacre; (5) financial support for anti-Palestinian
hate groups, such as Kach and the Jewish Defense League, needed to be investigated; (6)
Israel and the PLO should reiterate their commitment to the Fourth Geneva Conventions;
and (7) "the goal of these processes should lead to an internationally sanctioned State of
Palestine based upon international law.

12. Accounts of the massacre differ wildly due to partisanship and to the panic and
mayhem at the time. The author's description of the massacre is based on conversations
with dozens of Palestinians and Israelis, as well as on her reading of different accounts.

13. To those unaware of the realities of military occupation, "curfew" summons up
images of teenagers having to be home at a certain time. In Hebron, "curfew" means
that soldiers will not let Palestinians leave their homes, even to buy food or for medical
emergencies. A Mennonite missionary in Hebron told team members that when Israel
imposed a curfew on Palestinians during the first Gulf War in 1990, the Palestinians
knew it was going to be imposed and were able to stock up on food supplies. But since no
Palestinians anticipated the Goldstein massacre, two months of curfew meant that many
families went hungry.

as much bitterness about the collective punishment imposed upon them as they did about the massacre.

In the winter of 1995, CPT sent Kern and Lehman as part of a delegation—requested by Palestinian Christians and Non-governmental Organizations (NGOs)—whose purpose was to document a burst of settlement expansion around Jerusalem.[14] Since the Oslo Accords were signed in 1993, Israeli confiscation of Palestinian lands around settlements had increased dramatically. The Accords had had the effect of neutralizing the Israeli left and international opinion, which allowed the Israeli government to grab as much land as it could around key settlements close to Israel before final status talks. When Palestinians protested, Israel and the US told them that they would need to make some sacrifices if they wanted a state. Israel had also invested itself with the sole authority to decide who was and was not violating the Oslo Accords.[15]

After the rest of the delegation returned to North America, Kern and Lehman remained until the first week of April 1995. Basing themselves in the Bethlehem home of Zoughbi and Elaine Zoughbi, the two women traveled throughout Israel, the West Bank, and Gaza talking to Israeli, Palestinian, and international peace and human rights organizations.

A number of factors kept pulling the women back to Hebron: 1) The January/February 1995 delegation had visited Hebron and seen the hysterical outrage of Hebron settlers when the delegation's Palestinian driver had attempted to enter the Ibrahimi Mosque/Cave of Machpelah.[16]

14. Some of these contacts included Don Wagner of Mercy Corps (later director of Middle Eastern Studies at North Park College in Chicago), Naim Ateek of the Sabeel Liberation Theology Center, and Zoughbi Zoughbi of the Wi'am Center in Bethlehem. In a February 13, 2004, phone interview with the author, Gene Stoltzfus said that since the 1990s he and others on the Steering Committee had been putting out feelers as to whether there was a place for CPT in Israel and Palestine to various organizations working on peace and justice issues in the region. The initial delegation in which Kern and Lehman participated was in the region from January 29–February 12, 1995, after which they began their exploratory project.

15. For more background on the Oslo process, see Ashrawi, *This Side of Peace; Israeli-Palestinian Interim Agreement*; Chomsky, *World Orders Old and New*; Said, *The Politics of Dispossession*; Savir, *The Process*. Those with access to back issues of *PS: The Intelligent Guide to Jewish Affairs* may wish to find Gush Shalom's article in the May 13, 1998 issue, "Who's violating Oslo." *PS* ceased publication in 1998. See also Gush Shalom, "Who is violating the Agreements?"

16. A May 1994 CPT Middle East delegation also visited Hebron and reported on the reign of terror that settlers there imposed on their Palestinian neighbors. Kern had seen the CPT Steering Committee member Dale Aukerman's slides from that delegation's

2) Zoughbi Zoughbi had a friend in Hebron, Hisham Sharabati, who was active in organizing grassroots efforts against the Occupation. Sharabati, a journalist imprisoned during the first Intifada, had broad connections with both Israeli and international peace activists. When Kern and Lehman spent an evening in his home, he understood precisely how a small group of internationals could work in Hebron to deter and document violence. He would become CPT Hebron's earliest friend and most trusted advisor. 3) On February 25, 1995, an organization called the Hebron Solidarity Committee (HSC), comprising Israeli and international Jewish activists, held a vigil in Hebron to commemorate the slaughter in the mosque one year earlier. Kern and Lehman came down to Hebron for the demonstration and had a chance to talk to the activists. The fact that they were publicizing the systemic brutality imposed on the Palestinians in Hebron and trying to organize solidarity visits seemed in line with much of CPT's mandate. In a meeting with some of the HSC members in March, Kern and Lehman noted that CPT would be receiving invitations from Palestinian groups to set up a project in Hebron, and that it would be helpful for the HSC to issue an invitation for CPT as well. Lehman and Kern, thus, could write in their proposal that CPT would be working with both Israelis and Palestinians as they set up in a violence-deterring project in Hebron. The HSC members said they would be happy to work with CPT, but they believed they had no right to invite internationals to come stay in the Palestinian territories. They maintained that only Palestinians had the right to issue such an invitation.[17]

Prior to the meeting with the HSC activists, Kern and Lehman had met with the Public Relations director of the Hebron municipality, Ahlam Muhtasib. She asked about CPT's work on other projects. When Kern explained what she had done with CPT in Haiti, Muhtasib exclaimed, "That is just what we need here, people who will live in the Old City and report what the settlers and soldiers are doing there." She gleefully described

---

visit to Hebron, and his report on the thuggish behavior of settlers in Hebron made an impression.

17. HSC members also had strong negative reactions to Kern and Lehman referring to them as an "Israeli" group, since several of their members had made decisions not to become citizens for reasons of conscience. They further stipulated that they would not work with CPT if it endorsed the Oslo Process. See HSC, *Apartheid in Hebron: The True Face of Oslo*.

what it would look like if Americans dressed as Palestinians documented the behavior of soldiers and settlers.

Lehman and Kern told Muhtasib that in order to set up a project in Hebron, they would need an invitation from a local group. Accordingly, on April 3, 1995, the Mayor of Hebron, Mustafa Al-Natshe, faxed this invitation:

> April 3, 1995
>
> Dear Sir,
>
> As mayor of Hebron city, I'd like to express the wish of our citizens to receive a team of your [illegible] to accompany the people here as they struggle with the daily violence caused by the Israeli occupation. We hope that the team will report the truth of what it sees to the people in Canada and the United States. Thank you for your cooperation and understanding.
>
> Yours Sincerely,
>
> Mayor of Hebron
> Mustafa Natshe[18]

In their proposal drawn up at the Zoughbi home in Bethlehem, Lehman and Kern suggested that CPT send a team of four people to Hebron from June 1995 until October 1995. Since Israeli Prime Minister Yitzhak Rabin had scheduled a pullout of Israeli troops from Hebron in late summer or early fall, and since it was unclear whether the Israeli government would remove the Hebron settlers, Kern and Lehman suggested that CPT stay for a period of five months. They reasoned that having international observers for a month or two after the army redeployed might make the transition smoother. As was the case with Haiti, CPT ended

---

18. Natsche, fax, April 3, 1995. Given Natsche's role as a member of the establishment in Hebron, this invitation came from the least "grassroots" source of any CPT project. However, Lehman and Kern viewed Muhtasib as the real source of the invitation. She put them in touch with many families in Hebron who were losing their lands to settlement expansion and who were facing soldier and settler violence on a daily level. Although the team in Hebron as of 2008 still makes regular visits to the Hebron municipality to report on events happening in their neighborhood, the municipality could not be called precisely a "partner" in the same way that the Hebron Rehabilitation Committee, Sabeel, Holy Land Trust, the Hebron Land Defence Committee or the Israeli groups Ta'ayush, Israeli Coalition Against House Demolitions, and Bnei Avraham/Breaking the Silence are partners.

up staying far longer than originally intended—thirteen years, as of this writing.

In late May and early June, Cliff Kindy, Kathleen Kern, Wendy Lehman, and Jeff Heie set up the project in Hebron. Later in the summer, Kathy Kamphoefner, a communications professor at Manchester College and Carmen Pauls, who had worked with Mennonite Board of Missions in the Galilee, joined the team.[19]

The team spent most of the summer building relationships with Palestinians whose proximity to settlements in Hebron and on the outskirts of Hebron left them vulnerable to attack. They also developed significant relationships with Palestinian journalists and Hebron University students and professors.

Hebron University

The relationship with Hebron University students and professors led to the first "official" arrests of team members in July.[20] During the first Intifada, (1987–1993), the Israeli military sealed the front gates of Hebron University with concrete and metal. Even after Arafat, Rabin, and Peres signed the Oslo Accords in 1993, the Israeli authorities refused to allow the University to open the gate, claiming that doing so would allow students to throw stones or Molotov cocktails at passing Israeli jeeps. However, the University was nowhere near the Israeli settlements in Hebron or official checkpoints, so patrols rarely passed it.[21] Keeping the front gate

19. Kindy had not yet gone through training in 1995, but served on the CPT Steering Committee and had been part of a two-month CPT presence in Gaza in 1993 (see chap. 13). Kamphoefner had lived and studied for some years in Egypt and could speak conversational Arabic. She went through CPT training in 1997. Pauls would later work for MCC in Jerusalem and Iraq and also spoke some Arabic. Given that the team expected the project would last for only five months, the others did not put serious effort into learning the language, other than as a method of socializing. (Asking for help with a language is a good way of building relationships in almost any culture. Given the fact that Arabic is considered a difficult language even by Arabs, Palestinians are especially pleased when internationals make an effort to learn it.)

20. A week earlier, Cliff Kindy and Jeff Heie were detained by Israeli soldiers while accompanying a truck bringing water to Palestinian families living near the settlement of Tel Rumeida. That incident is described more detail below in the discussion of settler violence.

21. Lost in this concern for soldiers' safety was the fact that settlers had attacked the university in 1983, killing three students and wounding thirty-three students, teachers and staff. After the attack, Hebron settler Moshe Levinger said, "Whoever did this has sanctified God's name in public." Friedman, *Zealots for Zion,* 29.

closed meant that students, staff, and teachers had to climb over the fence or walk to the back campus entrance, a considerable distance from the main road. The closure seemed to serve no other purpose than collective punishment.

After the team made contact with professors at the University, one of them volunteered to help team members set up their computer. Upon hearing about CPT's work in Haiti, he spoke with students and other professors and then approached the team, asking if they would help take down the gate.

CPTers met up with the Hebron Solidarity Committee in Jerusalem to finalize plans for the July 22, 1995 action at the Hebron University gate. Hillel Barak and Maxine Kaufman from the HSC came to participate. Originally, for reasons of safety, Palestinians organizing the event planned to provide the tools and let the Israelis and CPTers do all the work, but when no Israeli patrols showed up, students joined them in chiseling through the welds on the metal gate and breaking the concrete seal with sledgehammers. When the army did arrive an hour later, students and staff fell back and soldiers under the command of Captain Eyal Ziv arrested Cliff Kindy, Kathy Kamphoefner, Wendy Lehman, and Maxine Kaufman. The police took the women to Abu Kabeer prison near Jaffa, and Kindy to the Russian Compound in Jerusalem, where he spent the night in a cell next to a Hebron settler youth who had been arrested for assaulting a police officer the day before.[22]

Linda Brayer, a lawyer who had put her services at the disposal of the team after the water truck incident at Tel Rumeida (see below), once again represented the team members and got them released. Yochanan Lorwin of the Alternative Information Center—an organization committed to publishing information about Israel and the Occupied territories censored or overlooked in the mainstream media—posted their bond. All four of the arrestees arrived in shackles for their hearing. A representative of the American Consulate in East Jerusalem vigorously intervened when an officer refused to uncuff Lehman long enough for her to use the bathroom. Later, referring to the arrests at Tel Rumeida ten days previously,

---

22. This incarceration happened after Kindy had begun receiving death threats from the Hebron settlers, because they thought he was a member of Hamas. See the section "Interactions with Hebron settlers" under "Issues" at the end of chap. 6.

the chief officer at the Consulate told team members, "Try to wait at least another couple of weeks before you get arrested again, okay?"[23]

Lehman noted in her unpublished report about the action and the arrests, that Captain Eyal Ziv repeatedly told them that the students at the University were angry with the CPTers and HSCers for destroying the gate. However, the students and faculty gave the team members who had not been arrested a tea and cookie reception at the University to thank them for their efforts and told them that a chant— "Jeff and Cliff did better than TIPH"—was circulating in their honor.[24]

Later, Lehman and Kern visited Captain Eyal, as he said they should call him. They told him what CPT had done in Haiti and why they were in Hebron. When they asked why the army wanted the gate closed, he smiled tolerantly and said essentially that the closure was for security reasons that Lehman and Kern could not understand. He also told them that representatives of the University had been in dialogue with the Israeli Civil Administration about opening the gate and that CPT had ruined negotiations. The team's contacts at the University later told them that Captain Eyal was lying. Administrators had never come to the Civil Administration hat in hand to ask for the doors to be opened. "It is not for them to give permission. It is our right," one of these administrators told them.

Bus bombings by the militant group Hamas in spring 1996 led to a closure of Palestinian universities throughout the West Bank. Despite the fact that no faculty, staff, or students from Hebron University were ever implicated in the bombings, the Israeli government sealed the University on March 5, 1996, forcing students to meet in schools and other buildings scattered throughout the city of Hebron. The rents for these spaces pushed Hebron University to the verge of bankruptcy

23. The Hebron team would continue to have a cordial working relationship with representatives of the American Consulate in the years following. Since they dealt with the rights of Palestinian Americans as well as Israeli Americans, consulate members were generally sympathetic to the team's work. They especially appreciated CPT funneling information about land confiscation and settlement building to them. However, meetings in which controversial issues were discussed generally happened in secrecy, and team members were never permitted to quote Consulate representatives.

24. Lehman, "Arrest Report." TIPH is an acronym for Temporary International Presence in Hebron, a group of European observers who set up a monitoring presence in Hebron after the Goldstein massacre. The Israeli government refused to renew their mandate after three months, claiming they were biased toward the Palestinians. However, after the Hebron Accords were signed in 1995 TIPH returned as part of the agreement, and remain in Hebron as of this writing.

CPT began meeting regularly with students and faculty throughout 1995 and 1996 to discuss strategies for re-opening the University. On December 9, 1996, after the Israeli military extended the closure of Hebron University without giving reasons for doing so, the students began a concerted campaign to end the closure. After an initial occupation of the campus on December 9, they began meeting every day outside the gates from about 8:00 a.m. to 11:00 a.m. Some of the slogans on their signs included, "We only want to study," and "We did not kill Yitzhak Rabin," referring to the fact that Bar Ilan University, Yigal Amir's school, remained open after he assassinated Rabin in 1995.

Student organizers maintained careful control of participants in their witness, limiting the numbers who were present and restraining those who responded to soldier provocations by yelling at them. When the soldiers were behaving in a particularly insulting manner, the students would sit down to defuse the tension.

The Hebron team accompanied the students every day, but did not participate much in the planning, with one important exception. One of the organizers, as the soldiers became more aggressive each day of demonstration, asked if the team had suggestions for responding to the soldiers' provocation. The team suggested that the organizers include more female students and put them in front of the men. The male students were shocked at the idea of putting women in danger and said they thought the women would refuse. Later, with excitement and bemusement, they reported to the team that the female students were eager to stand in front.

The strategy worked; soldiers were indeed much more reluctant to push the women around. On December 28, 1996, Hebron University re-opened. Whether the students' public witnesses were the main reason for the re-opening is unclear. Netanyahu was facing international pressure to finalize redeployment in Hebron and criticism of his hard-line policies in the Occupied Territories. A Palestinian journalist told the CPTers that it was the negotiations for redeployment—to be finalized on January 17, 1997—that had caused the Israeli authorities to "permit" the University to open, since the University was in H-1, the area for which the Palestinian authority would take control. On the other hand, at the time the demonstrations began, the students, faculty, and staff did not know when—or if—redeployment would occur. They decided to resist whatever the consequences, and the administration followed the students' lead by terminating the leases on rented classrooms.

On the day the University re-opened a student told the team, "This is the result of our peace."[25]

Settler Violence

The most pressing work that the team undertook in the summer and early fall of 1995 revolved around street violence committed by both Israeli settlers and soldiers.

On July 1, 1995, Palestinian witnesses from the Tel Rumeida neighborhood told the team that Hebron settler Baruch Marzel and an Israeli soldier had assassinated sixteen-year-old Ibrahim Khader Idreis. The boy, who lived with his family in Jordan, was visiting relatives near Tel Rumeida. The extended family ran out of bread at breakfast and sent him to buy more at a shop around the corner. He slipped on his aunt's shoes for the short errand. Palestinian witnesses said that the boy refused to stop when Marzel called to him and was subsequently shot once in the leg and once in the chest. A soldier then shot him again in the stomach. The Israeli military told an uncle visiting from the U.S. that his nephew had attempted to stab a soldier, but soldiers produced no knife as evidence. When Idreis' uncle picked him up to take him to the hospital, he saw that the shots to the leg had nearly amputated it below the knee. The boy died in the car on the way to the hospital.

Lehman, who went to investigate after hearing of the incident, saw soldiers and settlers laughing together as one settler, Noam Federman, pushed a baby stroller through a large smear of the young man's blood. Two days later, Lehman interviewed the uncle, Yunis Idreis. He told her the family had not responded as quickly to the gunshots as they might have otherwise, because they never dreamed Ibrahim would be a target. If he were going to attack someone, the uncle asked, why would he do it

---

25. For a more thorough discussion of the Hebron students' resistance, see Kern and Lehman, "Teaching Nonviolence in Hebron." This article also describes the team's experience teaching about nonviolence to Palestinian boys in a putative conversational English class in the summer of 1995. One of the boys, Osaid Rasheed, eventually became a regular translator for the team. See also "Collective Punishment," 2, and the following CPTnet releases related to the university witnesses: "Christian Peacemaker Team to hold teach-in," Apr 4, 1996; "Hebron: Soldiers Attack University Sit-In," (no date for release, but event occurred on Apr 9, 1996); "Hebron: Conversations with Soldiers," Apr 10, 1996; "CPT Conducts Teach-in," Apr 10, 1996; "Hebron: CPT Accompanies University Students," Apr 17, 1996; CPT Hebron: Five Frequently Asked Questions," Apr 19, 1996; "Open Hebron University Now" May 20, 1996. "Urgent Action Appeal Update," Sept 8, 1996.

in broad daylight in front of a soldier camp and in shoes four sizes too small? He told the CPTers that he did not think people would believe his story when he returned to his home in Seattle, Washington.[26]

Another family living in the Tel Rumeida neighborhood, the Abu Haikels, would develop an especially warm relationship with the team that first summer and in subsequent years. One could write a full-length book describing the assaults and the indignities this family has faced since the settlement of Tel Rumeida moved in next door in the mid-1980s.[27] The family resisted these pressures with a certain *joi de vivre*. Once, after settlers hit his mother in the head with a rock, Hani Abu Haikel called the Israeli police, who refused to come out. He then walked over to the soldiers' camp with a metal pipe, told the soldiers there that he intended to hit a settler with it and then walked back to his house and waited for the police to arrive. They took him and his mother to the police station where he was able to make a statement. The Shin Bet officer who took his statement appeared sympathetic to the Abu Haikels and wanted more information on the settler attacks. Hani Abu Haikel had also established meaningful relationships with Hebron Solidarity Committee members.

The delivery of water in the summertime is a pressing issue for all families in Hebron who live on hills. The Israeli government diverts most of the water from the West Bank aquifers to Israel and Israeli settlements in the West Bank.[28] Consequently, for five months out of the year, the pipes do not have enough water pressure for people living on hills (which is the situation of most of the Palestinians in Hebron) to have running water. Those who can afford to do so buy water from the municipality or private sources. The Abu Haikels paid about $28 for each water truck delivery to their home on the summit of Tel Rumeida.

However, after settlers had broken one too many windshields on water trucks coming up to Tel Rumeida, the municipality announced it would no longer deliver water there. The team told the Abu Haikels they

26. See two unpublished reports written by Wendy Lehman, "Israeli settler and soldiers assault Palestinians" and "Uncle of slain Palestinian teenager talks." The comment regarding how people would respond in Seattle is from author's memory.

27. See, for example, CPTnet, "Israeli police slow to respond," Oct 11, 1995; CPTnet, "Christian Peacemaker Team members accompany school girl," Oct 17, 1995.

28. See CESR, "The Right to Water in Palestine: A Background" and "The Right to Water in Palestine: Crisis in Gaza." See also Tolan, "Mideast Water Series: Collision in Gaza" and "Mideast Water Series: The Politics of Mideast Water."

would be happy to accompany the truck. On July 12, 1995, ten days be-fore the team worked on opening the gates of Hebron University, Cliff Kindy and Jeff Heie received the call that the water truck was ready to go. Soldiers at the checkpoints detained them both, emphasizing that they meant "detention" and not "arrest."[29] As they stood in the sun for an hour, two settlers walked past and threatened to kill Kindy.

The police eventually took Kindy and Heie to the Civil Administration and questioned them further. Kindy tried to explain to the officer interro-gating him that the Abu Haikels had been without water for over a week.

The officer said, "But why do you care? Why are you doing this?"

Kindy told the officer that if he had been in Germany during the time of the Third Reich, he would have done the same thing on behalf of the Jews.

"Are you calling me a Nazi?" the officer asked.

Soldiers later told the two men that they were being held on charges of entering a closed military zone, assaulting an officer, and calling sol-diers Nazis.

Israeli friends from the Hebron Solidarity Committee called the team to tell them that they, too, had been arrested for making statements nearly identical to the one Kindy made about the Third Reich. Kern was touched and surprised by their concern, not realizing the impact the Nazi remark would eventually have.

The official IDF report on the incident said that Kindy and Heie had called the soldiers Nazis and "cursed them in every known language." In the following weeks, if settlers saw team members having friendly conversations with soldiers, they would draw them aside and tell them something involving the word "Naziim"—presumably informing them that these were the people who called soldiers "Nazis."

Three positive things happened because of the water truck incident.

---

29. The distinction is important. Arrests generate paper work and a record that Israeli authorities can use later to deny internationals entry into the country. Detentions are more common. Before the outbreak of the Al Aqsa Intifada in September 2000, soldiers would detain CPTers and then hand them over to the civilian police. The police in turn would hold the CPTers for hours, or even overnight, and then release them. Generally, the civilian police worked hard *not* to arrest CPTers and other internationals if possible. After the outbreak of the Al Aqsa Intifada, the Israeli authorities began using a record of detentions as a reason to deny internationals entry into the country.

1. Linda Brayer, a lawyer who had founded the Society of St. Yves in Jerusalem, volunteered to represent CPT. She and her legal staff also eventually provided free legal help to several of the families in Hebron that team members knew.

2. A *Washington Post* reporter came to spend the day with the team (Heie had worked on CPT's Washington DC project and the reporter's editor told him to work the local angle).[30] One of the Israeli settlers living at Tel Rumeida approached the reporter and told him, when Kindy was out of earshot, that he had not wanted to talk to him in front of Kindy because Kindy was a Muslim-American activist who had come to raise money to kill Jews. "That's funny," John Lancaster told him, "he told me he was an organic farmer from Northern Indiana. He's Christian." "Church of the Brethren," Kern chimed in, handing the man a CPT business card. The settler, a British immigrant whom the Abu Haikels said was not involved in violent attacks on Palestinians in the neighborhood, looked stunned. He had obviously believed the information about Kindy, who had an Amish-style beard similar to those worn by religious Muslims. The conversation thus dispelled rumors about Kindy being a Hamas activist, and the sporadic death threats that the team had been receiving became less frequent.[31]

3. The subsequent publicity drew both Israeli and international attention to the water shortage in Hebron. Many in the Israeli public expressed outrage when they saw footage of the settlements in the West Bank with swimming pools and well-watered lawns and then learned that Palestinians in Hebron did not have enough water for drinking and washing. Prime Minister Rabin sent a fact-finding mission to Hebron to determine the extent of the problem—even though the West Bank cities had complained for years of water shortages.[32]

30. Lancaster, "Hebron Daunting for Ex-DC Activist." See also Lehman, "Military Detains Two American Members."

31. See the section "Interactions with Hebron Settlers" under "Issues" at the end of chap. 6. Hani Abu Haikel found the idea of Kindy being a member of Hamas hysterically funny. When team members told him that the settlers had told Lancaster that Abu Haikel was also a member of Hamas, however, he became highly indignant. "I am Fatah!" he said, "I used to be part of Arafat's bodyguard."

32. See Kern, "From Haiti to Hebron," 189–90, and also Lehman, "Military Detains Two American Members."

By far the team's biggest exposure to settler harassment and intimidation happened on Dubboya Street, which ran by the settlement of Beit Hadassah. Every Saturday afternoon, male settlers would march up the street attacking Palestinians and breaking anything they could. By the time team members became aware of the problem, neighbors had stopped replacing glass in the windows. Hisham Sharabati introduced the team to the neighbors at an evening meeting. One family brought forth a four-year-old boy who had stitches near his eye from a metal projectile that a settler had launched at him with a slingshot. Another family introduced the team to a twelve-year old son in a full-leg cast. He told the CPTers that settler boys had pulled him to the ground and jumped on his leg until it broke.

The meeting convinced the team to begin a Saturday afternoon presence on Dubboya Street that lasted for several months. They recorded what they observed and when possible, stood between Palestinians and settlers in order to prevent assaults.

These Saturday afternoons took on a surreal quality, which Kern wrote about in an article for *The Link*, a magazine put out by Americans for Middle East Understanding:

ONE SATURDAY AFTERNOON ON DUBBOYA STREET[33]

by Kathleen Kern

Early in the afternoon, I was sitting outside an Arab home on Dubboya Street. At any given time, there are twelve or more children in the three-story house, many of whom peer through the bars of a small bay window and drop things—sometimes by accident and sometimes to see if the people below will pick them up.

As three adult male settlers were passing by on the opposite side of the street, one of the children dropped an empty plastic soda bottle from the window. It landed directly under the window, about twenty feet from the settlers. Nevertheless, one of them hailed a passing military jeep, pointed at the bottle on the ground and insisted the soldiers do something about it. Reinforcements arrived about four minutes later, and eight heavily armed soldiers

---

33. Kern, "Hebron's Theater of the Absurd," 11–13. The descriptions of the September 23, 1995 interactions with settlers appeared in a form closer to Kern's original account in her novel, *Where Such Unmaking Reigns*. Hisham Sharabati was the "journalist friend" referred to in the original piece, so the author has substituted his name for "journalist friend" in this chapter.

got out of their jeeps and sent a young man who lived there inside to fetch his father. The father came to the window to speak to the soldiers, which seemed to satisfy them. They left after barking what sounded like a stern warning.

II

Two male settlers in their late teens or early twenties walked past singing in Hebrew, with mocking expressions on their faces. One then began singing in nearly perfect English, "All we are singing is 'Give war a chance.'" When he passed by again about two hours later, he sang, "If I had an Uzi, I'd shoot 'em in the morning. I'd shoot 'em in the evening, all over my land." Then, speaking, he said, "It's MY land. It's not their land. "It's MY land." He later identified himself as Azrael ben Israel.

III

Between 2:00 and 2:30 pm, a confrontation occurred between Palestinian youth and Israeli soldiers near the checkpoint at one end of Dubboya St. This was one of several clashes that erupted after the settler attack on Qurtuba girls' school.[34] As I watched, some soldiers shot in the air and threw sound bombs [percussion grenades]. One soldier smiled and waved at two settlers who approached the checkpoint. A few minutes later, Azrael ben Israel walked past me briskly, muttering, "There should have been fifty or sixty dead Arabs by now."

IV

Another young Israeli also became interested in events at the checkpoint and asked me about the explosions. "They were sound bombs," I said. He asked for a definition of sound bombs and then

34. On the first day of school, September 10, 1995, Qurtuba, a Palestinian girls' school across from the settlement of Beit Hadassah, raised a Palestinian flag—as did all the other Palestinian schools around the city. Prior to that time, the Israeli authorities forbade the display of the flag and could impose harsh consequences on Palestinians who chose to do so. Enraged by this negotiated accommodation to the Palestinians, settlers attacked students and teachers. Many of the girls fainted, and ten went to the emergency room to receive treatment for minor injuries. As it happened, a friend from Hebron University insisted that the team take their first day off as a team that summer, and took them to Jericho, so they were not in Hebron when the attack happened. See CPTnet releases: "Israeli Settlers attack Palestinian elementary school," Sept 12, 1995; "Israeli soldiers remove Palestinian flag," Sept 12, 1995. See also HSC, "Second Anniversary of Oslo," Sept 13, 1995.

inquired whether the army or the Arabs had thrown them. I told him that only the army uses sound bombs. "It doesn't matter," he said. "Pretty soon the Mashiach [Messiah] will come and [the Arabs] will all move to Jordan. I'm not like the others," he continued. "I don't want to kill them. I only want them to leave."

Then he asked, "Are you Jewish?"

"Christian," I replied. His face stiffened. "The Messiah will come and kill all the goyim—Arabs and Christians—and drink their blood," he said as he walked away.

V

The young messianic hopeful was joined by Ben Israel. He noticed a group of Palestinians watching him and his friend. "Why don't we invite ourselves for coffee?" Ben Israel asked. "I hear they are very hospitable people." Abruptly changing his tone, he pointed at them and said, "First, we'll deal with you and then we'll deal with the Germans."

"They are the same people," his friend said.

"Let's go," Ben Israel said. "It's making me sick to look at them."

As he walked away, he called over his shoulder, "Go back to Greece."

VI

Around 3:45 pm, about eight girls walked onto the street from the settlement of Beit Hadassah and began yelling insults at Palestinians watching from balconies across the street. Several began throwing stones at their homes. A soldier tried to cajole the girls into leaving. They ignored him and continued shouting and throwing stones.

They were joined by several small boys and a teenager in a prayer shawl who began reading from a prayer book. Another soldier approached the group, and the two of them ordered the children to leave. They ignored both soldiers. The girls began chanting the name of Baruch Goldstein [the man who committed the massacre in the mosque in February 1994] and saying, "Goldstein is our father" in Hebrew. Then they began throwing rocks and spitting in our direction.

A visiting Quaker professor engaged one of the settler men who was watching the children, and told us later, "I asked him how he, as a parent, felt about the children throwing rocks at Arabs and yelling, 'Goldstein, Goldstein.' He spent the next twenty minutes not answering my question."

VII

After the girls dispersed, Carmen Pauls, Wendy Lehman, Hedy Sawadsky, and I sat near the Beit Hadassah checkpoint. Ben Israel and the young man who had talked about the Messiah again passed the group. Ben Israel proclaimed loudly, "We should gas them all. Does anyone know where we can get Zyklon B? I heard you can get it in Germany. I think we should take some Zyklon B, put all these—I don't know what you call them—they're not human. Take all of them and put them into little camps and gas them."

Joe, the visiting Quaker professor, asked, "So you think what the Germans did to the Jews justifies the Jews using the same tactics against the Arabs?"

"Absolutely. We've learned our lesson. I'm a member of the Jewish Nazi party." His friend tried to hush him. "I'M not," the friend said. "Well, I am," Ben Israel said. "I'm a Jewish Nazi."

He then told the CPTers that he had no particular desire to kill Arabs. "We'd be much happier shooting Rabin and Peres."

After a pause, Ben Israel told us that the people living on Dubboya Street had roots that went back only about 100 years. "They're not from Ishmael. They're mixed. Mostly they're from Greece. The Ottoman Turks brought them over."

"Where are you from?" Wendy asked.

"I'm from here," he said.

"I mean, where were you born?"

"I was born in Romania," said Ben Israel, "but I don't see what that has to do with anything." . . .

VIII

A young man dressed like the settlers had watched quietly while the girls from Beit Hadassah had shouted insults and thrown rocks. He came over to a group of Palestinians on the street and began talking to them in fluent Arabic. At first skeptical, the Palestinian young people began asking him rapid-fire questions. Hisham Sharabati, interpreting, told us that he was telling the group that his family had come from Iraq, but that he had been born in Jerusalem. A young woman brought a newspaper out of her house and asked the young man to read aloud to test his Arabic.

Sharabati shouted, "What do you think of the situation in Hebron?"

"It is very beautiful here," he said. "But Nablus is more beautiful."

Soldiers approached and tried to drag the young man away. I called out "Shabbat shalom."

"God helps you," he called back.

He resisted the soldiers' attempts to remove him. "But they're my friends!" he protested. As the two soldiers each took one of his arms and physically forced him to walk away, he called back to the assembled Palestinian young people, "Come visit me in Jerusalem."

It was the only time that long afternoon that the soldiers intervened to prevent an Israeli from making contact with Palestinians.

Sharabati, as he watched the young man being dragged away, said, "He was very crazy."

IX

At 4:35, four male settlers walked past. One of them has become known to CPT members as the "Kill the Arabs" guy.[35] As is typical, he shouted these words as his group walked past.

Another of the men called, without waiting for a response, "Why are you interviewing Arabs when you should be interviewing Jews?

"Kill the Arabs," the first man said.

"Thank you very much," Sharabati responded.

"F— you," one of the men said. CPTers witnessed this particular settler assault a seventy-five-year old man ten minutes later, after the man became angry at comments this settler was making about the reputations of the old man's wife and daughters.[36]

On September 30, just hours before Kern was scheduled to leave the country, Lehman and Kern arrived early for the Saturday afternoon presence on Dubboya Street. Lehman heard shouting coming from around

---

35. The team later found that this man was Avishai Raviv, an agent the Shin Bet sent to infiltrate the settlers. After the Rabin assassination he was investigated for not having reported Yigal Amir's intentions to kill Rabin. The Israeli left pointed out that perhaps the Shin Bet should not use agents sympathetic to the settlers' agenda if it wanted reliable information.

36. When Kern and Lehman accompanied the old man, Mahmoud Al-Bayed, to the police station later, they were interviewed separately by the same Shin Bet agent who had assisted Hani Abu Haikel after settlers attacked his mother (see above). When he asked Kern to tell him more about CPT, she told him that the organization had received an invitation from mothers of Russian soldiers and Chechen women's groups to go to Chechnya. "Don't go to Chechnya," he said to her, "We need you here."

the corner, went to investigate, and saw some teenage settlers throwing bottles at people in the marketplace. She called for Kern to follow her. As Kern turned to walk in her direction, she heard people further up the street calling, "Kathy. Don't go. They are coming."

Kern turned and saw about twenty men appearing to range in age from mid-twenties to early forties walking purposefully up the street. She began walking up the street toward the people who had called her. A cry went up behind her and she heard running. Someone yanked at the red-checked keffiyah[37] Kern had tied to her backpack, pulling her over onto her back. Several men spit on her and kicked her as she lay on the ground.

The men ran past and began breaking the windows on all the cars parked on the street. When Kern began taking pictures, a very large man turned around and shouted, "No. No pictures."

Five or six men tried to grab her camera. One of the men punched her in the ear and knocked her to the ground. As the men dragged Kern around on the ground by the camera strap, she noticed that the there were no soldiers at the Beit Hadassah checkpoint, and she began screaming in order to attract attention.[38]

Lehman returned from around the corner, snapped a picture of Kern's chief assailant and joined her in trying to retain the camera. They both were pushed to the ground again. Lehman was kicked in the back and head and the man who had socked Kern stomped hard on Lehman's hand, which made her let go of the camera. He ran toward the settlement of Beit Hadassah, holding the camera high above his head. His co-assailants ran with him, laughing and cheering.[39]

37. Many of the settlers had strong reactions to them. One woman said wearing keffiyehs was the equivalent of wearing gang colors. Even one of the team's Israeli peace activist friends told them he felt uncomfortable with them when team members displayed them. He said it showed CPT had "sided" with the Palestinians. CPTers eventually decided to stop wearing them, because they felt they had built enough trust with Palestinians and they were unnecessarily alienating to soldiers and settlers. See the section "Partisanship Issues" at the end of chap. 6.

38. Kern later regretted screaming. Palestinians watching from their homes on Dubboya Street could not see her because of all the settlers clustered around her, and thought she was being tortured in horrible ways. Years after the incident, neighbors on Dubboya kept expressing sorrow that they had called her to come toward them, because they assumed settlers would not attack her.

39. See "Hundreds of settlers rampage." In May 1996, Kern and Lehman gave early testimony in court against the man who had assaulted them, Natan Levy (of whom Lehman

A little over a month later, on November 4, 1995—the same day Yigal Amir assassinated Yitzhak Rabin—CPTer Dianne Roe was also assaulted by settlers on Dubboya Street. Roe, who would go through training in January 1996, had befriended a Palestinian teenager, R., and agreed to meet the girl's sister, W., in front of Qurtuba school, so she could see W.'s scrapbook on Bosnia.[40] Settlers were threatening the children in Qurtuba—preventing them from leaving school—as often happened on Saturday afternoons. Wendy Lehman was videotaping them when a settler kicked W. As Roe attempted to intervene, settlers knocked her down. When R. came to her aid, settlers knocked her down as well. Then they began dragging R. along the ground by her hair braid. The young settlers kicked her as she screamed until an Israel soldier rescued her. After the situation had calmed down, an adult settler who had threatened Lehman earlier told her, "You will pay a very high price if you help these Nazis," and gestured toward the Palestinians, "This is my country and any foreigner who comes to be with these Nazis will pay with their life."[41]

The *New York Times* later conflated the two attacks in an article about Yigal Amir, the young man who assassinated Prime Minister Rabin on November 4, 1995:

> Such trips to Hebron were one of the [Amir] brothers' frequent activities. Several weeks ago, witnesses say, the two swaggered in the lead of such a group, some of whom broke ranks and attacked a line of Christian women peace activists who regularly placed themselves between the Jews and Palestinians, knocking two of them down and dragging them by their hair.[42]

---

had taken a photo). The police wanted him for violent assaults in other locations as well. After seeing how the lawyers, judge, and translator treated him, the team realized Levy was mentally slow and had probably been manipulated by more intelligent people, such as Baruch Marzel, who was standing with Levy when Lehman and Kern walked into the court that day. Later, after the Rabin assassination, Lehman read in the *Jerusalem Post* that Levy was Avishai Raviv's roommate (see note 36). Levy told the Associated Press that he would turn himself in only if he could see a lawyer immediately, "not after 48 hours," and would be questioned without physical violence (Lehman, e-mail, Nov 12, 1995). Neither Kern nor Lehman ever found out what came of the court proceedings against Levy.

40. Since the girls' family was very sensitive about their coming to public notice, the author has used initials instead of names. They later forbade the girls from associating with CPT because CPT had introduced them to some young Israelis.

41. Roe, e-mail, Nov 22, 2003. See also CPTnet, "Israeli Settlers attack Palestinian Girls," Nov 5, 1995.

42. Kifner, "The Zeal of Rabin's Assassin." Since the article notes this attack as happen-

Several hours after the assault on Roe and the two girls, more than one hundred thousand people rallied at Kings of Israel Square in Tel Aviv in support of the Rabin government's policies, which entailed removing some settlements from the Occupied Territories. The organizers felt they needed to respond to the numerous settler rallies and demonstrations, some of them violent, that had taken place that summer against the Oslo Accords. The turnout was beyond what any of the organizers had imagined, which affirmed that the majority of Israelis supported Rabin's policies. As Rabin left the rally, Yigal Amir shot and killed him.

The assassination had immediate consequences for the Hebron Team's work. Since Amir had strong ties to the Hebron settlers, public outrage was directed toward them and other right-wingers who had called for the death of Rabin and Shimon Peres.[43] The Israeli police and prosecutors, who had watched the complaints filed against the Hebron settlers go down a big black hole for decades, suddenly had the green light to follow through on charges pressed. Several of the Hebron settlers, as well as other settlers who had conspired against the government and carried out violent attacks on Palestinians, were put under administrative detention.[44]

---

ing some weeks before Rabin's assassination, it probably refers to the assault on Lehman and Kern.

43. The Hebron Jewish community immediately went into spin control mode and issued the following statement:

> The Jewish Community of Hebron renounces all acts of violence by Jews and Arabs alike, against all people of all races and religions. The murder of Prime Minister Rabin is a continuation of the violence commencing with the outbreak of the Intifada, that has peaked over the last year and a half, since the signing of the first Oslo Accords.
>
> The Jewish Community of Hebron joins all Am Yisrael in calling for national unity. The sad and tragic events that have culminated with the killing of a nationally elected leader by one of his countrymen demands a public accounting by the national leadership, whose decisions and declarations have led to overwhelming despair among large segments of the Israeli population. This has resulted, unfortunately, in an unwarranted and unjustified act of aggression and desperation by a lone gunman.
>
> The Jewish Community of Hebron sends condolences to Mrs. Lea [sic] Rabin and the entire Rabin family. We hope and pray for an end to all killing and violence. ("The Jewish Community of Hebron condemns the murder of Prime Minister Yitzhak Rabin")

44. Right-wing Sen. Jesse Helms, in an interview with a journalist from the settler news venue Arutz-7, spoke out against these detentions as a violation of democratic

With Amir in jail and Israeli public opinion having turned against them, the Hebron settlers and their supporters no longer conducted the Saturday afternoon rampages. This lack of activity led the team eventually to modify the Saturday afternoon presences. Instead of remaining in one place on Dubboya Street, they made a point of patrolling the area on Saturday and visiting the people who lived on the stretch of road between the settlements of Beit Hadassah and Tel Rumeida. The team also sought to build on Israeli and international outrage at the Rabin assassination by calling attention to settler violence against Qurtuba Girls' school, the Abu Haikel family, and the Shakr Shukri Da'na family, whose home near the Kiryat Arba settlement settlers had stoned repeatedly, causing severe psychological and economic damage to the family of fourteen.[45]

1996

Although the team no longer had to deal with frequent, egregious street violence, the winter and spring of 1996 was a busy time. In consultation with Gene Stoltzfus, Hisham Sharabati, and Fahmi Shahin (a journalist active in the Palestinian People's Party), the team decided to formally extend the project until, as Sharabati and Shahin suggested, the Israeli government definitely decided to remove the Hebron settlers or leave them in place.[46] The decision meant that CPT-Hebron was to keep running, as of this writing, for another twelve years.

Even though the settlers remained more or less entrenched, new opportunities for violence prevention kept cropping up. On January 7 and 8, team members assisted a semi-spontaneous effort of people living in the old city to remove the turnstile gates that the Israeli military had installed for crowd control. Soldiers grabbed two Palestinian boys in the crowd

---

rights. Kern sent him a letter saying she was glad to hear that he felt so strongly about such detentions and hoped that he would also speak out against the administration's detentions of the more than three thousand Palestinians currently in Israeli jails. She later received a letter from Helms' office saying he was glad to know they were "on the same team." See also CPTnet, "Police Arrest Settlers," Nov 9, 1995; CPTnet, "Hebron Action Alert," Nov 13, 1995.

45. See CPTnet releases: "Life in Hebron," Aug 1, 1995; "Hebron Action Alert," Nov 13, 1995; "Hebron Urgent Action: Stop demolition," Apr 26, 2003.

46. At the time, the Haiti team and DC project were still operating. As the team discussed what to do with Hebron Cole Hull said, "We've got to start learning how to close down projects." Instead, CPT began extending projected times or leaving project proposals more open-ended.

who had been watching the action, Cole Hull, who had been videotaping the event, Art Gish, and Cliff Kindy. Gish remained in prison for three days, during which time he refused to eat or drink. After he finished interrogating Gish on the first night, an Israeli officer told him that he would be deported the next day. Instead, the authorities released him without further charges.[47]

Captain Eyal told the team that although the Oslo II accords signed by Israel and the PLO in Washington on September 28, 1995, had stipulated that the gates in the market should be removed, the gates would now be reinstalled. Like his assertion that the Hebron University students were angry with CPT for breaking the seal of the main entrance to their campus, this information was not true. The passageways into the Old City would remain open until another commander ordered new gates installed in 2003, during the Al Aqsa Intifada.

On January 20, CPTers helped monitor the first Palestinian elections, which would ultimately have little effect on the lives of Palestinians. As Cole Hull said in an article about the event:

> As redeployment approaches, the Hebron settlers' belligerent rhetoric is increasing. Permanent military checkpoint buildings are replacing temporary tents. Bypass roads are being constructed right through some of the most productive grape vineyards in the West Bank . . . Confiscation of Palestinian homes and land continues. Intimidation and harassment persist. The construction crane for [Beit Romano—a yeshiva school] is still in place, despite the Oslo Accords, which call for the school's closure.[48]

On February 9, 1996, to mark yet another stipulation of the Oslo Accords left unfulfilled, the team sold tomatoes in the vegetable market near the team apartment and the settlement of Avraham Avinu.[49] People

47. Art Gish, "Hebron: Opening Gates to Freedom," 1–2. A more detailed account of the incident can be found in Gish's book, *Hebron Journal.*

48. "Signs of the Times in Hebron," 3. See also CPTnet, "Residents of Hebron respond," Oct 12, 1995.

49. The team sent out the following press release prior to their action:

OSLO II MARKET GRAND OPENING SALE

"Measures and procedures for normalizing life in Hebron's Old City and on the roads of Hebron will be taken immediately after the signing of this Agreement, as follows:

from the Hebron Solidarity Committee and various press agencies came down and surrounded the CPTers as they plied their wares in the "Oslo II Market." Pressure from the Hebron settlers on the Israeli military had kept the vendors from selling vegetables there since the Goldstein massacre. The team ran out of tomatoes to sell just as the army moved in to stop the action, which received good coverage in the Israeli and Palestinian media.

Several weeks later, on February 25, 1996, the Palestinian militant group Hamas blew up the No. 18 bus in Jerusalem as well as a bus in Ashkelon. The bombings marked the anniversary of Baruch Goldstein's slaughter in the Ibrahimi mosque and the forty days since the assassination of Yihye Ayyash, "the Engineer," who had masterminded several other bombings.[50]

---

a. opening of the wholesale market - Hasbahe as a retail market"

These are the words of the Oslo II accords, ratified by then Prime Minister Y. Rabin and Y. Arafat on Sept. 28, 1995.

In the interest of helping the peace process move ahead smoothly, and in recognition of the tremendous overwork and backlog of duties that the local authorities must attend to; and realizing too that the Accords, at over 400 pages of small type, and summaries and maps is a difficult document to wade through, the local members of the Christian Peacemaker Team will seek to assist in the transition to compliance with the Oslo Accords.

As such, the Oslo II market stand will begin operation this morning at 11 am, accepting all customers without regard to ethnicity, religion or historical origin . . .

The market will be located as specified on p. 53 para. 1 of the Accords (English copy: Article VII: Guidelines for Hebron) in the old city area of Hebron adjacent to the current vegetable market, the IDF checkpoint, and the Avraham Avinu settlement.

We invite your patronage. (CPTnet, "Oslo II Market," Feb 9, 1996)

Immediately following the action, settler news releases condemned the "Arab demonstration" instigated by several Americans from a Christian group sympathetic with Hamas tactics. The issue of the Oslo Accords was never mentioned, and the demonstration was described as more of an effort to block access to the Avraham Avinu settlement (which never occurred). The settler releases also condemned the complicity of "hundreds of Arabs." See the above CPTnet release and "Update from Hebron," Feb 17, 1996. The team and CPT delegations would repeat the tomato actions several times over the next seven years as the military periodically closed the market at the insistence of the Hebron settlers. The closure became permanent during the Al Aqsa Intifada.

50. Shimon Peres obliquely admitted to ordering the assassination. A Palestinian col-

On February 28, the Wednesday after the bus bombings, Yiphat Susskind of the Hebron Solidarity Committee called the team and said she had heard that the Israeli military was demolishing homes between the Israeli settlements of Kiryat Arba and Givat Ha Harsina on the outskirts of Hebron. The team wandered around the area for almost an hour and a half until they came to a house that had furniture, appliances, and sleeping mats strewn around the yard. They did not know it then, but finding that house would inaugurate a new phase in the Hebron team's work—preventing the demolition of Palestinian homes near settlements.

Two brothers and their families—twenty-two people in all—lived in the five-room house—a house the Zalloum brothers had built in 1991 because of impossible overcrowding in their parents' home. Soldiers had given them one hour to remove their possessions before they returned with a bulldozer to destroy their home. One of the brothers gave team members Anne Montgomery, Dianne Roe, Bob Naiman, and Kathleen Kern permission to climb up on the roof of the house along with a couple of BBC and AP journalists. A Palestinian journalist, Kawther Salam, told one of the sons to hide the ladder in the vineyard.

Soon, people from the Hebron municipality, including the mayor, showed up soon along with the neighbors. By the time the soldiers arrived with their jeeps and bulldozer, dozens of people surrounded the house. An Israeli friend gave Cole Hull, who was videotaping from the roof of another house, the number of an official from Meretz, one of Israel's most progressive political parties, who said he would pressure Shimon Peres to call a halt to the demolition.

Eventually, the military said that anyone who did not come down from the roof immediately would be arrested. The journalists left. A dozen or more soldiers climbed on to the roof.

"Why are you doing this?" Kern asked them. One told her that the demolition was happening "because of what they did to us in Jerusalem and Ashkelon, " another told her, "Because it's our land and we can do

---

laborator handed Ayyash a cell phone, saying he had a call, which then exploded. The Palestinian Authority, Hamas, and Israel had been observing a ceasefire since December 1995 when the Palestinian Authority and Hamas conducted negotiations in Cairo. Hamas used the assassination as proof Israel could not be trusted and began attacking civilians inside Israel once again. See "The loosing of the hounds," 1–4.

whatever we want," another said. A third soldier told her, "Because they built without a permit."[51]

One by one, the four CPTers, Bob Naiman, Dianne Roe, Anne Montgomery, and Kern were carried off the roof. The soldiers pushed Bob Naiman's head into the ground and told him to eat dirt. The soldier who approached Kern, was the last person left on the roof, had tears in his eyes.

The team watched as the bulldozer plowed into a corner of the house. As the roof slowly wilted to the ground, the women of the household likewise crumpled to the ground sobbing, and the soldiers standing around the CPTers broke into ululations and laughter.

The police arrested Roe and Naiman when they followed a young Palestinian man whom police were taking away. They charged the CPTers with incitement. To bolster the charge, the police kept asking Roe if she had made eye contact with any Arabs in the course of the three hours team members were up on the roof. The police told them that normally Arabs did not become so upset when their houses were demolished, so the team must have caused the resistance. The police charged Naiman with being a member of Hamas when he attended Bir Zeit University in the 1980s. This accusation was ridiculous for a number of different reasons, not the least of which was that Hamas had not existed when Naiman had attended Bir Zeit.

The team found out later from friends at the Hebron municipality that the Meretz pressure on Israeli Prime Minister Peres had been successful. He had called to issue a desist order on the demolition of the Zalloum family home. But Captain Eyal refused to take the cell phone call until his soldiers completed the demolition.

The rooftop witness tied up the Israeli military for long enough that they were not able to destroy six more houses in the area scheduled for demolition that day. The action also alerted a number of Israelis—who had no idea these demolitions were happening—to the problem. Their pressure on the government caused Prime Minister Shimon Peres to call an end to all home demolitions in April 1996.[52]

---

51. Since 1967 the Israeli authorities have not issued building permits for Palestinians with the bad luck to have Israeli settlements built near their land. This situation led to impossible overcrowding for families living on that land.

52. See "Collective Punishment," 1–2, and also "Confiscation Protest," 14–15.

On the day of Naiman and Roe's hearing, the police never showed up—possibly because of a torrent of e-mails and faxes from the CPT constituency—so the judge dropped all charges.[53]

Then, on the Sunday after the Zalloum's house went down, Hamas bombed the No. 18 bus in Jerusalem again, at approximately the same time in the morning. The following Sunday, the team decided to undertake a witness against this violence by riding the No. 18 bus during the hours that the other No. 18 buses had been bombed. The week before, the team sent press releases out to all of the Arab and Israeli newspapers in the region saying that they had been in Hebron the past year to serve as a violence-deterring presence and that they were riding the bus that morning to reaffirm that they were adamantly opposed to all forms of violence.[54]

The spring 1996 bus bombings in Jerusalem, Ashkelon, and Tel Aviv were to have fateful consequences for Israelis, Palestinians, and the work of the team. Binyamin Netanyahu of the Likud Party used footage from the bombings on TV and in movie theaters to convince Israeli voters that Shimon Peres and the Oslo process had brought these calamities to Israel. Israeli Arab voters boycotted the elections for several reasons: Shimon Peres had ordered the assassination of Yihye Ayyash in Gaza at a time when Hamas was observing a ceasefire, thus causing the chain reaction that led to the bus bombings. He had authorized the bombing of the U.N. compound in Kana, Lebanon that killed hundreds of Palestinian refugees and, as was true for all Israeli governments, he had generally ignored the needs of the Israeli Arab sector.[55] Thus, Binyamin "Bibi" Netanyahu—who,

53. CPTnet, "Hebron Urgent Action: CPT Threatened with Deportation," Mar 1, 1996.

54. See CPTnet releases: "The Day of the Bus Bombings," Feb 25, 1996; "CPT Condemns Jerusalem Bus Bombing," Feb 25, 1996; "One Palestinian journalist's response," Feb 26, 1996; "A prayer to beget peace," Feb 29, 1996; "Hebron: Clarifying the Status," Mar 6, 1996; "CPT Hebron Vows to Ride Bus #18," Mar 6, 1996; "Christian Peacemaker Team—Hebron Responds," Mar 7, 1996; "Personal Reflections on Recent Events," Mar 8, 1996; "Bus #18 Ride for Peace," Mar 10, 1996. The day after the team rode bus #18, Israeli plainclothes authorities ransacked the office of Defense for Children International in Hebron, taking the files of juvenile clients. Anne Montgomery connected the two events in CPTnet, "Lessons from the Children," Mar 12, 1996.

55. The amount of money Israel allocates to Arab towns and neighborhoods for schools and infrastructure is far lower than amounts allocated to Jewish areas. See Nir, "Anti-Arab Policy bias worsens"; Cook, "'Democratic' racism"; HRW, "Second Class: Discrimination." In general, Palestinians have told CPTers they see no difference between

in 1989, had complained at the time of the Tiananmen Square massacre that the Israeli government had lost a chance to conduct mass expulsions of Palestinians from the Occupied Territories—won the election.[56]

For much of December 1996, Netanyahu and Arafat were negotiating what would become the "Protocol Concerning the Redeployment in Hebron." The Protocol divided the city into H-1 and H-2. The Palestinian authority would govern H-1; the Israeli military would control H-2, the area around the Old City where the CPT apartment was located. Although the parties involved called the removal of an Israeli military presence in H-1 "redeployment," the number of Israeli soldiers in Hebron remained about the same; they were just more concentrated in the Old City.

Despite a shooting attack on January 1, 1997, by Noam Friedman, an Israeli soldier in the market near the Hebron team's apartment,[57] the redeployment of Hebron followed through as planned on January 17, 1997—ten months after the date stipulated by the Hebron Accords. In the part of Hebron handed over to the Palestinian Authority, H-1, Palestinians filled the streets waving Palestinian flags—forbidden by the Israeli occupation authorities in the past—and welcomed the newly arrived Palestinian police force. In H-2, which remained under Israeli control, boys began throwing stones at soldiers stationed in front of Avraham Avinu settlement and the military immediately closed the produce market and placed all Palestinians under curfew.[58]

Campaign for Secure Dwellings

In spring 1997, the team, along with Israeli and Palestinian groups, began a major initiative that was to become the primary focus of the Hebron team until the Al Aqsa Intifada broke out in September 2000. After Peres' defeat, the Netanyahu government instituted a new campaign of home demolitions. Houses that were "saved" because of Meretz pressure on Shimon Peres

---

Likud and Labor governments. Both have supported the expansion of settlements and the confiscation of their land. Some even say they prefer Likud governments because Likud leaders are at least open about their intentions. Although this opinion is largely valid, CPTers have found that Labor governments usually have progressive parties like Meretz in their coalition, which creates more avenues for appeal.

56. Benjamin Netanyahu to students at Bar Ilan University, cited in Drake, "A Netanyahu Primer."

57. Lehman, "Israeli Soldier opens fire," 3. See also Contreras, "Radicals in the ranks."

58. Rempel, "Redeployment and division of Hebron," 2.

in the spring of 1996 were now under threat of demolition again. Hundreds of other families received additional demolition orders. For nearly all the homes, the legal reason for their demolition was that they had been built without a permit.[59] The actual reason was that they belonged to Palestinian families who had had the bad luck to have an Israeli settlement move in nearby. Settlements expanded onto Palestinian farmland and confiscating this land was easier when houses were not on it.

Terry Rempel, Art Gish, Dianne Roe, Mark Frey, and Cliff Kindy initiated the Fast for Rebuilding to impress upon the North American churches the urgency of the issue. Originally, the team decided to fast for seven hundred hours—one hour for each house threatened with demolition in the West Bank[60]—and end it on Easter Sunday. "We have stood with Palestinian families as the bulldozers reduced their homes to rubble," wrote the team members. "We know what demolitions will mean for these 700 families [with demolition orders] and feel keenly their despair and hopelessness." Fasting, they said, was a way to "move to deeper levels of spiritual nonviolence, to embody solidarity with the Palestinian people, and to allow an inflowing of God's spirit to provide clarity of vision and

59. Before Israeli groups had done their work educating the Israeli public, a large portion of the Israelis believed that all home demolitions occurred because the residents had been involved in some sort of Palestinian military operation. The team witnessed one such demolition on June 29, 1995, when Israeli soldiers destroyed two Palestinian homes at the entrance to Hebron after discovering Palestinian militants in a vineyard nearby. CPTnet, "One Man Killed. Two Houses destroyed," June 29, 1995.

60. Someone told them halfway through the fast that the number was closer to 1500. According to the Israeli Committee against House Demolitions, during the Oslo negotiations (1993–2000) some 740 homes were demolished. Another 5,000 homes were demolished from the start of the second Intifada (October 2000) through 2004. See ICAHD, "Frequently Asked Questions." Amnesty International noted in its 1999 report about home demolitions in the West Bank:

> The number of demolition orders in force in March 1997 was 850. Despite many requests Amnesty International has been unable to obtain more recent figures from the authorities. Since that date, many more orders have been issued than houses demolished, and about 1,300 houses may be under threat of demolition at the present time. These might have a population of perhaps 9,000, or almost a quarter of the entire Palestinian population of Area C.

The same report said that twelve thousand homes in East Jerusalem were under order of demolition. AI, "Israel and the Occupied Territories."

direction."[61] Later, when Sara Reschly and Anne Montgomery joined the team, they participated in the fast as well.

Friends of the team set up a fasting tent in H-1, the Palestinian-controlled area of Hebron. In addition to providing a shelter for the public witness, the tent symbolized the Red Cross/Red Crescent tents that Palestinian families received after the Israeli authorities demolished their homes. Palestinian, Israeli, and International groups began making solidarity visits to the tent. Scores of villagers came to share their own stories of house demolitions, land confiscations, arrests, and raids on their homes by the Israeli military. An Israeli friend, Harriet Lewis, witnessed a home demolition while she spent a week visiting and fasting with the team. She went on to mobilize Israeli groups around this issue and planted the seeds for what became the Israeli Coalition Against House Demolitions. Thousands of people from at least eight different countries fasted in solidarity with the team in Hebron.[62]

The fasting tent also resulted in the team developing new and valuable contacts in Hebron. A group of young men put themselves at the service of the team, providing invaluable help with the logistics of life in Hebron and Arabic-English translation.[63] Through the fasting tent, the team also came to know members of the 'Atta Jaber family, who would become some of the team's closest friends.[64] Zleekha Muhtasib, a teacher who spoke nearly fluent English, and Abdel Hadi Hantash, the cartogra-

61. "Peacemakers fast for 700 hours."

62. Ibid. Rich Meyer, who would later direct the Campaign for Secure Dwellings, did a parallel fast in Lafayette Park outside the White House. He became part of a community of "chronic" protesters in the park, who helped watch each other's exhibits to prevent the National Park police from confiscating them. On March 20, 1997 Art Gish, Wendy Lehman, Bob Naiman, and Jeff Heie accompanied Meyer to the US State Department, bringing rubble and photos from demolished homes. They asked an official there why the US had vetoed the UN Security Council resolution calling on Israel to halt settlement expansion. "They essentially said that for policy to change we should be directing our appeal to Congress," said Rich Meyer, in a January 18, 2005 phone interview with the author. "The guy we were talking to spent 45 minutes agreeing with us about what we were saying and then sighed and said, 'It's sometimes hard to defend US policy in this area of the world.'"

63. They were also very helpful in dealing with a young man who sexually harassed Reschly continually and egregiously.

64. During the fast, the team heard that his home was about to be demolished in the Beqa'a Valley, east of Hebron, and headed out to the place. Frey, Anne Montgomery, and Kindy stayed with the Jabers, while the rest of the team followed the bulldozer to another family's house, which the Israeli military demolished instead.

pher of the Hebron district, turned from casual acquaintances of the team into friends and co-workers.

At the end of the Fast on March 29, 1997 (Good Friday), the team and about forty Palestinians, Israelis, and other internationals cleared rubble in preparation for rebuilding the Zalloum family home that the team had unsuccessfully tried to save a year earlier. Israeli police arrested Cliff Kindy, Rabbi Arik Ascherman, co-director of Rabbis for Human Rights, and two nineteen-year-old Palestinian youths, Imad Mohammed Shawer and Mamdoh Abd Al Asem Zaatari. The young men were held for a week in prison and tortured. Ascherman's wife bailed him out so he could perform Shabbat services that evening, and Kindy remained in jail for four days until his departure date. Israeli police drove Kindy out onto the tarmac of Ben Gurion airport, dumped the contents of his backpack on the ground and gave him barely enough time to scoop them back inside the pack before they escorted him onto the plane. The rest of the team broke their fast on Easter Sunday with friends from Sabeel, a Palestinian Christian organization, in Jerusalem.[65]

As houses continued to go down, CPT started sending Rebuilders Against Bulldozers (or RAB) delegations to the West Bank, the first ones occurring in June and October 1997. Participants in these delegations spent the first week touring Israel and Palestine and the second week in Hebron, meeting people facing demolition or whose homes were already demolished. When possible, these delegations assisted families in rebuilding the homes or agricultural terraces destroyed by the Israeli military.

In the fall of 1997, CPT launched the Campaign for Secure Dwellings (CSD) to address the growing number of demolitions under the Netanyahu government.[66] It did so in coordination with the Israeli

---

65. Anglican priest Naim Ateek had founded Sabeel in order to put Liberation Theology—developed in Africa, Asia, and Latin America—into a Palestinian context. The team regularly participated in discussion group organized by Sabeel, held after worship at St. George's Cathedral on Sundays until nasty church politics removed Ateek from his position at St. George's.

66. The name comes from Isaiah 32:16–18:

> Then justice will dwell in the wilderness, and righteousness abide in the fruitful field.
> The effect of righteousness will be peace, and the result of righteousness, quietness and trust forever.
> My people will abide in a peaceful habitation, in secure dwellings, and in quiet resting places. (NRSV)

Committee Against House Demolitions (ICAHD) and the Palestine Land Defence Committee. Congregations participating in CSD were matched with Palestinian families in the Hebron area facing home demolition. The congregations and families exchanged profiles, letters, and photographs. The North American families wrote letters to their representatives, the Israeli government and the US State Department describing the threat that their partner family faced. Canadian and U.S. churches also held vigils and witnesses outside Israeli Consulate offices and the local offices of their senators.

As thousands of Israelis became more aware of this issue, the pressure on the Israeli government likewise grew. ICAHD made a provisional commitment to Palestinian families facing these demolitions that it would rebuild the demolished home of any family if the family requested such assistance. The provisos were that the Palestinian Land Defence Committee had to authorize the rebuilding; the rebuilt homes would be simple cinderblock structures, and the rebuilding had to be a public act of resistance. Most families did not make the request because they feared reprisals from the military.

Home demolitions proved to be an effective entry issue into the Israeli-Palestinian conflict for both internationals and Israelis. Some people might have believed the Israeli government's propaganda about Arafat and demanded "balance" when referring to the culpability of both Israelis and Palestinians for perpetuating the conflict. But almost no one thought demolishing Palestinian homes so that Israeli settlements could expand was a good idea.[67]

During this period, team members became especially involved with the Jaber family and the Al Atrash family and the families living near them on the eastern and southern borders of Hebron respectively.

Jeff Halper, head of the Israeli Committee Against House Demolitions used the case of the Al Atrash family as a template for the issue of home demolitions in a letter to the British Ambassador to Israel at the time:

67. As noted earlier, the Israeli government's ostensible reason for demolishing homes was that they were built without a permit. Faced with impossible overcrowding, some families took the risk. Jeff Halper, the director of ICAHD, told Kathleen Kern and several delegations she led that the demolitions were like a reverse lottery: demolishing one house among many built without permits made other families decide not to take the risk.

To: His Excellency the British Ambassador, Mr. David Manning

A Protest Against the Brutal Treatment of the Al-Atrash Family of Hebron by the Israeli Authorities

The Israeli Committee Against House Demolitions wishes to register its protest against the brutal treatment, going back over ten years, of the Palestinian Al-Atrash family of Hebron by the Israeli authorities . . .

There cannot be a better example of arbitrary and completely superfluous cruelty as this case. Here is a family with 10 children, reduced to poverty by what is euphemistically called "the closure," the forbidding of most Palestinian workers to come into Israel during the day for purposes of employment—even though Israeli policy of the past 30 years was designed to transform them into a work-force completely dependent upon Israel by preventing the development of Palestinian industry, agriculture, business or even an adequate infrastructure in the West Bank and Gaza. Yusef Al-Atrash, an experienced construction worker, now sews boots in Hebron for a salary of $350 per month. All he wanted to do was build a house for his family ON HIS OWN PROPERTY which has been in his family since Ottoman times (and for which he has all the proper documentation.) No politics involved, in a rural area far from any Israeli settlement, army base or by-pass road, yet on a hillside from which he could point out another eight or nine houses also slated for demolition, and a school building the Israelis will not allow to be completed.

Why was he denied the permit? Well, the reason given by the Civil Administration was that only one house was permitted on "his" property according to the 1942 British planning policy—and a relative of his had already built one. But what is "his property?" The Mandate plan was intended to ensure that agricultural land was not overwhelmed with building—although the Al-Atrash property is on a steep and rocky slope that has never been cultivated. As time passed fathers passed on their holdings to their children, thus subdividing the land as happens naturally in every country. Yusef inherited his plot of six acres from his father, had it carefully surveyed and marked with border markings and officially registered with the authorities. When he travelled to the Israeli Civil Administration to obtain a building permit, however, he was told that the boundary is not recognized and that all the land going back 100 years was recognized as one undivided unit, upon which a house had already been built, thus foreclosing any other building in the future. Taking out his maps, Yusef protested that his plot was legally marked and registered, but was waved out of the office of the Israeli clerk Yossi Hasson (who has a reputation of dealing curtly with Palestinian petitioners seeking permits), who told him: "I don't care." The trek to the Civil Administration north of Jerusalem, the wait to see Hasson and the trip back took between 7–8 hours; the meeting with Hasson took less than a minute . . .

The Israeli Committee Against House Demolitions protests this action on the part of the Israeli authorities and calls on people and governments of good will to raise their voices as well. Indeed, we should together raise the issue of mass house demolitions—a cruel and completely unnecessary application of a Kafkaesque policy of planning in which Palestinian homes are demolished because they are "illegal" yet making it virtually impossible for Palestinians to obtain building permits—onto the international agenda. Over 1000 Palestinian families on the West Bank and in Jerusalem face the loss of their houses in this increasing aggressive campaign to clear most of the West Bank of its Palestinian residents.

Simply on a human level it is one of the most shameful aspects of Israeli occupation, one that violates fundamental rights of people to decent shelter as guaranteed in human rights covenants signed by Israel itself. And it victimizes primarily the poor and defenseless, causing untold suffering as it destroys any possibility of reconciliation between Israelis and Palestinians.

We call on you and your government to aid us, Palestinian and Israeli together, in combatting this inhumane policy that only undermines any chance for peace. Protesting the brutal and arbitrary treatment of the Al-Atrash family is a place to start.

THE ISRAELI COMMITTEE AGAINST HOUSE DEMOLITIONS[68]

As the family tried to rebuild, the team began sending one member every night to stay with them. Rich Meyer spent several weeks camping with the family in a large tent supplied by the Red Cross.

Continuing a twenty-four-hour presence with the Al Atrashes, however, proved stressful for the team. By 1998, the team's work had expanded to include visiting dozens of other families who belonged to the CSD network. The team was also conducting regular tours for Israeli, Palestinian, and international delegations, and individuals seeking to understand the situation in Hebron and the rest of Palestine. They had to visit regularly

68. Halper (under the auspices of ICAHD), e-mail, Mar 23, 1998. Also reprinted in Kern, *Where Such Unmaking Reigns,* 111–15.

with families affected by soldier and settler violence and conduct regular patrols past military checkpoints in their neighborhood. Daily meetings and writing required a significant block of time. Team members had begun establishing relationships with Palestinians, Israelis, and internationals in Jerusalem and Bethlehem; they also had begun taking Arabic lessons from Selwa Awad in Bethlehem.

On March 22, 1998, the team received a phone call from Bassam Eid. Eid, who worked with the Israeli Human Rights organization B'tselem at the time, told them that soldiers had arrived at the Al Atrashes, assaulted, and then arrested the parents, Yussuf and Zuhoor Al Atrash, and their two oldest children, Hussam (18) and Manal (17). They also confiscated the cement mixer the family was using to rebuild.

Not only had the Israeli military performed these strong-arm tactics in the presence of Eid, they did so in front of Gideon Levy, a journalist for the Israeli newspaper Ha'aretz. Levy posted bail for the Al Atrashes and wrote a stinging article entitled, "The cement mixer is in our hands"— meant to evoke the radioed message that Israeli forces sent when they captured the Western Wall in Jerusalem during the 1967 war.[69] Video of the Al Atrashes that showed Zuhoor and daughter Manaal being dragged along the ground in a way that exposed their bare stomachs—extremely shameful in conservative Palestinian culture—appeared on Israeli television and drew offers of help from sympathetic Israelis. On June 11, 1998, when team members were not present, the Israeli military demolished the Al Atrashes' partially rebuilt home again. The Al Atrashes asked the Hebron team to stop calling attention to their situation, because they thought that the attention had caused the Israeli military to target them.

Partly because the team was no longer spending as much time with the Al Atrashes, the team began spending more time as a violence-deterring presence with 'Atta Jaber's extended family. The Jabers had warmly welcomed a wide array of Israelis and internationals, including CPTers, into their homes, and team members developed affectionate relationships with family members.

In June 1998, the Israeli military built a road through the land of Abdel Jawad Jaber, Atta Jaber's father, destroying two and one half acres of terraced orchards. Three months later, they uprooted one hundred more

69. Levy, "The cement mixer." Israeli activist Harriet Lewis told Kern what the title meant in Hebrew. In the English edition of *Ha'aretz* the article appeared under the title, "All in order."

olive and fruit trees. On August 4, 1998, when the Israeli military arrived to remove irrigation hoses from the families' tomatoes, they detained CPT reservist Jim Satterwhite as he tried to collect the hoses and return them to the families.

The Israeli military destroyed the home of Atta and Rodeina Jaber's family, along with eight other homes at disparate locations in the Hebron District on August 19, 1998. The catastrophic effect the demolition had on the Jabers was a huge emotional blow to the team. Israelis, Palestinians, and internationals flocked to the Jaber land to help them rebuild, but less than a month later, on September 16, the military demolished the Jaber home once again. Soldiers arrested 'Atta Jaber when he tried to get his five-month-old son Rajah out of the house (see this chapter's opening quotation). They damaged his windpipe when they put him in a choke-hold, for which he sought medical treatment in Jordan. Rodeina Jaber suffered blinding headaches for weeks afterwards because of injuries sustained when soldiers beat her. The couple's oldest daughter, Amooni, became withdrawn and depressed.

Since the Jabers had welcomed so many people into their home and served dinner to numerous CPT delegations, the team's subsequent campaign, "Reduced to rubble. Whom shall I send?" garnered numerous responses. CSD coordinator Rich Meyer sent photos of two-year-old Dalia Jaber, the couple's second child, with her three-day-old brother, Rajah, to U.S. constituents. These constituents then sent them to congressional and state department representatives with the message, "Because you have not demanded an end to the Israeli policy of home demolitions, these Palestinian children were made homeless on Wednesday, August 19, 1998 and again on September 16, 1998 in the Beqa'a Valley east of Hebron."

Jaber began rebuilding his home for yet a third time in 1999, but did so quietly, asking that CPT not draw attention to him anymore, so the team stopped using the family's name in their releases and engaged in no more public witnesses on Jaber family land. Although the settlers took over the house over in 2001 (see next chapter), the house remains standing as of October 2008.[70] The Jabers' friendship with the Hebron team also continues.

70. Sara Reschly, in her comments on a draft of this chapter, wrote:

> Apparently one of the ICAHD folks was good friends with the Heb district commander's wife. She became aware of Atta's situation, was moved, and advocated on behalf of him to her husband, who made a

Amid the gloom of these demolitions, the pressure on the Israeli and American governments from letter writing and fax campaigns—undertaken by people who were part of the CSD and ICAHD networks—began to have an effect. Friends from the ICAHD reported that a contact in the U.S. State Department told them that the Department received more letters on the issue than it did for any other issue in the entire Middle East. Secretary of State Madeleine Albright began to put great, though unpublicized, pressure on the Israeli government to stop demolishing homes.

The Campaign for Secure Dwellings celebrated its first anniversary in December 1998. In total, fifty-eight churches had been matched with families who had experienced or were facing home demolition. Many of the matches had their roots in the participation of church members in CPT-RAB delegations. These people helped to rebuild homes or farming terraces that the Israeli military had destroyed. Then they went home and persuaded their churches to join the Campaign for Secure Dwellings.[71] A surprising number of people whose churches were matched with CSD families sight unseen also eventually participated in delegations to visit these families with whom they and their churches were matched.

On February 4, 1999, the Israeli military demolished the homes of Fayez Jaber in the Beqa'a Valley and Leyla Sabarneh in Beit Ummar (a village north of Hebron). In both cases, the team arrived too late to intervene. As a response to these demolitions, the team again initiated a "Tent for Lent" campaign on March 9, 1999, to call attention to the issue of home demolitions. Using materials from the Coordinating Committee of the Campaign Against the Permanent Occupation,[72] the team noted that the Netanyahu government had accelerated the demolitions of Palestinian homes and the confiscation of Palestinian land since the signing of the Wye River Memorandum in October 1998. They encouraged their constituents to set up tents in their homes and at church, and outside

---

deal with Atta—that his home would never be destroyed. Who knows if the agreement will be honored, but it is there. I'm not sure if it was ever written down or if it was just verbal.

71. Two rabbis (without their congregations) also participated in the Campaign for Secure Dwellings.

72. Groups belonging to this umbrella organization included ICAHD, Rabbis for Human Rights, Gush Shalom, Peace Now, Bat Shalom, Yesh Gvul, Netivot Shalom, Alternative Information Center, HSC, the Student Committee of the Hebrew University, Campus Tel Aviv, and Green Action.

the offices of legislators whose policies supported Israel, and hence home demolitions.

On May 19, 1999, Dianne Roe, Bourke Kennedy, and Jamey Bouwmeester arrived at Ramadan Rajabi's home, just as the Israeli military was about to demolish a reservoir he used to irrigate his fields. Bouwmeester sat between the reservoir and the front-end loader.

After a soldier told him, "Get up. Go. Leave here," Bouwmeester told him, "I'll leave after you, okay?"

The soldier once again ordered him to leave and Bouwmeester pointed to Rajabi's elderly father, who had smiled approvingly and told Bouwmeester "Tamam, tamam," (perfect) when he first sat in front of the machinery. "Do you see that man over there?" he said. "I get my orders from him."

Four soldiers grabbed each of Bouwmeester's limbs and a fifth jerked him up by his ears. In the process of dragging him away, one of the soldiers knocked Roe over and damaged the digital camera she was holding.

After the soldiers finished demolishing Rajabi's reservoir, they moved in a convoy to the home of Kaied Jaber and began again. Jeff Halper, head of the Israeli Committee Against House demolitions arrived, spoke to the officer in charge, handed Bouwmeester his camera and said, "Jamey, I think it's time for a little civil disobedience."

Bouwmeester reported that he felt a "sense of *deja vu*" as he watched Halper sit in front of the loader. After a short argument in Hebrew, soldiers handcuffed Halper, dragged him back up the hill, and dropped him in the dirt. Later, they stuffed him on the floor of their jeep. When Bouwmeester tried to help him onto the seat, a soldier elbowed him in the gut and two others pushed him back on the ground.

The loader and bagger then moved on to demolish Ismael Jaber's reservoir.

As it happened, a camera crew from BBC was following Halper around that day and documented the destruction of Kaied Jaber's cistern and the cistern of Ismael Jaber, cousin and neighbor of 'Atta Jaber. In a subsequent documentary, *Reservoir Raiders*, released in 2000, the documentary-makers noted that all three cisterns were built with funds donated from the European Community. It included an interview with Peter Lerner, the spokesperson for the Israeli Civil Administration, who said that the owners were "stealing water" by tapping into the nearby water main. However, when the camera people asked him to show them where pipes were connected to the cisterns, he was unable to do so.[73] Given that the military had confiscated the Jaber's irrigation hoses, leaving them to rely on rainwater, the destruction of the cisterns meant to catch the rainwater seemed egregiously nasty.

The next day, the team issued an Urgent Action calling for an end to "Lame Duck" demolitions. They asked their constituents to write Prime Minister-elect Barak and ask him to call for an end to land confiscation and home demolitions ordered by the defeated Netanyahu government.[74]

The election of Barak as Prime Minister in the summer of 1999 had inspired hopes that he would roll back the expansion of settlements in the West Bank. However, the building of roads and settlement housing on land already confiscated actually increased and the military continued to hand out demolition orders.[75]

This ongoing settlement expansion did not satisfy the Hebron area settlers, however. They began staging nightly demonstrations in the Beqa'a valley for two weeks—beginning on November 30, 1999—near the home of CSD family Omar and Lamia Sultan. Like the Al Atrashes and the Jabers, the Sultans had documents for their land dating back to the time of the Ottoman Empire. However, in their vigils, the settlers demanded that the Israeli government demolish the Sultan house, where fifteen people lived.

On December 21, 1999, the settlers began a twenty-four-hour presence near the Sultan home, after taking over an unoccupied neighboring house. One settler tried to enter the Sultans' home and pushed Lamia Sultan. Israeli police took Omar Sultan and his son to the police station after they tried to intervene and the settler claimed they had struck him. Two days later, the team put out an Urgent Action asking that constituents

73. CPTnet, "Hebron: Time for a little civil disobedience," May 19, 1999.

74. Team members also mentioned that the team's digital camera had been irreparably damaged when Israeli soldiers pushed Dianne Roe to the ground and asked for donations to replace it. They encouraged people to send checks to ICAHD if they wanted to support rebuilding efforts. CPTnet, "Hebron Urgent Action: Stop 'Lame Duck' Demolitions," May 20, 2004.

75. In his article, "In Sharm's Way," Jamey Bouwmeester reflected on the the Barak government's lack of progress toward a peaceful resolution. "Sharm" refers to the Sharm al Sheikh Memorandum signed by Arafat and Barak, which basically updated the Wye Memorandum, which had been unilaterally halted by Israel. See also Meyer, "Bulldozers and Steamrollers."

write to Ehud Barak and Canadian and U.S. diplomatic officials concerning the settler harassment. Art Gish and Kathy Kapenga, a friend who attended the Lutheran church in Jerusalem that the team attended, moved into the Sultan home to establish a twenty-four hour CPT presence in the area.[76]

The settler presence took a scarier turn on December 25 when about one hundred settlers charged up the hillside to the Sultan home with flaming torches, destroying property, and frightening the family. They announced they would return the following Tuesday (December 28) to demolish the house, confiscate the property, and start constructing a settlement there—theoretically an extension of Kiryat Arba/Givat Ha Harsina complex, although the Sultan home was more than two kilometers away from the inhabited area of Kiryat Arba.

Monday evening, the day before the threatened demolition, several Israeli peace activists joined the team and spent the night at the house. The next morning, soldiers told the Israelis and CPTers to leave. When they refused, the soldiers told the oldest son, Fahed, that if the peace activists remained in the "closed military zone" around the house, the settlers could insist on remaining, too. "These are our guests," Fahed Sultan responded. "Our culture does not allow us to ask guests to leave."

Busloads of sympathetic Israelis arrived with signs and banners to show solidarity with the Sultans. Settlers showed up later in the afternoon and exchanged words with Israelis who had remained.

Shortly after CPTers left the next day, a busload of settlers set up banners on an old Palestinian house near the Sultan home. They then rushed the Sultan house, but soldiers stopped them from reaching it.

Two weeks later, Rich Meyer posted a thank-you note to those who had responded to the Urgent Action. He told them that because of the international letter writing, the Israeli government promised the Sultans that their home would not be destroyed and that it would thwart the attempt of the settlers to establish a new settlement near the Sultan home. Meyer also noted that the campaign around the Sultan home had brought Jews, Christians, and Muslims together in a show of solidarity. However, the prefatory comment attached to Meyer's posting noted that the Israeli

---

76. Kapenga became a CPT reservist after going through training in 2003.

government continued to refer to the Sultans' land and the rest of the Beqa'a Valley as part of the municipality of Kiryat Arba.[77]

The travails of the Sultan family illustrated that families living near settlements at the end of 1999 still lacked real security. However, Rich Meyer, in the fall 1999 *Signs of the Times,* noted that under Barak's administration the Israeli authorities had demolished only four homes in the Jerusalem area and none in the West Bank.[78] Unwittingly, Interior Minister Natan Sharansky provided proof that the efforts of CPT, the Israeli Committee Against House Demolitions, and the Palestine Land Defence Committee had influenced Israeli government policy. The December 1, 1999, *Jerusalem Post* quoted Sharansky as complaining, "Every house demolition becomes an international incident."[79]

By 2000, many CPTers working in Hebron felt that the Campaign for Secure Dwellings had stagnated. Families with whom the team had worked most closely—and who had suffered the greatest losses in terms of home demolitions and harassment of the Israeli military—no longer wanted their names used in releases. They felt that if they rebuilt furtively, their houses might have a greater chance of remaining standing. Communications between Palestinian families and North American churches seemed to be mostly one-way, from North America to Palestine, which made congregations less likely to participate. Since threats to homes in the Beqa'a Valley, Qilqis/Al Sendas (where the Al Atrashes lived), and Beit Ummar, north of Hebron, seemed less imminent under

77. See CPTnet releases: "Hebron Urgent Action: Family Under Siege," Dec 23, 1999; "Prayers and Speeches, Destruction and Hope," Dec 26, 1999; "House under siege in the Beqa'a Valley," Jan 2, 2000; "Hebron: A Big Thank-You," Jan 13, 2000. See also Art Gish, "Love Overcomes Fear in Hebron." The College Mennonite Church of Goshen, IN, partnered through CSD with the Sultan family, sent about seventy-five faxes to Israeli prime minister Ehud Barak.

78. Meyer, "Bulldozers and Steamrollers." The lack of demolitions probably had more to do with the pressure of progressive parties in Barak's coalition, like Meretz, than Barak's own convictions.

79. Cited in "Demolition Season Reopened." The quotation appeared in a story about the demolition of two East Jerusalem homes at the end of October. A third was also scheduled to go down, but Israeli activists mobilized a worldwide protest against the demolitions, and Meretz Party whip Zehava Gal'on was able to persuade Barak that the protests from grassroots organizations and representatives of the European Union were a good reason to halt further demolitions.

the Barak government, the team began to focus more on ongoing land confiscation.[80]

A small legal victory at the end of March 2000 helped team members feel that their efforts and those of their Palestinian and Israeli co-workers, had made a difference for villagers in the southern part of the Hebron district. Members of the team were present at the Israeli Supreme Court in Jerusalem when a judge handed down a decision stipulating that seven hundred Palestinians, whom the military had expelled from their homes in November 1999, could return.[81]

The families had lived in caves near the town of Yatta for hundreds of years, but the caves lie in an area that the settlement of Susia wanted to confiscate.[82] Intense lobbying on behalf of the families by Israeli groups like the ICAHD and Rabbis for Human Rights finally paid off. On April 9, 2000, the families killed a sheep and invited their Israeli friends and CPT for a feast.

In an April 10 reflection on the court ruling, Dianne Roe wrote,

> "The other peace process" has not been taking place in fancy re-
> sorts in Sharm El Sheikh or Wye River. These meetings have been
> taking place in Red Cross tents set up after a house demolition, or
> in cinder block shells. Or in a cave warmed by a small wood fire.
> The security interests of this "other peace process" are not served
> by walls of separation, by checkpoints, by closures or by weapons.
> Instead this security will be one of friendship and mutual trust.
> Amos Gvirtz, an Israeli activist who worked tirelessly on this issue,
> had tears in his eyes as he embraced us.
>
> Later, as he introduced CPT to author David Grossman, Amos
> credited CPT with providing the inspiration that led to the forma-
> tion of the Israeli Committee Against House Demolitions. Activist

80. See CPTnet, "Hebron: Buckets of Soil Campaign," Feb 11, 2000; CPTnet, "Hebron Urgent Action: Send packets of soil," Feb 11, 2000.

81. For the of the cave-dwelling families, see CPTnet, "Hebron District Urgent Action: Stop the expulsion," Mar 23, 2002.

82. The Hebron team had contacts with Palestinians facing settler violence and land confiscation in the southern Hebron district since 1996. See CPTnet releases: "Hebron District: August 1997," Sept 8, 1997; "Hebron: Delegation Rebuilds," Dec 29, 1997; "Hebron: Update December 24 [1997]–January 4, 1998," Jan 6, 1998; "Hebron/Yatta: Between Settlers," Apr 18, 1998; "Hebron: Yatta Farmer," June 27, 1998; "Hebron Update: October 27–31, 1999," Nov 9, 1999. Transportation difficulties and the needs of families living closer to Hebron prevented the team from sustained humanitarian interventions on behalf of the families living in more remote areas of the Hebron District.

Beate Zilverschmidt added that CPT had provided a framework for them to meet Palestinians. "There have been dialogue groups before," she said. "But CPT found the burning issues and put them on our table.

"Thank you for having that table," we said.[83]

The Bill Clinton-sponsored Camp David negotiations between Barak and Arafat began on July 11 and lasted until July 27, 2000, at which point the parties broke without having come to an agreement. Arafat's refusal to sign the agreement—which would have left the largest settlements in Israeli hands and solidified Israeli control of Jerusalem—was depicted by the U.S. press and government as yet another example of Palestinian intransigence and refusal to compromise.

In an August 2 Urgent Action, the team encouraged its constituents to write a variation of the following letter:

Dear Editor,

At Camp David, President Clinton and Israeli Prime Minister Ehud Barak pressed Palestinian leader Yassar Arafat to agree to a settlement reflecting Israel's superior power, not an agreement based on principles of justice. While Israel talks about making concessions for peace, they [*sic*] continue to flout international law, creating facts on the ground that make a just and lasting peace more and more difficult to envision.

Today, Israel continues to build new settlements and expand those that already exist. Not only is Israeli settlement expansion illegal according to international law, but it results directly in land confiscation and home demolitions for Palestinians in the area. While Israel continues to build new Jewish-only settlements on occupied territory, the Israeli army bulldozes Palestinian homes, evicts entire villages from their ancestral homesteads and uproots olive trees and grapevines.

In the Beqa'a valley east of Hebron, more than 50 families have been issued home demolition orders. More than a dozen homes have been razed by the Israeli military. Palestinians are forbidden to cultivate and irrigate farmland that has belonged to their families for generations. At the same time, the Israeli settlement of Kiryat Arba/Harsina is in the process of building more than 200 new housing units on land confiscated from these same

83. CPTnet, "Hebron: The Other Peace Process," Apr 10, 2000. Four years later, the team would have a project in this area accompanying children to school in the village of Al-Tuwani.

Palestinian farmers. In currently existing settlements, the residents lounge on green lawns and swim in private pools while some of their Palestinian neighbors are not given enough water to drink.

Israel fails to implement U.N. Resolutions, ignores world opinion and pursues unjust policies that would give a fraction of the Palestinian people a fraction of their rights on a fraction of their land. Future negotiations between Israel and the Palestinians must be based on International law and the principles of justice.[84]

The Camp David negotiations set off a surge of street violence that summer of 2000, which shifted the team's focus away from home demolitions and land confiscation for the first time in several years. As Palestinians heard that Arafat might sign an agreement that would make aspects of the Occupation permanent, they stepped up street clashes, throwing stones at soldiers stationed on the border of H-1 and H-2. Soldiers generally responded by shooting rubber-coated metal bullets.[85]

The Camp David negotiations may have been responsible for an upsurge in settler violence as well. On August 10, Amos Harel wrote in *Ha'aretz*, the Israeli "newspaper of record," that according to the Palestinian press, Barak offered to evacuate the settlements in Hebron as a concession to the Palestinian authority. (Barak denied the allegation.)

Whatever the reasons for the settlers' behavior, the team increasingly found themselves standing between settlers and Palestinians in an effort to prevent assaults in July, August, and September 2000. Hebron Updates covering the period from July 18 through August 15 record eight instances in which settlers attacked Palestinians, CPTers, or both.[86]

The venue for many of these assaults was often the vegetable market around the corner from the team's apartment. When the Israeli authorities allowed the market to open over the years, it became a particular target for settlers any time a settler or soldier was attacked by Palestinians. Although no vendors were ever implicated in these assaults, the common settler response was to enter the market, physically abuse the vendors, and overturn vegetable carts and stands. Usually settler women and chil-

84. CPTnet, "Hebron Urgent Action: Telling the truth," Aug 2, 2000. For a progressive Israeli perspective on the Camp David negotiations, see Gush Shalom, "Barak's Generous Offers."

85. Clashes were a feature of life in Hebron from the beginning of CPT's Hebron project, but were not a central focus of the team's work. See an analysis of these clashes under the "Palestinian violence" section of "Issues" at the end of chap. 6.

86. See, for example, CPTnet, "Hebron Update: July 18–30, 2000," Aug 7, 2000.

dren carried most of the attacks, because male soldiers had to wait for female civilian police or female soldiers to arrive and deal with them. Attacks in the market became more frequent as the summer passed. In one such attack on August 19, the team spent several hours maintaining a presence there after settlers assaulted vendors because a taxi driver had allegedly hit a settler boy. Soldiers pushed Natasha Krahn and Jeremy Bergen to the ground as they moved Palestinians back with their rifles. After a soldier had told Bergen, Michael Goode, and Bob Holmes several times they would be arrested if they did not leave the area, Goode told the soldier that the team needed to be there. "I'm concerned that the IDF's response here is provoking more violence," he said. Soldiers then detained Goode for "inciting a riot," but released him five minutes later. More settlers joined in the melee and Palestinian children began throwing fruit and stones. The *Jerusalem Post* reported three settlers and ten Palestinians were arrested by the end.[87]

During this period, settlers also began frightening the residents of the Beqa'a Valley by holding regular demonstrations near the homes of the extended Jaber family and demanding that the IDF close the road to Palestinian traffic. Since the team felt at a loss regarding how they should respond to settler violence on the street and outside of Hebron, they decided to fast and pray on six successive Saturdays and invited their constituency to join them.

"Fasting and praying have often led to direction in CPT's work," the team wrote,

> Therefore, CPT in Hebron has decided to fast and pray on Saturdays for the next six weeks as a response to the violence, and also as a way of being open to the Spirit's guidance in this troubled time.
>
> We will have a peace candle burning all day and continue with our patrols in Hebron, being aware of what is happening on the streets. We will be breaking our fast on Sunday morning with communion at the church where we worship ... Let us call on the power of these two important spiritual disciplines not only to move our own hearts and minds, but also to transform the atmosphere of violence and fear pervasive in Hebron.[88]

87. CPTnet, "Hebron: Settler violence," Aug 16, 2000; CPTnet, "Hebron: Violence in the market," Aug 23, 2000.

88. CPTnet, "Hebron: Calling on the Power of God," Sept 22, 2000.

In an accompanying release, Bob Holmes noted that incidents of settler violence on Saturdays in September had decreased in comparison to Saturdays in August. He wrote that the Israeli military had told settlers that it would not tolerate further attacks, according to some newspaper accounts. However, Holmes wrote, the newspapers also reported that the IDF was assisting the settlements in acquiring more arms to counter anticipated Palestinian violence following either the completion or the collapse of the peace process.

"My prayer is that my next few weeks in this holy and conflicted city will not be a repeat of my first few weeks," wrote Holmes, in a release posted on September 22, 2000.[89]

Seven days later, Ariel Sharon visited the Temple Mount in Jerusalem, setting events in motion that created an outcome breathtakingly different from the one for which the Hebron team was praying.

89. CPTnet, "Hebron: Shabbat Shalom?" Sept 29, 2000.

5

"Things Fall Apart"—The Al-Aqsa Intifada

2000–2006

Things fall apart; the center cannot hold;
Mere anarchy is loosed upon the world,
The blood-dimmed tide is loosed, and everywhere
The ceremony of innocence is drowned;
The best lack all conviction, while the worst
Are full of passionate intensity.
Surely some revelation is at hand . . .

—W. B. Yeats, "The Second Coming"

W. B. YEATS' "THE Second Coming" evokes the Israeli-Palestinian
conflict for many people who have lived in the region. The poem
captures their feelings of powerlessness as they watch the peace and reconciliation work undertaken over the years recklessly destroyed by of
craven politicians.[1]

Such a political moment occurred on Thursday, September 28, 2000,
when Ariel Sharon, surrounded by hundreds of riot police, visited the
Haram al-Sharif compound, which includes the Al Aqsa mosque—Islam's
third holiest site after Mecca and Medina.[2] The visit was in keeping with

---

1. Israeli writers make frequent reference to the poem, e.g., Elon, *A Blood-Dimmed
Tide*; Rubinstein, "Slouching toward Jerusalem" and "Things fall apart"; J. Stein, *The
Widening Gyre of Negotiation*.

2. Muslims believe that Muhammad made a journey from Mecca to Al-Aqsa ("the
farthest") in a single night on a winged steed brought to him by the angel Gabriel. From
a rock there, he ascended to heaven, accompanied by Gabriel, received the command-
ments—including the traditional Muslim five daily prayers—before returning to Mecca
and communicating them to the faithful.

141

Sharon's historic bent for displaying flagrant domination in Palestinian areas.[3] To Palestinians in Jerusalem, the September 28 visit clearly signaled Israel's intent to assert sovereignty over the Haram al-Sharif/Temple Mount, and rioting erupted.[4] By the time Sharon left, hundreds of Israeli police officers and Palestinian worshipers had sustained injuries. The next day, September 29, 2000, riots broke out after Friday prayers in the Old City that resulted in the deaths of five people—shot by Israeli forces—and two hundred injured by rocks that Palestinians threw down on people by the Western Wall.

Although many pointed to Sharon's Temple Mount visit as "the start" of the Intifada, in reality Sharon merely threw a figurative match on a pool of gasoline. Israeli settlement expansion and land confiscation had continued throughout the Oslo, Wye, Sharm al Sheikh, and Camp David negotiations. Israeli checkpoints had increasingly made travel more difficult and humiliating for Palestinians. Israel had closed Jerusalem, the commercial and religious center of Palestine, to all but a few Palestinians who had Jerusalem identity and continued to hold political prisoners in its jails. Furthermore, U.S. President Bill Clinton had pushed an agreement through at Camp David that would have made no provision for refugees, would have allowed Israel to annex large settlement blocs, and legalized Israel's hegemony over Jerusalem.

By signing the Oslo Accords, Arafat had essentially signed over 78 percent of historic Palestine to Israel, so Palestinians felt they had already made great compromises. Sharon's visit to the Temple Mount was one more proof to Palestinians that Israel was negotiating in bad faith.

The clashes that began in Jerusalem on Friday spread to the whole of the West Bank and Gaza by Saturday.

3. For example, his house in the Muslim Quarter of Jerusalem's Old City—in which he spent little time—boasted a two-story Israeli flag draped out of the window and a giant Menorah on the roof. For more insights into Ariel Sharon's character, see Benzimann, *Sharon: An Israeli Caesar.*

4. Jews view the area of Al-Aqsa and Haram al-Sharif as the location of Herod's temple, of which only one wall—popularly called "The Wailing Wall"—remains. When Israel captured East Jerusalem in 1967, the government left the administration of the Muslim holy site in the hands of Muslims, fearing further attacks from the entire Arab/Muslim world. Since that time, right-wing Jews and their Christian Zionist sidekicks have advocated removing the Muslim structures, which they call "the abomination on the Temple Mount," by violence, if necessary.

Natasha Krahn wrote the first CPTnet release describing the change in Hebron's status quo, entitled "Fury, Fear and Faith."[5] In it, she reported hearing gunshots and percussion grenades in the distance, and settler youth attempting to smash the windshield of a van parked just outside the team apartment. This ambience was to mark the team's life in Hebron for the next year, as team members were forced to switch from the long-term strategizing they had done as part of the Campaign for Secure Dwellings to confronting one new crisis after another.

As time passed, however, the team's work during the Al Aqsa Intifada, which continues as of this writing, broke down into several basic categories.

Clashes

From the beginning of the CPT project in Hebron, clashes were a regular feature of life. Usually occurring on the border between H-1 and H-2, they often happened after a particular incident—such as when settlers attacked the Qurtuba Girls' School in 1995 or when a young Israeli woman hung flyers depicting the Prophet Muhammad as a pig writing the Quran in 1997. They also occurred after Israeli and Palestinian negotiators set up agreements detrimental to Palestinian residents of Hebron. The clashes lasted hours, days, or weeks, depending on the degree of anger simmering within the populace.

The team had learned early on that standing between soldiers and stone-throwing shabab (young Palestinian men) did not prevent a clash. Often, Palestinian women and children trying to move out of the clash zone were hit by rocks and bottles thrown by other Palestinians. The team tried to deal with the clashes obliquely, by noting that while they made good news footage, they distracted from the real issues of Occupation and the reconciliation work that Israeli and Palestinian activists were doing.[6]

---

5. CPTnet, "Fury, Fear and Faith," Oct 3, 2000.

6. Kern, "Sobbing on the Stairs":

> "When the Al Aqsa Intifada broke out in the fall, most representatives of the Israeli peace groups stopped coming to Hebron. But after a few weeks, Israeli women from Bat Shalom began visiting—often riding alone in Palestinian taxis to visit Palestinian families like the Abu Sharabatis [Kern gave Atta and Rodeina Jaber pseudonyms in the article.]

All clashes contained a certain degree of predictable theater. Young men would begin taunting soldiers at a checkpoint and throwing rocks, bottles, and Molotov cocktails. Soon, younger boys would join in. Soldiers would send for reinforcements and then begin shooting percussion grenades, tear gas, or rubber-coated metal bullets (called "rubber bullets") into the crowd, not necessarily in that order. Bystanders, shoppers and passersby often suffered injuries.

With the advent of the Intifada in September 2000, daily clashes went on for months and the rocks and glass shards on the streets near the border of H-1 and H-2 literally became ankle deep at times.

As clash after clash dragged on, their predictable theatricality became more surreal. Team members trying to get through a clash zone experienced the shabab and soldiers pausing, gallantly waving them through and then resuming their stone throwing and shooting. Zleekha Muhtasib, who translated for the team, told team members she had tried to get to the city center from her home in the Old City and realized she would not be able to get through. She and several other women turned to go back to their homes when one of the soldiers shouted to the young men in Arabic, "You stupid people! Can't you see there are women trying to pass?" The boys stopped and the soldiers allowed the women to cross the clash zone before they resumed their firing positions.[7]

Although some of the clashes seemed to start spontaneously, after awhile, the team began to wonder if the Palestinian Authority (PA) was, to some extent, encouraging and directing them. When shop owners near the H-1/H-2 boundary told the PA that they were suffering staggering financial losses because of the clashes, and when there seemed to be some progression in negotiations between Barak and Arafat, the Palestinian policemen came in to prevent the stone throwing.[8]

I think these visits are big news. But showing Israeli and Palestinian women sitting together drinking tea is not as "hot" as stone-throwing, so the women remain invisible.

7. CPTnet, "Hebron Update: November 8–11," Nov 17, 2000. On October 3, 2000 the team also observed soldiers telling a group of about twenty-five young Palestinian men and boys who were calmly watching the clash from the sidelines that they could join the stone throwers on the other side. Soldiers called for a brief cease-fire so that some of the boys could cross over. A Palestinian journalist told the team that soldiers had allowed the young men to cross so they could shoot at greater numbers of shabab. CPTnet, "Hebron Update: September 30–October 6, 2000," Oct 9, 2000.

8. Rich Meyer and Osaid Rashid, a translator for the team, once watched young Palestinian men making Molotov cocktails at the edges of a clash. Rashid told Meyer the

CPTers and the observers from TIPH found the clashes dispiriting and detrimental to the Palestinian cause. However, given the ongoing soldier and settler violence and land confiscation, they understood the rage as well. Anita Fast, in a reflection written on the team's third Saturday of fasting in October (see previous chapter), spoke of neighbors in the Old City going hungry because of the curfew the Israeli military had imposed on the thirty-five thousand residents since the beginning of the Intifada. When Hebron municipality workers tried to deliver emergency food aid to these families, soldiers denied them access. Krahn, Fast, and Holmes took the food and delivered it.

"My own hunger vanished as I took the small offerings of food to those who really needed it," Fast wrote,

> But the joy of fulfilling the one family's need was diminished by other hungry eyes, children watching from windows of homes for which we could not supply food.
>
> Knowing first-hand the suffering of those under curfew in H-2, it is easy to get angry at those Palestinians in H-1 who are throwing stones at soldiers and shooting at Jewish settlements, thereby providing justification for the curfew. I mourn the choice of many Palestinians who respond to violence with violence. Yet as I laid in bed Saturday night, the words of Jesus from the Gospels echoed in my mind: which one of you, when someone asks for bread, would give them a stone? And I remember that the Palestinian people have long been asking for bread—for the ability to live lives of dignity, self-determination, safety and freedom. Yet Israel, the U.S. and to a large extent, the entire international community has given them stones instead: hardened promises; firm and inflexible ultimatums; uncompromising policies of home demolitions and land confiscation; collective punishment; severe restrictions on movement . . .
>
> I have never, nor God willing, will ever condone the use of violence, even in revolt, but I wonder, what right has the hand that gives stones in the place of much needed bread to condemn and demonize God's children when they take the stones they have been given and begin to throw them.[9]

young men were receiving orders from above to make them. CPTnet, "Hebron Update: October 28–November 1, 2000," Nove 7, 2000.

9. CPTnet, "Hebron: Calling on the Spirit of God," Oct 16, 2000. In a letter to family and friends, Kathleen Kern recorded that Fast, during another worship session, had reflected on Amos 5:24: "Let justice roll down like waters and righteousness like an ever-flowing stream." Fast noted Amos' proclamation described a scary image:

Once, while Rich Meyer and Osaid Rashid—a nurse who sometimes served as team translator—observed young Palestinian men making Molotov cocktails, Meyer asked him about ways to promote nonviolent direct action. Rashid told him, "That would be like trying to teach breathing exercises to a woman in labor. She can't hear you. You needed to do that two months ago."[10]

The major daily clashes began to peter out in 2001. In later years, when team members did record these clashes in their Updates, they usually connected them to specific events. For example, when Israeli forces for the first time used American-made F-16 warplanes to bomb Palestinian population centers—Nablus, Gaza, Ramallah, and Tulkarem—clashes on the border of H-1 and H-2 lasted for a couple of hours the next day, May 19, 2001.[11] In 2006, clashes occurred after the Israeli military dropped a bomb on a beach in Gaza, killing nineteen men, women, and children.[12]

Invasions and Occupations of Palestinian Homes and Schools

Because of the clashes and nightly shooting, the Israeli military occupied homes, rooftops, shops, and schools situated near the H-1/H-2 border or at other strategic vantage points.

These rooftop outposts caused significant disruption in the lives of the families living in the homes. Some Israeli military units confiscated the upper floors of buildings, crowding the families into one or two rooms below. Soldiers often broke furniture, cut lines connecting satellite dishes to TVs, defecated and urinated on roofs (and sometimes in families' water tanks), shouted sexually suggestive remarks at the women in the

---

Justice is like a flash flood causing chaos and destruction in its path. Maybe that is the way to look at the recent violence. The false peace of the Oslo Accords that institutionalized Israeli economic, political and military hegemony of the region and facilitated the ongoing confiscation of land, had to be crushed and destroyed and swept away. (Kern, "Rage Rocks Hebron")

10. CPTnet, "Hebron Update: October 28–November 1, 2000," Nov 7, 2000.

11. CPTnet, "Hebron Update: May 16–29, 2001," June 5, 2001. The team mentioned only bombings of Nablus and Gaza, but the planes bombed Tulkarem and Ramallah also on May 18. On May 19 planes bombed Tulkarem once again and Jenin. The attacks were retaliation for the suicide bombing, which earlier that day killed five Israelis and injured ninety-six in Netanya's central shopping mall. See also CPTnet, "Hebron Update: July 30–August 11, 2001," Aug 26, 2001.

12. CPTnet, "Hebron: CPT observes protest," Nov 7, 2006.

household, and made insulting comments about Islam and the prophet Mohammed.[13] Having a soldier outpost on the roof also made the house the target for stones and Molotov cocktails thrown by youth during clashes. Some Palestinian families thus had rooms facing the street ruined by other Palestinians.

The Israeli military took over eight schools in Hebron to use as military outposts. The school takeovers resulted in the displacement of thousands of children. Other schools in Hebron began teaching in shifts to accommodate the teachers and students displaced from their former schools.

In 2005 and 2006, the team witnessed a resurgence of home invasions—most of them in their own neighborhood. Soldiers would sometimes break in, lock the families in a room, steal their valuables, and hangout to watch TV or otherwise enjoy themselves. After team members intervened in and documented several of these invasions, soldiers invaded the team apartment on December 29, 2005.

In a release about the incident, the team wrote,

> Walking around the apartment, the soldiers showed interest in a bowl of old sound grenades, used tear gas canisters, rubber-coated bullets and shells that CPTers picked up from the streets in the past. The soldiers passed these items around, and then one decided that the two or three dented cartridges constituted weapons. He explained that possession of weapons in this part of Hebron is prohibited, but when questioned by a CPTer the soldier corrected himself that Israelis are permitted to carry weapons in this part of Hebron. CPTers pointed out that it would be dangerous or impossible to place those bullets into a gun.
>
> A second patrol of six Israeli soldiers, including the captain, arrived. The captain collected the passports of all five CPTers present, and called the Israeli police. The police collected the display casings, shells and bullets and arrested John Lynes, Sarah MacDonald, Rich Meyer, Grace Pleiman and Harriet Taylor.

Although the team members locked the door behind them, and the captain assured them that no one would enter the apartment in their absence, when Kathie Uhler and Art Gish arrived at the apartment later, they

13. See CPTnet releases: "Hebron Update: September 1–15, 2000," Sept 26, 2000. "Hebron: The Martyrdom of Innocence," Oct 4, 2000; "Hebron Update: September 16–29, 2000," Oct 9, 2000; "Hebron Update: October 17–19 [2000]," Oct 22, 2000. "Hebron Update: January 6–11, 2001," Jan 23, 2001.

found the street door unlocked, the door to the office apartment forced, and the team's cameras, computers, and cell phones stolen. (A Palestinian American computer store owner later recovered one computer for the team, when a Palestinian man came in to hock it.) The police formally arrested Lynes, MacDonald, Meyer, Pleiman, and Taylor, drawing up the required paperwork and having them sign a statement saying the would appear in court if called to do so. Afterward, the police released them on their own recognizance, and never contacted them further regarding a court date.[14]

Later, that summer and fall, soldiers conducted another series of home invasions, which were possibly related to the war with Hezbollah in Lebanon. Dianne Roe took footage of soldiers traumatizing a family in their home. She and John Lynes then went to the police station near the mosque to show the officers her footage. When Roe refused to surrender the camera or the film, she and Lynes were taken to the Kiryat Arba police station, where police forced them to relinquish both and questioned them for five hours.[15]

As of this writing in the eighth year of the Al-Aqsa intifada, home invasions continue to occur in spates, as IDF brigades cycle in an out of Hebron. How often these occupations occur relates mostly to the caprice of brigade commanders, some of who are more respectful of Palestinian human rights than others. The team continues to monitor soldiers' behavior in this regard, as a December 2007 Hebron Update records:

> At dusk, [Jessica] Frederick and [Lorne] Friesen encountered a group of ten soldiers diligently studying maps as they walked about the Old City. The soldiers said that they were just orienting some of their number. One soldier asked Friesen why the CPTers were following them. Friesen replied that he was hoping that the soldiers would not do a house invasion this evening, to which the soldier replied, "We are too tired tonight." The soldiers stood on

14. CPTnet, "Hebron: Israeli military invades CPT apartment," Jan 8, 2006. CPTnet, "Hebron: Good Samaritan alive," Mar 1, 2006. See other CPTnet releases: "Hebron: Israeli soldiers occupy homes," Sept 14, 2005; "Hebron: Say it with a home invasion." Dec 21, 2005; "Hebron: Soldiers or Settlers?" Feb 3, 2006. See also Rich Meyer, interview, Feb 5, 2008. For an example of soldiers invading a home in a more considerate way, see, CPTnet, "Hebron Update: 6–12 August 2005," Aug 23, 2005.

15. See CPTnet releases: "Hebron: CPTers monitoring home invasion," Aug 12, 2006; "Hebron: Update on CPTers detained," Aug 15, 2006. See also CPTnet, "Hebron Reflection: Strangers in my home," Nov 2, 2006.

the roof of a house for ten or fifteen minutes before coming down. One of the soldiers, seeing that the CPTers were still there, asked if they had been standing there the whole time. Friesen said yes, and the soldier responded, "That's perseverance."[16]

Gun Battles, Snipers, and Military Invasions

Although Israeli soldiers and settlers and Palestinian gunmen in Hebron had shot at each other sporadically since the Hebron Project began in 1995, the Intifada brought nightly pitched gun battles between gunmen and soldiers for the first time in the history of CPT's Hebron project, as well as assassinations on the street by Israeli snipers.

The barrages usually started late afternoon or early evening and followed a predictable progression. The team would hear sporadic gunfire from the light weaponry of Palestinian militants firing at settlements and soldier encampments. Israeli soldiers responded from fixed machine gun posts and then the team would hear the loud boom of tank fire.

Israeli soldiers who served in Hebron at this time later described receiving nightly orders for "punitive fire." Unable to gun down or apprehend Palestinian gunmen who would squeeze off a few shots from residential neighborhoods and then duck behind houses, the Israeli soldiers received orders to rake the house fronts, water tanks, streetlights, and cars on the opposite hillside with "punitive fire." Although Palestinians slept in the lower floors and rear of their homes, several fatalities resulted.[17]

Sometimes Israeli forces shot into neighborhoods without any precipitating Palestinian fire as retaliation for violence that had occurred elsewhere. In one such case on November 1, 2000, Israeli peace activist

16. CPTnet, "Hebron Update: 3–16 December 2007," Dec 22, 2007. The entry for December 15 continues:

> Frederick said to a soldier that they would be welcome to drink tea in the CPT apartment, but they could not bring their guns. The soldier indicated that he needed his gun for safety, that he would be killed if he did not have it with him. Frederick said, "I'm sorry you feel that way. We walk [through the city] every day without guns." The soldier responded, "You are not a Jew." Frederick said, "We work with Jews, and Palestinians work with Jews." The soldier explained that a Palestinian could work for someone for twenty years, and then strap a bomb to his chest and blow himself up. Then the soldiers moved on through the Old City.

17. CPTnet, "Hebron Update: 2–15 December 2005," Dec 27, 2005. The soldiers were part of an organization called "Breaking the Silence." See below.

Adam Keller called the team at 12:30 a.m., saying, "I want to make sure you know that the Israeli military has told Palestinians to evacuate the neighborhoods of Haret i-Sheikh and Abu Sneineh. They are threatening retaliation because three Israeli soldiers were killed today." Two of the three soldiers killed were engaged in a firefight at Al Khader, near Bethlehem, and one was killed in a battle near Jericho.[18]

In the first few nights of shooting, the team huddled in the windowless kitchen of the apartment. Gradually, they realized that since they lived in a neighborhood with Palestinian families, Palestinian gunmen were unlikely to shoot at them. Since they had an Israeli soldier camp on one side of their apartment and the settlement of Avraham Avinu on the other, soldiers were unlikely to shoot at them. As the nightly shooting continued over the next months, the team and their neighbors began going up on the roof of the apartment building to figure out the locations from which Palestinians and Israeli soldiers were firing the shots. Children living in the team's apartment building played and rode bicycles on the roof as the adults chatted amicably with each other about the exchanges of fire.

Some of these snipers and gun battles claimed as casualties people team members knew personally. On October 9, 2000, Israeli snipers shot the brother of Tarik Sharif, one of the team's translators in its Campaign for Secure Dwellings, as Shehab Sharif walked home through the neighborhood of Haret iSheikh in the H-1 section of Hebron.[19] The next morning, shots fired from the settlement of Beit Haggai hit Ibrahim Abu Turki, uncle of CSD participant Nabil Abu Turki as both were returning from Hebron to their homes in the Qilqis/Al Sendas area with bread for their families. On the same morning in downtown Hebron, team friend Hani Abu Haikel emerged after a clash from his shop in the Al Andalus mall to deliver coffee when Israeli snipers shot him in the foot. A twenty-two-year-old father of three, who had also been waiting for the clashes to end, left the mall at the same time that Abu Haikel did, and an exploding bullet hit him in the abdomen. Abu Haikel told the team he heard nothing before he felt the pain in his foot and saw the young man, Mansour Saied Ahmad, fall. Soldiers would not allow an ambulance from Ramallah

18. CPTnet, "Hebron Update: October 28–November 1, 2000." Nov 7, 2000. Bethlehem, Beit Jala, Beit Sahour, and Jericho also underwent heavy bombing that night.

19. CPTnet, "Use my name, Mom," Nov 8, 2000.

through a checkpoint to bring blood to Hebron's Alia Hospital—blood that could have saved his life.[20]

On October 23, an Israeli sniper shot taxi driver Fayez Mohammed Al-Qemari—who had often driven team members out to the Beqa'a Valley—as he washed his vehicle. Andrew Getman and Dianne Roe saw pieces of his brain lying in the street.[21] Soldiers shot a relative of another CSD family in Beit Ummar on October 25, 2000.[22]

On the mornings after heavy gunfire barrages, team members would walk around the neighborhoods of Haret iSheik and Abu Sneineh to document the damage done there. In homes and shops, they saw burned bedding and furniture, shattered mirrors and windows, and bullet holes through steel doors and concrete and marble walls. Rockets left holes a foot in diameter. Bowls on coffee tables that used to hold flowers, cookies, or fruit now held a variety of bullets and other projectiles that had hit the houses. One family in the Old City made a necklace of hundreds of spent M-16 cartridges that fell into their courtyard because of Israeli soldiers firing from their roof into Abu Sneineh.[23]

After the team made several visits to the Qawasme family in the Haret iSheik neighborhood, one of the men in a household particularly hard-hit by Israeli barrages suggested that team members spend the night to get an idea of what life under fire was like, and perhaps prevent the shootings. Accordingly, the team delivered the following letter to the soldiers' camp

20. CPTnet, "View from Within," Oct 30, 2000. See also CPTnet releases: "Hebron Update: October 13–16, 2000," Oct 17, 2000; "Hebron: Calling on the Spirit of God," Oct 20, 2000; "God's Tears," Oct 18, 2000.

A settler youth had killed the brother of Ibrahim Abu Turki, the man bringing bread to his family, two years earlier along the same stretch of road by putting a board out the window of a car as it whizzed past him.

See also Ben Lynfield, "In Mideast, crossfire more careless," Lynfield covered the shooting of Ibrahim Abu Turki and the army's lack of interest in pursuing the matter. He noted that during the first Intifada, the Israeli military investigated every death—of Palestinians not classified as terrorists—at the hands of Israeli soldiers.

21. CPTnet, "Tonight it will be worse," Oct 23, 2000.

22. CPTnet, "A Spiral of Violence," Oct 31, 2000. See also CPTnet, "Hebron Update: October 23–27, 2000," Nov 2, 2000. Residents of Hebron actually sustained fewer casualties than Palestinians living in Gaza, Nablus, Ramallah, and Jenin. However, Hebronites participated in the agony of other Palestinians as they watched the deaths and the funerals replayed on Palestinian television.

23. CPTnet, "Hebron Update: October 7–9, 2000," Oct 9, 2000. See also Kern, "Hebron—H-2."

next to their apartment, shortly before Dianne Roe and Kathleen Kern went to spend the night in Haret iSheik:

> November 2, 2000
>
> To Noam Tibon, Commander of Hebron District:
>
> The Christian Peacemaker Team in Hebron, which has had a continuous presence here since June 1995, is saddened by the many deaths this month; whether Palestinian or Israeli, armed or unarmed, we believe that each killing destroys part of God's good creation, each killing is a loss for the entire human family. We are appalled by the dramatic escalation of violence the Israeli military is engaged in with indiscriminate fire from heavy weaponry in Bethlehem, Beit Jala, Beit Sahour, as well as throughout the neighborhoods of Hart-iSheik and Abu Sneineh here in Hebron. Accordingly, members of our team will be staying with families in the Hart iSheik neighborhood this evening, Thursday, November 2. As pacifists, we have asked the families to assure us there are no guns in their homes and they have done so.
>
> We are aware that the authorities of the Israeli occupation may accuse us of shielding terrorists, and we know there have been shots fired from these neighborhoods over the past month. However, no one from these neighborhoods has strafed Israeli neighborhoods with missiles and automatic weapons fire, and the vast majority of people in these neighborhoods are not gunmen. We believe that collective punishment against a whole people, whether they be Israeli or Palestinian, is morally wrong. In 1996 we rode the #18 bus in Jerusalem on the third Sunday after it had been bombed the two previous Sundays to protest the collective punishment of Israeli civilians. Tonight, we are staying in the Hart iSheik neighborhood to protest the collective punishment of Palestinian civilians. By the time you receive this, members of our team will be in this neighborhood and our consular representatives will have been notified.
>
> With hopes for a just and lasting peace for both Palestinians and Israelis,
>
> Christian Peacemaker Teams[24]

The team's overnight visits, which involved calling the US consulate to inform personnel that they were under fire, did not appear to protect

24. CPTnet, "CPTers Stay in Neighborhoods," Nov 2, 2000; CPTnet, "A night in Hart iSheik," Nov 6, 2000.

the neighborhoods in which they stayed. Most families involved, however, appreciated the gesture of solidarity. They understood the accompaniment was an experiment, and did not blame CPT when its presence did not prevent Israeli military fire on their neighborhoods.

Although gun battles in Hebron happened with less frequency in 2001, they still racked up a significant death toll. CPTers found themselves pinned down by gunfire several times, both in Hebron and as they traveled to and from the Jerusalem and Bethlehem areas.[25]

Of particular consequence to Hebron residents was the March 26 shooting of ten-month-old Shalhevet Pass, the daughter of Hebron settlers Yitzhak and Oriya Pass. Yitzhak Pass was also shot as he was pushing her stroller in the Avraham Avinu settler enclave. The IDF retaliated by bombarding houses in Abu Sneineh for two hours while settlers ransacked the Palestinian market, closed because of a curfew. The next morning, settlers invaded homes on Abu Sneineh. When the army turned them around, the settlers began shooting randomly into the neighborhood.[26]

After months of Hebron CPTers assuring family members and supporters that their apartment was quite safe from all the shooting, bullets finally hit their building on July 19, 2001. Several CPTers and their upstairs neighbors were, as usual, on the roof, chatting and listening to the shooting. A bullet hit the wall—against which Rick Polhamus was propping his chair—inches away from his shoulder, covering him with

25. See CPTnet releases: "Wedding Bells and Bullets," Feb 16, 2001; "Hebron Update: February 14–20, 2001," Mar 10, 2001; "Hebron: CPTers caught in crossfire," Apr 19, 2001; Nicole Mortellito, "Bethlehem District: CPT Delegation under fire," Aug 19, 2001; "Hebron: The Women and Children Weren't Shooting," Jan 14, 2001. See also HRW, "Israel/Palestine: Armed Attacks."

26. CPTnet, "Hebron: Baby killed; Army and settlers retaliate," Mar 27, 2001.

The Arab-American Institute published a report comparing media coverage of Shalhevet Pass's murder with that of a four-month-old Palestinian girl killed by Israeli troops in Gaza on May 7, 2001. It noted that *The Washington Post* and *New York Times* invariably write more sympathetically about Israeli victims of Palestinian violence than they do about Palestinian victims of Israeli violence. Morey, "A Tale of Two Killings." Shalhevet Pass's photo was prominently displayed on a banner at the Avraham Avinu settlement for many months afterward.

Four months after the killing of Shalhevet Pass, a seven-year-old girl in Abu Sneineh—a relative of the team's friend Nisreen Abu Mayaleh—died when an Israeli bullet hit her in the head during a shooting exchange. The team later learned that the girl's grandmother died of heart attack one hour after she left her dead granddaughter in the hospital. See CPTnet, "Hebron Update: August 12–19, 2001," Aug 30, 2001. The fact that the team consigned the girl's death to an update shows to some extent, the sheer amount of suffering that the team had been recording.

concrete dust. The next morning women on the team found six bullet holes in their apartment. One pierced the metal door and went through boxes and sheets stacked on a nearby shelf. When they looked through the bullet hole in the door, team members saw that it framed the roof of Avraham Avinu. A low caliber bullet shot from the roof of Avraham Avinu went through the glass in the door on August 20, 2001.[27]

Releases and updates from the spring and summer of 2001 reflect growing anguish, anger, and a sense of powerlessness within the Hebron Team about the relentless juggernaut of violence crushing both Israelis and Palestinians. Greg Rollins, in a September 15, 2001 release described following the drops of blood leading to the house where a seventeen-year-old boy had been shot in the head. He passed crying children running away from the house. "The moment I saw the children running down the street, I knew there was nothing we were going to be able to do," he wrote. "Part of me still wishes I had followed them to wherever they were running."[28]

The team began to look for new, creative ways to throw a wrench into the cycle of violence or at least hold warmongers accountable. On April 11, 2001, the team hung a banner on top of Abu Sneineh moun-

---

27. CPTnet, "Hebron: Christian Peacemaker Team Apartment," July 21, 2001. The release incorrectly reports the date the team found the hole on June 20, 2001. CPTnet, "Hebron: More settler attacks," Aug 21, 2001. Interestingly, Polhamus almost getting shot did not make it into the team's update or merit a special release. The author contacted him about the date and he said he had photos dated June 19 showing him with dust on his back and holding a shell fragment. When she asked if he remembered why the team had not written about it, Polhamus (known for his twisted sense of humor) responded in a May 11, 2004 e-mail:

> •We weren't sure if that shot was Palestinian or Israeli. •It was just a stray shot for sure while the ones to the women's apartment were from the settlement area and were probably deliberate. •It would just disappoint many people to know the shot came close but missed me. Take care, Rick."

28. CPTnet, "Hebron: Finding the Dead," Sept 15, 2000. See also CPTnet, "Hebron: More than watchmen," Sept 16, 2001; CPTnet, "Hebron: 'Israelis and Palestinians must stop,'" Aug 10, 2001. In this last release, Kern quoted Atta Jaber (anonymously) as saying:

> I am so sad. I was just watching the television and 19 Israelis are killed [in a Jerusalem suicide bombing.] I want to call all my Israeli friends and make sure they are all right. I want to run into the streets of Jerusalem and shout that the killing must stop. Maybe people will think I am crazy, but I just want to keep shouting that Israelis and Palestinians must stop killing each other.

tain reading, "The Veto Kills," referring to the U.S. veto of a December 2000 UN Resolution calling for unarmed observers in the West Bank and Gaza Strip. In June, the team called for a July 27 through August 8, 2001, Emergency Peacemaker Witness delegation to the West Bank to serve as a violence-deterring presence in locations around the West Bank suffering most from Israeli assassinations, shellings and full-scale military invasions. [29]

The assassination of right-wing Israeli Minister of Tourism, Rehavam Ze'evi, by the Palestinian Front for the Liberation of Palestine on October 17, 2001, prompted fresh invasions into Palestinian cities.[30] Hebron was spared from invasion initially, but the team's friends in the Bethlehem district reported their dire predicament as tanks fired into civilian neighborhoods, hotels, and hospitals. The team put out an Urgent Action, asking its constituents to demand that President George W. Bush, Secretary of State Colin Powell, Canadian Prime Minister Jean Chrétien, and Canadian foreign minister John Manley call for Israeli troops to pull out of Palestinian cities. Further, the team asked constituents to appeal for the implementation of the provisions in the Mitchell report that would reduce violence (e.g., placing unarmed observers in the Territories and freezing settlements). [31] "You may note," the team wrote, "That the U.S. war against Afghanistan is giving Prime Minister Sharon both cover and a precedent for increased attacks on Palestinians."[32]

The winter and spring of 2002 saw dozens of attacks and incidents of retaliation by Palestinian militants and the Israeli military. The Israeli

---

29. CPTnet, "Hebron Update: April 3–15, 2001," Apr 30, 2001; CPTnet, "Chicago: CPT calls for Emergency Peacemaker Witness," June 12, 2001. See also Mortellito, "West Bank: Under Fire."

30. As far as killings go, the Ze'evi murder was a measured response. The PFLP specifically stated that they killed the cabinet minister in retaliation for Israel assassinating the PFLP's Secretary-General, Abu Ali Mustapha, on August 27, 2001. Ze'evi was notorious for advocating that Israel expel Palestinians from the Occupied Territories, and was considered an extremist even by many right-wing politicians. Yasser Arafat outlawed PFLP and arrested thirty-three PFLP militants after Ze'evi's death, but Sharon invaded because Arafat did not turn over the men wanted for Ze'evi's death to Israel.

31. The Mitchell Report was a document published on April 30, 2001 that contained the findings of an American committee, led by former US Senator George J. Mitchell, regarding the first stages of the al-Aqsa Intifada. See CMEP, "Text of the Mitchell Report."

32. CPTnet, "Hebron/Bethlehem Urgent Action: Stop the Israeli Invasions," Oct 22, 2001.

military continued to besiege Yasser Arafat in his Ramallah compound and a debate raged within Israel about whether the IDF should enter and kill him. Israeli soldiers also regularly raided the Gaza, Balata, and Jenin refugee camps to kill militants suspected of attacks on Israelis. They killed dozens of Palestinian civilians as well.[33] Suicide bombings within Israel and near settlements also ratcheted up, killing dozens of Israeli civilians.

In one particularly gruesome attack, a suicide bomber killed nineteen Israelis at a Passover celebration in a Netanya hotel on March 27, 2002. Two days later, tanks and bulldozers attacked Arafat's compound as the next stage, according to Ariel Sharon, of a "long and complicated war that knows no borders."[34] Suicide bombers subsequently struck in Tel Aviv and Haifa the next two days.

Some West Bank cities experienced pitched battles in their streets for the first time since 1967. One contact of the team told them that Ramallah looked like Beirut at the height of Israel's invasion of Lebanon. A friend of Le Anne Clausen in Bethlehem told her that the family was out of food, water, and electricity; a tank had run over the family car and the stench of bodies lying in Manger Square had become unbearable.[35]

Hisham Sharabati arranged a meeting with the team after Ramallah and Bethlehem were invaded. He told the team that in those cities, the Israeli military had destroyed radio stations and made it impossible for the wounded to get to hospitals. Accordingly, Sharabati, along with a committee of journalists and medical personnel, divided Hebron into sectors and arranged to have a makeshift clinic and radio transmitter in each sector. (A great deal of panic happened in other West Bank Cities when the Israeli military took out the radio and television stations. With the Hebron settlers poised to take over uninhabited parts of the Old City, Sharabati and the other organizers wanted to make sure that people stayed in their homes as long as they could safely do so.) Sharabati asked the

33. Dianne Roe and Kathleen Kern visited the Al Aroub refugee camp, north of Hebron, on March 12 because of team concerns that the Israeli military might invade there, as it had other refugee camps. Residents of the camp told them that unlike the Balata and Deheishe refugee camps, Aroub was in Area C. It had never passed out of Israeli control, so there was no need for the Israelis to invade. "Hebron Update: March 7–12, 2002," March 21, 2002.

34. Goldenberg, "Israel turns its fire on Arafat."

35. CPTnet releases: "Hebron: Brief report on the current situation," Apr 2, 2002; "Hebron Update: April 7, 2002," Apr 7, 2002; "Jerusalem: Massacre in Jenin," Apr 15, 2002.

team to talk to Doctors Without Borders to get their assistance and told team members to be ready to disperse to the various sectors of the city when they received a call, so that each sector would have international accompaniment.

On April 29 at 4:00 a.m., after several false starts,[36] Israeli forces entered the H-1 area of Hebron, bringing to an end the control of the Palestinian authority in that part of the city. Compared to the bloodshed in Jenin, Nablus, and Bethlehem, the number of casualties was light: the military killed eight Palestinians and wounded twenty-five. CPTers visited one family who reported that when they heard screaming coming from cars that had been hit by shells and appeals for assistance on the radio, brothers Faris and Ibrahim Shaheen, and their cousin Nader, ran to help. All three died from helicopter missile gunfire. Soldiers destroyed several buildings, including the local television station, and arrested suspected Palestinian militants.

Over the next weeks, the team visited various locations in and around Hebron that had sustained damage during the invasion from shelling and soldier raids, including Haret iSheik, Abu Sneineh, Beit Ummar, and Shuyoukh (where the military blew up the communications center, causing considerable damage to surrounding homes and buildings).[37] Particularly hard hit was the Dweiban neighborhood, which Israeli tanks shelled on May 5, 2005, leaving ten families homeless. Soldiers also conducted room-to-room searches for militants, using a local blacksmith and a fourteen-year-old Palestinian boy as human shields to protect themselves from booby traps and gunmen. After another suicide bombing, the following morning soldiers blasted open the gate of a textile factory, starting a fire that destroyed the factory and several residential apartments. The soldiers later claimed the factory had been making weapons.

Le Anne Clausen accompanied Hisham Sharabati and some international human rights lawyers to Dweiban on May 13, 2002, to take testimonies from the residents there. They told the investigators that the soldiers

36. Rumors that Hebron was about to be invaded had been circulating since March. See CPTnet releases: "Hebron News Brief: Invaded or not," Apr 4, 2002; "Hebron Update: April 7, 2002"; "Hebron Update: April 19–24, 2002," Apr 27, 2002.

37. See CPTnet releases: "Hebron Update: April 29–May 3, 2002," May 10, 2002; "Shuyoukh: Disneyland," May 14, 2002; "Hebron Update: May 25–31, 2002," June 17, 2002; "Hebron Update: June 2–7, 2002," June 21, 2002.

had not confiscated anything from inside the factory, as they presumably would have if they had found weapons.[38]

Israeli troops eventually withdrew from the H-1 section of Hebron, and after 2002, Hebronites would not have to deal with pitched gun battles and full-scale invasions by the Israeli military. However, over the next years of the Intifada, Hebronites had no illusions about the authority that was in control of their lives and livelihoods. They understood that the brief period of the Palestinian Authority actually governing most of Hebron was over. They were still under Israeli military occupation.

Curfews and Closures

The clashes and the shooting led to the imposition of curfews on the Palestinian residents of H-1 that lasted for weeks. The military had little incentive to lift the curfew, because imprisoning the residents of the Old City in their homes made their jobs easier. They did not have to worry about settler/Palestinian altercations or someone attacking them from within a throng of civilians.

Sometimes, the military would lift curfew for a few hours, so people could buy food, but as time passed and people were unable to get to their jobs, they had no money with which to buy food. Team members often found themselves negotiating with soldiers at checkpoints, persuading them to allow residents of the Old City to pass through who had not gotten back before the military imposed curfew again.

The team also intervened when people told them they needed to get to the hospital. Whether soldiers let people pass for medical treatment generally depended on the unit staffing the checkpoints. In one case, soldiers told a woman whose daughter was having severe abdominal pain that they would not permit an ambulance through and that she must watch her daughter die. The mother hailed a garbage truck, which soldiers let through because trash collectors picked up both soldier and Palestinian refuse as well as Palestinian garbage. She and the driver laid the sick woman on top of the garbage and the man took her into the Palestinian-controlled section of Hebron, where she found a car to take her to the hospital in Jerusalem.[39]

38. CPTnet, "Hebron Update: May 11–17, 2002," May 31, 2002.

39. CPTnet, "Hebron Update: October 20–22, 2000," Oct 25, 2000. The team found out about this incident after it happened.

On November 1, Israeli journalist Amira Hass wrote a story about the curfew in Hebron, beginning,

> How perfectly natural that 40,000 persons should be subject to a total curfew for more than a month in the Old City of Hebron in order to protect the lives and well-being of 500 Jews. How perfectly natural that almost no Israeli mentions this fact or, for that matter, even knows about it. How perfectly natural that 34 schools attended by thousands of Palestinian children should be closed down for more than a month and their pupils imprisoned and suffocating day and night in their crowded homes, while the children of their neighbors—their Jewish neighbors, that is—are free to frolic as usual in the street among and with the Israeli soldiers stationed there. How perfectly natural that a Palestinian mother must beg and plead so that an Israeli soldier will allow her to sneak through the alleyways of the open-stall marketplace and obtain medication for her asthmatic children, or bread for her family.[40]

Hass claimed that the curfew in Hebron was a microcosm of the Occupation as a whole, showing that the Israeli public could accept with ease the intolerable suffering the Occupation imposed on Palestinians. On the day her article appeared in Ha'aretz, Israeli military officials told her that it had lifted the forty-day curfew on Hebron. She called the team in Hebron to see if it had indeed been lifted. Had she known the article would be so effective, she told them, she would have written it much sooner. In Spring 2002, as curfew was again imposed for great lengths of time, she would apologize to the team for not being able to write another piece about it, given the current Israeli government's assassinations of Palestinian militants and siege on Arafat's compound in Ramallah.[41]

Road closures between Palestinian neighborhoods and towns had effects similar to those of the curfews on Palestinian lives. Harriet Taylor wrote in July 2001,

> While the international community congratulates Israel on its "restraint" (i.e., no shelling of Palestinian areas) after the suicide bombing of the disco in Tel Aviv on June 1st, the Israeli government has imposed even more egregious measures of collective punishment and control on the Palestinian people in the Occupied Territories.

40. Hass, "The Mirror Doesn't Lie," Nov 1, 2000.
41. CPTnet, "Hebron Update: March 7–12, 2002," Mar 21, 2002.

Villages and towns are under siege, completely closed off by
barricades, often made more intimidating by the presence of the
Israeli military. Palestinian workers are forbidden to go to Israel
to their jobs and are subject to arrest and imprisonment if they
are caught trying to do so. Although settler roads remain open,
there are checkpoints every few miles; and since no one except
certain taxi drivers are permitted to leave their home territories,
Palestinians found traveling in private cars or taxis are forced from
their cars and stranded wherever they happen to be. International
borders are closed, and international mail and money transfers
into the West Bank and Gaza are cut off. Many Palestinians receive
financial support from family members abroad, without which
they may literally starve ...

While the world looks for images of bomb damage and tank
fire, which have been largely absent for the last several days, the
Israeli Knesset on Saturday tightened the silent, virtually invisible
noose of control and deprivation that is the occupation. When will
the world hear the strangled cries of the Palestinians?[42]

Families and shop owners with the financial means or family outside of
H-2 began to leave *en masse*.[43]

By the summer and fall 2002, the team's interventions switched to
survival mode. Several updates record the team delivering food to people
trapped in their houses by the curfew or accompanying representatives
of the Red Cross and Doctors Without Borders as they tried (and often
failed) to make these deliveries. After a fatal November 15, 2002 attack
on Israeli soldiers (see below, under "Home Demolitions"), the curfew
imposed was especially tight. Soldiers threatened to shoot representatives
of the Hebron Municipality if they attempted to deliver food. The team
noted in their update covering November 18, "According to the Fourth
Geneva Convention, occupation forces must guarantee occupied populations access to food, medical aid and humanitarian aid."[44]

42. CPTnet, "Hebron: The Strangulation of the Occupied Territories," July 2, 2001.

43. See CPTnet releases: "Hebron Update: August 29–September 3, 2004," Sept 14,
2004; "Hebron Update: July 22–28, 2001," Aug 16, 2001; "Hebron Update: August 20–28,
2001," Sept 4, 2001; "Curfew Babies," Sept 14, 2001; "Hebron Urgent Update: Pressure
Israeli authorities," Dec 13, 2001; "Hebron Update: March 7–12, 2002," Mar 21, 2002;
Hebron Update: August 20–28, 2001," Sept 4, 2001.

44. CPTnet, "Hebron Update: November 13–22, 2002," Nov 28, 2002. See also CPTnet
update releases covering June 23–29, November 13–29, December 6–19, 2002.

Curfew on the residents of the Old City and even the Bab iZawiyya area continued to intensify in 2003. The team began to see the resulting flight of Palestinians from these areas as a policy of the Israeli government, rather than an unintended side effect of military "security" operations. A family living near the Ibrahimi mosque reported to the team on January 8, 2003, that soldiers had invaded their home ten times in the previous twenty days. When the family complained to the local commander about soldiers abusing them during the raids, he said, "If you die, you die. If you live, you are lucky. You should move out of the Old City." In a January 16, 2003, release, Art Gish noted that extreme right-wingers had begun calling again for the transfer of Palestinians out of the West Bank. He then listed ways in which this transfer was effectively occurring in Hebron because of curfews, soldier raids, shop closings, and children falling behind in their education.[45]

In 2003, for the first time, the Israeli military ordered team members to abide by the same curfews and closures that it had imposed on their neighbors for years. Shuhada Street became entirely off limits to the CPTers as well as Palestinians in contravention of the 1997 Hebron Protocol.[46] At first, these restrictions seemed to operate at the level of individual soldiers who told team members they could not pass through checkpoints into the Old City or could not accompany children to school during curfew.

On May 18, 2003, the restrictions became official. That morning at 6:00 a.m., a Palestinian militant blew himself up on a bus in Jerusalem, killing seven people and wounding twenty. When Mary Lawrence, Diane Janzen, Chris Brown, Germana Nijim, Harriet Taylor, and Greg Rollins attempted to do school patrol, soldiers refused to let them leave the Old City. Rollins, Brown, Lawrence, and Janzen went through the tunnel network in the Old City to get to Bab iZawiyya. Seeing soldiers detaining about thirty Palestinian men at the Beit Hadassah checkpoint, Rollins and Brown went over to observe. Soldiers took Brown's passport and the ID of

45. See CPTnet releases: "Hebron Update: January 3–12, 2003," Jan 23, 2003; "Hebron: Population Transfer," Jan 16, 2003; "Hebron Update: February 28–March 10, 2003," Mar 22, 2003; "Hebron: The Shopkeeper," Mar 27, 2003; "Hebron Update: March 18–30, 2003," Apr 9, 2003; "Hebron Update: October 16–22, 2003," Nov 1, 2003.

46. See CPTnet releases: "Hebron Update: February 28–March 10, 2003," Mar 22, 2003; "Hebron Update: April 7–20, 2003," Apr 25, 2003; "Hebron Update: May 5–18, 2003," June 3, 2003; "Hebron: Turquoise awnings," July 22, 2003.

a Palestinian municipal observer. Unfortunately, Rollins had washed his passport in the laundry and was waiting to receive a new one from the Canadian Embassy. After three hours, the soldiers released Brown and most of the Palestinians. They took Rollins to the police station where the police put him under arrest and ordered his deportation. Rollins would remain in jail for three weeks, longer than any other CPTer who had served on the Hebron project.[47]

The day after Rollins' arrest, May 19, 2003, six Israeli soldiers searched the team's apartment. When the team asked why they had entered the house with guns, the soldiers told them that it was a "matter of life and death." (In her journal, CPTer Germana Nijim noted, "We are one step closer to being full-fledged Palestinians.")[48] The next night, soldiers again entered the apartment. They examined the passports and visas of the CPTers present, photographed the apartment and individual team members, studied the maps and pictures on the wall, and scrutinized the contents of the filing cabinet. The soldiers then verbally issued the following orders to the team:

1. CPTers were not allowed in H-1—the area of Hebron formerly under Palestinian control. If Israeli troops caught CPTers in H-1 they would arrest and deport them.

2. No internationals or Israelis were allowed in H-1 except those working for NGOs recognized by the Israeli government.

3. CPTers were not to go anywhere near an Israeli settlement (all of which were in H-2).

4. CPTers were not to accompany children to school in H-2.

5. CPTers would not be allowed back into H-2 if they left (e.g., to go to Jerusalem).

The team continued to conduct their morning school patrols, but more surreptitiously. On May 27, 2003, David Glass, the Israeli military Liaison to non-governmental organizations (NGOs), met them at the

47. Although the courts later overturned his deportation order and stipulated that no restrictions should apply to his entering the country again, when he arrived in Israel on March 11, 2004, the Israeli government denied him entry. Nijim, "The Saga of Greg Rollins"; CPTnet, "Hebron: Israel Cracks Down," May 20, 2003; CPTnet, "Hebron Reflection: Greg Rollins writes about his weeks in an Israeli prison," June 7, 2003.

48. Nijim, "The Saga of Greg Rollins."

locked gate recently installed in the alley where the team's apartment was located. Through the bars, he showed them a paper in Hebrew, which he said barred them from H-1, the area of the city formerly controlled by the Palestinian authority. No one on the team read Hebrew, but they saw clearly the date "2001" written on the paper. Glass refused to give them a copy of the order.[49] Yoav Hass, an Israeli conscientious objector, buoyed their confidence when he told them that for these orders to be legal, the military would have to write them in English and give the team a copy. He also told them that showing people papers purportedly containing orders that they could not read was a standard tactic of the military.[50]

The "virtual" closures imposed on the team were followed up by actual physical barriers in the Old City market area and areas leading from H-1 into H-2. In July 2003, the military began installing a "separation" fence from the Ibrahimi mosque to the gated entrance of the Old City market facing Shuhada Street. Jerry Levin noted in a release that when the gate was completed a soldier's key would trap the Palestinian residents of the Old City in a mini-ghetto—as the gates that the team helped take down in February 1996 had (see chapter 4). The Israeli authorities continued to install barriers throughout the Old City over the ensuing years.[51] A 2005 map of Hebron's Old City put out by the UN Office for the Coordination of Humanitarian Affairs (OCHA), notes seventeen checkpoints in the H-2 area, seven inner city gates, and seventy-six road blocks composed of iron fences and gates, concrete blocks, barrels, and earth mounds.[52]

Barriers and checkpoints continued to prevent Palestinians and CPTers from traveling between cities in 2003.[53] Trips out to the Beqa'a Valley—even on foot—became difficult. Curfews and closures began to

49. See CPTnet releases: "Hebron: Israel Cracks Down," May 20, 2003; "Hebron: Urgent Action and Update," May 21, 2003; "Hebron Update on Deportation," May 22, 2003; "Hebron: Update on restrictions," May 28, 2003; "Hebron Update: May 5–18, 2003," June 3, 2003.

50. Rollins, e-mail, June 2, 2004.

51. See CPTnet releases: "Hebron Update: June 9–20, 2003," June 24, 2003; "Hebron: Israeli army increases its chokehold," July 8, 2003; "Hebron Update: June 29–July 6, 2003," July 19, 2003; "Hebron Update: July 30–August 13, 2003," Aug 18, 2003; "Hebron Update: November 13–21, 2003," Dec 1, 2003; "Hebron Update: November 22–23, 2003, Dec 6, 2003. Several updates also record helpful soldiers telling CPTers routes they could take where no soldiers would stop them.

52. OCHA, "Special Focus, the Closure of Hebron's Old City."

53. CPTnet, "Hebron Update: August 25–September 2, 2003," Sept 9, 2003.

apply to areas inside H-1 in 2003, not just the entrance and exit points to the city.

The Al-Manara market area (where the team had had its first apartment in the summer of 1995) was particularly hard hit. On January 30, the military put all of Hebron under curfew and leveled the vegetable stalls in Al-Manara with tanks and bulldozers. In June, the army dug trenches into the five major roads that enter Al Manara, thus effectively cutting off all traffic into Bab iZawiyya, Hebron's primary commercial district. They ordered the municipality not to repair the roads.[54]

Bab iZawiyya, Hebron's city center that bordered H-2, also increasingly found itself under the same restrictions imposed on Palestinians in H-2. Soldiers set up huge cement block barricades that essentially extended the border of H-2 to encompass the once-bustling market area and began imposing curfews there, as well.

"Not that anyone was surprised by this latest land grab," wrote Jerry Levin in July 2003,

> The Israeli Army had been telegraphing its intentions fiercely and meanly for several weeks late last year. During the busiest part of the day, tanks would suddenly come tearing into the intersection, crushing or upsetting the portable stands, scattering goods and shoppers as they went. They would knock over and chase off not just those in the streets, but the ones on sidewalks, too. At other times, squads of Israeli soldiers would come dashing into the area, arbitrarily declaring curfew, gruffly shouting at shoppers to leave and ordering all business [sic] to shut down.[55]

54. See CPTnet releases: "Terrorists among the apples," Jan 30, 2003; "Hebron Update: January 30–February 4, 2003," Feb 10, 2003; "Hebron Update: February 5–9, 2003," Feb 25, 2003; "Hebron: Is this on the Road Map?" June 14, 2003; "Hebron Update: June 9–20, 2003," June 24, 2003.

Art Gish, in an August 9, 2004 e-mail, said that soldiers told him they needed to clear the area of stalls so they could get tanks and other vehicles through the intersection.

55. CPTnet, "Hebron: While you were gone," July 26, 2003. See also CPTnet releases: "Hebron Update: February 10–15, 2003," Feb 25, 2003; "Hebron Update: August 25–September 2, 2003," Sept 9, 2003; "Hebron Update: September 3–16, 2003," Sept 18, 2003.

Soldier Assaults

Violence from gun battles and invasions diminished significantly after 2001, but the team still had to challenge the more mundane ways soldiers harassed and abused the Palestinian residents of Hebron.

Soldiers told CPTers that all Palestinians were terrorists and needed to be beaten and humiliated. One soldier told Kristin Anderson and Mary Yoder that by helping Palestinians under curfew get food they were helping terrorists. "These people should all starve and you should go back to America," he said.[56] Several times, soldiers threatened to shoot CPTers if they continued to protect Palestinians or assist them as they entered and left a curfew area. On one such occasion, Rick Polhamus told the soldier, "Maybe you will, but ten others will take my place."[57]

The worst abuses often happened after a suicide bombing had killed Israeli soldiers and civilians. In October 2002, suicide attacks killed civilians in Haifa, Tel Aviv, and the Ariel settlement, as well as civilians riding a bus from Kiryat Shmona to Tel Aviv. On November 4, 2002, three Israeli soldiers entered a shoe factory in Hebron, vandalized it, beat the manager, and then made the employees and manager sit in a row. They said, "Because these people consider those who bomb to be martyrs, we will make them all martyrs. We will start with the manager first, then finish them off one by one." The brother of the manager pretended he was mentally ill and began shouting, which made the other employees shout, "Allahu Akbar!" (God is greater). Neighbors heard the shouting, opened the door to the factory, and the soldiers ran away. One of them dropped a flashlight, which later made identifying them easy. When the brothers filed a complaint with an Israeli officer at the District Coordinating Office (DCO), a commander told the brothers, "These are crazy soldiers. They did this by themselves and without orders." The soldiers tried to enter the factory again on November 5, but someone spotted them and the employees locked themselves inside. On the second visit, the soldiers questioned

56. CPTnet, "Hebron Update: December 13–19, 2002," Dec 26, 2002.

57. CPTnet, "Hebron Update: December 20–27, 2004," Dec 29, 2004. On another occasion, a soldier referred to an incident in which Greg Rollins, Greg Wilkinson, and a member of TIPH had intervened to stop a young woman from stabbing a soldier, pushing her against a wall, while soldiers wrested the knife from her grip (see CPTnet, Hebron Update for August 8–10, 2002). The soldier told Rollins, "If I'd have been there, I would have shot TIPH for trying to help a Palestinian. When Rollins told him he had also been involved with the incident, the soldier said, "I would have shot you, too." CPTnet, "Hebron Update: August 22–24, 2002," Sept 13, 2002.

neighbors about the "crazy" man. "We are concerned if he is in the hospital and would like to visit him," they reportedly said.[58]

During a follow-up visit to the area between Bab iZaweyya and Al Manara after the destruction of the fruit and vegetable stands, Sue Rhodes, Art Gish, Tracy Hughes, and Kathy Kapenga noticed an Israeli military jeep stopping to let a Palestinian man vomit. When the CPTers asked why the soldiers had detained the man, they did not answer and the man, with tears in his eyes, shook his head. The soldiers drove around for another half hour, stopping occasionally and then released the man. Afterward, he told a reporter that soldiers had beaten him for nearly two hours in the jeep.[59]

The team did not know it at the time, but they had witnessed an incident for which the soldiers would later be prosecuted. On May 1, 2003, Israeli courts indicted four border police officers on charge of manslaughter in the death of 'Imran Abu Hamdiya, a seventeen-year-old youth from Hebron, whom they had thrown from a jeep. They were also charged with brutality, theft, and obstruction of justice.

B'tselem, the Israeli human rights organization wrote,

> According to the indictment, the four border police officers set out on a journey of abuse and cruelty against residents of the city [Hebron], in which they misused their authority, by committing violent acts intended to cause bodily injury and damage to property and whose purpose was to humiliate and harass . . . During their travels throughout the city . . . the defendants put local residents whom they located by chance into the jeep and ordered them to jump from the jeep while it was moving. One of the local residents refused to jump while the jeep was moving at great speed, and the defendants pushed him out. He fell onto the road and struck his head, which led to his death . . . In addition, the defendants abducted other local residents and beat them, at times with a club and rifle butt; robbed property, and also hurled tear-gas grenades and percussion grenades at local residents for no reason whatsoever.[60]

58. CPTnet, "Hebron: Acting on Their Own," Nov 27, 2002.

59. CPTnet, "Hebron Update: January 30–February 4, 2003," Feb 10, 2003. See also CPTnet, "The Things You Don't Want to Hear."

60. B'tselem, "Border Police Trial on Suspicion of Killing 'Imran Abu Hamdiya."
On April 28, 2008, one of the Border policemen, Yanai Lalza, was sentenced to six-and-a-half years in prison for the murder of Hamdiya, robbery, destroying evidence and obstructing justice. The judge noted that the fact the Border police had photographed

After Israel fenced in Wadi Ghroos to confiscate the land in that valley, soldiers assaulted two sons of the Zalloum family, whose home CPTers tried unsuccessfully to save in 1996. Soldiers picked up the eight-year-old by his head, lifted him high up in the air, and slammed him to the ground. Then they knocked the six-year-old boy down and kicked him. Their father, Waheed Zalloum, complained to the police. When the police asked the soldier why he had done it, he said, according to Zalloum, "They will grow up to be terrorists, so it's better if we kill them now, while they're small."[61]

Interactions the team had with soldiers were not always negative. Soldiers frequently told team members they had no sympathy for the settlers and were appalled by the restrictions imposed on Palestinians in Hebron. When members of a February 2002 delegation asked a soldier on the eve of 'Eid al Adha (one of the busiest shopping days of the Muslim calendar) how long curfew would be imposed, he told them he hoped it would be lifted soon. "I know tomorrow is a feast day," he said. "I have Arab friends in my village and they have told me about their feast. I know how important it is to them." He then explained the significance of the Muslim Feast of the Sacrifice to the delegates. Mark Frey saw soldiers marching three young Palestinian men wearing blindfolds to a checkpoint on April 8, 2002 and learned that the soldiers had come across two Palestinian men beating their younger brother and intervened to prevent the abuse. On April 12, 2002, Mary Lawrence chatted with some soldiers about the meaning of Easter and Maundy Thursday, which coincided with the celebration of Passover/Pesach in 2002. The soldier ran up to his guard post and brought back matzo for the team to use during their Maundy Thursday communion and foot washing service.[62]

---

the incident "reflected the officers' immense moral and ideological deficiency." Lis and Edelman, "Border policeman convicted."

For other examples of soldier violence see CPTnet releases: "Hebron Update: January 3–January 12, 2003," Jan 23, 2002; "Hebron: Terrorists among the apples," Jan 30, 2003; "Hebron Update: January 24–29, 2003," Feb 5, 2003; "Hebron: Prayer requests," Feb 6, 2003; "Hebron Update: January 30–February 4, 2003," Feb 10, 2003; "Hebron Update: February 5–9, 2003," Feb 25, 2003; "Hebron Update: February 10–15, 2003," Feb 25, 2003; "Hebron Update: February 18–27, 2003," Mar 3, 2003; "Hebron Update: October 30–November 5, 2003," Nov 17, 2003; "Hebron Update: November 22–23, 2003," Dec 6, 2003; "Hebron: 'This Time They Meant to Destroy Me,'" Feb 14, 2003.

61. CPTnet, "Hebron: Israel fences in Wadi el-Ghroos," Sept 12, 2003.

62. See CPTnet releases: "Hebron Update: February 19–22, 2002," Mar 12, 2002; "Hebron: Just a Domestic ..." Apr 8, 2002; "Hebron: Sharing the Bread," Apr 12, 2002.

Janet Shoemaker and delegate Bret Davis attended a Peace Now rally in Jerusalem in March 2002. A young soldier stationed in Hebron approached them and introduced himself as Yehuda, then he introduced them to another friend who was a conscientious objector, Shabtai Gold. At the end of a two-hour conversation, the young soldier told Davis and Shoemaker that he dreaded going back to Hebron, because the settler presence made the treatment of Palestinians there worse than anywhere else in the West Bank.[63] Yehuda Shaul would go on to set up an exhibit and organization called "Breaking the Silence" that informed the Israeli public about the abuses that soldiers and settlers in Hebron perpetrated on Palestinian civilians.[64] In subsequent years, Shaul and other Israelis who had served in Hebron would conduct "Breaking the Silence" tours of Hebron for interested Israelis.

Settler Assaults

The settlers' assaults on Palestinians and team members that the team sought to address pre-Intifada continued in ebbs and flows over the next six years. In the first months of the Intifada, after the Israeli military lifted curfew, settler women and children would rush into the busy vegetable market near Avraham Avinu settlement, overturning stalls and stealing merchandise until the military declared curfew again. Ultimately, the settlers won what they wanted on November 27, 2000, when the military cleared away the stands from that portion of the market. Although most of the soldiers told CPTers they did so to create a "buffer zone," another soldier told CPT delegation members that the military was confiscating the market "to build offices and apartments." After the murder of Shalhevet Pass in 2001 (see above), settlers began turning garage-like structures that Palestinian vendors had leased from the municipality to sell their wares into split-level apartments. In 2005, the Israeli courts ordered the government to evict the settlers by January 15, 2006. When the police moved to accomplish this task, settlers and supporters who had come to join them rioted and pelted the officers with stones. Ultimately, the families living in the market agreed to move out, after the government told them it would

---

63. CPTnet, "Hebron: Conversations with soldiers," Mar 20, 2002. Shoemaker told Kern that Gold, given the pseudonym "Arik" in the release, told her, as part of his praise for the CPT website, that it "kicked ass."

64. CPTnet, "Hebron/Tel Aviv: 'Breaking the silence,'" June 28 2004.

take over the properties, void the Hebron municipality leases, and legally lease their apartments back to the settlers again in one year.[65]

Settler youth intensified their physical and verbal assaults on team members after the outbreak of the Intifada (e.g., youth from Beit Hadassah told Holmes and Getman on October 10, "Why don't you go home? You are Nazis. We are Jews. We killed Jesus." The youth then pushed Getman and kicked Holmes before soldiers intervened).[66] Settlers also threw rocks and shot marbles with sling shots at the team's windows, occasionally cracking the glass. They punctured the PVC-plastic water pipes that ran up the sides of a building near the CPT apartment.[67] In the first months of the Intifada, they cut the phone lines leading into the Old City, which made getting releases out difficult.[68]

The settler violence on the outskirts of Hebron also increased as settlers sought to close Bypass Road 60 to Palestinian traffic—even to Palestinians through whose land the road passed. Beginning in November 2000, hundreds of settlers began massing nightly on the road in front of the homes of the extended Jaber family, throwing rocks at their houses and setting fire to their vineyards.[69] Police and soldiers, more or less, kept

65. CPTnet, "IDF closes vegetable market," Nov 27, 2000; CPTnet, "Hebron Update: 30 January–5 February," Feb 13, 2006. See also *Ha'aretz* articles: "Police launch 'zero tolerance policy,'" "Hebron hooligans," "Settlers complete Hebron wholesale market eviction."

66. CPTnet, "Hebron Update: October 9–13, 2000."

67. CPTnet, "Hebron Update: December 11–14, 2000," Dec 16, 2000. USAID had installed water infrastructure in 1997 to fulfill a U.S. commitment stipulated in the 1996 Hebron Protocol (see chap. 4). Water poured out of the punctured pipes for days before the team thought to call the USAID representative who attended the Lutheran church in Jerusalem. As it happened, the engineer, David Muirhead—who had originally supervised the USAID renovations on Shuhada Street—happened to be in town, and he put in an irate call to the Israeli military, who immediately had the pipes fixed. Muirhead had come to Hebron in 1997 with the cheerful plan of hosting a barbecue for both the Jewish and Palestinian residents of Hebron once he finished the renovations. With the frequent closures the Israeli military imposed on the West Bank, and settler attacks on his Arab workers and construction equipment, he soon had a different perspective on the situation. The project, which turned Shuhada Street into a boulevard and upgraded the electrical and water infrastructure for the Old City, ended up with a 200 percent cost overrun. See CPTnet, "CPT Hebron Update: August 29–September 2, 1997," Sept 8, 1997; CPTnet, "Hebron: Turquoise awnings," July 22, 2003.

68. CPTnet, "Hebron Update: December 1–10, 2000," Dec 11, 2000; CPTnet, "Hebron Update: December 29, 2000–January 4, 2001," Jan 15, 2001.

69. See CPTnet releases: "Hebron Update: November 2–3, 2000," Nov 7, 2000; "Hebron Update: November 8–11, 2000," Nov 17, 2000; "Hebron Update: November 12–15, 2000," Nov 19, 2000; "Settler Attack," Nov 27, 2000.

these demonstrations contained until December 8, 2000, when Palestinian gunmen shot and killed settlers Rina Didovsky and Eliyahu Ben Ami on the bypass road near the village of Bani Naim, several miles away from the Jaber families. After the killings, Israeli settlers invaded Atta and Rodeina Jaber's home, burning most of their possessions, including photo albums and important documents. When team members, watching events unfold from the home of Abdel Jawad Jaber, asked why the police were not removing the settlers, an officer replied, "The army is in charge here and the army says they can stay." The next day, more settlers streamed up the hill to the house for Saturday prayers. Then, around 10:00 a.m., settler men and youth began fanning out to the other Palestinian homes and bombarding them with stones. One settler shot thirteen-year-old Mansour Jaber, a nephew of Rodeina Jaber, in the stomach. At that point, the police did move in and arranged for an ambulance to take the boy to Jerusalem. The settlers, still under the protection of the Israeli military, returned to Atta and Rodeina Jaber's house. Later in the day, four members of the Israeli Committee Against House Demolitions arrived with court orders for the army to remove the settlers. After they did so, they told Atta Jaber that his home was a closed military zone—meaning the family could not return to it—until March 2001.

Later, Atta Jaber told the team that the Israeli Druse officer who had protected his house from the settlers during the previous month had been on leave the weekend that settlers had occupied his house. When the officer returned on December 10, according to Jaber, he had wept when he saw the damage.[70]

Although the Israeli police and military continued to protect Atta Jaber's house because of a lawsuit that ICAHD had helped him bring against the Israeli military and police, settlers continued to hold demonstrations, attacking Palestinian cars and homes in the Beqa'a over the next months.[71]

<hr>

70. CPTnet, "Hebron Update: December 11–14, 2000," Dec 16, 2000. The military allowed Atta and Rodeina Jaber to move back into their home in January 2001.

71. See, for example, CPTnet, "Hebron: Donkeys and Bulldozers," Dec 29, 2000. Team members were able to stay out in the valley for short periods of time, but found they could not keep people there indefinitely and deal with disturbances in the city at the same time.

All but one of the team's CPTnet updates for 2001 contains some incident of settler violence.[72] These incidents included attacks on Palestinian homes and cars in the Beqa'a Valley.[73] In one particularly egregious example, a settler drove his car into four-year-old Mahmoud Jaber—son of CSD partners Ismael and Fatmi Jaber—crushing both of his legs. The settler also killed three sheep that the child was shepherding across the road, and then drove into the gate of Kiryat Arba without stopping.[74] Many of the updates have accounts of settlers attacking the homes of the Sharabati family next to Avraham Avinu, and the Abu Haikel and Baatch family homes on Tel Rumeida. Settlers threw Molotov cocktails into homes in the Old City, in one incident nearly killing a newborn and during another narrowly missing an old woman (who was a neighbor of the team).[75] Repeated assaults on vendors in the marketplace near the team's apartment continued as well as assaults on pedestrians—including women and children—and shooting into Palestinian neighborhoods.

Team members found themselves the target of attacks more often than in previous years and, depressingly, found that their presence with journalists and other visitors to Hebron sometimes made these visitors the target of attack instead of protecting them. [76]

Police and soldiers rarely intervened during or after these attacks, which team members often found more distressing than the attacks themselves. When settlers began pelting CPTers with rocks on several occasions, soldiers blamed CPTers for being present. "Don't you know they

72. The lone exception, covering February 7–12, 2001, contains the following entry for February 9: "Field workers from Human Rights Watch interviewed CPTers for a report that will be presented to the U.N. The interviews focused on how CPTers are treated by Israeli settlers and soldiers."

73. See, for example, CPTnet, "Hebron: Settler Security Officer killed," May 29, 2001; CPTnet, "Hebron: CPT delegation witnesses settler attack," Sept 6, 2001.

74. CPTnet, "Hebron Update: October 22–29, 2001," Nov 23, 1001.

75. See CPTnet, "Hebron: Israelis and Palestinians," Aug 10, 2001; Barr, "'Aggressive pacifists.'" Barr based his article on several visits to Hebron and interviews with the team.

76. See, for example, the attack on Angie Zelter who had taken photos of settler children who had hit an old man in the head with a rock. Zelter had come over under the auspices of the International Solidarity Movement (see below) and was exploring the possibility of setting up an all-woman team at some other location in the West Bank suffering violent confrontations. CPTnet, "Hebron: Settler assaults guest," Sept 1, 2001. The outcome of Zelter's complaint against the settlers is recorded in PHRMG, "Settler Violence Hotline."

hate you?" one soldier told them. "Why don't you leave and they won't throw stones at you."[77]

After several weeks of daily attacks on their persons, neighbors, and apartment in 2001, the team sent a letter—accompanied by nineteen photos documenting settler attacks on people and property—to the Commander of the Hebron Police Force, the National Police in Jerusalem, the State Comptroller, and the Israeli Ministry of Justice. It concluded,

> We understand that settlers are citizens of Israel. Are we correct in assuming that damaging private property, throwing stones at people, trespassing on private property, and making violent threats to people are infringements of Israeli law, as they most assuredly are in most countries worldwide? If Israeli settlers are subject to Israeli law, why were no arrests made?
>
> We will appreciate any information you will give us concerning these questions.
>
> Sincerely,
>
> Christian Peacemaker Team in Hebron

They followed up with an Urgent Action two months later, asking its constituents to question the Civil Administration about why they allowed these attacks.[78]

In September 2001, after an assault on Kathleen Kern and Anne Montgomery, the team tried a more light-hearted approach and put out a release entitled, "The Difference between Nazis and CPTers":

> By now, getting called "Nazi" or saluted with "Heil Hitler," by the Hebron settlers and their sympathizers has become a daily event. Since 1995, we have not taken this slander seriously, because, well,

---

77. See CPTnet releases: "Hebron: Let's Play 'Dodge Stones,'" Dec 29, 2001; "Hebron: Settlers attack CPTers," July 19, 2001; "Hebron: CPTers Anne Montgomery and Kathleen Kern," Sept 8, 2001; "Hebron Update: July 8–15, 2001," July 26, 2001; "Hebron Update: November 5–11, 2001," Nov 26, 2001. After a settler assaulted Mary Yoder in 2003—which led to her needing neck surgery—police asked her if she would drop charges if the settler apologized. In his apology, he told her that his twenty-six year old brother had been shot two weeks earlier and was paralyzed from the waist down. She later wrote a letter to him giving him information on the Christopher Reeves Foundation, which researches treatment for paralysis. CPTnet, "Hebron Update: January 3–January 12, 2003," Jan 23, 2003. See also CPTnet, "Hebron Reflection: Thoughts upon recovering," Apr 27, 2004; CPTnet, "Hebron Update: January 3–January 12, 2003," Jan 23, 2003.

78. CPTnet, "Hebron: Are Settlers Above the Law?" June 11, 2001; CPTnet, "Hebron Urgent Action: To the Israeli Civil Administration," Aug 27, 2001.

we're not Nazis and no Israelis who have spent any time talking with us (as opposed to yelling at us) think of us in those terms.

However, we also did not take seriously the threats to kill Yitzhak Rabin and Shimon Peres we heard on the streets of Hebron in the months leading up to Rabin's assassination. Recent attacks against our team in Hebron and members of the Temporary International Presence in Hebron have made us wonder whether we should respond to these efforts to demonize us by associating us with the Third Reich. So, in the interests of setting the record straight:

NAZIS were members of the National Socialist Party in Germany in the first half of the twentieth century.

CPTERS are Christians committed to nonviolence, who have, since 1992, provided violence deterring presences in Haiti, Gaza, the West Bank, Washington, DC, Richmond, VA, Bosnia, Chiapas, Mexico, Barrancabermeja, Colombia and with indigenous peoples in North America.

NAZIS worshipped themselves as the master race.

CPTERS worship God and believe God loves every human being on this planet equally.

NAZIS believed they had the right to dominate, exploit and murder people whom they considered inferior.

CPTERS believe that no person has the right to dominate, exploit, or murder any other person.

NAZIS encouraged street hooliganism of party members and young people as they consolidated their hold on power in Germany.

CPTERS recognize that state toleration of street violence ultimately leads to massive abuses of human rights and genocide on the part of that state.

NAZIS brainwashed their children into believing it was acceptable to regard certain people as subhuman.

CPTERS believe that teaching children to hate others or regard others as subhuman is a form of child abuse.

NAZIS slandered Jews by recirculating the myths of the Protocols of the Elders of Zion and describing Jews as akin to vermin.

CPTERS report what they see and what they hear.

NAZIS: Right-wing

CPTERS: Not

> We believe that referring to every person who does not agree
> with one's political or theological position as a Nazi hideously
> cheapens the tragedy of the Holocaust. We commit ourselves to
> fighting everything the Nazis stood for, wherever we encounter
> it.[79]

Over the next years, for the residents of the Old City and those living near settlements outside of Hebron, harassment continued in waves.
Settlers stoned and shot at their homes, threw trash in their courtyards,
shouted death threats, killed their pets, stole produce from gardens as
well as household items, and cut their phone and electricity lines. While
Palestinians were under curfew, settlers pried off locks and bars and stole
chickens, peacocks, clothing, and other items. Settlers in Beit Romano
broke a hole into an adjacent jewelry store and stole $50,000 to $60,000
of gold jewelry.[80]

On several occasions, settlers went on rampages following the
deaths of other settlers. One occurred after a settler who had grown up
in Hebron, Elazar Leibovitz, was killed in a Palestinian ambush while on
duty as an IDF sergeant in the southern Hebron District. The vigilante
revenge attacks on Palestinians in the Old City shocked a minister's aide
who was in Hebron for the funeral. The Israeli newspaper Ha'aretz covered the rampage as follows:

> Col. (res.) Moshe Givati, an adviser on settlement security for
> Public Security Minister Uzi Landau, yesterday termed the riot-
> ing that took place during the funeral of Elazar Leibowitz, "a po-
> grom against the Arabs of Hebron, with no provocation on the
> Palestinian side . . ."

79. CPTnet, "Hebron: The difference between Nazis and CPTers," Sept 11, 2001. The
reaction and discussion the team hoped the release would engender never materialized,
because the team put it out on September 11, 2001, and world events overshadowed issues
of petty harassment on the street. See also Kern, "Settler Violence and September 11."

80. CPTnet, "Hebron: Legal Breaking and Entering," Aug 10, 2002. Most of the updates from March–June, 2002 have some reference to settlers looting shops. For the case
of shops invaded and looted near Beit Romano, see CPTnet, "Hebron Update: July 21–27,
2002," Aug 4, 2002; CPTnet, "Hebron Update: August 25–30, 2002." This last update recorded a shopowner showing the team a copy of the complaint he had filed with the
Civil Administration. The Israeli officer to whom he submitted the complaint had put no
file number on the copy, which (the team assumed intentionally) meant the shop owner
would not be able to follow up on his complaint.

The violence began already on Saturday night, he says, when a group of Jewish youths invaded a Palestinian house in the city, and burned and vandalized the possessions inside ...

He said that "the Palestinians did not throw any rocks or boulders at the funeral procession ... I saw everything from very close range. There were long bursts of fire by the Israelis—into the air and at the houses."

It was during that fire that 14-year-old Nibin Jamjum was killed by a bullet to her head, and a Palestinian boy was stabbed. IDF sources say that these two and the other wounded—15 Palestinians in all were reported wounded, and an equal number of police were hurt—were casualties of the Jewish violence. "Dozens of thugs, including youths from Hebron, burst into Arab houses for no reason. They broke windows, destroyed property and threw stones. These people were there for the purpose of making a pogrom," said Givati.[81]

Since the team lived in an area where the settlers attacked, they responded to calls nonstop for most of the weekend. They learned later that settlers in the Beqa'a had thrown rocks down into the yard of Abdel Jawad Jaber, 'Atta Jaber's father. Settlers hit him on the back with a rock and he slipped on the steps of the veranda, fracturing his left leg near the hip socket and leaving him with a permanent limp.[82]

Sometimes the verbal harassment could hit as hard as physical attacks. Settlers covered homes and shops with vicious graffiti like, "Watch out Fatima, we will rape all Arab women," "Exterminate the Muslims," "Die Arab sand-niggers," and "Mohammed was a pig."[83] In the summer of 2003, while African American CPTers Chris Brown and Paul Pierce were working on the Hebron team, Brown discovered "WHITE POWER KILL NIGGERS" scrawled on the building opposite his bedroom.[84] After a settler told Maureen Jack that he hoped she would get cancer, she said, "Please don't say that. My husband died of cancer six years ago." "I am

81. Harel and Lis, "Minister's aide." The Israeli human rights organization B'tselem took testimonies of people attacked by the settlers between July 26–28, reported in "Standing Idly By."

82. CPTnet, "Hebron: Settler rampage kills one," July 28, 2002; CPTnet, "Hebron: Settler women attack CPTers," July 30, 2002; CPTnet, "Hebron Update: July 28–August 3, 2002," Aug 13, 2002.

83. CPTnet, "Hebron Update: April 29–May 3, 2002."

84. CPTnet, "Hebron: A settler greeting card," July 13, 2003.

happy about that," he responded.[85] CPTer John Lynes, who grew up Jewish, wrote a poem in 2006 about what it felt like to hear the ubiquitous "Nazi" epithet from settlers:

> A Jewish child, I hid my eyes
> from the pictured corpses of Belsen and Buchenwald.
> There but for the grace of God—
> Resurrection was not a word I knew.
> How could I believe I would live to see
> children and grandchildren of the Holocaust
> crossing the fields of the Promised Land
> to synagogue on Shabbat?
> Could there be a more heavenly vision?
> But surely not for this world?
> Yet two by two, there they walk as I write,
> not to any old shul:
> to synagogue on the very spot where Abraham, Isaac and Jacob,
> Leah, Rebecca and Sarah, lie buried.
> "Shabbat shalom," I greet the worshippers.
> Some have learned to recognise my red hat
> the mark of a Christian Peacemaker in Hebron,
> and they spit at me
> and they curse me as a Nazi. And it hurts.
> It hurts.
> You must forgive an old man—old enough to recall real Nazis.
> Today I pray for a miracle.
> I long to be part of that miracle, whatever the cost.[86]

International Accompaniment Movements

Starting in the summer of 2001, groups seeking to do violence-deterring work in the Occupied Territories from France, Italy, Denmark, and Holland visited the team. Groups of international Jews wishing to do work similar to CPT's under the auspices of the 2001 "Olive Tree Summer" also made connections with the team, sometimes putting members to work with the team for several days. The team later hosted delegations sponsored by Rabbis for Human Rights, Global Exchange, Junity (a progressive Jewish group), the Christian Accompaniment Program (Denmark and Iceland), Civilians for Peace (the Netherlands), the Quaker Peace Team (United

85. CPTnet, "Hebron Reflection: On hatred," Nov 24 2005.
86. CPTnet, "Hebron Poem: Shabbat patrol," Jan 21, 2006.

Kingdom), and the Fellowship of Reconciliation. Team members also provided nonviolence training for Palestinian students and Fatah youth in Bethlehem, International Checkpoint Watch, the Quaker Peace Team, and the Service Civile Internationale.

More significantly, representatives from the World Council of Churches visited the team in 2001 and later set up the Ecumenical Accompaniment Program in Palestine and Israel, (EAPPI) based on the CPT model.

Rick Polhamus attended the February organizational meetings for EAPPI in Geneva, which focused on the 'Draft Proposed Model . . . For Discussion':

> [World Council of Churches] WCC announced the official cre-
> ation of Ecumenical Monitoring Programme in Palestine and
> Israel (EMPPI) on October 20, 2001, after the WCC Executive
> Committee meeting of September 11–14, 2001 unanimously called
> for the WCC to develop an accompaniment program that would
> include ecumenical presence similar to Christian Peacemaker
> Teams in Hebron and called on member churches to join in acts
> of non-violent resistance, boycotts of settlement goods and prayer
> vigils to strengthen the chain of solidarity with the Palestinian
> people as part of a special focus of the Decade to Overcome
> Violence.

Following this announcement, WCC study groups visited Israel/Palestine and spent time with the Hebron team to see how CPT worked. Polhamus writes,

> The most significant thing in my opinion, that came from the
> meeting was the recognition that more than a monitoring pres-
> ence was needed. I told them of Yusef Al-Atrash saying, 'We don't
> need more people to come and tell me my son is being beaten and
> my home destroyed. We need people to come who will do some-
> thing.' This became a main theme in the discussions of what the
> EAPPI's role would be.[87]

87. Polhamus, email, June 10, 2004. The excerpt from the "Draft Proposed model" comes from this email rather than from an official WCC press release.

Polhamus also noted that CPT was instrumental in calling for WCC volunteers to "ac-company" rather than "monitor" (reflected in original "EMPPI" designation). Polhamus and Anne Montgomery participated in an EAPPI organizational meeting in Jerusalem where participants affirmed that WCC volunteers needed to work on teams, like CPT, rather than as individuals stationed with various organizations. CPTnet, "Hebron Update: November 30–December 5, 2002," Dec 10, 2002.

WCC organizers would choose Rebecca Johnson, a CPT reservist, to coordinate twelve EA (Ecumenical Accompanier) teams in the West Bank and Gaza. EAPPI began working in the Occupied Territories in August 2002, focusing particularly on accompanying Palestinian children to school.

Members of the International Solidarity Movement (ISM) were by far the most famous group of internationals to pour into the Occupied Territories in the summer of 2001.[88] Three of the young people most responsible for organizing the ISM volunteers, Neta Golan, George Rishmawi, and Huwaida Arraf had had extensive contacts with Hebron team members before they prepared to bring volunteers over. George Rishmawi had brought international tour groups to visit the team in Hebron and had helped the Beit Jala team significantly as they set up the project there (see next chapter). He was also active in the Palestinian Center for Rapprochement, which for years had organized nonviolent demonstrations in which Hebron team members sometimes participated. Golan had responded to emergency pleas for help from the Hebron Team when the Jaber family had come under assault from Israeli settlers. She was also instrumental in placing CPT's first "emergency" delegation in homes in Beit Jala on the night of July 31, 2001, when homes there suffered serious bombardment.

Members of the Hebron team began participating in ISM actions, when possible. Releases and updates from 2001 record team members traveling to ISM actions in Rantis, Nablus, Jerusalem, Bidya, Mashka, Bir Zeit, Ramallah, and Gaza. During a June 15, 2001, witness against expansion of the settlement of Efrat over the lands of Al-Khader, Anita Fast, and

---

WCC, "First group of ecumenical accompaniers." See also WCC releases "Ecumenical solidarity and action" and "Ecumenical efforts towards peace." As of 2008, EAPPI was continuing its work in various locations around Israel and Palestine, and had been mentioned frequently in the Hebron team's updates.

88. When asked about CPT's influence on ISM, Huwaida Arraf wrote in a May 23, 2004 e-mail that she had been active in mobilizing internationals to support Palestinian nonviolent resistance long before she heard of CPT. She said further:

> We consider CPT amongst the founding members of the ISM. CPTers did the trainings for our first campaign and continued to help us out with trainings and be an active part of our organizing, especially LeAnne Clawson [sic]. I would say the biggest influence the CPT had on the ISM was in the field of training. And of course, when the contact was a little stronger between CPT and ISM, the sharing of ideas, tactics, etc. made our efforts stronger, I believe.

Neta Golan tried to protect two elderly village women whom the police were assaulting, and were beaten and injured by the police as well, with Golan sustaining a broken elbow.[89]

The high-profile nonviolent interventions of ISM volunteers in Ramallah, Bethlehem, and Nablus provoked a crackdown by the Israeli government on many internationals entering the country and the deportation of others. In their Update covering April 2, 2002, the team noted,

> Although the Israeli Minister of the Interior had issued orders to prevent "leftist extremists" from entering the country and issued deportation orders for dozens of French and Italian activists, the seven-member CPT delegation entered Israel at Ben Gurion airport without incident.[90]

The Hebron team would not remain unscathed by the crackdown, however. Three CPTers, Michael Goode, Kurtis Unger, and Kathleen Kern were denied entry into Israel on June 23, August 30, and October 23, 2002, respectively. None of them had ever been formally arrested—the ostensible cause for Robert Naiman, Wendy Lehman, and Cliff Kindy being barred from the country in 1996 and 1997.[91] To address the issues of these deportations, CPT launched a fax campaign to Israeli consulates and embassies. The organization asked its constituents to tell the Israeli authorities they were monitoring the case and to express concern about what it meant when the Israeli government denied entry to committed peace activists. The Urgent Action included a portion of Kern's letter to Rafael Barak, Israel's Deputy Chief of Mission, whom the State Department told Kern to contact at the Israeli Embassy:

> Given that Christian Peacemaker Teams and I are absolutely committed to nonviolence, I am certain that we do not represent a security risk to the state of Israel. I believe that we actually enhance

89. CPTnet, "Bethlehem District: CPTer Anita Fast beaten," June 16, 2001. Bob Holmes, in a February 8, 2004 e-mail, wrote that the complaints of Golan and Fast that he filed, along with photos of the incident, appeared to have an effect on police behavior the following week: "[A] week later, in the same location, when arrests were made gently, we were kept in an air-conditioned room at the Efrat police station and even given lunch!"

90. CPTnet, "Hebron Update: March 26, April 3, 2004," Apr 4, 2002. CPT delegations during this period often plugged themselves into actions planned by ISM and other activist organizations.

91. See "CPTers Imprisoned"; CPTnet, Chicago/Hebron: CPTer denied entry," May 30, 2000.

Israel's security, by connecting the Palestinians we work among with Israelis who care about their human rights . . .

It is in the best interests of the Israeli public that internationals trained in nonviolent theory and practice live among Palestinians in the territories and support Palestinian grassroots nonviolent resistance to the Occupation. It is in the best interests of the Israeli public for nonviolent activists to intervene when they see settlers and soldiers brutalizing Palestinians, because these interventions help decrease the feelings of helplessness and rage that can be channeled into violent resistance.

If Palestinians believe their goal to end the Occupation can be accomplished nonviolently, there will be many fewer dead Israelis. And fewer dead Israelis and Palestinians is something that my co-workers and I truly yearn for. [92]

On March 16, 2003, an Israeli military bulldozer crushed ISM activist Rachel Corrie as she was trying to prevent it from demolishing a Palestinian home. Corrie, 23, from Olympia, Washington, had been part of an ISM team in Rafah (Gaza Strip) for the previous two months. Israeli forces in Jenin shot American ISM volunteer Brian Avery in the face on April 5, 2003—as he stood with other ISMers in front of an Armoured Personnel Carrier—for which he required several reconstructive surgeries. Five days later, Israeli soldiers shot British International Solidarity Movement volunteer Tom Hurndall in the head. Hurndall had been shepherding a group of Palestinian children out of a narrow passage where they had been playing when shooting started. Soldiers opened fire from a tank-mounted machine gun. Hurndall had just taken the hand of a little girl when the bullet hit him in the head. He remained comatose until his family disconnected him from life support in January 2004. Corrie, Avery, and Hurndall were all wearing fluorescent orange or red vests identifying

92. Although the fax campaign referred to Kern's deportation specifically—given her high profile as CPTnet editor and co-founder of the Hebron team—the campaign was meant to address the larger issue of deportations of peace activists as a whole. Kern met with Rafael Barak in November 2002, who told her that she should send him references of Israeli friends and that he would get back to her once he heard something from the Israeli Ministry of the Interior, which was on strike at the time. As of May 2004, the Interior Ministry had still not responded to Barak's query, according to his May 5, 2003 letter to the author. See CPTnet releases: "Chicago: CPTer Michael Goode refused entry," June 25, 2002; "Chicago/Toronto: Unger denied entry," Sept 4, 2002; "Christian Peacemaker Denied Entry," Oct 24, 2002; "Urgent Action: Support CPTer Asking for Review."

them as human rights accompaniers when the Israeli military killed or injured them.[93]

These attacks hit everyone who had worked on the Hebron team hard. Corrie, Avery, and Hurndall had all participated in the trainings led by the Hebron team. Furthermore, many Hebron team members, as well as their Israeli, Palestinian, and International friends, had stood between bulldozers and their designated targets as a part of their work.

An Urgent Action put out on April 12, 2003, quoted Le Anne Clausen as saying,

> It feels like open season on peace activists. It's been open season on Palestinians all along, now the lack of accountability in the Israeli military has reached a new level. For Palestinians, the threat of "transfer" (ethnic cleansing) looms large; the Israeli attacks on human rights workers accompanying them seem to be part of a move by the Sharon administration in this direction. If the internationals can be chased away, what will happen to the Palestinian civilians?[94]

Land Confiscation and Wall Building

The guns, missiles, and assassinations of the Intifada provided cover for Israeli settlements to confiscate enormous amounts of land. The team's first Urgent Action for 2002 described Israeli bulldozers plowing a road that totally encircled the Beqa'a Valley. The excavations were more than two kilometers away from the boundaries of Kiryat Arba at that time. The team asked U.S. citizens to contact Secretary of State Colin Powell, ask-

93. Joe Carr, who went through CPT training in 2004, was an ISM volunteer who witnessed the deaths of both Corrie and Hurndall. His sequence of photos showing Corrie's death and trip to the hospital were widely circulated on the Web. See Carr's reflection and eyewitness account, and "A Dove's Last Song," a rap song about Corrie.

94. CPTnet, "Urgent Action: Hold Israeli government accountable," Apr 12, 2003. The team soon adopted the new ISM policy stipulating that they would always place at least three workers in front of a bulldozer in the future. After Hurndall was shot, Israeli forces raided the ISM office in Beit Sahour, confiscating the organization's computers, photographs and CDs. They also arrested an American volunteer and a worker for HRW. They then moved on to the Palestinian Center for Rapprochement and confiscated its computer as well. Eight days later, soldiers in Hebron arrested Greg Rollins and searched the team's apartment, so the May 2003 arrest and restrictions on the Hebron team (see above) may have been part of a larger push on the part of the Israeli government to get rid of human rights and peace activists—however, the connection is speculative. CPTnet, "Hebron Urgent Action: Stop Israeli attempts," May 10, 2003.

ing him to affirm previous declarations that settlement expansion must stop, and to impose logical consequences, such as the withholding of U.S. aid to Israel. "Emphasize that the subsistence farmers of the Beqa'a Valley deserve security too," the team wrote.[95] In February 2004, the team put out another Urgent Action to the CSD network noting that proposed expansion plans for Kiryat Arba and Givat Ha Harsina would double the size of these settlements.[96] While the world focused on the Israeli government's removal of settlers from Gaza in 2005, it confiscated the largest tract of land ever in the history of the Hebron District.[97]

The Separation Barrier (also referred to as the Security Fence or the Apartheid Wall, depending on one's political leanings) that Israel began building in 2003 resulted in the confiscation of massive amounts of West Bank land and the destruction of hundreds of thousands of olive trees and other crops. According to the Sharon government, Israel built the wall to prevent terrorists from entering Israel. However, instead of Israel building the wall along the 1967 border, Israel, beginning in the northern West Bank, constructed the wall so that it made deep incursions into Palestinian territory, sometimes encircling entire villages or even cities like Qalqilya.[98]

Team members began participating in joint Israeli, Palestinian, and international demonstrations against the wall and tours of the wall's route as it cut through the northern West Bank. They also began participating in strategy meetings with students and other local activists confront the building of the wall in Hebron. According to Abdel Hadi Hantash, the chief cartographer of the Hebron District, Israeli officials had drawn up plans to divide Hebron and connect Beit Hadassah, Beit Romano, Tel Rumeida, and Avraham Avinu to Kiryat Arba. Connecting the settlements would result in the confiscation of the entire Old City, along with the Ibrahimi mosque/Tomb of the Patriarchs. In an October 2003 report on

95. CPTnet, "Hebron Urgent Action: No More Settlements!" Oct 8, 2001.

96. CPT Hebron, "CSD—Sample Urgent Action appeal."

97. CPTnet, "Hebron Urgent Action: Largest tract of land," July 8, 2005. See also CPTnet releases: "Hebron Urgent Action: Stop confiscation," Jan 26, 2002; "Hebron: Further Land Confiscation," Jan 25, 2002; "Hebron Update: January 21–31, 2002," Feb 4, 2002; "Hebron: Settler Security destroys Palestinian orchards," July 20, 2002; "Hebron District Urgent Action: Stop the expulsion," Mar 23, 2002.

98. See maps in ARIJ, "The Segregation Wall" and CPT Hebron, "Dividing Walls." The initial plan for the barrier was approved by Ehud Barak's government in 2000. See Jaradat, "Hebron: Another Apartheid Wall."

the approaching wall, Kathy Kamphoefner noted that the Israeli army had fitted gates across all the eastern exits of the Old City, fenced off Shuhada Street, and restricted all access to it and the Old City via Beit Romano. The military had also, by October 2003, forced hundreds of shops near the settlements to close—in some cases welding the doors shut. "In the big picture," Kamphoefner wrote, "The planned separation Wall will encircle the entire Hebron district . . . Only a narrow gap will exist at the northern end of the district, shaped like a bottleneck, at the Gush Etzion checkpoint."[99]

Jerry Levin, in a 2003 release, "HEBRON: Catch-22," noted that the confiscation of farmland followed a basic pattern: settler security guards forbid Palestinians to enter their vineyards. Soldiers affirm the right of the Palestinians to work in their fields, but prevent farmers from entering, "to protect them from the settlers." The Civil Administration, after the farmers complain, tells them they are in the right, but that it is the soldiers' job to keep the settlers in line. After two to three years of preventing farmers from working in their fields, the Israeli government confiscates the fields, under the pretext that no Palestinian is working in them.[100]

As a response to this confiscation, the team went on an "information offensive" in 2001 and 2002, inviting European, American, and other international diplomats to tour the Hebron area and showing them the extent of the land-grabs by settlers. Since the European community had invested heavily in Palestinian aid and development projects, the team thought Europeans needed to see how settlement expansion was destroying the projects they had funded. Although the consulate representatives expressed outrage at the devastation caused by settlement expansion and promised to bring the matter to the attention of their governments, the tours did not appear have much of an effect on the confiscation process. Given the weaponry used by soldiers and settlers to oversee and maintain the confiscation of land, the residents of the Beqa'a and the Hebron team were almost literally fighting a losing battle.

99. CPTnet, "Hebron: Wall slated to divide Hebron," Oct 31, 2003.
100. CPTnet, "Hebron: Catch-22," Aug 2, 2003.

Home Demolitions

Home demolitions, which had almost ended under Barak due to sustained grassroots resistance, also resumed during the intifada.[101]

After fifteen homes fell in the southern West Bank, the team speculated in an Urgent Action that the Sharon government felt free to resume demolitions because President George W. Bush had vetoed a U.N. Security Council resolution calling for international observers in the Occupied Territories. The Urgent Action noted,

> In the words of the Israeli peace group Gush Shalom, "The houses destroyed yesterday and today belong to ordinary Palestinian citizens whose only crime is the wish to have a roof over their heads. In this case, there isn't any pretence of 'security interests' or 'military targets.'" This is the consequence of [the] willingness of the world to tolerate (and of the U.S. Congress to support) the violence of continued Israeli military occupation.[102]

As a result of the April 2001 demolitions, the Campaign for Secure Dwellings sought more North American congregations to match with families facing home demolitions. Because the team had found family-to-family matches too difficult to keep up, the new Campaign for Secure Dwellings matched newcomers with villages and neighborhoods, specifically, those in the Beqa'a, Beit Ummar, and the Al Sendas/Qilqis area.

In Hebron, on October 10, 2002, the Israeli military destroyed seven homes in the Al Sendas/Qilqis area and four homes in a neighborhood near Kiryat Arba. None of the homes had received official home demolition orders. An Israeli friend from Peace Now speculated that the demolitions had occurred in response to a bus bombing in Tel Aviv on the previous day. The military had also evacuated several settlement outposts on October 10, 2002, and the team noted, "In the past, the Israeli military

---

101. CPTnet, "Hebron/Jerusalem: Eight homes destroyed," April 4, 2001. Demolished for the third time on April 4 was the home of Salim Shawamreh, which had become the highest profile house in the movement to end demolitions. He and Jeff Halper, director of the ICAHD, had done several speaking tours in the US, and Shawamreh had dedicated the house as a "House of Peace" where Israelis and Palestinians could meet. The Hebron team helped rebuild the Shawamreh home in 1998, 1999, and 2003.

According to the Palestinian Centre for Human Rights, from the beginning of the al-Aqsa Intifada until March 31, 2003, Israeli occupying forces demolished 1064 Palestinian houses in the Gaza Strip. PCHR, "Uprooting Palestinian trees."

102. CPTnet, "Hebron Urgent Action: Fifteen homes demolished," Apr 4, 2001.

has demolished Palestinian homes in conjunction with evacuating settlements to assuage Israeli settlers."[103]

A different sort of home demolition crisis in Hebron began on November 15, 2002, when Palestinian gunmen opened fire on a group of Israeli settlers and soldiers who were walking from the Ibrahimi Mosque/ Tomb of the Patriarchs to Kiryat Arba after Shabbat services. Nine Israeli soldiers and Border Police, and three settler security people died as well as three of the gunmen who initiated the attack. Colonel Dror Weinberg, commander of the Israeli forces in Hebron, was one of the dead.[104]

The military responded to the attack with several hours of firing into Palestinian areas from machine guns, tanks, and helicopters. They also demolished two houses near the site of the shooting and gave other houses in the area demolition orders during the following week.

Prime Minister Ariel Sharon told Ha'aretz newspaper that the time had come to create a "zone" between the Old City of Hebron and Kiryat Arba exclusively for Jewish use, "An opportunity has been created and facts have to be created in the coming 48 hours," he said. These facts included the demolition of dozens of Palestinian homes along the corridor.[105]

Accordingly, the team put out an Urgent Action on November 19, 2002, asking its constituency immediately to fax or call the Canadian and American ambassadors to Israel, and the Israeli ambassadors to the U.S. and Canada. "Ask these officials to make urgent, strong and clear representation to the government of Israel opposing new settlements/ settlement expansion in general and the Kiryat Arba/Hebron expansion in particular," the team wrote. Three days later, after more homes had received demolition orders, the team followed with another Urgent Action, requesting that U.S. citizens fax Senator Richard Lugar of the U.S. Senate

103. CPTnet, "Hebron: Israeli Bulldozers," Oct 11, 2002. The team also noted at the beginning of the report that "American-manufactured Caterpillar bulldozers" destroyed the homes. This specification reflected a growing movement among NGOs in Israel and Palestine to pressure Caterpillar into inquiring how the Israeli government was going to use its bulldozers before the corporation sold them the equipment.

104. CPTnet, "Hebron: Fifteen Killed," Nov 16, 2002. The release included a letter of condolence the team sent to the IDF, in which the team noted, "Our hearts are heavy with the losses of soldiers and civilians, and particularly Colonel Weinberg whom our team met on several occasions. We wish to extend our thoughts and prayers to families and loved ones of those who died. May the God of all comfort give you strength and hope during this time . . ."

105. Ben and Alon, "PM demands 'quick' changes."

Foreign Relations committee, asking him to challenge the Israeli government's demolitions of these homes. They quoted another Ha'aretz article that began with the sentences,

> The one and only meaning to the creation of 'territorial contiguity' from Kiryat Arba to the Tomb of the Patriarchs is expulsion. The expulsion of thousands more Palestinian residents of Hebron, people who were unlucky enough to find that their homes, shops and gardens are in the area meant for 'contiguity.'[106]

Team members also spent several nights with families living in the Jabel Johar neighborhood to protect the homes.[107] Eventually, the number of homes facing demolition dropped from twenty-two to thirteen or fourteen and the Israeli courts reduced the number to three. The reduction further demonstrated that "security" had, in fact, been a pretext for the demolition of twenty-two houses that stood in the way of territorial contiguity between the Old City and Kiryat Arba.[108]

106. CPTnet, "Hebron Urgent Action: Next 48 hours critical," Nov 19, 2002. CPTnet, "Urgent Action—Stop home demolitions," Nov 22, 2002.

107. In a memorial to Hebron team member Sue Rhodes, who died of liver cancer in 2003, Greg Rollins referred to a night that Rhodes had spent with the family in Jabal Johar:

> One night Sue and several others were sleeping in a house that had already had its kitchen destroyed by an Israeli bulldozer. There was a fear that the Israelis would return at any moment to destroy the rest of the place. Sue had trouble sleeping so she got out of bed and stared out the window. Not far away from the house, the Israeli army was bulldozing the land. Sue stood and watched as the bulldozer tore up an old olive tree. As the bulldozer tore the tree's roots from the earth, Sue heard the tree scream.
>
> The next morning Sue told her hosts what had happened during the night. How she watched the tree torn out of the earth and how she heard it scream. The family fell silent. One of them then told Sue that when their ancestors had planted that olive tree years and years ago, they said that if that tree were ever pulled from the earth, it would scream. After that, the family called Sue "The Women who Heard the Tree Scream." (CPTnet, "Hebron: Remembering Sue Rhodes," Dec 3, 2003)

108. See also CPTnet releases: "Hebron Urgent Action: Stop demolition," Apr 26, 2003; "Hebron: The scenery," Apr 26, 2003; "Hebron Update: April 21–27, 2003," May 2, 2003; "Hebron Urgent Prayer Request: Hold Dana families," May 16, 2003; "Hebron Update: May 5–18, 2003," June 3, 2003.

School Patrols

When the Intifada started in September 2000, the education of thousands of Palestinian students was put on hold. Children living in the curfew areas of Hebron's Old City were particularly affected, as were children living near the settlements of Givat Ha Harsina and Kiryat Arba.

The Hebron District Minister of Education told a November 2000 CPT delegation that of the 170 schools and 80,000 students in the Hebron district, 32 schools and 15,000 students were under curfew. Three schools had been turned into military camps, leading to impossible overcrowding in other, unoccupied schools.[109] Fariel Abu Haikel, headmistress of Qurtuba School, which stood across the street from the Israeli settlement of Beit Hadassah, told the same delegation that when the curfew ended, her students would study Arabic, English, and mathematics only. They would not receive any instruction in art, music, geography, or history for the next months, depending on when the curfew ended.[110]

Under pressure from TIPH and the Palestinian Ministry of Education, the Israeli military acknowledged its obligation under international humanitarian law to allow children to attend school even under curfew.

For some reason, however, these orders often did not filter down to the soldiers in the street—even on September 1, 2001, the first day of school. Thus, a big part of the team's work for the rest of 2001 involved accompanying children on their morning and afternoon trips to school and convincing soldiers to confirm this understanding with their commanding officers. Sometimes soldiers would then let the CPTers and students from H-2 pass and sometimes they would not. On one occasion, Lawrence attempted to call the DCO in Hebron to inquire about the new orders, but the DCO refused to talk with her.[111] This scenario, including the call to the DCO was to be repeated several times over the next months. Even when the most persuasive CPTers were able to get children

109. Just before the Intifada began, the Director of Education for the Hebron District told Gene Stoltzfus and Bob Holmes that thirty-four new schools were needed to accommodate the growing numbers of children in H-2 and area C, and that the Israeli authorities refused to give permits for even one. CPTnet, "Hebron: Lessons learned," Apr 10, 2001.

110. CPTnet, "Hebron Update: November 20–23, 2000," Dec 2, 2000. The Minister of Education also expressed concern about internationals believing that Palestinian parents deliberately put their children in harm's way.

111. CPTnet, "Hebron Update: October 22–28, 2001," Nov 23, 2001.

past the checkpoints in the 2001–2002 school year, soldiers often went to the schools in H-2 after the teachers and students had entered and forced them to evacuate. CPTers then escorted the frightened students past the checkpoints on their way home.

The school year of 2002–2003 was a particularly difficult one for the children of Hebron and consequently for the team. Team members repeatedly told soldiers about the agreement stipulating the children could go to school and soldiers repeatedly checked with their commanders who then acknowledged that there was such an agreement. However, these orders never seemed to carry over from day to day, leaving the impression that the Israeli military preferred not to allow children to go to school. One soldier told Dianne Roe and Kathleen Kern on March 5, 2002, that the orders to close Qurtuba School were coming "from very high up."[112] By the end of October 2002, soldiers had closed the schools thirteen times. Between November 15 and December 11, the military allowed schools to open only twice.[113]

More disturbing than the refusal of soldiers to let children travel to school were actual attacks by soldiers on the schools—particularly the Ma'aref Boys' School and the adjoining Khadijaa Girls' school.[114]

The updates for the first half of 2003 cite many incidents of abuse when soldiers enforced the curfew on the students, including the following:

1. Soldiers used teargas and percussion grenades on students who were already returning home after soldiers told them they had to leave.

2. Soldiers charged at children in their jeeps.

3. Soldiers screamed at children and using obscene language as they closed down schools that had opened for the day—considered particularly offensive when done in the presence of female

112 Technically the DCO served as a liaison between Israeli and Palestinian Authority security forces, but by this time the Palestinian Authority barely existed anymore, due to Israel's assaults on its infrastructure and police forces.
"Hebron Update: March 1-6, 2002," Mar 18, 2002.

113. CPTnet, "Hebron Update: October 28–November 15, 2002," Nov 21, 2002; CPTnet, "Hebron Update: December 6–13, 2002," Dec 19, 2002.

114. CPTnet, "Hebron Update: March 18–21," Apr 4, 2002; CPTnet, "Hebron Update: August 25–30," Sept 17, 2002.

students and teachers—and accusing children of being suicide bombers and terrorists.

4. Soldiers kicked water from the gutter into the faces of schoolgirls.

5. Soldiers aimed their rifles at young girls to scare them. (In a February 17, 2003, incident, Art Gish stood between the soldiers and the girls at whom they were pointing their guns and said, "Aren't you ashamed of threatening little girls? Just let the girls go to school.")

6. Soldiers shot rubber bullets at the children. In one case on February 19, they said they would shoot CPTers as well, if they tried to accompany the children.[115]

Chris Brown wrote a report in 2003 describing the trials of the 2002–2003 school year. At the beginning of the report, he noted that Israel is a signatory to the Fourth Geneva Convention. Article 50 of the convention reads as follows:

> In an occupied territory, the Occupying power must facilitate the proper working of all institutions devoted to care and education of children. It may not, under any circumstances, change their personal status or enlist them in formations or organizations subordinate to it. Should the local institutions be inadequate for the purpose, the Occupying Power shall make arrangements for the care and education of children who are orphaned or separated from their parents, if possible by persons of their nationality, language, and religion.

The report then included testimonies taken by fieldworkers for B'tselem and CPTers from students, teachers, and principals in Hebron. These testimonies described physical assaults by soldiers and settlers on students and teachers, the long, roundabout routes to school students

---

115. See CPTnet releases: "Hebron Update: December 27, 2002–January 2, 2003," Jan 11, 2002; "Hebron Update: January 30–February 4, 2003," Feb 10, 2003; Art Gish, "Hebron: No School Today," Feb 17, 2003; "Hebron Update: February 5–9, 2003," Feb 25, 2003; "Hebron Update: February 10–15, 2003," Feb 25, 2003. "Hebron Update: February 18–27, 2003," Mar 3, 2003; "Hebron Update: March 18–30, 2003," Apr 9, 2003; "Hebron Update: April 7–20, 2003," Apr 25, 2003. The autumn 2003 releases record many fewer incidents of soldiers harassing students and the CPTers accompanying them, but see CPTnet, "Hebron: Army tear-gasses children," Oct 15, 2003; CPTnet, "Hebron Reflection: The fire next time," Nov 4, 2003.

and teachers had to walk in order to avoid soldiers and settlers, declining student enrollment because of the harassment, the vandalism of school buildings, and the detentions of teachers while soldiers checked their ID's. Toward the end of the report, Brown listed sobering statistics: the military closed schools for 19 percent of February 2003; 22 percent of March 2003; and 80 percent in April 2003. During the 2002–2003 school year soldiers arrested ten teachers and twenty-two students. From September 2002 through March 2003, twenty-eight students and teachers filed complaints for injuries sustained at the hands of the Israeli military (most injuries went unreported). Of those injuries, twenty-seven happened to minors, one only eight years old.[116]

For the next years, accompaniment of students and teachers would continue to be the primary focus of the Hebron team and later, the At-Tuwani team in the South Hebron Hills. (See next chapter.) Even though this daily chore seemed mundane and often tedious to Hebron team members, school accompaniment proved to be an effective entry issue into the Israeli-Palestinian conflict for the CPT constituency. People might feel confusion about the borders of Israel and Palestine; they might not know what to think about the right of Palestinian refugees to return to their homeland, or whether Israeli military reprisals against a civilian population for acts of Palestinian terrorism were justified. However, just as almost no one thought demolishing Palestinian homes so settlements could expand was a good idea, almost everyone thought that Palestinian

116. Brown, untitled report. It includes a quotation from an IDF press officer on February 2, 2003, regarding the imposition of curfew on students:

> Terrorism is illegal under international law and somehow something has to stop it. And you cannot remove a curfew because children have to go to school, because if you have information about the terrorists coming out of a city, the children inside Israel will die, okay? They won't just not go to school, they won't go anywhere anymore. So we have to make the decision, what's the primary thing in your mind. And of course its Israeli citizens, it's the safety and security of Israeli citizens, okay? And when you have information about terror infrastructure you will do everything in what's possible of course and everything in the, uh, in the legal point of view to try and stop this terror act and try and ensure the safety of Israeli citizens. Even if it's not allowing school day for a group of Palestinian youth.

Brown's report cited both that twenty-four school days in April were lost to the curfew and 11.5 percent of school days were lost. In a July 8, 2004 e-mail to the author he said that twenty-four days (or 80 percent) was correct.

children and teachers should be able to attend school without fear of assault or harassment.

Conclusion

By the end of 2006, most of the positive advancements the team had seen take place in Hebron since 1995 had disappeared. The Old City market, once the heart of Hebron's economy, had become a ghost town; the team's upstairs neighbors who had doggedly remained in the Old City on principle (although they had the financial resources to move) left in March 2003. The military reinstalled the gates to the market that the team had helped Palestinians remove in 1996. The vegetable market where the team had sold the Oslo II tomatoes (see previous chapter) had become a settler parking lot. The Dana family in Jabal Johar—whom the team had accompanied in 1995 and connected with Israeli human rights organizations—again began living with daily attacks by soldiers and settlers as did Palestinians who remained in the Old City. Home demolitions were once again a fearsome reality for residents living on the outskirts of settlements, as was the confiscation of their land. Perhaps most sadly, many relationships between Israelis and Palestinians the team had helped develop collapsed, because most Israelis were too scared to visit Hebron and because anger at the daily violence caused both Israelis and Palestinians to retreat behind a wall of resentment.

Additionally, the wall or "security barrier" was heading inexorably toward Hebron, heralding the confiscation of ever greater amounts of land, and the further diminution of civil rights for those trapped behind it.

In 2001, Wifa' Obeidat, the public relations director for the Hebron municipality summarized the helplessness most felt:

> Our hopes are getting smaller and smaller. First, we wanted to end the Occupation. Then we just wanted them to clear the rubble away. Now we just want electricity. Soon, it will be just to see our children.[117]

For the next five years, hopes continued to dwindle.

117. CPTnet, "Hebron Update: July 15–18, 2001," July 28, 2001. She was telling the team about how the municipality was having to alternate current to different parts of the city because the Israeli military kept shooting out the transformers during nightly gun battles.

6

Other West Bank Projects

"Where is the Intifada? Israel and America talk about the Intifada.
There is no Intifada. Israeli tanks and soldiers roll into Nablus,
Jenin, Bethlehem and Hebron, no one does anything. The Israeli
soldiers shoot, kill people and demolish houses. Where is the
Intifada?"

> —A resident of Beit Ummar to CPTer JoAnne Lingle,
> August 15, 2002.[1]

CPT CHOSE HEBRON AS a project location partly because addressing
soldier and settler violence in the Old City and surrounding areas
provided a relatively narrow focus for the work. Since it could supply only
a four-person team in 1995, it needed to have such a focus, rather than
taking on multiple tentacles of the Israeli Occupation. At the outbreak of
the Intifada, it was no longer the small struggling organization it had been
in 1995. By 2000, it had more than one hundred reservists and dozens
of full-time workers it could draw on and had developed working relationships with Palestinians, Israelis, and internationals working throughout Israel and the Occupied Territories. So, when invitations to address
Intifada violence came from contacts in the Bethlehem District, Beit
Ummar, Jerusalem, and the South Hebron Hills, CPT stretched its human
and financial resources to set up satellite projects in those locations.

BEIT JALA

The team had had a special relationship with people in the Bethlehem area
since Wendy Lehman and Kathleen Kern did the exploratory work for the
Hebron project in the Winter and Spring of 1995. Zoughbi Zoughbi, one
of the people who had invited CPT to become involved in the Israeli-

---

1. CPTnet, "Beit Ummar Update: August 4–21, 2002," Sep 12, 2002.

Palestinian conflict, had his home there, as did many internationals working for various relief and development organizations.

The magnitude of the Israeli military's shelling of Bethlehem and the adjacent villages of Beit Jala and Beit Sahour in the first months of the Intifada far exceeded the shelling in Hebron. CPT received repeated requests from their contacts to put an emergency team in that area. Beit Jala was especially hard hit by Israeli shelling because it sat across a valley from the settlement of Gilo, built between 1973 and 1979 on land confiscated from Beit Jala residents.[2] Palestinian gunmen armed with light weaponry shot from the neighborhoods of Beit Jala at Gilo and the Israeli military fired tanks in response.

The team's goal in Beit Jala was thus more nuanced than in Hebron. Although they condemned all the shooting, they sought to publicize that Israeli retaliation to Palestinian gunfire was grossly disproportionate. One of the most technically savvy militaries in the world with the capacity to pinpoint gunmen at night was collectively punishing entire neighborhoods. Like the residents of Haret iSheik and Abu Sneineh in Hebron, the residents of Beit Jala sincerely wished that gunmen would not shoot from their neighborhood, but were nearly powerless to stop it.

Anne Montgomery and Pierre Shantz were the first CPTers to staff the house of Umm Elias Kunkar at the corner of Intifada and Martyr (in Arabic "Shaheed") Streets in Beit Jala. The basement apartment had three bedrooms that faced the settlement of Gilo. The most serious attacks on their neighborhood happened on December 5 and 11, during which shells gouged holes in the streets and damaged three sides of the team's house.[3]

Initially, Montgomery and Shantz spent their days networking with residents of Bethlehem, Beit Jala, and Beit Sahour. After nights of heavy

2. Part of a ring of Israeli settlements built around Jerusalem, Gilo is referred to by politicians and even progressive Israelis as "within the consensus," meaning that they no longer view it as a settlement, but part of Israel proper. Israeli sources generally call it a "neighborhood" of Jerusalem. Palestinians, of course, were not included in the consensus.

3. CPTnet, "Bethlehem District Update: December 1–14, 2000" (The team wanted to say that the releases came from Beit Jala. The Chicago Office wanted to say they were from Bethlehem—in order to tie constituent churches to the project during the Christmas season—so they compromised by saying the releases were from the Bethlehem district). Some details are from an undated note that Montgomery sent the author in 2004 after she read a draft of this chapter. See also Hauser, "U.S. nun plays witness."

shooting, they visited homes that the Israeli military had shelled, helping residents put sandbags in their windows and sweep up glass.

They also tried to address the problem of Palestinian gunmen shooting from Beit Jala. They accompanied Beit Jala residents to one meeting on December 5, 2000, in which they met with the mayor of Beit Jala and demanded that the local police stop gunmen from shooting at the settlements. Shantz accompanied neighborhood patrols that Beit Jala residents organized to get the shooters out of their neighborhoods. These met with mixed success. After a while, the gunmen started coming out at odd hours, like 4:00 a.m., and once, gunmen threw rocks at the neighbors who were yelling at them to get out of the neighborhood.[4]

Perhaps the most significant work of the Beit Jala project was supplying eyewitness accounts of what was happening to international media. On December 18, 2000, Zoughbi Zoughbi warned the team that the American and Israeli press were trying to put the shootings into the context of Christian-Muslim tensions. Many gunmen were Muslim residents of the heavily bombed Aida refugee camp in Bethlehem. The homes in Beit Jala sustaining the worst damage belonged to affluent Palestinian Christians. Thus, tensions resulting from class differences did enter into the situation in a small way. However, three days later, when a reporter from the *New York Times* called to ask Kern and Montgomery about the Christian-Muslim tensions, they told him what most Palestinians believed: gunmen chose to shoot from locations where they had the best vantage point to aim at settlements and soldier outposts. The situation of people living in the all-Muslim neighborhoods in Hebron did not differ significantly from those of the people living in Beit Jala. Muslims in Hebron never talked about the Israeli military shelling "Christians" in Beit Jala. They viewed them as fellow Palestinians suffering the same collective punishment for the actions of gunmen who did not live in their neighborhoods.[5]

---

4. The stories of these patrols did not appear in the Beit Jala updates. Kathleen Kern referred to them in a response to an e-mail query from Rabbi Yehudai-Rimmer (a progressive British Rabbi normally supportive of CPT's work) in the *Signs of the Times* 11:1. Her account was based on what Shantz had told her. She concluded the response by saying, "There are a lot of rumors about [the gunmen] being collaborators or even Israeli secret police. I think it's just too many guns in too many hands."

5. William J. Orme Jr. quoted Kern about the Christian vs. Muslim issue in Orme, "Jerusalem Christians."

The team put out one Urgent Action regarding the shellings and devastation of the economy in the Bethlehem District that December,[6] but by January most of their neighbors left at night to sleep in a safer location. The project thus lost its raison d'être: accompaniment of people under fire. After four weeks in which no shelling occurred, Jamey Bouwmeester, Bob Holmes, and Anne Montgomery closed down the Beit Jala project on January 12, 2001. Members of the Beit Jala team rejoined the team in Hebron, where shelling of neighborhoods had stepped up.

BEIT UMMAR

Beit Ummar is an agricultural village of about twelve thousand people located in the northern part of the Hebron district. The Hebron team became involved in the lives of Beit Ummar's residents in 1997 after more than a dozen families received home demolition orders. Dianne Roe, in particular, developed a network of friendships in the village, and when the Campaign for Secure Dwellings began in 1997, Beit Ummar, along with the Beqa'a Valley and the Al Sendas/Qilqis area, became a focal point. Team members often brought Israeli and international Jewish visitors there, because they knew that the inhabitants of Beit Ummar would treat them with less suspicion or reserve than a typical family in Hebron might. In particular, Edna Sabarneh, an Israeli of Iraqi-Kurdish descent who converted to Islam and became the second wife of her Palestinian husband, provided hospitality for dozens of visitors. Ghazi Brigith, an employee of the Beit Ummar Municipality, was a member of the Bereaved Families Network—a joint Israeli and Palestinian group comprising those who had lost family members to violence—and as such, also welcomed sympathetic Israelis.

On April 8, 2002, Dianne Roe, Mary Lawrence, and JoAnne Lingle moved into an apartment in Beit Ummar, shortly after the Israeli military had killed two young men from the community. At the time, Israeli soldiers had been making almost nightly incursions into Beit Ummar. They shot up the village; vandalized cars, water tanks, and houses; conducted midnight raids into various homes; and rounded up men at random for questioning and beating.[7] A May 27, 2002, roundup was especially brutal.

6. CPTnet, "No Christmas in Bethlehem: CPT Call for Solidarity," Dec 3, 2002.

7. An incident relayed to the team by ISMer Caoimhe Butterly testifies to the randomness of this violence. She spent a night in Beit Ummar with a family whose son

The Israeli military went door-to-door, ordering eighty-five men between the ages of sixteen and seventy to report to the checkpoint and forced them to remain there all night. Soldiers beat many of them, including a mentally retarded man, and broke the arm of another man. They also shot up two homes. When the women of the village approached to check on their husbands, sons, and fathers, the soldiers tear-gassed them. The mayor went to the checkpoint the next morning to intercede for the captives, and the soldiers forced him to stand in the sun for three hours, kicked him, and struck him with a gun butt. One of the team's Beit Ummar translators later told the team, "They spoke to us like we were insects ... There aren't enough words to express how disrespectful they were."[8]

On July 14, 2002, soldiers shot out the village's telephone connections box, which cut all phone service between Beit Ummar and Hebron. They also detained thirty-two men from 10:00 p.m. to 3:00 a.m. and kept them standing in a 3x5 meter iron cage opposite the checkpoint on Road 60. They threatened the men with teargas and the arrest of their wives and children if they complained. Two days later, soldiers moved through the town shooting out the town's electrical transformer, streetlights, and water tanks on houses and the school. While the soldiers shot up another area of town, Dianne Roe and Greg Rollins provided accompaniment for a municipal employee while he fixed the transformer.[9] For the next weeks, the team recorded many incidents of apparently random shooting by soldiers in the village.

Possibly the most significant help the Hebron and Beit Ummar teams provided to the residents of Beit Ummar and surrounding villages between April and November 2002 involved accompanying farmers as they harvested their crops—the main source of revenue for Beit Ummar residents. The previous summer, the Israeli military had prevented farmers getting their produce to the market, barricading the road between the market and Bypass Road 60 and shooting at farmers in the market. Beit

soldiers had taken on the previous night. A daughter of the household who understood Hebrew learned from the soldiers' radio conversation that they realized they had entered the wrong house. Nevertheless, the soldiers began interrogating her brothers, and took one into custody. When she asked why, they told her, "Because we want to." When she implored them not to beat her brother, another soldier said, "We're not animals." CPTnet, "Hebron Update: February 14–18, 2002," Mar 9, 2002.

8. CPTnet, "Hebron District: Israeli army rounds up eighty-five men," May 27, 2002.

9. CPTnet, "Hebron District: Israeli military shoots up Beit Ummar," July 17, 2002.

Ummar Mayor Rashid Awad estimated that farmers and the municipality had lost five million shekels.[10] On August 9, 2002, the Beit Ummar team put out an Urgent Action, asking constituents to write to Canadian and American legislators regarding Israel's refusal to allow the farmers of Beit Ummar to reach their land.[11]

The Beit Ummar project closed for the winter in 2002, because farmers no longer needed accompaniment to their fields, orchards and vineyards. Additionally, the soldier brigade that replaced the brigade that had conducted the random shootings did not abuse the human rights of village residents as much. More importantly, Hebron was in crisis following the shootings of the soldiers and settler security guards on November 15, 2002, (see previous chapter) and the Hebron team needed extra people. Although the team maintained the option of reopening the project when the weather got warmer, autumn 2002 marked the end of the Beit Ummar project.[12]

RAPID RESPONSE TEAM 2002

The Rapid Response satellite project set up in Jerusalem on October 4, 2002, was less successful than the Beit Ummar and Beit Jala satellite projects. Its original intent was to have CPTers on hand as a violence-deterring presence in other cities hard hit by the Israeli military rather than just reacting to and documenting this violence after it happened. Because the International Solidarity Movement was already covering the northern West Bank, CPT began exploring possibilities for presences in Bethlehem, Beit Sahour, Jerusalem, and Gaza.

Team members eventually decided to base themselves in Jerusalem. Factoring into the decision was the reality that CPT had been providing eyewitness accounts of Palestinian civilian suffering for years. As bombings of Israeli civilian sites increased, many CPTers felt they needed to provide similar eyewitness accounts of Israeli suffering. A release announcing the beginning of the project quoted Rich Meyer as saying,

10. CPTnet, "Beit Ummar Update: May 13–19, 2002," May 25, 2002.

11. CPTnet, "Beit Ummar Urgen Action: Allow Palestinian farmers," Aug 9, 2002. See also CPTnet, "Hebron Update: June 2–7, 2002," June 21, 2002; "Hebron: Farmers, CPTers negotiate," July 4, 2002.

12. Holmes, e-mail, June 15, 2004; Roe, e-mail, June 17, 2004; Rollins, e-mail, June 18, 2004.

> Each Israeli helicopter missile shot into a Palestinian home and each Palestinian suicide bombing is another step up the ladder of escalating violence. We cannot predict these attacks in advance. The Rapid Response team will try to get to the scene as quickly as possible to offer a pastoral and compassionate presence.[13]

CPTers in Jerusalem responded to one suicide attack there, but after hanging around the scene for thirty-five to forty-five minutes did not see much opportunity to help. Most often, CPTers in Jerusalem simply supplied bodies for organizations such as Rabbis for Human Rights who were helping Palestinians living near settlements pick olives. In February 2003, the team closed the apartment in Jerusalem, because the Hebron project needed the human and financial resources more.[14]

AT-TUWANI

In September 2004, the Hebron team set up a new project in the southern Hebron District, when CPTers began accompanying Palestinian school-children from the village of Tuba to a central school in the village of At-Tuwani. The dedicated nonviolent resistance of the villagers in the area, the involvement of Israeli activists in the region, and the ongoing need for international accompaniment would turn At-Tuwani into a CPT project independent of the Hebron team over the following year.

At-Tuwani and a dozen other small villages in the South Hebron Hills housed mostly shepherds whose families did subsistence farming. Because the villages lay within a few miles of the Green Line, and the Israeli government had sought to make the lives of the villagers miserable for decades so they would leave and Israel could annex their land. Settlers from Maʼon, Susia, and settlement outposts abetted this goal by regularly raiding the villages, burning crops, and attacking people and animals.

CPT had had relationships with inhabitants of the region since 1996, when they had helped a Hebron University professor cut a fence that settlers had erected around his wheat field and later participated in an ill-fated attempt to replant olive trees that settlers from Susia had planted in the same field.[15] In subsequent years, they would help the villagers in

13. CPTnet, "Jerusalem: CPT Rapid Response," Oct 4, 2002.
14. Rollins, e-mail, June 18, 2002. Montgomery, e-mail, June 20, 2004.
15. Following the lead of an eccentric American woman who also taught at Hebron University, the team accompanied her for the fence cutting under the agreement that they

the region harvest crops, rebuild homes and walls destroyed by the Israeli military, and make solidarity visits to people who had their homes demolished. The team also documented the expansion of settlements in the region onto Palestinian lands and damage settlers had done to Palestinian crops, wells, and animals.

Israeli friends of the Hebron team had for some time been anxious about the people living in these villages, because of their remoteness. They knew the Israeli military could easily evacuate villages of less than two hundred inhabitants as had happened to the villagers of Susiya in the summer and fall of 2001. Additionally, the settlers in the region were able to commit egregiously nasty acts against the Palestinians in the region with impunity. CPTers were present at one of these attacks near At-Tuwani village January 18, 2003. They had accompanied members of Ta'ayush, an Israeli-Palestinian peace group founded at the beginning of the Al-Aqsa Intifada, to protect farmers while they worked in their fields. As the farmers started plowing, the settlers began shooting from an outpost overlooking the fields. Some of the settlers charged down the hill, still shooting or hurling rocks from slingshots. When they saw CPTer Lorne Friesen taking a picture, they knocked him down, smashing his camera and destroying his film. They then struck the side of his head. CPTer Greg Rollins came to Friesen's aid and a settler's punch sent Rollins' glasses flying. Settler security personnel arrived at the scene, detained a Palestinian who had thrown stones at the settlers, shifted the tractors into neutral, and pushed them down the hill so they flipped over.[16]

Settlers also targeted children who had to walk several kilometers from the village of Tuba to the central school in At-Tuwani. Accordingly, Ta'ayush, which had developed significant relationships with villagers in

---

would not publicize the action. The team also helped the professor's family harvest wheat, which they described in the CPTnet release, "The Wheat Harvest," May 13, 1996. See CPTnet releases: "Hebron: CPT Team Arrested," May 30, 2996; "Urgent Action—Hebron CPTers Arrested," May 30, 1996; "Update: Hebron CPTers," May 31, 1996; "Hebron: CPT Members Released," June 2, 1996; "CPTer Released," June 2, 1996; "Hebron CPTers Arrested," June 3, 1996; "CPTers Resume Work," June 17, 1996.

16. CPTnet, "Hebron Update: January 13–23, 2003," January 31, 2003. The Israelis from Ta'ayush attacked by the Ma'on settlers filed complaints with the police in Jerusalem. Diane Janzen, in her comments on a draft of this chapter sent on October 25, 2007, noted that settler security people have no authority to arrest Palestinians or anyone else. Rollins, in an October 27, 2005 e-mail, wrote, "I am pretty sure the settler security let the guy go before the Israeli police arrived. To be honest with you I don't recall the details about settler security that day but I do recall that no one was taken away from our group."

the region, consulted with their Palestinian contacts, and then approached the Italian peace group Operation Dove[17] and CPT in 2004 to see if they could together supply a small team in At-Tuwani to accompany the school children and other Palestinians needing to work in their fields. A full-time team began its presence in the area on September 27, 2004.[18]

On September 29, masked settlers attacked the children from Tuba and the CPTers accompanying them. They threw rocks at the children, causing minor injuries, and left Kim Lamberty with a broken arm and a knee injury that made it impossible for her to walk. The same masked attackers whipped Chris Brown with chains and kicked him when he fell, causing head injuries and a punctured lung. Ten days later, the settlers struck again, attacking Diane Janzen, Diana Zimmerman, and an Operation Dove member, whose kidney they injured, as well as an adult from At-Tuwani, two adults from Tuba, and two fieldworkers from Amnesty International, Donatella Rovera and Maartje Houbrechts.[19]

Because of the international and Israeli outcry against this thuggish behavior, the Israeli military met with villagers in the region and tried to persuade them to ask CPT and Operation Dove to leave the area. Instead, the community presented the military with a list of demands they wanted met if they were not going to continue making a more public outcry. These demands included:

- Water: the villagers wanted to tap into the Ma'on settlement's water line, given that the small spring in the village only provided enough for drinking and cooking. Rainwater trapped in cisterns provided a limited supply of water for washing.

- Clinic: The village wanted to finish building their clinic, upon which the Civil Administration had put a stop-work order.

- Safe passage to the At-Tuwani primary school for the children of Tuba

17. See its Web site, http://www.operationdove.org. Because Operation Dove could not supply number of people to the At-Tuwani Project that CPT did, it requested that CPT not use the names of its workers in the At-Tuwani releases.

18. For more background on the history of At-Tuwani and the At-Tuwani project, see CPT At-Tuwani, "At-Tuwani Media Packet."

19. See CPTnet releases: "Hebron District: CPTers Kim Lamberty and Chris Brown," Sept 29, 2004; "Hebron District: Israeli military and settler security," Oct 5, 2004; "Hebron District: Settlers again attack CPTers," Oct 9, 2004"; Hebron Urgent Action: Tell Israeli government to stop," Oct 9, 2004. "Hebron District: Kim Lamberty's report," Oct 11, 2004; "Hebron District: Joe Carr's letter," Oct 13, 2004; "Hebron/At-Tuwani Urgent Action: Stop Extremist Violence," Feb 20, 2005. See also CPT At-Tuwani, "At-Tuwani Media Packet."

- Electricity: At-Tuwani got its power from a diesel generation the village could only afford to run for a few hours each evening. Villagers wanted to connect it to the same grid from which Ma'on got its power.

- Road access to Karmil: The villagers wanted the Israeli military to remove three dirt barricades blocking the road from At-Tuwani to the larger Palestinian population centers of Karmil, Yatta, and Hebron. These barricades prevented access to the hospital, secondary schools, and stores located there.

- Improvement of the road to Mufakara and villages to the south: Five years earlier, Israeli authorities denied villager requests to improve the path.

The official told the villagers that Israeli soldiers would accompany the children; they should go ahead and build their clinic and that questions about the road would be studied. A village leader told the At-Tuwani team,

> This meeting today didn't just happen. We have had these problems, and many attacks by settlers for years, but no one outside knew. Thank you for being here; you have brought us attention. Please thank all the people who have helped us—the media, the US consular officials who visited, and the Israeli and international peace groups. Your help made this visit happen.[20]

After the meeting, Israeli soldiers and police began accompanying the children of Tuba village to and from school; families from the nearby village of Maghayir Al-Abeed also began sending their children with the soldier escort.[21] The Israeli military predicated the accompaniment on the internationals not accompanying the children, so the CPTers and Doves began watching the patrol from a distance at each end of the route, noting, among other things, whether the soldiers arrived on time, whether they walked with the children instead of making them run behind the jeep,

---

20. CPTnet, "At-Tuwani, Hebron District: At-Tuwani villagers," Nov 1, 2004.

21. The Israeli Knesset Committee for Rights of the Child held hearings, instigated by the Israeli group Machsom ("checkpoint") Watch after the beatings, and then ordered the army to accompany the children See CPT At-Tuwani and Operation Dove, "Report on the Israeli Military." Doug Pritchard wrote in a November 21, 2007 e-mail, "I was struck at the time that they didn't order a stop to the settler activity or arrest of the perpetrators but rather ordered the much more expensive and time-consuming army accompaniment."

and whether they protected them from settlers.[22] The At-Tuwani team then summarized this information in a spreadsheet about every four weeks and submitted it to Ta'ayush and Machsom (Checkpoint) Watch, who submitted it to the Israeli Knesset Committee on the Rights of the Child.[23]

The soldiers were not consistent in their protection of the children. Some took their duty seriously—in one case, a soldier fired into the air to scare away settlers after they ambushed the children at a roadblock the settlers had installed to block the path of the escort jeeps. At other times, they did nothing to intervene as settlers threatened or attacked the children.[24] However, between 2005 and 2006, the accompaniment made it possible for fifteen to twenty-nine children to attend school in At-Tuwani.[25]

Accompaniment of Shepherds

While the children were in school, and during school vacations, team members accompanied shepherds from the villages as they grazed their flocks near settlements in the region or planted and harvested food and fodder crops. Regaining grazing and farmland, from which settlers had driven them, sometimes for years, became one of the key goals of the NVDA campaign waged by the South Hebron Hills villagers.

As had happened with the school accompaniment, the settlers pushed back when the shepherds attempted to graze their flocks with international accompaniment. On February 16, 2005, settlers came out of the Havat Ma'on (Hill 833) outpost[26] while Diana Zimmerman and a Dove were accompanying the shepherds and trained a gun on the two in-

22. A complete list of data collected on the school escorts is available in CPT At-Tuwani and Operation Dove, "Report on the Israeli Military," n. 23.

23. According to the At-Tuwani team, as of this writing in 2007, they still send the reports to Ta'ayush and OCHA.

24. CPTnet, "At-Tuwani: Tuba children and soldier," May 7, 2006; CPTnet, "At-Tuwani: Despite Defence Ministry orders," May 25, 2006.

25. In a November 18, 2007 e-mail the team noted that the numbers of children participating in the escort had decreased for the 2007 school year, mostly due to the graduation to high school of some of the older children.

26. The Israeli groups B'tselem and Peace Now have encouraged the team to use the latter designation, possibly because using settler terminology would grant it a legitimacy it did not have, even under Israeli law. From Diane Janzen's comments on a draft of this manuscript.

ternationals until the Israeli army arrived. Soon afterwards, when CPTer Sally Hunsberger and two Doves came over the hill, the same settlers saw their video camera and attacked the Doves. A karate kick broke the jaw of one of the Doves, causing blurred vision and short-term memory loss.[27]

A worse attack for the villagers occurred in March 2005 when settlers laid poison-covered barley around Ma'on, under bushes where sheep usually graze and near one of At-Tuwani's water sources. Since the villagers' flocks not only represented their main source of income, but was also a staple of their diet, the loss was catastrophic. At first the poison was identified as 2-Fluoroacetamide, a rat poison banned in several nations because of its toxicity and because it remains for a long time in soil and water. Prospective buyers in Israel must get special authorization from the Israeli government. Later, in April, a second type of poison was found, which a representative from the United Nations Office for the Coordination of Humanitarian Affairs (OCHA) said was called Brodifacoum. Israeli groups and the At-Tuwani team assisted the Palestinians in picking up the tiny poison pellets. Given the size of the pellets, the vast expanse of the land they covered, and the interference by Israeli settlers and soldiers, cleaning the ground sometimes seemed like a futile effort. For the next six weeks, shepherds continued to find poison throughout the hills and valleys around the Ma'on settlement. Sheep, goats, and wild gazelles continued to die; in the end, the villagers from At-Tuwani and Mufakara lost more than one hundred animals.[28]

During this period, Ta'ayush was creating relationships between the villagers of the region and Israeli lawyers, including two who worked with Rabbis for Human Rights and the Association for Civil Rights in Israel (ACRI). The ACRI lawyer filed a petition in the Israeli courts, asserting Palestinian ownership of the land in the Khoruba Valley. In the fall of 2005, an Israeli judge ruled that the valley was indeed owned by Palestinians and the Israeli military could protect them from settler attacks when they worked there.

Although the shepherds conscientiously notified the DCO every time they knew they would be grazing or working in the valley, the mili-

27. CPTnet, "At-Tuwani: Settlers Attack," Feb 16, 2005.

28. CPT At-Tuwani, "At-Tuwani Media Packet." See also CPTnet, "At-Tuwani: Shepherds Confront Police," Apr 7, 2005; CPTnet, "At-Tuwani: The little one," June 9, 2005; Lamberty, e-mail, Nov 9, 2007.

tary often failed to show up or showed up late.[29] However, the court's decision and the persistence of the shepherds to work in their fields, even when their phone calls to the military produced nothing, paid off. Settler attacks in Khoruba began diminishing.

Throughout 2005 and 2006, however, settler assaults on shepherds still occurred around settlements in the region. CPTers regularly accompanied shepherds to police stations to make complaints. These visits were often frustrating experiences. Barbara Martens wrote,

> Justice in Palestine operates by two standards. At the police station, the line of response to the death threat went like this: "Did you say there was only ONE youth? Did he take his gun (they are all allowed to be armed) and point it at you? No? He only held up a stone? Did he strike you with it? No? Well then, you weren't really hurt, were you? He's just a youngster. He probably meant no harm."
>
> We know of Palestinian youth who have been beaten and thrown into jail for throwing a stone at a settler, let alone uttering a death threat.[30]

Israeli Military Harassment and the Wall

Despite the assurances of the Israeli commander at the October 31, 2004, meeting mentioned above, residents of the South Hebron Hills faced ongoing harassment from the Israeli military when they tried to make improvements on the roads connecting the scattered villages, build their clinic, replant olive trees that settlers and soldiers had uprooted, and graze their flocks on land for which they had deeds and which other military commanders had told them they could use.[31]

---

29. Janzen, e-mail, Nov 28, 2005.

30. CPTnet, Martens, "At-Tuwani: Settler attacks shepherd," Feb 4, 2005.

31. See CPTnet releases: "Hebron/At-Tuwani: Palestinians and internationals," Dec 7, 2004; Carpenter, "At-Tuwani: Israeli authorities halt," Jan 10, 2005; Art Gish, "At-Tuwani: Two roads to At-Tuwani," Jan 19, 2005; Art Gish "At-Tuwani Reflection: A rocky road," Feb 3, 2005; Art Gish, At-Tuwani: Israeli Soldiers Drive Shepherds," Feb 24, 2005; Art Gish, "At-Tuwani: Hard Day," Feb 26, 2005; Art Gish, "At-Tuwani Reflection: Hungry sheep," Mar 4, 2005; Lamberty, "At-Tuwani: Israeli military commander," Mar 11, 2005; Zimmerman and Lamberty, "At-Tuwani: Ma'on settlers invade," Apr 7, 2005; Jack, "At-Tuwani: Sheep killed," Apr 28, 2005; Anderson, "At-Tuwani: Israeli military, police and settlers," May 24, 2005.

In May 2005, the military demolished nine homes in three of the villages. During the same month, settlers destroyed wheat and lentil crops and stole livestock belonging to the villagers. Then the Civil Administration and police had the chutzpah to meet again with the villagers and ask that they tell the internationals to leave, promising they would be more helpful with the settler violence. The villagers told them their officers wished the internationals to remain.[32]

Further military harassment occurred in 2006, when the military began building a low concrete wall the length of Route 317 (an Israeli bypass road from the Green Line to Hebron) that would effectively cut off the entire South Hebron Hills region from jobs, schools, and hospitals in Hebron and Yatta. The original plans for the Separation, or Apartheid, wall through the West Bank showed the barrier running along Route 317, rather than along the 1949 Armistice Line. When the Israeli cabinet moved the road back to the Green Line in 2004, the military decided to build the low wall instead.

Since the wall was only eighty centimeters high, and thus easily climbed over by hypothetical terrorists, making life difficult for the Palestinian residents of the area seemed to be its only function. The At-Tuwani team, working with the villagers, and Israeli activists thus initiated a letter-writing and public witness campaign, hoping to bring international pressure to bear on the wall. In 2006, the Israeli High Court ordered the military to create breaks in the wall so that villagers in the region could move freely, and then, in 2007, ordered the military to dismantle the wall entirely after it had disregarded the court's decision. The Nonviolence Coordinator in At-Tuwani told the team, after the wall was dismantled, "The IDF routinely disregards Israeli court decisions. We believe what happened is a success for the people's nonviolent resistance. This is a very important step."[33]

32. CPT At-Tuwani, "At-Tuwani Media Packet."

33. CPT At-Tuwani and Operation Dove, "Immanent Peril"; CPTnet, "At-Tuwani: Israelis and Palestinians arrested," Apr 24, 2006; CPTnet, "At-Tuwani Urgent Action: Tell Israeli government to halt," Apr 26, 2006; CPTnet, "At-Tuwani: 'Security' wall" Aug 20, 2007; "At-Tuwani: Parting the Wall." See also, ACRI, "HCJ Orders State."

In her comments on a draft of this chapter, Diane Janzen wrote, "the organization of resistance to [the low wall] was the start of the internal push among the villagers for a nonviolence committee among the South Hebron Hills villages—and the success of the various efforts in the removal was huge for the villagers in the area."

As of 2008, the At-Tuwani team remains in place, and the villagers continue to initiate nonviolent direct actions to reclaim their land and dignity. Hundreds of Israelis and internationals come to support these initiatives, making the region one of the few places in Palestine where the transforming power of nonviolent resistance is evident in the eighth year of the Al Aqsa Intifada.[34]

ISSUES ARISING FROM WEST BANK WORK

Culpability of the United States in the Israeli-Palestinian Conflict

The predominant grievance the Arab/Muslim world holds against the United States is its default and overt support of Israel. Although the U.S. State Department has given lip service to the principle that settlement

34. Dianne Janzen noted in her November 28, 2007 e-mail that the CPT At-Tuwani releases sometimes do not adequately communicate the degree of cooperation between Israelis, internationals, and Palestinians regarding the nonviolent resistance in the South Hebron Hills:

> Of course there are times of frustration and mis-communication, but for the most part, the cooperation has been quite remarkable . . . In general I would sum it up as something like:
> The internationals living in At-Tuwani provide daily accompaniment to the Palestinians shepherds and farmers in the area. Several Israeli peace groups support the work of the internationals and the non-violent resistance of the Palestinians by joining them on occasion in the accompaniment or in solidarity actions. The Israeli peace groups also have made connections with Israeli lawyers willing to take on cases in the area (sometimes the Israeli peace groups arrange the funding necessary for the lawyers) and the internationals have provided valuable documentation of incidents of attacks or harassment and property damage done by Israeli settlers or soldiers. This cooperation among the various groups has resulted in several non-violent victories for the Palestinian villagers including the continued use of the old Palestinian road between the villages of Tuba and At-Tuwani by school children, the removal of the barrier along Route 317 as well as regaining access to land previously claimed by settlers through violence." We've provided video and pictures to lawyers working in the area, to OCHA, to B'Tselem, to Machsom Watch, to Peace Now and to Ta'ayush. I think the naming of more Israeli peace groups working in the area is important—it's not just all Ta'ayush and us (CPT and the Doves).

She also mentioned in the e-mail that with the villagers' rights to Khoruba Valley secured, the Nonviolence Committee in the South Hebron Hills had begun focusing on regaining rights in Mashakha, the next valley to the north. B'tselem donated a video camera to the villagers of Tuba so they could document settler harassment occurring there.

expansion is detrimental to peace, the government has continued to send massive amounts of aid to Israel that have enabled it to continue building settlements and confiscating land.

Jeff Halper, the director of the Israeli Committee Against House Demolitions, has said that the U.S. Congress is the institution most responsible for keeping the Israeli occupation of the West Bank and Gaza in place. U.S. presidents and the U.S. State Department have understood that Israeli settlements are the primary obstacle to peace in the region. More than half of the Israeli electorate thinks that Israel should get out of the West Bank and Gaza. However, the political power of the right-wing partisans of Israel is enormous. Congressional representatives who have dared to criticize Israel for its abuses of human rights or ask that it abide by United Nations resolutions and pull out of the Occupied Territories have lost their seats due to the power of the Israeli lobby.[35]

Hebron team members have watched the American participation in the 1995 Oslo II accords, the 1997 Hebron Protocol, the 1998 Wye River Memorandum, the 1999 Sharm el-Sheikh Memorandum, the 2000 Camp David II negotiations, the 2001 Taba talks and Mitchell Report, and the 2003 "Roadmap to Peace" proposed by the "Quartet" of the European Union, Russia, U.S., and United Nations. None of these negotiations really addressed Israel's determination to hold on to settlements in the West Bank.

Likewise, when Arabs see U.S.-built Apache and Blackhawk helicopters killing Palestinian civilians and U.S.-built Caterpillar bulldozers demolishing Palestinian homes, U.S. advocacy for "peace" negotiations rings hollow.

In the first months of the Al-Aqsa Intifada, Dianne Roe and Kathleen Kern were hurrying to the neighborhood of Haret iSheikh so they could

---

35. Halper made this statement several times when Kathleen Kern brought delegations to meet with him. The defeat of Georgia Congresswoman Cynthia McKinney in the 2002 election is an example of how partisans of Israel influence congress. Israeli peace activist Uri Avnery wrote at the time that McKinney "had dared to criticize the Sharon government, to support the Palestinian cause, and (worst of all from the Jewish establishment's standpoint) had gained the support of Israeli and Jewish peace groups." "Manufacturing Anti-Semites." See also Tivnan, *The Lobby*. For other sources on the US political relationship with Israel, see Bookbinder and Abourzek, *Through Different Eyes*; Chomsky, *The Fateful Triangle*; Green, *Living by the Sword*; Novick, *The Holocaust in American Life*; Quandt, *Peace Process*; Rubenberg, *Israel and the American National Interest*; Findley, *Deliberate Deceptions*; Ball and Ball, *The Passionate Attachment*.

spend the night with a family there whose home the Israeli military had shelled (see chapter 5). Roe picked up a bullet as they walked down Shuhada Street. A soldier demanded that she give it to him, as well as others she had collected earlier. Roe wrote that she wished she had said,

> Excuse me sir, but I think those are mine. You see I come from the United States. It is my country that has paid for your army. It is my country that vetoed UN resolutions and thus enabled your country to carry on this brutal occupation. It was my congressman who joined over 400 other congressmen in supporting your country's assault on the people in these neighborhoods.
>
> I could have said, "These bullets are mine. They were paid for with my taxes. I want to return them to their rightful owner." But I did not need to argue with him. There are hundreds more on the street. I will see to it that some of them are returned to their rightful owners in Washington, DC, wrapped in a photo of one of the children who received it as a gift from America.[36]

In later years of the Intifada, the U.S. boycott of the democratically elected Hamas government, which included desperately needed aid to pay salaries of teachers and medical personnel, aroused much bitterness among Palestinians. The boycott confirmed what they had suspected—that "democracy" to the U.S. means that Palestinians should vote for the candidates the U.S. supported.[37]

Partisanship Issues—"Balance"

Related to the U.S. culpability is the issue of "balance" in the discourse about the Israeli-Palestinian conflict. In the U.S. (and to a lesser extent in other western nations), any remark construed to be sympathetic to Palestinians must be "balanced" by the Israeli view or by the views of Israel's partisans.

The "Israeli" view does not include those Israelis who care about the human rights of Palestinians and who are ardent foes of the Occupation. It includes only the view that Israel has a right to do whatever it wants to Palestinians. However, when pro-Israel views are widely discussed in

---

36. CPTnet, "Hebron: Whose Bullet Is This?" Nov 16, 2000.

37. The consequences of the boycott on team friend Abdel Hadi Hantash and other Palestinians working in the public sector were detailed in CPTnet, "Hebron Urgent Action: Tell U.S. Senate to stop," June 22, 2006.

the mainstream U.S. media, opposite "balancing" views that express what Palestinians suffer do not need to appear.

CPT does not claim to be neutral in any conflict with which it is involved. Teams live with people whom those in power oppress and exploit. Rather than neutrality, the CPT model is more like "guests in the house of the disenfranchised." Within that role, CPTers find themselves better able than their hosts to greet the oppressors at the door. Using active non-violence as a means of communication, they confront and engage those in power, making it clear that they will tell the truth about what CPTers see them doing; physically lay down their lives to prevent them from harming CPT's hosts; and treat them—the oppressors—with the respect and love to which they are entitled as children of God.[38] These tenets applied to Haiti, Washington DC, and later CPT projects did not provoke much controversy. When applied to Israel and Palestine, however, they only enrage Israel's partisans, particularly when CPTers speak in U.S. communities with significant Jewish populations. Although, as of 2008, wider access to alternative views in the media has made speaking about the Israeli occupation of the West Bank and Gaza less controversial, accusations of providing unbalanced, pro-Palestinian viewpoints continue to dog CPTers in their writing and speaking.

Interactions with Israeli Soldiers

Just as it had in Haiti, the question of how to interact with soldiers in Hebron caused considerable disagreement within the Hebron team over the years. Palestinian contacts of the team would have preferred that CPTers not talk to soldiers at all, unless they were intervening to help a Palestinian. Arguments then arose within the team about whether CPT was more than a Palestinian solidarity group.

Most Israeli citizens, with the exceptions of Palestinian citizens of Israel and ultra-orthodox Jews, go into the army for two to three years and remain on call as reservists until they are in their fifties. Since almost all Israelis serve in the armed forces, the soldiers that CPTers encountered in Palestine expressed a wide variety of political opinion (although the most dovish soldiers usually managed to avoid getting stationed in the West Bank and Gaza).

38. Kern, "From Haiti to Hebron," 199–200.

The team's first "relationship" with an Israeli soldier began when a young border police officer named Meron approached members of the Hebron team as they were conducting morning worship in the park across from the Ibrahimi Mosque. On the strap of his automatic weapon, he had written "R.E.M."—the name of an American alternative rock group—and the title of one of its biggest hits, "Losing My Religion." He revered American music and wanted to talk with the team about his favorite bands. Meron, who was obviously ill-suited to military life, would continue talking with the CPTers even after his commanding officer had shouted orders for him to stop. He expressed appreciation for the work of the team and hatred of the Hebron settlers, one who had called him a Nazi when he refused to let her park in front of the Ibrahimi Mosque. Coming from a mixed Arab/Jewish neighborhood in Tel Aviv, he said he saw no reason why Palestinians and Israelis could not live together.

One day, a Palestinian friend of the team who worked in a pottery shop adjacent to the grounds of the Ibrahimi Mosque told the team that the soldier he had seen the team talking to the other day had shoved him and verbally abused him. When the team mentioned this to Meron, he looked deeply embarrassed and said that if he did not hassle the Palestinians the other border police in his unit made life miserable for him.

This relationship with Meron characterizes the difficulty the Hebron team has had coming to consensus about the "right" way to interact with soldiers. Israeli soldiers in Hebron are mostly young and unhappy to be working there; they are anxious for contact with civilians, especially women.[39] Relating to them on a friendly basis arouses suspicion or causes pain for Palestinian friends of the team. On the other hand, CPTers have also helped humanize soldiers for Palestinian contacts, especially when these soldiers believe that the settlers should be removed from Hebron and that Palestinians should have the same civil rights as Israelis (a view held by most soldiers in the Nahal Brigade). Soldiers have stopped CPTers accompanying Palestinians at checkpoints and in the ensuing conversations, Palestinians have found that these soldiers would prefer to relate to them as equals rather than as a conquered people. Having a conversational relationship with some soldiers also provided leverage for CPTers when they saw soldiers with whom they had had friendly contact abusing

---

39. Interestingly, age does not seem to make a difference to soldiers; they have related equally well to most CPT women, whether they are the ages of their sisters, girlfriends, mothers, or grandmothers.

Palestinians; the prior relationship sometimes shamed the soldiers into behaving better

As of this writing, CPT has been in Palestine twelve years, and team members still have not achieved consensus regarding the "correct" way to relate to soldiers.

Interactions with the Hebron Settlers

In 1995, when Jeff Heie, Kathleen Kern, Cliff Kindy, and Wendy Lehman set up the Hebron project, they knew that having dialogue with the settlers there would be risky, and possibly harmful to the development of close working relationships with Palestinians in Hebron. However, they also believed that the team should look for opportunities to engage in low profile dialogue with settlers to be true to their peacemaking calling.

What they did not understand at the time was the degree of comfort some of the Hebron settlers felt with spreading whopping lies. After they learned about the rumors accusing Cliff Kindy of being a Hamas activist raising money to kill Jews (see chapter 4), Kindy talked with a settler, Eli, who had previously spoken in a non-hostile way with CPTers on the street. The rumors continued. Kindy and Art Gish then spoke with Hebron settler spokesperson Noam Arnon in the winter of 1996 about the work of CPT and the pacifist beliefs of Mennonites and Church of the Brethren. They also gave him a copy of Kathleen Kern's *We Are the Pharisees,* a book that deals with the history of anti-Semitism in Christianity. Still, the lies continued, and the team largely gave up trying to relate to the Hebron settlers, choosing instead to chat with settlers from outside of Hebron who occasionally visited the city to show support for the Hebron settlers. (The Hebron settlers were often less likely to attack people on the street when these outside visitors were present.)

In 1998, settlers went on the verbal offensive to get CPT removed from Hebron, by putting out the following release:

Date: Mon, 4 May, 1998 6:12 AM EDT

HEBRON—PAST, PRESENT AND FOREVER
By David Wilder

The Jewish Community of Hebron CPT—
Squalor on the Face of the Earth[40]
May 3, 1998

CPT is the abbreviated name of Christian Peacekeeping Teams. This primarily Mennonite group ends each of its internet postings with the following signature:

"CPT Hebron has maintained a violence reduction presence in Hebron since June of 1995 at the invitation of the Hebron Municipality."

Hebron Municipality = Arab Mayor Mustepha Natsche

What does CPT really stand for? On February 18, they posted the following: "CPT calls on Christians committed to stop hostility towards Iraqi people to wear ribbons with the words FOOD NOT MISSILES inscribed on them. The ribbons will signify our faith that food for people in Iraq rather than missiles represents the deepest will of God."

Blatant, official support for Saddam Hussein.

Members of CPT have been arrested and imprisoned in the United States following violent and illegal demonstrations.

These people preach peace and non-violence. In fact, they implement the exact opposite.

Fact: Art Gish from Athens, Ohio was detained in Hebron for attempting to aid a Palestinian terrorist who had just stabbed a 14 year old Jewish girl. According to eye-witnesses, he stepped on the knife used in the attack in order to hide the evidence from the IDF.

Fact: A number of CPT members have been deported and/or denied entry into Israel. Others have been arrested for participating in violent confrontations with the Israeli Defense Forces and other Israeli security forces. . . .

What do these people spend their days doing? Adorned in red baseball hats, they walk the streets of Hebron, looking for trouble. They have even begun giving 'tours' of Hebron to unsuspecting Christian groups, spreading their venomous duplicity. History takes a back seat to falsehood—Jewish property is 'occupied Arab land.'

40. Israeli friend of the team Ya'alah Cohen, who had a background in linguistics, was visiting at the time they received the release. She frowned as she read it, saying, "I think he meant to say 'filth.'"

On April 18, 1998, THE DAY BEFORE Dov Dribin was murdered, CPT members visited Arabs living in the vicinity of Maon. They posted an article specifically mentioning and vilifying Dov Dribin.

On April 26 they posted:

"Another visitor in the hospital room shared some of the following details. Ahmed, a Palestinian from Yatta was traveling near the area last Sunday. He reported that he left the car and walked along the rocky goat paths of the grazing land. Driben and the other injured settler had already been lifted by helicopter and taken to a hospital in Beersheba. Dabadseh was lying motionless on the ground and bleeding from bullet wounds to his chest, below his right shoulder, and in his right arm. Israeli soldiers, police and settler security paid no attention to Dabadseh. Ahmed picked up the injured Dabadseh and put him on one of the many donkeys that were nearby. As he put it, "I stole him from the soldiers so I could take him to the hospital.""

On May 1, they posted "Hebron: A Short Concise Background:"

"Since the early 1980s, this quiet land of shepherds has become dotted with Israeli settlements. These settlements are built and subsidized by the government of Israel in arrogant disregard for international law, under which they are illegal. They are built on Palestinian land confiscated by the Israeli Defense Force (IDF, the army). Recently 100 families in the area were given eviction notices by the IDF to make room for more settlements. Israelis living in these settlements that look more like military camps than residential communities are well armed and given free reign by the IDF to terrorize the local Palestinians. For years the most infamous of these settlers has been Dov Dribin. We have heard countless first hand accounts of Dov's brutality, including two execution style murders in which he tied the hands of his victims before shooting them. Dov and the other settlers in this area have romantic visions of themselves as cowboys, claiming the land for Israel and exterminating the 'savages' who inhabit it.

On April 19, Dov and several others blocked a group of unarmed Palestinians who were trying to get to their fields. According to eyewitness accounts, Dov and one of the Palestinian farmers began to struggle. Dov yelled to one of his settler friends, 'Shoot him! Shoot him!' The settler shot, missed the Palestinian and killed Dov."

Of course, the libelous allegations in these reports are pure, unadulterated lies.

1. Dov Dribin never killed anyone—he was never investigated, indicted, or tried for murder.

2. Dov Dribin was shot at least five times in the chest and once in the head. He was not shot by one of his friends. He was murdered by an Arab who grabbed a weapon from one of Dov's friends. Dov was unarmed and was known not to carry a weapon.

3. Eye witnesses at the scene of the murder have given detailed accounts of what actually happened. No Arab was left lying, bleeding, in the field. All the Arabs involved fled, including those who claim to have been shot.

4. The community of Maon was legally established by the Israeli government over a decade ago. The small farm being developed by Dov Dribin and his friends is located on land officially belonging to the State of Israel. Dov and his friends were never asked, or ordered to evacuate the farm.

5. In the vicinity of the murder, there are not any 'Arab fields.'

6. International law disallows the use of murder and terrorism, the likes of which have been perpetrated against Israelis by Arabs in all parts of the country, including Judea and Samaria. CPT seems to have forgotten this.

7. International law does not prohibit Jews from living on their own land in Eretz Yisrael.

Under a guise of 'violence reduction presence' this group of anti-Semitic Israel-haters continues to incite Arabs in Hebron, and in the Hebron area, against Israelis living here. This incitement may very well have been instrumental in Dov Dribin's murder. Those responsible should be arrested and imprisoned. As for the others, it is time for Israeli security and legal forces to take all measures necessary to evict this squalor from Hebron and from Israel before they do any more damage.

In the mean time, anyone desiring to express opinions directly to CPT is invited to write to them at: cpt@igc.apc.org (Christian Peacemaker Teams, Chicago, IL).

The Chicago office was not inundated with hate mail, as the team feared it would be, after the release. However, an aide to Senator Joseph

Lieberman did request a response to the accusations. Below is a draft of that reply (italics added for clarity):[41]

> On May 3rd, David Wilder of Hebron's settler community widely distributed a release that contained some serious accusations against our organization, Christian Peacemaker Teams (CPT). We have written the following for our supporters and interested observers who have asked for clarification regarding these accusations
>
> *DW (David Wilder): "CPT Hebron has maintained a violence reduction presence in Hebron since June of 1995 at the invitation of the Hebron Municipality.*
>
> *Hebron Municipality = Arab Mayor Mustapha Natsche"*
>
> CPT: Yes, we were invited by the mayor of Hebron, and yes, his name is Mustapha Natsche. [The final draft read, "Yes, he is Arab."] As the project has developed, we have also established relationships with other groups. Presently, as part of our Campaign for Secure Dwellings, we work most closely with The Israeli Committee Against House Demolitions and The Palestinian Land Defence Committee.
>
> *DW: "What does CPT really stand for? On February 18, they posted the following: to wear ribbons with the words FOOD NOT MISSILES inscribed on them. The ribbons will signify our faith that food for people in Iraq rather than missiles represents the deepest will of God."*
>
> CPT: Yes, we believe that food for the people of Iraq is more conducive to peace than bombing is.
>
> *DW: "Blatant, official support for Saddam Hussein."*
>
> CPT: No, we do not support Saddam Hussein; we just don't want the Iraqi people to starve. We also wish to point out that Saddam Hussein's actions against Iranians, Kurds and other Iraqis were just as vile when the U.S. considered him an ally.
>
> *DW: "Members of CPT have been arrested and imprisoned in the United States following violent and illegal demonstrations."*

41. Kern would meet the aide in 1999 at a conference, when he no longer worked for Sen. Lieberman. He gave her his card and asked her to give it to team members so they could contact him if they needed assistance in the future.

CPT: Members of CPT have indeed been arrested for participating in demonstrations at the U.S. Navy's ELF [extremely low frequency] facility in northern Wisconsin, a giant antenna for signaling Trident submarines in a first strike capacity. CPTer Anne Herman, a 64 year old grandmother, is serving a six month sentence in Danbury Federal Correctional Institute because she trespassed on the School of the Americas [SOA] property to protest the SOA's training of Latin American soldiers to torture, kill and generally abuse the human rights of people in their home countries.

In the witnesses at both ELF and the SOA, the demonstrations were strictly nonviolent. Because both institutions generate the possibility or reality of enormous violence against innocent people, CPTers felt that it was worth getting arrested in the course of demonstrations there. We believe this puts us in good company with Gandhi, King, and other nameless heroes who have committed their lives to nonviolent social change.

DW: *"Fact: Art Gish from Athens, Ohio was detained in Hebron for attempting to aid a Palestinian terrorist who had just stabbed a 14 year old Jewish girl. According to eye witnesses, he stepped on the knife used in the attack in order to hide the evidence from the IDF."*

CPT: Gish came upon the scene of a stabbing and stood between angry settlers and innocent shopkeepers, thus preventing an escalation of the violence. The police took him away for his own protection, because they were afraid settlers would kill him.[42]

DW: *"Fact: A number of CPT members have been deported and/or denied entry into Israel. Others have been arrested for participating in violent confrontations with the Israeli Defense Forces [sic] and other Israeli security forces."*

---

42. Regarding the rumor about Art Gish and the knife, he wrote in an August 23, 2004 e-mail:

I first heard the story about the knife when I returned to Hebron a year later. I then went to Noam [Arnon] and told him that the story was not true. He acted like he knew nothing about it, but said that he would check with others about the story. I am not sure, but I think we never talked about that again. I have no memory of meeting David Wilder the first few years I went to Hebron. About 4 years ago I approached him on the street and he spewed out a lot of anger toward CPT. I listened. He brought up the knife story. I said I was the person who was accused and told him it was not true, and that the Torah forbids making false accusations against others . . . The subject keeps coming up. Occasionally soldiers still repeat the story to me. Shalom, Art

CPT: No one has been deported. Two have been denied entry into Israel. Several have been arrested for being present at violent confrontations and refusing to leave when asked to.

By "*other Israeli security forces*," Wilder may be referring to the private armed settler security personnel. In May 1996 when CPT members accompanied a Palestinian landowner to harvest his wheat, armed settler security at Susia settlement threatened to shoot them if they did not leave the land. CPT members have never responded violently to these or any other threats.

DW: "*What do these people spend their days doing? Adorned in red baseball hats, they walk the streets of Hebron, looking for trouble. They have even begun giving 'tours' of Hebron to unsuspecting Christian groups, spreading their venomous duplicity. History takes a back seat to falsehood—Jewish property is 'occupied Arab land.'*"

CPT: There is occupation all around us. And yes, we are often asked to give tours to international groups and introduce visitors to Palestinian families. We take them to families like the Al Atrashes who had their home demolished by the Israeli military on March 3, 1998. They meet other children who have been made homeless by Israel's home demolition policy. This is not "venomous duplicity"; this is painful truth.

DW: "*On April 18, 1998, THE DAY BEFORE Dov Dribin was murdered, CPT members visited Arabs living in the vicinity of Maon. They posted an article specifically mentioning and vilifying Dov Dribin.*"

CPT: It is a tragedy when anyone dies whether it be in military conflict, paramilitary activity, "friendly fire" or in normal everyday life activities. On April 18th, we talked with families whom Dov had threatened to kill. While we were there, Dov released his horses into the families' wheat fields. We reported that in our release. Several Israeli and Palestinian organizations who are better equipped to do so have offered to assemble various records and affidavits testifying to Driben's history of harassing his Palestinian neighbors. We would be happy to share those when they become available.[43]

DW: "Under a guise of 'violence reduction presence' this group of anti-Semitic Israel-haters continues to incite Arabs in Hebron, and in the Hebron area, against Israelis living here. This incitement may very well have been instrumental in Dov Dribin's murder. Those responsible should be arrested and imprisoned. As for the others, it is time for Israeli security and legal forces to take all measures necessary to evict this squalor from Hebron and from Israel before they do any more damage."

CPT: We would suggest that those who are concerned about these accusations contact Israelis who have worked with us and know us personally for their opinion.[44]

After several settlers had threatened to kill members of the team, particularly Kindy, in 1995, the team put out a "Statement of Conviction" that future teams adapted and recycled several times in subsequent months or years as new threats from different sources appeared.[45]

43. Much to the team's chagrin, they found out later that they had reported false information regarding Driben's murder. In a November 23, 2004 e-mail message, Mark Frey wrote:
This is what I remember: Dov was killed by a Palestinian. [A journalist, name withheld] told us she interviewed people involved and while she wrote something along the lines of what CPT reported, she said she made it up because she didn't want to write that Palestinians killed him. So much for journalistic integrity. She was probably our main source for the release we put out. We were shocked when she told us.

44. CPT Hebron, draft of e-mail to Sen. Joseph Lieberman's office.

45. The most recent use by the Hebron team, as of this writing, was in August 2001, after verbal threats and physical attacks by settlers on the team had increased, and bullets fired from the settlement of Avraham Avinu had hit the women's apartment. See CPTnet, "CPT Hebron Statement of Conviction," Aug 29, 2001.
The Colombia team adapted the statement after they learned that paramilitaries had plans to kill a member of the team. See chap. 10 and CPTnet releases: "Colombia: CPT

STATEMENT FROM HEBRON CPT TEAM

In response to death threats the Christian Peacemaker Team in Hebron, West Bank Israel has called for the rejection of the use of violence in the settlement of all disputes including punishment of anyone who would be responsible for casualties to members of the Christian Peacemaker Team itself.

On July 11, two members of the team were detained by Israeli security forces while they tried to help a Palestinian move water to his home. The team has enjoyed positive relationships with most people in the tense city of Hebron including selected members of the Israeli Defense Force. Militant Israeli settlers have accused the team members of membership in Hamas, a Muslim grouping.

The statement calls for the removal of all persons who have guns and encourages an end to all U.S. aid to Israel. The team urges all persons committed to nonviolence to take the same risks that soldiers are asked to take in order for peace to be established.

HEBRON CHRISTIAN PEACEMAKER TEAM'S STATEMENT OF CONVICTION

Two members of our team have recently received death threats from several of the local settlers here in Hebron. While we do not wish to blow these threats out of proportion, they have prompted us to consider the consequences of being attacked, injured, killed or kidnapped. We would like our wishes, as stated below, to be respected in the event such a crisis occurs.

We utterly reject the use of force to save our lives should we be caught in the middle of a conflict situation or taken hostage. In the event that we die as a result of some violent action, we reject the use of violence to punish the people who killed us.

Should our deaths come as a result of attacks by soldiers or settlers in Hebron, we ask that our deaths be regarded as no more tragic than the murders of dozens of Palestinians who have died here in the last decade. We ask that all legal nonviolent means be

---

learns of alleged paramilitary plan," Aug 12, 2002; "Colombia: Statement of Conviction" Aug 13, 2002; "Colombia: CPT calls on all armed actors," Aug 17, 2002.

The Iraq team, in 2004 also adapted portions of the statement when they returned to Baghdad, after having left because their Iraqi coworkers deemed the situation too dangerous for the team to be able to work. They reissued the statement in 2005 after Iraqi militants kidnapped two CPT delegation members, Norman Kember and Harmeet Singh Sooden, and CPTers Tom Fox (who signed the statement in 2004, a year before he was murdered) and Jim Loney. See CPTnet releases: "Iraq: Christian Peacemaker Teams to Return," and "Iraq: Christian Peacemaker Team in Iraq," Nov 29, 2005.

taken to ensure that these deaths do not continue. We ask that the government of Israel follow the principle of logical consequences. People with guns who kill other people should be removed from society for that society's protection. Whether those people are soldiers, rabbis or students should make no difference.

We ask that the United States, which has funded the militarization of this society, immediately cut all aid to Israel that is used for the manufacture and purchase of weapons and for the expansion of settlements in the West Bank and Gaza.

At present, we feel much safer walking through Palestinian neighborhoods than we do when we walk past the Israeli settlements in Hebron. However, should our lives be threatened by Palestinians, we ask that they be treated by the authorities in the same way as those authorities would treat Israelis intent on harming us. If more Palestinian blood is shed by Israelis on our account, then our deaths will indeed be in vain. We think it is possible that a collaborator or unstable individual could be encouraged by Israeli intelligence to harm us, and ask that this possibility be investigated in the event of our death. We also ask that the people who care about us look into the root causes of violence found amongst oppressed peoples struggling for liberation.

All of us who joined Christian Peacemaker Teams recognized there are certain risks inherent in this work. We believe that until people committed to nonviolence are willing to take the same risks for peace that soldiers are willing to take for violence, people will always choose violence as the most viable solution to their problems. If our deaths promote the sort of soul-searching that leads to a rejection of armed conflict characteristic of this occupation then our deaths will indeed have redemptive value. Following the central tenet of our faith, we do not hate the people who have harmed us (Matthew 5:44–45). We believe that those best able to love their enemies will ultimately emerge the victors in this bloody conflict

Cliff Kindy, North Manchester, IN
Kathleen Kern, Webster, NY
Wendy Lehman, Kidron, OH
Jeff Heie, Washington DC
Kathy Kamphoefner, N. Manchester, IN[46]

---

46. CPTnet, "CPT Hebron Defines Nonviolence," July 20, 1995 (dated July 16).

Anti-Semitism

The last week of December 1996 closed with Christian Peacemaker Congress in Washington DC issuing a call for Christians to sign the "Pledge by Christians to our Jewish Neighbors." The pledge developed as a way to deal with charges of anti-Semitism leveled at CPT because of its work in Hebron. Those who signed promised not to allow contempt for Jews and Judaism to go unchallenged. "However," concluded the pledge,

> Because of our concern for human rights, inspired by the Jewish prophets and a Jewish carpenter from Nazareth, we cannot pay the price exacted by some people for meaningful Jewish-Christian dialogue—that of silence regarding Israel's human rights abuses. We believe that silence makes us complicit in the injustices at work in Israel and Palestine.
>
> We realize our intention to confront Israeli abuses of power may mean that we cannot have harmonious relationships with some of our Jewish friends. We will mourn the loss of these relationships. We will also pray for the eventual restoration of these relationships as we pray for a just peace between Israelis and Palestinians. And

until such time as the restoration of these relationships occurs, we will celebrate those Palestinians and Israelis, Jews, Christians and Muslims who have worked diligently and self-sacrificially for justice in the Holy Land.[47]

In the next several months of 1997, approximately 150 people requested the pledge and signed it. Charges of anti-Semitism, however, would continue to dog the Palestine teams, as of this writing, for the duration of the Hebron and At-Tuwani projects, both in Palestine and when team members gave talks in their home communities. [48]

In later years, team members would have an easier time dealing with these charges because of their close working relationship with groups like the Israeli Committee Against Home Demolitions, Bat Shalom, Rabbis for Human Rights, and Ta'ayush. A large percentage (relative to the number of Jews in the world) of International Solidarity Movement volunteers (see chapter 5) was Jewish and many volunteers made their way to Hebron to visit or work with the team. When confronting charges of anti-Semitism, team members could simply refer people to the Israelis and Jewish friends with whom they had worked, celebrated, and mourned over the years.

47. CPT, "A Pledge by Christians." See also the CPT Steering Committee's CPTnet release, "A letter to our churches about anti-Semitism," Apr 27, 1999.

48. On November 22, 2004 the author posted a query on GITW asking non-North American CPTers who had worked in Hebron whether they had had similar experiences in their own countries. British citizen John Lynes responded in an e-mail the same day:

I don't suppose my reply is worth much because I always declare "Hebron is where one of my ancestors was buried: his name was Abraham." I was born a Jew, so am unlikely to attract accusations of anti-Semitism. My (Jewish) cousins understandably disapprove of my Christian/Quaker position, and working with CPT in Hebron has confirmed their worst misgivings. (Too bad, but it's fun being in the same position as the authors of the Gospels and Acts). Hebron settlers have called me a Nazi, but I can't take this seriously, being old enough (76) to remember real Nazis. [However, See Lynes's CPTnet release, "Hebron POEM: Shabbat patrol," January 21, 2006."]

In reply to your specific question, I have never been accused of anti-Semitism in the UK. The only formal complaints (including one from the Israeli Embassy!) came from people who were not actually present at my talks.

Right now I'm teaching for a month in Nova Scotia. I've experienced just one vehement attack over here on me and CPT, and have met several fellow-Quakers in Canada who have been accused, grotesquely, of anti-Semitism. So I'm inclined to suspect that charges of anti-Semitism are more likely to be met in North America than in the UK. That's sad.

More difficult than dealing with anti-Semitism charges against themselves was dealing with Palestinian friends and acquaintances that used anti-Jewish rhetoric. As some Palestinians explored why settlers, soldiers, and the Israeli public regarded them with contempt, why they destroyed their homes and confiscated their land, rhetoric from the Protocols of the Elders of Zion began to make sense to them. When the team challenged these Palestinians about their anti-Jewish rhetoric, citing Israelis and other Jews who genuinely cared about their human rights, Palestinians often would say, "Of course, some are good," but maintained that in general, Jews were greedy and did not care about human rights.

As the al-Aqsa Intifada escalated, so did the anti-Jewish rhetoric. However, many Palestinians suffering in Hebron still wanted to believe the best of people. During the siege of Arafat's compound in Ramallah, a neighbor of the team whose business curfews and closures had decimated, greeted Kathleen Kern in the market on April 3, 2002. His face was alight as he described the Jewish International Solidarity Movement volunteers entering the compound and serving as human shields. Referring to Adam Shapiro, a Jewish organizer of ISM who spoke at a press conference, the shop owner told Kern with great earnestness, "And he said many, many good things."[49]

Christian-Muslim Issues

Many CPTers experienced both meaningful Christian-Jewish dialogue and Christian-Muslim dialogue for the first time as part of their work in Palestine.

Since Islam, like Christianity, is a proselytizing religion, their friends, acquaintances, and sometimes strangers in Hebron tried to convert them. In 1995, Ahlam Muhtasib, the public relations director for the Hebron Municipality, told Wendy Lehman and Kathleen Kern, as they talked about setting up a project in Hebron, "Wouldn't it be wonderful if you became Muslims!" Others over the years would approach CPTers on the street, assure them they cared about them, and then tell them how sad they would be if the CPTers died that night and did not make it to Paradise.

---

49. CPTnet, "Hebron Update: March 26–April 3, 2002," Apr 4, 2002. The team took several months in 1995 figuring out that "the Jewish" meant soldiers and settlers in Hebron, not Jews and Israelis in general.

Demystifying the western bogeyman of Islamic fundamentalism was a positive outcome of these encounters (in general, CPTers who have worked in the West Bank encounter much more anti-Muslim rhetoric in their home countries than anti-Jewish rhetoric). The team found out through their work in Palestine that Islamic fundamentalists were not that different from Christian fundamentalists. They also gained Muslim friends who were serious about their religion but valued the Christian principles that undergirded the work of the teams in Palestine. From these friends, they learned about Islam's commitment to hospitality, mercy, and caring for the poor—values that the western media rarely mentions. Team members were "rescued" from difficult situations numerous times in the first years of the Hebron project by Muslim strangers who saw them looking bewildered on the street or in crowds and helped them as an expression of their faith.

Christian Zionism

Christians have slaughtered and persecuted Muslims and Jews in crusades, inquisitions, and pogroms for more than a thousand years.[50] Working effectively for peace in Palestine requires an awareness of this history of persecution, and this awareness has constrained members of the Palestine teams from speaking about current Jewish and Muslim practices that contribute to the violence they wish to deter.[51]

---

50. On their way to the Holy Land, European crusaders killed most of the Jews living in the Rhineland. After they reached Jerusalem, Fulk of Chartres wrote that the crusaders

> joyfully rushed into the city to pursue and kill the nefarious enemies, as their comrades were already doing. Some Saracens, Arabs, and Ethiopians took refuge in the tower of David, others fled to the temples of the Lord and of Solomon. A great fight took place in the court and porch of the temples, where they were unable to escape from our gladiators. Many fled to the roof of the temple of Solomon, and were shot with arrows, so that they fell to the ground dead. In this temple almost ten thousand were killed. Indeed, if you had been there you would have seen our feet colored to our ankles with the blood of the slain. But what more shall I relate? None of them were left alive; neither women nor children were spared. (Fulk of Chartres, "Gesta Francorum Jerusalem Expugnantium")

51. These practices include using the Holocaust to justify persecution of Palestinians and referring to militants involved in violent assaults on civilians as martyrs.

Christian Zionists, however, are another matter. Very generally speaking, Christian Zionists believe that in order for Jesus to return all Jews must return to Israel, where two-thirds will die in Armageddon and one-third will convert to Christianity (see Zechariah 13:7–9). Rather than condemning this philosophy as fundamentally anti-Semitic, the Israeli government and the Israeli settler movement have gladly received Christian Zionist money and political support. As Christians, CPTers have felt free to criticize Christian Zionism and make their church constituency aware of the threat they believe it poses for prospects of peace in the Middle East. Kathleen Kern, in particular, did significant amounts of writing on the topic between 1995 and 1997.[52]

In May 1998, a small CPT delegation attended the Christian Zionist celebration of Israel's fiftieth birthday in Orlando, Florida. They wanted to provide an alternative Christian witness to what was happening in Palestine/Israel. Probably the most encouraging news coming out of the delegation was that less than half of the expected participants attended, and they had to move into a smaller hall for the main assemblies.[53] Given the influence of the religious right on the U.S. political system in the early twenty-first century, however, Christian Zionism is still a force affecting U.S. government policy toward Israel.

Gender Issues

Traditional Arab culture observes strict gender segregation. Boys and girls attend separate public schools, and at large gatherings, men usually go into one room and the women and children into another. These realities made life difficult for the initial work of the team in the summer of 1995, since Cliff Kindy and Jeff Heie would occasionally talk about work strategies for the team with the men and Wendy Lehman and Kathleen Kern had to hear about these strategies second-hand. As time passed, however, and their Arabic language skills improved, women on the Hebron team found that spending time with the women and children was actually more interesting than remaining with the men. Palestinian women tended to

52. See Kern, "Ambassadors for the End Times"; "Crossing the Weirdness Threshold"; "Under-cover with Christian Zionists." See also CPTnet, "Blessing Israel?" Oct 28, 1997; CPTnet, "Blessing Israel? Christian Embassy Responds" Nov 2, 1997.

53. See CPTnet, "Orlando FL: Christian Alliance," Apr 30, 1998; CPTnet, Orlando FL: Worshipers Celebrate Israel," May 15, 1998.

converse more, while men on the team often found themselves lectured in Arabic at gatherings by groups of Palestinian men.

The team also found that the fact that both male and female team members lived in the same apartment in their first year was disturbing to many of their neighbors. Dr. Deborah "Misty" Gerner gave the team some money to rent an upstairs apartment for the women after these neighbors moved out, and the team found that this separation made their neighbors feel much more comfortable. Unfortunately for men on the team, the amenities of the upstairs apartment were nicer than the original apartment, and the original apartment also contained the office, so the men on the team did not have the "retreat" that the women did.

On the other hand, men did not have to deal with sexual harassment. Young women on the team were almost inevitably sexually harassed in Hebron or Jerusalem by a minority of Palestinian men who considered them fair game for groping in taxis or on the street. As time passed, they began to follow the lead of Palestinian women and take precautions not to sit next to men, when at all possible. Some women on the team also began to consider slapping someone's hand and loudly calling attention to the groping of a Palestinian male an acceptable form of nonviolent resistance.

Palestinian Violence

One of the iconic images of the al-Aqsa Intifada was a little boy in Gaza standing in front of a tank, winding up his arm to sling a rock at it. For most Palestinians, the picture symbolizes bravery in the face of overwhelming odds. Indeed, most Palestinians view throwing rocks at Israeli soldiers and settlers as nonviolent resistance, since they do not expect to kill the people at whom they throw rocks and bottles.

CPTers, Israelis, and most of the world do not perceive stone throwing as nonviolent. For CPTers, the rock throwing is especially painful because they see the excuse it gives for soldiers and settlers to shoot Palestinians—some of whom are not even participating in the clashes.

In the summer of 1995, CPTers made a few futile attempts to stand between stone throwers and soldiers, but found these attempts ineffective for a small group of people.

Interestingly, Hebron team updates did not often record why a clash was happening, although team members usually knew the reason, e.g., the signing of agreements detrimental to the residents of Hebron or the circulation of a poster depicting Mohammed as a pig writing the Quran. At times, the clashes seemed like a force of nature, the product of two storm fronts colliding.

Still more painful was the lethal violence Palestinian militants committed—especially against Israeli civilians. After the team rode the No. 18 bus in 1996, no more incidents of "predictable" terrorism occurred. The best the team could do was to publicly condemn the violence, but such condemnations seemed paltry. Sometimes the best answer team members could give for how they prevented violence against Israelis was that by diminishing the systemic brutal violence against Palestinians, they were diminishing the rage that led suicidal young men to turn themselves into human explosives.[54]

Wasta

Much of traditional Palestinian society operates on the principle of *wasta*. That is, people from humbler stations in life appeal to people with more influence, or *wasta* to get something done. CPT's accompaniment ministry has borne some similarities to this system.[55] CPTers often have the ability to intercede with soldiers or other Israeli authorities more effectively than Palestinians do. On the other hand, CPT's guidelines also prohibit CPTers from becoming involved with aid and development work so Hebron team

54. One of several examples of the team's attempt to connect and condemn both Israeli and Palestinian violence appeared in a release put out after Palestinian militants killed two soldiers and the military demolished six Palestinian homes in response: "The Christian Peacemaker Team in Hebron strongly condemns the evening of violence, along with the violence of home demolitions, and calls for both sides to end the cycle of revenge." CPTnet, "Hebron: Two Soldiers Killed," Dec 16, 2002.

55. In later years CPT began to re-evaluate its attachment to the principle of accompaniment because of its racist overtones. See the "Issues" section of the chapter on the Colombia project.

members have experienced painful moments telling Palestinian friends they do not have the *wasta* to procure funds for them.

Particularly in the case of the Campaign for Secure Dwellings families, CPTers found that their *wasta* only extended so far. The Al Atrash and the Jaber families (see chapter 4) had hundreds of people visiting them, advocating for them and donating money toward the rebuilding of their homes through the Israeli Committee Against Home Demolitions. Their high profile brought with it extra persecution from the Israeli Civil Administration, and in 1998, they asked the Hebron team not to put their names in any more releases or Urgent Actions. By that time, both families were also deeply in debt. The Israeli Committee Against Home Demolitions (ICAHD) had decided the Palestine Land Defense Committee (LDC) would allocate funds to families participating in the Campaign for Secure Dwellings and ICAHD. The LDC felt that the Al Atrashes and Jabers had already received the lion's share of the funding and wanted to distribute monies more evenly to other families. Although ICAHD and CPT pointed out that the Al Atrashes and Jabers had also suffered more than other families, they had to respect the wishes of the LDC organizers. They thus demonstrated to these families that CPT had no *wasta* even with their friends and co-workers.

Collaborating with Other International NGOs

Many Israelis, Palestinians, and internationals working for non-governmental organizations in the region take a jaundiced view of starry-eyed activists who waltz in with the intention of getting everybody to "kiss and make up." Such people do not last long, unless they acquire some humility along the way. The conflict has a way of wearing out even sober and practical activists.

Deciding which groups would make useful allies, and which might harm their work, has been an ongoing issue for Palestine team members. In general, the team has erred on the side of openness, possibly because more experienced inhabitants of the region once viewed CPT as a group of starry-eyed activists.

The issue of working with the International Solidarity Movement (see chapter 5) was of special concern. On one hand, the team had wished for years to have hundreds of people coming to the region to do mass nonviolent direct action. On the other hand, many of the volunteers who

7

Chiapas: "A Struggle of Peaceful Stings"

"We look for the good path of peace without arms. We welcome those of all faiths to join us in a path of nonviolence. We do not know where this path will lead; we are creating it as we go."[1]

—A member of Las Abejas ("The Bees") 1998

O N NEW YEAR'S DAY 1994, the North American Free Trade Agreement (NAFTA) went into effect in spite of popular opposition from Canadians, Mexicans, and Americans.[2] On the same day, a group of Mexican indigenous militants calling themselves the Zapatistas began an armed rebellion demanding equal rights for indigenous peoples.

The timing of both events was not coincidental. Article 27 of the Mexican constitution protected the rights of indigenous peoples to own their land communally, as they had for centuries. By signing the NAFTA agreement, Mexico agreed to do away with the communal land ownership of indigenous peoples, opening those lands to foreign investors. Zapatista spokesperson Subcomandante Marcos described NAFTA as a "death sentence" for indigenous peoples.[3]

1. O'Hatnick, "Las Abejas: Nonviolence on the Line." See also Lehman, "Part of the Hope of God."

2. Ralph Nader writes, "True free trade would take only one page for a trade agreement. How come there are hundreds of pages, and thousands of regulations? It's corporate-managed trade." PBS Frontline, "Ralph Nader on Free Trade."

According to Noam Chomsky, free trade pushes for "unsustainable non-development" (see title so named).

3. Landau, "Five Years After Mayan Uprising."

Marcos is a *mestizo*, i.e., from a mixed Indian/European background, as the majority of Mexicans are, but declared himself "reborn" as an indigenous person. He chose to call himself "*Sub*comandante," because the "Comandante" was the people. His ski-masked, pipe-smoking image was ubiquitous in San Cristobal de Las Casas—where the Chiapas team apartment was located.

229

The casual disposal of indigenous land rights was typical of the way the Mexican government had treated indigenous Mexicans for centuries. Although Chiapas is the Mexican state richest in natural resources, and supplied 35 percent of Mexico's electrical energy, as of 1994, 34 percent of its population had no access to electricity. Nearly 60 percent of school-age children had no access to schools; 30 percent were illiterate and only 57 percent had access to potable water. In Chenalhó county, where the Chiapas team would spend most of its time, and where more than 98 percent of the population was indigenous, the numbers were yet more stark: 75 percent had no access to electricity; 80 percent of the population were malnourished; about 85 percent earned less than the Mexican minimum wage of $3 a day.[4] Racism against indigenous peoples was considered acceptable. Until the 1960s, indigenous peoples were legally not allowed to walk on the sidewalks of San Cristóbal.[5]

The Mexican government reported that 145 people died in the twelve-day armed Zapatista uprising. Zapatistas estimated that more than one thousand died. Accepting the Bishop of San Cristóbal de Las Casas, Samuel Ruiz, as a mediator, the government then declared a ceasefire and agreed to open dialogue with the EZLN (Ejercito Zapatista de Liberacion Nacional—Zapatista Army of National Liberation). In February 1996, the government and the EZLN signed what came to be called the San Andres Accords, which upheld the civil rights of Indigenous people.[6] Over the next months, the government reneged on most of the agreements it made with the Zapatistas, sending ever-greater numbers of Mexican troops into the region and arming paramilitary groups. The EZLN withdrew from negotiations. Ruiz dismantled CONAI (Comisión Nacional de Intermediación—the National Mediation Commission) in June 1998, demanding that the federal and state governments end their violent strategies and demonstrate their willingness to resolve the conflict.

---

4. Sipaz, "Brief history of the conflict in Chiapas, 1994–2003"; Weaver, *Restoring the Balance,* 69.

5. Teresa Ortiz, who coordinated the early CPT Chiapas delegations, told Kathleen Kern about the sidewalk law in 1998. It is verified on various websites, although some say it was the 1970s before the indigenous could walk on the sidewalks. A Mexican army officer told CPTers in 1999, "These indigenous people are very, very bad just like the Indians in your country; like the Sioux." CPTnet, "Chiapas: A Meeting with the General," July 6, 1999.

6. For a complete text of the Accords, see "San Andres accords."

Two organizations with which CPT's Chiapas team would have an ongoing relationship, sought to address this violence and its underlying causes. CDHFBC (Centro de Derechos Humanos Fray Bartolomé de Las Casas), informally referred to as "Frayba," was a human rights organization affiliated with the Catholic diocese in San Cristóbal. It coordinated "peace camps" staffed by Mexican and international volunteers who provided protective accompaniment to indigenous communities living in the conflict zones and documented human rights abuses.[7] SIPAZ (Servicio Internacional para la Paz—International Service for Peace) was founded in 1995 by a coalition that grew to include over fifty groups from North America, Latin America, and Europe. SIPAZ began with the belief that solidarity groups—international organizations that had come to support the Zapatista movement and its goals—already existed. What Chiapas and Mexican society really needed was dialogue. In its Statement of Purpose, SIPAZ said it was "a response from the international community to the shared sense among many Mexican sectors that international opinion can contribute to the search for peaceful solutions, through dialogue, to the conflict."[8]

Delegations

Several people involved with the beginning of CPT had significant Latin American experience, and many of its early supporters had been active in Latin American solidarity movements during the 1980s. Training coordinator Kryss Chupp had worked for four years in Nicaragua, and Gene Stoltzfus had been part of a delegation to Nicaragua that had resulted in the formation of Witness for Peace. The 1986 "Christian Peacemaker Teams: a Study Document" (previously cited in chapter 1) attests to an organizational interest in Latin America with its proposals for possible interventions in Nicaragua, Guatemala, and Chile (see chapter 1). These interests thus made many within CPT focus on the conflict in Chiapas and propose involvement with groups who were resisting the systemic oppression of the Mexican government in Chiapas.

---

7. Enlace Civil, a secular organization affiliated with the Zapatistas, did similar work. It was run mostly by non-Indigenous Mexicans. Although team members had friendly relationships with people at Enlace Civil, they worked more closely with Frayba and Sipaz.

8. Weaver, "Restoring the Balance," 232.

Wes Hare, who had worked within the Latino community in Texas, led the first CPT delegation to Chiapas in June 1995. The delegates' goal was to explore ways to support people in Chiapas who were seeking non-violent means of attaining justice. The report from the delegation urged North Americans to examine "how they are linked to NAFTA . . . and unfair practices in Mexico." Delegation members also urged CPT to place a team in the Chiapas region. The *Signs of the Times* article about the delegation concluded with the paragraph, "Persons with Spanish language skill and experience in Latin America are invited to communicate their readiness to participate, with the understanding that any new project will require special financial support."[9]

CPTer Val Liveoak participated in the 1995 delegation and then visited Chiapas on her own in summer 1996. Working with SIPAZ, she was part of a human rights presence in northern Chiapas where between two thousand and seven thousand indigenous people had been expelled from their communal lands. In an article that appeared in the fall 1996 *Signs of the Times*, Liveoak noted that almost all the parties involved were indigenous people, and most were armed. In broad terms, one side represented PRI (Partido Revolucionario Institucional—Institutional Revolutionary Party) supporters, the part that had ruled Mexican politics for seventy years and tended to be evangelicals (as most non-Catholic Christians are referred to in Latin America). The other side represented leftist opposition PRD (Partido de la Revolución Democrática—Party of the Democratic Revolution) supporters and tended to be Catholics. One paramilitary group in particular, Paz y Justicia (Peace and Justice), had locked the Catholic chapel in one community and set up roadblocks denying its opponents entry or exit from their communities. Evangelical churches in the area had broadcast over their loudspeakers the names of Catholics and PRD members and linked them with the Zapatistas.

"As we know from Guatemala, El Salvador and other countries, accusations linking people to so-called subversive movements have been

9. "Delegation to Chiapas." In a February 23, 2005 e-mail, Wes Hare noted that the delegation had visited with MCC representatives in Mexico City, who were afraid CPT might jeopardize MCC's status in the country. However, when CPT finally set up its Chiapas project, team members had a close and positive working relationship with Eduardo Rodriguez, the MCC representative there. Martin Shupack, an MCC human rights worker with whom the team talked in Mexico City, was part of an exploratory delegation earlier that year that led to the founding of Sipaz (see above). At his urging, CPT would become a member of the Sipaz coalition. Weaver, "Restoring the Balance," 121.

widely used to undermine nonviolent work for human rights," wrote Liveoak. She concluded her article,

> Over half of Mexico's army is currently stationed in Chiapas and the U.S. is offering Mexico more military assistance, including helicopters. In the name of the anti-drug campaign, Mexican Army and police officers are being trained in the U.S. and the U.S. has placed advisors with units in the field in Mexico. Recently the U.S. Ambassador to Mexico offered military help to the government in its campaign against another rebel group, the EPR (Popular Revolutionary Army.) With the political, economic, religious and ideological pressures, the tolerance for dissent has greatly diminished. The situation is ripe for violence, and one that calls out for active nonviolent change to avert a bloodier uprising and even more oppressive response by those in power.[10]

The reports and articles that came out of four subsequent delegations in 1996 and 1997 record an ever-deteriorating human rights situation. Mexican immigration authorities prevented an April 1997 delegation from traveling to a remote village in the state of Oaxaca where CPT had heard that torture and arbitrary detentions were "commonplace." The Mexican government then forced the delegates to leave the country under "Voluntary Departure Status," saying that by inquiring about conditions in Mexican prisons, they had violated the terms of their tourist visas.

Three weeks after a December 1997 CPT delegation returned home to report on increased displacement of indigenous peoples, paramilitaries slaughtered forty-five pacifist Christians who called themselves Las Abejas at the Acteal refugee camp.

LAS ABEJAS (THE BEES)

> Las Abejas explain their name in this way: "We came together in 1992 because we are a multitude and we want to build our house like the honeycomb. Here we all work collectively, and we all enjoy the same thing, producing honey for everyone. So we are like the bees in one hive. We don't allow divisions, and we all march together with our queen [reina], which is the reign [reino] of God, although we knew from the beginning that the work would be slow but sure." There is another interpretation of the symbolism

---

10. Liveoak, "Low Intensity Civil War in Chiapas." Liveoak worked as a nurse in El Salvador for four years.

of the bee: "It is a very small animal that stings. Our struggle is a struggle of peaceful stings."[11]

As tension between religious groups in Chiapas increased, the Ecumenical Bible School in San Cristóbal de Las Casas sought to bridge the gaps. Both Protestant and Catholics spent ten years under the auspices of the school translating the Bible into Tzotzil, one of approximately thirty Mayan languages. In 1992, a group of Protestant and Catholic Mayans formed a Bible study group using the new translation. Their understanding of the Gospel led them to conclude that Jesus would not support any sort of violence. In 1992, five members of this Bible study group from the community of Tzajalchen—in the municipio (county) of Chenalhó— were arrested and falsely charged with murder. Several hundred people in the community began a campaign that included a pilgrimage, a vigil at the prison, disseminating information, prayers, and penance. Because the press and government had claimed that the Mayans organizing this campaign belonged to PRI, the group decided to begin calling themselves "Las Abejas" (The Bees) for the reasons mentioned above.[12]

After they successfully freed their companions, Las Abejas decided to continue as a justice-promoting organization. When the armed Zapatista uprising began in January 1994, they decided to promote peace and dialogue. In their history, they wrote,

> When the armed uprising of the Zapatista Army of National Liberation (EZLN) happened, we didn't know who they were nor why they fought, nor against whom they fought. Eight days later, we found out that they were against the poverty of Mexico, for national liberation, and for the ten demands: land, housing, food, health, education, independence, freedom, democracy, justice and peace. Then we realized that we the bees were in agreement with their demands. But we are civil society, pacific and not armed and

11. Sipaz, "Las Abejas (the Bees) Continue to Fly."

12. The dispute was between a brother and his sisters, who disagreed about dividing their land inheritance equally. The brother sought support from a paramilitary group affiliated with PRI, and the sisters sought support from the Peasant Legal Solidarity organization. Ultimately the conflict escalated to the point where the brother and the paramilitaries ambushed the women's husbands. Members of the Bible Study group counseled the two groups to reconcile and then provided aid to those injured and killed in the shooting. Four of the five men arrested were evangelicals, which the *Abejas* would point to when people tried to divide the conflict along religious lines. Las Abejas of Chenalhó, "Our word to the UN" and "History of the birth of 'Las Abejas.'"

that we are not in agreement with the armed path but instead with the political and peaceful path.[13]

By 1997, tensions in the district escalated to the point where paramilitaries, who tended to be PRI supporters, organized to "exterminate" those whom they viewed as Zapatista sympathizers, which included the Bees. Rather than take up arms for personal defense, the Bees displaced themselves to safer areas. The paramilitaries then burned their homes and confiscated their crops.

The Bees began holding special days of prayer and fasting, asking God to end the violence. On December 22, 1997, some members of the Bees who had been forced to work for PRI supporters (called Priistas) in the village of Los Chorros escaped and told the Bees in Acteal that the Priista paramilitaries were planning to attack them. The Bees in the camp began to pray and fast to hold back the attack.

Meanwhile, according to one report, the paramilitaries had received arms from the Mayor of Chenalhó a week earlier. They rejected the 22 caliber guns he offered, taking automatic rifles instead. They allegedly told the mayor, "We only want guns that kill a lot of people."

The morning of the massacre, the paramilitaries gathered in the village of Pechiquil to coordinate the assault. Before leaving for Acteal, the paramilitaries allegedly prayed for protection in the Presbyterian church.

Around 11:00 a.m., the Bees in the Acteal refugee camp heard gunshots. The catechist in the chapel where they were praying calmed the group, but then the bullets came into the chapel and the people began to run. An eleven-year-old girl reported later that she had recognized some of the attackers as residents of the towns of Pechiquil, La Esperanza and Acteal. Some wore black, and others, the ones who appeared to be in charge, were wearing military uniforms. She saw them kill the catechist and shoot women and children in the back. For the next several hours, the paramilitaries hunted down and killed those who fled. Some sliced the breasts off the dead women with machetes. According to one report, paramilitaries allegedly said they needed to "finish off the seed," and opened the wombs of the pregnant women, removed the fetuses and passed them around from machete to machete. Despite pleas from various church leaders in the Diocese that they intervene to halt the killings, scores of Chiapas state police stood on the road above the camp and refused to stop

13. Cited in Weaver, "Restoring the Balance," 87.

the paramilitaries. Their only intervention was preventing people living in the nearby Zapatista camp from coming to aid of the Abejas.

After they had looted the refugees' possessions (stored in the church to protect them from the rain), the paramilitaries went back to their villages to celebrate. In Pechiquil, they killed a cow for a feast, and elders of the village conducted a ceremony of Thanksgiving to God for having kept paramilitaries safe.[14]

The massacre of pacifists as they prayed shocked Mexican civil society and the rest of the world. Most Mexicans thought that their country could not descend into the genocidal brutality they had witnessed in El Salvador and Guatemala during the 1970s and 1980s. Acteal served as a wake-up call.

Six days after the massacre, the Vicar of the San Cristóbal de Las Casas, Oscar Salinas, preached the a homily tying the slaughter of Las Abejas to the slaughter of children in Bethlehem ordered by King Herod (see Matthew 2:16–18):

> Today we celebrate the Day of Holy Innocents . . . An innocent is literally "one who does no harm,"—those of Bethlehem, because they were under two years old; these of Acteal (Chenalhó'), some not yet even born, others, already grown adults, because they had made a decision to be innocent, not to harm, as a form of struggle.
>
> . . . They said, as many other Mexicans have: "We are in absolute agreement with each and every cause in the Zapatista struggle. All the same, we cannot agree with the chosen method of taking up arms." So when the Zapatista movement asked of the nation's civil society, "If there is another way, show it to us," they, Las Abejas took it on as a challenge. They said, "We are prepared to die for this cause, but not to kill."
>
> . . . They have been unjustly accused of being "neutral" in this polarized society because of their nonviolent stand. Today we must shout: By no means are they neutral! Their option is very clear and radical . . . A group like this, armed only with love and truth is the most dangerous and threatening to defenders of the system because it most effectively unmasks their injustice.

14. Ibid., 61–62; Garza, Hernandez, Figueroa, and Olivera, "En Acteal Micaela oyo que gritaban"; Cuevas, "Queremos de las Armas"; Las Abejas of Chenalhó, "Our word to the UN" and "History of the birth of 'Las Abejas.'" The reference to police preventing the Zapatistas from helping the Abejas is from the author's memory of conversation with an Abejas leader, confirmed by Wendy Lehman in a March 2, 2005, e-mail.

These brothers and sisters of ours, like the Suffering Servant of Yahweh, decided to suffocate with their own blood the brewing spiral of violence that is unleashed in our state. Interceding they died. Fasting they died. This was the death they chose, "the Holy Innocents of Acteal." With them has been planted the seed of peace.[15]

Thousands of Mexicans and internationals subsequently responded to the call from the Diocese to come stay in the camps to provide protective accompaniment for the Las Abejas.

The massacre also shocked CPT and its constituency—particularly those who had met the Bees during a December 1997 CPT delegation. Rusty Curling, who would go through training in December 1998–January 1999 wrote of "falling in love" with the Bees and their profound faith:

For several days after the killing, I could hardly speak. I broke down and wept several times while leading worship and preaching in the following weeks.

My church struggled to understand the profound pain I was feeling, but it was hard for them to understand why their deaths would cause the pastor of a small church in western Ohio so much pain. I eventually became numb, not allowing myself to feel anything. This contributed greatly to a rift between me and my congregation, eventually leading to my leaving.[16]

15. Lehman, "Prepared to die, but not to kill." Duane Ediger provided the translation of Salinas' sermon. Salinas would become an important contact for CPT's Chiapas team.

16. CPTnet, "Mourning and healing in Acteal," Mar 26, 2001. In this reflection, Dinkins-Curling writes of what it was like to attend a memorial mass for the victims on February 22, 2001. He concludes:

At the end the worship leader passed out the 45 candles burning in front of the altar. We arrived at the grave and a time of prayer was announced. As we knelt on the concrete floor, I began to sob uncontrollably. I set my candle on the floor and went to the other end of the room as quickly as I could, leaning against a window and weeping again. A little girl looked up at me with both compassion and puzzlement. It was as if her eyes said, "Why do you weep so? We are healing our wounded hearts here. Is it not time for your heart to heal as well?" And so it was time for my healing. Almost instantly, my bitter tears of sorrow mixed with sweet tears of release, even joy.

There is still a part of my heart that is broken, and I suppose that will never go away. Should our hearts not be broken over the suffering, oppression and death of these people, and many, many others? Yet, I

Although the massacre brought the world's attention to Chiapas and caused widespread sympathy for Las Abejas, the situation in Chiapas continued to deteriorate. Thousands more indigenous people displaced themselves into refugee camps to escape attacks by paramilitaries. By June 1998, the Mexican daily *La Jornada* estimated that eighteen thousand people had been displaced in Chiapas. The Mexican military also began pouring troops into the state—some estimated the number as high as seventy thousand, or one-third, of the entire Mexican army.[17] Many people believed that the massacre had given the government the excuse it wanted to invade Chiapas for reasons of "security."

As the crisis deepened, CPT sent two more delegations in Spring 1998 with somewhat firmer intentions of setting up a project there, despite the fact that doing so would stretch its resources: not only had CPT just met the goal it had set for itself in 1993 for twelve full-time Corps people, but also the home demolition crisis in the Hebron area had peaked.

After the May 24–June 4, 1998, delegation ended, CPT full-timers Cliff Kindy, Wendy Lehman, and Kathleen Kern and reservists Pierre Gingerich and Esther Ho stayed on for the next month scoping out the possibilities for setting up a project.[18] As they met with SIPAZ and other

---

hear the music coming from the church now, not music of mourning and sadness, but dance music.

Thank you, Lord Jesus, for the profound example of faith and joy these people have become for me. I think I will go down and dance now.

See also Duane Ediger's CPTnet reflection, "Dallas, TX: An Open Letter to 'the Bees,'" Jan 8, 1998. Ediger also wrote a "Reflection for the Body of Christ" five days after the massacre that appeared in a December 27, 1997 CPTnet release. In it he connected the situation in Chiapas with the broader geopolitical situation:

Just as the body of Christ unites followers throughout the world, the coordination of those arrayed against the faithful has broad connections. The military commander of the Northern zone of Chiapas (including the massacre site) recently returned from official assignment in Israel, a country known for sophisticated "counterinsurgency" training. Just two weeks before the massacre, FBI personnel entered a training relationship with police from the conflictive states of Chiapas, Oaxaca and Guerrero.

17. Sipaz. "Summary: The Uncertainty of Peace."

18. The previous delegation, led by Duane Ediger and Wendy Lehman, had recommended that CPT send "two or more people for up to six months" to document human rights abuses, write reports for CPTnet and build relationships. Because the Northern Zone at that point was seeing the most paramilitary activity, they recommended travel-

human rights organizations in and around San Cristóbal de las Casas (SCLC), they realized that something they could bring Chiapas was "deportability."

In 1997, the Mexican government had begun a campaign of deporting foreigners with pro-Zapatista sympathies and NGOs who had established a longer presence in Chiapas had become extremely nervous. As was the case for CPTers working in the West Bank, internationals usually had only a tourist visa option when they entered Mexico. The Mexican government decided that any human rights observation done by people on tourist visas constituted "interfering in the internal affairs of Mexico." As international workers repeatedly told the 1998 delegation that they could not do the work they wanted to because they feared deportation, the CPTers on the May and June 1998 exploratory project began to think immigration issues was one area that they could push the envelope. CPTers could travel to places that the Mexican government had forbidden internationals to enter. If they did so and Mexico deported them, little harm would result, because they did not have the deep ties in the community, and local people were not depending on them. The people at Frayba, in particular, were excited by the prospect of challenging the Mexican government's expulsion of foreigners in court.

Another, more significant outcome, of the May and June exploratory project was a closer working relationship with Las Abejas and the Catholic diocese. For the first time, a team of CPTers would be working closely with a Christian group who had a profound commitment to nonviolence and to Christian spiritual disciplines such as prayer, fasting, and pilgrimage.[19]

In their conversations with the Bees during May and June, the exploratory delegation learned that 850 of them, accompanied by all four thousand Abejas, planned to leave the refugee camps and return to the villages of Ybeljoj and Los Chorros. They had arrived at this decision, after three days of fasting and prayer because of water and food shortages in the camps. CPT publicized their letter to the international community in which they asked for accompaniment, food, tools, and household goods

---

ing there, but proceeding with caution. CPT, "Christian Peacemaker Team Report."

19. When the seven-member exploratory group met with Diocesan Vicar, Father Oscar Salinas, he told them that perhaps CPT could undertake some nonviolence training and education for The Abejas. Team members, taken aback, told him that The Abejas seemed to have a firm grasp of the subject matter already. Salinas responded by saying that if CPT taught them about other nonviolent movements The Abejas might feel less alone.

to rebuild their lives. The Abejas asked CPT to include in the appeal, "It is important to say this is an initiative of Las Abejas because the government has not helped or protected us. Therefore, we must take the initiative to return to our home and heritage."

On the day in question, paramilitaries from Los Chorros (some of whom had participated in the Acteal massacre) threatened to harm the Abejas and take Bishops Samuel Ruiz and Raoul Vera hostage. Las Abejas thus decided to walk only part of the way back to the two villages, turning the journey into a pilgrimage of sorts. They walked in three lines that stretched for perhaps half of a mile holding a string that surrounded the entire group. Hundreds of children led the way singing; musicians played an accordion and guitar, and periodically the group waved white peace flags together.[20]

The majority of the Bees would not return to their villages until autumn of 2001. However, in anticipation of that return, Pierre Gingerich, Cliff Kindy, Wendy Lehman, and Esther Ho did the necessary logistics to set up the Chiapas project after this symbolic 1998 pilgrimage.

June 1998–December 1999

As was the case with the Haiti project, most of the team's work in Chiapas would involve simply being present with people. While team members were in the refugee camps [usually Acteal and X'oyep (pronounced show-YEP), with shorter stays in Nuevo Yibeljoj, and Tzaljachen] the daily routine included breakfasts, lunches, and suppers of tortillas and beans with no seasonings. (After a while, team members began bringing bottles of condiments with them to the campo.) In between meals, team members visited with camp residents, worked on learning Tzotzil, played volleyball and basketball with the men, and participated in the "security belts" around the camps. These belts—in both the Abejas and Zapatista camps—consisted of unarmed indigenous people, mostly women, who

20. See CPTnet releases: "Chiapas, Mexico: The Return," June 11, 1998; "Chiapas, Acteal, Chenalhó: An Urgent Call," June 14, 1998; "Chiapas, Mexico: Urgent Action," June 18, 1998; "Chiapas Mexico: The Bees walk freely," June 26, 1998. In an October release, the team noted that The Abejas were in the process of working on a document that would specify the conditions necessary for them to return to their communities. They planned to present the document to the Mexican government and ask them to comply with these conditions. The official government position at the time was that the communities were perfectly safe for The Abejas to return to and they could come back whenever they wanted. CPTnet, "Chiapas, Mexico: Update on the Bees," Oct 9, 1998.

surrounded the entire perimeter of the camps to keep out soldiers. An iconic photograph of the struggle in Chiapas was taken by Pedro Valtierra of a thirteen-year-old Abeja girl, black hair swinging below her waist physically pushing back a soldier armed with an automatic weapon who was trying to enter the Bees' camp in X'oyep.[21] Team members regularly visited the military bases near Acteal and X'oyep as well.

Team members also participated in the daily worship lives of the community, especially the afternoon prayers at 5:00 and they attended daylong community meetings during which the Abejas usually supplied someone who could translate Tzotzil into Spanish for them. Occasionally men in the camps let CPTers help build houses.

In San Cristóbal de Las Casas (abbreviated in team communications as SCLC), team members met with other NGOs and Mexican immigration officials, and wrote releases. They also gardened, did their laundry—which usually had gained a thick layer of mud during the time in the campo (a Spanish word that refers to rural areas), and took Spanish lessons.

Trips between SCLC and the campo were often projects in themselves, because CPTers and other internationals had to pass through immigration checkpoints. X'oyep and Tzaljachen, at the time that the CPT project opened, were reachable only on foot, so time in the campo often involved many hours of hiking between refugee camps.[22]

Challenging Immigration 1998–1999

After Ho, Kern, and Lehman returned to the United States, Gingerich and Kindy found a house to rent in SCLC. When CPTer Lynn Stoltzfus joined them, the three men went to Acteal on July 22, 1998, to participate in the memorial service that took place the 22nd of every month.[23] As they returned to SCLC on July 23, soldiers stopped them at a checkpoint and told them that they had "broken the law" by going to Acteal. The soldiers then issued an order for Kindy and Gingerich to report to an immigra-

21. The picture appears in Weaver's dissertation, "Restoring the Balance," 1.

22. Summary of e-mails from Sara Reschly, Claire Evans, Scott Kerr, Jerry Stein, Kryss Chupp, Carl Meyer, and Lynn Stoltzfus sent March 3–6, 10, and 22, 2005. Sickness and trips to the camp latrines also figured heavily in these e-mails.

23. Chiapas CPTers found these memorial services profoundly moving. At each one, participants lit forty-five candles—one for each victim—and let them burn out and melt onto the ground. Pierre Shantz would observe these monthly memorial services in Hebron, as well, letting the candles burn out on the stone floors of the team's apartment.

tion hearing in SCLC on Monday, July 27. Since the Mexican authorities inevitably deported foreigners who appeared before Immigration, most internationals either never showed up at the mandated time or simply left the country. Gingerich and Kindy decided instead to confront the issue. They asked a human rights lawyer from Frayba to accompany them and an Associated Press reporter.

Additionally, they asked the CPT constituency to contact their legislators. When the two men appeared on Monday at Immigration in SCLC, the officer interrogating them had a pile of faxes on his desk. "You have a lot of friends," he told them.

After three hours of grilling, during which Kindy told the officer that Americans had much to learn from the Abejas about the theory and practice of nonviolence, the officer told Kindy and Gingerich to return the next afternoon. At that time, the officer informed them that their activities had fallen within the boundaries of what was permitted by a tourist visa.[24]

Team releases from the summer and fall of 1998 reveal the anxiety that the Chiapas team experienced when traveling from SCLC to the campo. The Chiapas CPTers traveled in the very early hours of the morning, hoping to get in or out of Chenalhó County before the Mexican military set up their checkpoints.[25] Despite their precautions however, Lynn Stoltzfus and Anne Herman received citations in September 1998.

By February 1999, the team decided to confront the Mexican military's intimidation of "foreigners"—which included Mexicans from other parts of the country who were in Chiapas as an expression of solidarity with the indigenous peoples. Team members began openly telling Mexican security personnel where they were actually going in the campo and refusing to show their passports to Mexican soldiers, who had no legal authority to demand that CPTers present them. Instead, CPTers would offer their bags to the soldiers so they could search them for weapons and drugs—the ostensible purpose for the military checkpoints.

24. CPTnet, "Chiapas: CPTers threatened," July 25, 2005; CPTnet, "Chiapas, Mexico: CPTers permitted to remain," July 28, 1998.

25. For example, see CPTnet "Chiapas Mexico: Small Miracles," Aug 3, 1998. When asked why the team became less confrontational re: immigration toward the end of 1999, William Payne responded in a March 12, 2005 e-mail: "My recollection was that we had both things in mind: one, that part of our work was challenging the threats of deportation, but that there were other valuable parts to our work as well, so we didn't want that one to take over more than was necessary."

Scott Kerr in an interview with Paul Neufeld Weaver said,

> All the foreigners ... say they're going to Pantelhó, which is a near-by city, to buy artisans' crafts. Well if you've ever been to Pantelhó, there's no artisans' crafts to buy there. You know. That's the line. I mean immigration knows what they're doing. They may not know exactly where they're going, but they know what's happening. And CPT has really taken the initiative in telling them what's going on and to try and confront those things, and the soldiers as well, the soldiers will ask for passports and IDs, and CPT has taken the pol-icy we're not going to show them these things, because they don't have the right to do that. That's the way that [they try to restrict] the travel of human rights observers.
>
> So, if we tell the soldier no, they can't have our passport, hope-fully the next time a foreigner comes through who's not a CPTer they won't ask them ... If you have a law that says you can't have internationals visit Acteal, that's fine. But then we're more than willing to walk through that process with you, go through citation hearings and we're going to expose these laws to the world, and to other Mexican groups, to Mexican civil society, to the Mexican press, to our group of supporters. Because if your laws are just, you should not be ashamed of these laws.[26]

By 1999, the team developed a strategic routine for when soldiers stopped them at checkpoints. They informed immigration in advance about their plans, refused to show documents to soldiers or give any information about the people they were visiting, and engaged in active dialogue with soldiers and immigration officials. A March 1, 1999, re-lease recounts CPTers lighting candles at each checkpoint where soldiers stopped them and inviting soldiers and immigration officials to join a circle of prayer.[27]

Although other internationals feared that CPT's confrontational stance would make traveling more difficult for them, their fears were nev-er realized. Despite some team members receiving immigration citations and appearing before Mexican immigration authorities over the next few years, no CPTer was ever expelled from the country.

Director Gene Stoltzfus told Paul Neufeld Weaver,

> [In Chiapas] the NGO culture said, "Be careful, and never tell them what you're doing." And the most important decision that

26. Weaver, "Restoring the Balance," 127.

27. CPTnet, "Chiapas, Mexico: Light into the darkness." March 1, 1999.

we made in CPT was that we're no longer going to be careful, we're going to tell them everything we're doing, and we're going to be brutally honest, and we're going to do it in the spirit of prayer and confrontation. . . . From that time on we could talk about the work of nonviolence with much more boldness. We could enter into conversations with the Abejas and others about how to support the work of nonviolence with much more candor. We could initiate many projects in nonviolence. We could test out ideas, we could do a lot of things, that we couldn't do before. And that is sort of the paradigm of the contradiction that we always live with in CPT, where the dominant development philosophy of our global culture, which informs the work of peacemaking, sets limits on the things which you as a person from the outside should be able to do.

In August 2001, Weaver asked a Mexican immigration officer why he had expelled scores of other internationals but not CPT. The officer, after complaining about CPT's public witnesses at military bases, told Weaver,

I have personally greatly respected CPT's attitude because we know that they do not interfere in favor or against. They do not counsel the people to rebel against the government. Because they dedicate their efforts to prayer and fasting. They approach the permissible limit. . . . Ideology and faith do not have borders, but countries do, for better or worse, that is what allows us to live in harmony.[28]

Public Worship and Witnesses 1998–1999

Perhaps no CPT project has put out so many releases about public worship as the Chiapas project did.[29] In the camps, the Abejas had daily times of worship and prayers, and every month on the 22nd, they had a service commemorating victims of the massacre which internationals and people from all over Mexico attended. Most of the public witnesses taken

28. Weaver, "Restoring the Balance," 127–29.

29. However, when the author asked Chiapas veterans whether Chiapas was the most "spiritual" project they had worked on, only one, Scott Kerr, thought that was the case. (See e-mails sent by Kerr, Sara Reschly, Matthew Bailey-Dick, William Payne, and Erin Kindy, dated March 15, 2005, and the e-mail from Lynn Stoltzfus dated March 30, 2005.) Others said they had equally spiritual experiences working in Hebron, Colombia, and in North American indigenous communities. Payne, in a March 16, 2005 follow-up e-mail, speculated that the releases covered spiritual matters so heavily because there was not much else to write about.

on by the Bees also had a strong spiritual component—which might be one reason why spiritual matters figured so heavily in the Chiapas team's releases.

In a May 1999 reflection, Pierre Shantz wrote of his first participation in a 22nd memorial service:

> In this particular service, they honored the children who survived the massacre and brothers and sisters of the 17 children who died. The children did a processional at the beginning, and midway through the service the priest invited the children to come forward again and they where given a special blessing. In the front of the altar there were 45 candles lit, one for each of the persons killed. Every time the wind would blow one of them out, someone would light it again keeping that person's memory alive....
>
> Towards the end of the service, the name of each person killed was called out. As each name was called, the congregation responded, "She is living with us! He is living with us!"[30]

On the second anniversary of the massacre, Claire Evans described a worship service in which more than two thousand people participated. Mock paramilitaries with wooden rifles set off firecrackers that symbolized the destruction the paramilitaries had caused, and mock "public security" police in dark suits fled after them. Then, small white flags waved by hundreds of people on the hillside and the priests in the front appeared, signaling hope, strength, and new life. The Choir of the Displaced began singing.

Evans reported feeling a little jolted by the feasting and dancing with five bands that followed the three-hour Mass. As she thought about what the people were celebrating, she wrote,

> Two years ago, Acteal was unknown to the world. The people were in fear, having fled violence in their home communities. There were no internationals present for protection or documentation; no photos recorded the magnitude of the slaughter. Today, hundreds of people were waving white flags on the sun-filled hillside. Many foreigners were the eyes and ears of the world. Music, dancing, and feasting testified to the resilience of life. Words of hope were proclaimed from the pulpit. Not to say that the massacre was good. Most assuredly not! It was a tremendous individual and commu-

---

30. CPTnet, "Chiapas: Reflections on Acteal service," May 6, 1999.

nal tragedy that still scars the people of Acteal. But God has a way
of turning sorrow into joy, death into resurrection.[31]

Because the Abejas had an intensely spiritual lifestyle, the public
witnesses they developed in coordination with the Chiapas team had
liturgical dynamic. The first major witness in which the Chiapas team
participated occurred during Holy Week 1999. The Abejas wanted to
call attention to the increased militarization of Chiapas and Chenalhó
County in particular. The Mexican army had established twenty military
bases in the county and two thousand soldiers—one soldier for every
twelve inhabitants. These "Civic Action" or "Social labor" camps offered
medical and dental care, free meals, haircuts, and a host of other services
to community residents as ostensible proof that the military was there for
the well being of the indigenous residents. Few residents, however, had
any illusions as to their real purpose.

On Palm Sunday, March 29, 1999, the team and the Abejas prayed
at the foot of three Mayan crosses located on a ridge between the refugee
village of X'oyep (Show-YEP) and a nearby military base. When soldiers
interrupted the worship circle, the Abejas asked them to leave.

"Since you are not angels, you have no right to be here by our sacred
crosses," they said. As soon as the prayer service concluded, the soldiers
went back to the base. Over the next week, team members and Abejas
continued to hold vigils and fast—and on Maundy Thursday wash each
other's feet—in a small hut at the entrance to the military base. Those
participating in the vigils prevented a supply truck from entering the base
and prayed inside a small building ("casita") erected by the military as
an observation post. On Good Friday, the worship service and Stations
of the Cross procession connected Jesus' arrest and crucifixion to events
that had happened to the refugees in X'oyep. After soldiers refused the
group entry into the casita, on Holy Saturday the team and sixteen Abejas
surrounded it, reflected on Scripture, sang, and prayed. The soldiers left
and the group holding the vigils proceeded down the hill into the Social
Labor camp. When soldiers stopped the procession partway down, one of

31. CPTnet, "Chiapas, Mexico: They will be called 'Oaks of Justice,'" Dec 22, 1999
(dated Dec 27, 1999). For examples of how the Abejas connected their suffering with
the Catholic liturgical calendar, see CPTnet releases: "Chiapas, Mexico: Hundreds commemorate Acteal," Nov 25, 1998; "Chiapas, MX: St. Peter the Displaced," July 17, 1999;
"Chiapas, Mexico: Prayer Alert," Oct 28, 1999; "Chiapas: Tears and Coca-Cola," Nov 6,
1999.

the Abejas told about the action in January 1998, when women and children had pushed the soldiers away, preventing the military from setting up base even closer to the community.

On Easter Sunday, the vigilers broke their fast at 6:00 a.m. and then proceeded to the observation post. After worshiping for an hour there, they once again entered the Social Labor camp. Soldiers asked where they were going, but made no attempt to stop them. The Abejas planted corn—sacred to the Mayan people—there without interference by the military, and the team then left X'oyep, accompanied by its lawyer who made passing through the Immigration checkpoints relatively painless. On May 31, several Abejas, team members, and a CPT Pentecost delegation traveled back to the base to weed and water the corn, now two feet high. Team member Lisa Martens wrote about the event:

> Abeja women filled the entire road as we all paused to continue the ancient tradition, murmuring individually and simultaneously to God; calling for justice in Mexico. Soon after beginning, a green military jeep roared up and halted directly behind the women, who refused to be interrupted. A high-ranking official, flanked by two subordinates stepped out of the vehicle to the immediate salutes of nearby soldiers. The three paused for a moment; knowing that on either side of the narrow road were steep declines. Finally, stepping slowly, and brushing the skirts of unflinching, praying Abeja women, they found their way to the checkpoint.
>
> Three minutes later, a man leading a donkey piled high with firewood came from the opposite direction. He also wanted to pass, and in seconds, Las Abejas gave him more than enough space to comfortably continue along his way.[32]

The Feast of the Holy Innocents (slaughtered by Herod, see Matthew 2:13–18) on December 28, 1999, provided the inspiration for a fifteen-mile pilgrimage through Chenalhó County. Four CPTers and one thousand Abejas stopped at four military installations in the county and called

32. See CPTnet releases: "Chiapas, Mexico: Palm Sunday Prayers," Mar 29, 1999; "Chiapas Update: March 30–April 10," April 14, 1999; "Chiapas Update: May 23–June 3, 1999" June 18, 1999; "Chiapas: Slow Earthquakes," June 29, 1999. Three CPTers also accompanied six Abejas to the corn patch on April 29, 1999. They lit a candle and for twenty minutes "prayed that the transformation of the base into a place of peace might continue." See CPTnet, "Chiapas Update: April 27–May 3, 1999," May 12, 1999. On September 17, 1999 seventy-five Abejas, along with Anne Herman and William Payne, saw the corn was gone and planted more. See CPTnet, "Chiapas Update: September 5–29, 1999," Nov 11, 1999.

on soldiers to "transform their hearts from ways of war and injustice to ways of life and peace."

At the Majomut "Social Labor" camp near Acteal, a spokesperson for Las Abejas read the following release:

Pilgrimage for the Renewal of Our Hearts
God said to the people: Come, let us walk together in the light of the Lord. (Is. 2:5)

Holy Ground of the Martyrs of Acteal, Chenalhó, Chiapas
December 28, 1999

FEAST OF THE HOLY INNOCENTS

To the national and international press; To all the peoples of the world—brothers and sisters, indigenous, peasants, workers, teachers, professionals, homemakers, Mexican Army, elected officials, business people, students, criminals, and even drug traffickers; To all Chiapans and other Mexicans, from the poorest to the wealthiest:

We remember on this day the Feast of the Holy Innocents. From the moment of Jesus' birth during the reign of King Herod, he was persecuted. Herod ordered the death of many children because he was thought that the Savior Jesus would be among them (Mt. 2:13–16).

Today God speaks to us. This pilgrimage is for the renewal of our hearts, so that there will be no more deaths of innocents. How many innocents have died, how many displaced people have abandoned their belongings and suffered throughout the last 2,000 years of history.

Our friends, today we look back over our lives and acknowledge our attitudes and our actions. We remember that we are all children of the same God, that we are brothers and sisters, and that each of us is but a sojourner living on borrowed time in this world so that we may work for good and not evil. We are called to work for peace (Mt. 5:9). Let us be builders of truth, not violence, of peace, not of hostility.

We believe that peace is only possible through dialogue. We cannot talk of peace and want war. We cannot seek reconciliation and provoke violence with the presence of weapons. We cannot live in a land of justice while militarization increases. We want to plant and harvest the fruit of our mother earth in peace, free from military camps.

Let each of us do what we ought to do. Let us renew our hearts; let us be born again as Jesus said in John 3:3. It is time for us to correct each other with respect in the presence of friends and colleagues regardless of where we are from, our religion, our political party, our language, color, people or culture.

By the Civil Society Organization Las Abejas

After planting corn on the base, members of Las Abejas surprised the soldiers by handing them lighted candles and a leaflet. The text of the leaflet was a direct challenge to an assertion made by an officer at the Majomut camp to CPTers that the local people appreciated the role of the military in keeping peace and providing social services:

Mexican Soldier:

We ask you to join us in learning to walk in the way of life, of justice, of right and of peace. Together let us create the pathway that leads to the house of our Lord God. Our brothers and sisters, we have asked for the demilitarization of the region but the government does not listen.

You should not learn to think like them. That's why we are asking you now to leave this military camp. This is not the only way to make a living. There are many kinds of work to achieve a just and pleasant life. The evil spirit, the spirit of war, of injustice, of violence will be quite happy with us if we don't do what is necessary for peace to come to our land. Think hard about this. While we live, we have the opportunity to build the Reign of God.

You have walked through our region. You are familiar with our area. You know that there is no peace while you walk around provoking fear with your weapons. You have introduced weapons to the paramilitaries. With your checkpoints, you have harassed us and those who come to visit us. How does your heart feel?

Don't shed the blood of your brothers in the land because when you kill a person, you are killing God.

Civil Society Las Abejas

Accompanied by guitar, accordion, and song, the procession continued to three other bases in Yabteclum, Las Limas, and the town of Chenalhó, where participants repeated the corn planting and liturgy. They concluded the witness in the town of Chenalhó's plaza, and then went inside the church to pray. The band continued playing outside for those who wished to dance.[33]

Other joint CPT/Abeja witnesses did not directly connect with the liturgical calendar, but had a strong spiritual component, nevertheless. In early June 1999, after the arrest of Victorio Arias, an accused leader of the December 1997 massacre, the Abejas again began receiving death threats. "There are rumblings that local paramilitaries are reorganizing to eliminate the nonviolent opposition of the Bees so they will cease their demands that those responsible for the massacre be brought to justice," the team wrote in a "Call to Prayer." The Abejas thus invited the team to join in a prayer circle surrounding the entire community of Acteal (not just the refugee camp) to create a spiritual barrier. On June 4, 1999, team members and 250 Abejas walked through and around Acteal in a five-hour prayer procession. Participants prayed and read from Luke 4:16–30, Jesus' inaugural address before beginning his ministry. When the procession came close to the "Social Labor" base and the homes of paramilitary supporters, the head catechist spontaneously reread the passage, saying, "The Priistas (government party supporters) and soldiers need to hear this."

In November 1999, after eight families who joined the Bees fled their homes because of paramilitary threats, the Chiapas team and members of a CPT delegation discussed the situation with the Abejas in X'oyep. They all agreed that conducting a prayer service on the grounds of the base near X'oyep was in order. Within four hours of the team and delegation's arrival in X'oyep, more than one hundred Bees joined them in singing, "We are marching in the light of God"[34] as they slipped down the gooey

33. CPTnet, "Chiapas: One Thousand Witness," Jan 18, 2000; CPTnet, "Chiapas, Mexico: *Las Abejas,*" Feb 18, 2000. Note that releases about the December 28 witness appeared on CPTnet in January and February. The Chiapas team often sent releases describing events that had happened weeks earlier. In a March 18, 2005 e-mail, Anne Herman wrote:

> While there were times the people of the team just [did] not like to write, that was not always the case. It was extremely difficult to get e-mail out when we were in the campo. We were finally able to sometimes get mail out from Acteal, but when we were in X'oyep that meant someone had to walk between the two villages. In addition, there were at least two occasions when the fluctuations in electricity in the campo burned out a part to the computer that took at least a week to replace.

34. The South African freedom song "We are Marching in the Light of God" is often sung at CPT functions and public witnesses. As new CPT projects evolved, team

mud path to the base. Soldiers in the base fled to their bunkers, and the people gathered near the corn that had been replanted in September (see n. 32) while Cliff Kindy and delegate Karis Engle explained the nature of the action to the officer. The group hung a hand-woven bag—used by indigenous people to gather crops—on a post as they left. It symbolized the few belongings that people take with them when they flee their communities.[35]

Violence 1998–1999

While most of the Chiapas team's efforts in 1998 and 1999 involved socializing with and participating in the worship life of the Abejas, as well as networking with other NGOs, they continued to respond to sporadic outbreaks of violence. did occur. More often, the team found themselves dealing with threats and rumors of violence. The possibility of "another Acteal" was regularly voiced by the indigenous inhabitants of communities that were perceived as sympathetic to the Zapatista cause.

CPTers visited the community Union Progreso in December 1998, which had been the target of a vicious raid by Mexican soldiers, police and paramilitaries the previous June while the CPT exploratory delegation was in Chiapas. After another invasion by the armed groups, the community had fled to the hills and wanted accompaniment back to their village, which the team did through the auspices of Frayba.[36] The team visited the community of Magdalena in early 1999 after a contingent of five hundred Mexican soldiers, accompanied by journalists, entered it at 3:00 a.m., ostensibly to search for drugs. The soldiers did find some stands of marijuana on lands belonging to Mexican government supporters, Priistas, but most of the people involved assumed that the army was looking for the justification to establish another military base there—something that none of the local residents, including the Priistas, wanted. The accusations that their supporters might be growing marijuana was particularly onerous to the Zapatistas, because they had imposed an absolute prohibition

---

members translated the words into Haitian Creole, Arabic, and Tzotzil. Weaver notes in "Restoring the Balance" that the song became an unofficial anthem for joint CPT/Abejas witnesses (123, n. 72).

35. CPTnet, "Chiapas: Prayers Offered," Nov 15, 1999.

36. See CPTnet releases: "Chiapas, Mexico: Another Acteal?" Dec 19, 1998; "Chiapas, Mexico: Away in a forest," Jan 1, 1999; "Chiapas, Mexico: Alvaro Obregon Christmas," Jan 8, 2005; "Chiapas, Mexico: Embers by the Path," Jan 12, 1999.

on drugs and alcohol in the Zapatista autonomous communities. CPTers always had their bags searched for alcohol, guns, and drugs by community members upon entering Zapatista enclaves like Polo.[37]

In August of 1999, the team put out an Urgent Action after observing significant increases in "acts of violence, aggression and public rhetoric" that included the deployment of six thousand to ten thousand troops into Chiapas on top of the seventy thousand stationed there. On August 12, the army had invaded the town of Amador Hernandez, cordoning it off with razorwire. On August 21, paramilitaries detained, beat, and sexually assaulted a Mexican doctor and two Spanish human rights observers. Paramilitaries kidnapped and interrogated three members of Frayba on the same day. Both incidents occurred near military camps. The Mayor of SCLC put out statements in response, calling for the removal of "outsiders," which included both international and Mexican human rights volunteers—from the region.

Two days later, three CPTers, seven local indigenous men, and a Catholic priest found themselves surrounded by thirteen members of the Chiapas State Police, pointing their machine guns at them as they were traveling from a town that these police and Mexican military troops later invaded.[38]

The massacre predicted by the Chiapas team's Urgent Action never materialized. The team's closest brush with lethal violence happened in October 1999 when they accompanied a human rights lawyer to the village of Arroyo Graniso, where the lawyer was investigating the disappearance of an elderly man two months earlier. When Lynn Stoltzfus, Pierre Shantz, and Mark Frey arrived in the village they saw the body of another man, whom a local paramilitary had shot, loaded into the back of the truck. His granddaughter and daughter-in-law had also been shot but lived to identify the gunman.

As for the elderly man who had gone missing, Lynn Stoltzfus wrote that he was last seen walking toward his community to raise money for the release of two other men with whom the authorities had arrested him:

> Did Juan, who was over 70 years old, die of exhaustion on the long
> walk home through the heat of the jungle? Or was he picked up by

37. CPTnet, "Chiapas, Mexico: Marijuana in Magdalena," Jan 15, 1999; CPTnet, "Chiapas, Mexico: Drugs in the Chiapas Highlands," Feb 10, 1999.

38. CPTnet, "Chiapas Urgent Action: International Pressure Needed," Aug 27, 1999.

the military, police or members of a paramilitary group? Is he still alive and being held somewhere or was he killed weeks ago? No one really knows the answers to these questions.

In Mexico, there are no laws for dealing with cases of "disappearances" like Juan. Unless his body turns up, there will never be an investigation. Throughout Latin America, such "disappearances" have been commonly used during times of social unrest to get rid of people that are working for social change.

When people are "disappeared," you don't know whether to grieve or to hope, to wait expectantly or to say goodbye.[39]

Talking to the "Other Side" 1998–1999

CPTers from the Chiapas project were possibly the first to make consistent efforts to interact with the actors belonging to the oppressing power structure on a project location. In Haiti and Hebron, contacts with the military and paramilitaries (which includes Israeli settlers) usually occurred when the team was trying to be a violence-deterring presence or in response to some crisis. The Chiapas releases reveal a more concerted effort to reach out to factions in Chiapas that supported Mexican government policy. Team members met several times with the commander at the Majomut military camp near Acteal. Most of these meetings involved the military officials telling CPTers that the military bases were in the area for the benefit of the inhabitants and pointing out the medical services they provided for the locals. In one such meeting, a General Smith in the Majomut camp compared the Social Labor camps favorably with the "Civic Action" camps the U.S. set up during the Vietnam war to win the "hearts and minds" of the local population.

Smith also told them that none of the surrounding communities liked the Abejas because they were "dangerous." Cliff Kindy pointed out that the Abejas had no weapons. Smith responded,

> Yes they don't have arms, but they use their tongues as a weapon; they spread lies and rumors and provoke the others. They complain to everyone that they are suffering and that they are victims, but this is not the reality. They are living in their fantasies—it is all in their head. They just say these things to get pity from internationals and to get material benefit. Look at everything the International Red Cross has given them.

39. CPTnet, "Chiapas, MX: Disappearance or death?" Oct 25, 1999.

When Kindy pointed out that the massacre at Acteal had indeed happened, Smith claimed reports of the massacre were distorted. He then backpedaled and said that the massacre had happened but that it was in the past and that, "we must live in the present and move forward if we really want peace."

By July 1999, CPT's persistence had raised the hackles of the officials at the Majomut military base, and members were no longer treated as cordially. During a July 6 meeting, the team reported to General Mejia that displaced people in the region continued to hear gunshots and see armed men in the distance as they worked in their fields. They also brought up reports that people were selling the land of displaced people in Tzanembolom. The General responded that those who complained were the only ones who had heard these shots and that since Mexicans are good business people "of course they like to sell land." When the team mentioned that the military was taking pictures of indigenous women without asking their permission, General Mejia told them that indigenous women did not mind having their pictures taken. He continued to assert this willingness to be photographed was true despite the fact, as the team pointed out, tour guides warned people visiting the region not to take pictures. The July 6 meeting ended with a Colonel Villalobos pulling Kryss Chupp and Lisa Martens aside, telling them, "These indigenous people are very, very bad, just like the Indians in your country; like the Sioux."[40]

The July 6 meeting did bear fruit, however. Following the encounter, a Lt. Colonel Luna introduced the CPTers to two PRI leaders of the Majomut community. Feeling somewhat uneasy for their own safety, team members listened to Norberto and Juan Gutierrez Guzman tell them that paramilitary groups did not exist; people had just armed themselves for self defense. They said that the Acteal martyrs had died in crossfire between Zapatistas and civilians "armed to protect themselves." They also reported stories of Zapatista atrocities, which included Zapatistas tying people up and throwing them off cliffs and even eating one victim. When team members pressed them to verify these stories, the two men generally responded with "Well, we weren't there, but we heard. . . ."

40. "Chiapas, Mexico: Meeting with the military," Jan 25, 1999. "Chiapas Update: March 10–24, 1999," Mar 29, 1999; "Chiapas: A Meeting with the General," July 6, 1999); "Chiapas Update: July 3–17, 1999"; "Chiapas Update: December 5–26, 1999," Jan 6, 2000. General Smith's comments come from notes taken by Mark Frey on November 19, 1999, which he sent to the author in an April 2, 2005 e-mail.

When team members left Majomut and returned to Acteal, they found out that Norberto and Juan were major leaders of the paramilitaries there. Wendy Lehman wrote later,

> During the meeting with Norberto and Juan, I recall thinking "Is it possible that these two could have killed someone?" With the horrific stories we hear of paramilitary violence, it becomes all too easy to demonize their members. Yet this meeting made clear one of the truths of the conflict: that even the paramilitary members are in many ways victims. They come from low-income, indigenous families and communities and have faced racism and discrimination. Although clearly responsible for their activities, they are manipulated [by large landowners and PRI party leaders] through offers of small monetary gifts and by warnings of the "dangers" of opposition groups.
>
> Both Juan and Norberto and displaced people we talk to bemoan the fact that they used to live as neighbors and family members yet now are in conflict. The violence inflicted by paramilitary members is horrific-particularly as culminated in the massacre of men, women and children at Acteal. Yet, I was reminded of one displaced woman CPTers met about a year earlier. Despite all the violence she encountered at the hands of paramilitary members, she was still sympathetic to the poverty and the difficulties they, like she, faced, as she said, "Those poor people."[41]

On November 25, 1999, the team traveled to another Priista stronghold in Canolal. Nine families had fled Canolal on November 7, 1999, after paramilitaries threatened them for reporting on weapons caches to the authorities. They joined Las Abejas in Acteal.

When CPTers walked into the village, they saw several houses with PRI graffiti on them. One home proclaimed "Cristo es PRI" ("Christ is PRI"). Public Security officers approached the group and took their names. A school teacher from the community, later identified as a paramilitary leader, told them, upon learning the group's intention, that they could not enter the community to pray without permission from the local authorities. While waiting for the local governing council to arrive, the group lighted a candle and prayed for a "disarming of hearts" in the community.

The council members then informed them that in order to pray in Canolal, the President/Mayor of Chenalhó must give them written per-

---

41. CPTnet, "Chiapas: A Visit to 'the Other Side,'" July 14, 1999.

mission. The CPTers proposed that the entire group pray before they left. Some of the Canolal men (not including the school teacher) joined hands with them and after the prayer, appeared to have visibly softened.[42]

2000–2001

In the last two years of the Chiapas project, the overall threat of physical violence against the Abejas and Zapatistas began to diminish. However, after Vincente Fox won the July 2, 2000, presidential election—reputed to be the cleanest in Mexican history—rumors of paramilitary attacks increased for a brief period. Fox, belonging to the conservative PAN party,[43] brought to an end seventy-one years of continuous PRI rule. After his election, he announced that he would begin pulling military bases out of Chiapas. In preparation for his December inauguration, the Federal government began sending police to disarm paramilitary groups in Chiapas. PRI supporters in the community of Los Chorros fired on the police when they came to disarm them and drove them out of town. PRI paramilitary groups then set up blockades, and rumors of attacks on refugee camps again began circulating. After a Sunday worship in the Zapatista community of Polhó, one of the members told CPTers that the paramilitaries were saying, "If the government is going to come and arrest us anyway, we might as well do one more job like Acteal before they come and get us."

Because of specific threats by local paramilitaries, the Abejas asked for observers from the National Human Rights Commission to come stay with them in the camps, but the government told them they needed to enter into negotiations with the government. Team members joined the

42. CPTnet, Evans, "Chiapas: 'Cristo es Pri,'" Jan 14, 2000. When the team asked General Smith about what had happened in Canolal, he said, according to Mark Frey:

> [N]othing happened in Canolal. There is no danger there, no arms, and no problems. That the families left voluntarily. When asked why they would do this, he responded that they saw the material benefit the people in Acteal were receiving and they wanted it. That work in their field is hard labour and that by going to Acteal they would have it easy because the IRC gives the community food, water, and other material aid.

April 2, 2005, e-mail message from Mark Frey to author.

43. PAN stands for "National Action Party." "Conservative" and "liberal" are, of course, subjective terms. PRI, the Institutional Revolutionary Party, adopted rhetoric from the Mexican revolution 1910–1920, but governed in ways similar to right-wing governments in other Latin American countries.

Abejas in X'oyep and Nuevo Ybeljoj—the latter serving as a camp for recently displaced refugees—and participated in night watches along the trails leading into the camps. The level of anxiety felt was expressed by one man who told them, "I was awake until 2:00 a.m. last night thinking about what would happen to my children if I was killed."

On November 15, the team put out the following announcement:

November 14, 2000

OPEN LETTER TO THE PUBLIC

The Christian Peacemaker Team in Chiapas, which has had a continuous presence in Chenalhó County since June 1998, is concerned by the newly heightened tensions in this area in the last several days. We highly affirm as correct and worthy the Mexican government's public goal of disarming paramilitaries in this region, and recognize that the process of disarmament will take long and careful work.

At the same time, we know, from being present in the situation, that tensions, threats, and rumors are increasing and that the paramilitary groups in this region are on alert. Paramilitary radio activity has been high in recent days, in addition to frequent meetings taking place in communities in this area that have been known to be paramilitary strongholds.

In particular, new threats have emerged against La Sociedad Civil de Las Abejas, with particular reference to their displacement camps in X'oyep and in the newly established camp in the area of Yibeljoj.

In the face of this situation, members of our group, Christian Peacemaker Teams, will be present in these two camps beginning November 13 and during the following days. As pacifists, we refuse the use of weapons for the resolution of conflicts. As Christians, we put our faith in the Spirit of God, which is present in everyone in this situation, and which can cause new and unexpected things to flow forth.

We continue to hope and pray for the well-being of all those involved in this complicated situation: soldiers, paramilitary civilians, and the thousands of internally displaced.
With hopes for a peace with dignity and justice for all,

Christian Peacemaker Teams, Chiapas

Once again, the massacres never materialized. When Pablo Salazar Mendiguchia became the first non-PRI governor of Chiapas, his first action after taking office, was visiting the Abeja camp in X'oyep. The possibility for change began to seem real.[44]

Chiapas team releases for the next two years reflected this diminished fear of physical violence. They mostly covered the public witnesses conducted by the Abejas to remove military bases from their regions, the return of some of the Abejas to their home communities, and a growing awareness of economic violence replacing physical violence in the region.

Public Witness 2000–2001

Lent 2000 provided another spiritual venue for the Bees to challenge the militarization of the area, including the presence of "Social Labor" camps. On March 19, the Bees in X'oyep helped the team construct a tent using wooden poles and blue plastic on the grounds of the Mexican Army camp located one kilometer from X'oyep. The structure resembled the makeshift shelters most of the displaced in Chiapas had to use during their first months in refugee camps. They then strung a banner that read, in Tzotzil and Spanish, "Lent: Return to God's Path." For the next thirty-five days, team members fasted and took turns sleeping in the tent along with several Abejas every night. Every four hours the people in the tent prayed for peace.[45]

The day before Easter, "In a spirit of resurrection and hope," four hundred Abejas from X'oyep, Catholic nuns and priests from the SCLC diocese, students from Mexico City, and the team converged on the helicopter pad on the Social Labor military base near X'oyep. They transformed the pad from a circle of white stones surrounding a large, white painted "H" into the word "Paz" ("peace"). The Abejas then carved into the ground a large sun and moon as symbols of the Creator. On the other side

44. See CPTnet releases: "Chiapas Update: June 25–July 2, 2000," July 8, 2000; "Chiapas: Move Against Paramilitaries," Nov 13, 2000; "Chiapas: CPTers present," Nov 15, 2000; "Chiapas Update: October 30—November 17, 2000" Nov 24, 2000; "Chiapas: Update Nov. 30–Dec 24," Dec 26, 2000. Salazar's coalition, the Alliance for Chiapas, was perhaps the most diverse in Mexico's history. Made up of eight parties, the coalition included the conservative National Action Party (PAN) and the center-left Democratic Revolution party (PRD), two parties that do not often have a common agenda. But, this campaign proved to have a powerful uniting theme: the defeat of the PRI.

45. CPTnet, "Chiapas: "Tent for Lent Campaign," Mar 16, 2000; CPTnet, Frey, "Chiapas: CPTers Erect Tent," Mar 20, 2000; CPTnet, Reschly, "Chiapas Tent for Lent," Mar 27, 2000.

of the camp, people took down the tent for Lent, replacing it with peace flags and banners. They thus symbolically transformed the social labor camp into a space where God's peace could reign.

The next morning, when the team returned to the base for Easter Communion, all the symbols had been removed and the helicopter pad returned to its previous state.

But that was not the end of the story. Scott Kerr wrote in July 2000,

> I remember feeling empty inside returning to the same base the day after the action for a communion service and seeing all of the symbols of peace removed and "the base restored," as the commanding officer of the base put it.
>
> Upon subsequent visits to the base and neighboring community, I have been given hope that actual transformation took place that day, and is still taking place. The military had placed two rows of barbed wire around the helicopter pad. After a month, the pad became overgrown with high-grasses and other vegetation to the point that on my last visit there it was impossible to make out the encircled "H" within the pad.
>
> So many times the work of CPT and other activist communities is symbolic and seems to change nothing, but sometimes these symbolic actions have very real consequences. In X'oyep, it means that there is no longer a functioning helicopter pad.[46]

The Lenten presence of the CPTers in the tent next to the base gave them the opportunity to get to know soldiers in the base and have productive conversations. Some of the soldiers earnestly believed that they were in the region to help the local inhabitants. When a CPTer told a Mexican army nurse that the military had to bear blame for arming and training paramilitaries, she said, "That hurts." Other soldiers had a more realistic view of their presence. Asked by William Payne, "You know your gun won't bring peace, right?" one soldier nodded. Payne also challenged a Major General Enrique Canovas, who shared with Payne a deep Catholic faith, by saying, "You need to choose between your work and your Christianity. The two cannot go together." When Canovas told him that popes led crusades and that the Bible had a lot of violent stories in it, another CPTer told him that the Abejas made a better Christian example

---

46. CPTnet, "Chiapas: Death and Resurrection," Apr 20, 2000; CPTnet, Scott Kerr, "Chiapas: Military Base Transformed," Apr 24, 2000; CPTnet, Scott Kerr, "Chiapas: Transformation of military base," July 17, 2000.

to follow—modeling the love of God through suffering rather than using violence.

Abejas present during the conversation told Canovas, "People are afraid. They are not used to seeing people with guns here in this area. Never before were there guns of high caliber. Now, in every community there are guns. We don't know where they are from, but they are the same as the soldiers carry." (Many of the Abejas were displaced from their communities for refusing to purchase weapons for paramilitaries to use.) Canovas said that the paramilitary groups "use guns from Czechoslovakia or China, and we don't use these guns." A CPTer present during the conversation noted that the military had confiscated very few weapons, and no official declaration had been published about where the paramilitary guns came from, so how did the military know the type of guns paramilitaries carried?[47]

Another fruitful conversation happened one month into the fast after the Lenten fasters publicly read the "Litany of Resistance" written by CPT reservist Jim Loney.[48] Major Gregorio Mejia approached the group of four CPTers, a Jesuit priest, three nuns, and ten indigenous women after they finished the Litany. He told them he was a Christian and a pacifist, too, who had grown up as a poor farmer. He told the women that his General had ordered him to increase the numbers of local people using the camp's services. "We refuse to eat or go to the health clinic," one indigenous woman told him, "because we are afraid of guns and cannot be bought." Sara Reschly wrote in a reflection piece that the Major's comments about how he and the indigenous people were in a similar situation and how he wanted to help make one of the lines in the litany stand out for her: "With the hypocrisy of political maneuvering—we will not comply." Reschly then told him, "We invite you to put down your weapons and leave the military. Come with us. Join us in the path of peace."

Major Mejia said he could not leave his profession and then appealed to the priest for support. The priest, Father Pedro, told him, "Because you are in the army, you have allegiance to your superiors. You need decide

47. CPTnet, Frey, "Chiapas: CPTers Erect Tent"; CPTnet, "Chiapas: "Tent for Lent Presence," Mar 23, 2000.

48. Loney, "Litany of Resistance." CPTers have used the litany on several projects and have adapted it to fit specific situations over the years.

who you will obey—human law or God's law, because you cannot serve both."[49]

These conversations appeared to have an impact on the team. In a release written at the end of the Lenten fast, team members noted, "During the last five weeks, members of [CPT and the Abejas] have urged soldiers to imagine a way of life outside of the army. It is hoped that the individual soldiers realize how much they are a part of this system of violence that has . . . resulted in so much suffering, displacement and loss of life."

They found out a year later that their efforts had borne fruit. William Payne encountered two young soldiers, one in SCLC and one in the state capital of Chiapas, Tuxtla Gutierrez, who approached him to tell him he had quit the army. One of them, a quiet young man with glasses who used to sing hymns during guard duty, told Payne he still had the leaflet that Sara Reschly had given him urging him to quit.[50]

Over the following months, the Chiapas team participated in several public witnesses after violent deaths in the region, including two instances in which people from PRI factions and Public security police were killed.[51] They also marked Pentecost by praying at three military bases for the power of the Holy Spirit to enable soldiers to envision a world in which weapons of warfare would be discarded.[52] On August 10, 2000, the team accompanied the Bees on a march through San Cristóbal de Las Casas to publicize demands they were making of the government. These demands included disarming the paramilitaries, demilitarizing Chiapas, honoring the San Andres Accords, holding government officials accountable for the crimes that led up to and culminated in the Acteal massacre and the immediate payment of damages by the Chiapas state government to the Abejas. (The Mexican government had remitted the money to Chiapas state officials after a court found it liable.)[53]

49. CPTnet, "Chiapas: 'We will not Comply,'" Apr 12, 2000.

50. CPTnet, Payne, "Encounters with Ex-Soldiers," Mar 3, 2001. The text of the flyer handed to soldiers during the Lent 2000 witness was not preserved. But see CPTnet, "Chiapas, Mexico: Las Abejas," Feb 18, 2000.

51. CPTnet, Arbour, "Chiapas, MX: Pain on all sides," May 31, 2000; CPTnet, "Chiapas, Mexico: CPTers Pray," June 20, 2000.

52. CPTnet, "Chiapas: Pentecost Actions," June 17, 2000; CPTnet, "Chiapas Update: June 11–24, 2000."

53. CPTnet, "Chiapas: Bees to march," Aug 10, 2000.

262 In Harm's Way

The most notable public witness in which the team participated was Abejas' pilgrimage to Mexico City. Along with two other pacifist Mayan groups, the Xi'nich ("Ants") and Yomlej, the Abejas walked the nine hundred miles from Chiapas to the Basilica of Our Lady of Guadalupe in Mexico City. They began their march in Acteal on October 12—the anniversary of when the European invasion of the Americas by Christopher Columbus began—and ended on December 12, the anniversary of the appearance of our Lady of Guadalupe to Mexican peasant children. Since the legend of the apparition held that Mary appeared to the Mexicans as an indigenous woman, Our Lady of Guadalupe is venerated by subjugated peoples as someone who intercedes for them within the western-imposed religious structure.

Catholic churches provided food and floor space for sleeping along the way. Oscar Salinas, the Vicar of SCLC celebrated mass every evening with the pilgrims and their hosts, during which the Gospel passage was read in Tzotzil, Tzeltal, and Ch'ol.

The official prayer of the "Jubilee Pilgrimage" recited every evening at Mass, ran as follows:

> Leader: We ask Santa Maria of Guadalupe, Queen of Peace, for her maternal intercession for our needs.
>
> Response (follows each prayer): Santa Maria of Guadalupe, intercede for the indigenous people.
>
> For an end to the paramilitary groups acting in Chiapas.
>
> For the demilitarization of Chiapas and all of Mexico . . .
>
> For reconciliation in our communities.
>
> For liberty for indigenous political prisoners.
>
> That all women, men, and children in our indigenous communities enjoy conditions   For our full human development.
>
> That we might see our mother earth freed from the profanation of the market.
>
> That we might overcome all forms of racism and discrimination between the peoples and cultures that form our Mexican nation.
>
> For the fulfillment, on the part of all its signers, of the San Andrés Accords.
>
> That Congress pass a Law on Indigenous Rights and Culture that satisfies the real needs of the 56 indigenous groups in this country.

That a way might be found to continue the dialogue between the EZLN and the government.

That our Zapatista brothers and sisters be taken seriously, so that without abandoning the just causes of their struggle, they might be able to lay down their weapons.

That in this period of social change in Mexico:

The people might not fall into the temptation of violent insurrection; and the government might not return to the temptation of violent repression

That the Mexican people learn and practice ethical and pacifist methods of social change...

Father of Mercy, who has put these your people under the special protection of the always Virgin Maria of Guadalupe,

Mother of your Son, allow us by her intercession to deepen our faith and to seek the progress of our nation in paths of justice and peace. By our Lord Jesus Christ, *Santa Maria de Guadalupe, intercede for the indigenous* people. Amen.[54]

The team was not able to accompany the Mayan pacifists for the entire journey. The threats against people in X'oyep and Nuevo Ybeljoj (see above) claimed their attention, and they thought the pilgrims would be relatively safe given their large numbers and the number of internationals and non-Indigenous Mexicans accompanying them. Kerr accompanied the pilgrims for forty-five kilometers from X'oyep to San Andres—the site where the Mexican government and Zapatistas had signed the unimplemented San Andres Accords. Anne Herman and Carl Meyer walked with them between October 25 and 27. William Payne and Lynn Stoltzfus traveled to Mexico City to meet the pilgrims at the end of the pilgrimage. They participated in an all-night vigil in the Basilica of the Virgin of Guadalupe with tens of thousands of indigenous people and supporters from all over Mexico. On December 15, 2000, team members reunited in Acteal, along with 1500 Abejas to welcome the returning pilgrims.[55]

54. CPTnet, "Chiapas: Pray with the Pilgrims," Nov 1, 2000; Weaver, "Restoring the Balance," 105–7.

55. Kindy, e-mail, April 1, 2005; CPTnet, "Chiapas Update: October 1–29, 2000," Nov 4, 2000; CPTnet, "Chiapas: Update Nov 30–Dec 24," Dec 26, 2000.

In 2001 most of the team's public witnesses happened on a smaller scale.[56] The most controversial of these 2001 witnesses (and possibly of the entire three-and-a-half years of the Chiapas project) was the team's fast at the Guadalupe Tepeyac military base. The Vincente Fox government removed several other bases in Chiapas immediately after he was elected. (He had said during his campaign that he could end the Chiapas conflict "in fifteen minutes.") He also removed nearly all the checkpoints in the state and offered to meet with Subcomandante Insurgente Marcos. However, the military was reluctant to relinquish control of the Guadalupe Tepeyac base because of its strategic location. The base also possessed symbolic value. The Zapatistas had established its first "Aguascalientes" there—safe meeting spaces where Mexican civil society could meet with the Zapatistas.

CPT sent a letter to Fox on January 3, reminding him that the families from Guadalupe Tepeyac were still displaced and began a three-day fast in front of the base on January 5. As with the Lenten fast in Majomut, team members—Erin Kindy, William Payne, and Carl Meyer—prayed every four hours. They set up their tent facing the main gate of the base and displayed two banners: "The World is Shamed by the Displacement" and "Fast for Demilitarization." At 8:00 every evening, they lighted eighty candles every night for each family displaced from Guadalupe Tepeyac.

In a release about the fast, Erin Kindy wrote,

> During this extended Christmas season, we remember that Jesus Christ was born in a stable because there was no room at the inn. He was not born into a rich or powerful family, but of poor parents. He and his family had to flee to Egypt because of the violence of the government. These days in Chiapas many children are born like Jesus, poor and displaced, suffering in inadequate housing, because their parents had to flee the militarization and para-militarization of their lands. Today we say that the time has come to end the military occupation of the indigenous lands of Chiapas, so

56. See, for example, CPTnet, "Chiapas: CPT witnesses during Lent," Apr 12, 2001. On January 20 the team also vigiled outside the SCLC prison as an observance of the International Day of Nonviolent Action, which commemorates the anniversary of Mahatma Gandhi's assassination. At that time, ten people inside were identified as political prisoners. Pablo Salazar, the new governor of Chiapas, had already released some political prisoners, and the team prayed for the new President Vincente Fox to release federal prisoners as well. CPTnet, "Chiapas: "CPTers vigil," Feb 17, 2001.

that the displaced of Guadalupe Tepeyac and other communities
can return to their houses and lands."

The release went on to note that the three fasters recognized the U.S.
and Canadian governments' complicity in creating conditions that caused
the militarization of indigenous communities in Chiapas.[57]

The Mexican press covered the public witness widely and printed
editorials denouncing the foreign interference in Mexican affairs. Bishop
Arizmendi, who had replaced Samuel Ruiz in SCLC, condemned the witness, saying that fasting should be done in secret (a possible dig at Ruiz
who had carried out a high profile fast in 1994, calling for military disen-
gagement between the Mexican and Zapatista armies). More important
to CPT was the objection of SIPAZ, one of the NGOs they worked with
most closely (see above), who referred to the fast as "a terrible error," not
driven by local actors and done without consideration of the larger political framework.

In response to some of these criticisms, the team put out "An Open
Letter to Mexican Civil Society" on January 20, 2001. They praised the
changes that the Federal and state governments had already implemented
and stated their awareness of the "long and terrible history of foreign intervention into Mexican affairs by foreign powers." They then noted that as
citizens of countries that, along with Mexico, were signatories to NAFTA,
they felt compelled to challenge the interventions their governments had
made in Mexican political and economic affairs because of NAFTA. They
also noted their countries had provided aid, training, and equipment that
the Mexican military had used to repress civil society in Chiapas.

The team concluded their release,

> We are part of a filthy, rotten system that has led to so much suf-
> fering and violence, particularly here in Chiapas. We do not come
> here as people with great solutions, but as humble people who
> believe that it will be the power of prayer and a commitment to
> nonviolence that will lead us to more just relationships throughout
> our respective countries.
>
> The repression and injustices suffered by Indigenous peoples
> in all three of our countries do not know borders. The response
> of our Christian faith and consciences to their suffering must be

57. CPTnet, "Chiapas, Mexico: Your action invited," Jan 3, 2001; CPTnet, "Chiapas,
Mexico: Pacifist Christians fast," Jan 5, 2001; CPTnet, "Chiapas, Mexico: Fast for
Demilitarization," Jan 9, 2001.

just as universal. If the people of faith in Mexico, Canada and the United States were to all join together in the solidarity of conscience, as the civil society of Mexico did in January of 1994 to stop the war, and in defense of human rights, our governments would have no choice but to comply.[58]

Despite the criticisms from Mexican individuals and groups, CPT continued to consider the action at Guadalupe Tepeyac a success. Claire Evans noted in an interview with Paul Neufeld Weaver that the action gave the base high visibility in the press. By the spring, Mexican troops had pulled out of Guadalupe Tepeyac. Evans said that the press was still referring to the action when three CPTers joined the walk from Yabteclum to Acteal (see above).

The team met with SIPAZ twice to discuss their differing interpretations of the action. CPT agreed that they could have done more checking with partner organizations before the fast, but still considered the action a positive one. SIPAZ continued to think of it as a "reckless and irresponsible mistake which could have had very negative consequences both for foreigners working in Chiapas and for the peace process as a whole." However, Weaver noted in a February 20, 2005, e-mail to the author that he was struck by the friendship that continued between the two groups, despite their differing perspectives.[59]

58. CPTnet, "An Open Letter to Mexican Civil Society," Jan 20, 2001.

59. Weaver, "Restoring the Balance," 138–40. Weaver devoted an entire chapter of his dissertation to the differing approaches to nonviolent intervention undertaken by Sipaz and CPT, using the Guadalupe Tepeyac action as a case study. In the team's "CPT Log and Debrief—Guadalupe Tepeyac Action—January 4–8, 2001," they included sections on "What worked" and "What didn't work." Under the latter, they included"

Be more sensitive to the issue of us being internationals, 'meddling in Mexican politics.' Address it early on . . . should have focused our action more on displacement and lessen military presence, would have been harder to frame us as 'political'—Don't use the word 'demand' (exegir) in our press release. Gave the whole thing a more political and less religious tone and Is generally not in CPT's character.

Under a "Questions" section, the team wrote:

Did we do consultation widely enough ahead of time (for instance with the diocese, with the people from Guadalupe Tepeyac community, other NGOs in town, Onesimo Hidalgo, etc)? Thoughts: maybe not, but it's also tempting to get so caught up in consulting and analyzing that we never do actions—let's not let that happen. We did lots of notification, if not lots of consultation.

The Return 2000–2001

From the beginning of the project in Chiapas, CPT hoped to accompany the Abejas who had displaced themselves because of paramilitary violence back to their home communities. CPTers continued to discuss the possibility with Abejas over the next years.[60] In August 2000, the Abejas requested that the international community send faxes demanding that the Chiapas state government create conditions necessary for a safe return of the displaced. The Chiapas government had received indemnities from the Mexican government to pay survivors of the Acteal massacre, but the state government had decided in June it would only pay displaced members of the Bees when they returned to their home communities. The Abejas felt they could not do so as long as the government did not disarm the paramilitaries still present in the communities.[61]

In September and October 2000, approximately ninety-four families left the X'oyep refugee camp for Ybeljoj, the village from which they had fled, because food, water, and firewood in the camp were running low. They resettled in a location near Ybeljoj that would enable them to work their lands. However, the families erected a sign at the entrance of the new camp, Nuevo Ybeljoj, that read, "We continue to be displaced"—and families continued to feel threatened by the active paramilitary presence in Ybeljoj.[62]

Close to a year later, another exodus occurred from X'oyep. Fifty-nine families who had fled from the villages of Yaxjemel, Chuchtic, and Puebla in 1997 announced in August 2001 that they would return to their villages. Again, the reasons for the return were that the firewood was disappearing, the women had to walk one and a half hours to get water, food supplies were inadequate, and the housing was overcrowded—rather than the families feeling their old communities were safer. In an August 24 meeting moderated by the new governor, Pablo Salazar, a hundred Abejas

60. See, for example, a conversation that William Payne had with an Abeja man in X'oyep in CPTnet, "Chiapas: One Displaced Person's Story," Apr 15, 2000.

61. CPTnet, "Chiapas: Bees request international faxes," Aug 4, 2000.

62. CPTnet, Scott Kerr, "Chiapas, Mexico: Going Home," Oct 10, 2000; CPTnet, Kindy and Herman, "Chiapas, MX: Moving again," Oct 24, 2000; CPTnet, "Chiapas: Team corrects AP and Prayers," Oct 31, 2000. The team's CPTnet update covering September 29–October 22, 2001 reported that the residents of Nuevo Ybeljoj celebrated the first anniversary of their return with a mass, baptisms, speeches and the blessing of a new school.

came face to face with Chenalhó municipal authorities and some men who had run them out of their communities at gunpoint. Initially the event was meant to include the signing of a "Non-Aggression Pact," between the Abejas and local government authorities, but the Abejas insisted they had never committed any acts of aggression. The negotiations thus resulted in a retitled, "Accord of Mutual Respect" in which the government agreed, among other actions, to prohibit the possession of firearms in the villages and ensure the safety of those returning home. CPTers maintained a prayerful presence for six hours outside of the convention hall where the meeting was taking place. Abeja friends told them later, "We have a lot of experience with broken promises. We hope and pray that this time the authorities will keep their word."

After a farewell Mass for the three communities on August 25, the families, accompanied by seven CPTers returned to their homes in Yaxgemel, Chuchtic, and Puebla on August 28, 2001. In a report about the entire congregation of the church in Chuchtic meeting again for the first time in four years, Lynn Stoltzfus wrote, "As of this writing, the return has gone smoothly and there haven't been any incidents of violence. There is, however a lot of tension in some of the communities, where there hasn't been much interaction between the returnees and the others in the community." In Puebla, where much of the initial paramilitary organizing in Chiapas took place, the nine Abejas families reported that some of their neighbors had "a change of heart." Many non-Abejas children came to a celebratory dance at the Catholic Church and local members of the PRD—all of whom used to belong to PRI—came with a welcome banner.[63] In Puebla, Matt Guynn, Charles Spring, and Keith Young met a man who had been a paramilitary and they set up a meeting for the next day. An Abeja man accompanied them. After the former paramilitary spoke of how he and his people had "gone off the path" in 1997 and wanted to find out where they went wrong, the Abeja told the CPTers that he believed the man had sincerely repented.[64]

63. CPTnet, Lynn Stoltzfus, "Chiapas: Tears and Smiles," Sept 4, 2001; CPTnet, Stoltzfus, "Chiapas: Stories," Sept 13, 2001.

64. CPTnet, "Chiapas Update: September 4–9, 2001," Nov 8, 2001. The team kept three separate logs as they separated to accompany The Abejas in the communities of Puebla, Yaxgemel, and Chuchtic. In the September 10–28 update, which appeared on CPTnet on November 15, 2001, each group reported having heard about the September 11, 2001, al Qaeda attacks on either that day or the following.

On September 30, 2001, the team accompanied Abejas from X'oyep and Acteal back to Los Chorros. The last of the displaced Abejas returned to their homes in Canolal, Centro Quextic, Tzajalhucum, Poblado Quextic, and Acteal Alto on October 22, 2001. On that day, the monthly Mass commemorating the Acteal martyrs served as a send-off for eighty-seven families—almost five hundred men, women, and children. Thirteen mock coffins lay in the center of the chapel, each representing a family member who was not returning home because of the massacre. Bishop Arizmendi and Chiapas Governor Pablo Salazar accompanied the procession of one thousand people to Acteal Alto, then down muddy trails and across streams and rivers to Poblado Quextic and then farther down the valley to Quextic Centro, home of forty-seven of the returning families. There, the participants celebrated Mass. Bishop Arizmendi preached a homily on hope and reconciliation; the president of the Abejas reminded everyone that the returns had occurred without justice having been done and Governor Salazar acknowledged that the struggle for justice needed to continue. "With symbolism more than he may have realized," wrote Bob Holmes, "[Salazar] helped raise the white peace flag over the newly returned community." After the Mass, the procession then returned the final nineteen families to Tzajalhucum in the late afternoon.

Keith Young noted in a follow-up release that three months earlier neither the Mesa Directiva—the governing body of the Abejas—nor CPT would have foreseen that almost all the Abejas would shortly return to their home communities. The government had not met the conditions the Abejas had set for their return—disarmament and disbanding of paramilitaries and the implementation of the San Andres Accords. However, the fact that recently elected Governor Pablo Salazar had so openly supported indigenous rights indicated a shift in the political situation. Also, the Priistas in the Abejas' home communities were consolidating their political power and the Abejas felt they ought to return to participate in the governing of these communities and report on paramilitary activity.

Young concluded his piece,

> CPT must reevaluate its role now in Chiapas and in Chenalhó county. One discussion led to the idea of an "emergency response team" that could respond to violent or potentially violent situations in Abejas communities, ideally within a couple of hours. As long as Chiapas is militarized and paramilitaries are being armed, a repeat of expulsions and killings is very possible.

> CPT could also become a part of a non-violent direct action team, coordinated with another non-governmental organization and Las Abejas. However, now that the Abejas returns have taken place, and people are back in their home communities, the negative consequences of such direct action could be greater. The returned Abejas are no longer in large supportive communities of like-minded people, but are back in areas where their views and actions may be viewed as threatening to the status quo.[65]

The final updates from the Chiapas project further indicated that the raison détre for the CPT presence in Chiapas had changed. Splitting up between the villages of the returned communities, the team mostly recorded social visits with people who told them about what life in their villages had been like before the displacement. They also described to team members the current relationships between the Abejas and those who had remained in the communities. Without much else to do, team members helped with rebuilding homes and working in the fields. Occasionally the returnees spoke of threats they had heard or about the presence of plainclothes policemen and Public Security police. When they found out that six of the people who perpetrated the Acteal massacre had been released from prison and returned to Los Chorros, the team made a point of visiting the community. They recorded that the ex-prisoners were afraid to leave their houses and that "the whole community was scared."[66]

Closing the Chiapas Project

The fact that Abejas in Los Chorros and X'oyep expressed their concern to team members about the U.S. going to war with Afghanistan in fall 2001 and encouraged team members to visit nonviolent groups such as the X'inich (Ants) in other parts of Chiapas is perhaps significant. Both concerns suggested that immediate fears for their own safety had subsided.[67]

As with the Haiti project, the team in Chiapas saw that the worst violence with which their Chiapan partners had to contend was economic.

65. See CPTnet, "Chiapas: Six displaced communities," Sept 25, 2001. See also CPTnet, "Chiapas, Mexico: Abejas March," Oct 6, 2001; CPTnet, "Chiapas: Returned," Nov 12, 2001.

66. CPTnet, "Chiapas Update: November 11–December 10, 2001," Dec 20, 2001.

67. CPTnet, "Chiapas Update: September 29–October 22, 2001," Nov 23, 2001; CPTnet, "Chiapas Update: October 23–November 6, 2001," Nov 26, 2001; CPTnet, "Chiapas Update: November 11–December 10, 2001," Dec 20, 2001.

As was also the case in Haiti, the team in Chiapas recognized that CPT's mandate and structure was not set up to deal effectively with economic violence. Additionally, the Mennonite Church in Colombia had issued an invitation for CPT to set up a project there, so the Spanish speakers from the Chiapas team were needed to deal with overt lethal violence in that country. Thus, the team in Chiapas, in consultation with other partners and CPT staff decided to put the Chiapas project on hold for three months. The team never returned, although CPT did send a delegation in March 2002, which, along with thirty Abejas, issued "exit visas" to soldiers still stationed at the Majomut military base. A member of the Abejas, Antonio Gutierrez, also participated in CPT's first North American delegation to Colombia in April 2002.

In December 2001, the Chiapas team and the Mesa Directiva of the Bees met for the last time and conducted a ceremony that marked the end of CPT's Chiapas project. As they lit each other's candles, wrote Angie Freeman, "we shared in that moment the realization that we had done good work together and there will always be a connection to each other, as we all strive for peace." Given that the Abejas' demands for justice had not been met, the team invited constituents to pray on December 22, 2001, the fifth anniversary of the Acteal massacre, for those still experiencing threats and violence in Chiapas and "for those who feel the economic oppression more strongly now that the guns are lifted."[68]

ISSUES ARISING FROM THE CHIAPAS PROJECT

Secrecy

When CPT first began exploring the possibility of opening a project in Chiapas, the Mexican government's deportation of internationals it perceived as pro-Zapatista had paralyzed most of the NGOs in the area. Thus, when taking public transportation into the Zapatista areas, internationals or Mexican accompanistas often told soldiers at checkpoints they were on their way to see Mayan ruins in Palenque or to buy artisan crafts in Pantelhó. Although CPTers at the beginning of the project had decided to be open about where they were traveling, when people became more dependent on them for accompaniment, they felt they had to be more

68. CPTnet, "CHIAPAS: A light on the future and an invitation to pray," December 10, 2001.

circumspect. Maintaining positive relationships with other NGOs working in the area also required the team to take the other NGO workers'
fears of deportation into account. Accordingly, they would ask taxis to
drop them off some distance from their house in San Cristóbal, "so that
people who knew where we had been did not see where we were going,"
wrote Christopher Buhler.[69]

As this chapter has described, the team eventually moved to a proactively open and honest approach with soldiers at military checkpoints,
but not without a good deal of discussion about the consequences. These
consequences could have included deportation, leaving the Abejas without accompaniment and the alienation of groups in Chiapas with whom
the team wished to have a cooperative working relationship.

Partisanship

CPT does not claim to be neutral on any project location. In aligning
itself with the Abejas, CPT indicated its support of reforms the Zapatistas
were demanding. However, aligning with the Abejas also meant a refusal
to sanction violence directed against any of the parties involved in the
Chiapas conflict.

Mexican society has been fractured along various fault lines for
some time. These fault lines include those between indigenous and mestizo Mexicans, political parties, urban and rural inhabitants, and religious
groups. In the religious arena, which was of greatest concern to CPT and
the Abejas, the Mexican government exploited these fault lines. It told the
world that the conflict had to do with religious infighting, rather than the
government supplying its indigenous supporters with guns and material
aid.

Given the intensely spiritual worldview of the Bees and CPT's own
Christian orientation, the CPTers who first came to Chiapas paid close
attention to religious divisions. Since many of the Acteal murderers
had been evangelicals, and paramilitaries in the Northern Zone tended
to be Presbyterian evangelicals, CPT initially sought out contacts with
church leaders in these areas with limited success. When they talked
about their affiliation with the Abejas, the conversations generally halted.[70]

69. Buhler, e-mail, Mar 17, 2005.

70. Eduardo Rodriguez, the MCC representative in Chiapas, in an interview with
Paul Weaver, specifically noted that evangelical *Priistas* did not "have a good image of

Complicating the situation was the fact that Evangelicals in several communities, most notably San Juan Chamula, had been driven from their homes by PRI supporters because of their religious beliefs.[71]

However, the division between Evangelical and Catholic was not absolute. The Abejas themselves refused to divide people along those lines. During the spring 1998 exploratory project, when Kathleen Kern mentioned that she had heard most of the paramilitaries who had committed the Acteal atrocities were Presbyterian, an Abeja on the Mesa Directiva interrupted her, saying, "The paramilitaries are people who like to take up arms"—thus rejecting the framework of her question.[72] In the Zapatista community of Polhó was a Presbyterian congregation whose congregants considered themselves entwined with the Catholics and Pentecostals in the same community. "Here, we are united in our practice of justice," one of the Presbyterian elders told the team.[73]

Four of the five members of the proto-Abeja Bible study group arrested in 1992 (see above) were evangelical. Some Protestants and practitioners of traditional Mayan religion had joined the Bees, whose worship life centered around prayer and catechism conducted by lay leaders. (Although the evening prayer service was called "Mass" by the Abejas, Eucharist was rarely served.)

When the team accompanied the Abejas back to their home communities, they made a point of interacting with the Evangelical pastors in the communities from which the Abejas had been driven. In Puebla, especially, religion was an issue, given that the town had several Presbyterian, Baptist, and Pentecostal denominations. It had also been the site where much of the paramilitary organizing in Chenalhó started. In 1997, when Abejas in the community refused to sell their land to buy guns, the municipal government arrested six, publicly interrogating them and beating them. When they still refused to cooperate, one of the Abejas said they

---

CPT, because they say they have come to support just one side." Weaver, "Restoring the Balance," 125.

71. For a more in-depth analysis of how religion factored into the Chiapas conflict, see Weaver, "Restoring the Balance," 70–73. The PRI leaders who expelled the evangelicals in Chamula also expelled those Catholics who expressed loyalty to the Bishop Samuel Ruiz and the Diocese of SCLC. Ruiz denounced the expulsions and the Diocese aided both Catholics and Protestants whom paramilitaries had forced to leave their homes.

72. Kern wrote about the conversation in "The Bees Set Nonviolent Example."

73. CPTnet, Martens, "This time 'Divide and Conquer' failed," July 20, 2001.

were not paying for guns because they were following the Word of God. A pastor then told him that in a time of war, they should not follow God.[74]

On September 8, 2001, team members attended an ecumenical prayer service that included all the churches in Puebla, Bishop Filipe Arizmendi and Presbyterian minister Al Schreuder. "At one point," an update describing the event noted, "Al Schreuder shared his Tzotzil hymnal with Bishop Arizmendi and they sang together."[75] The prayer service thus indicated that something significant had changed in Puebla.

U.S. Culpability in the Chiapas Conflict

As mentioned at the beginning of this chapter, the Zapatista uprising occurred in response to the implementation of NAFTA that the U.S. was

74. Presbyterian CPTers Charles and Carol Spring, who would later become part of the Colombia team, had some interesting interactions with Presbyterian paramilitaries in the communities to which the Abejas had returned. Charles wrote in an April 17, 2004 e-mail:

> Our sub-team did visit the Presbyterian pastor in Puebla and I identified myself as Presbyterian. Our first meeting, he didn't have much time, but he introduced us to a couple of other leaders who were at the church. We visited with them over refrescos. (With us was one of our Abejas hosts, who didn't say anything once we all got introduced.) In Keith Young's entry on this meeting in the log (which I copied for myself), he said "I thought the fact that Charles is Presbyterian and had been an elder in his church really helped a lot in giving an entrance. Charles really knew the structure of the Presbyterian Church fairly well. Everyone there seemed interested in talking with him. At the same time, I think they knew quite well who we were staying with and the basic reason of why we were now here, and these issues were skirted around very theatrical like. We more or less skirted around them as well." In our conversations with them and with the pastor later, it was basically relationship-establishing conversations and did not involve challenging them or the church or its members over the conflict. I wanted to attend a worship at the church, but the first Sunday we were there, a PRI candidate was going to be there and I thought that would not mesh well with my presence. The other Sundays it just didn't work out for other reasons. I did get to attend a planning meeting at the church that involved several Presbyterians, a couple of Abejas, and folks from other churches as well. The meeting was to plan an ecumenical day of prayers for peace in Puebla, which was a pretty big deal . . .
>
> I don't remember any Abejas becoming reserved with me because of my denomination, but of course is was hard to interpret reactions being only there for 3 weeks.

75. CPTnet, "Chiapas Update: September 4–9, 2001," Nov 8, 2001.

pushing through despite widespread opposition from the Canadian, U.S., and Mexican public. In the years that followed, the specter of U.S. interests could be seen in nearly every aspect of the Chiapan conflict.

The ascendancy of paramilitary violence in Chiapas, for example, echoed the paramilitary violence in El Salvador, Guatemala, and Nicaragua that the U.S. had supported and encouraged. Although FRAPH members in Haiti and settlers in Hebron fit the definition of paramilitaries, Chiapas was the first experience that CPT had with the classic Latin American counterinsurgency campaigns. In Guatemala, El Salvador, and Nicaragua, paramilitary death squads often conducted the most despicable work of the militaries in these countries, and they often did so with U.S. support. When congress debated giving these countries military aid, the militaries in these countries could say that most of the violence occurred at the hands of non-military people over whom, they claimed, they had little control.

In Chiapas, much of that funding was sent ostensibly to fight the "War on Drugs." In a December 1998 release, the team mentioned coming across a military base on a Sunday outing filled with U.S.-supplied military vehicles and a radar tower.

> "Mexico's National Institute To Combat Drugs (INCD) issued a report covering the period, Nov. 16, 1995–April 30, 1996, in which the Institute identified the 10 Mexican states in which the most drugs had been found and destroyed. The southern state of conflict-ridden Chiapas was not mentioned." (The Slippery Slope/U.S. Military Moves Into Mexico, S. Brian Willson, Updated, April 1998)
>
> Why are United States tax dollars being used for a radar installation and for military equipment in a Mexican state that apparently has little if any connection to drug production or activity? Is this equipment being used to intimidate Mexican citizens who are seeking a role in the democratic processes of their government?[76]

By the time CPT set up its Chiapas project, a third of the Mexican army, seventy thousand troops, was in Chiapas, along with U.S. military advisors.[77] Because the military buildup and counterinsurgency strata-

76. CPTnet, "Chiapas, Mexico: Picnic in the Park," Dec 15, 1998.

77. In an update that never appeared on CPTnet, the Chiapas team recorded a visit to a Presbyterian missionary who had a son in the Mexican army. The son had reported the presence of US military advisors at a base near Tuxtla Gutierrez, the Chiapas state capital.

gems in Chiapas so closely resembled the brutal situations in Central America in the 1970s and 1980s, CPT began to participate actively as an organization in the November School of the Americas Watch (SOAW) demonstrations at Fort Benning, Georgia.[78]

In a release about the August 1997 delegation praying in Mexico City for an end to paramilitary violence in the Northern Zone, Kryss Chupp noted that the military general in charge of Chiapas, Mario Renan Castillo, was trained at the SOA. This information turned out to be incorrect, but Renan Castillo did receive training in counterinsurgency at Fort Bragg—home to the U.S. Special Forces, with whom CPT's Haiti team had dealings.[79] In his Tuxtla Gutierrez office Castillo displayed two posters promoting the "Paz y Justicia" paramilitary group and served as an "honorary witness" when Chiapas Governor Ruiz Ferro formally turned over 4,600,000 pesos (nearly $600,000 U.S.) to "Paz y Justicia" on July 4, 1997.[80]

In the November 1997 SOAW witness, Anne Herman—who would go through the January 1998 training and become a member of the Chiapas team—crossed the line onto Fort Benning's base for the second time. She received a six-month sentence. A CPTnet release noted that Herman was "serving the first six months of her three-year term with CPT at Danbury Federal Prison Camp in Connecticut." Nearly fifty people affiliated in some way with CPT participated, along with seven thousand others, in the 1998 November vigil at Fort Benning. CPTers associated

---

The same update also had the following entries:

Wednesday, August 5

The new [U.S.] ambassador to Mexico, Jeffrey Davidow, said that the Pentagon committed an "error" when it said that two US military personnel were detained by paramilitary members in Los Platanos (several hours north of San Cristobal) on July 26. He also denied the existence of paramilitary groups . . .

Sunday, August 9

Newspapers quote US Ambassador Davidow as saying that there are no US military personnel advising the Mexican government.

78. School of the Americas Watch maintains the "SOA Graduate Database," in which people can search for graduates by name, country of origin, rank, and SOA courses in which they participated. SOA later changed its name to Western Hemisphere Institute for Security Cooperation (WHINSEC), possibly because of the bad publicity.

79. CPTnet, "Prayers for Peace amidst Vigilante Violence," Aug 29, 1997.

80. Willson, "Section IV: Militarization and Repression."

with the Chiapas project continued to participate in the annual SOAW witness until the project closed down in 2001. Some—Cliff Kindy, Bob Holmes, Sara Reschly, Esther Ho, and Scott Kerr—were arrested or issued five-year "ban and bar" letters prohibiting them from crossing onto the base again.[81] Because Colombian officers implicated in atrocities had also graduated from the School of the Americas, CPT has continued to send people to the November vigils.

Economic Issues

When William Payne encountered Gutierrez, a soldier in Tuxtla who had left the army because of the Abejas and CPT Lenten witness in 2000 (see above), the young man asked Payne, "What do you counsel that I do now? Payne, who noted that the young man was barely literate when they exchanged addresses, wrote,

> What do I counsel? What are the options for a poor, Christian young man who has decided that in spite of his poverty, he does not want to carry a machine gun anymore? What are the options when minimum wage here is 30 cents per hour and the only realistic way to get more than that is to sneak into the U.S., and risk getting killed by some racist rancher?[82]

This anecdote illustrates that economic violence haunted every aspect of the team's work. As had been the case in Haiti, team members found themselves working with people whom economic realities had condemned to a life of malnutrition, grueling work, and early death. These realities were evident from the beginning of the project. In August 1998, the team visited La Revolucion in the Northern Zone. Seventy families had moved on to a coffee plantation in 1994 and begun a cooperative, with the agreement of the former German owners. Families

81. See CPTnet releases: "Washington, D.C.: Rally to Close the School," Apr 22, 1998; "For Benning, GA: CPTers participate in vigil," Nov 24, 1998; "Fort Benning, Georgia: I Carried a White Cross," Dec 7, 1998; "Ft. Benning, GA: CPT at SOA," Nov 19, 2001; "CPTers Join Call," Nov 21, 2000; "FT. Benning, GA: CPTers arrested," Nov 22, 2001. Ed Kinane, who worked with CPT in the Cry For Justice Coalition (see chap. 2) and would later do so in Iraq, was also arrested in 1997 along with Herman. Because he had been arrested in 1996 and September 1997 for "editing" the SOA sign to read "Home of the School of the Americas, School of Shame" and "SOA=Torture," he received a fifteen-month sentence.

82. CPTnet, "Chiapas: Encounters with Ex-soldiers," Mar 3, 2001.

fleeing attacks from the Mexican military and the paramilitary group, Paz y Justicia, also settled in La Revolucion. At the time the team visited, the community was expecting a violent invasion by the same paramilitaries. The team wrote a release putting the violence within the context of global economic change:

> The old plantations are dying out. There is a struggle going on concerning whether the indigenous people, the former workers, will be able to rebuild a communal way of life on the land, or whether the land will be turned over to large, often foreign interests. These interests want to develop large scale mechanized agribusiness operations as is already happening in western Chiapas and elsewhere in Mexico.
>
> Also, the tie of the indigenous people to their lands impedes other transnational exploitations such as timber and mineral development. In fact, recent reports indicate that the Mexican government's plan for the area includes turning it into another big 'maquiladora' region because of the potential for cheap labour, if only the indigenous people can be moved off their land.[83]

A Mexican major made the connection between economic and military violence explicit when he told Aaron Blythe and Cliff Kindy that foreign countries were interested in Chiapas's land and mineral resources. "The Mexican government is weak and, since the army is a political tool, we often get used to open areas we would not choose," he told them.[84]

In the final year of CPT's Chiapas project, economic issues came to the forefront of the team's work. The plight of small coffee growers in particular affected the team, given that many of the Abejas had depended almost entirely on coffee for their income. Because of the International Monetary Fund and World Trade Organization regulations, the price of coffee had decreased significantly. William Payne noted in a March 2001 release that small growers were currently making thirty cents for a pound of coffee that sold for $5.50 in the U.S., and for which they would have earned $1.25 six years earlier. The Lent 2001 resources from the Chiapas Team were entitled, "Who will roll away the stone . . . of economic injustice?" They encouraged constituents to pray at least once a week for impoverished coffee farmers—suggesting that they place coffee beans or ground coffee beside a prayer candle to "keep in mind the economic

83. CPTnet, "Chiapas, Mexico: A community lives in fear," Aug 25, 1998.
84. CPTnet, "Chiapas: The Mexican Major," Nov 28, 2001.

importance of this product to the displaced people." In Chiapas, on Ash Wednesday, the team had a prayer vigil at the Nestle's plant near Tuxtla Gutierrez, dumping coffee on the ground to protest the low coffee prices. They prayed,

> Dear Lord, this coffee that we pour into the ground represents the sweat and labors of thousands of poor coffee farmers in Chiapas. We see that the fruit of their labors is not valued in the market-place of the world economy. In your grace, O Lord, liberate us from these systems of domination. Let us help to bring in your reign, an economy of grace in which debts are forgiven, prisoners are freed, and all have sufficient food. Amen.[85]

The other major economic issue on which the team focused in 2001 was "Plan Puebla-Panama,"—designed to create a "Free Trade" zone between Puebla, just south of Mexico City all the way down through Central America. "'Free Trade," as one release noted, meant "free reign for corporations like Nestle, which nearly single-handedly bottomed out the price of Mexican coffee this year by threatening to import mass quantities from Asia and Africa." The same release noted that the displacement of indigenous people in Chiapas also opened up opportunities for maquiladoras—sweatshops paying minimum wage where workers are not allowed to organize unions.

In June 2001, CPTers Matt Guynn and Diego Mendez attended the Forum on Cultural and Biological Diversity, dressed in corn costumes that had served the team and delegations in other previous public witnesses. The forum was designed to deal with the damage that NAFTA had already done to Mexican agriculture and environment, which Plan

85. See CPTnet releases: "Chiapas Lent Resources," Mar 5, 2001; "Chiapas Update: Jan. 21–31, 2001," Feb 14, 2001; Payne, "What's in a cup of coffee?" Mar 1, 2001; "Chiapas: March 13 vigil," Apr 2, 2001; also Peters, "Chiapas: Paying the Price of Justice," Dec 3, 2001; "Chiapas: From Los Chorros to Nestle," Dec 7, 2001; "Chiapas Update: November 11–December 10, 2001." This update noted that the action at the Nestle's plant was not covered because former Beatle George Harrison's death dominated Mexican television.
In the summer of 2000, when a woman who had bought more than $100,000 worth of coffee from the Abejas refused to pay them as she had promised, the team responded to the Abejas' request that it launch a fax campaign to Sra. Juana Zoe Castro Rodriguez to make the payments. CPTnet, "Chiapas: Bees request faxes," Aug 21, 2000; CPTnet "Chiapas Update: August 6–20, 2000," Sept 2, 2000; CPTnet, "Chiapas Update: August 22–September 2, 2000," Sept 12, 2000. In an April 21, 2005 e-mail, Abeja José Alfredo Jiménez Pérez said that Maya Vinik had never received payment and that the police had never arrested her for stealing the coffee.

Puebla Panama would exacerbate. Under NAFTA, Mexico began importing corn from the U.S., causing the price of Mexican corn to drop, further impoverishing Mexican farmers. A Dutch corporation had patented the traditional indigenous corn drink, posol, which technically meant that Chiapan peasants might have to purchase the right to consume their own food. "As a symbolic act of resistance," the update noted, "the Forum began with posol being (illegally) served to all participants."[86]

When a CPT delegation came to Chiapas three months after the project shut down, they ended a release about a public witness as follows:

> "CPT ended its full-time presence in Chiapas last December and will look for ways to maintain relationships with nonviolent groups like the Abejas as Chiapas lives through the shift from the violence of the bullet to the violence of the empty stomach."[87]

Conclusion

In 1999, Pierre Shantz came back to the Hebron project after a stint in Chiapas and observed a funeral in Hebron for a local man who had been killed by Israeli soldiers during a military operation. As Shantz watched a group of Palestinian militants in black ski masks strutting with automatic weapons, he thought of the Abejas. Comparing these militants to the Abejas, with their patient resistance and Christ-like attitudes toward their enemies, he told the author that he realized he never wanted to return to Hebron. His heart was with the Abejas.[88]

Shantz's feeling about the Abejas was shared by most of the CPTers who worked in Chiapas. The Abejas had, on their own, decided that the following Jesus meant loving their enemies, and resisting injustice through prayer, fasting and pilgrimage. Their theology resonated with CPT's own: "We know we cannot carry out violence. Therefore, we are not taken into the world, but can save ourselves for heaven. This is why we are training

86. See CPTnet releases: "Chiapas Update: June 13–June 29, 2001," July 5, 2001; "Chiapas: The Prayer of Elders," July 9, 2001; Chiapas, Mexico: Plan Puebla-Panama," July 18, 2001; Rusty Curling, "Chiapas: It's the violence," Oct 9, 2001.

87. CPTnet, "Chiapas: Abejas Women Issue Exit Visas to Soldiers," Mar 8, 2002.

88. From a conversation Shantz had with the author while working with her in Hebron. In an April 19, 2005 e-mail, Shantz confirmed that the author's memory was accurate. In 2000 Shantz did return to set up the Beit Jala project (see chap. 6). Old friendships drew him back to Hebron, where he spent some time after the Beit Jala project closed.

people not to take up arms, to pray, to take up only the Bible. That is our weapon."[89]

Paul Neufeld Weaver noted in his dissertation that after the Acteal massacre, the Abejas gained the sympathy of the world, which regarded them principally as victims. "What CPT saw in the Bees," Weaver wrote, "was a movement which was, like them, committed to nonviolent action. CPT's identification of the Abejas in this way encouraged their self-identification as pacifists, and their recognition of a sense of being actors in the conflict."[90]

As one Abeja described it,

> Before and after the massacre, we felt very sad, forgotten, totally excluded, that no one was going to console us, but it wasn't like that. A few days later, the world heard about what happened here in Acteal. And then it was a surprise that in this moment, it was a miracle for us to see many people, not just from Mexico, but people from other parts of the world where there is a lot of violence, there is a war, that the government always oppresses the poor, then we saw all of this, that we aren't alone, that not just the Bees, nor just CPT which we met at that time also, but in fact there were other pacifist people that struggle for a better life, and also we saw the history of Mahatma, of Martin Luther King, in truth it was very interesting! This history inspired me a lot.[91]

The Bees, in turn, taught CPTers the process of loving one's enemies as they prayed for specific paramilitaries who had kicked them out of their homes, yet continued to demand that the government hold the unrepentant accountable for what they had done.

Eduardo Rodriguez, the Mennonite Central Committee representative in Chiapas, told Weaver that the Abejas considered CPT to be a part of the Abejas. Perhaps in no other project, would CPT experience that level of acceptance. As a minor, but not trivial, example of this closeness, CPTers taught the Abejas a South African hymn that CPTers often sing at official CPT functions. "We are marching in the light of God," translated into Tzotzil and Spanish, became the "theme song" of joint CPT and

89. Kern, "The Bees Set Nonviolent Example."
90. Weaver, "Restoring the Balance," 123.
91. Ibid., 98.

Abejas' public witnesses.[92] As of 2005, the Abejas choir in Acteal was still singing it.[93]

92. Ibid., 123–25.

93. Jiménez Pérez, e-mail, Apr 23, 2005. His uncle was the choir director in Acteal at the time he sent the e-mail.

8

"All My Relations": CPT's Work with Indigenous Communities

'Mitakuye oyasin' meaning 'all my relatives' is something Lakota people say when we pray. Do we really mean it? Our words are being poised in front of us as we contemplate this horror that happened on the East Coast. The pain, the fear, the anger, and thirst for revenge are causing many to contemplate more violence. Then there are those who say the United States is only getting what it has handed out. Are any of these emotions suited to 'mitakuye oyasin?' How many of our relatives, innocent people, were killed in the last 10 years in the bombing of Iraq? How many bodies of our relatives will be pulled from beneath the rubble of the World Trade Center? Is there any difference between one set of relatives and another? Are they all human beings? They each have different religions. Some are Christians. Some are Moslems. Both have spiritual beliefs that are different than the Lakota way of looking at life. Yet when we pray we say all of them are our relatives whether Christian or Moslem or Jew or someone who follows other beliefs. So a body pulled out from the rubble in one part of the world, or a body pulled from the rubble in another, are they still our relatives?

Were those sailors killed at Pearl Harbor our relatives? Were the people who died at Nagasaki and Hiroshima our relatives? If we are truly Lakota and we really mean what we say when we say 'mitakuye oyasin,' then the answer is yes. . . .

It is this understanding of 'mitakuye oyasin' that the world needs, especially now, especially in the United States. How do we teach this understanding? We are so tiny, and poor in money. But we are rich beyond belief because we have this understanding of 'mitakuye oyasin.' We have something the whole world needs.

—CPT advisor, Charmaine Whiteface, following Al Qaeda attacks on the World Trade Center and Pentagon, September 2001[1]

1. Whiteface, "We have another chance."

Because CPT had its origins in North America, early supporters paid particular attention to the policy of their governments toward the First Nations in the United States and Canada.[2] Unlike the projects in Haiti, the West Bank, or Chiapas, most North American CPTers were directly culpable in the oppression and dispossession of the First Nations because they lived on land from which the governments of Canada and the U.S. drove the indigenous inhabitants.

In what a CPT chronology calls the "first CPT conference,"[3] people interested in developing the fledgling CPT listened to Chief Carl Roberts of the Roseau River Indian Band (Anishinabe nation) talk about land claims in January 1988. The conference passed two resolutions: one reaffirmed the December 1986 Techny consultation (see chapter 1). The other urged local congregations to continue to explore ways of supporting Roseau River Band as they pursued "justice with treaty land entitlement issues."[4] Although CPT recorded no further interactions with the Roseau River Band, this early meeting set a direction, particularly for Canadian CPTers, toward issues facing indigenous communities, particularly rights guaranteed them in treaties by the U.S. and Canadian governments.

2. How people of European ancestry refer to indigenous peoples in North America is of huge concern to these indigenous and the European Canadian/American people who work with them. Nomenclature will be dealt with in the "Issues" section at the end of this chapter. In general this chapter will follow NAHO, "Terminology Guide," National Aboriginal Health Organization, www.naho.ca/english/pdf/terminology_guidelines.pdf. The author will, whenever possible, use names that peoples use to describe themselves, e.g., "Innu," "Lakota," and even "Indian," where applicable. She will use "First Nations" to refer to all indigenous groups in North America, although Canadians use that name more often than US residents do.

3. Formerly on the CPT Web site until 2007. CPT, "Christian Peacemaker Teams Activities 1984–2000."

4. The Canadian publication, *Mennonite Reporter*, called the event a "seminar" rather than a "conference," and reported that twenty people attended. Roberts reviewed the 117 years of unfulfilled promises regarding the land guaranteed the Band in treaties. He told the people attending "We do not want land which has been in your family for generations; we would not want to do to you what you do to us." "Christian Peacemaker Teams: New wine in old wineskins?"

In March 1996, a Treaty Land Entitlement settlement was reached between Canada and the Roseau River First Nation. It included a payment of $14 million, with which the Roseau River First Nation would purchase a minimum of 5,861 acres (including mines and minerals) for reserve. INAC, "Facts on File."

THE INNU NATION IN LABRADOR

The Innu may have been the first people of "Turtle Island" (a.k.a. North America) to encounter European explorers—probably the Vikings who briefly settled in Newfoundland around 1008 CE. However, because they were nomadic people who spent most of the year in the interior of Quebec and Labrador, which they called Nitassinan, they ultimately had less contact with European settlers than had other Nations in Canada.

As they did to other First Nations over the centuries, the British and later Canadian governments imposed what they thought was a "proper" way of life on the Innu. This policy fostered a dependency on government services that restricted Innu to government-recognized villages, and, beginning in the 1960s, forced children to attend schools that belittled Innu language and culture.

The forced settlement of the Innu into villages left the land they had used for hunting and trapping open to mining interests. Canada then put restrictions on hunting and trapping—which had been the Innu's main source of sustenance and income—for the benefit of sportsmen. The government also flooded traditional Innu hunting grounds, without warning, when it opened the Churchill Falls Dam in 1969. Many families lost all their trapping and hunting equipment as a result.[5]

CPT became involved with the Innu because of NATO low-level training flights over Labrador. Canadian, U.S., and European militaries used Labrador airspace to practice low-level flights in fighter planes and bombers. They chose the location because Labrador was "uninhabited," i.e., inhabited only by Innu.

The Innu maintained that the low level flights were not only frightening to them and their children, they were damaging the environment and harming the caribou and other animals they depended on for food.

More than eight thousand low-level flights between April and November 1989 ripped through the Nitassinan environment. Canadian Minister of Defense, John Crosby, then announced that his government would spend $93 million dollars to expand the Goose Bay military base for NATO trainings that would increase low-level flights to one hundred thousand a year. The Innu went on the offensive with Nonviolent Direct

---

5. Tanner, "Innu History"; Backhouse and McCrae, "Report to the Canadian Human Rights Commission."

Action (NVDA), occupying runways and military bases. By the summer of 1989, the Canadian government had arrested more than 250 of them.[6]

In May 1989, Dutch Mennonite Maarten van der Werf attended CPT's First Annual CPT Training/Action Conference in Chicago. He proposed joint Europe-North America CPT attention to NATO air forces training in Labrador and causing destruction of Innu peoples' lands. Accordingly, CPT sponsored a "consultation," in Ottawa, Ontario, entitled "The Innu Crisis and the Call of Christ," on the weekend of February 23, 1990, in Ottawa, Ontario. Gene Stoltzfus served as a resource person, as well as Steering Committee members Bob Bartel, who had served with Mennonite Central Committee (MCC) in Labrador, and Hedy Sawadsky.[7]

A brochure from the event, in which eighty-five people participated, noted,

> The consultation will be a time of listening, prayer and discernment as to how Christ is calling people of faith to respond to the crisis of the Innu of Labrador and Quebec and Canada's native peoples generally with respect to land and militarism.
>
> The event will provide opportunity to interact with Innu and others intimately familiar with the militarization of Nitassinan, the Innu homeland. It will draw together people from across Canada as well as from the U.S. who are committed to answering the call of Christ in the voice of Canada's native peoples.[8]

The statement drawn up after the consultation expressed solidarity with the Innu struggle and noted the resource people all cited the low-level flying in Nitassinan as "a reprehensible affront to the environment, the health of it its people and the sovereignty of the Innu." It called on churches to place nonviolent pressure on the Canadian government in

6. LaDuke, "Innu Women and NATO." See also PBI, "Justice and Healing in Sheshatshit."

7. Other resource people included Innu representatives Daniel Ashini, Elizabeth and Francis Penashue, Rich and Louise Cober-Bauman from MCC Labrador, Menno Wiebe, MCC Native concerns, Bill Janzen, MCC Ottawa, Lorna Schwartzentruber, ARC/Project North, Ernie Regehr, Project Ploughshares, and Lawrence Hart, a Cheyenne chief and Mennonite pastor. The conference was endorsed/supported by the General Conference Mennonite Church, Conference of Mennonites in Canada, Conrad Grebel College's Institute of Peace and Conflict Studies, Mennonite conference of Eastern Canada Peace and Justice Commission, MCC Canada Native concerns, MCC Ontario and Stirling Avenue and Olive Branch Mennonite churches (from Kitchener-Waterloo, Ontario).

8. CPT, "The Innu Crisis and the Call of Christ."

support of "Innu brothers and sisters." People who attended the conference committed themselves to sharing the Innu story in their congregations.

Notes from the strategy sessions reveal much brainstorming over how to educate constituents about the Innu's struggle and acts of public witness that participants could undertake on the Innu's behalf. Some creative suggestions for the latter included playing the noise made by low-level jet fighters in public and collecting litter from military exercises and leaving them in the yards of military authorities. Consultation participants held a public prayer vigil on the steps of the Department of National Defence.[9]

The Innu representatives told the participants that their biggest need at that time was fundraising and education of European Canadians about the disruption that the low-level flights were causing in their communities. Those present believed that these activities fit better under the purview of congregations and solidarity groups than they did under CPT's mandate.[10]

Had the Innu wanted CPT with them on the runways and bombing ranges, CPT's first accompaniment project might very well have been with them. The low-level flights over Labrador and the Innu's resistance to them would have fit CPT's mandate well on several different levels: U.S., Canadian, and European governments were all culpable in the oppression of the Innu; the flights tied into a larger issue of governments considering their military hardware more important than the welfare of human beings and the environment; the Innu had already organized themselves and were committed to Nonviolent Direct Action.

One consequence of the consultation was the organizing of an Innu solidarity group that would eventually become CPT-Ontario. Early members included Doug Pritchard—who would go on to become the coordinator of CPT-Canada and then co-director of CPT after Gene Stoltzfus retired—Hedy Sawadsky, Murray Lumley, and Lena Siegers.[11]

9. Except for the Innu resource people, all of the presenters and sponsors were in some way affiliated with Mennonites. Future projects show a noticeable shift toward a more ecumenical focus for CPT.

10. Notes attached to brochure that the author received from Bob Hull. Steering Committee member Bob Bartel would be arrested in 1992 for accompanying Innu in a sit-in on the runway.

11. Leis, letter to Pastors Peace and Justice Coordinators (lists Doug Pritchard as contact). Schirch-Elias, letter to June Schwartzentruber Fund Committee.

The organization of CPT-Europe did not fare as well as CPT-Canada. Dutch Mennonite Maarten Van der Werf and German Mennonite Wolfgang Krauss tried to get German and Dutch Mennonites more involved with the issue—given that German and Dutch military planes would use Labrador airspace. They expressed the hope that European CPTers could undertake NVDA and civil disobedience by accompanying the Innu. However, their constituents, as Van der Werf reported, liked "the idea 'peace' rather than the dirty work of struggle."[12]

THE KAHNIAKEHAKA (MOHAWK) NATION IN QUEBEC

The Mohawk Nation is part of a six-nation confederation called the "Haudenosaunee," or, "People building a longhouse." People of non-indigenous descent commonly refer to this entity as "the Iroquois Confederation." In this confederacy, the communal long houses used by the different nations had served as a template for the nations' roles. The Mohawks became the "Eastern Doorkeepers." The Seneca the "Western Doorkeepers" The Onondagas in the middle were the "Firekeepers" while the Cayugas and the Oneidas were the "Younger Brothers" and the Tuscarora, who joined the confederacy in the eighteenth century, were the "Adopted brothers."[13] Benjamin Franklin used The Great Law of Peace—the "constitution" of the Haudenosaunee Confederacy—as a pattern upon which he based the U.S. Constitution.

Founded some time between 1000 and 1450 CE, according to oral tradition, this confederacy predated the establishment of the United States and Canada. Its territory extended as far west as the contemporary state of Ohio and as far east as Quebec. At Fort Stanwix in 1784, the U.S. recognized the independent lands of the Haudenosaunee and established a formal boundary line.[14]

---

12. Van der Werf, letter to Gene Stoltzfus, Jan 26, 1990. In "CPT Update (from Europe)," dated Jan/Feb 1990, Van der Werf noted mournfully, "The European CPT activities have been reduced to having a mailbox and sending out once in a while a news sheet. This was decided in the EMFK (Europaiesches Mennonitisches Friedenskomitee—European Mennonite Peace Committee) board meeting in September 1989."

13. Knockwood, "Mohawk History, Thoughts and Wisdom." CPT would later become involved with the Oneida Nation, another member of the Haudenosaunee Confederacy. See chap. 9.

14. "Treaty with the Six Nations, 1784," 5–6.

The Oka crisis evolved from the municipality of Oka expropriating Mohawk lands in 1947.[15] The Quebec legislature in 1959 passed a bill that enabled the municipality of Oka to build a golf course on land that the Mohawks used as a burial ground. After trying and failing to have their claims recognized in court by the Department of Indian Affairs and Northern Development (DIAND) in 1975, 1977, and 1989, the Mohawks erected a peaceful barricade on a side road within their cemetery on March 11, 1990. Negotiations between the Mohawks and Oka could not resolve the situation and the Quebec courts and provincial government came down squarely on the side of the town of Oka. In July 1990, the provincial government gave Oka permission to remove the Mohawk barricade, by force, if necessary. A SWAT team and the Mohawks exchanged fire on July 11, resulting in the death of Quebec provincial police officer, Corporal Marcel Lemay.

MCC-Canada responded to a request by the Mohawks to become involved with the issue by urging the federal government to negotiate peacefully with the Mohawks. The Canadian government subsequently announced that it would not interfere in Quebec's provincial affairs.

The Mohawks, on July 20, 1990, announced four conditions that needed to be met before they ended the blockade:

1. Oka must abandon the plan to expand the golf course

2. Police forces must withdraw

3. Police blockades in Kanesatake and Kahnawake must be removed

4. The government must allow forty-eight hours after signing an agreement for people to leave the two Mohawk territories without being searched

John Paul Lederach, an internationally known mediator and head of Mennonite Conciliation Services, received an invitation to mediate from the Mohawk Nation office in Kahnawake on July 24 and left Mennonite

---

15. France had claimed Mohawk's land at Kanesatake in 1608 and granted them to the Sulpician Order of Priests. The British government, following the conquest of the area, reaffirmed the Sulpician Order's trusteeship of the lands. A 1912 ruling upheld the Sulpicians' ownership, but left unclear the division between church lands and those of the Kanesatake community. In 1945, the Canadian government then bought the land from the Sulpicians. Robert Hull, "Kanienkehaka Chronology," 105.

290 IN HARM'S WAY

World Conference to do so.[16] Two days later, he contacted Robert Hull, the chairperson of CPT, to see if CPT could provide the bodies for his proposal, endorsed by the Mohawks, that he called "Options for NGO/ Civilian Nonviolent Equivalent to United Nations Peacekeepers."

As proposals and counterproposals between the federal government, Quebec provincial government and the Mohawks went back and forth, Lederach strongly urged that the parties to the conflict send these proposals through private channels rather than the media. Meanwhile, Hull (representing CPT), the Montreal Center for Nonviolence, and the Montreal Mennonite Fellowship discussed ways of intervening. The Mohawks asked that CPT cooperate with the Paris-based Federation for Human Rights (FIDH) by putting people at the Sureté (police) checkpoint.

On August 17, after outbreaks of vigilante violence and a military buildup of 2600 personnel and twenty armed personnel carriers in the area, Hull faxed the names of eleven internationals in North America to replace the FIDH observers at the Sureté barricades. The Mohawks had specifically requested internationals to emphasize that the conflict was a dispute between sovereign nations. Quebec premier Robert Bourassa accused the Mohawks of "negotiating in bad faith," dismissed the FIDH observers and ordered the military to move into Kanesatake.

The Mohawks asked the army to allow Mohawk elderly, women, and children to evacuate. While the Quebec provincial police stood by and watched, local Quebecois vigilantes at the exit from the Island bridge pelted them with stones and chunks of asphalt; one elderly resident of the Mohawk reservation later died of his injuries. The same vigilantes also pelted the vehicles of FIDH with rocks and hit them with bats, again without the promised intervention of the Quebec and Canadian authorities.

The Mohawks asked Hull to find a way into the Kahnawake village so they would have an international observer present, should the military invade. He was not able to do so, but organized local Mennonites to participate as observers the following week. They reported numerous abuses of the Mohawks' civil rights by the Quebec provincial police.

On September 4, Hull received a phone call from the Mohawk Nation office in Plattsburgh, New York, who told him that the military

16. After Lederach's departure, three hundred people attended a workshop about the crisis and more than one thousand Mennonites signed a petition calling on the Canadian government to resolve the conflict in an honorable and just way. Hull, "Kanienkehaka Chronology," 108.

had invaded the Kahnawake Longhouse—a religious sanctuary—the previous evening. The military claimed to have found a cache of weapons there. Robert Hull and Menno Wiebe (director of Native Concerns for MCC Canada) discussed asking local Mennonites to form a choir to sing at the barricades to reduce the tension and present positive images for television. The Mohawks, in turn, would gather to sing on the other side of the barricade. Organizers of the event, however, did not reckon with armed and drunken vigilantes who tried to attack the choir on September 5. The Mennonites left when the Canadian army asked them to.

In his chronology of the events at Oka, Hull noted that on September 7, after a discussion with Debby Martin-Koop co-pastor of the Montreal Mennonite Fellowship, the Mennonites who had intervened in the crisis concluded that the "time is past for outside CPT intervention, especially from non-Quebec Anglophones."[17]

Although Hull was not able to muster an official CPT delegation to Oka, the Mohawk standoff proved to be educational for the people developing CPT in its early years. If, the CPT steering committee speculated, a group of trained CPT workers had been available for the singing at the barricade rather than local church people who had brought children and picnic baskets, they might have had better success dealing with the Canadian military and the vigilante violence. Thus the Oka crisis, like the 1992 Los Angeles insurrection, helped push CPT in the direction of training a team of full-time workers.

John Paul Lederach's interaction with CPT was also significant. By 1990, Lederach had already achieved international fame in the field of Conflict Resolution (which Lederach later renamed Conflict Transformation). Inviting CPT to participate in the Oka standoff accorded with Lederach's principle that sometimes an "insider partial" approach to mediation can do more good in a conflict situation than a neutral mediator. That is, sometimes a person or team that clearly sympathizes with and is trusted by one party, but wants to keep a conflict from escalating into violence, can do more good than someone who is neutral. Lederach believed a team of Insider-Partials representing the Mohawks, Oka non-natives, Quebec government, etc. would have greatly benefited the situation. He wrote,

17. Ibid., 112.

> A balanced team with clear accessibility and accountability would
> have reduced the potential for violence by improving communi-
> cation. It would also have increased the changes that negotiated
> settlement to the crisis could have been attained by creating and
> sustaining a clear and fair process and empowering people to
> identify and address short-a and long-term issues.[18]

Lederach clearly saw the potential for CPTers to function as insider-
partials in crisis situations as well as serving as a violence-deterring presence. For this reason, he specifically asked CPT to contribute a chapter to
his book, *From the Ground Up: Mennonite Contributions to International
Peacebuilding*.[19] For Mennonites uncomfortable with NVDA, who associated "peacemaking" with conflict resolution, Lederach's "seal of approval"
lent legitimacy to Christian Peacemaker Team's mission in its early years,
when CPT's constituency was largely Anabaptist.

AAZHOODENA/STONEY POINT NATION IN ONTARIO

Aazhoodena (also called Stoney Point) lies on the beach-ringed south-
eastern shores of Lake Huron. In 1942, the Canadian government seized
the land of the Aazhoodenaang [Ah-jhoo-DEH-nang] Nation—an
Anishinabe people—for an army base, promising to return it after the
war. The government failed to do so and fifty-one years later, in 1993,
a group of Aazhoodenaang re-occupied the land. In September 1995,
some of them occupied the adjacent Ipperwash Provincial Park, after it
had closed for the season, because the province had neglected to protect
traditional burying grounds there as it had promised.

Although the earlier occupation of the army base occurred peacefully, and although they had no evidence that the Aazhoodenaang were
bearing firearms, the Ontario Provincial Police (OPP) responded to the
occupation of Ipperwash Park by sending in four hundred officers on
September 6, 1995, and opening fire on unarmed men, women, and children. According to Aazhoodenaang people present there, police beat an
elder from a nearby First Nations community who had approached them
to calm the situation. During the fracas that followed, Acting Sergeant
Kenneth Deane shot and killed Dudley George. The Ontario Provincial

---

18. John Paul Lederach, "Facing the Oka Crisis: A Conflict Resolution
Perspective," 124.

19. Kern, "From Haiti to Hebron," 183–200.

police prevented George from receiving immediate medical attention and George died of his wounds. An Ontario provincial court found Deane guilty of "criminal negligence causing death" and sentenced him to two hundred hours of community service.

Aazhoodenaang people, along with other First nation groups, faith groups, community groups, and political parties, as well as Amnesty International and the United Nations Human Rights Commission called for a public inquiry into the attack.[20]

By the time CPT-Ontario became involved with the Aazhoodenaang Nation, the CPT Steering Committee had authorized, in October 1997, the establishment of a CPT Ontario office in Toronto with Doug Pritchard as a part-time staff person. One of CPT-Ontario's first official actions was to consult with First Nations people about the conflict at Ipperwash in November 1997.[21]

In April 1998, CPT-Ontario was present at the hearing in which Warren George, a cousin of Dudley George, was convicted of "Criminal negligence and assault" for driving into police lines during the Ipperwash confrontation. He had come to rescue Kettle Point Band Councillor Bernard George whom the Provincial police were beating.

Unlike Police Officer Deane, who had received a sentence of community service for deliberately killing Dudley George, an unarmed man, Warren George received a six-month jail sentence, a two-year suspension of his driving privileges, and a ten-year ban on owning firearms. The judge noted that Warren George had a clean record and was not a danger to the public, but that the court had "to send a message to the community." At the request of George's family, CPT-Ontario participated in a prayer circle with other First Nations people while the judge was considering the sentence.

On September 6, 1998, members of CPT-Ontario participated in a sunrise ceremony on the third anniversary of George's death at

20. "In Depth: The Ipperwash inquiry"; CPTnet, Klassen, "Stoney Point, Ontario—Sunrise," Sept 15, 1998; "Ziisbaakdoke-Giizis"; AI, "Canada: Why there must be a public inquiry."

21. In March 1999, CPTers in Canada organized a Consultation at the Conference of Mennonites in Canada offices in Winnipeg, MB to discuss a proposal for Christian Peacemaker Teams Canada. Consensus regarding next steps for CPT's development in Canada included establishing a "Canada office" accountable to CPT with responsibility for organizing regional CPT groups, recruitment, constituency development, and lobbying Canadian governments. Doug Pritchard, comments on draft of this chapter.

Aazhoodena. A month later, on October 12, 1998, they formed a mile-long "human billboard" alongside Highway 401 in Cambridge, Ontario to call for a public inquiry into Dudley George's death. The participants, each with a single word, held them up to compose the following poem:

> Ipperwash:
> Stoney Point is native burial land
> Dudley George died there 'cause he took a stand
> The province resists an inquiry still
> Who put our taxes to work to kill?[22]

In 2003, the George family settled a wrongful death lawsuit with the Ontario Provincial Police and dropped their suit against Ontario Premier Mike Harris—who had refused to authorize an inquiry into Ipperwash incident—after the newly elected Liberal government promised to call an inquiry, which opened in June 2004. Justice Sidney Linden, the commissioner of the Inquiry into the death of Dudley George ruled in May 2007 that the Ontario Provincial Police, former Ontario premier Mike Harris, and the Canadian government all bore responsibility for events that led to George's death. Particularly significant was the November 2005 testimony of former attorney general Charles Harnick, who said Harris had told him, "I want the f—ing Indians out of the park," during a meeting about the Ipperwash occupation just hours before the fatal shooting of George.[23]

22. See CPTnet releases: Doug Pritchard, "Sarnia, Ontario: 'Two Circles,'" April 3, 1998; Joel Klassen, "Stoney Point, Ontario—SUNRISE AT AAZHOODENAANG," Sept. 15, 1998; "Kitchener, Ontario: OCT. 12 Oct. 12," "CPT WITNESS FOR DUDLEY GEORGE," October 12, 1998; "Waterloo, ON: Human Billboard Calls for Inquiry in Ipperwash Tragedy," October 16, 1998.

The report following the witness referred to highway 401 as being the "North America's busiest highway." Oddly, this remark generated the most criticism of CPT that had appeared to date on the CPT discussion group (menno.org.cpt.d@mennolink.org), as trivia buffs argued about which highway was busiest.

23. CBC News, "The Ipperwash Inquiry." "In Depth: The Ipperwash Inquiry," CBC News Online, Updated May 31, 2007, http://www.cbc.ca/news/background/ipperwash/ (accessed April 28, 2008).

CHIPPEWAS OF NAWASH UNCEDED FIRST NATION
IN ONTARIO

When MCC-Ontario's Native Concerns staff suggested in 1997 that CPT-Ontario become involved with the Ipperwash incident, they also suggested that the organization look into recent violence toward the Chippewas of Nawash First Nation. Clashes had erupted during the fishing season in 1997 between Nawash fishers and non-native fishers. Additionally, a private developer had plans to build cottages on the Nation's burial grounds.

Like the Aazhoodenaang, the people of the Nawash First Nation were members of the Anishinabe people. In most of their publications, however, they referred to themselves as Chippewa, an Anglicization of Ojibwe—the language of the Anishinabe. On their website they refer to themselves as "The Chippewas of the Unceded First Nation." In the nineteenth century, their nation had given up land in a series of treaties that reduced their territory from 1.5 million acres to reserves of a few thousand acres on the Saugeen (Bruce) peninsula. Non-natives then expropriated much of those acres without informing the Nawash they had done so.

The 1998 CPT-Ontario regional training group visited the Chippewas of Nawash First Nation in February 1998. CPT-Ontario hurried to complete the regional training by May 1998, so they would have people on hand to deter the violence that could happen with the opening of the fishing season. However, by that time, Nawash had come to a satisfactory fishing agreement with the government of Ontario and did not require the CPT presence.

However, CPT-Ontario reservists did attend the 11th Annual "Salmon Spectacular" in nearby Owen Sound, Ontario. The salmon fishing was a concern to the Nawash because it involved stocking non-native salmon species in Lake Huron, which threatened the native trout species that the Chippewas fished commercially.

At the derby, officials from the Ontario government and the Sportsmen association reminded the anglers not to tamper with the Nawash's nets. Their message of tolerance and respect, however, did not make it down to the rank and file sports fishers. In a release about the Derby, Doug Pritchard recorded one sportsman telling him (as he weighed in his catch of five large Chinook salmon), "There aren't any fish left here. The natives fished them all out. They oughta take all them Indians out in the woods and shoot them."

CPT-Ontario also attended the October 1998 Nawash Fisheries Conference held in Owen Sound. The conference organizers invited CPT to participate as "security" for the weekend in case non-natives showed up to harass conference participants, but no untoward incidents occurred.[24]

CALDWELL NATION IN ONTARIO

The Caldwell Nation also belongs to the Anishinabe people. In 1999, the Caldwell Band of Point Pelee and Pelee Island, was the only federally recognized Indian Band in southern Ontario without reserve land of its own. Because the Caldwell Nation of Point Pelee had no reserve land, they had no access to most federal government programs available to other native communities. In 1951, the Minister of Indian Affairs put the Caldwell Band under the Indian Act "elective" system of government, which stipulated that only reserve residents may vote. Since Canada also maintained that the Caldwells had no reserve, the move effectively blocked the formation of a recognized band government.

After years of legal wrangling, the Caldwell Nation once again made a formal claim on Point Pelee and Pelee Island in 1987. The Canadian government reached an agreement-in-principle with the Caldwell to provide $23 million over a twenty-five period for the purchase of land in an area around Blenheim, Ontario. Once land was part of the Caldwell Reservation, it would no longer be subject to municipal zoning or municipal taxation.[25]

The agreement stipulated that the Caldwell nation would not expropriate land from Canadians of European descent. The Nation also agreed to pay for municipal services such as fire protection and garbage collection and to maintain environmental standards on reserve land at least as high those on municipal lands.[26] Nevertheless, the Canadian govern-

24. Pritchard, e-mail, Sept 12, 2005. See CPTnet releases: Pritchard, "Cape Croker, Ontario—Unceded," Feb 25, 1998; Pritchard, "Cape Croker, Ontario—Place of Healing," Mar 1 1998; Pritchard, "Owen Sound, Ontario—Shoot," Sept 9, 1998; Pritchard, "Owen Sound, Ontario—Laws and Nets," Oct 20, 1998. See also *Chippewas of Nawash Unceded First Nation.*

25. Caldwell First Nation, "History of the Caldwell Band."

26. Caldwell First Nation, "Caldwell Present Info"; INAC, "Negotiations on the Caldwell First Nation's Specific Claim"; INAC, "Backgrounder: Caldwell Claim and Additions."

ment's decision was deeply unpopular with the local Euro-Canadians. Almost every home within a ten-kilometre radius of the band office put up "NOT FOR SALE" signs.

CPT-Ontario became involved with the Caldwell after a January 28, 1999 incident when someone entered the Caldwell property, spiked the tires of a vehicle, cut through supports on the baseball backstop and sprayed graffiti on a new barn reading "CONDEMNED" and "Abide by the LAWS!" Chief Larry Johnson invited MCC-Ontario and CPT to be a violence-deterring presence on the property shortly after. A release about the overnight vigils quoted CPT reservist Benno Barg as saying, "We recognize we cannot solve the root issues here, but we can act to reduce tension so the involved parties have space to work toward resolution." The CPTers encountered no hostility in the evenings and ended their two-week presence on February 27, 1999. Chief Johnson said that the presence had allowed the band to "recover some peace of mind" and arranged for band members and other supporters to carry on nightly watches.[27]

In the fall of 1999, CPT-Ontario sought to address the reaction of the Euro-Canadian settlers to the Caldwell land purchase. They knocked on the doors of houses whose mailboxes bore the "not for sale" signs and asked them why they had put them up. Some had done so simply because their neighbors asked them to. Others had more blatantly racist reasons: "You know what the reserves look like—full of junk and shacks and dirty kids. They'll drive the price of my land way down." Others cited concerns about the Caldwell driving up the price of the land.

In a second round of CPT door-to-door visitations in December, local people living near the Caldwell territory expressed more frustration with the Canadian government than with the Caldwell Nation and expressed sadness about the deterioration of relationships between native and non-native residents. Theresa Johnson, a Caldwell leader, told the team that many signs had come down since the September visit.[28]

---

27. CPTnet, "Blenheim, ON: CPTers Accompany," Feb 20, 1999; CPTnet, "Blenheim, ON: CPT Completes Nightly Vigils," Mar 22, 1999; "Blenheim, Ontario: CPT Keeps Watch," 5.

28. CPTnet, Pritchard, "Blenheim, ON: Who is my Neighbour?" Oct 9, 1999; CPTnet, Morton, "Blenheim, Ontario: Making Little Ripples," Nov 20, 1999. The dates for the actual visitations do not appear in either release, but the second refers to the first visitation as happening in September.

Pritchard noted in "Who is my Neighbor?" that Chief Larry Johnson of the Caldwell put his own sign on his mailbox: "Canadian racism can be beaten."

THE OCETI SAKOWIN ("SEVEN COUNCIL FIRES")
ENCAMPMENT IN SOUTH DAKOTA

The Lakota, Dakota and Nakota nations—called the "Great Sioux Nation" in broken treaties—have perhaps the highest profile of all the First Nations in the continental United States. Hollywood movies such as *Little Big Man* and *Dances with Wolves* romanticize Plains Indians.[29] Non-native Americans know the names of Sitting Bull and Crazy Horse and have heard about the rout of General George Armstrong Custer and the Seventh Cavalry by Sitting Bull and his coalition of First Nations. Fewer learn about the Seventh Calvary massacre of 150–350 men, women, and children encamped at Wounded Knee Creek (one of many massacres of Plains Indian civilians by European-American soldiers and settlers). Lakota spiritual leader Black Elk said of the event,

> I did not know then how much was ended. When I look back now from this high hill of my old age, I can still see the butchered women and children lying heaped and scattered all along the crooked gulch as plain as when I saw them with eyes still young. And I can see that something else died there in the bloody mud, and was buried in the blizzard. A people's dream died there.[30]

Eighty-seven years later, Wounded Knee again reached the radar of European-Americans when activists affiliated with the American Indian Movement (AIM) and people still pursuing a traditional Oglala Lakota way of life occupied the town of Wounded Knee on the Pine Ridge reservation. They did so to protest the corrupt policies of tribal President Richard Wilson. Declaring the birth of the Independent Oglala Nation, the AIM activists remained in a standoff between the FBI Federal Marshals and Wilson's Guardians of the Oglala Nation (GOONs) for seventy-one days. Heavy fire from automatic weapons killed AIM activists Frank Clearwater (Cherokee) on April 17, 1973, and Buddy Lamont (Oglala) on April 27. After the activists occupying Wounded Knee surrendered on May 7, 1973, three years of what the local people call the Reign of Terror followed in

---

29. Most of the indigenous people CPT worked with in South Dakota preferred the name "Indians" to "Native Americans"—some because they considered themselves a sovereign nation and therefore no more "American" than residents of India, and others because they were just comfortable with the term. Also, the American Indian Movement still commands respect among Indians in the region.

30. Neihardt, *Black Elk Speaks*, 207.

which Wilson's GOONS attacked, raped, and killed their opponents on Pine Ridge.

By 1975, many AIM leaders were in jail or underground due to the FBI hunting them down and tying them up in court. AIM activists were thus keeping a low profile on Pine Ridge. On June 26, 1975, two FBI agents came onto the Jumping Bull property, near the village of Oglala, ostensibly in search of a man who had stolen a pair of cowboy boots.[31] A shootout followed between the FBI and AIM activists staying on the property. Two FBI agents and AIM activist Joe Stuntz Killsright, were killed. Leonard Peltier and AIM members Dino Butler, Bob Robideau, and James Eagle (the accused boot thief) were indicted for the deaths of the two agents.

Peltier fled to Canada, which extradited him after the U.S. government supplied the courts there with a false affidavit. In the meantime, an all-white jury had acquitted Peltier's co-defendants Robideau and Butler in 1975. The jury—after hearing about the deaths of fifty-seven members and supporters at the hands of the FBI and the paramilitary GOONS aligned with the FBI—concluded that Butler and Robideau had a right to defend themselves.

According to an official memo obtained under the U.S. Freedom of Information Act, the FBI dropped charges against Jimmy Eagle in 1976 "so that the full prosecutive weight of the Federal Government could be directed against Leonard Peltier." Leonard Peltier remains in Leavenworth Prison, as of this writing in 2007.[32]

The fact that the case against Peltier, Robideau, and Butler rested on the testimony of the Federal agents against the testimonies of Indians was one of several factors that led to an invitation for CPT to accompany the Oceti Sakowin encampment on LaFramboise Island in the spring of 1999.

In early 1999, a delegation of First Nations Mennonites from North America came to visit the team in Hebron and learn about what CPT was doing to address the issues relating to Israeli confiscation of Palestinian

---

31. In a June 25, 2005 e-mail, CPTer Carl Meyer, then working with MCC on Pine Ridge, noted the search was "a ridiculous pretext, since the FBI is only responsible for major crimes on the reservation; a theft of cowboy boots doesn't come close to FBI jurisdiction."

32. A good source for the shootout and events leading up to it is Matthiesen, *In the Spirit of Crazy Horse.*

land.[33] Delegation members, including MCCer Harley Eagle of the Dakota Nation, asked the team why they had come halfway around the world to address issues of land confiscation in Palestine when the U.S. government and the state of South Dakota were in the process of confiscating land from the Lakota, Dakota, and Nakota people.

Several months later, a group of First Nations men affiliated with the Lakota Student Alliance began an encampment on La Framboise Island near Pierre, South Dakota. The island was a part of the two hundred thousand acres at risk for confiscation—land twice promised to the "Great Sioux Nation"[34] in the Fort Laramie treaties of 1851 and 1868. The legislation authorizing the confiscation was called informally the "Mitigation Act"[35] and represented the largest transfer of Federal land to a state in U.S. history. Senator Tom Daschle and Governor William Janklow had enlisted the help of collaborators from the Cheyenne River and the Lower Brulé tribes to sign the bill, so that they could say they had the support of the Sioux. Those taking a public stand against the transfer, most of them Oglala Lakota, noted that an 1868 treaty with the U.S. government stipulated that three-quarters of the men in the Sioux Nation had to sign agreements that would have changed the treaties, so the acquiescence of the two bands did not legitimize the transfer.[36]

The origins of the Oceti Sakowin encampment lay in a gathering of "Great Sioux Nation" to protest the Mitigation Act on March 22, 1999. While they were on LaFramboise Island, seven Lakota men decided to stay and keep a sacred fire burning at the camp as a "reminder that the aboriginal and Treaty rights of the Sioux Nation are not extinguished." The fire would remain alight for the next seven months, even through violent thunderstorms when water swamped the tipi that housed it and

33. MCC had also organized a delegation of Palestinians to visit First Nations reserves in North America.

34. The term "Sioux" derives from an Anishinabe/Ojibwe term, *nadewisou*, which means "snakes," and can also mean "enemies." The French shortened the name to "Sioux." Sultzman, "Ojibwe History." One Lakota Web site notes, "The name was never meant to be a compliment, since the French were at war with us at the time." Tasnaheca, "History of the Sioux."

35. The full title of the act was "Cheyenne River Sioux Tribe, Lower Brule Sioux Tribe, and State of South Dakota Terrestrial Wildlife Habitat Mitigation Act."

36. Dobbs, "Visions of a new future."

the "Warriors" literally lifted the fire up to keep it burning.[37] They vowed to remain until the government met three objectives:

1. A test of the legality of the "Mitigation Act"
2. An environmental impact statement conducted by the Army Corps of Engineers
3. Proper congressional hearings on the bill

Several of the warriors had lived on Pine Ridge in the 1970s and remembered well the persecution of the AIM members at the time. Robert Quiver, head of the Lakota Student Alliance, told John Lurie, a reporter for *Indian Country Today,*

> Our house became an AIM house: The AIM people would come over for a shower, something to eat, or to rest. We always had tight security in case the GOONs came around. But one day we were on the road and we came up behind a really slow-moving truck. Another truck full of GOONs was suddenly on our tail and we were forced to stop. They got out, put a gun to my father's head and ordered two men onto the road. My dad pleaded with them not to shoot because we were there. My baby brother and I were scared and started to cry. Those GOONs aimed their guns at us and said, 'If you don't shut those kids up we're going to blow their heads off.' The GOONs were death squads, just like they had in El Salvador and Guatemala.[38]

Harley Eagle and his wife Sue called the CPT Chicago office after the encampment began and said that the situation called for international observers to prevent another incident similar to what happened at Wounded Knee in 1973 and at the Jumping Bull compound in 1975.[39]

37. Kaufman, e-mail, June 27, 2005. See also her CPTnet release, "South Dakota: Pray with your Heart," May 25, 1999.

The founders of the encampment used the Lakota term "Warriors" to describe themselves. Harley Eagle, a Dakota, told the team on May 19, 1999 that "it was the way of the warrior to do whatever was necessary to protect his people" and that white men had given it the violent interpretation. "To be a warrior means that you will lay down your life for your family, not that you will take another person's life," he told them. He also said that the leadership of the encampment had strongly resisted suggestions from older AIM members outside the encampment that "other tactics should be considered." CPT Oceti Sakowin Encampment, "Update from Pierre last week."

38. Lurie, "A Life or Death Last Stand."

39. Jeanne Kostner of the South Dakota Peace and Justice Center also issued the invitation on behalf of the Great Sioux Nation's tribal leadership; the Chicago office clarified

As had happened at Wounded Knee and the Jumping Bull compound, FBI agents staked out at the Oceti Sakowin encampment in its early days. When participants walked across the causeway to run errands, the Pierre police and South Dakota highway patrol stopped them and checked their records.

CPT responded to the invitation and set up a project on La Framboise Island in April 1999.[40] Rick Polhamus, Gene Stoltzfus, and Joanne Kaufman set up a tent on La Framboise Island—connected to Pierre, South Dakota by a causeway—with the Oceti Sakowin encampment on April 1, 1999. Shortly afterwards, Kathleen Kern and Lisa Martens replaced Stoltzfus. Given access to office space, electricity, and the Internet by the South Dakota Coalition Against Domestic Violence in Pierre (pronounced "Peer"), Kern and Kaufman put out four Urgent Actions between April 8 and May 14, 1999. The Urgent Actions asked constituents to send letters to Congress members, particularly those serving on committees with the power to change the status of the land transfer, and to Governor Janklow. They also designed a bulletin insert about the issue for CPT's constituent churches.[41]

While living at the encampment, the South Dakota team spent most of its energy listening to the stories of the Oceti Sakowin warriors and supporters and helping them maintain the camp by cooking, cleaning, and participating in night watches. They also spent time talking to government representatives in Pierre and environs. These included representatives of the FBI—whom the team felt it important to contact given its negative history on the Pine Ridge reservation—the Army Corps of Engineers and Governor Janklow's office. [42]

---

that the Nation had asked the center to do so before accepting the invitation. Kostner, "South Dakota Invitation to CPT."

40. Ibid.

41. See CPTnet releases: "Urgent Action Alert: Ask Senators," Apr 10, 1999; "Pierre, South Dakota: Continued Request," Apr 13, 1999; "Pierre, SD Urgent Action: Federal, South Dakota," Apr 17, 1999; "Pierre, SD, Update on La Framboise Island," May 14, 1999.

The bulletin insert, which gave a brief historical background, contact information, and suggestions for actions was titled "Taking Treaty Land by an Act of Congress: The 'Wildlife Mitigation' or 'Wildlife Restoration Act.'" See CPT Oceti Sakowin Encampment in Bibliography.

42. CPTnet, "South Dakota Update: April 16–26, 1999," May 9, 1999; "South Dakota Update: July 20–30, 1999," Aug 31, 1999. See also Lurie, "A Life or Death Last Stand."

The team also spent time visiting with First Nations people and sympathetic white residents living in Pierre. From them they learned that Governor Janklow exacted retributions from people who opposed him and his policies. Since the largest business in Pierre was the South Dakota state government, he could pull strings to see that people were fired, not promoted, or lost funding if they (including the local newspaper) defied his wishes.[43]

As the summer passed, people joined and left the encampment. Some First Nations people came from as far away as the Canadian Maritime Provinces to support the Oceti Sakowin. CPTers from the Boulder, Colorado regional training group were especially helpful in supplying reservists to maintain the project because full-timers were over-stretched. The warriors invited the team to participate in several official meetings to discuss the land transfer.[44]

Over the next months, no physical violence toward the Oceti Sakowin camp occurred, although people there did experience some harassment from non-Indians, who asserted that the island was the part of the State of South Dakota, called out "Get a job!" at those in the encampment or made Tarzan calls and shouted insults like "Prairie Niggers."

Some police harassment also occurred. On June 22, an off-duty Highway Patrol Officer called Pierre detective Mike Bucholz, saying that he smelled something funny coming from a "VW van with Utah plates, painted as a hippie van parked at Dairy Queen." Detective Bucholz found a white Mercury van with Utah plates at the Dairy Queen and searched it, finding nothing. When Lynn Stoltzfus and several members of the camp drove by the Dairy Queen in Stoltzfus' distinctively painted van (which did not have Utah plates), Bucholz followed it and approached Stoltzfus and the camp members after they arrived at their destination. With Stoltzfus' permission, the police officer searched the van and found no drugs; he

43. CPTnet, "South Dakota Update: April 16–26, 1999," May 9, 1999.

44. Some of the meetings to which CPTers were invited included one with Janklow, with the Pierre Sheriff's Office, several between the Black Hills Sioux Nation Treaty Council (BHSNTC) and the Army Corps of engineers (at one of which Janklow showed up and asked that the Corps give leases for all of the recreational sites to the state of South Dakota), at an Oglala Sioux tribal meeting, a Treaty Council meeting at Rosebud Casino, and between the Pierre Police, Sheriff's Dept., U.S. Attorney's Office, the COE and the Mayor. The Oceti Sakowin organizers also invited CPTers to particpate in a protest "reception" for President Bill Clinton at an Air force base near the Pine Ridge Reservation.

304 IN HARM'S WAY

ignored Stoltzfus and a white passenger, but arrested a Lakota passenger on an old Driving Under the Influence (DUI) charge.

An officer stopped Rick Polhamus just after he drove off the island and gave him a written warning for going 31 in a 35 mph zone, along with a verbal warning that "here in South Dakota you have to obey the law." Polhamus replied, "Where I come from in Ohio we get warnings for going above the speed limit, not below it." As it happened, he was on his way to the police station to talk with the chief about police harassment of the camp, so he took the warning along as physical evidence. The chief tried to take it from him, but Polhamus pleasantly refused to hand it over. Police also stopped Oceti Sakowin participants walking home to the encampment one night, claiming they smelled alcohol on his breath. The man noted wryly that he had not had a drink in six years and wondered how they could still smell it.[45]

At the end of July 1999, good news arrived. The U.S. House of Representatives voted to overturn the Mitigation Act. Members of camp had demanded an oversight hearing as one condition of their withdrawal, but its actual overturning was more than they had hoped. The repeal (called Section 505) was attached to an energy and water development appropriations Bill HR 2605 and still needed to pass the House and Senate Joint Committee, where similar bills are reconciled. The reconciled bill then needed to come to a vote before the House and Senate again.

As the time for the congressional vote approached, the South Dakota team enlisted the help of the CPT constituency in three Urgent actions. At the end of July, they asked constituents to fax their congressional representatives before 2:00 p.m. on July 27 when the vote was to take place, and urge him or her to vote for HR 2605 and in particular Section 505 of that appropriations bill that repealed the Mitigation Act. At the end of August, they asked constituents to contact representatives on the Joint Committee working on HR 2605 before Labor Day. The background information on the act that came with the Urgent Action included the following:

<hr/>

45. CPT Oceti Sakowin encampment, Letter to local law enforcement agencies (The copy of the letter in the Chicago office's South Dakota file bore the notation, "never sent-in computer"); CPT Oceti Sakowin encampment, "Report on harassment and arrest, Tuesday, June 22, 1999"; CPT Oceti Sakowin, "Memorandum re: events of Tuesday afternoon, June 22, 1999." The story about Rick Polhamus's citation by the police was from a June 23, 2005 e-mail sent by Carl Meyer to the author.

Urge the committee members to keep Section 505 in the Energy
and Water Development budget bill and repeal the first Title VI.

More importantly, also ask them to add language to the bill
which will also repeal Title VI of the Water Resources Development
Act (WRDA) of 1999. . . .

- Remind them that Title VI was passed in an underhanded manner
  after the WRDA bill failed to pass the House in 1998 because of
  treaty issues. Explain that it was passed twice under circumstances
  which make its legality suspect.

- Remind them that the U.S. is obligated to honor all treaties, including the Fort Laramie Treaty of 1868 under which the land in question should belong to the Lakota nation. Note that Article VI of the
  Constitution states that treaties are "the supreme law of the land."

- Remind them that Lakota people are concerned about two sections of Title VI which contradict each other: Sections 605A, which
  transfers the land to the state of South Dakota, contradicts Section
  605H, which gives Federal legal protection to Native American
  grave and cultural sites along the river.

- Remind them that Lakota people are so concerned about this bill
  that they have camped as a nonviolent witness since March on La
  Framboise Island, enduring racist heckling and sacrificing family
  time, jobs and education to ensure that there is land for future
  generations of Lakota.

On September 30, 1999, President Bill Clinton signed a bill that included the repeal of the Mitigation Act. Since, confusingly, the second
version of the Mitigation Act (605A) passed in August, the Oceti Sakowin
warriors decided to prepare for the winter. The South Dakota team asked
its constituents to contact Senators and representatives to (1) thank them
for keeping Section 505, (2) ask them to repeal the Mitigation Act attached to the Water Development Resources Authorization Act of 2000,
or (3) hold hearings on it so that Native Americans and others could register their concerns.[46]

---

46. See CPTnet releases: "Urgent Action: Urge Representatives," July 27, 1999; "Pierre,
SD: Small Victories at Seven Fires Camp," July 30, 1999; "South Dakota Urgent Action:
Support Repeal," Aug 25, 1999; "South Dakota: First Mitigation Act Repealed!" Oct 4,
1999.

U.S. Congress, *Making Appropriations for Energy and Water.* See also Harlan, "Land
transfer gets OK" and "WRDA not an appropriation." Harlan unravels the politics behind
the double-appropriation bills meant to expedite the transfer of the land in question.

As a last public action before CPT left the Oceti Sakowin encampment, Joanne Kaufman and Cliff Kindy accompanied fifty members of a Lakota delegation to Washington DC. The Lakota carried the sacred fire—representing the 1868 treaty that had still not been extinguished—in a stove on a pickup truck, stopping at Sioux City, Iowa City, and Indianapolis along the way. Participants intended the trek to bring visibility to treaty issues and the Oceti Sakowin encampment and to influence the legislation that could still transfer the land in question to South Dakota. Once in DC, they met with legislative assistance to discuss treaty violations with them [47]

On October 4, 1999, the team formally ended its presence in the camp. Charmaine White Face, a leader of the encampment and the Media Coordinator for the Black Hills Sioux Nation Treaty Council, said that the prayers for the repeal had been answered and that now the participants must work together to face other attacks on treaties the U.S. government made with the Great Sioux Nation.[48]

CPT would send a delegation the following year, March 25, 2000, to celebrate the anniversary of the camp's founding. Charmaine White Face, Media Coordinator for the Black Hills Sioux Nation Treaty Council recognized CPT as part of the celebration, for its role in reducing poten-

---

47. CPT Oceti Sakowin EncampmentPress release, "Celebrating Sovereignty,"; CPTnet, Chicago office archives."South Dakota: Sacred Fire," Sept 9, 2005; CPTnet, "South Dakota/D.C.: Sacred Fire," Sept, 1999; CPTnet, "South Dakota Update: August 18–September 11,1999," Sept 21, 1999. September 1999 CPTnet archives.

The Lakota and Dakota ran into some trouble with the D.C. Fire Department and Park Police because they kept the fire burning in a stove at the back of a pickup truck. Concerned that the authorities might douse the fire, the participants rallied around the truck with their signs as one man sang to the beat of a drum. However, once the fire fighters found out that the truck carried a fire extinguisher, the matter was resolved. Rick Polhamus tended the fire on La Framboise while the others in the encampment were in D.C.

48. CPTnet,"Pierre, South Dakota: CPT Presence," Oct 11, 1999. The unwritten reality of the end of CPT's presence was the belief that the Oceti Sakowin warriors had become dependent on CPTers to do key functions, such as political organizing and communications that Robert Quiver had done when he was at the encampment in the spring; the other warriors were not interested in that sort of work. Additionally, the campers asked Kaufman to carry the money on the trip to DC, because she was an "outside observer" and therefore more trustworthy. Kaufman, comments on draft of Oceti Sakowin section of this chapter.

tial and real violence against camp residents and supporters. The Treaty Council decided by consensus to keep the sacred fire burning.[49]

The real tribute to CPT had happened months earlier, in June 1999, when representatives of the Great Sioux Nation honored the Warriors of LaFramboise in a traditional Lakota ceremony. CPTer Bob Epp had accepted at that time a hand-lettered, framed buckskin plaque, reading, "Great Sioux Nation Certificate of Appreciation, Christian Peacemaker Team, Honoring your courageous and dedicated stand protecting Fort Laramie Treaty Rights at the Oceti Sakowin Camp on La Framboise Island."[50]

ESGENOÔPETITJ/BURNT CHURCH NATION IN NEW BRUNSWICK

Although the Innu and the Beothuks may have had the earliest contact with Europeans, the Mi'kmaq probably had the earliest routine interactions with Basque, French, Spanish, and Irish fishermen in the sixteenth century. They developed a special relationship with the French, intermar-

49. CPTnet, "South Dakota: Laframboise Anniversary Celebration," Apr 25, 2000. The delegation ended up participating in a more tumultuous event on the Pine Ridge Reservation on March 21, 2000, when they joined a blockade to keep out a Bureau of Indian Affairs official from the reservation offices. Citing corruption and financial mismanagement by the Tribal Council, more than one hundred Oglalas had taken over the offices on January 16, 2000 to safeguard financial records that they said documented the corruption. CPTnet, "South Dakota: Lessons in Listening," May 11, 2000.

50. CPTnet, "South Dakota: CPT and La Framboise Warriors Honored," June 14, 1999. The release noted that the seven Lakota men who had begun the encampment had been inducted into the Lakota "Most Dependable Warriors" society a month earlier The induction ceremony had not been performed for over a century. See also Whiteface, "Sacred Ceremony."

In the summer of 2006, CPTers returned to South Dakota for six weeks, to accompany an encampment on Bear Butte, a site sacred to the Plains Indians. The encampment, which included the Oceti Sakowin tribes, was protesting the establishment of a biker bar and amphitheater outside Sturgis, South Dakota. The owner, Jay Allan boasted that the venue would contain "over 150,000 s.f. of asphalt for semi-tractor trailers ... 22,500 s.f. of ...ice cold beer ... kick-butt music & oh yea, hot hot women!" Native activists said building this bar within sight and hearing of Bear Butte would be analogous to putting a toilet in the sanctuary of a cathedral. As it happened, most of the thousands of bikers coming to Sturgis for the annual motorcycle rally heeded the call to support the Bear Butte encampment by boycotting Jay Allan's bar. See "Bear Butte, South Dakota"; CPTnet, John Spragge, "Bear Butte, SD: Lakota people and their allies protest desecration of Mato Paha," August 6, 2006; CPTnet, "Bear Butte, SD: Update on Urgent Action Request; Congresswoman Herseth meets with Bear Butte encampment representatives, 8 August 2006."

rying with French traders and explorers. Most converted to Catholicism under the tutelage of French Jesuits in the early seventeenth century. The French built their homes near the sea, rather than clearing forest, so their presence did not disrupt the Mi'kmaq's traditional hunter-gatherer lifestyle as much as the British presence did in other colonies. As Catholics, the French largely abided by the Pope's ruling in 1610 that indigenous peoples of the New World had the right to choose Catholicism, traditional religions, or both and the 1639 ruling that indigenous peoples should neither be enslaved nor deprived of their property.

Their alliance with the French meant, over the next two centuries, that the Mi'kmaq became involved with the battles between the French and British for control of what eventually became the Canadian Maritime Provinces and northern New England. The same European epidemics that had killed most of the First Nations in New England, facilitating settlement of European colonists,[51] also devastated the Mi'kmaq who came into contact with them during these battles. After a second epidemic struck the Mi'kmaq, the French accused the English of deliberately infecting them. Whether or not the accusation was true,[52] the Mi'kmaq believed it and the fighting became more intense. The British began offering bounties for the scalps of Mi'kmaq.

In 1755, the British expelled seven thousand French Acadians from the Maritimes. Some managed to stay behind, hidden by the Mi'kmaq. The British attacked one Mi'kmaq village on Miramichi Bay where Acadians were hiding in 1758 with "red-hot cannonballs," destroying wigwams, houses, and the church, thereby giving the village its English name, "Burnt Church." Christian Peacemaker Teams was to set up its project there more than two hundred years later.

Some of the Mi'kmaq continued at war with the British until 1779 when they signed a peace treaty. The treaty, like others signed in 1752, 1760, and 1761, promised that in exchange for a cessation of hostilities, the Mi'kmaq could hunt and fish "free from any molestation of any of

51. In Loewen, *Lies My Teachers Told Me,* 81, Loewen notes that these epidemics "probably constituted the most important geopolitical event of the early seventeenth century. Their net result was that the British, for their first 50 years in New England, would face no real Indian challenge."

52. Documentation from primary sources exists for the British deliberately infecting French-affiliated First Nations during the Pontiac Rebellion in 1763–1766, so they possibly had done so earlier. See, for example, the sources cited in d'Errico, "Jeffrey Amherst and Smallpox Blankets."

His Majesty's Troops, or other his good Subjects."[53] Other First Nations in the region had signed earlier Peace and Friendship treaties with the British government guaranteeing similar rights to earn a livelihood by fishing. These treaties became the rallying cry for the indigenous people of the Maritimes when the Canadian government sought to restrict their fishing.

By the 1970s, Canada was beginning to take a serious look at the depletion of the North Atlantic fishing stocks by factory fishing trawlers. The government began passing laws restricting fishing to certain seasons and stipulated that all fishers needed to have a license to catch fish. These regulations systematically shut out native fishers from the fishery, restricting them to fishing for personal consumption alone. According to Janet Shoemaker, an Esgenoôpetitj elder told her at the time the licensing system for lobster went into effect, no one informed the native communities about it. Someone he knew at the Department of Fisheries and Oceans called him two hours before the deadline for buying a license and told him he needed to come if he wanted to fish for lobster. Only three people from Esgenoôpetitj were able to come into town that day.[54]

Under the auspices of the eighteenth century treaties, the Mi'kmaq and other indigenous nations in the North Atlantic asserted their right to continue fishing, regardless of more recent laws passed by the Canadian government. In 1990, with the Sparrow Decision, Canada's Supreme Court ruled that native people could fish for purposes of personal consumption. However, throughout the next decade the restrictions on amount of catch and amount of time they could fish kept getting tighter and tighter.

Treaty rights were further tested in 1993, when the authorities from the Department of Fisheries and Oceans arrested Donald Marshall Junior, a Mi'kmaq fisherman, and prosecuted him on three charges under the 1985 Fisheries Act: selling eels without a license, fishing without a license, and using illegal nets after the fishing season closed.

Marshall argued that treaties signed in 1752, 1760, and 1761 exempted him from the Fisheries Act regulations. When his case came before the Supreme Court of Canada in 1999, the court decided that Marshall, along with other members of the Mi'kmaq, Maliseet, and Passamaquoddy

53. Sultzman, "Micmac History"; Mi'kmaq Resource Centre at Cape Breton University, "Timeline from Mi'kmaw Resource Guide 2007"; Smith, *Charlotte Taylor, her Life and Times;* Comitas Institute for Anthropological Study, "Treaty of 1779."

54. Shoemaker, e-mail message to the author, August 31, 2005.

nations did indeed have the treaty right to secure a "moderate livelihood" from year-round fishing, hunting, and gathering.

Non-native fishers[55]—who were themselves struggling economically—responded to the ruling by staging a "protest" that involved their destroying three thousand lobster traps set by native fishers in New Brunswick's Miramichi Bay on October 3, 1999. Although the Department of Fisheries and Oceans, the Canadian Coast Guard and Royal Canadian Mounted Police (RCMP) were also on the water and had assured the Esgenoôpetitj community before the protest that they would be patrolling, they did not intervene to prevent the destruction.[56] Several weeks later, after some Mi'kmaq fishers put out lobster traps for a second time, DFO officers confiscated the traps, saying they were "saving" them from non-native fishers.

The Mi'kmaq fishers never received any compensation for the traps and only twenty-two of the white fishers were charged with "causing mischief" after pressure from the Canadian public. Esgenoôpetitj First Nation (EFN) members felt they were caught in a Catch-22 situation: "We go out to cut wood, they tell us we can't. We go out to fish, they tell us we can't. We go home, they call us welfare bums," one Esgenoôpetitj First Nation member told Shoemaker and William Payne during an exploratory CPT delegation to the region in January 2000.

In March 2000, just before the spring fishing season opened, Esgenoôpetitj and the other Mi'kmaq and Maliseet bands met with the DFO. As had happened in South Dakota with the Lower Brule and Cheyenne River bands, the government met with each of the bands separately, hoping to get one or two of them to agree to DFO regulations, so that it could impose them on all the Maritime First Nations. The DFO negotiator told the aboriginal fishers they would discuss compensation for the fishing equipment destroyed in the fall, but only if the various bands submitted their fisheries to government regulation. Esgenoôpetitj was the first of the bands to reject the DFO regulations.

CPT's initial intervention on behalf of the Esgenoôpetitj nation was an Urgent Action calling on its constituents to contact Canadian government representatives asking them to compensate the Esgenoôpetitj fish-

55. The team elected to use this term, because both men and women were involved with fishing in New Brunswick.

56. Shoemaker, e-mail message to the author, August 31, 2005. Shoemaker noted that the non-native fishers even had media on board with them to document the event.

ers for their losses and to assist new fishers in obtaining training in time for the spring fishing season. The Urgent Action asked its constituents to "emphasize the Canadian government's responsibility to deal with aboriginal people on the nation-to-nation basis enshrined in the treaties as new understandings are worked out for the conservation of fish stocks."[57]

At the invitation of the EFN, Lena Siegers and Janet Shoemaker arrived in April 2000 to set up the Esgenoôpetitj project. Among all of CPT's projects in indigenous communities, Esgenoôpetitj would prove to be the most eventful and the most violent.

On May 1, the opening of lobster season, European-Canadian fishers licensed by Canada's Department of Fisheries and Oceans began setting 240,000 lobster traps in the inner and outer parts of Miramichi Bay. Five days later, Brian Bartibogue, a band councillor from the Esgenoôpetitj First Nation, set out ten traps licensed by the authority of the EFN Fishery Act (a management plan that marine biologists determined was more conservation-oriented than the DFO plan).[58] DFO officers immediately

57. CPTnet, "Burnt Church, NB: The Minister Wanted One Dead Person," February 10, 2000; CPTnet, "New Brunswick: Hold Canadian Government accountable for attacks," February 15, 2000; "Burnt Church, New Brunswick: The Right to Regulate," March 24, 2000.

58. Ward and Augustine, "Draft for the Esgenoopotitj First Nation Fishery (EFN) Fishery Act (*Fisheries Policy.*)"

Canadian journalist Colman Jones, in his article, "Claws of Power," cited David Coon of the Conservation Council of New Brunswick and Ransom Myers, Killam chair in Ocean Studies at the Biology department of Dalhousie University as saying that Mi'kmaq fishers presented no threat to lobster stocks. "They are basically adopting all the conservation measures that commercial inshore fisherman have used for years," noted Myers (who had worked as a research scientist at the DFO).

Jones quotes Lloyd Augustine, an Esgenoôpetitj Band councilor with whom the team worked closely, as saying, "Our philosophy is that what we have or see or taste is something that has to be shared with the seven generations yet unborn, so with that kind of thinking we always try to find ways to conserve." Jones then cites Augustine as noting that traditional native fishing activities are divided into two seasons, spring and fall. "We collect only what is needed and essential for the community. Federal policy is based in economics, not conservation. Non-natives, if given the choice, would deplete the stock until nothing is left."

Jones included the following statistics in, "Claws of power":

- Number of licenses for lobster fishing in New Brunswick: 1,592

- Number of lobster licences belonging to commercial non-native fishers: 1,514

- Number of lobster licences belonging to native bands: 78

intercepted Bartibogue, confiscated his traps, threatened to seize his boat, and later charged him with "fishing without tags approved by the Minister of Fisheries and Oceans."

CPTers Bob Holmes and William Payne jumped into Bartibogue's boat as it was being taken out of the water onto a trailer and attempted to reclaim the traps. The Royal Canadian Mounted Police then arrested Holmes and Payne, detaining them until officers took the traps away. Later, the Department of Fisheries and Oceans charged them with "obstructing a fisheries officer," handing Payne a writ to appear in court when the team began a fast in front of the DFO office in Néguac, New Brunswick on May 23.[59]

The legal proceedings against Bartibogue, Payne, and Holmes would stretch out over the next three years. Meanwhile, the team participated with EFN members and Aboriginal Rights Coalition (ARC) observers in twenty-four-hour watches that proved exhausting for everyone involved. EFN fishers continued to set out their traps in Miramichi Bay and the DFO continued to confiscate them.

On May 18, the EFN fishers decided to confront the DFO. As the DFO was pulling up the last of eleven EFN traps, Brian Bartibogue went out in his boat with CPT Reservist Nina Bailey-Dick, and Lena Siegers went out in another boat with EFN people. The DFO boat fled the scene.

- Number of lobster licenses valid for Miramichi Bay: 200
- Number of those that belong to non-natives: 180
- Number belonging to natives: 20

In a July 12, 2005 e-mail message to the author, Doug Pritchard wrote,

> The areas where I recall EFN's plan being more conservative was that they had an upper limit on lobster sizes which the DFO regulations did not. EFN elders believed that the larger females were the main breeders of future stock and so had an upper limit on the size of lobsters which could be taken. I seem to recall that the state of Maine also has upper limits but that the Canadian DFO did not. The DFO regulations for corporate fishers also were in terms of tonnage rather than the number of traps and seasons and so taking a lot of big lobsters helped corporate fishers reach their tonnages quicker.

59. CPTnet, "Neguac, NB: CPTers arrested defending Mi'kmaq rights," May 6, 2000; CPTnet, "Neguac, NB: CPT Fast Calls on Canadian Government to Honour Treaties"; CPTnet, "Esgenoôpetitj (Burnt Church) Update: April 28–May 27, 2000," June 15, 2000. Christian Peacemaker Teams, *Gunboat Diplomacy*.

Although they were not able to retrieve the traps, the fact that the DFO left once the EFN boats came into the water inspired the EFN fishers and observers. For the next ten days, every time a DFO boat appeared, the EFN boats went out and the DFO left. On June 1, the DFO fought back. In a large pre-dawn raid, forty officers in eight DFO boats, two RCMP boats and six RCMP cruisers on shore seized thirty-five EFN traps.

The EFN continued to go into the water for the next two weeks every time a DFO boat appeared (the DFO was also using planes at this point). On June 12, the DFO ratcheted the violence up a notch. When CPTers Doug Pritchard and Chris Buhler, along with ARC observers, went out with EFN boats to confront three DFO boats confiscating traps, DFO officer Louis Breault attempted to swamp one of the EFN boats and threatened their occupants with arrest. Another boat nearly rammed the second EFN boat and then swerved and hit another DFO boat. CPTers Pritchard, Buhler, and Cliff Kindy then went to Néguac to intercept the DFO officers as they docked their boat. Breault threatened them with arrest for a second time. He refused to answer their question about why he spent so much time and so many resources on twenty EFN traps. When a European-Canadian fisher complained, in the presence of the CPTers, to Breault about certain DFO-licensed non-aboriginal fishers using illegal bait Breault told him, "the Department doesn't want us spending time on that."

Five weeks later, on July 17, 2000, two DFO officers appeared at Pritchard's home in Toronto, wearing bulletproof vests, carrying pepper spray and handcuffs. They came to charge Pritchard with "obstructing a fisheries officer." They charged six EFN fishers with obstruction as well, which carried a maximum fine of $500,000 Cdn. "It's a pattern of harassment," Pritchard said in a CPTnet release, "First they [the DFO] charge the people who go out to fish. Then they charge the people who go out to challenge the DFO officers. Now they are charging the people who go out to observe."[60]

In their February 2001 report, *Gunboat Diplomacy: Canada's Abuse of Human Rights at Esgenoôpetitj*, CPTers documented twenty-two incidents occurring June–October 2000 in which the Canadian government "violated the human rights of EFN members and failed to deal with EFN in a fair and honourable manner." These incidents included threatening

60. *Gunboat Diplomacy;* CPTnet, "Esgenoôpetitj Update: May 28–June 13, 2000," June 19, 2000; CPTnet, "Toronto: A pattern of harassment," July 28, 2000.

to shoot unarmed EFN members trying to protect their traps, beating and choking EFN members into unconsciousness, swamping dories so that those on board fell into the water, and then beating them with batons while they were in the water. Videotape showing the attacks on unarmed natives played on the Canadian news, evoking widespread condemnation of Canadian government tactics. One website lists the tape as one of the most historically significant uses of the "handicam" by amateurs along with the Rodney King footage (see chapter 1) and the fall of the World Trade Towers on September 11, 2001.[61]

Prior to citing the long litany of abuses, the report called on the Canadian government to stop their violence against the EFN, to negotiate in good faith with the Mi'kmaq people on a nation-to-nation basis, and to stop wasting resources on its disproportionate response to the EFN fishers. Regarding the last point, the report adds, "If this money were redirected to conflict transformation efforts and scientific research into lobster stocks, there would be significant progress toward a just and mutually satisfactory solution."[62]

2001

Although many people of the EFN community who had participated in the 2000 lobster fishing season were exhausted and traumatized by the end, overall they regarded it as a success and the people of Esgenoôpetitj extended an invitation to CPT for the second season in 2001.

Between the fall 2000 and spring 2001 fishing seasons, however, CPT and the EFN community were embroiled in a series of legal proceedings regarding the arrests of the previous summer. Trials were repeatedly postponed for a variety of reasons, and some did not take place until long after CPT closed its Esgenoôpetitj project in 2002.

---

61. Seeingisbelieving, "The handicam revolution."

62. CPT Esgenoopetitj, *Gunboat Diplomacy* In a January 15, 2001, e-mail message to the CPT-Ontario regional group, Doug Pritchard wrote,

> A little fact I gleaned from the DFO's website. Their whole flotilla for the Gulf region is 3 Coast Guard and 22 smaller DFO boats. So they must have had most of that flotilla at EFN for much of the fall. They could also have called on boats from the Laurentian (lower St Laurence) or Maritimes (Grand Banks, PEI, NF) regions. Underlines again how disproportionate the DFO response to the EFN fishery was and how they ignored the rest of the fishing region.

On May 18, 2001, more than a year after Payne and Holmes tried to recover Brian Bartibogue's ten lobster traps, Judge Henrik Tonning granted them an absolute discharge, which meant that the charges of obstructing a fisheries officer would not remain on their record. Interestingly, Tonning said he accepted the moral motivations, but not their legal arguments as justification for retrieving the traps—which he still considered an illegal act. However, he added that relations between the Canadian government and aboriginal nations might improve if more non-natives were active in opposing government action. In his sentencing, Tonning said he thought Payne and Holmes "were doing more good than bad, both in the local situation and elsewhere in the world," and that he did not want to impede the work.

Judge McCarroll of the New Brunswick Provincial Court ruled on May 16, 2001, that Crown prosecutor's assertion that the State should not have to pay for the defense of the EFN fishers—because the case was not serious—was in error. The outcome of the case was of "national importance" and would affect the defendant's ability to earn a living.

By the time Doug Pritchard visited Esgenoôpetitj in April 2003, Brian Bartibogue was still waiting for his trial for the May 6, 2000, charge. On April 17, 2003, in Federal Court, Miramichi, New Brunswick, McCarroll found Leo Bartibogue not guilty of obstructing a fisheries officer in the June 12, 2000, incident. In a related case involving EFN members Curtis and Dominique Bonnell Dedam, Judge William McCarroll challenged the Federal Crown Prosecutor Denis Lavoie from Halifax, Nova Scotia, as to why he was still proceeding with these cases from the 2000 dispute. He noted that EFN had signed a fisheries agreement with Canada in August 2002 and the subsequent lobster-fishing season in the fall of 2002 had concluded without incident. Nevertheless, the Crown insisted on proceeding. The Dedams, tired of the interminable proceedings, pled guilty. The Judge then fined them $1 each in February 2003.

Undeterred by this message from the Judge, the Crown proceeded with the case against Leo Bartibogue. Bartibogue was one of the EFN fishers who had gone out in a small dory to observe three Canadian Department of Fisheries and Oceans vessels as they were seizing his lobster traps. The case had already been held over many times and Bartibogue had appeared for every hearing. DFO officers testified that Bartibogue had yelled at them and that they "thought he might try to take his traps back," but they admitted he made no attempt to do so. Judge McCarroll ruled that those actions did not constitute obstruction and declared Bartibogue not guilty.

In total, roughly 160 charges were laid against forty EFN members as part of the 2000 lobster-fishing dispute. The EFN never got a chance to argue the fundamental issue of "illegal" fishing because those charges were subsequently dropped, or unrepresented individuals pled guilty.[63]

When Doug Pritchard, William Payne, and Bob Holmes visited Esgenoôpetitj in March 2001, the community had not decided whether they were going to begin fishing again during the spring lobster season. After the visit, Doug Pritchard wrote to the CPT-Ontario group:

63. See CPT Canada press releases: "Toronto Human Rights Workers and Mi'kmaq Fishers Charged in Lobster Conflict," August 1, 2000; "Toronto Human Rights Workers Call for an End to the Federal Harassment of Mi'kmaq Fishers," August 2, 2000; "Media Statement Re: Charges Laid in the Lobster Fishery," (William Payne) August 2, 2000; Judge Reserves Decision Until May 18 in Trial of Christian Peacemakers Defending Mi'kmaq Fishing Rights," March 15, 2001.

See also Pritchard, "Notes from a Trip to Esgenoôpetitj First Nation (EFN)."

See CPTnet releases: "Neguac, New Brunswick: CPTer William Payne appears in court," September 1, 2000; "Esgenoôpetitj: Fisheries Trials Held Over," September 8, 2000; Esgenoôpetitj Update: September 1–14, 2000," October 5, 2000; Esgenoôpetitj; Doug Pritchard, "Your Honour, I will not make a plea," December 19, 2000; "Neguac, NB: CPTers William Payne and Bob Holmes complete trial on obstruction charges," March 16, 2001; "Esgenoôpetitj, New Brunswick: Court Recognizes Canadian Government's Abuse of Mi'kmaq Human Rights," March 29, 2001; "Esgenoôpetitj (New Brunswick) Update: April 22–May 4, 2001," May 18, 2001; "Miramichi, New Brunswick: CPTers given absolute discharge by court," May 21, 2001; "Esgenoôpetitj Update: May 5–May 19, 2001," May 24, 2001; Natasha J. Krahn, "Esgenoôpetitj (New Brunswick): Community Service," June 7, 2001; "Corrections on Esgenoôpetitj 'Community Service' and Chicago 'Emergency Delegatio[n] to West Bank' releases," June 13, 2001; "Esgenoôpetitj Update: May 21–June 3, 2001," June 18, 2001; Doug Pritchard, "Miramichi, New Brunswick: Fisheries Justice?" April 24, 2003.

The difference between how the Canadian government treated natives and non-natives involved in the fishing dispute is illustrated by the case of Leigh Morrison, who had been part of the demonstration in October 1999 that had destroyed all of the EFN traps. Six EFN members had gone to Morrison's house to take some of his traps in compensation. Morrison had rammed the side of their truck with his van and then beat two of the injured passengers on the head with a baseball bat. The prosecutor noted all the run-ins with the law that the EFN victims had had since they were teenagers. Morrison was acquitted of all charges on October 11, 2001. CPTnet, "Esgenoôpetitj Update: September 27–October 24, 2001," November 17, 2001. In her August 31, 2005, e-mail message to the author, Janet Shoemaker notes Morrison's victims were each charged a $1200 fine for the same incident and put under two-year house arrest.

Hi CPTO

Will there be fishing at Esgenoôpetitj this year? We don't know. After our visits there the past couple of weeks, William, Bob and I have quite a mixture of impressions and feelings. Certainly the community is under intense pressure as the questions of fishing swirl around and as they face trials for 40 community individuals who have no money for lawyers. But the community is very determined to stay together and exercise their rights to fish....

The interim 1-year agreements with DFO all expire next week. DFO is putting immense pressure on all the Atlantic First Nations chiefs to renew the agreements for 3 years this time. So far, the chiefs say they will stick together and not sign....

If they begin to sign, then EFN will be watching to see how many sign this time. If a few more hold out and go fishing, inspired by the example of EFN and Indian Brook, that will spread DFO's enforcement operations more thinly and more people at EFN and elsewhere would consider fishing in the spring and fall.

If only EFN and Indian Brook refuse to sign again, EFN folk are wondering whether they have the stamina to hold a contested fishery from May all the way to October again. It was very draining for the community. The spring fishery was not very productive and was run mostly to assert their right to fish. EFN might choose to just focus on a fall fishery from Aug to Oct and forego the spring fishery....

So ... what do we do? My guess is we keep preparing to go April 18. If nothing is decided by then, we go anyway to learn first-hand what is happening and support EFN. If by early May, they decide they will not fish in the spring, we could go on to support Indian Brook if they are fishing. If no FN is fishing under its own regulations, and we find there is nothing else for us to do, we pack up and come home until August and the fall fishery.

We're CPT. We're flexible. Right?

Doug[64]

The team put out only three updates during the spring fishing season and in only one did they mention actual fishing happening. Their updates focused more on the trials and networking with other groups in the Maritime Provinces. An entry for June 18, 2001, records people spotting a DFO boat in the bay checking traps and confiscating nine without tags.

64. March 26, 2001, e-mail message forwarded by Janet Shoemaker to the author on July 13, 2005.

After this single incident, the June 18 entry reads, "Payne and Shoemaker closed up camp for the summer."[65] CPT also maintained an uneventful six-week presence with the Indian Brook Nation in Nova Scotia.[66]

The autumn 2001 fishing season was more active, although most actual violence or threat of violence occurred at the hands of the non-native fishers than at the hands of the RCMP or DFO.[67] On August 26, 2001, during the EFN's annual pow wow (a two-day festival of native culture and family reunions), about twenty-six non-native commercial fishing vessels circled the buoys marking the EFN lobster traps. The community immediately recalled the destruction of their three thousand traps in 1999 and headed out to the wharf. RCMP officers assured the team and a CPT delegation that they had the situation under control, but threatened Natasha Krahn with arrest when she asked him to repeat, as she videotaped, that the RCMP had thirty-five boats and two helicopters "out there." Some of the CPT delegation attending the pow wow heard non-native fishers watching on the wharf saying "I hope [the boats] cut their traps and "the Natives should get out of my yard." The community found out the next day that hundreds of their traplines had indeed been cut.

65. CPTnet, "Esgenoôpetitj Update: June 4–20, 2001," July 13, 2001.

66. See CPTnet releases: "Esgenoôpetitj Update: May 21–June 3, 2001," June 18, 2001; Joanne "Jake" Kaufman. "Halifax, Nova Scotia: One Day is Not Enough," June 26, 2001; "Indian Brook, Nova Scotia Update: June 10–24, 2001," July 3, 2001. "Indian Brook Update: June 25–July 2, 2001"; "Esgenoôpetitj Update: June 4–20, 2001," July 13, 2001; July 21, 2001; "Indian Brook, NS: Aboriginal Fisheries Management Plans—a Model for the Future," August 5, 2001; Indian Brook, Nova Scotia: Lawsuit questions DFO's concern for conservation," August 14, 2001. Indian Brook, Nova Scotia Update: July 2–28, 2001," August 22, 2001.

Janet Shoemaker, describing her visit to Indian Brook in May 2001, wrote in a July 28, 2005, e-mail message to the author,

> My impression in visiting them is that Indian Brook was much more unified in their struggle, and much more organized. But they had also been fighting some legal battles for several years relating to the issue, whereas Esg. had just started their resistance and weren't as well-versed in the legal case-making. They didn't observe fishing because (I think) that happened at the west end of Nova Scotia rather than in the community, and then the community called it off for the season.

67. The RCMP, however, did park a trailer at the wharf for the entire season and did not allow any native fisher to use it. Shoemaker, August 31, 2005, e-mail message to the author.

On September 16, 2001, an RCMP officer informed the EFN community that fifty non-native boats were coming into the bay for a "peaceful protest." Krahn went out with an EFN member in a boat that non-natives—driving a much larger commercial fishing boat—tried to swamp by circling around it, creating large swells. The EFN boat's propeller got caught in a lobster line and the non-native fishers began throwing beer bottles, rocks, and buoys from lobster traps they had cut at the boat Krahn was in and six other EFN dories. An RCMP helicopter flew overhead, but did nothing to intervene. Neither did the authorities intervene when shots were fired—according to the people observing on the land—from the water toward the shore. In her article on the incident, Krahn noted that these demonstrations had also occurred on two previous Sundays, with more non-native fishers participating each time. "One question I have heard over and over again from the members of this community," she wrote, is "how can people go to church on Sunday and then commit these kinds of acts on Sunday afternoons?"

The day after the incident, fifteen Big Cove First Nation (another Mi'kmaq nation in New Brunswick) commercial boats came into the bay to show support for the EFN. The RCMP responded to the Mi'kmaq fishers very differently. By the time they reached the Wharf, the RCMP had about six boats waiting for them, filled with heavily armed police in full riot gear. They refused to let the EFN people greet their guests, until some EFN rangers walked past the officers who told them to stop.

On other occasions during the fall season, non-native fishers cut the buoys marking EFN lobster traps or pulled the traps up and smashed them. EFN fishers lost hundreds of traps. The DFO and RCMP never pressed charges against any of the white fishers who destroyed the traps.[68]

The DFO continued confiscating EFN traps throughout the season. Conflicts with the DFO in autumn 2001 often revolved around an indeterminate boundary line of a small strip in the bay that the DFO had designated as an aboriginal "food fishery" zone. The zone produced very few lobsters, and different DFO officers gave conflicting designations of

68. CPTnet, Heather Toews, "Esgenoôpetij: To Serve and Protect," September 3, 2001; CPTnet, Natasha Krahn, "Esgenoôpetitj : Sunday Morning, Sunday Afternoon," September 19, 2001; "Esgenoôpetitj Update: September 12–25, 2001," October 26, 2001.

Regarding the question of whether the non-native fishers were arrested for the September 16, 2001, incident, Janet Shoemaker, in a July 20, 2005, e-mail message to the author, said that the RCMP told her that it was "too dark" for their officers in the helicopter to see the numbers of the boats.

where the boundary line was. After the DFO had told one EFN fisher that his traps were within the zone, another DFO officer had come along and pulled up the traps, despite the EFN fisher's willingness to remove them himself. Another EFN fisher approached the DFO boat that had confiscated the traps. "Just where exactly is this line I'm supposed to be observing?" he asked. The DFO officer then threatened him with arrest for "obstructing an officer in the line of duty."[69]

In August 2002, the Band Council of the EFN agreed to end the conflict with the DFO, and acquiesce to the Canadian government's right to regulate its fishery. The government stipulated that the EFN would fish in the fall for food and ceremonial purposes only, and their catch was not to exceed 13,500 kilograms. In exchange, the DFO gave the EFN community another twenty-two commercial licenses on top of the thirteen they already had, increased its quota of snow crab, and paid for some boats and training.

Bob Holmes, in a release announcing the end of CPT's work in Esgenoôpetitj, wrote,

> Is it a good deal or a bad one? Is it a re-negotiation of treaty rights or an extinguishing of Aboriginal rights? Will it bring peace or will the conflict continue—with angry non-native fishers, with dissident native fishers? Whichever, CPT respects the right of the members of the EFN community to decide their own future and is grateful for the opportunity we were given to stand with them in their lonely, courageous fight for their way of life.[70]

69. See CPTnet releases, Barbara Martens, "Esgenoôpetitj: Drawing the Line," October 4, 2001; "Esgenoôpetitj Update: August 30–September 10, 2001," October 16, 2001; Update: September 12–25, 2001," October 26, 2001; "Esgenoôpetitj Update: September 27–October 24, 2001," November 17, 2001.

70. CPTnet, "New Brunswick: CPT ends commitment at Esgenoôpetitj," August 15, 2002.

9

"Getting Out of the Way"—CPT's Continuing Work with Indigenous Communities

"This accompaniment touches the roots of life in N. America (Turtle Island)—it's OUR wounds, but also our collective healing that we (native and non-Native) are working out here."

—From the final evaluation of
the Asubpeeschoseewagong project, July 2005[1]

ASUBPEESCHOSEEWAGONG/GRASSY NARROWS NATION IN ONTARIO

THE PEOPLE OF ASUBPEESCHOSEEWAGONG call themselves the Asubpeeschoseewagong Netum Anishnabeck or "Grassy Narrows First Nation."[2] Like the Caldwell, Stoney Point, and Nawash nations, with whom CPT had previously worked, they are members of the Anishinabe people. In 1873, the First Nations in Northwestern Ontario signed Treaty 3 with the government of Canada, which guaranteed them the right to hunt and fish on their traditional lands, territory that the British and then Canadian government considered "Crown Land." However, the government felt no compunction about making this land unsuitable for hunting,

1. CPT Asubpeeschoseewagong, "Evaluation of CPT's Role."

2. Jessica Phillips, when asked about how the people in Asubpeeschoseewagong referred to themselves and whether the nation used ANA to the extent that Esgenoôpetitj used EFN, wrote in an August 5, 2001 e-mail:

From my perspectives or observations, people did at times use the ANA name, usually in talks that were about governance. Asubpeeschoseewagong Netum Anishnabek was like the entire full name (my name is Jessica Phillips), Asubpeeschoseewagong was used as the full first name (like my name is Jessica) and Grassy Narrows was used like a nickname (like people often call me Jess or Jesse).

321

fishing, or deriving any other kind of livelihood from it. This lack of concern about the environment and how altering it would affect the ANA, heaped a succession of traumas on the people for decades.

In the 1950s, Ontario Hydro built two dams up river of the ANA that flooded sacred sites, burial grounds, and wild rice beds. The dams made traveling on the river, which the ANA had done for thousands of years, unpredictable and at times, impossible. Also in the 1950s, timber companies began logging in areas around the ANA, which altered its residents' ability to live off the land. In 1963, the Canadian government forcibly relocated the nation from along the English River to a new community with soil too poor for gardening. The move split up family groups, a key part of Anishinabe identity.[3]

The toll on the ANA that Canadian government and corporate policy in the woodland region had taken hit the headlines in 1970. Japanese researchers conducted tests in the area and found alarmingly high levels of mercury in the water and fish on which the Anishinabe depended. The researchers thus tied a rash of neurological orders in the White Dog and Grassy Narrows reserves to mercury poisoning.[4] After paper mills stopped dumping mercury in the English and Wabigoon river systems, people expected the health problems to clear up. However, in 2003, the Japanese researchers returned, and found the people there still suffering from the same neurological disorders. The ANA claimed that the mercury poisoning was due to the clear-cut logging in the area. Researchers had established that mercury levels were up to 100 percent higher in heavily logged watersheds than in lakes where there was not logging nearby.[5] A member of the Grassy Narrows community told a September 1999 CPT delegation,

> At the environmental conference in Ottawa, they asked us to tell
> our 'success' stories. I told them that we hang our fish upside-down

3. CPTnet, Pritchard, "Grassy Narrows, ON: They moved the reserve instead," June 4, 1999.

4. Japanese scientists take a special interest in mercury poisoning because of an outbreak of neurological disease and birth defects in the 1950s among people who ate fish and shellfish caught in Mina Mata Bay. The scientist gave the syndrome the name "Minamata Disease." See Japanese Ministry of the Environment, "Minamata Disease."

5. Bueckert, "Mercury poisoning issue back." In the article Bueckert cited a theory that airborne mercury from coal-fired power plants and incinerators is held in the soil and foliage of an intact forest, but runs into waterways that have been clear-cut.

until the [thermometer] drops. When the mercury drops to the bottom, we cut their heads off. That is our 'success' story . . . There is 50 tons of mercury in our river and it took the government 30 years to even admit it. They have done nothing to remove it. We're worth nothing.[6]

To address the damage done to their community by flooding, logging, and mercury poisoning, the community had participated in mediation processes with the Ontario Ministry of Natural Resources, the paper company Abitibi-Consolidated, the federal Department of Indian Affairs and Northern Development (DIAND), and the federal Ministry of the Environment. The failure of this process and the lack of interest the Ontario provincial government had for ANA concerns became evident in February 1999 when Ontario renewed a twenty-year license to Abitibi-Consolidated that allowed the corporation to clear-cut the Whisky Jack Forest. The forest's boundaries were nearly identical to the ANA's traditional land-use area.[7] The clear-cutting would make deriving a livelihood from the forest impossible for members of Grassy. A 2003 CPTnet release records the mournful comment of a ten-year-old Grassy Narrows girl: "When I grow up, if I have a husband, he would like to hunt, but there will be no place to hunt. I would like to fish, but the fish will already be dead."[8]

To assert their rights to hunt, fish, and live off their traditional lands the ANA decided in 1999 to set up road blockades to prevent logging trucks from entering the traditional lands area of the Whiskey Jack Forest. At its invitation, CPTers Doug Pritchard, Wes Hare, and Cole Hull spent two weeks—May 13, 1999 through May 26, 1999—in Asubpeeschoseewagong and Kenora, the mill town about eighty kilometers from Grassy. In their delegation report, they recommended that CPT continue its involvement with Asubpeeschoseewagong Netum Anishnabek should it decide to set up the blockades and link CPT's involvement with the ANA to CPT's

6. CPTnet, Braun, "Grassy Narrows, ON: How much" Nov, 1999.

7. The Ontario Provincial government's licensing of the Abitibi's clear-cutting made "environmental" restrictions placed on the Anishinabe seem especially onerous. For example, in March 2004, citing environmental concerns, a provincial conservation officer put a "Stop Work" order on a trapper's shelter that Grassy Narrows resident Roberta Keesick had put up in a forest clearing, as well as trails she had made to her traps. CPTnet, Lisa Martens, "Asubpeeschoseewagong, ON: We've been self-managing."

8. CPTnet, Hookimaw (age 10), "Asubpeeschoseewagong, ON: The Blockade," Mar 18, 2003.

other work with First Nations in the U.S. and Canada. They also suggested that CPT support Asubpeeschoseewagong by posting an Urgent Action on CPTnet asking DIAND to intervene with Abitibi and Ontario to stop the clear-cutting, encourage churches to take up the issue with Abitibi, supply community with social action-organizing handbooks, and to undertake "any of the following:"

> ... assist those planning future actions; maintain observer/peace-keeper presence at blockade or other action; recruit/train other observers from outside the community; contact NOTO [Northern Ontario Tourist Organization] for supportive statements/actions; support Abitibi shareholder actions: presence at annual meeting, boycotts, pressure on other shareholders or funds; research the forest industry's impact on other nearby First Nations and their responses; organize a short-term CPT delegation from Manitoba or Ontario.[9]

As it happened, severe storms washed out the roads into the Whiskey Jack Forest and Grassy Narrows after the May delegation. The people at Grassy told CPT that their services as human rights observers would thus not be needed at that time because, "the Creator has set His own blockade."

As a way to maintain relationships with the Grassy community, CPT sent four small delegations of Winnipeg residents, led by Lisa Martens and Matt Schaaf, to Asubpeeschoseewagong between the fall of 1999 and the winter of 2002.[10]

On December 3, 2002, the ANA blockade of Jones Road, which led into the Whiskey Jack forest, began in earnest. In a flyer explaining the

9. CPT, "Report on CPT Fact-Finding Mission."

10. CPT Asubpeeschoseewagong, "Summary of Remembered History."

In 2002, CPT also sent a small delegation to the Secwepemc (Shuswap) Nation in British Columbia in 2002. Having heard of its work with other First Nations, the Secwepemc people asked CPT to consider sending human rights monitors to accompany them at sites where recreational resorts were encroaching on their traditional lands and during the fishing season on the Fraser River. CPT, "Report on Exploratory Trip"; CPTnet, Pritchard, "Secwepemculecw (Chase, British Columbia): Go Home!"; Shoemaker, e-mail, Aug 31, 2005.

In a September 12, 2005 e-mail, Doug Pritchard wrote:

> This really was an exploratory trip for us to get to know the lay of the land and to understand the VERY different legal situation in BC where virtually NO treaties have been signed. Secwepemc was the most public dispute at the time...

blockade, the community compared clear-cutting of their traditional land-use area to the devastation caused by clear-cutting in the Amazon Basin during the 1980s, referring to it a "cultural genocide." They responded to the criticism that the blockade would result in unemployment for the people of Kenora (a predominantly white timber and paper mill town) by saying that mechanization of the mills had already replaced half of the Kenorans who used to work there. "The environment and quality of life on the land does not appear to be a priority of the mill, rather to make a quick profit. This is the legacy of multi-national corporations," it noted.

The ANA flyer also pointed out that the Royal Proclamation of 1763 (cited by the First Nations in the Maritime provinces as well) was still in force. It also asserted that Treaty 3 protected the right of the Anishinabe to earn a livelihood from the forest.[11] In a November 27, 2002, letter to the Ontario Provincial government and Abitibi, the community, noted that the clear-cutting in the Dead Fish Lake area would "destroy wildlife habitat and undermine hunting and trapping success in one of their few remaining intact hunting grounds."[12]

Although the community had been talking about establishing blockades for some time, the initial blockade happened somewhat spontaneously, as an initiative of two ANA women in their twenties, Chrissy and Jessica Swain. Chrissy Swain had been involved with environmental activism in other locations and had returned to her home community to do some organizing there. Matt Schaaf—who would become the first member of the Asubpeeschoseewagong project—had just finished lead-

---

We continue to follow news here closely since it is a more conflicted and potentially volatile part of the continent with disputes over forestry, fishing, ski resorts etc in a legal vacuum.

11. The "official" written text of Treaty 3 appears on the INAC Web site at http://www.ainc-inac.gc.ca/pr/trts/trty3_e.html. However, the Anishinabe people assert that the verbal agreement with Her Majesty's government was changed in the written document. They thought they were agreeing to share resources with white settlers in exchange for economic assistance, protection of their villages and harvest areas, and guaranteed access to hunting, fishing and wild rice. They did not "cede and release" all their rights to natural resources. The Anishinabek's verbal understandings are preserved in the Paypom treaty. See INAC, "The Administration of Treaty No. 3"; Grand Council of Treaty No. 3, "Paypom Treaty." See also notes taken at the meeting by Treaty Commissioner Simon J. Dawson, a shorthand reporter, and the interpreter Joseph Nolin. Delegations to Asubpeeschoseewagong received a flyer put out by Treaty and Aboriginal Rights Research (TARR) titled, "'We have kept our part of the treaty.'"

12. CPTnet, "Grassy Narrows First nation: Blessing the Earth," Dec 1, 2002.

ing a delegation to Asubpeeschoseewagong and happened to be around when the blockade began on Monday, December 3, 2002. During the first days of the blockade, Anishinabe young people stood in the way of the Abitibi logging trucks. The loggers called the Ontario Provincial Police, who decided they would not intervene, which gave momentum to the blockade.

A few days later, CPTers Scott Kerr and Chris Brown joined Schaaf, and members of the Okiijida Warriors[13] arrived to protect the blockaders as they had in other indigenous communities who were trying to prevent the confiscation or abuse of their land. When a logging truck driver made an obscene gesture to a pregnant woman, a Mohawk warrior engaged the man in a heated interchange. Although no physical violence had occurred, the incident caused the community to reflect on what types of resistance they would support. According to Jessica Phillips, by the time she arrived to join the Asubpeeschoseewagong project in January 2003, the community had decided they were committed to Nonviolent Direct Action (NVDA). The warriors respected the community's decision, but reserved the right to act as they saw fit if women and children were attacked.

As had been the case in Haiti, Chiapas, and South Dakota, most of CPT's work at the blockade involved being present and relating to people. Simply gathering firewood to cook with and keep warm in the frigid climate filled many hours. (Early on, CPTers in Asubpeeschoseewagong decided that helping to tend the blockaders' sacred fire was inappropriate. They believed that doing so would be another example of non-natives usurping indigenous spirituality.)

According to Phillips, the first months of the blockade passed enjoyably, with people engaging in various winter sports, telling jokes, playing games, and even using a karaoke machine that someone had donated to the cause. Dignitaries from other First Nations, such as Matthew Coon Come (Chief of the Assembly of First Nations), visited. In the evenings, a Keeper of the Drum from Slant Lake beat the drum to accompany traditional Anishinabe tunes and taught the drumming to others at the camp. The CPTers and the Warriors slept in trailers around the blockade into the Whiskey Jack forest. During the day, thirty to fifty community members would come in bringing food and other items to make the camp more comfortable, such as a coffee urn. A contingent of students came every

13. See Alfred and Lowe, "Warrior Societies."

day after school and visited with the elders, who told them stories and taught practical skills from Anishinabe culture.

As the U.S. began to move inexorably toward war with Iraq in March 2003, the team began to feel uncomfortable with the idea of living in a trailer that depended on diesel generators for warmth. Grassy Narrows members helped them build an A-frame heated by a wood stove. It would prove to be less warm than the oil-heated trailer, but as CPT reservist Tricia Brown noted, "like all such spiritual sacrifices, this trade is bringing liberation to those of us at Asubpeeschoseewagong. For as we begin to loosen the grip our reliance on oil has over us, we find not deprivation, but freedom."[14]

When the April and May spring runoff came, people did not have to monitor the blockade, because logging trucks could not travel on the muddy roads. The Okiijida warriors left in May 2003 and did not return. That summer, the CPTers were the only people to spend the night at the blockade. Grassy Narrows residents came during the day and some women organized a summer camp for young people to teach them traditional Anishinabe skills. Other blockade organizers had work in area lodges that catered to summer tourists.[15]

The team also accompanied four "roving blockades," that summer in which people set up barriers at various logging roads going into the forest. People would arrive in their trucks, usually at night, pull brush from the surrounding forest, start a campfire in the road and begin making tea. When the logging trucks came in the early morning, community members would tell the drivers they could not go through the road while CPTers documented the interactions. Sometimes, the Abitibi loggers, who had been in the area before the blockade went up, worked all night. The blockaders allowed these loggers to leave when they were finished.[16]

The economic impact of the blockade began taking its toll on the logging corporations. Three times in the summer of 2003, about six months after the blockade began, representatives of logging companies approached the community. In the first instance, loggers were conciliatory, saying that they did not approve of clear-cutting either, and that

14. CPTnet, Brown, "Asubpeeschoseewagong Reflection: Spiritual sacrifices," Mar 21, 2003; Phillips, interview, Aug 5, 2005.

15. Phillips, interview, Aug 5, 2005.

16. Ibid., CPTnet, "Asubpeeschoseewagong Update: May 1–June 13, 2005," June 19, 2003; Erin Kindy, e-mail, Aug 14, 2005.

Abitibi had lied to them, too. The second time, loggers issued oblique threats, to which two blockaders said, "You can beat us up. You can even kill us, that doesn't make it right. We're unemployed and have nothing left to lose." In the third and final visit, the owner of the Devlin Timber Company spoke to Grassy Narrows Chief Simon Fobister and Deputy Chief Steve Fobister at the band office. The Devlin Timber representative seemed taken aback that the Grassy Narrows community meant literally its demand that clear-cutting in their traditional land-use area stop immediately. Jerry Stein, in a release about the visits quoted Grassy members as saying to the Devlin representatives, "We've been telling you what we want for 100 years. You know forestry science. You come up with a plan different from clear-cutting."[17]

In September 2003, leaders in the Grassy community were invited to Montreal to meet with John Weaver, the president of Abitibi. They explained how their struggle was one of economic values vs. spiritual and social concerns and reiterated their demand that Abitibi stop clear-cutting.

Because Weaver would not agree to stop clear-cutting or respect treaty agreements, the team members put out an Action Alert on November 3, 2005. They asked CPT constituents to write to the McClatchy Company—which operated nine newspapers and was the biggest customer for Abitibi paper products—recommending that writers close their letters to Gary Pruitt, the CEO of McClatchy with:

> As a Christian and a consumer of newspaper, I want to know that when I buy a paper it has been produced with as little damage as possible to God's Creation. Christian values call on all of us to ensure that our actions do not cause harm to our neighbours. My faith calls on me to encourage your company to actively take part in hearing from Grassy Narrows First Nation.

The team then put out a follow-up release, encouraging constituents living in areas served by McClatchy-owned newspapers (the largest being the *Minneapolis Star-Tribune*) to express their concerns about the newsprint coming from the Traditional Land Use Area of Grassy Narrows.

On November 11, 2003, Abitibi representatives met with Grassy Narrows leaders in Kenora, along with Schaaf and Phillips and an envi-

17. CPTnet, Stein, "Asubpeeschoseewagong, ON: Loggers Try Negotiation," Aug 8, 2003.

ronmentalist from Winnipeg. Abitibi presented a proposal that stipulated it would not log at all within a ten-kilometer radius around the reserve, co-manage cutting with Grassy Narrows within the next ten-kilometer radius and provide money for social programs. In response, one of the Grassy Narrows leaders noted that Ontario forestry policy required logging to occur in a manner acceptable to all affected parties. The government's inadequate consultation process in issuing the logging permits had served as a catalyst for the blockade. Abitibi should thus not consider the mutually agreeable ten-kilometer cutting zone a bargaining chip, but a right that already existed. The Grassy Narrows leadership then told Abitibi that they needed to bring the issue back to the community for a decision—a process that was to continue after CPT's presence at the blockade ended.[18]

That autumn of 2003, in a meeting under stars and aurora borealis, team members discussed their activities over the summer with their Grassy hosts, who asked them to continue accompanying the community and the blockades.

In a description about the meeting, the team articulated issues that were to dog the project until its conclusion in Winter 2004:

> Since the nature of the violence at this project is considerably different from that in other CPT locales, the team is constantly trying to discern its role in violence reduction at Grassy. One supporter framed the violence as "cultural genocide." While it may be slow and lethal, it is just as devastating as the violence inflicted by missiles and machine guns.
>
> Nevertheless, CPT supporters feel that the team has played a significant role in reducing the more overt violence commonly associated with CPT work. One individual at the meeting felt that without CPT's presence, the government and police would have forcefully removed the blockade and escalated the hostilities. While

18. See CPTnet releases: "Asubpeeschoseewagong Update: September 1–14, 2003," Oct 14, 2003; "Asubpeeschoseewagong Action Alert: Send letters," Nov 3, 2003; "Asubpeeschoseewagong Action Alert Update: Newspapers," Nov 25, 2003; "Asubpeeschoseewagong: Abitibi Talks," Nov 25, 2003; "Asubpeeschoseewagong Update: November 9–December 3, 2003," Dec 3, 2003.

Doug Pritchard, in his comments on a draft of this chapter, wrote that Joe Fobister and possibly other ANA members had already done some speaking in Minneapolis before the team put out the Action Alert connecting issues at Grassy with the *Minneapolis Star-Tribune* and McClatchy papers. He noted, "I think that this contact with Abitibi's customers is what finally prompted the [meeting with Weaver] after Abitibi had ignored the blockade for months."

the main blockade is currently in hibernation since active logging around Grassy has ceased for the time being, there is always the potential for roving blockades on roads where logging traffic continues. Therefore, while CPTers continue to discern how they can best respond to the structural violence against Anishnabe people, they are also ready to provide an immediate violence reduction presence should a roving blockade spring up. Now that school is back in session, the students who were so central the blockades of the past year may provide the impetus for more actions.[19]

Abitibi approached the Asubpeeschoseewagong community again in January 2004, repeating its offer not to cut in the immediate vicinity of the Grassy Narrows community and consult community members about further cutting in the area, if Grassy Narrows activists took down the blockades. Shortly after the meeting, logging contractors working for Abitibi clear-cut a stand of timber near Anishinabe Lake. In doing so, they destroyed the trapline[20] of Alex Fobister, including his access trail into the trapline, for which he had a license from the Ontario provincial government. He also found that all his boxes set out for capturing pine martens were missing. Since pine martens only live in deep forest, the logging contractors had essentially destroyed an important part of Fobister's livelihood.

The community took the destruction as proof that Abitibi was negotiating in bad faith. They immediately put up another blockade on Deer Lake Road and delivered the following eviction notice to loggers in the area:

> You are hereby advised that you have until 5:30 p.m. Friday, February 5, 2004 to cease all logging activities and vacate the Anishnabe Lake area and the whole Grassy Narrows Traditional Territory. Failure to comply will result in your workers and your equipment being blocked in the area.
>
> —Signed: X, Signatory Indians to Treaty #3 1873

19. CPTnet, "Asubpeeschoseewagong Update: September 1–14, 2003," Oct 14, 2003.

20. Traplines are not lines or a series of connected traps, but designated areas of the forest in which trappers have permission to trap animals. Each legal trapper has a license to set his or her traps in a parcel of the forest where no one else is allowed to set traps. Martens, e-mail, Aug 4, 2005.

CPT's Asubpeeschoseewagong team then put out an Urgent Action in support of the blockade, noting that both the federal government of Canada and the Ontario provincial government were new and both had promised "a new way of doing things." The team suggested that their constituents

1. Congratulate the new leaders on their election and their desire to do things in a new way

2. Let them know about the violation of treaty rights of the Grassy Narrows residents by Abitibi (operating under an Ontario license)

3. Ask that they intervene to stop treaty violations and the destruction of Grassy Narrows' means of livelihood

On February 4, 2004, the day after the new blockade went up, the Ontario Provincial Police announced they had begun an investigation on behalf of the Ontario Ministry of Natural Resources as to whether the Abitibi logging contractor that had destroyed Fobister's trapline had cut in an area for which Ontario had not licensed him. Abitibi was already facing twenty-two charges at the time for failing to comply with their approved Annual Work Schedule for logging, making false statements to the government, and failing to provide required information.

Despite Abitibi's decreasing credibility, its corporate representatives again asked for a meeting with the community on February 11, 2004, saying they wished to "build trust" and develop better communication. Some community members told them that no communication gap existed. They simply and unambiguously wanted the company to stop clear-cutting. They also wanted the provincial and federal governments to participate in future meetings, since they were the legal entities bound by Treaty 3.

At the conclusion of the meeting, the community was left with difficult decisions. Should they agree to rights and protections already granted them by Ontario law? Doing so would mean immediate economic benefits. If they rejected the proposal, they ran the risk of losing access to the land through unjust court rulings, but they would be upholding the principle their own sovereignty, of nation-to-nation negotiations outlined in legal precedents dating from the 1700s. The Grassy Narrows leadership began surveying the residents of Grassy Narrows residents, including children, about what they should do.[21]

As of 2007, the blockades (some merely sticks with signs on them across logging roads and some encampments or centers of community activity) were still in place. The Abitibi mill in Kenora closed in 2006. Ontario invited new companies to enter bids for the wood previously allocated to Abitibi without consulting the people of Grassy Narrows. On January 17, 2007, Grassy Narrows community leaders declared a moratorium on further industrial activity within their traditional territory carried out without community consent. [22]

Kenora

From the beginning of the Asubpeeschoseewagong project, the team understood that the paper and timber mill town of Kenora figured heavily in the lives Grassy Narrows community members. About eighty kilometers away, it was the closest municipality offering hospital and specialized medical care, groceries, recreation, and employment. Abitibi had a paper mill there, and its inhabitants—whose jobs would be at risk if the mill closed down—tended to view the Grassy Narrows blockaders with hostility.[23] CPT team and delegation members often chose to do their public witnesses in Kenora.[24]

---

21. See CPTnet releases: "Asubpeeschoseewagong Urgent Action: Stop the Clear-Cutting," Feb 6, 2005; "Asubpeeschoseewagong: You are hereby advised," Feb 11, 2004. "Asubpeeschoseewagong: Abitibi comes to bargaining table," Feb 14, 2004; "Asubpeeschoseewagong, ON: Abitibi breaks," Mar 18, 2004; "Asubpeeschoseewagong Update: January–March, 2004," Mar 20, 2004.

In an August 5, 2005 phone interview, Jessica Phillips told the author that what really brought Abitibi to the table was the fact that logging contractor Jim Ambs had thousands of dollars worth of lumber already cut, which the community would not let him collect.

22. Grassy Narrows Chief and Council . . . , "Re: Moratorium on industry." See also AI Canada, "Mission to Grassy Narrows."

23. In December 2005, Abitibi announced it would close its Kenora paper mills in October 2006. James, "Kenora paper mill closed"; "Abitibi cutting paper production."

24. For a description of these witnesses, see CPTnet releases: Lepp, "Asubpeeschoseewagong, ON: Residents protest," Mar 3, 2003; "Kenora, ON: CPTers hand out 'Treaty Cards,'" Nov 10, 2003; "Asubpeeschoseewagong, ON: High school students speak to Open House," February 14, 2005; Matt Schaaf, "Asubpeeschoseewagong, ON: Abitibi breaks," Mar 18, 2004; Enns, "Asubpeeschoseewagong: CPT dumps clear-cut mess," June 19, 2004; "Asubpeeschoseewagong/Kenora: What would you lose," July 19, 2004; "Asubpeeschoseewagong/Kenora: CPT Delegation," Sept 20, 2004.

The Asubpeeschoseewagong updates for 2003 record intentional efforts the team made to network with the citizens of Kenora, particularly white church members, many of whom had not heard before of the devastations suffered by the Grassy Narrows community over recent decades.[25]

In 2004, the team's releases about their work in Kenora contained grimmer emphases. On April 30, 2004, an indigenous man, Stewart Smith, was beaten nearly to death—probably at the hands of a gang called the Kenora Indian Bashers (KIB.) The police barely investigated the crime and charged no one. The beating reminded the community of another in 2000 when an Anishinabe man, Max Kakegamic, was beaten to death. Police charged one man and then released him. They did not arrest another suspect, who was a nephew of one of the investigating officers.

Grassy Narrows community members told other stories of the racist violence they encountered in Kenora, which highway signs proclaimed a "Designated Safe Community." One team contact called Kenora the "Mississippi of the North."[26]

"White youths beat native people when they are teenagers, then they grow up to become mayors, business people, city councilors, police officers. And their kids, the next generation of civic leaders do the same," one man told the team. Another woman told of her father and his cousin who had stopped to help four white strangers with their car in the 1970s. The strangers knocked him unconscious, and then they raped and beat his cousin, who later died of her injuries. Although they reported the incident to the police, they never heard of any investigation into the murder having taken place. Referring to her Kenora trips, she said, "I have a real deep-in-my-stomach, deadly fear. I'm scared for my kids." Other members of the Grassy Narrows community expressed fear that if the Abitibi mill closed down, Kenorans would take out their anger on indigenous street people.

Other, less violent, forms of racism on the part of white people in Kenora also chipped away at the souls of the Grassy Narrows community. These included police harassment and disrespectful treatment in local shops. CPT delegate Mary Ann Harder reported a conversation with a non-native trapper in a delegation release. He told her that he sometimes could not trap a profitable percentage of his beaver allotment because:

25. CPTnet releases: "Asubpeeschoseewagong Update: June 15–July 4, 2003," July 24, 2003; "Asubpeeschoseewagong Update: July 4–20," July 11, 2003; "Asubpeeschoseewagong Update: November 9–December 3, 2003," Dec 10, 2003.

26. Loney, James, "Confronting the Violence of 'Normal'," *Signs of the Times*, 11.

My trap-line is surrounded by Natives. They never trap there at all, just claim the line so no one else can use it. And the trouble is, they don't have to follow the rules like everyone else. They don't pay taxes. They don't work, just get their cheque, and they're always drunk at the mall. The police can't do anything about it. If they even touch them, they'll be charged with assault. They're not helping us to control the animal populations. They are just taking over all the territory. We're all going to get pushed out. Reverse discrimination, that's what it is . . .[27]

Then there were the statistics: 90 percent of the people in the municipal jail cells were aboriginal. The police were much less likely to solve murders of aboriginals than those of non-aboriginals. Several First Nations people had died in police custody.[28]

27. CPTnet, Harder, "Kenora: A Trappers' Workshop," Feb 25, 2005.

28. See CPTnet releases: Martens, "Asubpeeschoseewagong: Displacement," May 18, 2004; "Asubpeeschoseewagong Update: Spring 2004," May 25, 2004; Schaaf and Martens, "Asubpeeschoseewagong: Healing needed," July 9, 2004; Bender and Stutzman, "Kenora: Raising Questions," Feb 28, 2005; "Kenora, ON: CPT announces closure," May 3, 2005. See also GITW, posting by Loney, June 27, 2005."

The team connected these stories of racism and violence in Kenora with the August 26, 2003 killing of nineteen-year-old Geronimo Fobister at Grassy Narrows. Fobister, in a drunken stupor, had threatened two Grassy community members, who had called the Ontario Provincial Police (OPP). Initially, they fired at him with rubber bullets, hoping to incapacitate him long enough to get his gun away from him. When he pointed the shotgun at them, they shot him in the head with their revolvers, killing him instantly. The Special Investigations Unit (SIU) ruled that the officer was not criminally guilty.

After listening to the community's reactions to the SIU report, CPT put the following concerns and opinions into a July 1, 2004 release entitled, "Asubpeeschoseewagong: The Killing of Geronimo Fobister":

1. We are concerned that non-lethal options were not discussed with Geronimo's family or other community members before lethal options were used. The police did not consult with community members at all until around 1:30 in the afternoon and then it was the Chief of Grassy Narrows who took the initiative to approach the police.

2. Non-lethal options were available to the police. They could have used tear gas or shot him in the arms and legs.

3. Giving Geronimo more space, especially since he was lying down on his back for well over an hour, getting advice from community members and involving an Ojibway-speaker could have moved the decision-making process further away from split second life and death choices.

See also CPTnet, Martens, "Asubpeeschoseewagong: The killing of Geronimo Fobister, part two," July 2, 2004; CPTnet, Schaaf and Martens, "Asubpeeschoseewagong: Death of Geronimo Fobister," Dece 5, 2003.

Accordingly, Grassy community members closest to the team urged them to consider setting up a project in Kenora to address the racism there, once the threat of overt violence at the blockades had diminished.[29] The team moved into its Kenora apartment in August 2004. From the beginning of their time there, the team viewed their work as an extension of the Asubpeeschoseewagong project, since they were relating to many of the same people. They also made frequent trips to Grassy Narrows to visit and discuss strategy with the people there.

However, instead of the specific goal of accompanying a logging blockade, the amorphous goal of "dealing with racism" was harder to undertake strategically; the team had difficulty translating the goal into concrete actions.

Team members did meet frequently with the Anishinaabe Coalition for Peace & Justice to document police harassment and conducted an anti-racism workshop in Red Lake.[30] Mostly, however, the team focused on building relationships in the community. The question arose whether building these relationships should be an end in itself or a means to achieving the end of reducing violence. Like the later phases of CPT urban projects, which had the similarly vague goal of "dealing with violence," the Kenora project also had trouble attracting CPTers to work long-term. Team members wrote few releases about their work in Kenora, which probably also contributed to the lack of investment other CPTers felt in the project.

On May 3, 2005, the Kenora team and Jim Loney (who, along with Rebecca Johnson had replaced Doug Pritchard as CPT Canada co-Coordinator) announced the closure of the Kenora project due to a shortage of long-term team members. The announcement of the closure caused a flurry of vehement arguments on the intra-CPT discussion group, Getting In the Way (GITW).[31] Kaaren Olsen, an Anishinaabe partner of the team who had conducted Undoing Racism workshops in Kenora, begged the team to reconsider its decision to close. James Loney posted her letter on GITW, which read in part,

29. CPTnet, "Grassy Narrows Update: August–September 2004," Oct 15, 2004.

30. Schaaf, e-mail, Aug 24, 2005. Most of this writing was not for CPTnet.

31. The GITW list was started in 2002 as an internal venue for CPTers to talk about issues that affected CPT workers and teams.

There are so many people out there who are genuinely democratic and progressive and they are willing to learn and CPT is able to move them forward in such a gentle and profound way. I feel so abandoned that CPT is leaving just when it looks like they can make a difference here. It had taken me so much effort to overcome past experiences and prejudices to work with CPT and then it feels like it's happening all over again. Can we not ever trust Christianity when their words and teachings are so promising?

Is not the daily violence of genocide against the original people of this continent just as real as the physical violence of war? Why would CPT want to distance itself from the work against the violence and insidiousness of racism? I know that the struggle of undoing racism is even more difficult because of the insidiousness of its nature, where lines are ambiguous and there are no clear enemies. It is easier to discern who the enemy is when there are guns and bombs. Maybe people don't know that they are putting their lives on the line just as much when they are fighting racism as they are when they are face to face with a soldier. Maybe they don't realize that fighting racism is also saving lives, that someone may decide not to commit suicide because they feel hope when they see white people fighting racism. Not to understand this, ultimately, is racism.

Maybe the Kenora project of CPT should be doing de-colonizing workshops with the whole of CPT. I do think that if any work can be done, CPT is the natural leader. It is said that it is not the duty of the oppressed to teach the oppressor. I thought that CPT was beginning that journey and I am making the request that you continue on that journey.

Some CPTers suggested that CPT needed to rethink its modus operandi and accept relationship building as the most important work in challenging racism, which would eventually lead to the prevention of overt violence. Some suggested a regional training. Others argued that repairing the egregious racism in Kenora required a long-haul approach that was not in CPT's "repertoire." What Kenora needed was an intentional community of CPTers who would choose to live there, take on jobs (some suggested full-time and others part-time), raise children, and become part of civic life.

Ultimately the discussion, which became bitter at points, resulted in CPT Canada deciding to continue the Kenora project on a part-time basis. CPT would send teams to Kenora for two-month stints in autumn 2005 and spring 2006.[32]

The short-term teams produced mixed outcomes. The kidnapping in Iraq of Kenora Project Support Coordinator Jim Loney (see chapter 12) interfered with the team's focus, but nonetheless the teams and local partners, in a November 2006 evaluation session, identified some key areas in which the short-term Kenora teams had succeeded in their goals. These included maintaining relationships with Anishinaabe partners, local pastors, and other solidarity organizations, promoting dialogue between Anishinaabe and white inhabitants of the region, and hosting several delegations.

Anishinaabe partners cited CPT Reservist Esther Kern's delivery of vital supplies and calming presence in July 2006—when a number of Grassy Narrows friends were arrested by the Ontario Provincial Police for blockading a logging road at the Separation Lake Bridge—as particularly useful support from the Kenora team.[33] Maria Swain noted, "I felt safer because Esther was there and could tell the world if something happened." They also expressed appreciation for the delegations the Kenora team had hosted and the team's work to make sure Max Kakegamic's and Geronimo Fobister's murders were not ignored.

White church members and pastors in the area reported that the team's organizing of a dinner at the Baptist church, where Anishinaabe people told their stories, had been particularly effective, and that they especially appreciated CPT setting up a trip to Grassy Narrows for them, because they had no idea how to arrange the visit themselves.

The evaluation also contained a "What Didn't Work/What Could Have Been Done Differently" section. One Anishinaabe advisor felt the team had not taken seriously her suggestion that the team conduct a listening project among recently laid off Abitibi mill workers "with the goal of reducing antagonism that was being drummed up by the media and by the company against Grassy Narrows." Kenora team members also felt that they should have put more effort into teambuilding, communication,

32. GITW, postings April–June 2005.

33. CPTnet, Esther Kern, "Kenora, ON: Of Pampers and OPP," Aug 26, 2006. Kern responded to a call for accompaniment of this blockade, and Rebecca Johnson had accompanied a blockade of the Trans-Canada Highway in June 2006. Both events occurred outside of the designated stints for the Kenora team, but the blockaders still regarded their presence as part of the Kenora team's work.

and proactively addressing issues of racism and sexism that cropped up within the team. A project to document racist treatment of Anishinaabe people by the police was deemed unsuccessful, possibly because the idea had emerged from team members rather than a local partner. Living at the First Baptist Church also produced some concerns, given the lack of respect for Anishinaabe spiritual practices shown by some in church leadership. Members of both the Baptist and United Churches in town thought the team was not interacting in a balanced way with the Anishinaabe and white communities.

At the end of the November 2006 three-day evaluation in London, Ontario, Kenora CPTers and other CPTers involved with indigenous issues participants came up with the following recommendations:

1. That CPT enter into a discernment process to assess overall work on Aboriginal issues

2. That CPT seriously examine the issue of invitation or trusted welcoming body for future work in Northwest Ontario

3. That CPT find ways to clarify and communicate that CPTers are NOT third-party neutrals[34]

4. That CPT develop a plan of action for the establishment of a long-term local CPT presence in the Treaty #3 area

5. That CPT take concrete steps to assist future teams to engage the necessary internal work of undoing racism and sexism and in proactively addressing team dynamic issues

6. That mechanisms are put into place to maintain relationships in the region during periods when CPT does not have a team in the field

7. That CPT establish an "emergency response team" of trained CPTers who would be willing to travel to the region on short notice for crisis situations.

8. That CPT continue to organize delegations to the Treaty #3 area

9. That CPT continue to explore ways to engage the local churches, particularly the non-aboriginal members, and leaders, in the work of violence-reduction and undoing oppression

---

34. Maiese, "What is Neutrality?"

10. That CPT explore ways to respond to the repeated request from Anishinaabe partners to help facilitate nonviolence training in the region.[35]

ONYATA'A:KA (ONEIDA) NATION IN NEW YORK

Like the Kanien'kehake/Mohawks, the Oneidas are founding members of the Haudenosaunee (Iroquois) Confederacy (see previous chapter.) During the Revolutionary War, Oneidas and Tuscarawas fought beside the white colonists against the British (with whom the other Haudenosaunee nations had allied themselves). The grateful General Washington later recognized the contribution of the Oneidas to American Revolution by signing a treaty with the Oneida Nation to preserve its land in New York State.[36] New York promptly ignored Washington's promise and confiscated most of the Oneida homeland along with that of the other Haudenosaunee nations in the following decades. Seeking refuge from the white settlers taking over their land, most of the Oneidas left, beginning in 1820, for the contemporary London, Ontario area, the Onondaga territory south of Syracuse, New York and the Menominee Nation territory in eastern Wisconsin. A small group of Oneida refused to leave and held on to their thirty-two acres outside Sherrill, New York. Their descendants would be the group among whom CPT would work for a short time.

In 1985, the U.S. Supreme Court upheld a lower court ruling that the State of New York had unlawfully confiscated land guaranteed to the Oneida in treaties. The ruling acknowledged their ownership of 872 acres and opened the possibility for the Oneida to claim another 250,000 acres in central New York. Given that most of that land is now inhabited by people of European descent, how the Oneida will reclaim it or take compensation for it has been the subject of bitter dispute.

In 1977, the Grand Council of the Haudenosaunee and the Oneida Clan Mothers designated three individuals, Lyman Johns (Turtle clan), Richard Chrisjohn (Bear Clan), and Arthur Raymond Halbritter (Wolf Clan), as "messengers" for the people residing in Central New York. They did so because issues arising from gambling revenue had split the com-

35. CPT Kenora, "Evaluation of CPT's presence."

36. Oneida Indian Nation, "A Brief History." The Oneida also gave corn to Washington's starving troops in Valley Forge, and an Oneida woman, Polly Cooper, stayed to cook for them. Glatthaar and Martin, *Forgotten Allies*, 203–8.

munity into factions and the Council needed Oneidas who could serve as its "Eyes and Ears." The job of the three men was to observe and report back to the Council of Chiefs. They had no authority to speak on behalf of the Council.

With the death of Johns and Chrisjohn, Halbritter assumed unilateral powers and created an organization called the "Men's Council," a governing body foreign to Haudenosaunee tradition. He also appointed new clan mothers, which ran counter to Haudenosaunee tradition (the position of Clan Mother is hereditary).[37] He then informed the Bureau of Indian Affairs that he was now "Chief" of the Oneida.

After Halbritter concluded secret negotiations with New York Governor Mario Cuomo to open a casino on the disputed territory, the Grand Council of the Haudenosaunee stripped Halbritter of his status as an Oneida observer or representative. The U.S. Department of the Interior accepted the Council's verdict, and then rejected it one day later when New York congressman Sherwood Boelhert intervened on Halbritter's behalf.[38]

Halbritter proceeded to create a fifty-four-member police force, entirely composed of non-natives, and a tribal court with non-native lawyers and judges to consolidate his power in the Oneida Nation. Dissident Oneidas say that to mollify the critics within his Nation, he used funds from the U.S. government to build a housing project and provide social services.[39]

Halbritter also gained complete control of the revenue garnered by the gigantic Turning Stone Casino. He refused to supply the National Indian Gaming Commission (NIGC) with audits from 1993–1996 until the commission threatened to close the casino down. He also refused to let other members of the Oneida nation view the financial records from

37. See ""Haudenosaunee tradition and culture."

38. Anne Herman, in an August 29, 2005 e-mail, noted that various sources documenting the conflict at Oneida refer to the Grand Council and Clan Mothers making Halbritter, Johns, and Chrisjohn "representatives" or "spokesmen." These designations result from a mistranslation of the Oneida language. The Grand Council had long refused to accede to the Bureau of Indian Affairs' request that it appoint official spokespeople or "chiefs" for the Haudenosaunee nations.

39. CPT affiliated itself with these dissidents, and Halbritter's other actions seem to bear out this critique. However, he may also have had some genuine concern for the well-being of Oneidas living in substandard housing.

Turning Stone. Eventually, Halbritter changed the name of the Oneida Nation to Oneida Nation, Inc. and installed himself as CEO.

On March 20, 1995, members of the Wolf Clan critical of Halbritter's rule found they had been locked out of their Longhouse, the spiritual center of most Haudenosaunee communities. The non-native police officers had instructions to arrest anyone who tried to enter. The Traditional Oneidas moved the meeting to the cabin of Maisie Shenandoah—Wolf Clan mother and aunt of Halbritter—and voted to remove Ray Halbritter as their representative.

Halbritter responded by banning media coverage on Oneida property, meetings of more than five people, and traditional ceremonies taking place on the thirty-two-acre territory. In 1998, he bought the most widely-circulated First Nations' newspaper, *Indian Country Today*, to keep members of other Nations from hearing about the conflict in Oneida. He also disenrolled the dissident Oneidas from the Nation, which meant they lost employment, health benefits, educational benefits, and their quarterly allowance.

In one particularly poignant case, Halbritter's regime took away the benefits of a seventy-eight-year-old amputee, Liddy Wilson, because she had attended a press conference held by Oneidas who were demanding that Halbritter disclose what he promised Mario Cuomo in exchange for permission to open the casino. The bus that brought elderly Oneida into the community center for a daily meal stopped coming for Wilson. When a new well paid for by an Indian Health Service grant went through a salt vein, Wilson called the Health Service and asked how she would survive on a well full of salt. The people there laughed at her and said she would not have to add salt when she boiled her potatoes.

Halbritter's people told her that they would restore her benefits if she swore an oath of allegiance to Halbritter's government. She refused. Shortly afterwards, she had surgery on her unamputated foot. Left at home alone, she bumped the stitches, and the blood thinners she was on made her bleed uncontrollably. Her cordless phone was found in a pool of blood next to the wheelchair in which she had died. "With all of [the casino] money, couldn't the nation have paid for an attendant?" one member of the Wolf Clan sorrowfully asked Kathleen Kern.[40]

40. George-Kanentiio, "History of the Onyota'aka Oneida"; CPT Oneida, "Oneida Report"; CPTnet, Kern, "Oneida Territory, NY: What they did to Liddy," Dec 2, 2002. For a summary of the traditional Oneidas' initial legal challenges to Halbritter's rule, see the CCR, "Shenandoah, et al v. Halbritter."

Because Halbritter controlled the social services, the non-native police force, and tribal courts, the traditional Oneida felt they had no venue within the nation to express their grievances. When they appealed to federal, state, or local courts, Halbritter asserted that Oneida was a sovereign nation in which the U.S. courts should not interfere. Ironically, most of the traditional Oneidas agreed with him in principle, but felt they had no other recourse. Moreover, since he staffed the entire tribal judicial system with non-natives, the traditionals believed that gave them the right to appeal to non-native judicial venues.

In November 2001, "Hawk," a Shawnee observer at the thirty-two-acre territory contacted John Paul Lederach who encouraged reservists Rob and Patty Burdette—CPT supporters who had spent time on the LaFramboise Island and Esgenoôpetitj projects—to visit the territory.[41] They told the traditional Oneidas about CPT's work in South Dakota and New Brunswick, which led to a request from the traditional Oneidas that CPT send a two-week observer delegation to Oneida. In particular, the traditionals feared that Halbritter was about to evict them, demolish their homes, and set up another casino on the remaining thirty-two acres of the Reserve. Anne Herman, Rod Orr, and Cliff Kindy arrived at the thirty-two-acre territory on February 7, 2002. After visiting with traditional Oneidas, area pastors, and law enforcement, as well as Halbritter and members of his government, the delegation proposed that CPT be "on-call" as it had been in Vieques (see chapter 13) in case Halbritter moved against the traditional Oneida.[42]

In August 2002, Danielle Shenandoah Patterson's house became a target. Under the auspices of a "beautification program," Halbritter had

---

Ray Halbritter responded to the charges against his leadership by the dissidents—whose website is www.Oneidasfordemocracy.org—by starting the website oneidasfordemocracy.com (with the home page title "*The Real* Oneidas for Democracy"). His regime also operates the Web site oneida-nation.net ("The Official Website of the Oneida Indian Nation"). Halbritter has sought to frame the conflict in terms of a family dispute, with the Shenandoah family being the only Oneidas who are opposed to his leadership.

41. In e-mails sent August 25 and 26, 2005, Lederach wrote that he thinks "Hawk" (the only name Lederach and CPTers knew him by) got his name through Lederach's Mohawk contact, Dale Dionne. (Hawk writes about his involvement with Oneida in "Hawk's Letter," where he identifies himself as Michael Walking Thunder of the Black Panther Clan, Kispoko Band Shawnee Nation.)

Lederach was on his way to mediate a conflict in Tajikistan, which is why he called the Burdettes.

42. CPT Oneida, "Oneida Report."

already evicted thirteen other families on the thirty-two acres and demolished their homes. Patterson's home was next. She tried to prevent non-
native tribal housing inspectors from entering her home in November
2001. The officers charged her with assaulting a police officer and said
her home was uninhabitable. Prior to the inspection, Patterson had had
a New York State inspector examine her house trailer, who judged it to
comply with New York State regulations.

Over the next month, CPTers played tag team, coming for several
days or a week in hopes of preventing the demolition of the trailer. Some,
like Joel Klassen, Rusty Curling, Murray Lumley, John Finlay, Dianne Roe,
Kathleen Kern, and Anne Herman came by themselves for short stretches
of time. On several of her visits, Herman conducted Nonviolence training
for community members.

Patterson refused to appear in Tribal court in September 2002,
because she did not recognize the legitimacy of the legal system. She expected that the consequences would be her arrest and the demolition of
her home. CPTer Joel Klassen was among those who stood on the roof of
her home to prevent its demolition. (Awaiting the judge's verdict, one of
the role-plays Herman had conducted during the Nonviolence training
involved standing on the roof of the trailer.) The court, however, did not
send either arresting officers or bulldozers after the judge ruled that she
would be tried in absentia if she refused to appear again and adjourned
the trial.

The victory was short-lived. On October 18, 2002, the Oneida Nation,
Inc. police, arrested Patterson for contempt, taking her to a maximum-
security prison in Pennsylvania, where she had to undergo a body cavity
search. (The police from the non-native town of Oneida refused to allow
Halbritter's people to use the city or county jails for the purpose.) When
she appeared in Tribal Court on October 21, she accepted a plea bargain,
saying she would not interfere with the destruction of her home in order
to stay out of jail.[43]

CPT continued to have an intermittent presence at Oneida for the
next two years, with Anne Herman making visits most frequently. The
last release to appear on CPTnet about the project alerted the CPT con-

43. See CPTnet releases: "Oneida, NY: Time for Another Campaign" Mar 2, 2002;
"Oneida, NY Urgent Action: Stop demolition," Aug 27, 2002; "Oneida Territory, NY:
Tribal Court," Sept 30, 2002; "Oneida Update: September 17–30, 2002," Oct 7, 2002; Horst,
"Oneida Territory, NY: Another family homeless," Nov 1, 2002.

stituency that Oneida Nation, Inc. had just inspected Wolf Clan mother Maisie Shenandoah's home—the final home on the thirty-two acres to fall victim to the "beautification program." Halbritter's people gave families on that parcel of the territory until August 20, 2003, to move.

Anne Herman, via GITW, kept other CPTers updated about the suits that the traditional Oneida had filed in U.S. courts arguing that Halbritter was discriminating against them because of their political beliefs. In May 2005, they lost their last legal battle to save their homes when the U.S. Supreme Court refused to hear their appeal.

Just two weeks earlier, Halbritter's Oneida Nation, Inc. lost its case in another legal venue arguing that the land it had bought in the last decade be regarded as under Oneida sovereignty—and thus not subject to local or state taxation. Afterwards, Diane Shenandoah told a journalist, "we're hoping he has too many things on his plate to deal with us at the moment."[44]

ISSUES ARISING FROM CPT'S WORK IN INDIGENOUS COMMUNITIES

Colonizing and Defining First Nations

The deepest wounds that contemporary First Nations in North America have sustained are related to having their stories and names defined by European colonists and their descendants. For centuries, novels, textbooks and movies largely ignored the history of the First Nations or mentioned them only in passing. When various media did pay attention to them, they either portrayed the indigenous as bloodthirsty savages or noble children of nature, now extinct. For White North American CPTers, resisting the temptation to define indigenous people took much emotional energy and conscious effort.

Even citing the names of the communities with whom CPT has worked has taken conscious effort. When Joanne Kaufman and Kathleen Kern first came to the Oceti Sakowin encampment, they asked a local white woman sympathetic to First Nations whether they could refer to the camp members as Lakota, since all of the warriors there were not only Lakota but also Oglala Lakota, instead of always writing "Lakota/Dakota/

---

44. CPTnet, Kindy, "Oneida, NY: Shenandoah home inspected," July 7, 2003; Coin, "Families refuse to leave homes."

Nakota" people. Her response was firm. CPTers should always use the titles that the people at the encampment asked them to use, and so they included the Dakota and Nakota names as well.

For English-speaking CPTers, "Burnt Church" and "Grassy Narrows" are much easier to remember than "Esgenoôpetitj" and "Asubpeeschoseewagong." And indigenous members of these communities used the English names as well. However, given that North Americans of European descent historically could not be bothered to learn what the First Nations called themselves, stumbling through tricky pronunciation and spelling was a necessity for CPTers seeking to move away from the historic disrespect their ancestors had shown to indigenous communities.[45]

Matt Schaaf, with tongue-in-cheek, acknowledged the difficulties of learning unfamiliar indigenous names in his release, "Asubpeeschoseewagong: A Political and Pronunciation Guide":

> The various Ojibwa-speaking communities of northwestern Ontario, Manitoba and Minnesota make up the Anishinabe [Uh - nish - uh - naw - bay] Nation. The Ojibwa use the word Anishinabek to describe themselves. It means "natural people" or "human beings...."
> —Asubpeeschoseewagong (Grassy Narrows) is an Anishinabek community of 700 people located about 70 kilometres north of Kenora, Ontario. Asubpeeschoseewagong [Uh - sub - shko - see - wah - gongk] translates roughly to English as "web-like grass." Hunters, trappers, teachers, students and elders have lived here for as long as anyone can remember.
> —The young country of Canada [Ka - naw daw] was formed in 1867.
> —Canada and the Anishinabe Nation signed Treaty #3 [Tree - tee - three] in 1873. This international agreement allows Canada and the Anishinabek to share lands and its resources. The treaty has worked very well for white society but not for aboriginal communities....
> —The Ontario Ministry of Natural Resources [Em - en - awr] sets the standards for the timber industry and grants logging licences. MNR employs only one person to monitor whether or not timber companies comply with provincial environmental standards. MNR mostly lets companies police themselves.

45. Spelling was an issue when CPT worked at Esgenoôpetitj. The Mi'kmaq used no capital letters for proper names, e.g., miigam'agan and gkisedtanamoogk, two of the team's primary contacts in the EFN.

—Pulp and paper company Abitibi [A - bih - tih - bee] holds a Sustainable Forest Licence from MNR and employs contractors to clearcut in the Whiskey Jack Forest to provide spruce and pine for its pulp and paper mill in Kenora....
—The Ontario Provincial Police [Oh - pee - pee] patrol the blockade camp daily. OPP officers pledge their loyalty to the Queen of Canada....
—Members of Christian Peacemaker Teams [see - pee - tee] live at the blockade camp in order to reduce the possibility of violence between Asubpeeschoseewagong folks and loggers or police. CPT seeks to be a good neighbour and an honourable inheritor of the Treaty that allows us to live here.[46]

More seriously, CPTers learned that they should not serve as spokespeople—another "defining" activity—for the indigenous communities they were accompanying or talk about their affairs with outsiders unless given permission to do so. Non-indigenous journalists and civilians routinely approached CPTers at the camps in South Dakota, Esgenoôpetitj, Asubpeeschoseewagong, and Oneida for information. The Grassy Team conducted role-plays to practice referring non-indigenous inquirers to indigenous spokespeople.

In June 2000, an officer with the DFO drove onto Esgenoôpetitj territory and began questioning Kindy about a confrontation between an EFN boat and a DFO boat the previous day. Although Kindy told Officer Louis Breault that he did not want to have this conversation without an EFN member present, EFN members told him that he should not have spoken to Breault at all on their territory. Since the DFO was not technically allowed to be on the reservation, speaking to its officers might legitimate its conduct.[47]

46 CPTnet, Feb 15, 2003.

47. Additionally, speaking with non-indigenous people about the community-fed rumors, at least in Esgenoôpetitj, that CPTers were informers. See CPTnet, "Esgenoôpetitj, New Brunswick Update: June 13–28, 2000," July 7, 2000; CPTnet, "CPT Esgenoôpetitj Project: Project Evaluation," Oct 27, 2001. See also August 31, 2005 e-mails from Doug Pritchard, Jessica Phillips, Anne Herman, and Rusty Curling.
Regarding his experiences at Oneida, Dinkins-Curling wrote:

In Oneida there were often non-indigenous folks present with CPT being one of many groups. We were looked to for leadership by the Oneida there in keeping the other non-indigenous in line with what they were trying to do (training in non-violence etc.). On a few occasions the press wanted to talk to us to get the particular angle of CPT in the midst of the

Co-opting Indigenous Culture

Even sympathetic interest in and advocacy for indigenous communities can have colonial overtones. A critique of the genocidal behavior of European colonizers can sometimes lead people to believe that the First Nations of North America are extinct, when in fact their numbers have been growing steadily over the last century. Romanticizing the First Nations also objectifies them, as does co-opting their culture through dress and ersatz forms of spirituality.

One of the blockaders in Grassy Narrows had a dream about Matt Schaaf's name. She taught him the Ojibwe pronunciation and said it meant something like "Man who starts something" or "Man who is working." (Previously, she had joked that his name should be Tall Skinny White Man Who Turns Red.) Schaaf began introducing himself by that name in ceremonies and sharing circles. Several months later, a white man who was a longtime resident of Grassy Narrows gently pointed out to him that that the Anishinabe youth in the community had lost their own language and culture, and would never be considered white. Imagine, the man told Schaaf, how they felt when they heard him use his "spirit name." Once again, he told Schaaf, "the white guy" had taken something that belonged to the First Nations.[48]

Pushing CPT Values onto Indigenous People

Working in any culture other than one's own causes paradigm shifts. CPTers have worked in communities where patriarchy reigns, where homosexuality is considered abhorrent and where cruelty to animals is an unpleasant fact. Quite often, dominating powers responsible for oppressing these communities point to these realities as proof that the oppressed culture is inferior and needs to be controlled and subdued. CPTers thus

---

story. On at least one occasion it would have been better if I had referred a reporter, I played the old open mouth and insert foot game quite well. He got a great quote and I offended some people needlessly.

As a general rule we did refer people to the Oneida who were present though. At least that's what I recall. Why should I talk when there are people as bright and articulate and Diane, Danielle and Vicky [Shenandoah] present.

48. GITW, posting by Schaaf, "Blockade! Racism! Crazy Stuff!" May 25, 2005. The man concluded the conversation with, "You're a friend of the people here and I'm telling you this because we know you'll be around."

face a delicate task of upholding their ideals, challenging the oppression of the dominating culture, and examining the racism, homophobia, and sexism in themselves and their own culture while advocating for oppressed communities.

In general, working among First Nations caused less ideological conflict for most CPTers than on some other project locations. The tendency of these communities to care for the environment, advocate for the poor and put their life in a spiritual context resonated with most CPTers. Sometimes, however, cultural differences made gentle collisions on CPT's project sites in indigenous communities. CPTers tend to eschew nationalism, but have supported First Nations in their desire for sovereignty.[49] They have also supported First Nations' claim to have their burial sites respected, even though CPTers largely do not care what becomes of their own bodies after death. They know that when people have the luxury of choosing what happens to their bodies, they cannot judge those who have had the bodies and cultural artifacts of their people turned into museum exhibits and their graveyards sacrificed to non-indigenous development.

More serious is the issue of "pushing" the Nonviolent Direct Action model that CPTers have learned in training onto the indigenous peoples with whom they worked. As was true in Haiti and Palestine, some members of North American First Nations with whom CPT worked were not committed to nonviolence as a principle, but as a strategy. In Esgenoôpetitj, the indigenous community with whom CPT worked experienced the most physical violence at the hands of government authorities and vigilantes, these issues confronted CPTers most starkly. Once the DFO began to attack EFN members, several members of that community decided they needed to fight back. In one instance, after DFO officers pointed guns at one EFN fisher, he went back to the shore to get his own gun. Matthew Bailey-Dick told him that he would need to get out of the boat if the fisher chose to pursue this course, and the man told him that he understood. When they docked the boat, older members of the community talked the

---

49. CPTer Tricia Gates-Brown described what she sees as the qualitative difference between the two in a September 1, 2005 e-mail:

> To me, sovereignty implies autonomy/freedom from outside dictators, whereas nationalism implies supremacy over others. If I think of this on a personal scale, the distinction is even more clear. I feel justified asserting my own freedom from outside dictators, but do not feel justified asserting my supremacy over others.

young men out of getting their guns and said they would follow through on the threats by setting up roadblocks instead.

Janet Shoemaker wrote in a letter to her supporters about an incident that happened a couple weeks later,

> We believe that [the DFO] really wanted a confrontation in the dark—because they knew that no one could see it. But they didn't get it. So they waited until it was light. They seem to really want violence, for the native people to lose control, bring out the guns and kill or wound a "peace" officer so they can lay the blame on the Indians. The DFO has been getting some bad press up here because there are too many video cameras out there showing how they harass and attempt to hurt native fishermen. They are losing this battle, and they know it.
>
> —Please keep the prayers coming our way: that the native fishermen will continue to refuse to use violence in this struggle, that the DFO will recognize the treaties, and that the non-native fishers will recognize the lies the government feeds them about the lobster fishery and gain some peace of mind in this situation. And for the team that we can find creative ways to support this struggle and speak the truth in ways that the non-native community can hear it.[50]

At the Oceti Sakowin camp and Asubpeeschoseewagong, the teams encountered a similar reluctance about engaging in CPT's mode of Nonviolent Direct Action.

Joanne Kaufman wrote,

> . . . the camp's own sense of direction and strength wasn't geared toward action—but as one member put it: (not exact quote) "We are here to pray. If we are led to action, we will do it. But we aren't here to make trouble just to make trouble."
>
> . . . we North Americans are addicted to physical action that we see going on, whatever the amazing undercurrents (spiritual and/or emotional and/or building things that aren't tangible for people).

Carl Meyer took issue with the final evaluation written about the South Dakota project, which noted,

50. CPT Esgenoopetitj, Report describing events of August 13, 2000; CPTnet, Shoemaker, "Esgeno'petitj: Letter," Aug 29, 2000.

Aware that Native Americans are wary of non-Indian and especially Christian interference with or infiltration of their movements, CPT was careful not to try to impose an outside agenda. In retrospect, the team got somewhat sidetracked, focusing on simple presence, legislative follow-up and action, and responding to insensitive intervention by authorities and law enforcement. Opportunities for engaging in nonviolent direct action or brainstorming proactive nonviolent direct actions should have been more actively pursued.

Meyer responded,

The report basically said that CPT should have pushed more to engage in CPT-style direct action, and our mistake was in being too passive. I think exactly the opposite is true. Lakota people know what they're doing when they take actions like this, and they're being directed by the spirits and by their elders, wisdom at least as wise as that which guides CPT. If they want our accompaniment they'll ask for it (and they did), if they want our NVDA training they'll ask for it, but acting like we've got the "right" model for how they should address their issues (or unilaterally taking our own actions that might have consequences for the camp without taking direction from camp leadership) is, frankly, racist, and I think some CPTers at the camp acted that way (I remember that CPT was harshly reprimanded for that at one point by Charmaine White Face).[51]

51. Kaufman, comments on draft of Oceti Sakowin section of previous chapter; Carl Meyer, e-mail, June 25, 2005; CPT Oceti Sakowin Encampment, "CPT, Pierre, South Dakota." Polhamus responded Kaufman's and Meyer's comments in a June 28, 2005 e-mail:

In regards to the idea that CPT wanted to insensitively push its own agenda of NV I would like to add a couple of comments. I know that we did make mistakes but as Stella Pretty Sounding Flute told the warriors at camp one night, "Mistakes are part of the lesson." I think we tried to "repent" when we did make mistakes. I also think the sentence in the report "Aware that Native Americans are wary of non-Indian and especially Christian interference with or infiltration of their movements, CPT was careful not to try to impose an outside agenda" was not written just to make us sound good but from the truth that we tried to be sensitive to this issue. If we didn't act or were perceived not to act that way 100% of the time does not take away from the fact that this was talked about and efforts were made to avoid the imposing. I think most suggestions and discussions regarding NV were usually framed from the "what if" perspective and that we wanted to learn how these ideas of NV from other traditions fit into the Lakota. I agree with Joanne's comment, "one

The evaluation of the project at Asubpeeschoseewagong was even more blunt: "Sometimes CPTers try to push projects the community doesn't want. This happens when we need to feel busy or useful and don't know how to listen to local people's soft cues."[52]

How CPT'S Projects with First Nations Informed Each Other

In an early release about the Esgenoôpetitj project, a bracketed comment at the beginning noted, "CPT encourages our U.S. constituency to see the connections between its ongoing work with First Nations people in Esgenoôpetitj and its work with First Nations people in South Dakota and Chiapas." The team intended the note to help the U.S. constituency feel engaged with the dispute between the EFN and the Canadian government. However, it also highlights the inclination of CPTers to compare and contrast the characteristics of one First Nations community with others.

William Payne noted in a later article written from Esgenoôpetitj,

> A helicopter circles over our heads three times as we chat on the wharf. One man gets out binoculars to take a closer look, though we can almost see the faces without the help. For me, memories of being a human rights observer in a remote village in Chiapas, Mexico come back. Government surveillance feels the same in Canada, at least when you are in a First Nations Community.[53]

Most CPTers who had worked in more than one First Nations communities were struck by the similarities between these communities, even though their geographic, historic, and linguistic characteristics could be vastly different. In all indigenous communities, conversation tended to happen slowly, with First Nations people allowing a period of silence between speakers. First Nations people also had a certain patience to allow change to happen slowly and organically, rather than finding ways to make the process faster. Often communication was indirect, wishes and desires implied, rather than declared. As one Mi'kmaq woman told the Esgenoôpetitj team, "Don't expect a specific invitation because our people

---

of the amazing things also that happened was that our presence built bridges and built trust with Lakota people whose perspective on whites and especially on Christians was pretty jaded." Bridges and trust aren't made by people who feel that you are imposing your will on them.

52. CPT Asubpeeschoseewagong, "Evaluation of CPT's Role."

53. Payne, "Gunboat Diplomacy in Canada."

will not want to make you feel obligated in that way. Just come in the spring, and we will put you to work."[54]

Although making these comparisons are a type of non-native "defining" of the First Nations, it was a type of categorization that most of the First Nations with whom CPT worked did not resent. William Payne found that Mayans in the municipality of Polho loved seeing pictures of the EFN warriors. Participants at the South Dakota encampment were eager to hear about the Mayans in Chiapas (a conversation that started when Kathleen Kern took the ashes from the camp's [non-sacred] fire to put in the La Framboise Island latrine, as the Mayan refugees had in their refugee camp latrines).

Doug Pritchard wrote,

> . . . lots of interest at Esgenoôpetitj about what was happening in Chiapas since the projects were simultaneous and we had folk like Cliff, Janet(?), and William who had been in Chiapas. We found EFN folk VERY knowledgeable about the Zapatista movement but they had not heard much about the Abejas. We even proposed bringing two Abejas to EFN to be part of an even more international presence and we applied for a grant to bring them. We didn't get the grant, one of the Abejas decided he needed to stay in the community during the upcoming election(?) and the fishing season ended before we could take his idea further.[55]

All of the First Nations communities where CPTers had project sites were visited by people from other First Nations seeking to show solidarity. These visits illustrate possibly the most important similarity among the First Nations of the Americas: they were all survivors of brutal colonization. Had the Europeans never come to the Americas, the indigenous people of the Great Plains, the Haudenosaunee Confederacy, and the Incas, Aztecs, and Mayans almost certainly would have thought of each other as distinct and unrelated nations, just as Canadians would see very little relationship between themselves and, say, Bulgarians.[56] But colonization turned all the First Nations of the Americas into "Indians."

54. CPT "Proposal for a CPT project in Burnt Church," Feb 7, 2000.

55. Pritchard, e-mail, Sept 12, 2005.

56. James Wilson, in *The Earth Shall Weep*—his comprehensive history of the indigenous nations in what became the United States—noted on page 28 that just before the conquest of the Americas, Europe was a much more homogeneous political entity than the Nations of the Americas were.

As time passed, they began to feel solidarity with each other and learn from the ways other First Nations had resisted European colonization. In one particularly interesting encounter during CPT's early involvement with the ANA, a Kayapo Indian Chief from Brazil visited Grassy Narrows. He told the people there that the Brazilian government had actually protected Kayapo lands when people or corporations had tried to take the natural resources in these lands. The visit impelled Lisa Martens to write, "Imagine this: An indigenous nation, when encroached upon by loggers (or miners or hydroelectric developers), simply calls up the federal government's Department of Indian Affairs, and the government expels the intruders."[57]

The connections forged between First Nations in North and South America, in turn, taught CPTers working in disparate First Nations communities ways not to encroach on or define these First Nations. Given the number of invitations CPT has continued to receive from First Nations who have learned about CPT via word-of-mouth and the Internet, this training will prove useful as the organization develops and continues its work with indigenous people.

Internecine Struggles

One of the most difficult realities of CPT's work among the First Nations was the internal struggle within these communities. The "template" for these struggles usually involved tribal leadership recognized by the U.S. and Canadian governments giving away resources or Treaty rights while the people whom they claimed to represent demanded that the U.S. and Canadian governments adhere to treaties they had signed.

In South Dakota, two bands of the "Great Sioux Nation" gave up their claim to the land along the Missouri River in exchange for Federal funding. Senator Tom Daschle used their acquiescence to push "The

57. CPTnet, "Grassy Narrows, Ontario: Imagine," Sept 21, 2001. Another Latin American connection was the CPT Colombia team's involvement in the campaign to free the kidnapped Embera Katío leader, Kimy Pernia Domico, in Colombia. Pernia spearheaded the Embera Katío people's struggle against the Urrá Dam. After paramilitaries threatened his life and he was subsequently kidnapped, Colombian Mennonites asked the first team in Barrancabermeja to participate in a march with the Embera Katío in the department of Cordoba. See CPTnet releases: "Colombia Urgent Action: CPTers accompany search," June 15, 2001; "Colombia: Call for Prayer," June 22, 2001; "Colombia: Outcome of Embera Katío march," June 30, 2001. See also, Horst, e-mail, August 15, 2006.

Mitigation Act" through congress. Some of the two bands, protesting their leaders' decision, joined the Oceti Sakowin Encampment.

In June 1999, the Army Corps of Engineers told the two collaborating bands—Cheyenne River and Lower Brulé—that the promised congressional funding would go toward the costs of implementing the transfer first; the members of the two bands might have to wait for seven years before they received the money promised them for signing off on the transfer. Their dismay at this betrayal caused one of the La Framboise Island campers to leave the room. He later told Carl Meyer, "I just couldn't stand to stay in there and watch my brothers begging the wasicu [white man] for money."

In his release about the meeting, Carl Meyer noted that the U.S. government had long used the effective strategy of "divide and conquer" within the First Nations. In the early nineteenth century, promising guns, molasses, and whiskey, the U.S. would persuade chiefs of individual bands to sign away rights to their land. The U.S. would then claim that these minor chiefs were leaders of "The Great Sioux Nation," even though the L/D/Nakota people had never had a leader with that much centralized authority. Meyer concluded his release, "For traditional Lakota people struggling to protect their rights and their land, very little has changed since the days of Crazy Horse."[58]

Among some Mi'kmaq nations, band council leaders were willing to allow the government to regulate their fisheries in exchange for financial help. The rumor that EFN chief Wilbur Dedam had done so prompted an angry meeting in April 2000 in which Dedam assured the EFN members he had done no such thing. One of the nations that had signed, Big Cove, found itself in a situation similar to that of the Lower Brule and Cheyenne River bands in South Dakota. In exchange for Big Cove signing away its treaty fishing rights, the government promised them fifty boats, of which they had received only four at the time that CPT visited them.[59] In Asubpeeschoseewagong, certain members of the Grassy Band Council were ready to accept the terms that Abitibi offered (no cutting for ten kilometers around the Grassy Narrows community and cutting done in consultation with the ANA for the next ten kilometers) in exchange for ending the blockade, while most of the blockaders were not.

58. CPTnet, "South Dakota: Divide and rule," July 3, 1999.

59. CPTnet, "New Brunswick: Esgenoôpetitj Update April 4–27," May 8, 1999. CPTnet, "Esgenoôpetitj Update: October 1–31, 2000," Nov 21, 2000.

By far, the most difficult exposure to internecine struggles for CPT occurred at Oneida, where the self-appointed chief of the Oneida, Ray Halbritter, was a nephew and cousin to the Oneidas most active in their resistance to Halbritter regime. Early on, the team's reference to Halbritter as a "dictator" in a local paper, prompted Doug Pritchard to write the following:

> He may be a dictator, but I don't think CPTers have used that kind of dismissive labeling of other enemies in our work. It does imply we know all about this situation and have concluded we can add Halbritter to the list that includes Saddam Hussein et al. I don't know if that is true, or if it is wise to speak in these words. When Halbritter reads this article, I suspect that will be the end of any chances for further dialogue with him or his supporters. Our good friend Theresa Johnson, an Oneida married to Chief Larry Johnson at Caldwell First Nation, has counselled caution before we state our conclusions about the situation at Oneida. I agree and I don't think this quote helps the situation.[60]

Also complicating the intra-nation dispute was the alliance of Upstate Citizens for Equality with the Shenandoah women. UCE's *raison d'etre* was protesting the Haudenosaunee land claims that affected settlers of European descent. UCE, in effect, denied that First Nations had sov-

---

60. Pritchard, e-mail message to CPTers working at Oneida, Sept 10, 2002. Robin Buyers, who would later visit Johnson to discuss these concerns, wrote in a September 8, 2005 e-mail:

Gina [Lepp], Joel Klassen, and I drove down to Caldwell to speak to Theresa and, uncomfortably, arrived as a hotly contested band council election was taking place. Theresa spoke well of Halbritter, who is her uncle, and his work to improve the economic status of the community. She felt that he might be being unfairly attacked by members of the community. Her primary concern was with the nature of attacks within her own community on her husband, who only narrowly won the election. While Larry had fought hard to get the federal government to agree to a settlement in order to buy land for the community, other community members were arguing for cash settlements to be paid to individual band members. This was the primary issue in the election.

My concern, always, with the Oneida project was with the potential for taking sides in an internal conflict within an Aboriginal nation. I don't think this is where we, or any group of primarily settlers, belongs.

This is my quick reflection on this bit of CPT history, from an internet cafe in Santander de Quilichao in the north of Cauca, Colombia.

Robin

ereignty over lands promised them in treaties, and the corruption of the
Ray Halbritter government was a convenient chip they could use to dem-
onstrate that the Haudenosaunee Nations did not deserve sovereignty.
Thus, they took on the plight of the Oneida dissidents as a *cause celebre.*

When Kathleen Kern asked Diane Shenandoah about UCE taking up
her cause, she looked uncomfortable; she supported Oneida sovereignty
and the land claims that the Oneida were pursuing in court. However, she
also said that when the Oneida reorganized in the 1980s under the Clan
Mothers, the traditional leadership sought to assure white people living
in the area that the Oneida would not force them to leave their homes.
"We always told people that our disagreement was with the State of New
York, not the people living here." When Halbritter, under the banner of
sovereignty, began building on disputed land, thus driving down the tax
base of the small, economically struggling towns in the area, he polarized
factions, turning the conflict into a White versus Indian issue. The traditional Oneida would have preferred a more conciliatory approach.[61]

Given that most internecine battles in First Nations communities
involve how much these nations should collaborate with the Canadian
and U.S. governments, CPTers' work in First Nations will continue to be affected by these disputes. Whenever possible, however, CPT tries to follow
the sentiment expressed in the 2001 October Esgenoôpetitj evaluation:
"Do not comment on community politics or policies or get drawn into
conversations on internal community affairs. It is none of our business."

61. Most of the Haudenosaunee Nations have gone through struggles between designated leaders recognized by the US government and factions of these nations who
believe that this leadership is illegitimate or is squelching their right to express their
opinions. These disputes usually occur when the tribal leadership signs agreements with
state and federal governments. In the Onondaga Nation, some members were concerned
about the tribal government allowing Syracuse University Hospital to dump its waste on
Onondaga Territory, thus polluting the groundwater. One of the dissidents who high-
lighted this environmental abuse, Ron Jones, died in a suspicious house fire in 2000.
Kathleen Kern had met Jones and some Palestinian university students in Rochester
shortly before he died on the day that Rodeina and Atta Jaber's house was destroyed (see
chap. 4). She began weeping, and Jones joined her, sharing about his own experience of
the Onondaga leadership evicting him from and destroying his house.

When Kern told this story to one of the Shenandoah women, she learned that
Onondaga chief Oren Lyons, whose abuses of power seemed similar to those of Ray
Halbritter, supported the Shenandoahs, who obliquely sided with Lyons in his dispute
with Jones and other dissident Onondagas. Joanne Shenandoah received the first "Oren
Lyons Award" in 2001 and performed with him on stage.

Relationship with White Communities Bordering First Nations' Communities

Although not all of the CPTers who have worked in indigenous communities are of European descent, most of them have been, which has led to both difficult and rewarding relationships with the white communities located near the indigenous project sites. Most of the white communities neighboring indigenous communities were also economically depressed, with people feeling they needed to assert their right to make a living and survive in the communities where they had grown up.

When the team set up in Esgenoôpetitj, CPTers made an effort to network with churches and law enforcement organizations in the area to help defuse the violence during the fishing season.[62] However, from the beginning of the project in spring 2000, they found themselves encountering naked racism in the white communities around Esgenoôpetitj. One businessman told them that the local businesses would not sell traps to Aboriginals to replace the ones that white fishers had destroyed in the previous fishing season. After the close of the EFN fishing season in October 2000, the team conducted a "Listening Project" similar to the one they conducted with the neighbors of the Caldwell Nation. Often, once people they interviewed realized the CPTers were the "troublemakers" who had brought the unfavorable outside publicity, they had doors slammed in their faces. Those who spoke to them described EFN members as drunken, lazy, greedy, ungrateful, and "having no morals."

One man who had helped Leigh Morrison attack EFN members (see n. 63 in chapter 8) said,

> I have no use for them f—ing Indians. If I had a nuclear bomb, I would drop it on them, Basically, the reserve is a waste of air and space. I could shoot them all and piss on their bodies. . . . They were conquered so let's get on with it. . . . You don't hear the French complaining and they were conquered. How long do we have to keep giving them stuff?

More often, the negative responses from non-indigenous neighbors of the EFN seemed rooted in a fear of economic survival. Most fishers were

---

62. When Joel Klassen and Lena Siegers attended a United Church of Canada service in September 2000, they spoke with a woman who talked about the pain that the UCC had caused members of the church when it released a statement supporting the struggle of the EFN. CPTnet, "Esgenoôpetitj Update: September 1–14, 2000," Oct 5, 2000.

poor and targeting the EFN as a source of their problems was easier than blaming factory trawlers or Canadian policies that allowed the depletion of the fisheries.[63] People mentioned that the prices for housing around the EFN had decreased to such an extent that it would be impossible to sell them. One woman talked about how the stress had caused an epidemic of high blood pressure in the community, but that unlike the EFN, white people do not get free prescription medication. Most respondents wanted the EFN to have to pay for the expensive fishing licences and the taxes that the white fishers did. A few people expressed concern that there would be a "race war" in the future.[64] White fishers also seemed to have a distorted idea as to the size of the EFN fishery. One man told Natasha Krahn that eight hundred Natives had fished a total of five thousand lobster traps in the fall of 2000, when the number was closer to one thousand people fishing with 1300 traps.[65]

On the positive side, Lisa Martens noted in a 2003 Advent release that many Second Nations (non-aboriginal) people she met near Asubpeeschoseewagong had "a great deal of compassionate interest" in what was happening at Grassy Narrows and expressed a desire to visit. For a fall 2003 gathering at a United Church of Canada in Kenora, thirty non-natives showed up, earnestly desiring better relationships with their Grassy Narrows neighbors. One of the people who attended the gathering was a senior citizen who had worked on the hydroelectric project that had destroyed much of the Grassy Narrows traditional lands.[66] At the Oceti Sakowin encampment in South Dakota, CPTers also helped make connections between the La Framboise warriors and sympathetic churches in the area.

63. When the Indian Brook team celebrated National Aboriginal Day in Halifax on June 21, 2001, a non-Aboriginal woman joined their group with a sign saying, "First Nations were here First; They have First dibs." She said she supported their action because, "You don't see [Mi'kmaq] out with factory trawlers. They could teach us a thing or two about conservation." CPTnet, Kaufman, "Halifax, Nova Scotia: One Day is not Enough!" June 26, 2001.

64. CPT Esgenoôpetitj, "A Summary of Responses," Oct 12, 2000.

65. CPTnet, "Esgenoôpetitj Update: August 1–28, 2001." Sept 6, 2001. After reading a draft of this chapter, Doug Pritchard included in his editing (sent in an e-mail October 8, 2005) the notation, "I don't think this number is right. I think it was more like 400 people (adults) since the population of whole reserve, including children, was only about 1,000."

66. CPTnet, "Asubpeeschoseewagong: An Advent prayer," Dec 2, 2003.

Culpability of All Non-Native North Americans in the Dispossession and Destruction of Native Communities

William Payne, in a statement he read at a Toronto Press conference before the trial of EFN member Brian Bartibogue, said,

> My own people left Scotland and arrived in the Annapolis Valley in Nova Scotia in 1760. The land that they laid claim to—500 acres—was tainted, first by the blood of the Mi'kmaq people who had been displaced from it by the French and later by the blood of the thousands of Acadians killed and deported at this time.
>
> In an address given on the occasion of the Canadian government's response to its own Royal Commission on Aboriginal Peoples, past-Minister of Indian Affairs Jane Stewart says, "The seventh generation philosophy, a traditional way of thinking and decision-making, orients us between past and future. It tells us to be conscious of the lasting impact of our decisions today and to do the very best we can for coming generations." She goes on to remind us "We must proceed with care, because just as we are living with the past, what we do today will stay with us for generations." In a very real way, we are all part of the seventh generation and we must work to right the terrible wrongs that are part of our history.[67]

Even North American CPTers of European descent who could not trace their heritage in the New World as far back as Payne could had to face this daunting fact when they worked in First Nation communities: they and their ancestors benefited from their governments' confiscation of land and resources from the First Nations. They had to live with the definition given them by an Anishinabe man at an Un-Making Racism training: "that's what it means to be White—to say that you're standing on your own ground and standing on someone else's and then mystifying the whole process so it seems like you're not doing that."[68]

Sometimes CPTers who worked in indigenous communities felt an almost crippling guilt over the fact that they and their ancestors had easier, more comfortable lives than the indigenous people among whom they worked, because colonizers had not cared how European settlement had affected the First Nations. Truths they had believed all their lives, the ways

---

67. CPT Canada, "Media Statement Re: Charges Laid in the Lobster Fishery."

68. CPTnet, Martens, "Kenora/Anishnaabe Nation: Un-Making Racism," May 7, 2005.

they had lived and worked, looked different from a First Nations perspective. Yet, for most non-native CPTers, taking responsibility for how they had benefited from the dispossession of the First Nations did not leave them feeling guilt-ridden or paralyzed. The interactions between CPTers and First Nations people created a vision of ways white North American privilege could be turned back, ways that the disinherited and the inheritors could effectively challenge five centuries of genocide, occupation, exploitation, and humiliation.

CPTers came away from their time in First Nation communities feeling that such change could occur, because they had themselves been changed by First Nations friends and coworkers.

10

Colombia

Instructions to Self
Wake up again
Face the burning sun again
Hear the news of last night?
where the men with guns were
what they did
Open your fists
Quietly go and find them
Talk to the men with guns again
Note which ways they are carefully choosing to
terrorize your friends today
Believe what they say
And decide not to hate them again

—Lisa Martens[1]

I F ASKED TO NAME a chronic conflict dating from 1948, most informed people would immediately think of the founding of the State of Israel and the subsequent Palestinian refugee crisis. However, 1948 also marked the beginning of a bloody conflict in Colombia between the Liberal and Conservative Parties that was to continue under various forms until the present.[2]

In 1986, after continued repression by the government and the assassinations of their political leaders, all guerrilla groups formed in previous years called off a cease-fire negotiated between 1982 and 1984. Paramilitary groups armed by the Colombian military, began to carry out massacres against union members, civilians accused of being guerrilla supporters and "disposables" such as homosexuals, prostitutes, petty criminals, indi-

---

1. CPTnet, "Colombia: Three poems," May 18, 2002.
2. Of course, the conflicts in both locations had their origins in earlier events.

gents, and street children. Rightwing death squads murdered more than three thousand members of FARC's[3] political party, UP, (Patriotic Union), including its candidate in the 1986 presidential elections.

Liberal president Virgilio Barco fostered a peace process between 1986 and 1990, and stripped the military of its legal right to arm civilians. However, the power of the paramilitaries—still supported by the Colombian military and financed by drug money—continued to grow. In 1995, more than twenty-five thousand homicides took place in Colombia, making it the most dangerous country in the Western hemisphere. According to the Colombia Human Rights network, paramilitaries committed 60 percent of the political murders, the guerrillas 25 percent, and the Colombian military 10 percent.

From 1996 to 1998, paramilitaries and drug traffickers moved into FARC-controlled areas, trying to get control of coca-growing regions. To accomplish their aim, they began campaigns of terror against the civilian populations in these areas, displacing more than one million. FARC and the ELN[4] guerrilla groups stepped up attacks on the Colombian military and tried to prevent civilians from voting in the national elections.

After Conservative President Andrés Pastrana won the election, he signed the "Barrancabermeja Agreement" with displaced *campesinos*. The agreement was supposed to facilitate the return of the *campesinos* to their land under the protection of the Colombian military, but paramilitary attacks on civilians continued. In 1999, Pastrana ceded an area the size of Switzerland to FARC control, and the head of the AUC paramilitary group, Carlos Castaño, declared that human rights advocates were now military targets.

In spite of the enormous number of casualties, U.S. President Bill Clinton proposed a $1.6 billion military aid package for Colombia in January 2000. The U.S. Senate tried to shift some of the funds from military aid to human rights promotion, but the bill ultimately allowed the secretary of state to skip human rights certification if doing so was in the interests of national security. Clinton later waived all but one of the human rights conditions in the aid package.[5]

---

3. In English, "Revolutionary Armed Forces of Colombia."

4. In English, "National Liberation Army."

5. CHRN, "An Overview of Recent Colombian History."

Concerned by this massive influx of military aid and the violence it would inevitably foster in their country, leaders of the Colombian Mennonite church invited CPT to send an exploratory delegation to the country in April 2000.[6]

The April 2000 exploratory delegation accompanied Colombian Mennonites to several regions suffering most from violent conflict and recommended that CPT continue to explore the possibility of working in Colombia. During the subsequent Lent 2001 delegation, a wave of paramilitary violence in the city of Barrancabermeja (called "Barranca" by locals) helped convince the delegates—Cliff Kindy, Christine Forand, Duane Ediger, and Janet Shoemaker—that this location and the surrounding environs would be best suited for a CPT accompaniment project.

Over 80 percent of Colombia's oil is processed in Barranca's Ecopetrol refinery, but in spite of the wealth generated there, unemployment and poverty run roughly twice the national average. For decades, the city was under the influence of guerrilla groups, especially the ELN. In the early 1980s, a group of military authorities, business owners, ranchers, and representatives of Texas Petroleum set up structures that would lead to the formation of paramilitary groups, to protect their interests from guerrillas. The primary paramilitary group, Autodefensas Unidas de Colombia (AUC) became a major force in the 1990s. At the end of 2000, they had made a major incursion into Barrancabermeja, controlling 80 percent of the neighborhoods by April 2001. Paramilitaries killed as many as seven people a day without intervention by the Colombian police or military. They also imposed rules on appearance and behavior, such as not allowing men to wear their hair long. After terrorizing the population, they then began actively recruiting young men to join their ranks, promising them a $250/month salary, a cell phone, and a pistol—a lucrative lifestyle when compared to the majority of locals who lived in poverty.[7] At the end

---

6. In September 2000 the Colombian Mennonite Church put out a call to American churches asking them to redirect their taxes to "life-producing projects" because of the enormous suffering US military aid was causing in Colombia. See Esquivia and Stucky, "A Call from the Colombian Churches"; MCUSA, "Resolution on Colombia." Members of the April 2000 delegation included Jose Luis Azurdia (a Guatemalan Mennonite), Kryss Chupp (Chicago), Mark Frey (Newton, KS), Kathleen Kern (Webster, NY), Val Liveoak (San Antonio), Paul Neufeld-Weaver (Worthington, MN).

7. Wilson, "Colombian Right's 'Cleaning' Campaign." The team in later years was to encounter similar fascist impositions of "good" behavior in Barrancabermeja and the rural Opón communities. In Barrancabermeja, the coercion was referred to as "social

of 2001, the *Vanguardia Liberal*, the paper for the Department (province) of Santander, reported the murder rate in Barranca as being one per every five hundred citizens. Of the 203 murders committed by known perpetrators (half had unidentified perpetrators), 165 were attributed to the AUC paramilitaries. CPT chose to rent a house in the neighborhood with the highest mortality rate in the city.[8]

THE OPÓN

While the Lenten delegation was doing background research in Barrancabermeja, they were invited by the Programa de Desarrollo y Paz del Magdalena Medio (PDPMM—also known as Programa) to take a trip to the Ciénaga del Opón region. One to two hours south of Barranca by motor canoe, the area had seen some especially harsh paramilitary activity—largely due to the oil pipeline that runs through it. This violence had displaced many of the farming families along the Opón River to Barrancabermeja. The visit resulted in an invitation from local NGOs and the displaced farm families to set up an accompaniment project. For the next three years, accompanying the Opón communities would become the primary focus of CPT's Colombia Team.[9]

---

cleansing." In the Opón communities, a paramilitary commander justified the presence of his unit by saying they were going to force the community to have a work day to clean up the small school building and clear out plants clogging waterways. The team wrote in a 2003 release, "After the team explained that these orders would be a violation of the human rights of civilians and that the team intended to document it as such, the paramilitaries instead facilitated a community meeting the following morning regarding new rules about community life." CPTnet, "Colombia: Awakened at gunpoint," Aug 4, 2003.

8. CPTnet, "Colombia Update: December 17–25, 2001," Jan 12, 2002.

9. During the first month of the project in 2001, at the request of the Mennonite organization Justapaz, CPT participated in a campaign on behalf of indigenous leader Kimy Pernía Domico. Pernía had led the struggle of his people, the Embera Katio, against the Urrá Dam in the Department of Cordoba. The dam had flooded the homeland of the Embera Katio and ruined their fisheries. Because Pernía and the Embera Katio were impeding the functioning of the dam, AUC paramilitary leader Carlos Castaño threatened him. Several days later, Pernía was kidnapped by men on motorcycles.

For three days in June 2001 CPTers accompanied thousands of Embera Katio and other indigenous peoples in the town of Tierra Alta, where a shaman said the kidnappers had taken Pernía. The assembled people knocked on doors of residents and asked peasants, ranchers and passersby if they had seen Pernía. His body was never found. CPTnet, "Colombia: Call for Prayer," June 22, 2001; CPTnet, Horst, "Colombia: Outcome of Embera Katio march," June 30, 2001.

In 2006, paramilitary leader Salvatore Mancuso testified that army-backed paramilitaries has killed Pernía Domico as part of a controversial paramilitary demobilization

The CPTers who set up the first full-time project in Barranca established a routine that involved splitting the team. One part remained in Barranca and networked with human rights groups there and the other part traveled to the Opón communities of La Florida and Los Ñeques. These visits reassured frightened community members who had stayed in the Opón and facilitated the return of the villagers who had sought refuge in Barranca.

In their first trip out to the Opón, Scott Kerr and Benjamin Horst stopped to talk to three families who had been hiding near the banks of the Ciénaga del Opón ("Ciénaga" is usually translated as "swamp" or "marsh," but the body of water looks more like a shallow lake).[10] They had fled Barranca after losing family members to paramilitary killings. Because guerrillas had mined the area in which they were hiding, paramilitaries avoided it, but one of the young women had had half of her leg blown off by a landmine as a result. The families desperately wanted to get out of the swamp area and back to Barrancabermeja, where they could get a bus to a safer region, but feared passing through paramilitary checkpoints where they might be abducted and killed as guerrilla sympathizers.

Kerr and Pierre Shantz came back the next day and spent the night with the family, listening to machine gunfire in the distance. Shantz wrote about the accompaniment,

> We boarded the boat and off we went, I was sitting beside "Jorge" (not real name) a ten-year-old child who on the outside seemed

---

process that reduced legal penalties against paramilitaries in exchange for their testimony. Amnesty International Canada wrote regarding the testimonies,

> Amnesty International is concerned that this process—which is supported by Canada—may allow those responsible for crimes against humanity to escape justice and retain positions of power in Colombia. . . .
>
> Indeed, Amnesty International continues to receive disturbing reports of new paramilitary threats against Indigenous leaders and communities throughout Colombia. (AI Canada, "Colombia: Justice for the people")

See also Kairos, "Kimy Pernía Domicó was assassinated."

10. In an e-mail to his supporters on June 7, 2001, Pierre Shantz wrote:

> Once we got to one of the communities someone took us to a smaller river that led to what is called a swamp but it was a huge lake with clear water as hot [as] any bath I have ever taken. The vegetation was amazing and the wildlife is straight out of a National Geographic magazine. The whole trip down all I kept saying to myself was "And I call this work?"

happy and secure but on the inside, he was scared for his life. The reason they had fled the city was that two close relatives of the six had been killed and they had received a lot of threats. . . . For most of the trip, I joked around with "Jorge" and all seemed fine. Then as we [approached] the city a boat that is used for public transportation up and down the river came towards us. "Jorge" started crying and screaming "why why."

Looking back to where his mother was he [asked] her, "Why do they want to kill us?" As I looked around the boat all the women were petrified and in tears. I have never seen fear like that in someone's face as I did in the men's on the boat . . ."

We got to the rendezvous point and with luck, the others were there and waiting with taxi. . . . We came to a military checkpoint as we were leaving the city but passed through after they checked our bags and frisked us for weapons. As we arrived to the bus station where we could catch a bus back to Barranca the man who had been our main contact hugged me and said, "You saved our lives today. If you had not been there, they would have killed us, those men on those boats. And if you had not come with us here they would have killed us before we left the city." As I hugged "Jorge," I told him "God is watching over you and you will be safe where you go next. . . ." We are still awaiting a phone call from them when they get to their new places to say that all is well.[11]

The team was to agree to many more such accompaniments in the next months.[12] As the summer of 2001 turned into fall, paramilitary killings became more gruesome and hit closer to home. In August, three boat drivers were killed for bringing food and medicines to outlying communities along the rivers that flowed into Barranca. Matt Schaaf and Shantz, on a trip out to the Opón, learned that two people from the Opón communities had received "the call." Paramilitaries issued these calls for people to present themselves and explain their activities. People who responded to the call—believing that once the paramilitaries understood they had no connections to guerrilla groups they would be safe—often ended up dead.[13]

The team's first encounter with finding a body in the river happened that October. Shantz wrote about the incident in a letter to his supporters:

11. CPTnet, "Colombia: CPTers accompany," June 7, 2001.
12. See, for example, ibid.; CPTnet, "Colombia Update: June 7–16, 2001."
13. CPTnet, Shantz, "Barrancabermeja: The Call," Aug 12, 2001.

Well, last week was particularly hard for me because we (Jon [Horst] and I) found pieces of a body floating down the river. The first part we found was half of a man's torso with half his arm. Further down river we were told that there was another piece and we found the pelvis: no legs and cut off at the belly button. This is typical of paramilitary killing. . . .

We called the Colombian navy to come and get the body parts and they sent someone out but they did not come with every thing to collect them. So the parts were secured to the shore and we were asked to return the next day to show them where we had found them.

The next day when the authorities finally arrived (we waited 4 hours for them), one of the agents asked me to put on some gloves and give them a hand. Well, after watching the agent attempt to put the body part into the bag with a canoe paddle, I simply grabbed it out of frustration and threw it in the bag. We then went to get the second piece. . . .

People whom the paramilitaries declare as collaborators are killed and often find themselves floating down river in pieces like the ones we found.[14]

About two weeks later, friends from the displaced Opón communities came to the team's house in Barranca and told them that paramilitaries had kidnapped José Benito Jiménez in the port. "When they told us who he was," wrote Pierre Shantz, "We realized that he was "Thumbs up guy."

As part of our work, we travel up and down the river a lot and as we pass by people's homes, they wave at us and we wave back. But at one house in particular three brothers stand at the shore and enthusiastically extend their arms out with their thumbs up. We all hold our arms up until we finally disappear around the bend. We actually turned it [into] a competition to see who can wave as many limbs in the air at once (arms and legs). We in the team joked around that one-day we would come around the bend and see José and his brothers on their backs with arms and legs up in the air.

This morning, I was woken by a telephone call from the police to say that they had found someone that fit the description of José. They asked if we could or someone we knew could identify the body. . . . It was him. They said he had been found behind the municipal slaughterhouse (the current paramilitary killing grounds).

14. CPTnet, Shantz, "Columbia: Pieces of a body," Oct 18, 2001.

They say that the paramilitaries accused José's father of being a collaborator of the guerrilla and decided to kill his son to teach him a lesson.

Going past his home will no longer be the same. His two younger brothers will still be there to salute us and wave their arms and legs at us but José's smiling face will be missing. This morning my teammate Jonathan said "Next time when I go by there I will hold my thumb up and silently say a prayer." I said, "We should give him the 21 Thumb salute."

On the afternoon of October 29, Shantz and Erin Kindy took José Benito Jiménez's body up the river to his family. The Red Cross normally would have taken the body, but the volunteers told the team that doing so would have made them paramilitary targets. Since the US Congress was about to vote on military aid to Colombia, the Colombia team's release about Jiménez encouraged CPT's US constituency to contact their legislators within the next two days, asking them to make aid to Colombia dependent on an end to human rights abuses by the Colombian military and paramilitaries.[15]

In November 2001, paramilitaries waved William Payne, Matt Schaaf, and their boat driver over to the riverbank. Payne gave the men CPT literature and told them that CPT did not believe in weapons and was not connected to any armed group. The paramilitaries searched the canoe to verify these claims. "Apparently growing tired of their message of nonviolence," as Schaaf wrote in a release about the encounter, the men told the CPTers and their driver they could continue upriver. After dropping their driver in a safe place, Payne and Schaaf turned back to continue the discussion with the paramilitaries.

Before they could reach the armed men, however, a woman frantically waved them to shore. Her fifteen-year-old son had been working with three other young men to fix the electrical lines at the community school. Community members had heard four shots in the area where the young men were working just before the CPTers came into view.

Payne and Schaaf continued to the paramilitary checkpoint; all the men were gone. Locals told them that the young men had been return-

---

15. CPTnet, "Colombia: 21 Thumb Salute," Oct 29, 2001. The team later found out that Benito's family did have some connection with the guerrillas. In an August 12, 2006 e-mail Erin Kindy noted, "this in no way excuses José's assassination, but it may help to explain one kind of reasoning behind it."

ing to their homes in a canoe when the armed men appeared upriver in two motor canoes. Three leaped overboard and scrambled into the jungle. The fourth parked the canoe and ran to join them as the paramilitaries opened fire.

In the dark, Schaaf, Payne and community members guided their boat along the shore calling their names. Later they found out the young men had made their way home through brush and several river tributaries in the dark.

After the incident, the community members asked CPT to make an announcement saying the fishers and farmers along the Opón did not want armed groups in their lives and that fleeing meant only they were afraid, not that they were a member of an armed group.

Accordingly, CPT distributed an open letter over the next few days in the Barrancabermeja area, focusing especially on Barrio Arenal, known for its paramilitary presence, where they held a prayer service:

> November 29, 2001
> Open Letter
> To the leadership of the United Self-Defense Forces of Colombia
> [AUC is the Spanish acronym]
> Municipality of Barrancabermeja and surroundings
>
> ... By invitation of the villages of La Colorada, La Florida and Los Ñeques, all in the township of Ciénaga del Opón, CPT maintains an international and ongoing presence of human rights observation in the area.
>
> CPT is not connected to any armed group. The work of CPT includes calling on armed actors to transform their actions with regards to the civil population. Sometimes CPT publicly denounces cases of human rights violations committed by members of armed groups. To date CPT has denounced violations committed against civilians by members of the Colombian Navy, of the ELN and of the AUC.
>
> CPT uses the services of motorists who have been named by the community to provide transportation to CPT members. The leaders of the community have assured that the named motorists are not involved with any armed group and CPT has verified this with its own consultations. CPT is certain that our motorists have NO connections with any armed group. ...
>
> On November 24 at 5 p.m., two members of CPT arrived at a checkpoint of presumed members of the AUC. There was a group

of approximately 16 people, many of them armed, situated at the mouth of the Rasquia channel....

CPT subsequently learned from members of the community that a short time earlier shots had been heard in the mouth of the Colorada River and that there were four people missing including a minor. CPT returned to speak with the presumed members of the AUC but they had already left. A search was initiated for the missing persons. At this point CPT contacted the Colombian Armed Forces to help in the search for these missing and possibly seriously wounded people....

CPT asks the leadership of the AUC to explain to its members that neither CPT nor its motorists have any connection to any guerrilla group or any other armed group. Also, CPT asks that the leadership of the AUC require its members to leave the villages of the township of Ciénaga del Opón, including la Colorada, la Florida, loss Ñeques and the other villages, in peace. Finally, please explain that when country people flee it is not an indication that they have any connection to an armed group. It only means that they are afraid of guns.

Thank-you for your attention. In the unending love of God,
Erin Kindy William Payne Matthew Schaaf
Jacobus Vroon
Christian Peacemaker Teams (CPT)[16]

The team made several attempts to engage paramilitaries in the first year of the project. They brokered a soccer game between Puente Opón, firmly under the control of paramilitaries, and Los Ñeques, whom paramilitaries accused of supporting guerrillas, which helped residents of both communities realize that most of the inhabitants of both villages belonged to no armed groups.[17]

During a trip out to the Opón on "the line," a motorized canoe used for public transportation, paramilitaries searched Payne, Kerr, and the rest of the boat's occupants. CPTers returned to the same paramilitary checkpoint the next day for a prayer service, in which they invited the paramilitaries to participate. The time of dialogue and prayer effectively allowed

16. See CPTnet releases: "Colombia: Paramilitaries create fear," Nov 30, 2001; "Colombia: CPT's letter to AUC paramilitaries," Nov 30, 2006; "Colombia Update: November 18–December 2, 2001," Dec 15, 2001.

17. CPTnet, Kerr, "Colombia: Building peace," Oct 11, 2001; Payne, e-mail, Aug 16, 2006. Providing accompaniment for the occasional soccer game would continue to be part of CPT's work over the years. See below and CPTnet, "Colombia: Sacred Soccer," Oct 20, 2003.

civilian traffic to pass unhindered while they were there. On Christmas Eve 2001, as the team traveled out to the Opón to celebrate the holidays, they engaged the paramilitaries in dialogue at the fork between the Opón and Colorada rivers. Payne passed out maple syrup to the paramilitaries, offering to exchange syrup for guns. Christmas Day, when the team returned from the Opón, the checkpoint was gone.[18] Future conversations that Payne and Chris Schweitzer were to have with paramilitaries resulted in one AUC commander, called "Antonio" in CPTnet releases of 2003, laying down arms and leaving the group. Several men under his command left with him.[19]

Contacts with Military

Throughout the course of the project, the team also had contacts with the Colombian military—sometimes in official meetings and other times in surprise encounters in the Opón. The contacts were important for several reasons. As the only "legal" armed groups in Colombia, the military had official channels through which team members could report abuses. Additionally, the U.S. "War on Drugs" meant that huge amounts of tax revenue—some from the pockets of the CPT constituency—were going to the coffers of the Colombian military.[20] The US was also training Colombian officers at the notorious "School of the Americas," where over the decades some of the worst human rights offenders in the Western Hemisphere had matriculated. Perhaps the most pressing reason, however, that the team sought out encounters with the military had to do with its relationship to paramilitary groups. The military officially claimed that it had no contacts with paramilitary organizations and were, in fact, as committed to fighting them as they were to fighting guerrillas. However, the conventional wisdom of the people among whom CPT worked was

18. CPTnet, "Colombia: CPTers hear gunfire," Dec 26, 2001; CPTnet, "Colombia Update: December 17–25, 2006," Jan 12, 2006.

19. CPTnet, "Colombia: Letter from Duane Ediger," April 15, 2003; CPTnet, Holmes, "Colombia: Seeing the Face of Jesus," May 13, 2003. See the Chiapas chapter for other instances of Payne converting soldiers. When asked about this knack Payne seemed to have for influencing armed men, he responded in an October 16, 2006 e-mail: "Not sure if there really is enough data to say there is a pattern, but I do ask people directly to do what I think they should do . . ."

20. For a reflection on the connection between drug use in Colombia and the US, see CPTnet, Kingsley, "Colombia: On Drugs and Disillusionment," Dec 4, 2003.

that the military was in collusion with the AUC.[21] In a November 2001 letter to his supporters, Kerr noted that a paramilitary checkpoint was stationed fifteen minutes outside Barrancabermeja along the river in full view of a Colombian Navy checkpoint. "The links between paramilitary forces are not debated in this city, the lines are very clear," he wrote.[22] The team noted in releases over the years incidents that seemed to suggest that Colombian military and paramilitary groups might have been in communication with each other, but frustratingly, when they wrote about these encounters, the incidents hardly seemed like smoking guns.[23]

On July 4, 2001, Benjamin Horst and Kerr met with a military official who advised them to leave the Opón region because of an upcoming military operation in the area. On July 7, the team put out an urgent prayer request regarding the anti-insurgency operation the Colombian Army and Navy had begun two days earlier. It noted the team had held a press conference to denounce military operations that might endanger the lives of civilians. Four team members then went to the Opón. They encountered a five-hundred-soldier battalion and five heavily armed Navy speedboats. Kerr reported that the patrols he talked to were treating the civilian population with respect. "Please pray that the armed forces will respect their constitutional obligation to respect the lives of the civilian population," the release concluded. "Also pray for good communication skills, safety and calm nerves for members of the team as they face press conferences, a steady stream of news releases, communication with Army and Navy officials and an unsure situation during the operation."[24]

The next month, another military operation occurred without warning, while Robert Epp and Scott Kerr were in the Opón. About four hundred soldiers were in the area to look for a handful of guerrillas local people had spotted. Some of them wore yellow armbands that had identified paramilitary members. Kerr wrote a letter to his supporters about the event:

21. The Colombian military has also slaughtered civilians. In the team's Barrancabermeja neighborhood, a massacre had occurred nine years earlier, which local human rights organizations believed the Colombian Navy had committed. CPTnet, "Colombia Update: June 7–16, 2001," July 14, 2001.

22. CPTnet, Kerr, "Colombia: The SOA and the War on Terrorism," Dec 22, 2001.

23. See, for example, CPTnet, "Colombia: Navy and paramilitaries," Feb 2, 2002.

24. CPTnet, "Colombia: Urgent Prayer request," July 7, 2001; CPTnet, Colombia Update: June 7–16, 2001," July 14, 2001.

I believe that the soldiers were just as surprised to see a gringo in the middle of the jungle as I was to see 400 Colombian army personnel walking around our little farm. We passed the evening talking about the war and the prospects for a resolution. For the most part, they were very respectful of the people there, but some joked about massacres and tactics of this dirty war. The next morning at 8am all that remained of their presence was the Ready to Eat meal packages that lay strewn on the ground.

A few days later, I encountered a smaller platoon of this group at another farm down river. Again, they brought with them a careful balance between respect and intimidation, taking fruits of the trees without asking, and using water without helping to bring more up. This may not sound like a lot, but it adds to the hardships of the campesinos there. A handful of soldiers scribbled in the initials of the AUC prominently into a box that was set in the middle of the patio area....

Later that same night around 1 am while sleeping in a tent, I awoke to a light in the tent. When I went outside to investigate, two heavily armed guerrillas were at the farm looking for transportation out of the swamp. Separated by only a few hours the two groups continued to dance around each other. For the civilian population that lives out there, the tornado comes when any of these armed groups bump into each other.[25]

The team surprised the military again in early October 2001. Docking at the school in La Florida, Erin Kindy, Matt Schaaf, and William Payne saw three heavily armed Colombian Navy speedboats. Several soldiers were removing items from a nearby house. The residents said the soldiers had been friendly initially and then became more belligerent. They seized one fifteen-year-old boy, put him in a military uniform, forced him to take a gun and then used him as a human shield as they put him in front of a line of soldiers searching for guerrillas in the underbrush.

When the CPTers arrived, Navy personnel were accusing the men of being guerrillas, although one man showed them his hands and said, "You can see by the calluses on my hands that I am a fisherman." They were just about to whip one man to get information out of him when the CPTers showed up.

The soldiers then returned the items they had taken and left. The La Florida residents said the situation would have gotten much uglier if the

25. CPTnet, "Colombia: Soldier Occupation," Aug 7, 2001; CPTnet, Colombia: Letter from Scott Kerr," Aug 15, 2001.

CPTers had not showed up and asked them to spend the night just in case the Navy came back.[26]

Over the following years, the team would note official visits with Colombian Army and Navy personnel, and cite them by name when they denounced violence by all armed groups—which may have been partially responsible for the team's visa crisis in 2002 and 2003.

Contacts with Guerrillas

The brief encounter with guerrillas that Kerr mentioned in his August letter was one of only two recorded in 2001 releases.[27] The team, however, had more contacts with guerrillas when they accompanied people to and from the Cimitarra Valley (see below). Shantz and Jonathan Horst were returning from a trip during which they had accompanied a group of people to their Cimitarra village of Yanaquay, when they and their driver encountered two guerrilla checkpoints. At the first, the guerrillas just asked for vocal identification. At the second, they commanded the CPTers to come up the bank. Thinking they were at a paramilitary checkpoint, Shantz said that they had had recent contact with the Colombian Navy. After a brief conversation, the driver and guard began to laugh quietly, and it was then that the soldier in charge identified himself as FARC. The driver later explained that since he had been driving so fast, and since the FARC had heard them stop near a paramilitary checkpoint, (where their canoe had become stuck on a sandbar) the guerrillas assumed the driver was affiliated with paramilitaries.[28]

Often the accidental contacts the team members were to have with guerrillas were cordial. In two encounters recorded in team releases, the

26. CPTnet, Kindy, "Colombia: Interrupted Navy Operation," Nov 4, 2001.

27. In an August 22, 2006 e-mail, Pierre Shantz estimated that the team had five to ten encounters with guerrillas in 2001. Benjamin Horst, in an August 17, 2006 e-mail, said that at least twice in the Opón guerrillas passed the team's tents at night while team members slept, noting, "We would never have had a clue that they were there if locals hadn't told us about it the next morning." Erin Kindy, in an October 18, 2006 email, wrote:

> Probably the team ran into guerrillas a whole lot more than they noticed. That was during a time when the Opón was mostly controlled by the guerrilla, and even though they team probably didn't notice it, I'm quite confident the guerrillas appeared often, dressed in civilian clothes, and because the team didn't know all the residents of the rivers as well they didn't know who they were seeing.

28. CPTnet, Horst, "Colombia: Nighttime Encounters," July 24, 2001.

men put down their guns and joined the CPTers in prayer. The cordiality of these contacts, however, did not mitigate the threat their presence posed to the community.[29]

Other encounters with the guerrillas were more businesslike. In 2002, the team confronted the FARC commander in Valle Cimitarra (Cimitarra Valley) about putting civilians at risk during shootouts with paramilitaries in the Opón and documented other instances of FARC-initiated attacks that put civilians at risk.[30] They also denounced guerrillas along with paramilitaries and the Colombian military when they made public statements against the violence. (Noting, in a March 11, 2002, release, "CPT considers the lives of all—civilians, Army, FARC and paramilitaries—as sacred.") However, since the violence committed by paramilitaries was exponentially greater and more brutal, and the Colombian military represented an "official" channel through which CPTers could lodge their complaints about violence and human rights abuses, their relationship with guerrilla movements was usually minimal.

2002

Paramilitary violence in the Barrancabermeja and Opón area continued to increase in 2002. Because of paramilitary attacks in the Opón, already-displaced residents delayed their return and others became newly displaced.[31] CPTers had to turn down requests for accompaniment in various regions because of the heightened threat level. CPTers would also face consequences for their public witnesses denouncing the Colombian government's human rights record.

---

29. See CPTnet releases: Kingsley, "Colombia Reflection: Two fleeting moments," Oct 29, 2003; Buyers, "Colombia: Accompaniment with a funny nose," Nov 20, 2003; "Colombia Update: November 1–15, 2003"; "Colombia Update: November 15 to December 1, 2003," Dec 8, 2003.

30. See CPTnet releases: "Colombia Update: January 13–February 14, 2002," Mar 8, 2002; "Colombia: CPT statement regarding FARC," Mar 11, 2002; "Colombia: Spring and Martens," July 27, 2002; "Colombia Update: July 16–July 21, 2002," Aug 3, 2002. Carol Foltz Spring noted in a September 13, 2006 email that one July 2002 meeting with a FARC commander "was long and chatty and covered many subjects. [The FARC commander] drank several beers (fetched by young female FARC members) and philosophized extensively."

31. CPTnet releases: Holmes, "Colombia: A Dirty Stinking War," Mar 15, 2002; Kerr, "Colombia: Barranca update," Aug 20, 2002; "Colombia: Sheep in the midst," Nov 25, 2002.

Their first public statement of the New Year occurred after guerrillas and paramilitaries exchanged fire at the juncture of the Opón and Colorada rivers:

> The civilian population is tired of the war. They have made it clear to us that they do not want an armed presence of any nature in their communities. . . .
>
> We denounce the presence and shooting of firearms in the Ciénaga del Opón Township. We denounce any possible retaliation. We denounce the subjection of the civil population to checkpoints maintained by illegal groups. We denounce the lists of marked people maintained by illegal armed groups. We denounce the actions of any individual or group that puts the civilian population in danger or brings fear and uncertainty to the lives of the women, children and men who reside in this township.
>
> We lament the way things are. We lament the economic reality of the world where so many have so few choices. . . .
>
> To the members of armed groups, we plead with you to search for non-violent methods to resolve conflicts. We ask you to consider that the way of violence has been very costly for your families, your country, and in fact for the whole world. Consider all the pain and suffering that the violent "solutions" have brought to people you know. We invite you to consider a better way. As Protestants and Catholics, we try to follow the teachings of Jesus Christ—Love of enemy and forgiveness—and ask you to consider how these might have a place in your lives. You are, each and every one of you, children of God. God dwells within you and calls you to a life of love and respect for the dignity of all people.
>
> In conclusion, we beg the members of all armed groups, please leave the civilian population of the Ciénaga del Opón Township in peace. They are not responsible for your confrontations.
>
> Christian Peacemaker Teams[32]

Among paramilitary murders the team wrote about in their releases,[33] none affected the team more than the death of their neighbor, Nelcy

---

32. CPTnet, "Barrancabermeja: Leave," Jan 20, 2002; CPTnet "Colombia Update: January 13[–]February 14, 2002," Mar 8, 2002.

33. See, for example, CPTnet, "Colombia Urgent Action: Release Manuel," Feb 8, 2001; CPTnet, "Colombia: Manuel Francisco Navarro," Mar 13, 2001. In a February 2002 letter to his supporters, Pierre Shantz wrote, "One of the community leaders was kidnapped on Saturday and has not been found so we are very worried. His name is Manuel and we ask your prayers for him. I am doing ok but the last few days have been crazy running around trying to find him. It's pretty exhausting." CPTnet, Shantz, "Colombia: The soccer

Gabriela Cuesta Cordoba. A teacher and the president of the community action committee in the Valle Cimitarra village of Puerto Matilde, Nelcy was kidnapped at one of the paramilitary checkpoints blockading the valley on April 4, 2002, as she attempted to bring supplies to the village. Carol Spring and Sara Reschly traveled to the Valle Cimitarra village of El Tigre on April 6, and spoke to paramilitaries there, who insisted they had done nothing to her; they had just prevented her from entering the town. On April 7, the team received a call from a Colombian partner organization asking them to accompany one of Nelcy's family members to identify a body that someone had seen floating down a river. Carol Spring, Keith Young, and Scott Kerr accompanied "Manny" in their motor canoe to the place where people had reported seeing the body.

Young wrote about the incident,

> We scanned the riverbank, under overhanging limbs casting shadows. We asked people along the shore if they had seen her body and they would point further downstream, "She was working her way down at 9:30 this morning," they would say. Then we saw the vultures. We located the body, but it wasn't Nelcy.
>
> It was a young man with a bullet wound in his chest. A man and a boy arrived at the same time in their canoe. They seemed to have known the person in the water that once was alive, and so we continued down-river.
>
> Then, a man standing on the riverbank waved us to the shore. He knew where the body matching our description was. He got in the canoe and guided us to a small village. In the village, women were crying, and men were fretting. They believed the body they had pulled out of the river was a family member from Puerta Matilde, and they had just brought the mother in from another village to identify her, which was difficult. It would have been hard to identify even a family member in the condition the corpse was in. A call was made to Puerta Matilde using Kerr's cell phone, and to their relief, the woman was located and alive. Manny then looked at the body and identified it as Nelcy. He wept.[34]

---

game," Feb 6, 2002. Responding to a question from the author, Shantz wrote in an August 22, 2006 e-mail, "He is still disappeared." See also CPTnet, Martens, "Colombia: Letter to Gordo," June 24, 2002.

34. CPTnet, "Colombia: They found her body," Apr 10, 2002; CPTnet, "Colombia Update: April 1–15, 2002." Apr 26, 2002.

Throughout the spring and summer of 2002, paramilitary violence increased in Barrancabermeja as well as the Opón. In a letter to his supporters, Scott Kerr wrote,

> The Paras have brought in a new moral code that makes my stomach turn, with rules like hours of play time for kids, what color of garbage cans you can use, hours to illuminate your house, regulations on traveling in and out of certain areas, just to name a few. It seems like every week more mutilated bodies are pulled from the river with signs of torture. In the latest most brazen act, the Paramilitary have put on their death lists some girls between the ages of 12 and 16 that have been "unfaithful" to there paramilitary "boyfriends." Some girls have already been killed...
>
> Many Human rights leaders have been forced to leave, or live under continual threat. I have seen a lot of evidence that links the paramilitary and the state armed forces, but what may concern me more at this point, is what happens when the paramilitary no longer answer to the military as they have in the past.[35]

The team became involved in the struggle between trade unionists working in Coca Cola bottling plants in Barrancabermeja and the paramilitaries whom bottling plant managers allegedly hired to threaten and assassinate them.[36] They also began accompanying civilians threatened by paramilitaries in the Cimitarra Valley.[37]

A paramilitary blockade of that valley reached crisis proportions in spring and summer of 2002, so the team began regularly accompanying people needing medical treatment and human rights workers in and out of the valley. Because of the guerrilla presence in the region,[38] paramilitaries had established checkpoints on roads and rivers leading into the valley in order to prevent the guerrillas from obtaining food and supplies. Paramilitaries forced civilians to buy groceries at specific stores and pay a paramilitary "tax." Taxes on farming and construction supplies were

35. CPTnet, Kerr, "Colombia: Paramilitary oppression," July 29, 2002.

36. See CPTnet releases: "Colombia: Unionist attacked," Aug 30, 2003; "Colombia Update: August 2003," Sept 12, 2003; "Colombia: Delegation supports Colombian worker boycott," Aug 6, 2004; "Colombia Update: July 2006," Aug 11, 2006.

37. Horst, e-mail, Aug 17, 2006.

38. In one update, team members reported seeing AUC paramilitaries, FARC and ELN guerrillas and Colombian army and navy representatives on a single trip from the Cimitarra valley to Barrancabermeja. See also CPTnet, "Colombia: Letter," Feb 18, 2002; CPTnet, "Colombia Update: April 16–30, 2002," May 16, 2002.

much higher. Partly because cement is used in cocaine production, taxes on it sometimes came to 90 percent the cost of the cement.[39]

The team put out an Urgent Action in August 2002 noting that civilians in the valley were fleeing their homes for fear of becoming caught in the crossfire of a military operation. Fresh paramilitary graffiti on civilian homes where the army had been six hours earlier was also a possible cause of the panic. They quoted a farmer who told them he offered drinks to paramilitaries, guerrillas, and army and navy soldiers who passed his home. But, he added, since he lived in a guerrilla-controlled zone, he was falsely accused of being a guerrilla.[40]

Later in the month, paramilitaries invaded the Valle Cimitarra village of San Francisco. When Charles Spring and Scott Kerr arrived, the destruction was in progress. Cars, motorcycles, and fields were all burning. About half the village had left. As Spring and Kerr spoke to an AUC paramilitary, guerrillas began firing on the town. Kerr wrote of the event,

> Unfortunately, the man we were talking to had a very large assault rifle, so our place of cover was not ideal, but we hit the deck. After a few minutes the firing ended and we again began to walking around the village reassuring the people and inviting the AUC to leave the town, lay down their guns, and respect the civilian population.
>
> Later that day we traveled to [Puerto] Matilde where we connected with some partners, and strategized about our presence a bit. In the afternoon we went back with trepidation knowing that if the AUC was still in the area around the houses at night, the FARC and ELN guerrillas would most likely fire on the town with rifles and cylinders (home-made bombs). When we got back to San Francisco many of the AUC had left....
>
> That night we slept in a community area with many other families who remained.... During the night, the Colombian army/air force began flying overhead and shooting at some areas from the air....

39. CPTnet, Martens, "Colombia: Cement Saga," Aug 24, 2002. See also CPTnet, "Colombia Update: June 22–30 2002," July 9, 2002; CPTnet, "Colombia Update: July 16–21, 2002," Aug 3, 2002.

40. CPTnet, "Colombia Urgent Action: Ask Colombian military," Aug 7, 2002; CPTnet, "CPTnet Correction: Censored words," Aug 9, 2002. Erin Kindy wrote, in an October 18, 2006 e-mail, "the offering of drinks to armed groups is often coerced, or it can be just human to human hospitality in the super hot climate, but this is often painted as collaboration."

> The next day the plane came back again and fired repeatedly.
> . . . A few times the firing was very close to houses in the area. If
> this is not terrorism, I don't know what is. On Tuesday, the army
> arrived to occupy the town. In four days, this town has had large
> numbers of three different types of armed groups in their small
> village. Yikes![41]

The 2002 releases record that the team continued seeking creative ways in which they could humanize and reach out to paramilitaries, sometimes one-on-one and sometimes through public witness. Often the reaching out included asking paramilitaries to join the team in prayer.[42]

William Payne wrote up conversations with a young paramilitary who told him that his parents and brother had been killed in front of him. After several encounters, Payne brought a photo of a friend, Pablo, who was a member of the Abejas in Chiapas (see chapter 7). His wife and mother had died in the Acteal massacre in 1997. Payne had asked Pablo how he could forgive the paramilitaries who had killed his family. Pablo said, "As members of the Bees we have decided to forgive the perpetrators of that horrible crime. It is something I decide to do every day." At the conclusion of his piece, Payne wrote,

> I think of this young man who has seen so much violence. I re-
> member his loss of his parents. I also remember the people I know
> here who have lost children, siblings and parents to the group that
> Lucas has joined. God in your mercy free this young man from the
> horror he as lived.[43]

The team balanced these cautiously friendly and empathetic conversations with more strident challenges to paramilitary violence and the tacit consent to it by the Colombian and U.S. governments. Some of these witnesses were ad hoc. After hearing that the American ambassador to Colombia was in Barrancabermeja, the team washed an American flag—to protest the "dirty war" against civilians the U.S. was funding—outside a

41. CPTnet, Kerr, "Colombia: If this is not terrorism," Sept 16, 2002.

42. CPTnet, Shantz, "Colombia: The soccer game," Feb 26, 2002. For other examples of the team trying to humanize paramilitaries, see CPTnet releases: "Colombia Update: December 28–January 12, 2002," Jan 28, 2002; Martens, "Colombia: The grandmothers are watching," Jan 8, 2002; Martens, "Colombia: Letter to Gordo," June 24, 2002.

43. CPTnet releases: "Barrancabermeja:"Would you forgive?" Jan 21, 2002; "Colombia Update: August–October 2002," Nov 14, 2002, Foltz Spring, "Colombia: Bringing peace," Nov 5, 2002; Young, "Colombia: Sheep in the Midst," Nov 25, 2002.

new community center, called "the coexistence center," she was visiting.[44] When they learned that paramilitaries were assassinating homosexuals, street people, and prostitutes in "social cleansing" operations, William Payne, Scott Kerr, and Lisa Martens wore t-shirts proclaiming in Spanish, "I am homosexual" in around Barrancabermeja.[45]

The team planned other public actions more carefully. For Lent that year, the team chose to do a series of public witnesses that would denounce the "death lists" put out by armed groups. Although the release about the Lenten witnesses noted that the Colombian military and guerrilla groups also had death lists designating individuals as targets for assassination, paramilitary death lists were of most concern to the team and their local coworkers. CPTers had witnessed paramilitaries consulting one of these lists as they stopped people at checkpoints. As part of the Mardi Gras celebration, the team hung festive banners from community members expressing desires for peace. (Banners with messages promoting peace and human rights were to be a significant form of public witness for the team throughout the duration of the Colombia project.) In its Ash Wednesday service, the team used ashes from homes that paramilitaries had recently burned. For the rest of the Lent season, team members set up a camp in a space usually occupied by an armed group, such as paramilitary checkpoints, declared it a weapons-free zone, and conducted a weekly worship that concluded with participants burning a symbolic death list.

At 6:00 a.m. on Easter morning, CPTers and others in the encampment raised two seven-meter banners with "life lists" on them. The names on the list included "Civilians working their land, waiting for a better future; those who have been assassinated in battle; women threatened because of their commitment to life; guerrillas, paramilitaries, soldiers; displaced people; union members; disappeared people; and community leaders organizing for justice."[46]

44. CPTnet, Foltz Spring, "Colombia: CPTers confront," May 9, 2002; CPTnet, "Colombia Update: May 1–15, 2002," May 24 2002.

45. Payne, e-mail, Aug 22, 2006; Kerr, e-mail, Aug 25, 2006. Kerr reported meeting a Navy commander in a Barrancabermeja disco, who saw his T-shirt and "got a big kick out of it." CPTnet, "Colombia Update: May 1–15, 2002," May 24, 2002. The update did not mention the team response to the "social cleansing." Erin Kindy, in an August 22, 2006 e-mail, noted that paramilitary targeting of gays was still an active problem in Barrancabermeja.

46. See CPTnet releases: "Chicago: CPT Colombia and Hebron," Feb 12, 2002; Fitz, "Colombia: God's Kingdom Rising," Feb 22, 2002; Reschly, "Colombia: Planting New

382 IN HARM'S WAY

Several other highly confrontational nonviolent public witnesses over the next months[47] increased CPT's credibility with local peace and human rights organizations. However, they also had negative consequences. Through a Colombian coworker, they learned that paramilitaries planned to kill an unspecified member of the team in retaliation for denouncing human rights abuses, even though they denounced violence committed by all armed groups, including guerrillas.[48] In a release about the event, the team called on its constituents to write U.S., Canadian, and Colombian governmental representatives asking that nonviolent measures be taken to make life safer for the civilian population in the Opón and Cimitarra, and what the Canadian and U.S. Embassies are doing to protect nationals and internationals in the Barrancabermeja area. The release noted that newly elected President Alvaro Uribe had declared a state of emergency following violence that killed on hundred Colombians and displaced many more after his inauguration. "The inauguration of a new President has initiated a very deliberate moment of testing," the release read. "People living out the gospel in Colombia deserve the best that their sisters and brothers around the world have to offer."

The team also adapted, once again, the Hebron team's 1995 "Statement of conviction" (see chapter 4) beginning the statement with:

> We would like our wishes, as stated below, to be respected in the event that members of Christian Peacemaker Teams (CPT) in Colombia are harmed or killed by any of the armed groups currently targeting civilians. Whatever happens in the coming days or months, we believe life will ultimately claim victory over death, and what we are sowing in tears we will one day reap with songs of joy (Psalm 126).

Life," Mar 5, 2002; "Colombia Easter Action: 'Life Lists'," Mar 16, 2002; Holmes, "Colombia: Death and Resurrection," Apr 3, 2002; Colombia Update: March 1–15, 2002," Apr 18, 2002; Colombia Update: March 16–31, 2002," Apr 22, 2002. See also CPT Colombia, "Up from the Ashes."

47. See, for example, CPTnet, "Colombia: 'Paso de Esperanza,'" July 13, 2006. In an October 26, 2002 action release the team asked their constituency to write letters expressing their hope that the recipients would live free from the fear of weapons and violence. CPTnet, "Colombia: 'Child of God' letters." See also, CPTnet, "Colombia Update: November 2002," Dec 6, 2002. In their respective e-mails sent August 25, 2002, Pierre Shantz estimated that the team received 100–200 letters to pass out to armed groups, while Carol Foltz Spring estimated the number at approximately 100 or less.

48. The threat was reported to the team by the local government human rights ombudsman, the Defensor del Pueblo. Spring, e-mail, Aug 23, 2006.

Since the intended effect of the threat was to prevent CPT from continuing to denounce paramilitary abuses, the team, five days later distributed the following statement in Spanish to local media and organizations:

> The violent actions of armed groups have caused immense suffering to civilians in the Opón River region in recent weeks. We, members of Christian Peacemaker Teams (CPT) who maintain an international presence in the area, call on all armed groups to take courageous action by doing as Jesus instructed—to love their enemies. We call on all armed groups to stop killing their enemies and to leave the civilian population in peace.
>
> CPT denounces the actions of the FARC guerrillas (Revolutionary Armed Forces of Colombia) that occupied civilian homes without the owners' permission in the last days of July, disrespecting the rights of noncombatants in a zone of international accompaniment.
>
> CPT denounces the actions of the paramilitary group AUC (United Self-Defence Units of Colombia) who burned two civilian homes and attempted to burn a third on Wednesday, July 31.
>
> By means of this document, we, the members of CPT in Barrancabermeja, Colombia, express our profound concern for the civilian population of the Opón River region due to armed clashes between guerrillas and paramilitaries in this region on Wednesday, July 31 and Friday, August 2. We denounce the FARC and the AUC for bringing the armed conflict into civilian communities.
>
> We daily witness the tireless and nonviolent work for peace done by unarmed Colombian men, women and children. We call on the Colombian Army and Navy, the AUC, the FARC and the National Liberation Army (ELN—a guerrilla group also present in the zone CPT accompanies) to take a lesson from the courageous unarmed civilians with whom they share this country: To love each other and to be givers of life rather than death.[49]

Visa Crisis

The death threats in the end did not much interfere with the work of the team.[50] They were not nearly as draining on team morale as the crisis that

---

49. CPTnet releases: "Colombia: CPT learns of alleged paramilitary plan," Aug 12, 2002; "Colombia: Statement of Conviction," Aug 13, 2002; "Colombia: CPT calls on all armed actors," Aug 17, 2002.

50. Carol Foltz Spring wrote, in an August 25, 2006 e-mail:
"I think the threats had an impact only temporarily, probably making us a little more

began developing in spring 2002 when authorities at the Bogotá airport denied CPT reservist Murray Lumley entry into Colombia. The public denunciations that the team had done of the Colombian military and public witnesses—designed, after all, to capture the government's attention—had begun to backfire. The Colombian authorities would not grant CPTers another visa until September 2003.[51]

Later in the summer, after the team had twice published calls for all armed actors to leave civilian populations in peace and publicized the death threats against them, the government moved from refusing to grant visas to deporting CPTers already in the country. Scott Kerr and Duane Ediger were the first to receive the summons on 23 August when DAS (Department of Administrative Security) officers came to the team's house in Barrancabermeja. They took everyone's passports and visas, copying down the information, and then told Kerr and Ediger to come to their office the next day. After a brief interview, they received deportation orders. The authorities said that they had violated the terms of their tourist visa because their accompaniment of civilians constituted work. Chris Schweitzer and Ben Horst were called in two days later with similar results. After Kerr and Ediger (who were scheduled to leave the country anyway) and Colombian Mennonites met with various officials in Bogotá, the Colombian authorities gave a verbal assurance that the orders were revoked on September 6, 2002, and written assurance of the revocation on October 2.[52] However in September 2002, President Alvaro Uribe also signed "Decree Number 2002 of 2002" that stated the government

cautious for a few weeks or so." William Payne, in an email sent the same day, wrote

> My recollection is that the death threats didn't change my thinking at all regarding the work, etc.
>   Perhaps a rumour wasn't enough to do anything to me. In fact, I remember when I learned about the death plan (I was in the campo with Scott, deep in territory under control of guerrilla but which was subject to many para attacks), when we learned one evening that there was such a plan. We learned during our evening check-in with the team in the city. I went to bed shortly afterwards and slept well (I remember thinking later that was an interesting reaction).

51. Lumley had been active with the Canada Colombia Solidarity Campaign, which involved sending many letters to the Colombian government, so the authorities did have his name and address on record before he entered the country. However, Colombian Mennonites believed strongly the denial of entry was related to the work of the Colombia team.

52. In an August 30, 2006 e-mail, Duane Ediger wrote:

could control the movement of foreigners in areas where it has imposed martial law. An October Urgent Action noted that "The team's experiences at U.S. and Canadian consulates suggests that consular officials are reviewing meticulously CPTers' visa applications." It also noted that since May 2002, CPTers had been unable to get Religious Worker NGO visas. "Meanwhile," the Urgent Action noted, "the activity of illegal armed groups in the area CPT accompanies has increased; team members' endurance is being stretched and investigative/immigration officials have

---

The resolution revoking the deportation order is very interestingly written. It includes a lot of "legañol" (term I just invented for Spanish legalese), for which reason I feel unable to give a good translation into English legalese. Nevertheless, I would like to try my hand at a few phrases for you, starting with some of the "whereases":

Whereas in exercise of their rights under article 91 of decree 2107 of 2001, they traveled to Barrancabermeja to visit their colleagues who with legally authorized visas carry out their religious mission of humanitarian aid.

Whereas understanding that there are many forms of taking rest and recreation they did such activities accompanying their colleagues in visits to needy families in conflictive areas where they offer their services.

Whereas [these] religious human beings, sensitive to the human pain and violent conditions of life in these areas, upon return from these visits and being interviewed by the media about what they had seen, told the truth, for this reason, it is not an infraction for a tourist who has seen and heard these things to repeat them in an interview.

Whereas it is evident that the only sin they have committed is to accompany colleagues in their visit to areas of armed conflict and to tell the media a truth of which we are all aware.

Whereas [they] consider themselves as not having committed any infraction, for which reason [they] request revocations of the resolutions under which DUANE PETER EDIGER and STEVEN SCOTT KERR were deported.

THEREFORE BE IT RESOLVED:

... [that] this office reconsiders its initial position, taking into account that according to the what came out of the interrogation, it was not their intention to infringe on migratory dispositions, even though the accompaniment activity carried out should be supported by a visa, but upon considering that they referred to such activity as rest and recreation, in spite of the region and the public order situation that reigns in that place, for which reason it is incumbent upon the subjects and authorities that in future occasions in which they desire to enter Colombia to carry out religious or accompaniment activities, they seek and obtain the respective visa from any consulate of the Republic of Colombia, thus avoiding [future] incidents of this kind.

requested reports from the team's local partners about the activities of CPT and other NGOs.[53]

Five days after the team issued the Urgent Action, Colombian co-workers from the Valle Cimitarra called the team, asking them to accompany a woman and her recently deceased husband to the town of Yondó. Most of the team was in the Opón with a CPT delegation. Horst and Martens agreed to talk to the widow. When they met her, she was so distraught that they misunderstood her reply when they asked how her husband died and agreed to accompany her.

At one of the checkpoints, Martens told the officers that the man whose body they were accompanying had died of natural causes, at which point the widow whispered to Martens, "Bullet." After delivering the body, the widow reported to the National Police and the inspector in Yondó. The team later learned that it is illegal to move a body before the police have investigated a murder—a fact that the authorities were to cite as a reason for deporting team members or denying them visas.[54]

When Horst and Martens returned to Barrancabermeja, government officials told them they needed to go to the immigration office immediately. They were held there from 10:00 p.m. to 5:00 p.m. the next day. On October 12, Martens spoke at a press conference outside the Barrancabermeja City Hall. She described what happened and asserted that CPT was in the Magdalena Medio region by invitation of the civilian population. She further stated that as followers of Christ CPTers believed in compassion for widows and orphans and that they rejected "the claim made by mutually opposing groups around the world that the use of weapons is compatible with and facilitates such tasks." At the close of her statement, she said, "During the night and day of detention, Ben and I sang, prayed, and recalled the great cloud of witnesses that surround us (Hebrews 12:1) naming heroes of faith and peace throughout the centuries and from every corner of the word." It is our intention to follow all the administrative processes necessary to maintain our pres-

---

53. CPTnet releases: "Colombia: CPTers Ordered Deported," Aug 26, 2002; "Colombia: Deportation Update," Aug 30, 2002; "Colombia: Government broadens clampdown," Oct 3, 2002. See also Mencoldes, "Follow Up to Recommendations," 7.

54. However, the police often refused to come to the area where the deceased had been shot. Furthermore, the widow had moved the body, not the team, and she had taken it straight to a government morgue upon arrival in Yondó. Rose, e-mail, Sept 1, 2006.

ence here in Colombia and to continue our accompaniment of civilians in the region."[55]

Prior to the press conference, local media alleged that the deceased had had connections with the FARC, which handed the Colombian government another weapon it could use against the team in the matter of visas. The team put out another Urgent Action the end of November 2002, urging its constituency to write the Colombian Minister of Foreign Relations and their congressional and parliamentary representatives asking them to see that Scott Kerr, Erin Kindy, Jessica Philips, Matthew Schaaf, Stewart Vriesinga, Lisa Martens, and William Payne got visas.[56]

In the meantime, Keith Young, Carol Foltz Spring, and Charles Bunch Spring were the only CPTers remaining with valid religious worker visas. Recognizing their limitations, they, at the suggestion of Duane Ediger, the project support person at the time, proposed that CPT close the project in Colombia; their Colombian coworkers told them bluntly if they left, people would die. The three thus ended up staying on assignment long past the amount of time it would have been psychologically healthy to do so. Several updates mentioned the team having to turn down requests from local coworkers for accompaniment and that the team stopped visiting the Cimitarra Valley. Additionally, the team moved from doing its own denunciations to doing them through other groups, particularly through the government's Human Rights Ombudsman.[57]

The three-person team began looking for creative ways of making their presence known. They had had a flag made in the fall of 2001 that bore the logo ECAP (Equipos Cristianos de Acción por la Paz) that flapped in the breeze as their motor canoe went up and down the river. Intended

55. CPTnet, "Colombia: CPT workers detained," Oct 10, 2002; CPTnet, "Colombia: CPT Statement on detention," Oct 12, 2002; Foltz Spring, e-mail, Aug 31, 2006. The CPT delegation came in from the Opón while Horst and Martens were detained and were planning to do an action at the DAS office, but the two were released before the time the delegation planned to do the action.

56. CPTnet, "Colombia Urgent Action: Protest expulsion," Nov 28, 2006. Schaaf, Phillips, and Martens became the "core" of the Grassy Narrows team while they waited for their visas. See chapter 9.

57. Albrecht, e-mail, June 7, 2006; J. Klassen, e-mails, June 9 and Sept 4, 2006. Erin Kindy, in a September 6, 2006 e-mail, wrote that the shift "included signing on to a few, as well as publicizing others into our network. I think we still occasionally did our own denouncements, we just realized that over using that tool made it less useful for us." See also CPTnet, "Colombia Update: June 22–30, 2002," July 9, 2002.

as a response to flags flown by the armed groups to assert control over regions, the flag helped assert that "Peace" was in control of the Opón.[58] Now with the ranks of the team so decimated, the flag assumed a crucial importance as the team took the motor canoe up and down the river as a way of marking the "peace" territory. At one point, the diminished team even considered dressing up a mannequin in a red hat and blue t-shirt to be the second CPTer in the boat.[59]

The team also delineated the territory by hanging banners along the river and footpaths traveled by armed groups with Scripture verses and slogans such as "Peace without weapons. Peace without fear."[60]

Colombia Team members who could not get back into Colombia formed a "Team in Exile" (TIE) whose members strategized ways they could get back into the country. "We have to make it more difficult for the Colombian government to have us here working to cut off their U.S. government life-line than if we were advocating for human rights within Colombia," Scott Kerr was quoted as saying in a release about CPT participation in the annual November School of the Americas protest. Kerr, Erin Kindy, and Chris Schweitzer spent time in December meeting with congressional representatives and even did a few small public actions in DC. They also visited the Colombian consulate and U.S. Senators offices in Chicago.[61] Perhaps their most significant accomplishment was getting twenty-one members of the US Congress to sign a "Dear Colleague" letter, dated April 2, 2003, to Colombian President Alvaro Uribe that read, in part,

58. Originally, the flag was red with white writing. When Colombians told them those colors too closely resembled ELN colors, they changed it to white with red writing. Kerr, e-mail, Aug 7, 2006; Erin Kindy, e-mail, Aug 12, 2006. Pierre Shantz remembered Colombians telling them that red was the color of war. E-mail, Sept 6, 2006.

59. Carol Foltz Spring, Charles Bunch Spring, and Keith Young mentioned this idea to Kathleen Kern when she visited them in Barrancabermeja during in December 2002. CPTers first began wearing blue T-shirts in Chiapas, and this unofficial uniform—blue shirt with red hat—emigrated to Colombia when the Chiapas project closed. Most of the human rights organizations in Barrancabermeja had some sort of uniform. Kindy, E., e-mail, Sept 4, 2006.

60. CPTnet, Bunch Spring, "Colombia: Peace Begins Here," Nov 30, 2006. This information also reflects conversations Kathleen Kern had with Charles Bunch Spring, Carol Foltz Spring, and Keith Young while in Colombia during December 2002.

61. CPTnet, "Fort Benning, GA: Presente!" Nov 26, 2002; Erin Kindy, e-mail, Sept 4, 2006. See also "North American complicity in Colombia's violence," under the "Issues" section at the end of this chapter.

We are concerned about the pattern of increasing harassment and attacks on Colombian church workers. Faith based organizations, especially in war torn regions, provide necessary comfort to victims in the crossfire. CPT's ministry has allowed 100 displaced civilian families to return to their houses.

While we understand the Government of Colombia has the right to control its immigration policies, we are concerned about the inability of peace seeking religious workers to access their brothers and sisters in Colombia.

Your assistance in expediting visas to members of the Christian Peacemaker Teams would be appreciated.[62]

2003

The visa crisis was to continue until September 2003, when the Colombian government approved the visas of Elizabeth Garcia, Erin Kindy, Jim Fitz, Stewart Vriesinga, and Pierre Shantz. These approvals were the fruit of many months of meetings with Colombian government officials, advice from lawyers working for local NGOs, intercessions by the Colombian Mennonite Church, the PDPMM, and the above Congressional letter signed by twenty members of the U.S. House of Representatives urging President Uribe to expedite visas for CPTers.[63]

In the mean time, the team mostly continued to restrict its efforts to the Barrancabermeja and Opón region. To augment their numbers, three Colombians with Mennonite affiliations began working on the team.

62. CPT Colombia, Dear Colleague letter. Signatories included Lane Evans, Dennis Kucinich, Jan Schakowsky, Chris Smith, James Walsh, Sam Farr, Barney Frank, James McGovern, Edward Markey, David Wu, Frank Wolf, Todd Tiahrt, Tammy Baldwin, Barbara Lee, William Lipinski, Luis Gutierrez, Raul Grualva, Lloyd Doggett, Bernie Sanders, Anna Eshoo, and Charlie Norwood. See also CPTnet, "Colombia Action Alert Update: More visas denied," Mar 13, 2003; CPTnet, "Colombia: Progress on Visas," May 8, 2003. Because Christmas in the Opón had often been a time when people were vulnerable to attack, CPT sent a delegation during Christmas 2002 to support the three exhausted and depressed team members. Foltz Spring, e-mail, Aug 31, 2006; CPTnet, "Colombia: Colombian Mennonites," Dec 17, 2002; CPTnet, "Colombia: A Christmas Odyssey," Dec 25, 2002."

63. See CPTnet releases, "Colombia Action Alert: Support Congressional Letter," Mar 1, 2006; "Colombia Action Alert Update: More visas denied," Mar 13, 2006; "Colombia Update: March 2003," April 18, 2003; "Colombia: Progress on visas," May 8, 2003; "Colombia Update: April 2003," May 30, 2003; "Colombia Update: May 2003," June 17, 2003; "Colombia Bound: CPTer gets Visa," June 5, 2003; "Colombia Update: June 16–30," July 19, 2003; "Colombia: Visa victories," Oct 4, 2003; "Colombia Update: October 1–31," Nov 12, 2003.

Sandra Rincón, Adaía Bernal, and Julián Carréo participated in a 2002 Christmas Choir delegation to Barrancabermeja to provide support for the team and subsequently interned on the Colombia team. Rincón and Bernal would go through training in 2003. These Colombian CPTers, and the Colombian CPTers who followed them, were to change not only the work and character of the Colombia team but also the work of CPT as a whole. (See Incorporation of Colombians into team under the Issues section at the end of this chapter.)

Paramilitary violence continued to claim the most casualties in 2003, but the team releases reported more of it happening in Barrancabermeja than in the Opón. In February, the AUC-BCB (the AUC unit that controlled Barrancabermeja) released an e-mail saying that that it planned to cease hostilities and that the assertion it had targeted NGOs including CPT was "perverse, opportunistic and demagogical."[64] But killings attributed to the AUC continued in the city and human rights activists several times asked the team for accompaniment.[65] After paramilitaries killed the husband of an OFP (Popular Women's Organization) member, one of its members told the team. "It used to be we could call [the authorities] to accountability and they would at least try to portray the image of protecting human rights workers. Now they don't even do that."[66]

In September, after nine people had disappeared in the space of one month—including the husband of an other OFP activist—the team accompanied a demonstration of about three hundred people who gathered in a soccer field to call for the return of their loved ones. "They took them alive and we want them back alive," the crowd chanted. Local human rights groups had met with the Army and police in the city a few days earlier and demanded investigations into the disappearances. Dissatisfied with the authorities's response, the three hundred residents organized the demonstration and then went on a "busqueda," or search party, through

64. CPTnet, "Colombia: E-mailing the Paramilitary," Mar 11, 2003.

65. The team also reported that paramilitaries had been forcing people to pay "protection" fees—equivalent to an hour's wage every week— to keep their houses from being robbed. CPTnet, "Colombia: Letter from Duane Ediger," Apr 15, 2003; CPTnet, Young, "Methods of a Mafia," Apr 29, 2003.

66. CPTnet, "Colombia: Letter from Duane Ediger," Apr 15, 2003; CPTnet, "Colombia Update: April 2003," May 30, 2003.

neighborhoods in the northeastern part of the city demanding the return of the missing people.[67]

An October CPT delegation built on this witness by holding a demonstration at the paramilitary-controlled port in Barrancabermeja, calling out the names of those who had disappeared in the previous three months in Barrancabermeja. "Where is David?" "Who is responsible?" they proclaimed. Local community leaders accompanied the delegation in the neighborhoods around the port afterwards, handing out flowers and cards containing prayers for the disappeared.[68]

Two of the team's December 2003 releases mention reading about assassinations in every morning's paper, e.g., "Broad daylight, near downtown, a young woman between 23 and 25 years old, light brown skin, 168 cm tall, long black hair wearing light blue shorts, a white blouse and sandals." Reflecting on the killings both in Barrancabermeja and the Opón (see below), Barb Howe wrote, "If T. W. Eliot had lived in Barrancabermeja, Colombia he might have said that December, not April, is the cruelest month."[69]

Team releases about trips to the Opón in the late winter of 2003 record a heightened presence of guerrillas, Colombian military, and paramilitaries in the region, all of whom increased the threat to civilians. Ostensibly, the battalion known as Plan Especial Energetico y Vial No. 7 said they were in the region to get to know it and the inhabitants better. However, as one of the releases dryly noted, "Despite their stated objective, to get to know the region, the military had only minimal conversation with the farmers living there." Indeed, the only long conversations the soldiers seemed to be having were with men the CPTers recognized as paramilitaries.[70]

For most of 2003, the team's focus in the Opón continued to be monitoring paramilitaries.[71]

67. CPTnet, "Colombia: More disappearances," Sept 8, 2003; CPTnet, "Colombia Update: September 2003," Oct 7, 2003.

68. CPTnet releases: "Colombia: Breaking the Law of Silence," Oct 13, 2006; "Colombia: Where is our sister?" Oct 23, 2003; Colombia Update: October 1–31, 2003," Nov 12, 2003.

69. CPTnet, Erin Kindy, "Colombia Reflection: Worth more than sparrows," Dec 14, 2003; CPTnet, Howe (unattributed), "Colombia Reflection: The cruelest month," Dec 31, 2003.

70. CPTnet, "Colombia: Whom can the civilians trust?" Feb 13, 2003; CPTnet, "Colombia Update: January–February 2003," Mar 3, 2003.

71. They also discovered that paramilitaries had been monitoring them. In February a

After the three men, allegedly guerrillas, shot the president of the Ciénaga community in January, instances of lethal violence seemed to diminish in the Opón, although guerrillas, army, and paramilitaries continued to maintain a presence there.[72] The situation in June 2003 was stable enough that the remaining displaced people who had sought shelter in Barrancabermeja's Normal school decided to return to the Opón. Given that CPT's original decision to set up a project in the area related to the accompaniment of civilians from the Normal school back to the Opón, the closing of the shelter seemed to close a chapter in the history of the Colombia team. However, the displaced community insisted that the Colombian government allow international accompaniers, meaning CPT, to go with them as a condition of their return.[73]

Several violent incidents shattered the calm in the Opón at the end of 2003. After finding a body in the river near Los Ñeques on December 13, the team alerted authorities in the city. National and international human rights groups and the Defensoria, accompanied by CPT, went out to retrieve the body. Three days later, Opón community members reported the assassination of a laborer on a local farm as well as hearing an explo-

paramilitary had a long discussion with Sandra Rincón, saying that he had been observing her at several locations in the CPT accompaniment zone and that they were working with fishermen as a way of "supervising" the area. He told her that AUC respected the work of CPT and did not intend to harm the team. CPTnet, "Colombia Update: January–February 2003," Mar 3, 2003. Rincón said that at the time she did not know whether he had singled her out because she was Colombian and a native Spanish speaker or because he was attracted to her. The thought crossed her mind later that his comments may have been a threat. E-mail, Oct 11, 2006.

72. CPTnet, "Colombia Update: January–February 2003," Mar 3, 2003. The man was taken to the hospital and survived. In an October 14, 2006 e-mail, Sandra Rincón said he returned to Ciénaga, but stopped working as a community activist. An update also reported that two men from the Ciénaga community were "disappeared." CPTnet, "Colombia Update: July 1–15, 2003," July 22, 2003.

73. CPTnet, "Colombia: Normal Shelter closes doors," June 11, 2003. About the reasons for the shelter's closing, Pierre Shantz wrote in an October 12, 2006 e-mail:

> The conditions were so bad that people got tired of being there. The Gov. had fulfilled some of its agreements and so some people felt they could leave. Also the Gov. was closing it and it was almost a forceful removal of those who remained there. A National delegation met with the last leader to leave the day before they closed it for good. He said that a lot of people had allowed themselves to be bought by the gov. for a few handouts and so decided to leave. He wished that people had resisted longer and maybe they would have gotten more in the end.

sion near Los Ñeques. A tugboat had blown up after guerrillas allegedly attacked it. The four occupants died. The authorities checked the area and claimed they found no evidence they could use to prosecute. CPTers, checking the same area, saw bloodstains and evidence that bodies had been dragged to the river and dumped in it. On December 18, two bodies floated to the surface.

In a reflection about the killings, Barb Howe wrote,

The man in the river that day was only the first. By the end of the month, there were six people dead and one disappeared. Two lived in the communities we accompany on the Opón river. The others just died there. I got used to scanning the river for chulos (vultures) and corpses.

The first man lacked a face. The chulos had eaten it. We thought, at first, that he was a community member who had disappeared not long before. His family came out to try to identify him but were unable to recognize him. It's awful what floating in water for several days does to a human body.

Later tests in the city proved the corpse was not him. A teammate told me they never found out who he was and have buried him in the public cemetery.

I want to visit his grave. I want to tell him I'm sorry for what happened to him, for the way he died . I have read that human beings, like other animals, have a mechanism that kicks in during trauma and shuts down the part of your brain that registers pain. I hope that happened to him in the moments before he died.

I want him to know that I didn't think the smell was too terrible. I want to tell him that the way his body floated on the current was graceful and gentle and that I wasn't horrified or repulsed by him.

"Fear not, for I have redeemed you;
I have summoned you by name; you are mine.
When you pass through the waters I will be with you;
And when you pass through the rivers,
They will not sweep over you." Isaiah 43: 1–2

We lit seven candles for the six dead and one disappeared man on the day we found the last body. I made name cards for the lost men and on the one for the man without a face I wrote, "hombre desconocido." Unknown man.

...Someone loved him. And right now, someone is missing him. And even when his body is bloated and waterlogged, when his skin is gray or just gone and his bones shattered, I see the Christ stepping into the water with him, wrapping his arms around what's left of his broken body and saying "This one is mine." He is claimed, his name etched on the palms of God's hands.[74]

2004

Between 2004 and 2006, the Colombia team put out noticeably fewer releases. Already in 2003, the team had started writing monthly and bimonthly updates as opposed to weekly or biweekly. While the dearth of material had something to do with the aptitude and inclinations of people serving on the team and the difficulties of translating Spanish releases to English and vice versa, in reality the threat of lethal violence in Barrancabermeja and the Opón diminished. The team put out more releases reflecting efforts at community building in the Opón and, as the Haiti and Chiapas teams had done before them, taken a more serious look at economic violence.[75]

The threat of lethal violence had not disappeared, of course. A February 23, 2004, prayer alert noted that team members had seen guerrillas and the Colombian military traveling near each other in the Opón and asked that constituents pray that the movement of armed groups would not lead to violent confrontation. In April, such a confrontation occurred when armed men, presumably guerrillas, shot three Colombian Army soldiers who were in civilian dress as they boated down the Opón River near Los Ñeques. Many residents of Los Ñeques—described by Carol Rose and Duane Ediger in a release about the incident as "farmers, fishers, children, great-grandparents, chefs, singers, sharers of mangos, smiles and practical jokes"—fled to Barrancabermeja. In subsequent days, the area was flooded with Colombian soldiers. The team increased its presence in the area praying with soldiers, handing out fliers, and explaining that by hanging their hammocks and cooking in the homesteads of civilians, they were violating the Geneva conventions.[76]

74. CPTnet, "Colombia Reflection: Upon the palms of my hands," Jan 10, 2003.

75. The team also put out an Urgent Action early in 2004 when Ricardo Esquívia, one of the team's primary Colombian Mennonite advisors, came under threat. The Colombian government accused him of being a member of a guerrilla group to justify imprisoning him. CPTnet, "Colombia Urgent Action: Colombian government threatens," Jan 16, 2004.

76. CPTnet, "Colombia: Prayer Alert," Feb 23, 2004; CPTnet, "Colombia: Fears and prayers," May 11, 2004.

Paramilitary attacks also continued to claim victims.[77] During a June trip to the Opón, an eight-year-old girl ran toward team members screaming, "They're going to kill my Daddy!" They followed her back to her house and found AUC-BCB members threatening to execute the girl's father in front of his family. A guerrilla the paramilitaries had captured earlier said the man had collaborated with FARC. The paramilitaries left ten minutes after the team arrived, and the CPTers stayed with the family and prayed with them. The family told them that if they had not come, the paramilitaries would have killed the father. Later, the FARC and AUC members crossed paths and a shootout occurred. The people of Los Ñeques then asked the team to circulate a letter they had written, signed by forty-four residents, including eight minors, to local human rights organizations:

> Because of the events that occurred recently in our region, we, the civilian population, denounce the violence perpetrated against us and call upon human rights organizations and the responsible government authorities to come to our community and address our concerns. We are tired of threats, pressure, verbal abuse, and in some cases losses and deaths of people from our community. As we assert our insistence on respect for our status as civilians, we need your support, which will give us more strength to continue with our process. Right now, we are accompanied by God and the CPT team.[78]

The assassination of Ancizar Giraldo, a farmer with four young children, also had a huge emotional impact on the Los Ñeques community. The team put out two requests for prayers in subsequent weeks. The communities of La Florida and Los Ñeques also put out a letter decrying the assassination, describing Giraldo as "a man convinced of the value of life, liberty and dignity which caused him to be part of the process of the Humanitarian Space of the Ciénaga del Opón." After referring to other forced displacements, armed confrontations, disappearances, and assassinations inflicted since May 2001, the community wrote,

> Despite this fear, and strengthened by life, we have made the decision to not displace since we do not see it as an option of life

77. See, for example, CPTnet, Erin Kindy, "Colombia: Son of the community," May 14, 2004; CPTnet, Pritchard, "Colombia: CPT delegation witnesses aftermath," May 29, 2004.

78. CPTnet, Albrecht and Rincón, "Colombia: They're going to kill my Daddy," June 19, 2004; CPTnet, "Colombia: Letter from community," June 28, 2004.

such as we have been working toward through the Humanitarian Space. In light of the absence of the Colombian state, today more than ever we call upon the illegal armed actors to respect us, as organized civilians, because the only thing we want is to be rooted to our land in peace.[79]

The Opón communities' letter reflected a process of solidarity that the communities had intentionally begun developing in 2003 after visits by Colombian church, human rights and economic development organizations (most significantly the PDPMM). Called the "Process for Life, Dignity and Liberty," the program was designed to help residents ensure their own security by presenting a united front toward all the armed groups. "But armed groups should not be the only ones to hear the community say loudly, 'We are Colombians. You must respect us,'" said German Plata of PDPMM at a May 15 meeting of the community. The Process also involved helping people assert to the Colombian government their rights as tax-payers for education, health care, and land titles. Additionally, the process involved the communities undertaking economic development projects, such as planting African palms and improving cocoa cultivation.[80]

2005–2006

The Process for Life, Liberty, and Dignity was to continue throughout 2005 and 2006. Although acts and threats of violence continued to occur during this period,[81] the feelings of solidarity generated by the Process helped to keep most Opón residents from displacing.

79. CPTnet releases: "Colombia Prayer Alert: Assassination," Sept 11, 2004; "Colombia Action Alert: Send prayer," Sept 27, 2004; "Colombia: Letter from communities," Sept 27, 2004.

80. See CPTnet releases: "Colombia: Expanding Solidarity," July 9, 2003; "Colombia Update: January 2004," Feb 7, 2004; "Colombia: Spiritual Accompaniment," Feb 18, 2004; "Colombia Update: February 2004," Mar 19, 2004; "Colombia Update: March 2004," Apr 23, 2004; "Colombia Update: April 2004," May 15, 2004; "Colombia: 'Sing a new song,'" May 27, 2004; "Colombia Update: May 2004," June 29 2004; "Colombia Update: June 2004," July 7, 2004; "Colombia Update: July 2004," Aug 30, 2004; "Colombia Update: August–September, 2004," Oct 13, 2004; "Colombia Update: December 2004," Jan 12, 2005; "Colombia Update: July 26," Aug 11, 2006.

81. Erin Kindy noted in May 20 and September 15, 2005 releases that she had become so used to deaths that she skimmed over headlines about murders and massacres in the newspaper. "Colombia: Commonplace"; "Colombia Reflection: What do you get used to?" For other incidents of violence documented by the team during this period, see CPTnet releases: "Colombia Update: January 2005," Feb 12, 2005; "Colombia Update: February

Much of the team's focus at this time revolved around the Colombian government's Law of Peace, Justice, and Reparation, which encouraged the demobilization of paramilitaries.[82] On the surface, the law seemed a positive step toward ending Colombia's civil war. However, since paramilitaries could hand in their weapons without confessing any of their crimes, Opón residents did not express much enthusiasm for the demobilization. They remembered that during the time that Colombian President Alvaro Uribe was governor of the Department of Antioquia, paramilitary strength there increased dramatically.[83] Instead, at an Organization of American States (OAS) gathering in the Opón, community members expressed concerns that paramilitaries who had committed atrocities would not suffer any consequences for their actions, and that the government would move demobilized paramilitaries unwelcome in other parts of the country into their community. Further, since illegal armed groups, and not the government, had controlled the region for years, they wondered how effective the government would be at overseeing the region now. A community leader thanked the OAS for its efforts, but told those present that local people would have to work out their own security and that might involve entering into direct dialogue with the armed groups. He then asked the OAS to support the communities' efforts in the same way it was supporting the government's efforts. One of CPT's partner groups, the Popular Woman's organization (OFP) held a demonstration a month later at Barrancabermeja's DAS office to protest the impunity they thought the

2005," Mar 17, 2005; "Colombia: Wars and Rumors of Wars," Apr 1, 2005; Colombia: Paramilitary and guerrilla presence," Apr 25, 2005; "Colombia Update: April 2005," May 17 2005; "Colombia Update: May 2005," June 23, 2005; "Colombia Update: June 2005," July 18, 2005; Hughes, "Colombia Reflection: Dog days," Aug 17 2005; Hughes "Colombia Reflection: I prayed today," Aug 22, 2005; Erin Kindy, "Colombia: Voices from the Opón," Sept 13, 2005; "Colombia Update: November 2005–January 2006," Feb 8, 2006; "Colombia Update: February–March 2006," Apr 19, 2006; Collerd, "Colombia Reflection: 'Stupid fireworks,'" May 4, 2006; Rincón, "Colombia Reflection: The Flame of Life," June 29, 2006."

82. The government offered a similar amnesty to those involved with Colombian guerrilla movements. However, people who left the guerrillas found the government qualified this amnesty, withholding promised aid and protection until ex-guerrillas gave them information. See CPTnet, Stokes-Prindle, "Colombia: CPT Delegation meets," June 1, 2004.

83. In 2007, Uribe's government became embroiled in a scandal when the press revealed the connections of top military officials and right-wing congress people with paramilitary death squads. Forero, "Paramilitary Scandal." See also CPTnet, "Colombia: CPT joins call," May 2, 2007.

law promoted. They banged together rocks and held up photos of Opón community members who had been murdered or displaced since 2001.[84]

Throughout 2006, the team continued to hear reports of hypothetically demobilized paramilitaries operating in the Magdalena Medio region. Some took on work as security guards, which meant they were still armed and thus still a threat. Another group called "The Black Hand" appeared in Barrancabermeja as a "social cleansing" group, targeting street youth as well as social and human rights organizations.

A trip to the very small town of Pueblito Mejia in the Department of Bolivar gave the team its starkest encounter with the failure of the demobilization process. CPTers Suzanna Collerd and Julián Gutiérrez were part of a commission that included representatives of the Support Mission to the Peace Process of OAS and a representative from the Colombian Interior and Justice Ministry. The commission was responding to a call from the community of Pueblito Mejia to see that paramilitary activity was continuing as before. In a May 2006 release, Gutiérrez noted what was happening in the village encapsulated all major facets of typical paramilitary activity:

- Killing of civilians

  The community said there were hundreds of bodies buried in the environs of assassinated peasant leaders and paramilitaries who had left their units for reasons of conscience. The government mortuary and the Attorney General chose not to investigate these mass graves.

  Just twelve days earlier, a group of two active paramilitaries and three ostensibly demobilized paramilitaries kidnapped four young men who they said had stolen a barrel of chemicals needed to produce cocaine. "They planned to kill all of them if they were guilty and only one of them if they were innocent as a 'lesson' to the community," Gutiérrez wrote. Colombian soldiers had allowed the paramilitaries to take the men out of town and Colombian police allowed paramilitaries to pass a checkpoint without asking why the armed men were following a jeep holding the four detainees. Only

---

84. CPTnet releases: "Colombia: Little enthusiasm," Sept 9, 2005; "Colombia: Central Bolivar," Sept 16, 2005; Rincón, "Colombia: For Our Dead," Oct 30 2005.

organized resistance from the community stopped the paramilitaries from killing the young men.

- Territorial control

  Paramilitaries had also stolen the principle mine in the area and sold it to a company that employs demobilized paramilitaries. The Colombian government had taken six thousand hectares from the community and given it to a corporation to grow African Palm. The peasants thus had to choose whether to leave or cooperate with pro-paramilitary institutions that controlled the resources and work.

- Legitimization

  The government continued to give permission for the Central Bolivar Block of the AUC to carry guns.

Afterward the government and OAS representatives talked about the visit giving them hope. They also referred to the paramilitaries as victims and noted cases in which demobilized paramilitaries had successfully reintegrated into society.

"We asked ourselves if they had been in the same place we had been," wrote Gutiérrez, "Or if they had been in a parallel reality wherein the communities had not denounced the actions of paramilitary groups, the complicity of the State with paramilitaries, their extrajudicial penal system and the stolen mines."[85] Later in the summer, paramilitaries kidnapped and tortured a woman who worked locally with displaced women and pulled guns on people playing volleyball in the team's neighborhood.[86]

Reading through the 2005–2006 releases, one is struck by the institutional networking that had become a major focus of the team. The updates record numerous meetings the team had with peace and human rights groups in the Magdalena Medio region and other parts of the country. In November 2006, the Colombia team joined the Steering Committee of the Latin America Working Group (LAWG).

In 2006, Colombia Team members also began participating in meetings of the of the Americas Policy Group (APG), which included representatives of Amnesty International, the Canadian Labor Congress, United Church of Canada and Kairos, among other organizations. Since

---

85. CPTnet releases: "Colombia Update: April 2006," May 9, 2006; Gutiérrez Castaño, "Colombia: Pueblito Mejia," May 23, 2006; "Colombia Update: May 2006," June 15, 2006.

86. CPTnet, Dillard, "Colombia Reflection: The air here is hot," Nov 14, 2006.

Canadian oil, gas, and mining companies were operating in zones where the paramilitaries and the Colombian army were driving people off their land, a national roundtable of eight Canadian government departments as well as dozens of representatives from civil society organizations and industry met in September 2006 to examine the complicity of Canadian corporations in human rights abuses. Joel Klassen and Bob Holmes, representing CPT, testified at the Toronto and Montreal meetings respectively about abuses occurring in mining communities in the Department of Bolivar.[87]

Also indicative of the team's work becoming more structured were strategy meetings and retreats the team participated in under the facilitation of Colombia Team Support Coordinator, Robin Buyers. In these meetings, they evaluated their work of the current year and made plans for the following year. Following the SWOT (Strengths, Weaknesses, Opportunities, Threats) methodology, the team made conscious decisions in the 2005 evaluation process to reduce the time it was spending in the Opón, and evaluated requests for accompaniment from the Colombian Mennonite Church and the Micoahumado, Montes de Maria, Toribio-Cauca regions. Team members also decided to write more political analysis about the conflict and socioeconomic realities. In the write-up of the 2006 evaluation and planning, the team listed four goals:

- Understand structures of domination and oppression with attention to grassroots initiatives for justice and peace

- Work together on grassroots initiatives for justice and peace

- Make visible grassroots initiatives for justice and peace and the structures of domination and oppression as they relate to Colombia

- Transform structures of domination and oppression as they relate to Colombia

---

87 See CPTnet releases: "Colombia Update: May 2006," June 15, 2006; "Toronto: CPT Colombia Team," Sept 15, 2006; "Montreal, Canada: Government Roundtable," Nov 30, 2006; Buyers, "Cazuca, Colombia/Toronto, Canada: The price of bread," Oct 19, 2006."

PROJECTS OUTSIDE THE BARRANCABERMEJA/ OPÓN REGION

Micoahumado

Of all the areas outside of the Opón region visited by the team, Micoahumado in the southern part of the Bolivar province was the community visited most by the team as part of their work. The residents there had declared themselves independent of all armed groups and told the government that they would be willing to eradicate their coca crop by hand, if the government would stop fumigating their fields and help them find markets for their crops.

In the first year of the CPT's full-time team, Jonathan Horst accompanied a caravan to Micoahumado bringing food, medical supplies, and farm implements to the area, breaking a blockade imposed because the ELN controlled the region. Keith Young and Charles Bunch Spring traveled to the area in December 2002, accompanying Father Francisco de Roux who was negotiating on behalf of the community with paramilitary and guerrilla groups. Community members had signed a pledge of resistance against all armed groups and hung white flags from their windows as a show of solidarity. Team members would continue to visit Micoahumado and the other small mining towns in its environs regularly throughout 2005 and 2006.[88]

Other Communities

In 2004, team members accompanied a caravan with humanitarian aid to the northeastern part of the Department of Antioquia, where a military blockade designed to prevent campesinos from supplying guerrillas was causing a great deal of civilian suffering. They also accompanied organizations to other locations in the Department of Bolivar, such as the community of Alto Cañabraval. By 2005, these visits to other communities

88. See CPTnet releases: Horst, "Colombia: Communities in Resistance #1," Sept 10, 2001; Bunch Spring, "Colombia: Micoahumado Zone," Jan 9, 2003; Bernal, "Colombia: De-mining a road," Jan 31, 2005; "Colombia Update: May 2005," June 23, 2005; Klassen and Rincón, "Colombia Reflection: The town that would not be uprooted," July 15, 2005; "Colombia: Police arrest leaders," Oct 11, 2005; "Colombia Update: November 2005–January 2006," Feb 8, 2006; "Colombia Update: February–March 2006," Apr 19, 2006.

became part of the team's mandate, as recorded in the notes of their 2005 and 2006 evaluation and planning retreats (see above).[89]

Toward the end of 2006, the Colombia team began to pay special attention to the problems of mining communities in the southern part of the department of Bolivar. The communities had settled there relatively recently and mined on a very small scale. Within the space of a year, several families had dug four gold mining shafts with only picks and shovels. In total, about thirty thousand people derived their livelihoods from this small-scale mining. Because the Colombian government wanted to grant authorization for Kedahda—a joint venture of AngloGold Ashanti and Kinross Gold—to begin open-pit mining in the area, paramilitaries began threatening community leaders.

After the Nueva Granada battalion of the Colombian army assassinated community leader Alejandro Uribe on September 19, 2006, the team accompanied 1300 people to Santa Rosa del Sur, the local seat of government, who demanded a meeting with the federal government authorities and without the presence of the military. When the military showed up anyway, the community members refused to meet with the other members of the government. The Colombia team put out an Urgent Action asking the CPT constituency to urge the government to negotiate in good faith with the miners.

On November 5, the participants went home, accompanied by representatives of the Regional Office of the government's Human Rights Ombudsperson, the UN Human Rights Commission, and other civil society organizations, including CPT, after the government came to an accord with the miners. The journey back to the mining communities involved a two-hour ride in flatbed trucks and then several more hours of hiking

89. See CPTnet releases: Horst, "Colombia: Caravan brings hope," Sept 9, 2001; Horst, "Colombia: Communities in Resistance #2," Sept 12, 2001; "Colombia Update: February 2004," March 19, 2004; "Colombia Reflection: "Don't Abandon Us," March 13, 2004; Rincón, "Colombia: A complex conflict," May 19, 2004; Fitz, "Colombia: Documenting Colombia's civil war," Nov 18, 2004; Collerd, "Colombia Reflection: Yes, there are children," Oct 5, 2005; Buyers, "Colombia: Walking the Word," Oct 7, 2005; "Colombia Update: September 2005," Oct 13, 2005; Ediger, "Colombia Reflection: Operation Genesis," March 9, 2006; Gutierrez, "Cacarica, Colombia: The most important match," Apr 26, 2006; "Colombia Update: April 2006," May 9, 2006; Vriesinga, "Colombia: Third Annual Humanitarian Action," May 16, 2006; "Colombia: CPT accompanies human rights lawyers," Aug 15, 2006; "Colombia: CPTers participate," Aug 19, 2006; Brickner, "Colombia: Landmines," Sept 12, 2006; "Colombia: CPTers accompany mining region residents," Sept 29, 2006; "Colombia Urgent Action: Ask Colombian government," Sept 29, 2006.

along mountain trails to the mining villages. As the people began walking, Colombian soldiers surrounded a small group of people in a threatening manner, until hundreds of other people walking the same trail appeared. Other soldiers gave out leaflets to returnees that encouraged guerrillas to turn in their weapons. Many people ripped up the leaflets immediately, infuriated at the insinuation that they were guerrillas. These actions by the Colombian military fueled doubt about whether the government and Colombian military would honor the accord, which included the stipulations that the Colombian military would respect the distinction between civilians and combatants and that the government would respect the miners' Federation as legitimate.[90]

ISSUES ARISING FROM COLOMBIA PROJECT

Climate and Logistics

Most CPT projects have one or more stressors that are not intrinsically related to the work of the team, but impose significant hardships on team members. In Haiti, the stressor was extreme poverty and in the West Bank, it was relationships between genders. In Barrancabermeja and the Opón, the factor was the equatorial climate. Located at sea level in Colombia's interior, the region had neither the altitude nor the proximity to the ocean to relieve the relentless heat and humidity. North Americans and Colombians who lived at higher elevations often had difficulty adjusting to life there. During the wet season, the region could be a little cooler, but the mosquitoes were at their worst. Many CPTers fell victim to diseases such as malaria and dengue fever—so much so that the team joked about providing international accompaniment for the local hospital.[91] As a partial result of the climate's rigors, the Colombia team tended to have young, physically fit workers. Given that the best functioning teams often contain a mixture of ages and genders, homogenous teams of people in their twenties sometimes lacked the perspective of more mature CPTers.

90. See CPTnet releases: Klassen, "Colombia: "The South of Bolivar," June 10, 2006; Gutierrez "Colombia Reflection: The miners' wisdom," July 28, 2006; "Colombia: CPTers accompany mining region residents," Sept 29, 2006; "Colombia Urgent Action: Ask Colombian government," Sept 29, 2006; Braley and Klassen, "Colombia: Miners return home," Nov 9, 2006.

91. Kerr, e-mail, Aug 7, 2006. Pierre Shantz missed meeting Nobel Peace Laureate Rigoberta Menchú because he was hospitalized at the time with cellulitis, which he contracted while in the Opón. CPTnet, "Barrancabermeja: CPT Colombia," July 19, 2001.

Traveling in the area also presented a challenge the team had not experienced before. River transport was the primary method of getting to the areas in the Opón and Barrancabermeja most affected by violence. The team at first relied on "the Line" a community motor canoe that traveled between the Opón and Barrancabermeja about every ten days. For emergencies, they hired a boat and driver. The expense of the private rentals resulted in the team buying its own motor canoe (called "motors" by local people) in the fall of 2001. Some members of the team learned to pilot the canoe themselves, but for most of the time, the team hired local drivers who understood the moods of the river better and were less likely to damage the motor.

With the purchase of the canoe came the dilemma of how much the team would let their contacts in the Opón use it. People needing a ride into town sometimes couched their requests as a need for accompaniment. Opón residents, reasoning that the team was going to Barrancabermeja anyway, frequently asked team members to take goods such as catfish and plantains to sell and buy goods such as soap and cigarettes for them. Eventually, following the advice of Opón community leaders, the team instituted a policy stipulating that people needing accompaniment had to arrange their own transportation.[92]

Compartmentalization of Colombian Government

"In Colombia everyone is free to say whatever they want and anyone else is free to kill you for saying it," a Colombian Mennonite pastor told members of CPT's 2000 delegation. Javier Giraldo captured this idiosyncrasy of the Colombian government in the title of his book, *Colombia, the Genocidal Democracy* (1996). Scores of Colombian prosecutors, judges, and journalists have tackled the egregious human rights abuses of the Colombian government and armed groups. Many have been assassinated and many more have taken their places. The Colombian government actually has an official Human Rights ombudsman whose job it is to investigate the abuses committed by the Colombian government, but the Defensoria, as it is called, requires international accompaniment at times to investigate human rights abuses of the government that pays his or her salary. The

---

92. CPTnet, Gingerich, "Colombia: The Motor," Sept 5, 2001; Erin Kindy and William Payne, e-mails, Aug 11–12, 2006.

Colombia team has provided accompaniment for the Defensoria on more than one occasion.[93]

This compartmentalization of functions has enabled some branches of the government to encourage the worst abuses of the paramilitaries, while others categorize the paramilitaries along with the guerrilla groups as illegal.

Colombian and international human rights organizations are always looking for ways to make the government's connection with paramilitaries clear. Proof of the connection is elusive, and sound human rights documentation practices dictated that the team could only mention that paramilitaries and the Colombian military were in the same area, or note that individuals they had been told were paramilitaries were seen talking to soldiers. Some of the team's caution in "connecting the dots" appeared in a March 2002 correction of their Easter release:

> Our Easter Action Invitation, "COLOMBIA EASTER ACTION: 'Life Lists' and Tax Resistance" stated—about connections between paramilitaries and legal armed groups—that:
>
> "CPT members have been eye-witnesses to the cooperation between military and paramilitary forces."
>
> CORRECTION:
>
> Because use of information is extremely sensitive on this project, we want to correct ourselves by saying:
>
> "CPT members have witnessed one clear instance of friendly relations between paramilitary members and members of the legal armed forces, and have heard of other instances."
>
> CPT-COLOMBIA[94]

The mandate to provide a balance—which involved repeating the refrain that all armed groups committed atrocities—could be exasperating, given that the body count of paramilitary victims was exponentially higher and that the conventional wisdom of their contacts was that the paramilitaries were a greater threat. A letter Lisa Martens wrote to her supporters captured some of this frustration:

93. See, for example, CPTnet, "Colombia: CPT accompanies government," July 24, 2003.

94. CPTnet, "Correction on Colombia Easter Release," Mar 21, 2002.

You may have heard that those FARC / guerrilla / rebel-type people are being uncooperative in negotiations with the Colombian
government.

Lisa's analysis #1: True enough. FYI: The FARC controls roughly
half of the country, though the actual map of their control areas
morphs often. The FARC and other guerrilla groups are corrupt
and violent. I have no particular love for them except insofar as
I'm working on loving enemies, but note, re: lack of cooperation
in negotiations: You can believe the government hasn't been real
charming either.

Lisa's analysis #2: Guess who does about 80% of the violent political acts in this country (including massacres using chainsaws)? It's
NOT the FARC. It's the ultra right-wing paramilitaries. Though it
is veiled, there are connections between the paramilitaries and the
army / navy and therefore the government.[95]

Connections of Armed Groups with Civilians

If the connections between paramilitaries and the Colombian government were murky, the connection between the armed groups and the civilian population was also difficult to discern. In a response to the author's
question about which armed group controlled Puente Opón (see above),
Erin Kindy wrote,

The alleged or actual support of an armed group by people in a
community, at least in the Opón, changed a lot and back and forth
over time. The fact is that alleged support (even if it's not actually
true) carries the same risks for people as actual support. Rumors
carry a lot of weight and can cause things as drastic as death and
displacement. I guess I'm telling you this because the issues of who
controlled what and who supported whom are really sensitive and
complicated issues. I know people who within the span of a week
fed both guerrillas and paramilitaries and doing that is seen as
support of an armed group and can put people at a life and death
risk. How do you say in such a situation who they supported or
why they did what they did?[96]

The team thus had to weigh the costs and benefits of associating with
certain people, because association with certain individuals would tag

95. CPTnet, "Colombia: Letter from Lisa Martens," Mar 22, 2002.
96. Erin Kindy, e-mail, Aug 19, 2006.

team members themselves with the label of paramilitary or guerrillas supporters and thus cut off effective communication with some parties. Given that most of the leftwing guerrilla groups espoused a philosophy compatible with most of the social justice groups the team worked with, and given that these groups often had actual connections with guerrillas, the team had to be careful about how closely they worked with such groups.

Trauma

Not since 1993, when Bob Bartel and Joel Klassen had found the mutilated body of Madame Elwime after she was murdered by FRAPH (see chapter 2), had CPTers come close to the murderous malice they found in Magdalena Medio. Finding bodies and parts of bodies in the river, sometimes belonging to friends and acquaintances, took a deep emotional toll on the team, as did the realization that most of the Colombians they worked with might be targeted for this particularly gruesome form of violence. Some of this concern is evident in Lisa Martens' poem, "To God."

> To God
> [Regarding people under death threat who are not
> afraid to be killed quickly, but are afraid of being
> tortured to death or mutilated after death.]
>
> God, look at this one—his eyes, fingernails, good ears—
> who wants to live free like anyone would;
> Really lovely, this one.
>
> I wanted
> to draw to your attention
>
> that this one would die for his people.
>
> He's that sort.
> I figured you would understand that;
> and would at least pay some attention.[97]

When asked how these traumas had changed her and her work on other project locations, Erin Kindy wrote,

> I think the main thing I noticed is that working with and through
> trauma in Colombia taught me to be more aware of my own in-

97. CPTnet, "Colombia: Three poems," May 18, 2002. See also Martens' poem in CPTnet, "Colombia: No one has greater love," July 25, 2002.

ternal responses to the realities I work/live in. It also taught me to be attentive to the effect those realities had on teammates or other people I worked with.

I know that the risks of work in Colombia (primarily how risky it was for our partners) affected how I thought about what we were asking of partners in Grassy Narrows and the impact that might have on their lives. I also think it sometimes made the team hypersensitive to security risks, especially with information and names.

I know that I brought some of my trauma with me when I went to work in Grassy Narrows the second time. In some ways my time on the team during those summer months was a time of healing from my previous stint in Colombia. I think there were 2 primary links that helped make that possible: one was the presence in Grassy of friends and co-workers who were familiar with the Colombia work setting, the other was the presence of much water, just like in Colombia. Water continues to be very healing for me and is a link for me to Colombia and Grassy.

OK, so today I feel able to at least make a stab at the part about how working with trauma changed me. One of the primary ways is that I am a person with more depth now. I also feel like I'm more able to, in a very small way, identify with people all over the world who live in places where daily safety is not taken for granted as often is here in the US. Working with trauma has taught me tools I wouldn't have had to learn otherwise; about how to manage my own fears and how to support other people in the midst of their fears. I feel like my own view of the scale of relative danger was modified by seeing and living in the more dangerous setting of the Barrancabermeja team.[98]

Rethinking Emergency Room Approach to Team Work

Before CPT's work in Colombia, most team members stayed on projects for about three months—the usual amount of time for a tourist visa. Occasionally in Hebron and Chiapas, some people stayed longer, although the people who did so often suffered from burnout. Even if team life was uneventful, team members were always on call should crises arise. Once the Colombian government began denying visas to CPTers, the problems of this 24/7 approach to the work became apparent. At a time when the level of violence the team was encountering was acute, and team members

98. Erin Kindy, e-mail, Sept 16, 2006.

needed greater amounts of rest and retreat, those whose visas enabled them to stay in Colombia did so far longer than was emotionally healthy.

Colombian Mennonite advisors urged team members to stay in Colombia for longer periods, and adapt their lifestyle to provide the requisite time for relaxation and mental health. With addition of Colombian nationals to the team and the marriage of one long-time CPTer to a native of Barrancabermeja, CPT's Colombia team members have continued to reshape what it means to be "on assignment" and to explore ways that enable them to stay in Barrancabermeja and the Opón for longer periods.

Economic Violence

Colombia has an abundance of mineral and agricultural wealth, but like most other countries in Latin America, only an elite few profit from its riches. In areas where oil, gold, emeralds, timber, and plantations are found, paramilitary violence has often succeeded in driving small-scale farmers and miners off the land.

Wealthy individuals could turn the many subsistence farmsteads into gigantic cattle ranches or African Palm plantations. In 2004 Keith Young wrote a release noting that the Colombian government's anticipated amnesty for paramilitaries was leading some of them to ensure they had such ranches or plantations to fall back on for income. Dealing with one wealthy ranch owner who could pay "protection tax," was easier for paramilitaries than shaking down cash-poor farmers for small sums.[99]

Those that promoted the "Process for Life, Liberty and Dignity" in the Opón, understood the economic connection with massacres and displacements, and thus used economic development of the Opón region—by planting cash crops such as cacao and African palm—as a unifying force.

Matthew Wiens, after attending one of these Process meetings wrote,

> As I took in the various sessions, I thought about the similarities (and the drastic differences) between the struggles faced by these rural people and the rural communities in Canada. In Colombia, as in Canada, farmers are struggling to receive a fair price for what they produce. Young people from the Opón region are leav-

99. CPTnet, Young, "Colombia: Land, our daily bread," Apr 30, 2004; CPTnet, "Colombia Update: November 2004," Dec 10, 2004.

ing for the cities because they don't see a future for themselves in their communities—an all too familiar situation in the Canadian prairies.

As in many rural communities in Canada, the people of the Opón realize that they must work with their neighbours if they want to have any hope of surviving. I am thankful that in Canada, we are not in the midst of a civil war, but I wondered if the courage and determination evident in the Opón leaders stemmed from the fact that they face such overwhelming odds.[100]

As was the case in Haiti and Chiapas, releases written later in the life of the Colombia project reflected a deeper concern with economic issues, although not, as was the case in Chiapas and Haiti, because the threat of lethal violence had subsided. Perhaps the releases that described the negative effects of "free" trade agreements—such as flooding the market with cheap corn from the U.S. and selling of oil exploration rights to multinational companies—on Colombia's poor was a reflection of the increasingly structured approach the team was taking to its work. Having become part of the communities they accompanied, team members had established secure platform from which they could view the systemic causes of violence.[101]

U.S. complicity in Colombia's Violence

As U.S. Defense Secretary Donald Rumsfeld visits Colombia, members of Christian Peacemaker Teams Colombia project would like to add our voices to those clamoring for a climate more conducive to the growing of peace in Colombia. The seeds of military aid, weapons technology and combat training that the U.S. is currently planting only produce the bitter fruit of more war, making life increasingly difficult for campesinos in rural areas.[102]

So wrote the team regarding a 2003 visit by Donald Rumsfeld in which he praised President Alvaro Uribe for fighting "narcoterrorists" whom the Bush administration was trying to connect to Al Qaeda, the organization

---

100. CPTnet, Wiens, "Colombia Reflection: The painstaking struggle," Nov 5, 2004.

101. CPTnet releases: "Colombia Update: February 2005," Mar 17, 2005; "Colombia: Barrancabermeja marches," May 5, 2006; Gutierrez Castaño, "Colombia: Coca farmers," Aug 31, 2006; "Colombia: CPTers accompany demonstration," Sept 7, 2006.

102. CPTnet, "Colombia: 'Peace Doesn't Grow Here,'" Aug 20, 2003.

that had hijacked U.S. civilian airliners in 2001 and crashed them into the World Trade Center and Pentagon.[103]

The involvement of the United States in Colombian affairs was a key reason that CPT chose to set up a project there. Almost all the violence occurring in Colombia—physical, economic and otherwise—had some U.S. connection. Plan Colombia, which had as its purported goal the reduction of and eventually elimination of Colombia's production of illicit crops, was passed by the U.S. Congress in 2002. However, the billions of dollars of aid that the U.S. sent as part of the Plan, was quickly, and with the approval of the U.S., used for counterinsurgency purposes. Indeed, the entire heavily funded U.S. War on Drugs, became a tool to suppress guerrilla and civil society groups.

The fumigations that wrought so much ecological and economic havoc on small farmers were a part of this plan.[104] A measure of the U.S. control over the Colombian government can be seen in its response to a Colombian court that ruled these fumigations were illegal and ordered a moratorium on them in 2003. The U.S. insisted that they continue and President Alvaro Uribe obliged the U.S. by saying that the fumigations would not stop as long as he was president.[105]

The team put out two action alerts in 2004 asking their U.S. constituents to contact their congressional representatives and urge them to vote against an increase in U.S. military aid, which included sending more troops.[106] In 2005, after the Colombian authorities arrested two American

103. Gilmore, "Rumsfeld: Colombia Is Doing 'An Excellent Job.'"

104. The 2001 Lenten delegation had made fumigations one of its foci, and the Colombia team continues, as of 2008, to regard the issue as important. See CPTnet releases: Cliff Kindy, "Colombia: Cash Crop Coca," Feb 21, 2001; "Colombia: CPTers fast for peace," Mar 8, 2001; "Colombia Update: February 12–25, 2001," Mar 15, 2001; "Colombia Update: March 12–26," Apr 7, 2001; "Colombia: The Coca Lives," Sept 2, 2001; Schaaf, "Colombia: Plan Colombia's 'War on Farmers,'" Oct 1, 2001; Collerd, "'I am cold,'" Sept 3, 2005; "Colombia: U.S. 'War on Drugs,'" Sept 23, 2005; "Colombia Urgent Action: Call U.S. senators," Feb 7, 2006; Dillard, "Colombia: The sound of helicopters," Mar 18, 2006; "Colombia Urgent Action: Call U.S. Congress," June 7, 2006.

105. Rose, "A day in the life"; CPTnet, Schaaf, "Plan Colombia's 'War on Farmers,'" Oct 1, 2001; CPTnet, Dillard, "Colombia: The sound of helicopters," Mar 18, 2006. Also indicative of US control was Colombia's expressed "support" for the US invasion of Iraq in 2003, which garnered the Colombia government $104 million more in military aid. CPTnet, "Colombia: Letter from Duane Ediger," April 15, 2003.

106. CPTnet, "Colombia Action Alert: U.S. Congress to vote," May 5, 2004; CPTnet, "Colombia Call to Prayer," Aug 20, 2004.

soldiers for trafficking American military supplies to paramilitary groups, the team put out another Urgent Action. In it, they asked CPT's constituents to contact their elected representatives, Rumsfeld, and Senators on the Foreign Relations and Armed Services committee, asking that they demand a thorough investigation into American military involvement with Colombian paramilitary groups.[107]

The School of the Americas, renamed the Western Hemisphere Institute for Security Cooperation in 2001, was another repugnant contribution the U.S. made toward the violence in Colombia. CPTers had participated in the movement to close the school since 1994, because Haitian officers had been trained there.[108] Over the years, CPTers began participating in increasing numbers in the annual November mass witnesses at Fort Benning, Georgia, where the school was located (see chapter 8, under "Issues arising from the Chiapas project"). Two members of the first Colombia project team, Scott Kerr and Ben Horst, were arrested at Fort Benning in 2001.[109]

Canadian Complicity in Colombia's Violence

Because CPT has a large Canadian constituency, when the organization puts out Urgent Actions, it tries to find ways that both Canadians and Americans can participate. Sometimes this strategy has proven difficult when, for example, the U.S. invaded Iraq and Canada opposed the invasion. Likewise, Canada's involvement in Latin American has usually not had the negative consequences that U.S. involvement has, nor has it had the power to pressure the U.S. to conform to international human rights norms.

107. CPTnet, "Colombia Urgent Action: Demand a thorough investigation," May 8, 2005. The Colombian authorities deported the two soldiers who had been in the company of three Colombians with alleged paramilitary ties. According to a treaty ratified in 2000, the soldiers had diplomatic immunity and could not be tried in Colombian courts.

108. CPTnet, "School of the Americas fast ends," May 21, 1994.

109. CPTnet, "Ft. Benning, GA: CPT at SOA," Nov 19, 2001; CPTnet, Kerr, "Colombia: The SOA and the War on Terrorism," Dec 22, 2001. Reflecting on an incident that had occurred in 2003, Pierre Shantz wrote about staying up all night with Michael Goode to monitor a paramilitary encampment in the Opón. One of the paramilitaries who spoke good English said he had been trained at the SOA when he was in the Colombian army and then joined the paramilitaries when he returned to Colombia. CPTnet, "Colombia: CPT celebrates four years," June 20, 2005.

As CPT became more involved with mining communities in the Department of Bolivar, however, the role of Canadian corporations in the violence there became an issue. In 1997, the ominously named Conquistador Mines Ltd. expressed interest in Bolivar's Simiti mine, at which point paramilitaries arrived in the area. They killed at least nineteen people in towns around Simiti, beheaded one miner, and tortured and killed the vice president of a local miners association. Thousands of people fled the area.[110]

In February 2006, representatives of the Canadian Embassy visited the team in Barrancabermeja and told team members that they were open to hearing about any situations involving Canadian companies. Later in the year, Joel Klassen and Bob Homes represented CPT and members of Colombia mining communities at Toronto and Montreal roundtables held "to examine measures that could be taken to position Canadian extractive sector companies operating in developing countries to meet or exceed leading international Corporate Social Responsibility (CSR) standards and best practices." Klassen argued that in practice, corporations rarely meet CSR standards voluntarily. Furthermore, since they received Canadian government subsidies, they were making the government culpable in human rights abuses that took place in mining regions. "You don't deal with crimes against humanity by voluntary measures," Klassen argued.

"We must take seriously the stories coming out of mining zones around the world, stories of liberty denied far too often—the central question we are facing in these roundtables, in this laborious process of policy development, is, "Do we want to build policy with soul? Are we morally capable as a nation of taking the interests of others into account?"[111]

Incorporation of Colombians into Team

Perhaps no other factor changed CPT's Colombia project and CPT as an organization as much as the inclusion of Colombian nationals on the team. For the first time, the language used at team meetings was that of the local community. For the first time, instead of being consultants and coworkers, citizens of a non-North American country in which CPT worked took on leadership roles within the team.

110. Halifax Initiative, "Simiti Gold Mine"; Ismi, "Profiting from Repression."
111. CPTnet, "CPT Colombia Team brings case," Sept 15, 2006.

The team's working relationship with the Colombian Mennonite Church facilitated the development of trinational teams (Colombian, U.S., and Canadian.) The Colombian Mennonites had issued the original invitation for CPT to come to Colombia and Colombian Mennonites had already come in delegations to Barrancabermeja to support the team during its visa crisis, visit conflict locations, and participate in public witnesses.[112] The first Colombians to serve on the team in Barrancabermeja had Mennonite connections.[113]

Some of the issues involved with the change of nationalities on the team were minor. For example, once the Colombia team made Spanish its first language, timeliness of releases was affected, because they had to be translated into both English and Spanish.

Other changes involved radical paradigm shifts. CPT's principle of accompaniment, i.e., the presence of North Americans protecting threatened groups because North American lives were considered more valuable, came into question. Since most of the Colombians joining the team were educated urban professionals, they possibly possessed more privilege in the eyes of the Colombian military than the campesinos of the Opón. Nevertheless, they would not have had an embassy inquire about their injuries or deaths, and many other Colombians of their social class had been kidnapped, tortured, and assassinated. Ultimately, Colombia team members, both nationals and internationals, agreed that the benefits of having Colombians on the team far outweighed the possible increased risk.

The change that Colombian CPTers had wrought in the organization as a whole was evident in a September 2006 antiracism training held in Chicago after the biennial fulltimers' retreat. Participants noted that the CPT website was full of references to how North American privilege had protected the people among whom CPT had set up projects. Given the

112. CPTnet, Reschly, "CPT Colombia Fasts and Prays," Mar 29, 2002; CPTnet, Ediger, "Colombia: Holy Week delegation," Apr 22, 2003. The prominence of the Stucky family in the leadership of the Colombian Mennonite church also may have contributed to the tri-national makeover of the team.

113. Adaía Bernal and Julian Carréo were Mennonites. (Carréo was one of the conscientious objectors whose rights Justapaz represented. He did not go through training.) Sandra Milena referred to herself as "Mennonite-Catholic." Julián Gutiérrez Castaño, who went through training later, was Catholic. Gutiérrez Castaño, e-mail, Nov 28, 2006. As time passed, the team developed deep relationships with other Colombian churches, most significantly the Catholic Church in its Barrancabermeja neighborhood.

fact that Colombians on the team without this privilege had worked so effectively, and given that everyone in the organization wanted CPT to become more multinational and multiethnic, those present agreed that a change in the CPT attitude toward accompaniment was necessary.[114] This decision was not made without a sense of sacrifice. Having someone tell CPTers that their presence saved his or her life is a heady, energizing experience. However, most CPTers agreed that it was more important to accompany communities whose focus was building solidarity among their members as a way of protecting themselves.

Even though the Colombia team consciously moved away from the principle of "effective racism" as a factor in accompaniment, this decision did not negate the value of the accompaniment of the previous years. Indeed, accompanied Colombians, when speaking of CPT's work, tended to talk more about the emotional and spiritual benefits that CPT's presence had brought into their lives, rather than about physical safety, and how this presence had helped them reclaim their own dignity. The Barrancabermeja-based organization, CREDHOS (Regional Corporation for the Defense of Human Rights) told a May 2004 delegation that CPT's presence had encouraged them, in dangerous times, to keep working for human rights. This presence also emboldened a member of the Los Ñeques community to tell a member of an armed group in 2003, "Before CPT arrived, the guerrilla and paramilitary forces didn't respect us. The Colombian army never respected us. Now that the [CPTers] are here, they respect us more."[115]

---

114. CPTnet, Erin Kindy, "Toronto/Chicago: Structural racism," Oct 19, 2006. The author was present at the gathering, and as a result agreed to modify the section on "Effective racism" in the Haiti chapter.

115. The author replaced the original "gringos" with "CPTers" after Julian Gutierrez noted in a November 28, 2006 e-mail, that "gringos" as a "terrible connotation" in other parts of Colombia and most of the world. Duane Ediger wrote in a November 27, 2006 e-mail,

The appearance of the word "gringos" is quite deflating to read in the context of the rest—perhaps it is worth noting that people on the Opón jokingly/affectionately refer to [the team's] dark-skinned Colombian boat driver as "el gringo negro." Their use of that word in the 2003 quote is evidence that the challenge Colombian team members brought to oppression-tainted understandings of "accompaniment" extends beyond CPT to Colombians stratified by generations of racism, feudalism, and colonialism.

11

Iraq

When society goes mad, Christians should probably be where the consequences will be the worst.

—Cliff Kindy, letter to supporters, March 17, 2003[1]

BY THE TIME CPT set up a project in Iraq in 2002, members of the organization had realized that effective peacemaking was safer than its founders had originally thought. Participants in the 1993 training imagined it likely that one of their numbers might die or be seriously injured in the line of duty, and in the early years, single parents of young children were not encouraged to apply, nor were children admitted on project locations. As years passed, however, minor assaults by Israeli settlers and tropical diseases were the most physically dangerous crises that CPTers had faced.[2] The outcomes of death threats against the Hebron and Colombia teams were largely positive, i.e., they resulted in increased visibility of the teams' work and increased solidarity with grassroots organizations that spoke on their behalf. In every training, participants still planned their memorial services and made out their wills, but gradually, children, spouses, and other family members began visiting CPTers on location and teams made hosting international and national civilians wanting to know more about the team's work a priority.

1. CPTnet, "Iraq: Letter from Cliff Kindy," Mar 19, 2003.
2. The Israeli settler assault on Kim Lamberty and Chris Brown took place in 2004, two years after the establishment of the Iraq team. One might argue that team members who stayed in Hebron and Beit Jala homes while the Israeli military was shelling them in the early years of the Al Aqsa Intifada put themselves in jeopardy, but the families they were staying with always took them to safe places within the homes, out of the line of fire.

CPT's work in Iraq would snap it back to its original understanding of the danger to trained peacemakers stepping into the line of fire. By 2006, the Iraq team would experience two serious auto accidents, have friends and colleagues die in violence that spiraled out of control after the invasion of the Multinational Forces in 2003, be tied up and robbed by armed men, and have a delegation kidnapped. Two trained CPTers would die in Iraq, one in an accident and one in an execution-style murder.

HISTORY

Historians refer to Mesopotamia, which encompasses Iraq, as the "cradle of civilization." Mesopotamia boasts the first recorded instances of reading, writing, trade, urban centers, metallurgy, agriculture, and a legal system. The cities of Ur (birthplace of Abraham), Nineveh, and Babylon, among others, are mentioned in the Bible and their remnants remain in contemporary Iraq. Over the millennia, the Sumerian, Mittani, Assyrian, Babylonian, Persian, Seleucid, Ottoman, and British Empires ruled the region.

In 1979, after a brief period of stability and prosperity, Saddam Hussein took over the offices of both President and Chairman of the Revolutionary Command Council. He had been the de facto ruler of Iraq for some years before he formally came to power. Hussein launched the war against Iran in 1980 over disputed territories in the Persian Gulf region. When hostilities ceased in 1988, Iraq had the largest military in the region, but also faced a mountain of debt and an ongoing rebellion of Kurds in the north that Hussein's government brutally repressed.

A territorial dispute with Kuwait led to Iraq invading the country in 1990, because a section of Kuwait had been part of Iraq's Basra province during the Ottoman Empire. Kuwait had declared independence in 1961, over the Iraqi government's objections. In the months leading to the First Gulf War, Iraq accused Kuwait, more or less accurately, of "slant-drilling," i.e., drilling on the border in such a way as to pump oil from under Iraqi territory. The Arab League and U.N. Security Council condemned the invasion and four days later, the Security Council imposed an economic embargo on Iraq. Iraq responded by annexing Kuwait as its "19th province" on August 8, 1990.

In November 1990, the U.N. Security Council adopted Resolution 678, which authorized military action against the Iraqi forces occupying Kuwait and demanded a complete withdrawal by January 15, 1991.

CPT'S FIRST DELEGATION TO IRAQ

CPT first became involved with issues related to Iraq in October 1990, when it encouraged its constituent churches to participate in "Oil-Free Sunday" on October 21 (see chapter 1). In November 1990, it held its second CPT Training Action conference—a gathering that eventually developed into the annual Christian Peacemaker Congress. Participants in the Denver, Colorado, event took nonviolence training and attended workshops on the Persian Gulf Conflict. Five of them were arrested for trespassing at Lowry Air Force Base. Attendees also raised $700 for a CPT delegation to Iraq and commissioned Hedy Sawadsky and Gene Stoltzfus to lead the delegation by anointing them with oil.

This delegation, comprising thirteen Mennonites, Brethren, and Friends (Quakers) with backgrounds working in the Middle East then traveled to Amman, Baghdad, and Babylon between November 21 and December 1, 1990. Delegates hoped to persuade Saddam Hussein to release his western hostages, and to end the food and medicine blockade by the US-led coalition. They hoped that by doing so they would be able to "open up less emotionally-charged space for genuine dialogue leading to negotiations." While not successful in achieving these goals, the delegates made hundreds of public appearances in churches and the media after their return.[3] Additionally, Stoltzfus noted in his Iraq Peacemaker Team Activity Report, that the delegation had presented the Iraqi Minister without Portfolio a list of five western hostages whom the U.S. State Department had identified as having serious medical conditions. Later, the Iraqi government released those hostages and ten others to the care of boxer and humanitarian Muhammad Ali whose delegation had not provided any names to the Iraqi government.[4]

The delegation met with some of the forty plus hostages—most of whom were free to move about in Baghdad. They were nominally hostages

3. CPT, "Christian Peacemaker Teams Activities 1984–2000."

4. Ali and the delegation were staying in the same guest center. They went to events with him and his staff and shared ideas informally. The hostages were probably released to his care because of his higher media profile. Gene Stoltzfus, e-mail, Sept 11, 2007.

in that the Iraqi government would not give them an exit visa. Hussein's government forced others to stay in strategic locations, presumably to prevent western countries from bombing those sites. At the conclusion of the report, Gene Stoltzfus listed eight points under "Conclusion and Next Steps." The three he emphasized in bold text were,

1. Iraq was willing to come to the negotiation table. "As one Iraqi intellectual said, "If you come to us in anger, you will find the Iraqi a fierce combatant, but if you come kindly and respectfully, you will find that he will give you his house."

2. CPT urgently needs finances to fund a smaller team in mid-January.

3. Persons need to call the White House number to encourage serious negotiations and a lowering of the rhetoric. "Prayers are needed everywhere."[5]

After the delegation, the CPT Steering Committee circulated a call for CPT supporters to observe an "Emergency Sabbath," in which people would plan worship for, and participate in, peacemaking activities on the first Monday after hostilities began.

In the years between the first and second Gulf Wars, CPT maintained connections with Iraqi issues. A December 1991 *Signs of the Times* featured the efforts of early CPT supporters Cathy and Andre Gingerich Stoner who worked with Mennonite Central Committee in Germany providing counsel to personnel on military bases who wished to become Conscientious Objectors during the Gulf War. Veteran Chicago-based peace activist Kathy Kelly participated in most of the CPT trainings from 1993 onward. CPT officially endorsed her organization, Voices in the Wilderness, which publicized the human cost of the war and sanctions

5. Gene Stoltzfus, "Iraq Peacemaker Team Activity Report." The report also records a meeting with Joe Wilson, the Charges d'Affairs at the US Embassy in Baghdad. Stoltzfus described him as explaining U.S. policy "in a brisk [George H. W.] Bush style with a picture of Marilyn Monroe hovering over his head." However, as the conversation progressed, Wilson became genuinely interested in CPT's mission. Wilson would later write an op-ed in the *New York Times*, "What I Didn't Find in Africa," accusing the George W. Bush administration of using intelligence it knew was false to justify the second invasion of Iraq in 2003. Members of the administration then retaliated by leaking information to the press that Wilson's wife, Valerie Plame, was a CIA agent, which resulted, as of this writing, in a criminal conviction of Vice President Cheney's former chief of Staff, I. Lewis Scooter Libby.

regime on Iraqi civilians.[6] Palestinians in Hebron were concerned about the fate of fellow Arabs in Iraq under the sanctions regime. One family that the team visited frequently in the Hebron project's early years had pictures hanging on the wall of a sister-in-law and her five children incinerated in the Amiriya bomb shelter during the first Gulf war.[7]

As the George W. Bush administration looked for reasons to invade Iraq after the catastrophes of September 11, 2001, killed almost three thousand people, CPT began developing a response. The damage done to the Iraqi infrastructure in the First Gulf War and grievously exacerbated by the sanctions prompted CPT to begin sending delegations to Iraq in 2002 as a way of preventing such destruction from happening again.[8] By sending delegations in the months leading up to the war, CPT hoped both to educate people about the damage done by the previous war and sanctions and to evaluate the possibility of setting up a CPT project that might protect Iraqi civilians and civilian infrastructure.[9]

On one of these exploratory delegations the first of several tragic episodes in the history of CPT's Iraq team occurred. As the delegation was traveling in a three-vehicle caravan between Basra and Baghdad on January 6, 2003, the Chevrolet suburban in which seventy-three-year-old George Weber was riding blew a tire and rolled over, killing him instantly. (Other delegates sustained minor injuries, including a broken nose and broken rib.)

---

6. Gene Stoltzfus, e-mail, Sept 11, 2007. He noted that in CPT's early years, the organization did not endorse many other peacemaking ventures. He also wrote that he had wanted to send CPT delegations to Iraq for the entire sanctions period, but had to give up that idea because CPT lacked the staff to carry it out.

7. CPTnet, "Tea with the Muhtasibs," Dec 8, 1996. CPTer Jim Loney visited this shelter in 2003 and reported seeing images of bodies seared into the walls and floor. CPTnet, "Iraq: Things are not as they seem, part 1," Feb 17, 2003.

8. Before the first delegation in October 2002, CPT put out a "Wake Up Call" on Iraq, urging its constituent churches to bang pots and pans at federal buildings, among other acts of resistance, to alert people to the danger of the war. CPTnet, "Urgent Action: Wake Up Call," Sept 27, 2002.

9. Unicef estimated in 1999 that out of the one million Iraqis who died as a result of the sanctions, half were children. "Iraq surveys show 'humanitarian emergency.'" See also CPTnet, Jane Pritchard, "Mosul, Iraq: Children's Hospital visit," Feb 25, 2003. Delegate John Worrell wrote about a pre-war hospital visit in CPTnet, "Iraq: Why Don't They Hate Me?" Nov 27, 2002. A version of this article that appeared in the fall 2002 Signs of the Times was used by a US border guard as an excuse to deny CPTer Matthew Bailey-Dick, a Canadian citizen, entrance into the US. Bailey-Dick had been returning to seminary in Indiana after a speaking engagement in Ontario. See Kern, "A clash of views."

Weber, who had served as a reservist in Chiapas and Hebron, had become increasingly disturbed, as war with Iraq increasingly seemed to become inevitable. He told his wife, Lena, "I just can't sit back and do nothing. What would I say to my grandchildren?" In an interview with a local paper before he left, he said, "We are going to suffer along with the Iraqis. It's an opportunity to light a candle instead of cursing the dark."

His wife, Lena, said later that whenever they approached a taxi stand in Nicaragua and Mexico, he always chose the man driving the most dilapidated taxi, figuring that the driver was the one that needed the money most. In the same spirit of aiding the impoverished, Weber went to a tailor in Baghdad to order a new suit. Jim Loney picked up the suit and paid the tailor upon return to Baghdad and Weber's body was clothed in it for the funeral. Doug Pritchard wrote of the service:

> We have now accompanied our dear friend George Weber along another step of his journey home.
>
> Twenty-one CPTers and partners participated in the funeral service at his hometown of Chesley ON yesterday [January 13]. It was a very snowy, blowy day with all schools and some roads closed but most people were able to get there....
>
> The church was full with about 300 attending. At the front was the simple made-to-measure casket he had traveled in from Iraq topped by lovely photo of him and a green CPT Directory with the "Getting in Way" Logo prominent....
>
> After the service, the CPTers donned their red hats and formed one side of an honour guard from the bottom of the steps of the church to the hearse and George's Rotary Club colleagues formed the other side. The pallbearers brought the casket down the steps, through our honour guard, and into the hearse. We then followed the hearse on foot for several blocks through the snowstorm to the funeral home where his body would wait until the roads were clear enough to drive to the crematorium in Owen Sound.

Summarizing the impact Weber's death had on CPT as an organization, Gene Stoltzfus wrote,

> We all have known that this moment in our life together would come. We could not have predicted how it would come or that our

fallen brother could provide us with such a modest, mature and well timed witness to what all of us aspire to be.[10]

By March 2003, the invasion of Iraq by the George W. Bush administration was clearly going to happen. Working under the auspices of the Iraq Peace Teams[11]—which was an outgrowth of the Voices in the Wilderness organization—the team[12] sent out an Urgent Action on March 6, 2003, that listed the locations, e.g., water treatment and electrical plants, schools etc., where they and Iraq Peace Team members would be when the bombing started.[13] On March 15, the team put out the following letter, á la the epistles of the Apostle Paul, to churches in Canada and the United States.

> A Letter to the churches in Canada and the United States from the Christian Peacemaker Team in Iraq

---

10. CPTnet, "Basrah, Iraq: CPT reservist killed," Jan 6, 2006; CPTnet, "Chicago/Toronto: Memories of George Weber," Jan 17, 2002. See also CPT "George Weber Memorial." Initially, the UN sanctions against Iraq forbade the "export" of Weber's body. Canadian officials got permission, based on "humanitarian" reasons, to transport the body to Amman on January 9, 2002. See CPTnet, "Baghdad, Iraq: Body of CPTer killed," Jan 10, 2002. The Al Wathba water treatment plant in Baghdad, where CPT/IPT had encamped during the 2003 bombings, still, as of this writing, bears the plaque by a date palm planted there: "Tree of Life, in honor of George Weber, 1930–2003, CPT volunteer, and CPT presence here during 'Shock and Awe' March–April, 2003." CPTnet releases: "Iraq: Remembering George Weber," Jan 13, 2004; "Iraq Update: July 29–August 1, 2004," Aug 10, 2004; Peggy Gish, "Iraq Reflection: Progress with water and peace," Aug 24, 2004.

11. When asked how CPT came to work under IPT, Kathy Kelly wrote in a Jan 6, 2007 email:

> In August of 2002, a group of Voices activists met in Chicago and decided to move ahead with a commitment to form a team intent on remaining in Iraq throughout a war that we hoped we could prevent. We wrote documents seeking permission for the team and began building outreach, developing a careful screening process for potential participants ...
>
> In the fall of 2002, CPT decided to begin sending people recruited and prepared by CPT to join the Iraq Peace Team. CPT was reliant on Voices for visas, and it was important to understand that ultimately Voices would be responsible for anyone who came to Iraq and that it would be quite important to assure that people understood basic guidelines and were in agreement with them.

12. Cliff Kindy, Peggy Gish, Lisa Martens, Scott Kerr, Betty Scholten, and Stewart Vriesinga.

13. CPTnet, "Iraq Urgent Action: Write and/or call your Representatives," Mar 6, 2003.

...As members of Christian Peacemaker Teams, from both Canada and U.S., we have found a warm welcome in the homes of Iraqis. We have visited the institutions that shape this society. Iraqi people understand that the low intensity war of sanctions and bombings in the "no fly" zones is perpetrated by our very own government. Yet they seem to have the moral and spiritual resources to treat us graciously even though our bombings and sanctions have destroyed their economy for more than a decade, killing hundreds of thousands of people, many of them children ...

In order to live out our convictions, we will continue to be prayerfully present in Iraq and develop friendships with Iraqi people even in the event of an escalation of violence here. We don't know what we might experience in a bombing or occupation, but we plan to accompany civilians in specific places of our choosing. In an occupation, we will be on the streets, documenting and trying to prevent human rights abuses. At this time, the Iraqi government is not restricting us or determining where we go or what we do. We will continue to cry out against the apostasy of war in this setting of God's creation.

We invite you, sisters and brothers, to the nonviolent life of Jesus. From prayer and fasting, find the strength to stop paying for war. From joy in discipleship, hold fast to the evangelistic boldness to invite soldiers and corporate technocrats to abandon their posts. From the faith that teaches us that we are all sisters and brothers, believe in the reality of barriers broken down between all enemies. Live in Easter hope.

Then Jesus said to them, "Go out into the whole world and proclaim the Good News to all creation." Mark 16: 15[14]

At 4:00 a.m. on March 20, 2003, the deadline that U.S. President George W. Bush had given for Saddam Hussein and his sons to leave Iraq expired. The team in Baghdad celebrated communion and prayed for the security of all people. About an hour and a half later, team members began hearing aircraft overhead, sirens, and explosions. Within the first hour of the bombing, CPT Iraq team members Lisa Martens and Stewart Vriesinga were on CTV national television across Canada reporting live from Baghdad.[15]

14. CPTnet, "Iraq: A letter to the churches," Mar 15, 2003. See also the statement that CPT sent as part of the Iraq Peace Team to the US, Iraqi, and other governments (as well as "Supporters, Press, and interested parties"): CPTnet, "Iraq: Christian Peacemaker Team statement," Mar 17, 2004.

15. Doug Pritchard, who was CPT Canada Coordinator and the contact person for

Once the barrage was over later that morning, Peggy Gish, Betty Scholten, and Cliff Kindy set up a tent at the Al Wathba Water Treatment Centre, which was near an electrical plant and provided water to one sixth of the city, including a nearby hospital complex. The banner at the campsite read, "To Bomb this Site is a War Crime/Geneva Convention, Article 54.)" Scott Kerr, Lisa Martens, and Stuart Vriesinga and IPT member Father Jerry Zawada stayed at the Al Daar hotel in a civilian neighborhood. Martens concluded an e-mail reporting these events with, "Be outraged. Make Peace."[16]

Over the course of the next six days, eleven updates appeared on CPTnet, most based on phone conversations team members had with Gene Stoltzfus and Doug Pritchard about the force of the bombings, the presence of life on the streets and what sort of wounds local hospitals were treating. On March 26, after a communication center was hit, the coordinators lost phone contact with the team. CPTers and IPTers, who had intermingled in groups that were staying at different hotels, also lost contact with each other.

Because one group could not call a taxi, they walked to a team meeting and examined the site of the destroyed communications tower on the way, after checking with a police officer who said they could do so. They were taking pictures of a bombed-out restaurant across the street when Iraqi security personnel arrived and took them to a police station. They had to stay there for about five hours, whereabouts unknown to the increasingly worried CPTers and IPTers in other groups. A Mr. Zaid, the team's Iraqi government "handler" finally met the detained group at the station and ordered its members out of the country the next day.[17]

Iraqis had been burning oil around Baghdad to make U.S. reconnaissance photography more difficult and the security personnel may have thought the team was going to submit the photos to U.S. intelligence. Kerr

---

the Iraq Team at the time, wrote in his comments on a draft of this chapter:

> Providing this alternative media voice was a large part of the team's work with a couple people on the phone at all times doing interviews with media from around the world (although few from the US as I recall) while other team members were on the street gathering the latest info. It was at this time that we did a major overhaul of the CPT website with Diane Janzen's help in order to make it much more useful, informative and up-to-date for media and inquirers.

16. CPTnet, "Iraq: War report from team in Baghdad."
17. Cliff Kindy e-mail, Jan 8, 2007.

noted in a communication with the author that Iraqi government personnel might also have wanted to protect team members from someone who
had lost a house or family member from taking revenge.[18]

Zaid told the remaining CPTers, a recently arrived CPT delegation,
and IPTers they now had to stay all in the same hotel. Since part of the
Iraq team's *raison d'être* was to stay in as many places as possible to protect
vulnerable sites, some team members and delegates chose to leave with
those designated for expulsion on the morning of March 29, 2003.

Because the U.S. and British forces were actively bombing the road,
the drivers of the three vehicles in which delegates and team members
were riding decided to spread them apart and drive as fast as they could.
Once again, a tire blew in the third vehicle in the convoy and the driver
lost control.[19] Because of the distance between the vehicles, the people in
the first two did not observe the accident.

After the crash, Weldon Nisly and Cliff Kindy were bleeding heavily. Delegation member Doug Hostetter reported that they were "just
beginning to panic," when an Iraqi civilian car approached and the driver
packed them in and took them to the town of Rutba (population about
twenty thousand), about 140 kilometers east of the Jordanian Border.
Although the town had no apparent military structures, much of it had
been destroyed in the bombing, including a children's hospital in which
two young patients had died. At an approximately 20 x 20 foot clinic, the
town gathered to welcome their foreign guests and read the leaflets the
delegates handed out explaining who they were. A doctor who spoke perfect English diagnosed a broken thumb, several broken ribs and other
possible fractures in Weldon Nisly. He apologized that Kindy would have
to receive ten stitches to the head without anesthesia and that he could
not take them by ambulance to Jordan under the circumstances.[20] Later,
when the two other cars returned and found the group, the doctor and
clinic staff refused an offer of payment as the entourage left, saying, "We

18. CPTnet, "Amman, Jordan: Report from CPTer Scott Kerr," Apr 2, 2003; Scott Kerr,
e-mail], Feb 16, 2007; Cliff Kindy, e-mails, Jan 29 and Feb 17, 2007.

19. Gene Stoltzfus, in a September 11, 2007 e-mail, wrote that at the time he heard
that metal left on the road from the bombings had probably punctured the tire.

20. When members of the group resumed their trip to Jordan, they saw a bombed-out
ambulance not far down the road. CPTnet, Hostetter, "Welcome at Rutba," Mar 30, 2003.

treat everyone in our clinic: Muslim, Christian, Iraqi or American. We are all part of the same family, you know."[21]

On April 1, the remaining team and delegation members left Baghdad for Amman. In addition to their Iraqi handlers no longer allowing them to move freely, they realized that they were using food and other resources in short supply. "Everyone in Baghdad is making cutbacks, so we decided to cut back too," Scott Kerr told CPT staff in a phone report to CPT staff.[22]

Team members returned to Baghdad on April 16 and 18, 2003, and immediately began renewing acquaintances and assessing the damage. Via satellite phone, Scott told Doug Pritchard,

> It is terrible here. It is very sad. I couldn't believe the level of devastation as we approached the outskirts of Baghdad with destroyed vehicles and buildings everywhere. People are walking around dazed not knowing what to do. Every public building has been bombed or burned. I see buildings blown away or with holes right through them from one side to the other. All the records are gone—birth records, marriage certificates, school reports, hospital files. Some public buildings were bombed by the US. Some were

---

21. Ibid. Gene Stoltzfus, in a September 11, 2007 e-mail, wrote:

> CPT Chicago learned of the event during a Steering Committee meeting in Chicago. AP and Israeli Army news reported that people had been killed and hotel staff where CPT stayed in Amman called our office to say that something terrible had happened to the CPT vehicle . . . Because the trickle of news was already on the airways, we immediately called the families to inform them that there had been an accident; we did not confirm wounds or fatalities because we did not have confirmation. From approximately 4:30 in the afternoon until approximately 9:00 p.m., we worked the phones and prayed. Every hour I called the hotel in Amman to find out if they knew more or if the group had arrived. The Steering Committee continued to meet and pray. Finally, at 9 p.m. when I called the Hotel, the group had arrived and everyone was injured but alive. I asked to speak to Cliff Kindy who came on the phone to say that they arrived at the hotel to a feeding frenzy of the press from all over the world . . . [He] then proceeded to describe the accident, the help in Rutbah and the hard work of evacuating Weldon Nisly to Amman by using a series of four ambulances which either broke down, ran out of gas or had other difficulties. . . . We then called the families and prepared a press release profoundly grateful that we had been cautious, not gone with the reports that the press had sent out and stuck by our procedures of confirming all things as much as possible.

22. CPTnet, "Amman, Jordan: Report from CPTer Scott Kerr," Apr 1, 2003.

destroyed by Baath party officials covering their tracks. It completes the destruction of Iraqi history and culture. This started with the Gulf War and twelve years of sanctions, and now the rest has been destroyed. The history of the country and its people is gone. . . . Every day there are large gatherings of protestors outside the Palestine Hotel where the US administration is based. There are lots of street demonstrations elsewhere too and they are getting bigger. Some thank the US for coming but now they want the US to leave. People are tired and desperate. They are angry and explode at each other in a way I never saw before."[23]

The team's first focus in the conquest's aftermath was the piles of unexploded ordnance (missiles, bombs, grenades) left all over the city that were injuring curious children and other civilians.[24] When team members tried to alert U.S. forces so they could clean up the sites, or enclose them or mark them in some way, they received frustrating responses. "Each time, we have made the report, the Army personnel have said either we should make more reports, or that the munitions are partly burned and too dangerous for them to touch or that they have to wait for engineers or that the site is not a priority because the munitions are too unstable to transport or that we should make more reports," wrote Lisa Martens.[25]

After the team had spent almost two weeks in a fruitless effort to get the U.S. military to clean up these sites, they visited a four-year-old boy, Ali, whom a bright yellow cluster bomblet had blinded. A doctor who was treating the boy asked the team during their visit to the hospital why guarding the Oil Ministry was more of a priority for the U.S. than cleaning up the weapons sites. Since U.S. officers had told the team they could not mark off the sites because they did not have orange tape left, Lisa Martens wrote at the end of one release, "God help me, I would like to shut with bright coloured tape the mouths of Major Colin Mason, Lieutenant Wheeler, Jay Garner and several others, and sit them down in Ali's room for a while to listen."[26]

23. CPTnet, "Iraq Update: April 19, 2003."

24. For a more comprehensive list of their concerns, see CPTnet, "Iraq: Questions from CPT Iraq," Apr 30, 2003.

25. CPTnet, "Iraq: Not a priority," May 6, 2006.

26. Ibid. Wheeler's response to Martens, and her follow-up to that response, appeared in CPTnet releases, "Iraq: Letter from US Army Captain," Jan 2, 2004; and "Iraq: Letter from CPTer Lisa Martens," Jan 2, 2004.

Accordingly, the team's first action after the war was to encourage CPT's U.S. constituents to send pieces or rolls of brightly colored tape to their congressional representatives. In the accompanying letter, the team asked people to tell these representatives,

> I urge you to use your influence to ensure that international or locally-developed demolition teams are deployed to Baghdad and other areas in need, along with plenty of bright-coloured tape. This will assure Iraqis that the U.S. values their lives and the lives of their children more highly than Iraq's oil."[27]

THE OCCUPATION

The team soon found other reasons to intervene with the U.S. military. Between 2003 and 2004 they put out more than three hundred releases, documenting their accompaniment of Iraqis as individuals and during nonviolent demonstrations. As increasing numbers of Iraqis began approaching the team and telling them terrible stories of what coalition forces had done to their families during home raids, the team members also began documenting human rights abuses and atrocities[28] committed by coalition forces and their Iraqi trainees and the indifference of U.S. officers to Iraqis seeking redress. One officer, a Colonel Brennan, would tell them bluntly, "The U.S. Forces say no property was confiscated. I would trust an American soldier ten times more than any Iraqi." When they brought Iraqi human rights lawyers to talk to Colonel Nate Sassaman about abuses his unit had committed, he told CPTers the lawyers were frauds who were

27. CPTnet, "Iraq Action Alert: Send Coloured Tape," May 1, 2003. This release lists the efforts the team had put into getting one site taken care of since April 22, 2003. Prior April updates include information about other ordnance sites. The unavailability of the tape presaged the controversy Secretary of Defense Donald Rumsfeld was to ignite in December 2004 when he visited troops in Kuwait. Army Specialist Thomas Wilson asked him, "Why do we soldiers have to dig through local landfills for pieces of scrap metal and compromised ballistic glass to up-armor our vehicles, and why don't we have those resources readily available to us?" Rumsfeld replied, "As you know, you go to war with the army you have, not the army you might want or wish to have at a later time." See "Soldier's question puts Rumsfeld on spot."

28. See, for example, CPTnet, Holmes, "Iraq: U.S. soldiers kill four of their own," Dec 12, 2003; CPTnet, Cliff Kindy, "Iraq: CPTers investigate November 22 killings in Al Jazeera," Dec 27, 2003. See also Kern, "The rest of the story."

using team members. The day after the meeting, Sassaman's unit raided one of the lawyer's homes and detained him and his five brothers.[29]

In November and December 2003, the team began handing out leaflets to US soldiers they met with the following message:

> Like all human beings, Iraqis have a right to just treatment and respect. Yet many Iraqi families have shared with us their stories of U.S. troops violating their human rights and dignity. As a result, support is growing among Iraqis for violent resistance.
>
> If any Coalition soldier mistreats an Iraqi citizen, it endangers all Coalition soldiers. For your own safety and for the well being of Iraqi citizens, we invite you to abide by these principles taken from the Geneva Conventions, the Universal Declaration of Human Rights, and related humanitarian and human rights law:
>
> 1. Soldiers have a duty to protect civilians. Care must be taken not to harm those who are unarmed, or women, children, and the elderly or sick. Force should be used only when absolutely necessary and in proportion to the level of force threatened.
>
> 2. Coalition Forces, as the Occupying Power in Iraq, are ultimately responsible for ensuring that family members of detainees are notified as to where they will be detained.
>
> 3. It is against international law to punish a group of people collectively, (such as reprisal assaults on a family, neighborhood, or town) because individuals within that area have attacked Coalition Forces. Only those who have are guilty of wrongdoing should be punished.
>
> 4. Soldiers shall respect the property of civilians. If property is confiscated, a receipt must be issued with explicit instructions for how it may be retrieved.
>
> Iraqis detained by Coalition Forces have been held for months without charges, without legal counsel, and without contact with their families. The loss of husbands and fathers and the income and security they provide creates terrible hardship for families. Often men are detained on the basis of false information and malicious

29. CPTnet, "Iraq Update: January 1–17, 2004," Jan 23, 2004; Slater, e-mails, Jan 23 and 24, 2007; CPTnet, Cliff Kindy, "Iraq: U.S. military detains lawyer," Feb 10, 2004. Sassaman's career in the military would end after his superiors discovered he covered up evidence that men in his unit had thrown two captive Iraqis into the Tigris River and one of them had drowned. Chernus, "Is Anyone Responsible"; Filkins, "The Fall of the Warrior King."

rumors. Please remember that suspicion is not proof and that the men detained may be innocent of all wrongdoing....

You can be held liable for your actions in Iraq even if you are obeying orders from your commanding officer.

* * * * * * * *

When you return home, will you be able to tell your families that you acted with honor and compassion?[30]

2004

In the first week of 2004, the Iraq team released a sixteen-page report presenting seventy-two case studies of abuses that coalition forces had committed against Iraqi families during home raids that resulted in the detention of family members. The release announcing the availability of the report provides a good summary of the team's foci for 2003–2005: [31]

Violent House Raids

During these raids, soldiers seized men of the household almost indiscriminately and abused terrified family members. In a society where women covered their hair for modesty's sake, for a foreign soldier to see not only their hair but the women's bodies through their night clothes caused immense shame.

Family Visits with Prisoners

Many of the releases from 2003 and 2004 detail CPTers accompanying Iraqis to the U.S. authorities and trying to find out where the U.S. military was holding their family members. Often, the authorities gave the family wrong or misleading directions, and the families had no way to inquire about the detainees' well-being or whether they were getting necessary medications. Given that many detainees were injured during home raids, family members were especially anxious to know whether they were receiving treatment.

---

30. CPTnet, "Iraq: Text of Human Rights Leaflet," Dec 1, 2006; CPTnet, Milne, "CPTers leaflet," Dec 1, 2003.

31. CPTnet, "Iraq: CPT summary report," Jan 6, 2004; CPT Iraq, "Report and Recommendations."

Theft of Property

Confiscating jewelry and money from homes that Coalition Forces raided was one of the most underreported aspects of U.S. troop behavior in Iraq. In interview after interview, Iraq team members heard families tell about soldiers taking away their valuables. In one case, troops even sacked a church built in 1668, breaking the walls and taking church funds and the passports of the church workers.[32]

The Coalition Provisional Authority maintained soldiers had security reasons for confiscating property, and that owners would be recompensed after investigations, providing they had a receipt. In their report, team members wrote, "Team members have not heard of any instances in which Coalition forces gave the owners receipts for confiscated property." When they accompanied families to the Iraqi Assistance Center (IAC) to apply for compensation, the military authorities there would give them no proof that they had made the application, so they could not follow-up.

This callous disregard for the needs of already impoverished people inspired Allan Slater to do an ad hoc hunger strike at the Iraqi Assistance center. After U.S. military personnel closed the IAC an hour early on January 8, 2004—while twenty-four Iraqis were still waiting—Slater said he would refuse to leave the building until the soldiers helped them. Still waiting there at 1:00 p.m. the next day, he told the personnel that he would stay until he had a chance to talk to Coalition Provisional Authority administrator Paul Bremer or commander of coalition forces Lt. General Ricardo Sanchez about soldiers confiscating money, jewelry, and other property. Slater had been accompanying three men swept up in a September 30, 2003, house raid that Coalition Forces (CF) admitted later was a mistake. Despite that acknowledgement, however, the Coalition Provisional Authority (CPA) had not returned the Iraqis' property. Frustrated by how the IAC had been stringing the men along, Slater decided to fast until it addressed their concerns. However, once he realized he would not be able to do so outside of the IAC, he gave the idea up.[33]

---

32. CPTnet, Slater and Chandler, "CPT documents sacking of church," Nov 28, 2003. For other examples of looting, see CPTnet releases: "Iraq Update: May 13, 2003 10 p.m./2p.m. EDT," May 13, 2003; "Iraq Update: June 13–17, 2003," June 18, 2003; "Iraq Update: June 20–23, 2003," June 27, 2003; Milne, "Iraq: Operation Iraqi Freedom," Oct 6, 2003; "Iraq: Testimony of an Iraqi minor," Nov 3, 2003; "Iraq: Testimony of Saddam Saleh Al Rawi," June 2, 2004.

33. CPTnet, "Iraq: CPTer Allan Slater holding sit-in," Jan 8, 2004; CPTnet, "Iraq: CPTer

In its report, the team wrote,

> CPT urges Coalition forces to cease unnecessary confiscation of property, to issue receipts when confiscation is necessary, and to return all property that has been unjustly confiscated. . . . Many people who have applied for compensation for damaged and confiscated property have not received any written proof of their application. CPT urges the CPA to document and follow through on all requests for compensation, and to give families copies of all documents relating to compensation.[34]

Detentions of Innocent Persons and Mistreatment of Detainees

Often home raids resulted in coalition forces seizing every adolescent and adult male in a home or cluster of homes. In its report, the team noted that released detainees had reported that the military had put them in crowded tents without proper clothes or toilet facilities. CPTers had themselves seen soldiers leading handcuffed prisoners around with plastic bags over their heads.

The detainees and their families were especially bitter that the coalition forces were freeing ordinary criminals—who were taking advantage of the social upheaval to commit their crimes—to make space for the mostly innocent detainees.

Detainee issues would continue to be the primary focus of the team for the next two years.

PRISONER ABUSE SCANDAL

The January 2004 report about abuses committed during home raids received modest news coverage in the international media. Virtually no one came to the press conferences CPT held in Washington and Toronto to announce the availability of the report.[35] A team update covering the

Alan Slater begins hunger strike," Jan 10, 2004. In a January 23, 2007 e-mail, Slater wrote, "We were not aware of the interest the fast was generating in North America. That was unfortunate because I had been fasting long enough that my body had adjusted quite well. I was feeling fine."

34. CPTnet, "Iraq: CPT summary report," Jan 6, 2004. CPT Iraq, "Report and Recommendations."

35. Doug Pritchard, in his comments on a draft of this chapter, wrote:

> We also sent it to legislators and officials. Gene says a few US legislative aides began calling him about it. At this time, we learned later, the US

period January 1–17, 2004, mentions the *Toronto Globe and Mail, Toronto Star,* and ABC reporters interviewing the team about the report.[36] When Paul Bremer of the Coalition Provisional authority (CPA) announced that he would release 506 prisoners, some in CPT wondered if the report was partially responsible.[37] The team responded to Bremer's announcement by noting that of the seventy-two detainees in their report, only twenty-seven had been charged with a crime against the CPA and none had been charged with civil crimes. Furthermore, the team continued, the fact that families were unable to visit the detainees or get information on their whereabouts was especially troubling, as were the conditions under which the CPA was holding the detainees.[38]

As the team continued to accompany families seeking the whereabouts and conditions of their detained loved ones, they decided to employ what had become traditional CPT responses to injustice: letter-writing campaigns, fasting, and public witness. Accordingly, they posted the following release on February 10, 2004:

> Is this what you call a fast, a day acceptable to the Lord? THIS is the kind of fasting I desire: to loose the chains of injustice and untie the cords of the yoke, to set the oppressed free and break every yoke. Isaiah 58:5–6, 8, 12.
>
> . . . Mahmoud huddles beneath two blankets at Abu Ghraib prison outside Baghdad. U.S. forces raided his home by mistake last September. Aisha weeps for her imprisoned brothers and their

Army was doing its own internal investigations and so those aides may have been hearing about he problem elsewhere too.

Gene Stoltzfus wrote in a September 11, 2007, e-mail that he got calls every couple weeks beginning in January 2004 from national US media who had read the report and were interested in learning more about CPT's experience with detainees and their families. "Always the next question was 'Do you have photos?'" he wrote.

36. CPTnet, "Iraq Update: January 1–17, 2004," Jan 23, 2004. See Toronto Globe and Mail, "Report reveals humiliation of Iraqis at the hands of U.S. soldiers," January 19, 2004.

37. However, Sheila Provencher wrote in a January 26, 2007 e-mail:

> Honestly, I think that makes us sound presumptuous. I am sure that Bremer could not have cared less about CPT's report. The problems with detainee identification and location were severe, but the mistreatment we documented, while bad (thirst, hunger, sleep deprivation) was mild compared the extent of the revelations that eventually came out of Abu Ghraib. I don't think that anyone paid any attention to our report.

38. CPTnet, "Iraq: CPT responds to CPA's announcement," Jan 8, 2004.

4 IN HARM'S WAY

now-homeless wives and children. She has not seen them since June and cannot get permission to visit. A young soldier looks out at the night, haunted by what he has seen and done. . . .

No one knows how many Iraqis are being detained. The Coalition Provisional Authority is able to provide names and locations for 11,000 to 13,000 detainees, but human rights organizations estimate that there are over 18,000. Due process for the detained is unbearably slow or nonexistent, and many suffer abuse, hunger, and psychological distress in prison. Their families struggle to get by and wonder if their loved ones are dead or alive.

We fast to set the oppressed free and to break the yokes of injustice that keep thousands of Iraqis imprisoned without due process . . . We invite you to fast with us.

CPT members in Iraq will fast in a variety of ways (liquids-only, Ramadan-style dawn to dusk) and will engage in daily public witness in Baghdad.

Please JOIN THE FAST in whatever way you are able:

- Give up a meal, a TV show, or a favorite pastime each day during Lent. Spend that time in prayer for a detainee and their family . . .

- Write letters on behalf of Iraqi detainees and their families . . .

- Hold a public vigil to draw attention to the plight of Iraqi detainees. Possible symbols could include candles, posters of detainees, and wearing handcuffs and head-shrouds to graphically depict the situation of Iraqi detainees.[39]

The team launched its own forty-day public fast on February 26, 2004, appearing at Freedom Square/Tahrir Circle in downtown Baghdad on selected days with banners, fliers, and pictures of detainees. Some of those passing by expressed approval and reported on detained family members. Some were hostile, telling the team that the detainees were all criminals and the witness showed that CPTers were agents of Saddam Hussein. Other Iraqis and international journalists told the team they were in a dangerous part of the city controlled by gangs and thieves.

The team evaluated this feedback after several witnesses and decided to continue. To the question of whether the detainees for whom they were advocating deserved to be in prison, the team asserted that soldiers had rounded many of them up in indiscriminate neighborhood sweeps. They

39. CPTnet, "Iraq: Break Every Yoke—A Lenten Fast," Feb 9, 2004.

also noted that even criminals deserved to have their case settled through a fair judicial process.[40]

The Lenten witness had many positive outcomes for the team, including an understanding of the difference between Sunni and Shi'a Muslims, building solidarity with Iraqi human rights organizations—some of whom came all the way from Abu Ghraib and Karbala, gaining credibility with Iraqi religious leaders, and meeting the person who would become their most valuable translator. More than one thousand people from Canada, France, Germany, India, Israel, Nigeria, the Palestinian Territories, Sweden, Switzerland, and the United States would eventually participate in the team's "Adopt-a-Detainee" campaign launched at the time of the Lenten Witness.[41]

Unfortunately, these outcomes did not seem to have much of an effect on the problem of the ever-increasing detainee pool and lack of access detainee families had to their loved ones. Families began directing their anger toward the team and the Iraqi human rights lawyers who were trying to help them. Peggy Gish wrote,

> How should we respond? We can tell the families about our report on seventy-two detainee cases which we presented to policy makers under Bremer and high military officials in Iraq. We can tell them the lack of response has pushed us to use more confrontational actions. We can tell them about sending stories around the world, about our "adopt a-detainee" letter writing campaign and public Lenten fast and vigil. We can listen. We can report what the US government is doing here and say we are sorry. But basically, we have to tell them there is little we can do to change the system.
>
> We can walk away thinking that at least we have done what we could. They will continue to suffer the brunt of a violent and inflexible occupation system that has created the chaos and held back the desperately needed healing and repair.[42]

40. CPTnet releases: "Iraq: CPT launches 40-day public fast," Feb 26, 2004; Peggy Gish, "Iraq: Dangers and angels," Mar 6, 2004; "Iraq: Letter from Cliff Kindy," Mar 8, 2004.

41. Provencher, e-mail, Jan 26, 2007; CPTnet, "Iraq: CPT announces closure," Sept 21, 2005.

42. CPTnet, "Iraq: What we have and have not done," Mar 4, 2004. In her reflection, Peggy Gish wrote that an Iraqi human rights lawyer asked her if the team had achieved any results from its work with detainees. She asked what he thought, and he said, "I don't think so, but it's good for you to be here, for Christians and Muslims to work together." That comment reflects an underreported aspect of the Iraq team's work: supporting local Christians who were, at that time, about 8 percent of the population. Saddam Hussein's secular regime had provided some protection for religious minorities, but as Iraq be-

In the end, what brought the treatment of detainees to the attention of the international media was a factor outside the control of the team and their Iraqi colleagues. Spc. Joseph Darby stationed at the Abu Ghraib prison knew that a man in his unit, Charles Graner, was an amateur photographer and asked him if he could see photos of a shooting incident that had happened in Abu Ghraib while Darby had been on home leave. As Darby began looking through the digital photos, he was shocked to see pictures of U.S. soldiers abusing naked detainees. When he asked Graner, a Pennsylvania prison guard, about it he said Graner told him, "The Christian in me says it's wrong, but the corrections officer in me says, 'I love to make a grown man piss himself.'"

After Darby learned that Graner was returning to guard duty after an assignment to another job, he quietly dropped off the photos and an anonymous letter to the Criminal Investigative Division unit at the prison. General Antonio Taguba investigated the abuses and issued a secret report on February 25, 2004. The CBS news division acquired the report and the accompanying photos, but delayed their release at the request of the Defense Department. However, when CBS executives heard that the *New Yorker* was going to run the photos along with a report by Seymour Hersh, they showed them on an April 28, 2004, 60 Minutes II episode.

Hersh had won the Pulitzer Prize in 1970 for his reporting on U.S. soldiers committing atrocities in the Vietnamese village of My Lai. He also had interviewed members of the Iraq team in 2003 about abuses they would later include in their January 2004 report.[43] The resulting coverage made the media take a more serious look at this report. Although the team never put out an "I told you so" release, Americans for Middle East Understanding did devote an issue of its publication, *The Link*, to CPT's report, entitled, "Before '60 Minutes II, before the Red Cross Warnings,

came more Islamist after the invasion, Christians became a target. The teams worshipped regularly at local churches, brought delegations to meet Christian leaders, and kept warm relations with Christian clerics.

43. Provencher, e-mail, Jan 25, 2007. Hersh had heard reports of soldiers using dogs to intimidate prisoners at Abu Ghraib. The team had not heard of this happening at Abu Ghraib, but Cliff Kindy told him that US soldiers in the village of Ramadi had turned dogs on thirty handcuffed prisoners. Hersh's series of articles in the *New Yorker* on the Iraqi prisoner abuse scandals were incorporated into *Chain of Command*, which mentions Kindy and CPT on page 35. Later, during the 2005–2006 hostage crisis, Hersh referred to CPT's work as "cutting edge." Interview by Goodman, Nov 30, 2005.

before the Taguba Report, there was the CPT Report, and it went to U.S. Ambassador L. Paul Bremer III and U.S. Lt. General Richard Sanchez."[44]

Sheila Provencher authored the only team release specifically about the repugnant photos in which she asserted that the problem was not a "few bad people," but something systemic. She wrote,

> Every case I heard about abuse also included testimony about good and honorable soldiers. . . . However, most of the abuse we have documented—for which no soldiers will ever be court mar-tialed—is perpetrated by GOOD young men and women. These soldiers have somehow become dehumanized enough by training combat stress and neglect to deprive people of food, water and toilet facilities, to beat them and humiliate them. We need to ask, "How did this happen?" . . .
>
> The military ideology that separates the world into "good guys" and "bad guys" (I constantly hear this language) sees all security detainees as potential "bad guys." If a soldier who has watched his or her friends die and must take out his or her anger on someone, it is all too easy to abuse the closest "bad guy" although that "bad guy" might very well be a fifteen-year-old boy scooped up in a house raid because his uncle was a suspected Baathist. . . .
>
> Many Iraqis ARE guilty of terrible violence. One only has to watch the daily news to hear of regular, lethal attacks on young sol-diers. But by their own admission, military officials have chosen to cast a wide net when hunting for insurgents. . . . In order to capture one suspect, the Coalition forces arrest all of the male members of a household, during chaotic midnight raids that terrify entire families and sometimes end in the injury or death of women and children.
>
> And the devastation to Iraqis is only part of the suffering. What about the psychological and spiritual devastation to the soldiers who witness and perpetrate acts of violence upon Iraqi detainees?
>
> The number of soldiers who are becoming dehumanized by a system based on violent force is not negligible. We are all respon-sible for them. We are all responsible for these actions. And so we must all be part of the healing.[45]

---

44. *The Link* 37:3 (2004). The CPTnet release, "Iraq/Amman Update: May 3–6, 2004," May 14, 2004, does record Mark Frey in the Chicago office saying, "Is there a polite way of saying 'We told you so?'"

45. CPTnet, "Iraq: The Iraqi prisoner photos," May 4, 2004. A longer version of Provencher's release appeared in *America: The National Catholic Weekly*, under the title, "Responsibility and healing in Iraq."

The updates for May 2004 record many interactions with international media precipitated by the prisoner abuse scandal.[46] The disclosure of the photos made the families of the detainees increasingly frantic. Before, they did not know what was happening to the their loved ones. Now, they knew that they might be experiencing sexual abuse and other forms of torture. Friends of the team speculated that the U.S. had purposely released the photos to intimidate resistance fighters in Fallujah. Others expressed anger at the what they thought was a sham act of contrition on the part of U.S. authorities," [U.S. Secretary of Defense] Rumsfeld said he bears full responsibility for these acts," one man said, "So what? Was he raped? Was he naked? Was he dragged on the ground by a leash?"[47]

While the conditions for prisoners improved as a result of the prisoner abuse scandal,[48] the uproar over the abuses did not result in the release of prisoners whom the Coalition Forces were holding without charge. Although the Coalition Provisional Authorities announced that they released hundreds of prisoners every day, Greg Rollins wrote, "Inside the word 'release' there is still a prison." The CPA counted prisoners sent to the infirmary or to another detention center "released." And when they told the families of detainees that they had "released" the prisoner, the families became every more angry with the authorities and fearful that "released" could refer to the prisoner simply disappearing as many had

---

46. The sudden worldwide interest in the issue caused the team and the Iraqi human rights organizations with which they worked to do some awkward reporting. See for example, the CPTnet releases: "Iraq: CPT takes testimony from photographed detainee," May 12, 2004; "Iraq: CPT Iraq retracts prisoner abuse testimony," May 22, 2004; "Iraq: Testimony of Saddam Saleh Al Rawi," June 2, 2004.

Doug Pritchard, in his comments on a draft of this chapter, wrote:

> We began receiving lots of phone calls from journalists then saying, "You told us about this in January and we ignored it. Now can we interview some of these families you mention?" . . . The report added to our credibility with media and other international human rights groups like AI, HRW, and the UN. CPT was therefore among the first to report on this very big issue and I am glad it finally got the attention it needed. But we remain frustrated that the Administration was able to spin it that this was only a handful of low-ranking soldiers in one prison at one time who did this. Our experience . . . was that it occurred to every detainee in every holding facility across Iraq with authority from the highest levels, and even the US Army acknowledged that 70–90% of these detainees were innocent of any crime.

47. CPTnet, "Iraq/Amman Update: May 7–10, 2004," May 17, 2004.

48. CPTnet, Rollins, "Iraq: A ray of hope," June 17, 2004.

under Saddam Hussein's regime. When the team visited Abu Ghraib on June 16, they found no office for helping people find detained family members, which workers for the Iraqi Ministry of Human Rights (IMHR) had assured them was there. They saw three lines of visitors standing outside with no protection from the fierce Middle Eastern sun. A soldier who spoke no Arabic and had no translator provided security for the lines. He and a soldier at another entrance had no knowledge of an IMHR office. People waiting outside the prison told CPTers that they now could visit their family members more frequently, but the visits lasted for only fifteen minutes. Families could not bring clothes for the detainees—a real problem, because detainees were often arrested in their nightclothes. Muslim prisoners were still finding pork in their meals.[49]

Nevertheless, the team felt their efforts, and those of their constituents who had participated in the Adopt-A-Detainee campaign, had borne fruit. A low-ranking officer gave the team a list of about six thousand detainees that it used in helping families find their loved ones. Then after the Abu Ghraib scandal, the army put up a website listing thousands of the detainees as another resource for families.[50]

In a Campaign update, the team wrote,

> Your work has made a real difference, especially during the weeks of publicity surrounding the detainee abuse. U.S. legislators, international human rights associations, and other officials viewed CPT's research into the abuses of detainees and their families as more credible because all of you had sounded the alarm long before the scandal broke.[51]

OTHER TEAM ACTIVITIES IN 2004

Even without the work the team put into issues of detainees, 2004 would have been a notable year for the Iraq team. In February, two men claiming they wanted to know more about CPTers' work with detainees and nonviolence visited the team's apartment in Baghdad. After a short discussion,

49. CPTnet, Rollins, "Iraq: Inside the word "Release," May 27, 2004; CPTnet, "Iraq: June 16," June 26, 2004. For a description of the detainees' clothing situation, see CPTnet, "Iraq Update: June 12–15, 2004," June 23, 2004.

50. Pritchard, comments on a draft of this chapter. Regarding the Web site, Pritchard noted, "I think the website was taken down in Nov 2004 'for maintenance' and never restored but it was useful for awhile."

51. CPTnet, "Iraq: Detainee campaign update," July 1, 2004.

one of the men told the CPTers his friend had a bomb strapped to him that he would detonate if they did not cooperate. They then proceeded to tie up Jim Loney, Cliff Kindy, and Stewart Vriesinga with computer mouse cables and told Jane Wright and Peggy Gish to get the team's money and computer equipment. "We kept talking to them in caring ways," Peggy Gish reported. After taking about $800 in US currency and some computer equipment, the two men warned the CPTers not to leave the apartment or call for help. "I don't want to kill you, Jesus loves you people," said the man with the gun. "Jesus loves you too," Kindy told him.[52]

Officials who maintained the Shi'a Kadhum shrine in Baghdad, asked the team in March to monitor an annual pilgrimage there, because Sunni Muslim insurgents had made threats against the Shi'a Muslim community. On March 2, gunmen fired at an Iraqi police vehicle at 5:15 a.m. at the height of the celebration. Shrine officials told the team they believed other insurgents took advantage of the diversion to plant bombs with timers that detonated at 10:00 a.m. The windows of the hotel room where CPTers were monitoring the activity shattered at the explosion. The blood of the bombings's victims sprayed up three stories of a shrine wall. Helpless, the team could only document with their video camera the injured victims screaming among corpses and bystanders helping the Red Crescent ambulance workers collect body parts. They also began praying when a convoy of US army vehicles, including tanks and ambulances, arrived to help, unaware that someone had seized the mosque's microphone and blamed the attacks on the Americans and "the Jewish." The crowd began throwing shoes (a sign of outrage), rocks, and other debris at the soldiers, who responded by firing in the air. The Shrine's overseer, learning about the unauthorized announcement and the arrival of the troops called their base commander and told him to withdraw the troops for their own safety. He then used the loudspeaker to forbid revenge attacks on soldiers, police, and other authorities. At least thirty-eight pilgrims died.[53]

52. CPTnet, Peggy Gish, "CPTers physically threatened," Feb 13, 2004.

53. The annual religious observance commemorates the martyrdom of Hussein, the grandson of the Prophet Mohammed. Saddam Hussein's regime had forbidden the pilgrimage for thirty-five years. CPTnet, "Iraq: CPTers witness attacks on Shi'a shrine" Mar 5, 2004. Half an hour before the Kadhum bombing, militants had attacked a shrine in Karbala, a holy city to Shi'a Muslims, and killed more than one hundred pilgrims.

EVACUATION AND RETURN

In April, the bloody U.S. assault on Fallujah that killed numerous civilian women and children prompted the team to put out an Urgent Action asking U.S. citizens to contact their legislators and urge them to intervene. Canadian constituents were asked to contact Prime Minister Paul Martin and urge him to contact Canadian Brigadier General Walt Natynczyk, Deputy Chief of Strategy and Planning for Coalition Forces (CF).

"Ask Martin to tell Natynczyk that he needs to come up with a new strategy, because the current one the CF are using is getting a lot of people—soldiers and civilians—killed," the team wrote.[54]

The assault on Fallujah had other consequences for the team. Hearing reports that 60 percent of the fatalities were women and children, Iraqis began targeting their anger at all internationals connected in some way with the Multinational Forces. In early April, thirty foreigners were kidnapped in Iraq and several killed.[55] The team's most trusted Iraqi partners urged the team to leave for Amman, because in that climate, their work would become impossible, and their presence might actually endanger Iraqi coworkers and neighbors. They thus joined the thousands of Iraqis and other internationals thronging the airport on April 14, 2004. Most NGO representatives never came back to Iraq.

LeAnne Clausen and Stewart Vriesinga returned quietly to Baghdad on May 3, 2004, to assess the situation. "Given the special risks to foreigners in the past month as well as concerns of the team's family, friends, and colleagues," the team wrote in a May 1, 2004 CPTnet release, "members of CPT Iraq have prepared the following statement in preparation for their return. This release is being distributed to international and Iraqi media sources."

> CPT Iraq Statement of Conviction:
>
> CPT Iraq evacuated to Amman on April 14th, at the urging of our Iraqi partners and friends due to the deteriorating conditions within the country. Now, with support from our Iraqi contacts, we are returning to determine whether we can continue our work of witnessing to justice and peace where there is violence.

---

54. CPTnet, "Iraq Urgent Action: Stop excessive use of force," Apr 13, 2004. See also CPTnet releases,: "Iraq: Letter from Iraq team," Apr 10, 2004; "Iraq: CPT colleagues describe massacre in Fallujah," Apr 13, 2004; "Iraq: An open letter to Brigadier General Walter Natynczyk," Apr 22, 2004."

55. See LaMotte, "Iraq/Kidnappings."

We are aware of the risks both Iraqis and internationals face at this time. However, we are convinced that these risks are not disproportionate to our purposes in returning, nor greater than the risks faced by soldiers, other armed actors, or fellow human rights workers.

Iraqi friends and human rights workers have welcomed us as a nonviolent, independent presence. They ask us to tell their stories, since they cannot easily be heard, nor can most flee to a safer country. They ask us to be the eyes and ears recording the abuses of the occupation and the devastating effects of violence. Especially when other international monitoring bodies have pulled out, our presence provides a vital link between people in North America and Iraq....

We reject the use of violent force to save our lives should we be kidnapped or caught in the middle of a violent conflict situation. We also reject violence to punish anyone who harms us, and we ask that there be no retaliation against such a person's relatives or property. We forgive those who consider us to be their enemies. Therefore, any response should be in the form of rehabilitation rather than in the spirit of revenge.

We hope that in loving both friends and enemies and by intervening nonviolently to aid those who are systematically oppressed, we can contribute in some small way to transforming this volatile situation.

(Signed)

Christian Peacemaker Team in Iraq
Matthew Chandler (Portland, OR)
Le Anne Clausen (Mason City, IA)
Sheila Provencher (South Bend, IN)
Greg Rollins (Surrey, BC)
Stewart Vriesinga (Lucknow, ON)[56]

NAJAF

The release announcing the departure of the team from Iraq had noted, "... Iraqis are afraid that the residents of Najaf will soon experience the same treatments as the residents of Fallujah have." Given that Najaf contained the holiest Shi'a Muslim shrine in the world, the consequence of

56. CPTnet releases: "Iraq: CPT delegation and team leave Baghdad," Apr 14, 2004; "Amman: Letter from Greg Rollins," Apr 16, 2004; "Iraq: Christian Peacemaker Teams to Return," May 1, 2004.

an attack on that city would have inflamed Iraqi anger against American forces to an even greater extent. Thus, upon CPT's return, Najaf became a focus of the team. To pre-empt a battle between U.S. forces and armed militants under the authority of Shi'a cleric Moqtada al-Sadr, representatives of Iraqi Human Rights Watch-Kerbala,[57] the team's primary Iraqi partners—along with the principal Shi'a Cleric Grand Ayatollah Sistani—decided to organize a pilgrimage of sorts from Karbala to Najaf and asked CPT to accompany it. U.S. troops stopped the August 14, 2004, procession, which included 150 vehicles, ten kilometers outside of Najaf, and participants held a vigil there until the early evening. CPTers also participated with tens of thousands of Iraqis in another nonviolent procession to Najaf on August 26 that was organized by the Grand Ayatollah Sistani. He had issued an invitation to his followers to gather in Najaf to help find a peaceful solution to the conflict there and reclaim the holy site. After the throng had reached the checkpoint, Sistani, who had entered the city earlier to get opposing forces to talk, told them to go home. The Iraqi police had killed four people who had tried to enter two hours earlier. As the group left, streams of bullets began hitting the concrete in the lot where cars from the pilgrimage procession had parked. Nonetheless, a representative from Iraqi Human Rights Watch told the team that he thought the massive nonviolent turnout signaled a new beginning.[58]

2005

Taking the testimonies of detainees and their families continued to be a primary focus of the Iraq team until September 2005, when the team ended its Adopt-A-Detainee campaign. As one response to the Abu Ghraib scandal, the Multinational Forces began holding detainees on military base detention facilities instead of in "official" prisons like Abu Ghraib and Bucca. The detainees in these "hidden prisons" were not counted with the total prisoner population, making monitoring numbers and treatment of detainees difficult.[59] The updates record U.S. soldiers's treatment

57. This organization has no connection to the better known international organization, Human Rights Watch.

58. See CPTnet releases: "Iraq: Iraqis conduct vigil," Aug 13, 2004; "Iraq: Soldiers prevent Iraqi peacemakers," Aug 14, 2004; Rollins, "Iraq: the tightrope in Najaf," Aug 16, 2004. Milne, "CPTers participate in massive nonviolent procession," Aug 27, 2004; "Iraq Update: August 21–26, 2004," Aug 31, 2004.

59. CPTnet, Cliff Kindy "Iraq: Hidden U.S. prisons," Jan 14, 2004.

of prisoners's families as similar to pre-scandal treatment. One woman reported the guards having set dogs on the visitors and laughing as they ran or crawled to get away. After soldiers at the Scania military base told a mother whose son had been taken in a raid on April 26, 2005, that they could not tell her the charges, allow her to see her son or tell her when he would be released or transferred, she left weeping. Provencher, who had accompanied the woman, tried to explain to the soldiers the sorts of trauma that families of detainees experience when they cannot find their detained loved ones. One of the soldiers asked her, "What should we do—put a sticky note on the door, saying, "We took your son, here's where you can find him?"

On a return visit to the Scania military base on May 17, Greg Rollins and Joe Carr talked with two Iraqi men who had been released four days earlier and were now seeking compensation for property American soldiers had taken in a house raid. During the raid, one man saw them take a Quran from the top of his refrigerator and step on it. He said that the guards at Scania had given them only biscuits (cookies) and water, took them to the bathroom four times a day and allowed them to shower every two days (an issue when the temperature was often 120 degrees). Cells measuring 6 x 8 meters commonly held fourteen to fifteen detainees. Although American soldiers had not beaten him, Iraqi soldiers had. In other interviews at the base, CPTers heard of a man shot when an MNF convoy appeared on the wrong side of the street where the man was driving and thought he was a suicide bomber, of a landlord arrested and held because the forces were looking for his previous tenant whose current whereabouts were unknown to the landlord. One family had had soldiers repeatedly raiding their home for a father and son whom they were already holding at the Scania base; soldiers told another family that two sons had been "released" to Abu Ghraib.[60]

The team cited the unresponsiveness of the U.S. government to letter writers as the primary reason for shutting down the Adopt-a-Detainee letter writing campaign in September 2005. Prior to that announcement, Peggy Gish wrote about the visit of "Waleed." He had been searching for his nephew Yassar, who had been part of the campaign, since the US military took him away in spring 2003. "We suspect," Gish wrote, "that in

---

60. See CPTnet releases: "Iraq Update: 3–6 April 2005," Apr 19 2005; "Iraq Update: 1–5 May 2005," May 14, 2005; "Iraq Update: 17–21 May 2005"; "Iraq Update: 14–18 June 2005," June 24, 2005; Fox, "Iraq Reflection: Exit interviews," June 28, 2005.

most of these cases, the disappeared person is actually dead. Friends and family have said this to Waleed, but he, like many others has not had any evidence to give him closure . . . he knows we care, but we are also among the many in the past two years who have been unable to help him find the truth that can help him move on with his life.[61]

The team began hearing sinister stories in 2005 about Iraqi forces, to which the US had theoretically transferred sovereignty, committing egregious abuses and even assassinations of detainees. In particular, they began hearing stories of torture committed by an Iraqi police unit called "the Wolf Brigade." In November, they asked their constituents to join an Amnesty International (AI) letter-writing campaign, prompted by interviews that CPT facilitated between AI representatives and Palestinians tortured by the Wolf Brigade.

Although the Adopt-a-Detainee campaign ended, releases over the next months show that the treatment of detainees remained a primary focus of the Iraq team.[62]

Two elections were another focus of the Iraq team in 2005. In the first, held on January 30, Iraqis elected a Transitional National Assembly, provincial councils for each of Iraq's provinces, and Kurdistan Regional Government. The team noted a lack of enthusiasm on the part of Iraqi friends and acquaintances regarding this election. On January 5, a widowed neighbor with three children told them she was too afraid to vote, but said that if she did, we would say, "Give us electricity." Another neighbor told the team on the same day that only about half of the residents in the district had received ballots and voiced the suspicion that the ballots may have been stolen as part of an election fraud scheme. Sunni leaders were encouraging Sunnis not to vote, because they viewed the elections as a "tool of the Americans." An Iraqi Christian friend told them, "This will not be a perfect election. In fact, it will be the worst. But it is step one. I have never had the right to vote before, so of course I will use it." Given the team's positive relationships with both Sunnis and Shias, a representative of the Iraqi electoral commission asked them to serve as election observers. After some discussion, the team decided not to because of concerns about the U.S. influence on the election. They did, however observe the

61. CPTnet, "Iraq: Waleed's quest," Sept 2, 2005.

62. See CPTnet releases: "Iraq: Waleed's quest," Sept 1, 2005; Iraq Update: 26–31 August 2005; "Iraq: CPT announces closure," Sept 21, 2005; Rollins, "Iraq: A police state," July 20, 2005; "Iraq Action Alert: CPT and Amnesty Int'l," Nov 9, 2005.

election in Karbala under the auspices of an Iraqi human rights organization. Peggy Gish reported that the mood of the people in Karbala,
a mostly Shi'a city, was upbeat about the election. On the doorway of a
school that served as a polling place, a sign in Arabic read, "Today is the
real Iraq wedding." However, she noted at the end of the release that the
elections would probably not bring much change to Iraqis' quality of life.
If this quality of life did not improve, she wrote, "Iraqis will find their new
hope and excitement crushed again."[63]

On October 15, 2005, Iraqis voted to ratify the new constitution and
on December 15, 2005, to elect a permanent 275-member Council of
Representatives. Because half of the team was accompanying Palestinians
fleeing to Syria in October, the team mentioned the October 15 election
only in passing. Because team and delegation members had been taken
hostage before the December 15 election, it passed unmentioned.[64]

MUSLIM PEACEMAKER TEAMS

The team was not in Karbala in January 2005 only for the elections. They
were conducting a five-day training for a group that had taken the title,
"Muslim Peacemaker Teams." Some of the members were Iraqi human
rights lawyers that the team had met in the course of their work of the
previous two years. Appalled by the violence conducted in the name of
Islam around the world, the group wanted to promote nonviolence similar

---

63. See CPTnet releases: "Iraq Update: 9–16 January 2005," Jan 18, 2005; "Iraq Update:
16–20 January 2005," Jan 21, 2005; Provencher, "Iraq Reflection: The Daily Dance," Jan 24,
2005; Cliff Kindy, "Iraq: Election prelude," Jan 31, 2005; Peggy Gish, "Iraq: Observing the
elections," Feb 1, 2005; Slater, "A tale of two elections," Feb 1, 2005; "Iraq Update: 27–31
January," Feb 7, 2005. Doug Pritchard, commenting on a draft of this chapter, wrote:

> [T]he team has described to me Iraqis' anger at the form of elections
> imposed on them by Bremer as a major cause of the current sectarian-
> ism and violence. Because the country was declared as one electorate
> with proportional representation and little time for political parties
> to form and prepare platforms, people only had sectarian identities to
> use to distinguish among the 200 parties and coalitions who were on
> the ballot. Most voters therefore voted accordingly (Sunnis for Sunni
> parties etc) since that was all they knew about these parties. This has
> entrenched this new sectarianism into the parliament and govt in un-
> precedented ways. It is a complex but very powerful explanation for
> what has happened.

64. CPTnet, "Iraq Update: 26–31 August 2005," Sept 5, 2005; CPTnet, "Iraq Update:
September 28–30, 2005."

to that which CPT promoted, but grounded in Islam's tenets.[65] They also had all experienced significant trauma over the past two decades under the Saddam Hussein regime and the Iraq/Iran war, and were seeking ways to form a better society. "With MPT, we want to live the real Islam—the loving, the helping," one of the group told CPTers in December 2004.[66]

A particular concern of the newly founded MPT was healing the divide between Sunni and Shi'a, which Multinational Forces exacerbated when they wreaked havoc on Sunni cities like Fallujah. MPTers noted that in the 1960s, Iraqi Muslims, Christians, and Jews had lived together peacefully in Karbala; they wanted to devise strategies for making living that way again possible between Shi'a and Sunnis. After hearing Cliff Kindy describing Israeli groups rebuilding Palestinian homes that the Israeli military had demolished, MPT members began thinking about what sort of witness they might do in Fallujah.[67]

The team had been concerned about the plight of Fallujans for some time (see n. 55). An April 2004 U.S. invasion and bombing of the city killed hundreds of Iraqi civilians, left many more homeless and devastated the city's infrastructure. By December 2004, an estimated six thousand Fallujans had been killed by Coalition Forces. Eyewitnesses reported troops killing civilians waving white clothing.[68] A refugee crisis then resulted from Fallujans fleeing to surrounding villages and to Baghdad, where the local inhabitants had little in the way of food or money they could share with them.

Muslim Peacemaker Team members had already helped Fallujan refugees in the Ain Tamur refugee camp, but since the camp was in the district where most of them lived, they did not feel a particular threat. Actually going to the predominately Sunni city of Fallujah—whose citizens were enraged by the attacks they had suffered at the hands of Coalition Forces and what they saw as collaboration by Shi'a leaders—was another

---

65. The Shi'a founders of MPT noted that one of their leaders, Imam Hussein, had, like Jesus, sacrificed himself for others and shown love to enemies. See Sheila Provencher's CPTnet release, "Iraq: Kerbala's Pilgrims," Apr 23, 2005.

66. CPTnet, "Iraq Update: December 5–11," Dec 16, 2004. For accounts of the training see CPTnet releases: Cliff Kindy, "Iraq Reflection: A Trauma Story," Jan 27, 2005; "Iraq: Muslim Peacemaker Team training," Feb 2, 2005; "Iraq Update: 21–26 January 2004," Feb 4, 2004. See also CPTnet, "Iraq: Iraqis conduct vigil," Aug 13, 2004, which mentions Hussain il Ibrahimi, the director of Iraqi Human Rights Watch in Karbala. He and Sami Rasouli (see below) were probably the most instrumental in getting MPT off the ground.

67. CPTnet, Peggy Gish, "Iraq Reflection: Overcoming the Divide," Feb 2, 2005.

68. Project Censored, "Top 25 Censored Stories of 2006."

matter. However, after some exploratory visits to Fallujah by the team and Sami Rasouli—an Iraqi-American who was one of the movers and shakers behind the Muslim Peacemaker Teams—MPTers felt ready to conduct a joint action with CPT in Fallujah.

On May 6, 2005, the Shi'a MPTers traveled to the city with CPT to help clean up rubble left by the US attacks there. A Sunni cleric, describing the devastation of the city and lack of help from the Coalition Forces to repair infrastructure, told them, "It will take fifty years at this rate to return Fallujah to the condition it was in before the U.S. attacked us."[69] The CPTers and MPTers joined with employees from the Department of Public works to clean a street outside one of the largest mosques in the city. To those passing by, they handed leaflets saying, "Muslim Peacemaker Teams from Karbala and Najaf is pleased to be in Fallujah in order to assist in the ongoing clean-up efforts. We are among our brothers and sisters in the city of Fallujah to recognize our solidarity with you." Following the cleanup, the MPTers joined Sunnis in the mosque for Friday prayers.

The team returned to Fallujah with the MPTers in November to visit some of the contacts they had made there. Sadly, when one of the MPTers asked a cleric whether an MPT group might be started in Fallujah, he replied that most Fallujans trusted neither Shi'a nor U.S. citizens.[70]

ACCOMPANIMENT OF PALESTINIANS TO SYRIAN BORDER

Another joint venture of CPT and MPT was accompaniment of Palestinian Iraqis fleeing the country. The team had first learned about the plight of the Palestinians in 2003, shortly after the invasion. During his regime,

69. As of summer 2007, civilian infrastructure in almost all areas of Iraq was still not functioning as well as it had under Saddam Hussein. Team updates contain many references to lack of electricity. Doug Pritchard, in his comments on a draft of this chapter, wrote:

> This is something that continues to enrage Iraqis. They expected so much from the coalition but most of the billions seems to have been wasted on security contractors, corruption and boondoggles with no improvement in supplies of electricity, gasoline, water, sewage . . . Iraqis note that after the Gulf War, Saddam was able to get bombed power stations back on line within 6 months with local engineers and scrounged parts. But the mighty USA with its Haliburton engineers still have not increased electricity supplies after 4 years!

70. See CPTnet releases: "Iraq Update: 3–6 April 2005; "Iraq Update: 26–30 April 2005," May 7, 2005; "Iraq: CPTers and Shi'a MPTers," May 9, 2005; "Iraq Update: 1–7 November 2005," Nov 19, 2005.

Saddam Hussein had subsidized the housing of Palestinian refugees, but refused to increase the subsidy as years passed, which meant landlords lost money on them. After the fall of his regime, many landlords evicted their Palestinian tenants so they could charge market rates for their apartments. Two hundred evicted families eventually set up tents in a Baghdad sports stadium.[71] As the situation deteriorated in Iraq, the conditions for the Palestinians worsened. Even Palestinians born in Iraq had always had to reapply for residency permits every six months. Now they had to do so every month. When team members went to apply for their own residency permits, they were typically in a room full of Palestinians. The Wolf Brigade began targeting Palestinians, kidnapping them, and torturing them. Under the torture—which in at least one case involved boring through a man's leg with an electric drill—Palestinians would confess to acts of terrorism they had not committed. Later in the year, the Iraqi Minister of Immigration said that all Palestinians in Iraq should be forced to move to Gaza.[72]

By October 2005, the team may have been the only international NGO remaining outside the Green Zone in Baghdad. Exhausted by their work and Iraq's general slide into chaos, they had decided to take a spiritual retreat in the more stable zone of northern Iraq. The only safe way to get there was by plane, but the levels of fatigue and stress in the team were so great, CPT staff deemed the tickets for a Monday through Thursday retreat a necessary expense. On the Saturday before they were to leave, team members received a call from the Palestinian refugee camp in Baghdad. About twenty Palestinians were leaving for Syria on Tuesday and wanted CPT and MPT to help get them through the many checkpoints along the way.

That Saturday night, the team started what they assumed would be a long consensus process to discern whether they should go on their much-needed retreat or do the accompaniment. Tom Fox, at the start of the meeting, suggested having a time of silence for the team to search

71. CPTnet, "Iraq Update: June 17–20, 2003," June 30, 2004; CPTnet, Maureen Jack, "A new refugee camp in Baghdad," July 21, 2003.

72. See CPTnet releases: "Iraq Update: 16–27 March 2005," Apr 7, 2005; "Iraq Update: 23–24 June 2005," July 5, 2005; "Iraq Update: 13–14 July 2005," July 27, 2005; "Iraq Update 24–31 October, 2005," Nov 8, 2005. See also CPTnet, "Iraq Action Alert: Help Stop State-Sponsored Torture," Nov 2, 2005; "Iraq Action Alert: CPT and Amnesty Int'l," Nov 9, 2005.

their hearts, saying that by listening to the Spirit, they might find that the decision was not too difficult. After the time of silence, the team took ten minutes to come to a consensus that they should accompany the Palestinians.[73]

On October 4, Tom Fox, Sheila Provencher, and Beth Pyles, along with Sami Rasouli,[74] one of the leaders of Muslim Peacemaker Teams, boarded a bus early in the morning with twenty Palestinian refugees from Baghdad and traveled to the Syrian border.[75] However, upon successfully arriving at the border and passing through Iraqi immigration, the refugees found that Syria was refusing them entry. That first night at the border, the Palestinians and their accompaniers slept on the ground and in truck beds among honking horns and diesel fumes, not knowing what would happen to them the next day. Fox told Provencher, "I think Hell must sound like a truck stop." The Palestinians told Pyles it was the best night's sleep they had had in years. When Tom Fox asked one man what he would do if the UN and Syria were unable to reach a solution and told them to return to Iraq, the man replied, "We will either stay here or die before we return to the certain death of Iraq."

CPTers remained encamped with the Palestinian for thirteen days while the United Nations High Commissioner for Refugees (UNHCR) negotiated with the Syrian government over where the refugees could go. When Pyles, Provencher, Fox and Rasouli returned to Baghdad, they remained behind. On November 10, the team received word that the Syrian government had allowed the families to move further into Syria and they were now living in a refugee camp that provided houses instead of tents.[76]

---

73. Holmes, "Standing Firm." A shorter version of Holmes' eulogy appeared in CPTnet, "Toronto: Standing firm—Bob Holmes' eulogy," Apr 5, 2006.

74. When asked to describe Rasouli, Sheila Provencher wrote, in a February 12, 2007 e-mail:

> ... he makes everything happen, he is amazing at bonding with people and reaching across sectarian lines. he is full of ideas and drive and he will never give up no matter what suffering he endures. proof positive, he has stayed in iraq through all of this, he only leaves for two months in feb-march to give a vast speaking tour, often several talks per day.

75. Jordan, Kuwait, Turkey, Saudi Arabia, and Iran had closed their borders to Iraqi refugees by this time.

76. See CPTnet releases: "Iraq: Christian and Muslim Peacemaker Teams accompany Palestinians," Oct 5, 2005; "Iraq Update: 1–8 October 2005," Oct 18, 2005; "Iraq Update: 9–16 October 2005," Oct 27, 2005; "Iraq/Syrian Border: Iraqi Palestinians in No One's Land," Oct 24, 2005; "Iraq Update: November 8–10, 2005," Nov 26, 2005. See also Fox,

Rana Abdulla, of Ottawa, Canada, who had used her own money to bring more than fifty stateless Arab refugees to Canada in the past, wrote to CPT staff after reading team releases about the Palestinians' predicament. Tom Fox responded to her offer of help and she ultimately agreed to act as their sponsor. The first group of six arrived in Ottawa on June 20, 2007, fifteen months after Fox was slain in captivity. In honor of Fox's memory, Abdulla referred to the refugees as "Tom Fox's people."[77]

THE DOWNWARD SPIRAL

Taken as a whole, the updates and releases from 2005 reflect a continually deteriorating situation for everyone living in Iraq. Almost every update contained reports of the team hearing gunfire exchanges and explosions and experiencing electricity and water outages. In a reflection on how governments and soldiers demonize their enemies, Jan Benvie mentioned, almost in passing, waiting in a line of traffic when a car bomb exploded some meters ahead of her.[78] On November 13, a mortar landed on the roof of the team's apartment building, destroying four water tanks and four satellite dishes and blowing out many windows but, somewhat surprisingly, injuring no one.[79]

Not included in the releases was CPTer Justin Alexander's hasty departure from the team in April 2005 when an Iraqi friend told him that his name had appeared on an abduction list—possibly because he had given some television interviews after his friend Marla Ruzicka died in a car bomb explosion.[80] The team also did not publicize its accompaniment of a convoy bringing relief supplies to the city of Tal Afar, populated largely by the Turkmen ethnic group, which U.S. and Iraqi forces were besieging. Shi'a cleric Muqtada al-Sadr organized the convoy and accompaniment

"Snapshots from the Syrian Border"; Provencher, "Our Refugee Family."

77. CPTnet, Iraq/Canada: Iraqi-Palestinian refugees," June 24, 2007; Provencher, e-mail, June 25, 2007. Provencher took over as Abdulla's contact after Fox was kidnapped. "World Refugee Day highlights worsening crisis."

78. CPTnet, "The good, the bad and the innocent," Aug 29, 2005.

79. CPTnet, "Iraq Reflection: Normal," Dec 1, 2005. A note at the beginning of this release read, "The following reflection was written ten days ago by a CPTer no longer in Iraq," which indicates the team's awareness of the dangers they were facing. See CPTnet, "Iraq Update: 11–14 November 2005," Dec 6, 2005.

80. Alexander, e-mail, July 18, 2007. Ruzicka founded Campaign for Innocent Victims in Conflict (CIVIC), an organization that counted civilian casualties and assisted Iraqi victims of the 2003 U.S. invasion of Iraq.

by the (Sunni) Muslim Scholars Association and CPT. Other participants in the convoy were heavily armed, contrary to assurances made to the team when they agreed to accompany it. On the way back to Baghdad, the convoy was attacked by unknown armed actors. Iraqis riding in a black car were killed, and team members Maxine Nash and Jan Benvie were told that they, the "foreigners," who were also riding in a black car, might have been the intended targets.[81]

"As terrible as life was under Saddam," CPTer William Van Wagenen wrote in September 2005, " life for Iraqis is now much worse."

> In addition to the fear of terrorist bombings, Iraqi civilians suffer from mass detentions and torture at the hands of the Iraqi security forces, who are now engaged in a bloody counterinsurgency war. U.S. forces bomb populated urban cities (Fallujah, Qaim, and more recently Haditha) from the air, killing civilians and destroying homes, while the terrorists simply leave the area and regroup elsewhere. Crushing poverty, joblessness, and high child mortality rates compound the suffering yet further. Despite the disaster that the U.S. invasion and subsequent occupation of Iraq have brought upon the Iraqi people, President Bush insists we "stay the course," when the continuing occupation of Iraq is itself the problem.[82]

Greg Rollins, at the end of November 2005, wrote of an outing to the Baghdad Zoo at the invitation of the team's driver. He noted the sorry state of most of the animals, including a "depressed, almost comatose porcupine." Indignant at one man who was throwing rocks at the porcupine that landed amid garbage that other people had thrown at it, Rollins wrote that he wanted to ask him how he would feel if someone were treating him that way.

"Then I realized that the Baghdad Zoo mirrors the state of the country," Rollins wrote.

> Most Iraqis are caged in. They can't leave. And other people, whether they are foreign armies, foreign militants or foreign corporations, think of themselves and what they want from this place

---

81. Pritchard, interview, June 18, 2007; Benvie, e-mail, June 27, 2007. As was the case with the threat to Alexander, the team did not publicize the convoy for reasons of security.

82. CPTnet, "Iraq: 'These uniforms draw a lot of attention,'" Sept 2, 2005. Van Wagenen noted in this release that James Steele, who had overseen Salvadoran security forces' activities in the 1980s when they were committing unspeakable atrocities, was now an advisor for Iraqi commando units.

1 2

"A Great Hand of Solidarity": The CPT Hostage Crisis

A great hand of solidarity reached out for us, a hand that included the hands of Palestinian children holding pictures of us, and the hands of the British soldier who cut our chains with a bolt cutter. That great hand was able to deliver three of us from the shadow of death. I am grateful in a way that can never be adequately expressed in words.

There are so many people that need this hand of solidarity, right now, today, and I'm thinking specifically of prisoners held all over the world, people who have disappeared into an abyss of detention without charge, due process, hope of release—some victims of physical and psychological torture—people unknown and forgotten. It is my deepest wish that every forsaken human being should have a hand of solidarity reaching out to them.

—Statement by Jim Loney upon his arrival home, March 27, 2006[1]

As Iraqis continued to die by the thousands and internationals came under increasing risk in Iraq, the team and the CPT organization as a whole evaluated on an ongoing basis whether they should keep the team in Baghdad. In October 2004, Iraqi militants kidnapped British citizen Margaret Hassan, director of Iraqi operations for the relief and humanitarian organization CARE International. She had lived in the country for decades, spoke fluent Arabic, and was married to an Iraqi, so her kidnapping destroyed any remaining illusions CPTers might have had that they were perhaps safer than other internationals because they were living in solidarity with ordinary Iraqis.[2] After her kidnapping, Tom Fox wrote,

1. CPTnet, "Toronto: Statement by Jim Loney on his arrival home," Mar 27, 2006.

2. However, CPTer Justin Alexander wrote, in his comments on a draft of this chapter:

She lived a life of giving away the human need for security. She worked tirelessly for the people of Iraq coping with governments whose human rights record varied from somewhat intolerant to outright oppressive. She lived a life with the people of Iraq, not a life spent behind gates and walls. . . . She lived a life of courage in the midst of fear. We are called to do the same, no matter what the consequences.

CPT has had the privilege of knowing Margaret during the two years that CPT has been in Iraq. She met with a number of visiting delegations and shared with them her vision for the future of her country. One CPT member reflected on his experiences with her, "Margaret and her staff placed their energies into building the future for the people of Iraq. When attackers bombed their warehouse last year, they moved the operation, but continued their efforts with other Iraqis to improving life in this country. Margaret modeled an extravagant way of living for others."[3]

One year later, the Iraq team was hosting a small delegation led by CPT Canada co-coordinator Jim Loney.[4] Norman Kember from the United Kingdom and Harmeet Singh Sooden, a Canadian citizen and resident of New Zealand,[5] were the other two delegates. Sheila Provencher had just left the team in Baghdad to spend two weeks with Palestinians camped at the Syrian border before she returned home. Greg Rollins had originally been scheduled to accompany the three men to meetings on November 26, but needed to do laundry before he took the delegation to Karbala the day after. Fox volunteered to take the delegation to meetings in the morning and then switch with Rollins in the afternoon. Since one of the meetings ran long, Fox continued with the delegation to an afternoon meeting at the Muslim Scholars' Association.[6]

When I was on team in spring 2005, I think there was still an impression that CPT might be less of a target than other groups because of its work with detainees and other victims of the occupation. CARE was involved in relief & development, something that occupation was also involved in, dangerously blurring the NGO/military distinction in the eyes of some.

3. Fox, "Remembering Margaret Hassan." A shorter version appeared in a CPTnet release on November 20, 2004.

4. Rebecca Johnson was the other CPT Canada co-coordinator.

5. Singh Sooden was born and raised in Zambia to Sikh parents originally from Kashmir.

6. Rollins, e-mail, May 29, 2007.

Rollins initially thought the team's translator was joking when he called and said, "Greg, I have some bad news, man. The delegation has been kidnapped." Once convinced, Rollins wrote down the details: the four men, their translator, and their driver had just left the office of the Muslim Scholars Association—a Sunni organization—when two cars pulled up in front of and behind theirs. Gunmen forced the driver and translator out of the van, took their phones, and then drove away with the four CPTers.[7]

Thus began a four-month odyssey of fear, anguish, and grace as CPT traveled in unfamiliar waters to seek release of the four hostages. For the hostages, the kidnapping meant a four months of terror, loss of control over the most mundane matters of their lives, and excruciating boredom.

After the initial kidnapping, committed by men the four hostages never saw again, the CPTers had regular interactions with four captors: three guards whom they nicknamed Junior, Uncle, and Nephew, and their leader, whom they called Medicine Man, because he brought pills for Kember's high blood pressure. Of the four, Junior appeared the most devout, and Nephew performed some of the five daily Muslim prayers. Uncle sometimes had prayer beads. "They had a narrow view of their faith," Loney said, especially when it came to sectarian differences. "They believed the Shia were no good. They didn't see the Shia Muslims as Muslims really." Over time, Loney came to see them as "good people who had been infected with a toxic kind of religion."[8]

None of the four captors spoke English and none of the four captives spoke more than a few words of Arabic, but with what seemed like an infinite amount of time at their disposal, they nevertheless managed to communicate. The captors told the CPTers that they had been members of Saddam Hussein's army. Norman Kember speaking at a 2007 church peace conference in Northern Ireland, told participants, "They told us we

7. Although Singh Sooden and Kember had not gone through training, and never voiced an intention of joining CPT, throughout the hostage crisis members of CPT fell into the habit of referring to them as "CPTers" and "colleagues." Their willingness to enter a dangerous situation, and the consequences they suffered because they had joined the CPT delegation seemed to entitle them to the designation of honorary CPTers. The author, who was part of the crisis media team set up to address the kidnappings, also found herself thinking of Fox and Loney as "serving on assignment" in Iraq, and what they would need to do when they returned from their term "in the field."

8. Rhodes, "Hostage struggled with desire to escape."

were lucky to be kidnapped by that group, because if the Zarqawi group had kidnapped us, Tom Fox and myself would have been shot immediately because we were American and British."[9] On the first day of captivity, they showed the CPTers photos of friends and relatives killed by Coalition Forces in Iraq.

They told the CPTers that they were planning on releasing them quickly to show them they were "not like Al Qaeda." Early on, the hostages realized that their captors were lying to them. They continued to lie over subsequent months, telling the four men they would be released as a goodwill gesture during the Iraqi elections, then Christmas and then New Years.

For most of their captivity, the men were handcuffed and chained to each other and held in a small room. During the day, they sat in plastic lawn chairs and at night slept on a makeshift communal bed. The kidnappers took off their handcuffs so they could exercise for about a half hour in the mornings. Three times a day, the men received one *samoon* (an Iraqi pita) with a bit of potato or rice stuffed inside.

Like the captives, the captors too, became frustrated and bored as the captivity wore on and both sets of men attempted to relate to each other. Junior, who was about twenty-five years old, declared one day that he was going to blow himself up in an attack on U.S. forces. Disturbed, Loney began to think of ways to communicate "something of the goodness of his young life" so that he might re-think his intention. Because Junior complained constantly of neck and back pain, during exercise one morning, Loney offered to give him a massage.

Loney wrote in an e-mail to the author, "Although he was 25, Junior was more like a twelve year old boy in his emotional maturity, and like any twelve year old boy, you can never have too much of a good thing. So this strange thing happened where I would massage Junior rather frequently, every couple days. His back was full of knots and muscle spasms. I don't think the insurgent life agreed with him."[10]

The guards, in turn, gave the CPTers Christmas presents: underpants, socks, jackets, and jogging trousers. The CPTers used the packaging from these presents to make a deck of playing cards. Kember created a "Snakes

9. Huber, "Former Iraq hostage reflects on captivity."

10. Loney, e-mail, Aug 20, 2007. Loney wrote, "On the last night of our captivity . . . [Junior] asked me whether suicide was accepted in Canada. He seemed quite depressed. I was shocked and said, of course not, no, this is *haram*. And he said, 'This *haram* in Islam. Me no suicide.'"

and Ladders" game (called "Chutes and Ladders" in the U.S.) designating the ladders to apply to high points of their captivity, such as shaving, a Christmas cake, and killing mosquitoes, while the snakes (chutes) included times without electricity.

Other ways they passed the time without books or newspapers included conducting daily meetings to talk about their situation, worship, and Bible study, discussing passages they knew from memory. Sometimes, their captors showed them movies such as *Zorro* and a DVD set of the *Life of Christ*. Watching a convict springing his handcuffs with a nail in the movie *Con-Air* gave Loney the idea of using the nail from a shoe—early on, the kidnappers had taken the hostages's shoes and replaced them with cheaper pairs—to unfasten their own handcuffs so they could sleep more easily at night.

On February 12, the kidnappers told the four men that they would release them one at a time at the mosque in Baghdad where they had been kidnapped. Although Fox volunteered to be the last to go, the kidnappers said they were taking him first. Loney told CPTers at a full-timers's retreat that when he hugged Fox good-bye, he remembered thinking how boney he was; as the tallest of the four hostages, he had suffered the most from the scant amounts of food their kidnappers brought him. Later, he wrote that Fox had been the hostages's anchor in the early days of captivity, maintaining a calm, stoic presence, filling the other hostages in about Iraqi culture and the Iraqi kidnapping industry, and deferring comforts such as blankets and pillows to the others. Later, however, his psychological coping devices began to fail him.

"It's my hunch," Loney wrote,

> That Tom was haunted by the dread fear that the stresses and privations of captivity would irrevocably sever his connection to the divine, that he would eventually succumb to the temptation to hate and dehumanize his captors, and thus everything he worked for in the spiritual life would be lost. In our desperate circumstances, his answer was to strive harder, to hold fast with every last ounce of strength lest he fall helpless into the abyss of negativity. It pained me to watch him in this struggle. I wanted to tell him, "You don't have to fight. God loves you more than you can possibly imagine. You don't have to do anything. Your connection with God is permanent and irrevocable. You cannot not be in the Light.[11]

11. Loney, "No Greater Love," 212.

Days passed and the kidnappers did not release the remaining three men. On March 5, 2006, the kidnapper they called "Medicine Man" made a video of the remaining hostages and said the kidnappers would falsely claim that Fox had been killed in order to apply pressure on the three men's governments.

On March 10, the three went downstairs to watch an Arabic-language news broadcast. They saw a deserted road and Fox's picture, which first led them to suspect he had been murdered, although the kidnappers, lying to them once again, assured them Fox was still alive.

Two weeks later, on March 23, the men heard sounds of tanks moving on the street outside. Then they heard the thuds of boots and a soldier with a British accent shout, "Open the door!" After the British Special Air Service smashed the door, and fired a volley of shots, one commando called out, "Mr. Kember, are you there?" The soldiers then burst into the room where the hostages were chained, set them free with a bolt cutter and informed them, apologetically, that Fox was dead.[12]

In an Easter reflection for the *Toronto Star*, Loney wrote,

> On March 23, at about 7.30 in the morning, our tombstone was rolled away: not by angels garbed in heavenly robes, but by a unit of British Special Forces in full battle gear. There were the sounds of boots on concrete, the door being smashed open, gunfire, voices in English shouting, "Get down! Stay away from the door!" Then a roomful of commotion, soldiers telling us "You're free, it's okay,

12. Ibid., 213–17; Rhodes, "Hostage struggled with desire to escape"; Elvidge, "Captive of Conscience," interview with Norman Kember."

Some details are taken from the presentation Loney delivered at the CPT biannual retreat for full-timers in September 2006 at which the author was present.

The circumstances of how the rescue came about are still somewhat mysterious. Iraq Project Support coordinator Doug Pritchard wrote in his comments on a draft of this chapter

> We never got a ransom demand during the first kidnapping and the governments insist they paid no ransom. But we know that some kind of deal was done in the end. From the published reports and what the guys have said publicly—someone warned their guard to leave before the troops arrived, and one of the kidnappers was accompanying the troops. Why? Who arranged this? How? The US military spokesperson said at the time that they had had a lucky break in catching someone the night before, interrogating him, and found out where our guys were held. The UK spokespersons said at the same time something rather different, that this was the fruit of weeks of painstaking intelligence work. Which was it?

it's over." And hands, shaking with excitement, cutting us free with a bolt-cutter.

They led us past the smashed-glass threshold of our tomb and out. Out into blue! Beautiful all sky blue! Fresh flowing air and a palm tree and good morning sunlight! They led us through a smiling gauntlet of soldiers and, with a big step up and a big hatch down, we were entombed again.

This tomb was a bland desert-camouflage colour. It was squat, constructed of impregnable steel, moved on a rolling tread of metal plates. The passenger section was dark and cramped and crammed with carefully tooled metal shapes (each with an exact purpose) and little signs that told you things like what to do in the event of a rollover. A young soldier named Rob kept watch through a tiny slit of super-thick plate glass. Through it, you could see a small, distorted rectangle of the world outside. It brought us to a helicopter armed with a fixed, heavy-calibre machine gun, and the helicopter brought us to the Green Zone—the sprawling, blast-wall lockdown that houses the offices of the fledgling Iraqi government and the occupying forces of Britain and the United States.

Yes, we went from one tomb to another.

I am learning many things from my captivity, and have a universe of things to be grateful for. Among them is a new and deep appreciation for the women and men who wear the uniform of military service. I likely would not be writing this today if it were not for them. Thus, I am confronted with a great paradox. I, the Christian pacifist peacemaker, am alive, am free because of the very institutions I believe are contrary to Christian teaching.

Christ teaches us to love our enemies, do good to those who harm us, pray for those who persecute us. He calls us to accept suffering before we inflict injury. He calls us to pick up the cross and to lay down the sword.

We will most certainly fail in this call. I did. And I'll fail again. This does not change Christ's teaching that violence itself is the tomb, violence is the dead-end. Peace won through the barrel of a gun might be a victory but it is not peace. Our captors had guns and they ruled over us. Our rescuers had bigger guns and ruled over the captors. We were freed, but the rule of the gun stayed. The stone across the tomb of violence has not been rolled away. . . .

We must all find our way through a broken world, struggling with the paradox of call and failure. My captivity and rescue have helped me to catch a glimpse of how powerful the force of resurrection is. Christ, that tomb-busting suffering servant Son of God,

seeks us wherever we are, reaches for us in whatever darkness we
inhabit.

May we reach for each other with that same persistence. The
tomb is not the final word.[13]

Before Singh Sooden and Loney parted to return to their homes in
New Zealand and Canada, respectively, Singh Sooden showed Loney two
musical time signatures that Tom Fox had written in Singh Sooden's note-
book: 3/4 and 4/4. A professional musician, Fox had been teaching Singh
Sooden music theory to pass the time. Harmeet put his finger over the 3/4
and said, "In the beginning we were 4/4." Then he put his finger over the
4/4 and said, "Now we're this—3/4."[14]

RESPONSE OF IRAQ TEAM

After they heard news of the kidnapping, the team remaining in
Baghdad—Greg Rollins, Anita David, and Maxine Nash—began calling
members of the Muslim Scholars Association at the suggestion of one of
their Iraqi coworkers. Then they called personnel at the United Nations,
who offered to call the British, Canadian, and U.S. Embassies. The team
sent them the information they had gotten from their translator, asking
that they not release it for a couple of hours, because they wanted to assess
the information they had before governments and press became involved.
Their translator would stay with them for the next five days to field phone
calls, during which time Rollins came down with flu and David had a
constant migraine.

After Rollins called Provencher, encamped at the Syrian border, to
give her the news, she later wrote,

> Daily events took on the liquid unreality of nightmare. The adult
> refugees, already reeling from the stress of life with little food and
> no clear future, blanched when I told them. "No! Haram (forbid-
> den)!" they cried. The children wept. Their Amu Tom (Uncle Tom)
> so strong and tall, was now helpless somewhere, just like them.
> . . . "I will go back to Baghdad," Thaer declared seconds after we
> received the news. "I know Baghdad better than CPT, and I can
> help them." This was unthinkable. He had received a death threat
> before we left. The CPTers still in Iraq told me they did not want

13. "From the Tomb."

14. CPTnet, "Toronto: Statement by Jim Loney," Mar 27, 2006; Loney, "No greater
love," 217.

anyone to return at the time and I knew they would not want the refugees to risk their lives after working so hard to reach safe haven. Instead, Thaer called everyone he knew in Iraq who might have the ability to help.[15]

The days that followed passed in a blur of activity as the team held meetings every couple of hours to make decisions. "It seemed every decision before us had to be made in thirty seconds and new problems arose every fifteen," Rollins wrote. People inside and outside the country called constantly to offer advice; the press demanded interviews and the team called the CPT Toronto office several times a day to update CPT's support team (a term the organization uses for staff). Team members wrote statements for the press and statements aimed at the kidnappers, in case they were watching the CPT website. They made lists of people who could offer statements of support on their behalf and then tried to track them down; some were willing to make the statements and others took persuading. Finding local news outlets that would broadcast the team's statements proved challenging. Sometimes, even when these stations said they would do the broadcasts, they ended up not doing so.

Many Iraqi individuals and groups voluntarily issued public statements calling for the release of the hostages, despite the fact that their lives were much more at risk than those of the team. Two Iraqis actually appeared on television—an incredibly gracious and dangerous gesture—to make their appeals.

Mr. Sa'ad,[16] an Iraqi human rights worker, began making contacts with people he thought might lead to the kidnappers. A link presented himself, saying that he had contact with the men holding the CPTers. They did not want money, he said, but the link wanted $1000 for his troubles. Ali informed him that talk of money would come after the release. The team put together a CD containing pictures of the four men at demonstrations or doing other violence reduction work and their writings. They put together a second CD after the link informed Ali that the kidnappers thought Harmeet Singh Sooden was a spy, but the others were not.[17]

15. "One Family: From Syria to Jordan, Stories of Compassion," 47.

16. Name changed for security reasons.

17. Doug Pritchard wrote, in his comments on a draft of this chapter:

There was lots of evidence for Tom, Norman and Jim's anti-war work but there was much less info re Harmeet. And he could fit a "spy's" profile more readily—single, lots of [international] travel, multiple "home"

A British CPTer, Justin Alexander, who had previously worked on the Iraq team and had a network of contacts in the country, hired private investigators on his own initiative to locate the hostages and establish communication between the kidnappers and CPT. The investigators began work in early December, and delivered a range of confusing reports over the following months. They said there were in contact different times with possible intermediaries to the kidnappers. At one point in January 2006, they said that they had learned the kidnappers wanted a ransom of a million dollars for each person and would kill them if they did not receive this sum. Alexander had explained to the investigators from the outset that CPT opposed ransom, and hoped that if genuine contact could be established between the kidnappers, CPT, and the families then perhaps a peaceful release could be mediated. In one case, the investigators said they met with a masked man who they believed to be one of the kidnappers who made a call telling someone not to "kill the American." Like Mr. Sa'ad's link, they claimed to have established contact with the kidnappers, but were unable to provide proof that Singh Sooden, Fox, Kember, and Loney were still alive.[18]

Rollins wrote,

> Given a choice between this lead and Mr. Sa'ad's link, we preferred to pay closer attention to Mr. Sa'ad's link. Neither group had provided us with proof of life, but Mr. Sa'ad's connections were easier to listen to. They didn't threaten to kill our friends.[19]

The link turned out to be of little use and actually did some damage when he falsely accused one of the team's translators of complicity in the kidnapping. He never responded when the team asked for proof that the four men were still alive. When videos or other information about the hostages appeared, the team learned about it from neighbors and other people watching TV. Throughout the crisis, representatives of the kidnappers never contacted the team directly.

Adding to the stresses on the team were the repeated meetings demanded by representatives of the United Kingdom's Scotland Yard, who

---

countries, electrical engineer etc. So Mr. Sa'ad asked us to provide more evidence of Harmeet's bona fides.

18. Alexander, comments on draft of this chapter.

19. Rollins, "The Response from Baghdad," 40. "Mr Sa'ad" left his home in the south after an assassination attempt on him in July 2006. Pritchard, e-mail, July 26, 2007.

seemed to ask the same questions of the team at every interview and led the team to believe they were in charge of the investigation. Particularly distressing to the team was Scotland Yard's insistence that four Iraqis who had served as team drivers and translators give full statements to the Iraqi police. After western authorities assured team members that no harm would befall the men if they gave statements, team members persuaded the men to do so and were thus dismayed when the Iraqi authorities arrested and held them for sixteen days.[20] As weeks passed, the team continued to post letters to the kidnappers on the CPT website, addressing them—at the suggestion of Iraqi advisors—as "Our Brothers holding our colleagues." They also posted regular messages to the four men, using birthdays and holidays as a reason for the writing.[21]

Originally, Greg Rollins, Maxine Nash, and Anita David wanted no other CPTers to enter the country until the crisis had passed, but gradually, they realized they could not continue without help. Peggy Gish, Beth Pyles, Allan Slater, and Michele Naar-Obed joined them in December and January. Team members made efforts to continue the work they had been doing before the kidnapping. However, the increasing violence made team translators and drivers reluctant to leave their homes and team members reluctant to ask them to do so. Armed men had killed the translator for American journalist, Jill Carroll, kidnapped shortly after the CPT delegation's kidnapping, and the team's Iraqi colleagues believed that accompanying team members in public posed a real danger to themselves and their families. Nevertheless, during the crisis, the team still assisted Iraqis seeking detained love ones, and facilitated meetings between the US compensation committee and the director of the private university damaged by a 2004 bombing raid. They maintained contact with displaced Palestinians in Baghdad camps, and on March 19, they accompanied a convoy of eighty-eight Palestinian refugees to the no man's land between Iraq and Jordan. The team also strategized with Muslim Peacemaker Team members about ways to decrease the sectarian violence that had exploded after insurgents bombed the Al Askari shrine, one of Shia Islam's holiest sites on February 22, 2006.[22]

---

20. David, e-mail, June 30, 2007; Pritchard, e-mail, July 1, 2007. David wrote, "All four men were devastated by their experience."

21. See, for example, CPTnet, "Iraq: Message to missing CPTers," Jan 7, 2006.

22. Gish, "Continuing the work in Iraq," 15–31.

After weeks of preparation and aborted attempts, the team was able to arrange for a translator and driver to accompany Michele Naar-Obed and Anita David to the Baghdad morgue on February 28, 2006. The team knew that many unidentified bodies were there, and thought they ought to check and make sure Singh Sooden, Loney, Kember, and Fox were not among them. The two women dressed in the long black robes and head-scarves that Iraqi women wear and agreed with their translator that they would not talk in English while they were there.

The morgue was crowded with wailing women and other Iraqis pressed against a Plexiglas window where they could view photos of the unidentified dead cycling every three seconds on a computer screen. Naar-Obed later wrote,

> While I was waiting my turn, my eyes locked with the one other woman who was, at that time, wedged into a corner. She tried to speak to me in Arabic. I looked around for our translator who was milling about amongst the larger crowd. Conscious of my promise not to speak, I was unable to call for his assistance.
>
> The woman continued to speak and it seemed like she was pleading with me. I felt helpless and stupid and wished I could be one of the flies and fly away. I broke eye contact and looked down, choking back my tears. I tried to focus on our mission of looking for Tom, Jim, Norman, and Harmeet. I was acutely aware that I was not an observer, but a participant in this deathwatch. These were our colleagues, our family members we were looking for. I was no longer the CPT human rights worker observing and documenting abusive policies against Iraqis. I was another distraught human being caught in the ugly, bizarre, and inhuman consequences of war.

Naar-Obed noted that after viewing more than one hundred photos of bodies and parts of bodies, they all began to look the same. While she was there no one made a positive identification of a relative or friend.[23]

On March 10, 2007, CPT Co-director Doug Pritchard called the team in the evening, saying the Iraqi police had found Tom Fox's body near train tracks where the bodies of other murder victims had been dumped in previous months. Although the U.S. embassy said Beth Pyles could accompany the body home and provided transportation for her to the U.S. military base in Balad, the U.S. State Department in Washington

---

23. Naar-Obed, "The Baghdad Morgue," 81.

DC refused to allow her on the flight because she was a civilian. When they had not changed their minds after two days, she watched, early on the morning of March 13, as the unit of Puerto Rican soldiers in charge of the mortuary—who had treated Pyles with great kindness while she waited in Balad—loaded Fox's body onto the plane. In another casket was the body of an Iraqi detainee who had died in U.S. custody and was going to Dover Air Force Base for an autopsy. "I laugh through my tears," Pyles wrote, "to see that even in death, Tom is accompanying an Iraqi safely to his destination."

As soldiers saluted Fox's flag-draped coffin, Pyles, a Presbyterian minister, read from John 1, ending with "The light shines in the darkness, and the darkness did not overcome it." For the Iraqi man she recited what she could remember of the Muslim declaration of faith[24] and then read for both of them from Job 1: "Naked I came into the world, naked I will depart. The Lord giveth, the Lord taketh away, blessed be the name of the Lord."[25]

The team remaining in Baghdad began planning their personal commemorations of Fox. They held a memorial service at St. Raphael's Catholic Church, the team's primary place of worship; about fifty Iraqi Christians and Muslims attended. They read their eulogies, sang his favorite hymn, "Be thou my vision," and lighted candles, as well as making a time for silence—an integral part of Fox's spiritual life. After the service, the team shared regrets with an Iraqi friend, that any children Fox's son and daughter might have would never know their grandfather. The friend told them, "Tom is a hero. It will be an honor for those children to have a grandfather who died in this way and to tell their children about him. I never met anyone like you people, who would come here, at this time, to people whom you don't know. You are angels."

At the site where his body was found, the team, with the help of many Iraqi friends, erected black banners, according to the Muslim tradition, with messages in white script based on a passage from the Quran sent them in condolence by an Iranian Imam: "In memory of Tom Fox in this place. Christian Peacemaker Teams declares, 'We are for God and we return to God.' To those who held him we declare God has forgiven you."[26]

24. "I bear witness that there is none worthy of worship except Allah and I bear witness that Muhammad is His servant and messenger."

25. Pyles, "Practicing Peace," 199–202.

26. CPTnet, Pritchard, "Iraq: Tom Fox commemorated in Baghdad," Mar 25, 2006.

In addition to proclaiming the forgiveness that Fox's life embodied, the team hoped, to no avail, that the banners might encourage a witness to come forward with news of Singh Sooden, Loney, and Kember. However, the banners were left in place over the following weeks; in the midst of Baghdad's violent chaos, people seemed to respect them as holy.[27]

On March 23, after Gish and Pyles had accompanied the Palestinians to the Jordanian border (see above), Doug Pritchard called to say that coalition forces had released Singh Sooden, Loney, and Kember. David, Nash, and Gish visited Loney and Singh Sooden and briefly Kember, in the Green Zone. The next day, Kember traveled home to Britain and Singh Sooden and Loney met again with David, Nash, and Gish at the British embassy where they filled in the blanks for each other about what had happened during the period of the captivity. During the meeting, they celebrated Harmeet Singh Sooden's recent birthday with a Maple-leaf-decorated cake provided by Canadian diplomatic staff in Baghdad.[28] Back at the apartment, the team was inundated with phone calls from media and friends. When they turned their phones off, people showed up at their door.

Once Kember, Singh Sooden, and Loney returned to their home countries, Nash, David, and Gish began meeting with trusted Iraqi friends to discuss continuing the project. Almost all of them advised the team that remaining in Baghdad would be too dangerous for them and the Iraqis with whom they worked. The women left Iraq in April for a time of debriefing, healing, and discernment. After considering the danger the team's presence presented to Iraqi partners, the difficulty getting visas through Baghdad, as well as the hardships and dangers of continuing to work in areas they had covered for the previous three years, the team decided to pursue possibilities of working in northern Iraq.

RESPONSE FROM CPTERS SERVING ON OTHER PROJECTS

Although by 2005, CPT had grown past the point where all of its workers knew each other, every team had at least one person who knew Fox or

27. In her comments on a draft of this chapter, Beth Pyles noted that the team took one of the banners in Baghdad down to present to Fox's children, after the original banner commissioned for them was stolen from a CPTer's car in Chicago.

28. Loney, e-mail, July 3, 2007; Pritchard, e-mail, July 4, 2007. Since the team and former hostages had only a very short time together, the presentation of the cake was something of an intrusion, but they received it with good grace.

Loney well. But even those CPTers who did not know the two men had imagined what might happen to them should they be taken hostage.

Particularly in Colombia, where thousands of people had been kidnapped and murdered, or held awaiting ransom for years, the team felt acutely what might happen to the four hostages in Iraq.

Once the news of the kidnappings became public, friends of the Colombia team in the Opón and Barrancabermeja prayed and participated in vigils for the captive CPTers. At a December 2005 "Assembly of Victims of Crimes against Humanity by the State," mothers whose children had "disappeared" expressed a sense of solidarity with the team. After Tom Fox's murder, condolences from Colombia partners poured in to the team, and Sandra Milena Rincón wrote that they knew thousands of prayers were being whispered in memory of him and in supplication for Iraqi detainees.

Rincón concluded her essay about the hostage crisis:

> As accompaniers we were able to understand, perhaps for the first time, what the disappearance or kidnapping of a loved one means. We would always listen in a new way to the stories of communities, families, and individuals whose loved ones had disappeared— stories full of questions...
>
> I remember many conversations about our kidnapped friends in which we imagined them—especially Jim and Tom who we knew—having discussions about nonviolence with their captors. We imagined them as a group creating strategies to survive the hardship of captivity, strategies that revitalized their commitment to love even their enemies. And we imagined them celebrating Christmas, the New Year, and other special days seeing their captors in all of their humanity, fragility, and goodness.
>
> We needed to imagine our friends' well being, because it was too difficult and frightening to imagine otherwise. So we imagine that Tom died at peace. We imagine that the testimony of Tom's life left his captors with a new way of imagining their own lives and their world—imagining it at peace.
>
> We imagined these things in order to believe that everything would turn out well for the fourteen thousand detainees in Iraq. We imagined these things for three thousand two hundred kidnapped people, and the thirty thousand forcibly disappeared, in my country, Colombia.[29]

29. Rincón, "The Road Traveled in Colombia," 89.

In Kenora and Grassy Narrows, CPT partners knew Loney in his capacity as CPT Canada co-coordinator. Indigenous friends in Grassy and Sioux Lookout held their own vigils for the hostages. In Kenora, the team and local coworkers organized a vigil connecting the fates of the hostages with Iraqi detainees and the hundreds of indigenous women whose disappearances the authorities had never fully investigated.[30]

In a CPTnet release about the vigil, John Spragge wrote,

> Throughout these difficult weeks, the outpouring of solidarity, support, and love from an abused First Nations community continues to move me. However good our intentions, we have not done very much for them; surely our efforts fall far short of what they need, and what justice requires. Yet they give us unconditional support and love, and they grieve for Jim's predicament. The love that people all over the world have shown Christian Peacemaker Teams during this crisis boldly challenges the destruction done by armies, defence contractors, and the politicians they serve.[31]

The Hebron and Tuwani teams, having many Arabic-speaking friends and colleagues were in the best position (other than the Iraq team) to help during the hostage crisis. After the first video of the four hostages appeared on Al Jazeera, along with a note accusing them of being spies, Palestinian friends called to offer this help. For the next ten days, the teams in Palestine did little else but focus on ways they could secure the release of Kember, Loney, Fox, and Singh Sooden.

The team's lawyer, Jonathan Kuttab, began submitting stories about the work of the team in Hebron to Arabic media. As he had for the previous ten years of the Hebron team's existence, Hisham Sharabati jumped in to help them with the crisis. He and Hamed Qawasmeh from the Hebron District Governor's office began contacting all of the Palestinian political parties, and late the night the video appeared they had signatures from eight groups on a statement appealing for the release of the hostages.

The statement was read at a press conference the next morning in a local mosque. Westerners probably did not appreciate the dramatic symbolism of Fatah, Hamas, Popular Front for the Liberation of Palestine, and the other parties usually at odds with each other appearing on the same platform to call for the release of the hostages. Also speaking at the press

30. Mustus, "500 Missing Indigenous Women"; Ross, "Disappeared aboriginal women not forgotten."

31. CPTnet, "Kenora, ON: Vigil for missing people," Dec 5, 2005.

conference were Fariel Abu Haikal of Qurtuba Girls' school, Naim Daour from Hebron University, and Campaign for Secure Dwellings participant, Jamal Miqbal (see chapter 4). At the press conference, one of the political leaders in Hebron offered to go to Baghdad if the team thought it would help. Later in the day, a Palestinian National Authority official issued the following statement from the PNA Ramallah offices:

November 30, 2005

A PLEA TO THE IRAQI PEOPLE

From Palestine we call upon you to release the four from the Christian Peacemaker Teams who were kidnapped from Baghdad. This is an organization that has helped and continues to help our people living under Israeli occupation in the city of Hebron and in other regions throughout our occupied homeland. They expose themselves to danger in order to provide protection to our women and children in front of Israeli military checkpoints.

We urge you in the name of humanity and in the name of all peoples that have tasted bitter wars, violence and occupation . . . we urge you to release Tom Fox (American citizenship), Norman Kember (British citizenship), James Loney and Harmeet Singh Sooden (Canadian citizenship), all of whom insisted on helping our family in Iraq and living with our Iraqi brothers and sisters through the war and destruction, believing in the message that every human being has the right to live in freedom and with dignity and that occupation is wrong and must end.

We have faith that you will find that this group is among those working for peace and against occupation and that you will release them immediately, God willing.

Coordinator of the National Committee to Resist the Wall

Qadura Fares[32]

Qawasmeh would lose his job at the Hebron District Governor's office for complying with the team's request to hold the press conference in a place of Islamic religious significance. However, whenever the team tried to thank him or other Palestinians for their help, the uniform response was "No, don't thank us, we have to do this; it is our duty." The International Solidarity Movement (see chapter 5) also eagerly offered assistance. They organized press conferences and demonstrations, for which

32. PNA, "A Plea to the Iraqi People."

they produced expensive photo banners of the captives and obtained statements from Muslim clerics, and spokespeople from villages where Singh Sooden and Fox had participated in ISM actions.

These initial actions, covered by the Palestinian Arabic media, rapidly inspired other Arabs and Muslims around the world to speak out for the captive CPTers. The large banner of Fox holding a sign saying, "Stop the Wall" in particular seemed to produce a response. Local Palestinian friends called whenever they saw something about the hostages in the media and translated the team's releases into Arabic. Palestinian journalists went out of their way to publicize the press conferences, demonstrations, and calls from the Arab world to release the hostages. By the end of December 2005, CPT's Palestine project had added more than three hundred contacts to its e-mail list of Arabic language media.

After the Palestinian Prisoners' Society organized a demonstration that connected the hostages's ordeal to the administrative detention of Palestinian prisoners, the Palestine team thought of another angle to try. The kidnappers had called for the release of Iraqi detainees before they released Fox, Kember, Singh Sooden, and Loney: the very work that the hostages and CPTers in Iraq, Palestine, and Canada had been addressing. Again, a large photo banner of Loney calling for the release of post 9/11 Arab detainees in Canada proved useful. The Hebron team also decided that whenever they talked of Kember, Loney, Singh Sooden, and Fox to the Arabic media, they would use the opportunity to highlight the predicament of Iraqis detained by Coalition Forces.[33]

In Tuwani, the villagers's predominant reaction to the kidnappings was one of outrage. They remembered Tom Fox, who had worked in Tuwani for a few days. On November 30, 2005, the head of the village, Hafez Hereni, borrowed the team's video camera and took testimonies of local villagers. Speaking directly to "Iraqi brothers and sisters" who might be viewing them, the villagers described what their lives had been like before CPT and Operation Dove had sent workers to live in Tuwani and how they had changed once the Tuwani team began providing regular school escorts for their children. Hereni assured CPTer Kristin Anderson that when the kidnappers knew CPT, they would set the hostages free. Anderson found out later that Hereni had not gone to work for the first week of the hostage crisis. She knew that his wages were supporting his

33. Meyer, "With a Lot of Help from Our Friends," 63–70.

five children, wife, and mother, and that he was already overburdened with the unpaid work of nonviolence coordinator for the southern Hebron district villages. Wanting to acknowledge these responsibilities and affirm that the hostage crisis was not more important than the problems facing these villages, Anderson tried to ask about a recent Israeli high court case regarding the village's land. Hereni interrupted her, saying, "Really Kristin, I cannot think about anything else right now. Right now everything I am doing is for them."

On December 2, 2005, the people of Tuwani held a demonstration at their school calling for the release of the hostages. The children held photos of the four men, or had these photos taped to their chests. Mothers and grandmothers held signs they had made and the young men held banners professionally produced in Yatta. More than one hundred people gathered, including a shepherd who came from Jinba village, even though that day his lawyers and the Israeli authorities were meeting at his house to discuss land confiscation orders and plans for the construction of the Separation Wall on Jinba's lands. After processing the short distance between the village school and health clinic, the village inhabitants held a press conference. The speakers all referred to sacrifices CPT had made for Palestinians and Iraqis. Given all the injustices faced by Palestinians and Iraqis, the speakers said, they should make efforts not to be unjust toward those who were trying to help them.

When the people of the South Hebron Hills heard about the demonstration in Hebron organized by the Palestinian Prisoners' Society (see above), almost one hundred people, including half of the village of Tuwani came to march. For some, going to the demonstration was the first time they had left the isolated rural areas of the Hebron district.

In the intervening period between the demonstrations in December 2005 and Fox's death in March 2006, Anderson had dinner with Hafez Hereni and his family. His mother stood up and said the hostages had been held for too long, and that she was going to Iraq to get them, at which point she left the room. Amidst the laughter, Hafez Hereni translated for the team and added, "Really, she says she'll go." "We joined the laughter," Anderson wrote in a letter to the captives, "knowing that if anyone could march into Iraq to get the four of you, it would be Fatima."

Anderson concluded the letter,

That night, tucked in the moonlit hills of At-Tuwani, I considered
the distances between us. I considered the distance between me
and you. Tom, Jim, Norman, and Harmeet. I considered the distance between me and the village of At-Tuwani. I considered the
distance between me and the village, and you and your captors. I
considered the distance between the village and your captors.

In these distances, I found unexpected solace. I saw the beginnings and endings of each distance dissolve into likeness. I saw
through the lies of our separation.

I found us all so very close.

After Fox's death, the village descended on the team in Tuwani to
mourn with them, and assure them that those who had killed him were
not true Muslims. Fatima Hereni, who had never before come to the
team's house, said when she visited that she would plant an olive tree after
the forty-day Muslim mourning period and care for it as if it were one of
her children.

On March 26, 2006, Anderson wrote a letter addressed to all four
captives at the time of the three survivors's release:

> In between settlers killing two goats, settlers assaulting a young
> boy with spray resulting in temporary vision loss, settlers beating
> that boy's father, police arresting two shepherds, the death of this
> year's bee crop, other lost crops, and a worsening water shortage,
> the village celebrated your freedom.
>
> Though I wasn't there, others told me our neighbor fam-
> ily cooked a big meal the night they heard you were freed. Kiefa
> prepared the meal and Nasser encouraged overindulgence saying,
> "Eat, eat, this is a celebration!" Others offered thanks, and through
> wide smiles, conveyed their happiness. One man told a CPTer that
> he hoped the three of you would someday visit At-Tuwani.
>
> Days later, at a village meeting, the people again expressed
> their joy at your freedom, and their sadness over Tom's death.
> They spoke of the deepening trust between the village and CPT
> and saturated the room with "ilhumdulla's" ("thanks be to Allah").

Anderson closed her final letter with the story of Fatima and three
grandchildren planting the olive tree at the end of the mourning period.
"Before me, the hands of the Hereni family move in and through the

earth," she wrote. "I watch closely because in these hands, I see what has taken root."[34]

Rich Meyer, referring to Fatima Hereni at the end of his chapter on what the Palestine teams did during the hostage crisis, wrote, "I hope that someday Jim, Norman and Harmeet can meet her on their 'Thank you, Palestine' tour."[35]

RESPONSE OF THE WIDER CPT ORGANIZATION

CPT Co-Director Doug Pritchard was the project support coordinator for the Iraq team and was thus the first person in North America Rollins called after the team learned of the kidnappings. Pritchard, in turn, called Co-Director Carol Rose who was in California for Thanksgiving weekend, saying, "The Iraq delegation has been kidnapped. Crisis Team call in sixty minutes.[36] Need to be off the phone to get further information from the team in Baghdad."

For the next four months, in addition to juggling the routine work of supporting projects in Palestine, Iraq, Colombia, and Northern Ontario, CPT staff in Toronto and Chicago had two gigantic priorities: supporting the extended families of Fox, Loney, Kember, and Singh Sooden, and doing everything in their power to secure the safe release of the hostages. The "families" expanded to include Fox's Quaker and Mennonite communities, Loney's Catholic Worker community, Singh Sooden's friends in the Australian and New Zealand Peace Movements, and Kember's home church as well as his Pax Christi, UK, Fellowship of Reconciliation, Baptist Peace Fellowship, Anglican Pacifist Fellowship, and Campaign for Nuclear Disarmament networks.

Diplomats who had experience regarding kidnappings in Iraq advised that the CPT support team should avoid publicity for the first seventy-two hours, because doing so would make securing a quick release more possible. Thus, the Chicago and Toronto support teams told no one

34. Anderson-Rosetti, "Excerpts from Letters to Tom, Norman, Harmeet and Jim," 54–61.

35. Meyer, "With a Lot of Help from our Friends," 70.

36. Between November 2005 and March 2006, the Crisis Team comprised CPT Steering Committee members Ruth Buhler and Brian Young, CPT staff Robin Buyers, Kryss Chupp, Claire Evans, Rebecca Johnson, Doug Pritchard, and Carol Rose, and CPT reservists Jane McKay Wright and Kathleen O'Malley.

but the hostages's families. In a chapter covering their experience during the crisis, Pritchard and Rose wrote,

> This secrecy was a heavy burden for those of us who did know. It cut against the grain of CPT's culture of trusting, open teamwork. It inhibited the prayers of CPT's wide network of supporters and the actions they were ready to take on CPT's behalf. We now see this initial silence as a mistake.[37]

The release of the Swords of Righteousness Brigade's first video of the four men that Al Jazeera broadcast on November 29, 2005, was actually a relief for the support team in some ways. They could see the four men were alive and well and they could finally tell other CPTers and supporters who could organize prayers and vigils for the hostages.

Statements of support began pouring in from prominent Muslim, Jewish, and Christian leaders and organizations, as well as thousands of individuals who prayed, held vigils, and in general held the hostages "in the light." Ehab Lotayef from the Canadian Islamic Congress and Anas Altikriti from the Muslim Association of Britain traveled on their own to Iraq, at considerable personal risk, to try securing the release of the hostages. Without being asked, staff of the Electronic Intifada set up an online petition in Arabic and English eventually signed by more than forty thousand people—including luminaries such as Cindy Sheehan, Arundhati Roy, Noam Chomsky, Howard Zinn, and Daniel Berrigan—calling for the release of the hostages.[38]

Some statements of support came from highly unexpected quarters. Groups committed to the violent overthrow of Israeli and American occupations such as Hamas, the Al Aqsa Martyrs' Brigade, and the Muslim Brotherhood[39] called on the kidnappers to release the hostages. Muslim prisoners held in administrative detention following 9/11 in Canada and the United Kingdom also voiced their support. In one moving plea, three men detained without charges for whom Loney had advocated in Toronto put out the following letter:

37. Pritchard and Rose, "Unless a Grain of Wheat Falls," 3.

38. Electronic Intifada, "Sign the Urgent Appeal"; Ali Abunimah, e-mail, Dec 5, 2005. A list of "Persons and Groups Who Issued Support Statements or Appeals on Behalf of the CPT Four," appears in the appendix of *118 Days*.

39. Al Aqsa Martyrs Brigade, "Statement by the Al Aqsa Martyrs Brigades Palestine"; CPT, "Arabic Materials—Links."

6 December 2005

To the people holding James Loney and the other Christian Peacemaker Team Members in Iraq,

In the name of Allah, the Most Gracious and Merciful,

Our names are Mahmoud Jaballah, Mohammad Mahjoub and Hassan Almrei, and we have been detained without charge for between four- and five-and-a-half years. Some of us have spent as many as four years in solitary confinement as well. We are being held captive under security certificates because the government of Canada alleges we are linked to terrorist organizations and that we pose a threat to the national security of Canada. Allah is witness to our innocence of these allegations.

We are suffering a great injustice here in Canada because the government stereotypes Muslims and because of our strong faith and daily attendance to mosque....

James Loney of the Christian Peacemaker Teams is one of thousands of people who have been fighting to right this wrong. He is a person who has organized and motivated people to participate in this struggle for what is right. We have recently seen a photo of him in the newspaper and it has saddened our hearts to learn that he is being held captive in Iraq.

This is the same James Loney who has traveled to Iraq on more than one occasion to help the people of Iraq. This is the same James Loney who has reached out to the families of the Abu Ghraib prisoners. This is the James Loney who was against the US invasion and is against the US occupation of Iraq.

It pains our heart to know that a person of this calibre is being held captive. We care about his freedom more than we do our own.

If you love Allah, if you have goodness in your heart, please deal with this matter as righteous Muslims and not let these kind, caring, compassionate and innocent people suffer....

We hope and pray to see these captives freed as much as we hope and pray for our own freedom here in Canada, a freedom for which James Loney has worked so hard.[40]

---

40. CPTnet, "Toronto: Statement on behalf of missing CPTers," Dec 6, 2005; CPT, "Arabic materials—Links." In the United Kingdom, Abu Qatada al-Filistini, accused by a Spanish judged of being "Al Qaeda's Ambassador in Europe," released a video calling for the release of the hostages, as a "merciful act according to the principles of Islam." Judd, "Abu Qatada appeals for release of the hostages"; "Concern grows for Iraq hostages."

Two months later, an Iraqi group called "Independent Activates, a Society to Defend Human Rights," notified the Iraq team that they had been holding vigils calling for the release of the hostages. A visit from a member of the group provided much needed spiritual sustenance for the team after weeks had passed without news of the hostages.[41]

After the Swords of Righteousness Brigade released a second video, threatening to kill the hostages unless the Americans and British released all detainees and withdrew their troops, the CPT Crisis Team shifted its focus. Given that the Iraq team had been advocating for Iraqi detainees since 2003 and CPT now had use of a spotlight, the Crisis Team "felt the Spirit's call to let that same spotlight illuminate more clearly the plight of fourteen thousand Iraqis held by Multi National Force in Iraq" without charges or access to family and legal help.[42]

A Media Team spun off of the Crisis Team in December 2005. Public Relations professionals and political activists Alyssa Burgin and Wilson Tan volunteered their services. Colombia Team Project Support Coordinator Robin Buyers, a veteran activist and organizer—and later, while Buyers was in Colombia, CPT reservist Jane MacKay Wright—directed the Media Team. With CPTers Kathleen Kern and William Payne, they met in conference calls several times each week to discuss the coverage of the crisis and how to make inroads into the media, especially the Arabic media.[43] Sheila Provencher, Beth Pyles, Kim Lamberty, Jenny Elliot, Michele Naar-Obed, and Peggy Gish over the next months helped facilitate these inroads, tag-team style, in Amman, Jordan and also participated in the Media Team calls at times.[44]

As a secondary goal, albeit one with life and death consequences, the Media Team communicated with all CPT reservists and full-timers about

41 CPTnet, Naar[-Obed], "Iraq: Angels in 'Activates' clothing," Feb 24, 2006.

42. Pritchard and Rose, "Unless a Grain of Wheat Falls," 5.

43. An incomplete list of volunteers who monitored the Arabic and Farsi-language media includes Ali Mallah, Khaled Amayreh, Hassan Abunimah, Khaled Mouammar, Walid Husseini, George Rishmawi, Hossein Alizadeh, and Mohammed Shabluq. Reschly, e-mail, July 9, 2007.

44. Provencher, "One Family: From Syria to Jordan," 48–50. Provencher wrote of her arrival in Amman to do media work, and coming into the lobby of the Al Monzer Hotel in Amman, where Iraq team members had frequently stayed. The front desk attendant wept and hugged her, and another man at the hotel, a survivor of the Abu Ghraib detainee abuse, burst into tears when he told her what CPT had meant to him. Hotel staff members went out of their way many times to aid the team in their press work.

what they should and should not say to the media. A December 20, 2005, posting on the intra-CPT discussion group, GITW, provided guidelines that were adapted as the crisis wore on:

Current Core Messages

We are deeply concerned about Tom, James, Harmeet, and Norman. But we are equally concerned about the 14,000 to 16,000 Iraqis who are detained by both U.S. and Iraqi forces.

While we are waiting for the release of our friends, we are continuing to document and expose abuse of the human rights of Iraqis detained both by U.S. and Iraqi forces....

We have always opposed the war and the occupation....

DOs and DON'Ts

DO: Refer to Tom, James, Harmeet, and Norman by name.

DO: Refer to the longstanding commitment of each man to peace and social justice. Note that Tom and James have advocated for the rights of Iraqis and Palestinians in their work with Christian Peacemaker Teams; that Harmeet works with the International Solidarity Movement in Palestine and the peace movement in New Zealand; and that Norman has been a member of the British peace movement for 50 years.

DO: Use words like "missing," "gone missing," "taken," "being held," "concern for their safety," "safe return home," "hosts," "teammates," "friends," "colleagues..." DO NOT speculate about the demands.

DO NOT speculate about the group holding our friends, their possible associates, or their motivations.

DO NOT reveal details of marital status or orientation.

DO NOT mention the word "ransom." The team and their advisors insist that mention of the word "ransom" increases the danger to our friends. Please do not discuss CPT's thinking [against] ransoms publicly at this time.

CONTINUE to avoid words like "terrorist..."

The Media Team also became involved with publicizing public witnesses, such as the Shine the Light campaign in Washington DC, Toronto, and Chicago, highlighting the abuses of Iraqi detainees, always hoping that the publicity done around these witnesses would make it into the Arab media.[45] When cartoons insulting Islam and the Prophet Muhammad appeared in a Danish newspaper and sparked worldwide riots, the organization immediately put out a release condemning the cartoons to various Arab media.[46]

After a December 10, 2005, deadline passed,[47] the kidnappers put out no further communications for seven weeks. Doug Pritchard would later write,

> Early in the days of the crisis team we prepared draft news releases for best case and worst-case scenarios. We finished the best case one (hostages all released) quite quickly. It took quite a few more days to finish the worst case (one or more hostages killed by captors or would-be rescuers), reflecting our reluctance to think a lot about this scenario. But as the days went by, we began to feel that the worst worst case was having no resolution, having it go on for years, or maybe never knowing. We got a glimpse of what it must be like in every war for those whose loved ones are "missing in action" and never knowing what happened and whether they might still be alive somewhere or where their body is.[48]

With the hostages's families and the various governments involved, the Crisis Team continued to reiterate CPT's policies against ransom and use of violence in rescue attempts. Governments insisted that they could use whatever methods they wished to free the hostages. Talks with families regarding ransom were more difficult. However, the Crisis Team held onto the "no ransom" policy because paying the money would support the violence of armed groups and would jeopardize the lives of CPTers working in locations like Iraq and Colombia. In the end, CPT received no genuine ransom demands.

On January 28, 2006, a video of the men in beards looking thinner was broadcast, along with the statement that this was the "last chance" for the governments to comply with their original demands before they

45. CPTnet, "Chicago/DC Call to Action: Shine the light," Dec 30, 2005; CPTnet, Wilson-Hartgrove, "Washington D.C. Reflection: The dark before dawn," Jan 19, 2006. CPT, "Shine the Light Events."

46. CPTnet, "Iraq: CPT Iraq statement on anti-Muslim cartoons," Feb 5, 2006. The Activates mentioned earlier also helped distribute the team's statement.

47. The kidnappers said they would kill the hostages if the U.S. did not free all Iraqi prisoners by this date.

48. Pritchard, comments on draft of this chapter.

killed the hostages. The last video appeared on March 7, 2007. Ominously, Tom Fox did not appear with Kember, Loney, or Singh Sooden.

Two days later, Carol Rose received a call from the U.S. State Department asking for assistance in contacting Fox's daughter, Kassie, but refusing to give Rose further information. In Toronto for the semi-annual CPT Steering Committee meeting, Rose was able to meet with Doug Pritchard in person and speculate what the call meant. Minutes later, Pritchard received the call from the Canadian authorities saying a body believed to be Fox's had been found. After calling the team in Baghdad, co-workers in the Chicago office and Fox's family, the support team gathered in the Toronto office to pray. Pritchard read the Iraq team's statement of conviction that Fox had signed. Closing with the Lord's Prayer, members of the support team then marshaled themselves for the next round of team and media work.[49]

Although the U.S. military refused to allow Iraq team members to accompany Fox's body home, Rich Meyer and Anne Montgomery held a vigil outside the Dover Air Base in Delaware until the body arrived there on March 13. Carol Rose joined Fox's family and Meyer for a viewing of the body and brief memorial service.

Ten days later, Jim Loney's partner, Dan Hunt, called Pritchard at 3:00 a.m. to tell him that Loney, Kember, and Singh Sooden were free and that he had just talked to Loney on the phone. The Crisis Team and Media Team then went into overdrive as they kept open communications with the team in Baghdad, held press conferences, monitored the media, and planned homecomings and Tom's memorial services.

To some extent, all involved with the Crisis and Media teams had anticipated this whirlwind of activity. No one had fully anticipated, how-

---

49. This workload, and the added danger hanging over the remaining hostages (particularly Kember, since UK forces were in Iraq), short-circuited the grieving process for Fox. Many CPTers mourned Fox's death more deeply after the remaining hostages were released, because they empathized with the sense of loss that Kember, Loney, and Singh Sooden felt when they discovered Fox had died.

In an August 4, 2007 e-mail, Maureen Jack wrote:

> Somehow, after Tom's death our focus had to be on the other three. I remember fearing that they would kill them one by one and that the next one would be Norman. It was only once the others were free that it was possible to concentrate on mourning Tom. My euphoria at the release was very short-lived ... probably less than an hour ... and so it was hard to do radio interviews saying how pleased I was.

ever, the attacks and accusations the press began hurling at CPT as an organization and the hostages in particular.

The Arabic and international press had been generally sympathetic to CPT and its work during the hostage crisis. At CPT's request, they did not report the names of Iraq team members remaining in Baghdad nor describe the location of their apartment. They also withheld information about the captives's backgrounds that might endanger them such as Tom Fox's military service (which involved playing clarinet in the Marine Corps band at the White House), Harmeet Singh Sooden's work for a New Zealand defense contractor and Jim Loney's long-term same-sex partnership with Dan Hunt.[50]

After Fox's death, however, the attitude of the press began to change. Some pundits depicted him as deluded and naïve, without ever bothering to read his writings, easily available on the internet, which showed that he had a keen sense of the dangers that could befall him. Of more concern were the repeated references to Fox's body showing marks of torture. *Newsweek* insisted on printing that Fox's throat had been savagely slit, despite the fact that Rose and Meyer had seen no marks of torture or throat-slitting on the body and repeatedly called *Newsweek* to tell them so.[51]

---

50. The suppression of Hunt's identity was especially painful for those close to the couple, as was Hunt's struggle with Canadian government officials to be considered Loney's immediate family. The photo of Loney that became widely used in the media during the hostage crisis had shown the two partners together, with Loney's arm around Hunt's shoulders. Hunt was both literally and metaphorically cut out of the picture. Robin Buyers, who coordinated the Crisis Media Team wrote:

> The defining moment for me as a queer woman during the crisis was when Dan's image was cut out of that loving photo taken of Jim and Dan together the night before Jim's departure. I watched the process of the photo editing from my desk, and cried quietly. In the days that followed, I worked ferociously to protect Dan, and Jim and Dan's relationship, from an already knowledgeable media. At the same time, my active role in making Dan invisible broke my heart. (Payne, "On Silence, Closets and Liberation," 127)

See also Hunt, "Taken Twice," 90–101.

51. Pritchard and Rose, "Unless a Grain of Wheat Falls," 12. The autopsy showed that Fox died from six bullet wounds. Loney wrote, "[S]ix murderous instructions to an index finger, six separate emissaries of a singular intention to kill; mind steadying the hand, eyes directing the gun that ripped through Tom's emaciated body, releasing his soul into light" ("No Greater Love," 203).

The flurry of criticism that CPT dealt with following Fox's death turned into a tsunami when the other three hostages were finally freed. Without having all the facts, and before the CPT support team had time to talk at length with any of the men, they posted a response thanking God for their freedom and reiterating their stance about the occupation and the plight of Iraqi detainees.[52]

Following that posting, the "dominant narrative" of the media immediately became the following: brave soldiers, whose lives were imperiled by the foolish peace activists, succeeded in rescuing the three men and they and CPT callously refused to thank them. The media took CPT's use of the word "release" (also used by UK and US government spokespeople) instead of "rescue" as a sign they were not sufficiently grateful to the soldiers who freed them. Indeed, the UK press devoted two or three days of front-page headlines to this perceived ingratitude.[53] The accusation was not true. Loney, Kember, and Singh Sooden had all personally thanked the soldiers who rescued them, and later, when CPT knew more details about the capture, the Media Team posted an addendum to the previous statement:

> We have been so overwhelmed and overjoyed to have Jim, Harmeet and Norman freed, that we have not adequately thanked the people involved with freeing them, nor remembered those still in captivity. So we offer these paragraphs as the first of several addenda:
>
> We are grateful to the soldiers who risked their lives to free Jim, Norman and Harmeet. As peacemakers who hold firm to our commitment to nonviolence, we are also deeply grateful that they fired no shots to free our colleagues. We are thankful to all the people who gave of themselves sacrificially to free Jim, Norman, Harmeet and Tom over the last four months, and those supporters who prayed and wept for our brothers in captivity, for their loved ones and for us, their co-workers.[54]

However, this addendum did not suffice for one radio talk show host who encouraged his listeners to call the CPT office to protest the use of

---

52. Pritchard and Rose, "Update on Hostages"; CPT, "CPTers Freed."

53. Nafziger, e-mail, July 24, 2007.

54. CPT, "Addenda to Statement." The addendum also responded to the curious criticism that CPT had not mentioned *Christian Science Monitor* journalist Jill Carroll, also kidnapped in Iraq around the same time.

the word "release."[55] These calls put the phone lines of the CPT Chicago office out of commission for two days, at a time when legitimate journalists and other people required critical access to the CPT support team.

In subsequent months, when the mainstream media lost interest in Christian Peacemaker Teams, what remained was the coverage from sources like Ekklesia, a Christian think tank in the United Kingdom, *Democracy Now*, *Mennonite Weekly Review*, and *Sojourners*, who understood what the real story had been all along:

- Hostage taking happened much more often to Iraqis than internationals
- Violence on all sides was the problem, not the solution
- The US-led invasion and occupation of Iraq was the backdrop for the insurgency and civil war
- Conflict transformation was part of a "credible tradition of action and research"
- Christians, Muslims, and others were finding common cause in the CPT hostage crisis
- This common cause indicated that efforts to build peaceful relationships and to resist violence resolutions in a situation of escalating low-intensity war were not foolish, but offered hope.[56]

55. Claire Evans, who fielded the call from Neil Borst, wrote in a July 24, 2007 e-mail:
> [T]he talk show host (Neil Borst) called for this effort after he had talked with me on the phone. He was trying to press me to express gratitude to the soldiers and I would not do that. I said I did not have all the information about what had happened. (I don't remember if it was he or a subsequent caller that said, "What do you mean, you don't have the info? Its all over the media, have you had your head in the sand all day!?") I told him not to put words in my mouth and when he persisted along the same line I got tired of his rudeness and hung up. Evidently he also cited my "unchristian" behavior in hanging up on him as further ammunition against us (as that shocking behavior was mentioned by various callers to the office).

56. CPTer Tim Nafziger, and Ekklesia's Simon Barrow provided an excellent analysis of media issues that arose during the hostage crisis in "Writing Peace out of the Script." Curiously, the issue of CPT receiving statements of support from groups committed to violent resistance, such as Hamas, the Al Aqsa Martyrs' Brigade, and the Muslim Brotherhood, was not used as a weapon by mainstream media critics. CPT did not translate the appeals in Arabic from most of these groups on their Web site, reasoning that the

Those who had heaped scorn on CPT over the months of the hostage crisis and its denouement became an afterthought. Those who had been touched by the witness of Kember, Loney, Fox, and Singh Sooden, and the thousands of people who rallied to their support, forged enduring connections with CPT.

"People are hungry for alternatives to violence that has destroyed so much in Iraq," wrote Rose and Pritchard; they continued,

> The media served to open a much-needed debate. They voiced the worldly wisdom that says only violence and armed force can bring peace and security. We had an opportunity from our direct experience of the world to speak of fundamentally different possibilities.
>
> Many people, hearing about CPT for the first time, wrote to CPT about their concerns, questions, hopes. Many prayed who had not prayed before. Many wept at the news of Tom's death and then wept again at the news of the others' release. This kidnapping stimulated a vigorous public debate about the work of nonviolence. It provided an opportunity to lift up both the powerful writings and witness of Tom, Jim, Harmeet, and Norman, and the work of the CPT team in Iraq. An important public discussion was stimulated by this crisis, and it will continue long into the future.
>
> Jesus said, "Very truly, I tell you, unless a grain of wheat falls into the earth and dies, it remains just a single grain; but if it dies, it bears much fruit" (John 12:24). Our delegation was kidnapped and Tom was killed. Yet this crisis has already produced much fruit. We have no idea of the full extent of this harvest.[57]

At the end of 2006, the Multinational Forces in Iraq apprehended men thought to have been conspirators in the kidnapping of Kember, Loney, Fox, and Singh Sooden. After some discussion amongst themselves, the three surviving hostages held a press conference in London, England on December 8, 2006, and read a statement that included the following:

> We understand a number of men alleged to be our captors have been apprehended, charged with kidnapping, and are facing trial in the Central Criminal Court of Iraq. We have been asked by the police in our respective countries to testify in the trial. After much

---

Arabic-speaking people they were targeting would understand the importance of these appeals in a way that non-Arabic speaking Western media would not.

57. Pritchard and Rose, "Unless a Grain of Wheat Falls," 13.

reflection upon our traditions, both Sikh and Christian, we are issuing this statement today.

We unconditionally forgive our captors for abducting and
holding us. We have no desire to punish them. Punishment can
never restore what was taken from us.

What our captors did was wrong. They caused us, our families
and our friends great suffering. Yet, we bear no malice towards
them and have no wish for retribution. . . .

In our view, the catastrophic levels of violence and the lack of
effective protection of human rights in Iraq is inextricably linked
to the US-led invasion and occupation. As for many others, the
actions of our kidnappers were part of a cycle of violence they
themselves experienced. While this is no way justifies what the
men charged with our kidnapping are alleged to have done, we feel
this must be considered in any potential judgment.

Forgiveness is an essential part of Sikh, Christian and Muslim
teaching. . . . Through the power of forgiveness, it is our hope that
good deeds will come from the lives of our captors, and that we
will all learn to reject the use of violence. We believe those who
use violence against others are themselves harmed by the use of
violence.

Kidnapping is a capital offence in Iraq and we understand that
some of our captors could be sentenced to death. The death penalty is an irrevocable judgment. It erases all possibility that those
who have harmed others, even seriously, can yet turn to good. We
categorically oppose the death penalty.

By this commitment to forgiveness, we hope to plant a seed
that one day will bear the fruits of healing and reconciliation for
us, our captors, the peoples of Canada, New Zealand, the United
Kingdom, the United States, and most of all, Iraq. . . .

Harmeet Singh Sooden, Norman Kember, James Loney[58]

As of this writing in the summer of 2007, CPT is still in the process of learning how the 2005–2006 hostage crisis affected its workers,
constituency, and supporters around the world. One can tentatively assert

58. CPTnet, "United Kingdom: Statement by Norman Kember, James Loney, and
Harmeet Singh Sooden," Dec 8, 2006. See also Loney's piece, "'I won't testify against my
abductors'" (in which he described the impossibility of his captors receiving a fair trial in
Iraq), and Kember, "Christianity Is a Radical Call." In July 2007, Kember told a reporter
for *The Mennonite Weekly Review* that he might participate in the trial, but only if he
were assured the current Iraq government would not impose the death penalty. "I think I
have a responsibility to try to help those men in some way," he said. Huber, "Former Iraq
hostage reflects on captivity."

that the organization successfully weathered the trauma. The four brothers who endured the violence and boredom of captivity, and the three who survived and suffered the loss of Tom Fox, retained their commitment to the nonviolent resistance Jesus modeled. With all of the energy put into the hostage crisis, CPT as an organization still managed to hold its trainings, put out newsletters, and support the work of all its teams.[59] The "great hand of solidarity" extended by thousands of friends, strangers, and fellow activists to aid CPT in its time of need still remains a source of comfort and energy. Donations to the organization increased and the possible cost of service with CPT unveiled by the kidnappings did not appear to cause a decline in recruitment. However, the very act of evaluating what the organization learned from the kidnappings—and the pain and blessings that accrued because of it—has instilled in everyone closely involved with the crisis a certain anxiety: that a trauma equally or more agonizing may someday arise for the organization.

POST-HOSTAGE CRISIS WORK IN IRAQ

Despite the evident dangers, most of the CPTers involved with the Iraq project wanted to find a way to keep working in Iraq. A view from outside the Green Zone was desperately needed and the violence in Iraq had been so directly fostered by the U.S.-led occupation. After January 2006, the authorities in Baghdad would not approve the visas of rotating team members, but a Kurdish woman in Suleimaniya had offered to sponsor CPT, which would enable team members to get visas there.[60]

Accordingly, Jan Benvie, Peggy Gish, Anita David, and Maxine Nash began some background exploration in the Kurdish region of Northern

59. In an August 5, 2007 e-mail, Father Jerry Stein, who for the first weeks of the crisis stayed with Jim Loney's family in Sault Ste. Marie, ON, wrote of stopping in at the Toronto office on his way to and from the Loneys' home:

"I saw a great professionalism, yet the communication and caring of deeply loving people, intensely busy yet excruciatingly available. I saw Christian community working and loving as one in a way that was obviously letting the Spirit do more work than usually noticed."

60. Peggy Gish, in a July 16, 2007 e-mail, wrote: "We had even thought at the time that Suleimaniya might be an entry port from which we would move out to work in other parts of Iraq." CPT kept paying rent on its two apartments in Baghdad until Sept 30, 2006, and continues as of this writing in Summer 2007 to pay a reduced rent on one apartment where sensitive files are stored. The landlord and his family left Baghdad for Amman in July. Pritchard, e-mails, July 23 and 27, 2007.

Iraq in the summer of 2006, meeting with NGOs working in the region and listening to the traumas that people there endured under the Saddam Hussein regime.[61] They also expended great effort in jumping through the necessary bureaucratic hoops for finding a place to live and registering as an NGO.[62] In November 2006, the team officially moved to Suleimaniya, with some hope they could still make short visits to Baghdad and other areas of Iraq.[63] For the next three months, the team continued to focus on the rights of detainees. They also met with Kurdish governmental officials, lawyers and human rights groups and internally displaced people and. talked with Kurdish groups interested in nonviolence training.

In January 2007, Peggy Gish, Will Van Wagenen, and their translator made what they thought would be a three-day trip to a region in Northern Iraq that lay outside of the Kurdish Regional Government (KRG) area. A newspaper editor who was the leader of an educational center there wanted the team to witness and report on the Yezidi community, which was suffering religious persecution, poverty, and mass displacement. He also said organizations and people living in the area might be interested in nonviolence training or collaborating with MPT to build a nonviolence movement in Iraq. As they traveled back to Suleimaniya on January 27, 2007, armed men stopped the editor, translator, Gish and Van Wagenen and told them to follow another car into the desert. When they had not returned to Suleimaniya within the timeframe they said they would, team members immediately began contacting organizations that had connections in the region where they had been abducted.

Their captors permitted Gish and the translator to leave the village on Monday, January 29, 2007. After her return to Suleimaniya, Gish was

---

61. CPTnet, Breen, "Iraq: Azad's Story from Kurdistan," June 22, 2006 (a longer version appears on the CPT Web site); CPTnet, Benvie, "Iraq: Remembering Anfal," Sept 1, 2006.

62. See, for example CPTnet, "Iraq Update: 11–17 July 2006" July 26, 2006.

63. In his comments on a draft of this chapter, Doug Pritchard wrote:

> We initially hoped to get to Baghdad and other parts of Iraq from [Suleimaniya], if only for short visits, to renew residency permits, visit friends etc. But that quickly became quite untenable. I think it was only during the face-to-face team consultations in Michigan in Sep 2006 that we officially gave up on getting to any other part of Iraq again soon and so let the second apartment in Baghdad go etc. in order to focus more on a return to Kurdistan.

questioned by the Kurdish security police for four days. Six days later, on February 4, 2007, the kidnappers released Van Wagenen and the editor.

Four months later, after she had had time to reflect, Peggy Gish wrote of the experience:

> When our guard asked me if I was a Christian, I simply said, "yes." But after he repeated the question, I sensed a veiled threat in what he asked. Then I knew I needed to say more....
>
> "You are holding us here, and you would do us harm," I said, "I am a Christian, and because I am, I will forgive you!" Our guard seemed taken aback at first, and then responded defensively, "No, we will not harm you! You are like my mother ..."
>
> Since then, I have been walking on a path toward healing, which I believe includes forgiveness of all involved in the kidnapping. I want to be free of the burdens of resentment toward those who took us captive and threatened to harm us, yet allow room for a healthy anger toward injustice and abuse.
>
> Looking back, I see that the anger I felt during the kidnapping was a gift God gave me and has been part of the forgiving process. This anger helped me combat the feelings of helplessness encroaching on me at that time and made it possible for me to speak the truth about the harm our captors were doing.[64]

On February 28, 2007, Doug Pritchard posted a notice on GITW saying that after consultations among Kurdish friends and the wider Iraq team, CPT had decided, for the time being, to withdraw from the region. He cited continuing security concerns, limited prospects for CPT work, and the unwillingness of the Kurdish Regional Government to extend team members's visas or grant NGO status to CPT workers as reasons.[65]

Pritchard wrote,

> The team leaves with a heavy heart knowing that the Iraqis whom we have met and with whom we have worked over the past four and half years face an increasingly unstable situation which has made the building of civil society extremely difficult. Our Iraqi

64. Walch, "Kidnapped BYU grad home safe"; GITW, "A Letter to Fellow CPTers," Feb 23, 2007; CPTnet, Peggy Gish, "Iraq Reflection: Anger, forgiveness, and healing," May 31, 2007.

65. Beth Pyles, in her comments on a draft of this chapter, wrote on August 1, 2008: "To be precise—the team never asked for our visas to be extended—Peggy sought a permanent visa and this was denied—and in terms of NGO status, this was neither granted nor refused—to my knowledge, our NGO application continues to remain in bureaucratic limbo in the KRG somewhere."

friends still hold hopes for a better future and that gives us hope too.

ISSUES ARISING FROM THE IRAQ PROJECT

Logistics

CPT set up its Iraq project roughly ten years after the first trained CPTers opened the project in Haiti. Some of the difficult issues the Iraq team faced CPTers had faced on other projects before. As was the case in Barrancabermeja, Colombia, Iraq team members had to live with enervating heat (both Iraq and Colombia team members noted the phenomenon of taking a cold shower and then putting on clothes they had laid out that felt as though they had been in a very hot dryer). Some Iraq team members also had to deal once again with difficult economic issues and feelings of guilt arising from the knowledge that they could leave a desperate situation and the people they worked among could not.

However, the intensity of how these issues affected the team seemed ratcheted up a notch from how they affected other teams. CPTers had had trouble obtaining visas from the Colombian and Israeli governments, but they had never had to provide proof that they did not have HIV/AIDS, nor did they have to wait weeks to obtain a visa in another country.[66]

66. Kerr, Montgomery, e-mails, July 14, 2007. Members of CPT's short-term delegations had a considerably easier time obtaining visas than CPTers who arrived to work on the Iraq Team. Evans, e-mails, July 24, 2007. David Milne wrote in a July 16, 2007 e-mail:

> It may be important to note that for a long time after the occupation there were no controls at the border. This was quite striking given that under Saddam the controls were quite tight. I remember going into Iraq on September 11 of '03 and we were not stopped, questioned or searched on the Iraqi side at all though American troops were present.

Doug Pritchard made a similar observation in his comments on a draft of this chapter:

> This was another thing that outraged Iraqis, that the US maintained no border controls during the whole period from Apr 2003 until Bremer left in Jun 2004. Even US army officers like Col Nate Sassaman couldn't believe this when we told them. This decision must have been made at the very highest levels. When Gene [Stoltzfus] and I went to Kabul shortly after the Taliban left they already had border controls at the bombed out airport—a group of mujahaddin with big guns and an ink pad came onto the tarmac, checked our passports and stamped them, and you then had to get visas in town before you could leave. Yet here in

Some CPTers suspected that the U.S. and UK governments were actively trying to prevent team members from getting visas or permission to work in the Iraq. These officials gave as a reason for not helping with visas that the situation in Iraq was too dangerous for civilians. When team members pointed out that they helped civilian contractors enter Iraq, their response was, "Well, they work for us."[67]

Most CPT projects involved jumping through bureaucratic hoops but, with the possible exception of CPT's project in Washington DC, these projects never consumed the amount of team time that getting in and out of Iraq and later setting up in the Kurdish north did. And the bureaucracy CPTers faced barely compared to the US military bureaucracy put in place to deter the Iraqis the team was accompanying from finding detained loved ones or seeking recompense for theft and damage caused by soldiers.

CPTers had faced death threats before in Palestine and Colombia, but these threats never trapped them in their apartment the way dangers in Baghdad did at times. The restriction on their movements made exercise and time away impossible for the team, which added to the already great amount of stress resulting from fears of kidnapping or death from countless possible acts of random violence.[68]

In most of the countries where CPT has worked, the reigning governments had at least one or two branches that functioned as a police state. However, before Iraq, the team had never really worked in a country ruled by a dictator as organized and ruthless as Saddam Hussein. Prior to the US-led invasion in March 2003, if CPT wanted to be in solidarity with

---

Iraq with thousands of US troops everywhere none of this was necessary at any border. Iraqis assume that the US was deliberately letting in any foreigners who wanted to come for whatever purpose and the country has suffered the consequences ever since.

67. Doug Pritchard, e-mail, June 10, 2007. Elizabeth Pyles, e-mail, July 16, 2007.

68. Regarding these stresses, Doug Pritchard wrote in his comments on a draft of this chapter:

And we had some close calls: the car blown up in the Tel Afar accompaniment, the bombings of nearby churches while we were attending others in Aug 2004, the mortar which hit on our roof in Nov 2005, the bomb in the local market minutes after Allan Slater walked by in Feb 2006. This we shared with all Iraqis and there was no way to predict when it might happen. But this all wore our people out at a considerable rate. More full-timers became depressed and had to quit early or change projects than I think has happened in other projects.

Iraqis who had suffered from a decade of western-imposed sanctions and faced imminent bombing from western nations, the organization could not publicize the egregious, even genocidal human rights abuses of the Hussein government.[69] Nor could it publicly condemn Hussein's government—as it had the coup government in Haiti or the Israeli government for their human rights abuses—if it wanted to keep sending CPTers and CPT delegations to Iraq. Not testifying to Saddam Hussein's atrocities rubbed against the CPT mandate to shed light on situations of oppression and was emotionally difficult for some CPTers.[70] Furthermore, after Saddam Hussein fell, team members undertaking public witnesses sometimes faced hostility from Iraqis who asked where they had been when they were suffering under Hussein's regime.[71]

Dealing with Media

While a small portion of CPT's constituency and people active in Latin American, Middle Eastern, and Indigenous solidarity movements had always followed CPT's work with interest, historically, CPTers spent much time strategizing ways that they could pique the interest of the mainstream media regarding the realities of the locations where they worked. Often this work required great effort and achieved minimal results. Even in Iraq, team members did not always achieve the goal of making people more aware of unexploded ordinance, thefts of jewelry and money during

69. At home, CPTers and CPT delegation members generally felt free to speak and write about these abuses, but focused more on the complicity of their governments in the suffering and deaths of hundreds of thousands of Iraqis. Ordinary citizens could not do much about Saddam Hussein, but they could address the abuses their own governments were committing.

70. Regarding CPT's criticism of governments, Doug Pritchard wrote in an August 8, 2007 e-mail:

> We were fairly free with denunciations of the Colombian govt initially. Then after the visa crisis we became more selective and did not do as many denunciations of the govt itself and the ones we did had a slightly more diffuse focus . . . It does stick in our craw to have to turn a blind eye to some things in order to keep one seeing eye in the region, but in these situations (Saddam's Iraq, current Colombia) we have felt it better (for the time being) to have one eye in the region rather than none. I suspect the same will be true in Kurdistan . . . But our caution in speech is constantly under review and there could easily come a time where we MUST speak out, even if it means immediate deportation.

71. See, for example, CPTnet, Peggy Gish, "Iraq: Dangers and angels," Mar 6, 2004.

house raids or the reconciling work of Iraqi Sunni, Shia, and Christian activists.

However, because the ongoing war in Iraq was in the world news almost every night, the team largely did not have to get people interested in Iraq the way they had had to solicit interest in other projects.

At some point, when CPT became one of the only international NGOs based outside of the Green Zone, the Baghdad team turned into a magnet for media seeking unfiltered impressions of what life was like in the Iraqi streets.[72] Although their 2003 report documenting abuses during home raids did not achieve the initial attention they had hoped for, after the Abu Ghraib photos came out, suddenly their report was in much demand by the international media.

On principle, Christian Peacemaker teams in the field try to shift the attention of international media wanting to do human-interest stories on the teams to the local people and issues they are facing. When the 2005 kidnappings occurred, however, the team could no longer avoid becoming the story, as much as they tried to uphold the detainee issues. This notoriety did not always sit comfortably with CPTers in Iraq and those doing support work in North America and the UK, but overall, once Kember, Loney, and Singh Sooden were freed, most in the wider CPT organization felt they had used the platform they had been given to espouse the principles of justice, nonviolence, and love of enemies.

Another issue that arose out of CPT's dealings with the media during the hostage crisis was having to advocate for the hostages blindly. In Palestine, Iraq, and Jordan, CPTers working on the hostage situation had trusted advisors who helped them get word to the Arabic media. CPTers doing media work in North America and the UK did not have the same sense of guidance. No one knew what the kidnappers were watching or reading, so every attempt at publicity was undertaken with the question,

---

72. David Enders wrote, in "Amid Hostage Vigils":

> As my colleagues were increasingly forced by their news organizations into secure hotels and to rely on foreign security advisors to tell them where it was safe to travel, I became one of the last foreign journalists willing to travel to places like Fallujah or to drive to the south. The CPTers were the only other Westerners I could rely on for information on what I might expect. Going to visit CPT over the months in Baghdad often felt like finding an oasis of sanity in an ever-expanding desert of confusion, a light in the darkness. I was comfortable working the way I worked as long as I knew they were there as well.

"What would the kidnappers think if they saw or read this?" Thus the banners people used at demonstrations, whether teams could drum up a digital camera to record these demonstrations, and even what CPTers were saying to their small, hometown newspapers took on enormous significance for people on the Media Team. This focus caused a certain amount of stress and fractious interactions among the people involved. Underlying these arguments was fear, the unspoken thought, "If we don't get the digital camera for the 'Shine the Light' demonstration in DC, and thus can't get footage to Al Jazeera, Jim, Norman, Harmeet and Tom might die."

As for the media turmoil after the hostages had been freed, people who served on the Media Team thought they should have perhaps said at the beginning, "We have not had a chance to fully debrief with Loney, Kember, and Singh Sooden so we do not know what happened when they were rescued. We will release a statement after we have been fully informed."[73]

Working in an Environment Where CPTers' Governments Were Directly Waging War

In Haiti, Chiapas, Palestine, and Colombia, the U.S. supported militaries, proxy militia, and economic violence, directly or indirectly. CPTers could generally draw a clear line from U.S. support to the violence in these conflict regions. CPTers could also make clear connections between violence that happened to North American indigenous communities and the U.S. and Canadian governments.

In Iraq, drawing this line was unnecessary; U.S. and UK troops were in the same locations that CPTers were, shooting and bombing Iraqi civilians and militants.[74] The soldiers were also, most of them, homesick and unprepared for what they encountered in Iraq, and—as had been the case with enlisted soldiers in Haiti, Hebron, and Chiapas—eager to talk with people who were neither their superiors nor the "enemy." Many had gone into the military and National Guard as a way of paying for college or because of limited employment opportunities in their home communities.

73. However, note Claire Evans' comments in n. 54.

74. U.S. Special Forces were also in Haiti, but under an awkward "peacekeeping" mandate. See chap. 2.

Some soldiers from the Oregon National Guard told CPTers that when they joined, they had expected to fight forest fires.[75]

As had been the case in the past, CPTers who viewed themselves as choosing work that was the opposite of what militaries do, often found themselves feeling compassion for these soldiers, especially for the enlisted men and women. (Officers were more often a part of the inhumane and bureaucratic processes the team found frustrating.) Allan Slater wrote,

> Dealing with soldiers was the part of the Iraq experience that changed me the most. It took me at least two months working in Iraq before I could bring myself to speak to them at all. I simply generalized in my own mind that they were all the enemy. The team that I was working with in late 2003 eventually forced me to deal with that perception when it was decided that I should fa- cilitate a meeting with several officers in the Green Zone. On that day I met a colonel who completely supported the war, the violent mid-night house raids and the incarceration of tens of thousands of Iraqi civilians. . . . He had no clear, ready statement of just what that job was. That colonel was never going to risk his neck ventur- ing out of the green zone on to the streets of Baghdad.
>
> On the same day I met a sergeant-major who risked his neck to put lists of detainees on a flash disk which we were able to copy to CD's for Iraqi human rights lawyers we were working with. It was the only access these people had to that information. . . .[76]
>
> Then there were the ordinary soldiers patrolling on the streets of Baghdad. Those meetings with officers made me curious about what the young privates might think. So I started to talk to them when I thought it safe for them, and when I would not be per- ceived as a US collaborator. They could really open up to someone who spoke English with an accent close to theirs, especially when they learned that I was just an old farmer from Canada. Most were scared, tired, and homesick. They were worried about their mar- riages, their children, and their boy friends or girl friends. . . .

75. CPTnet, "Iraq Update: June 22–27, 2004," July 9, 2007.

76. In his comments on a draft of chap. 11, Gene Stoltzfus wrote, regarding the lack of help the U.S. military extended to families seeking news of detained family members and redress for damage done during home raids,

> While you refer to military people who stonewalled, there were also people who were nervous, concerned and admitted there was a prob- lem. The team was helped immeasurably by sympathetic and low level military personnel. I think that this . . . was very important for the future work [and] legitimacy of the team and contributed to the atmosphere of inquiry leading to Abu Ghraib.

> All this experience has led me to conclude that soldiers are
> the very first victims of war. Even before war starts, they are being
> trained to hate and mistrust a potential enemy.... Do our societies
> have a right to do this? If we are willing to send soldiers to war,
> what responsibilities do we have to heal their traumatized lives,
> their wounded bodies, souls, and minds? What responsibilities do
> we have to families?[77]

Working in Dangerous Situations

CPT's work in Iraq led CPTers into dangers the organization had not faced before and these experiences altered the work of the team. In an organization that valued transparency as an operating principle, Iraq team members had to become secretive, particularly after the kidnappings, because speaking with complete frankness could get them and their Iraq coworkers killed.[78]

The hostage crisis also depleted many in the organization emotionally and resulted in some of its Iraq team members leaving the organization. While many in CPT had anticipated this affect on CPTers, they had not considered the affect on constituents and those outside the organization who had expended great effort on the hostages's behalf. They were thus surprised when a representative of the Electronic Intifada, which had posted the petition for the hostages' release and kept its constituents updated on the plight of the hostages and world-wide support for them and posted the petition for the hostages's release, asked that CPT staff close the project, because of the emotional toll it had taken on EI workers.[79]

And even though the organization planned trauma counseling for all of the CPTers most closely involved in the hostage crisis situation, many are still, as of 2007, still struggling with grief and anger. Doug Pritchard wrote,

> One consequence for both Carol and I and many others in CPT
> has been the need to largely put aside our own rage (at Saddam,

77. E-mail, June 11, 2007.

78. For an illustration of this secrecy, see Sheila Provencher's CPTnet reflection, "Normal," which appeared on December 1, 2005, shortly after the hostages were taken, and was attributed to "a CPT Iraq team member" with the added note, "The following reflection was written ten days ago by a CPTer no longer in Iraq." Provencher, e-mail July 18, 2007.

79. Electronic Intifada representative, e-mail correspondence, Mar–Apr 2006.

the occupation, the kidnappers) and our grief (at the kidnapping, at Tom's death) in order to do what was most needed for CPT at the time. The various memorial services and trauma healing sessions gave us some opportunity to grieve, but again we, and many other CPTers, had organizing or other public roles during those events and so did not feel free to grieve fully. We also had no traditions to fall back on (other than what we had done for George Weber) and so had to make these up as we went along. I think we got a lot of things right, but not everything. And we are learning from our trauma counselors and our own experience about the cost that comes with unresolved anger and grief. One only needs to look at some of the atrocities committed within Iraq by all sides to know how bad it can go.[80]

Counting the Cost

As mentioned above, CPT's commitment to continue working in Iraq in spite of the increasing dangers was regarded as a sign of naïveté by the mainstream media after the kidnappings. But reading through the releases and letters of Iraq team members from 2004 to 2006 one is struck by two recurring themes:

1. Iraqis are in constant danger; they are being kidnapped and murdered in much greater numbers than are internationals in Iraq.

2. Part of what makes us CPTers is our willingness to place ourselves in jeopardy.

Indeed, the writings of Iraq team members show a keen appreciation of the dangers they faced. During the Lent 2004 fast on behalf of Iraqi detainees (see previous chapter), Cliff Kindy found himself thinking that a suicide bomber could easily enter the crowd during the team's public vigil on the busiest street in the center of Baghdad.[81] Also in 2004, Tom Fox wrote the following:

I have visual references and written models of CPTers standing firm against the overt aggression of an army, be it regular or paramilitary. But how do you stand firm against a car-bomber or a kidnapper? Clearly the soldier disconnected from God needs to have me fight. Just as clearly the terrorist disconnected from God needs

80. Comments on draft of this chapter.
81. CPTnet, "Iraq: Letter from Cliff Kindy," Mar 8, 2004.

to have me flee. Both are willing to kill me using different means to achieve the same end—that end being to increase the parasitic power of Satan within God's good creation.

It seems easier somehow to confront anger within my heart than it is to confront fear. But if Jesus and Gandhi are right then I am not to give in to either. . . . Does that mean I walk the streets of Baghdad with a sign saying "American for the Taking?" No to both counts. But if Jesus and Gandhi are right, then I am asked to risk my life, and if I lose it to be as forgiving as they were when murdered by the forces of Satan.[82]

Jim Loney wrote a piece in 2004 comparing his father's anxiety for him to the anxiety felt by an Iraqi father he met for his son detained in Abu Ghraib prison:

I first told him in September [2003] that I was planning to go to Iraq with a group called Christian Peacemaker Teams to do human rights work. He said, "Well James . . . wish you'd think of your mother and I when you do these things."

. . . I told him I was scared, but that I felt it was something I needed to do. I talked about how Rick Yuskiw—he was a year behind my brother Ed in grade school—was sent to Afghanistan as part of Canada's war against terrorism, and how one of his closest buddies was killed when a roadside bomb exploded next to his jeep. If Rick was being asked to risk his life as a soldier then I, as a pacifist Christian who believes that war is not the way to peace, should be prepared to take the same risks.[83]

Every CPTer has wondered at some point, how he or she would react in the face of ultimate danger. CPT's work in Iraq made the organization as a whole ask itself that question, along with such questions as, "Is our willingness to face death endangering the people we work among?" and "What if death is not the worst thing we could face?" Perhaps the yearning of several Iraq team members to return to the country after CPT withdrew in early 2007 is an indication that the organization passed the test of nonviolent love.

---

82. "Fight or Flight?" This reflection, posted on October 22, 2004 on Fox's blog, Waiting in the Light, also appeared that day on CPTnet, and later on November 30, 2005.

83. CPTnet, "Iraq/Canada: Jim Loney's reflection, "A tale of two fathers," Nov 30, 2005. The fact that Justin Alexander left Iraq immediately in April 2005, after his name appeared on an abduction list (see previous chap.), also rebuts the charge that CPTers did not take precautions.

Sheila Provencher summed up some of this thinking on the cost of CPT work when she wrote about the hostages,

> They believed that it was worth risking everything to come close enough to listen. They came close enough to experience the other's pain and joy as their own. CPT was and is in Iraq to work . . . But above all, we are there to listen. To just "be-with." And we all agree—it is worth our lives.[84]

84. Provencher, "Our Refugee Family: Al Hol, Syria."

13

Short, Intermittent, and Stillborn Projects

> I believe what is waiting to happen is more and varied experiments
> in peacemaking to be birthed in places of impending disaster
> around our world... [I]n the midst of the debacles people are wait-
> ing and asking, "Where are the people with a strategy and follow
> through of the things that make for peace?"
>
> —Gene Stoltzfus, CPT Director Emeritus, 2007.[1]

THE PREVIOUS CHAPTERS HAVE covered projects that have served as a sustained focus of CPT over a period of years.[2] During the period covered by those projects, the organization was always considering invitations from crisis locations—and turning the majority of them down. From this slush pile of invitations, however, CPT staff in the early years would select a few to investigate further, based on the critical nature of the violence there, the ability of CPT to provide a fresh approach to the conflict or because its constituent congregations had a deep concern about a particular region. After initial exploration, CPT decided that it could not sustain some projects like Chechnya and Afghanistan or find CPTers with the necessary skills to staff them. Some, like the Borderlands (and Kenora and Bear Butte) projects had seasonal emphases or, like Vieques, needed people who could drop everything on short notice to support local organizers planning Direct Actions. The axiom that no experiment is

---

1. Gene Stoltzfus, "Warrior Strategies."

2. Although some of CPT's projects in some Indigenous communities were both short and intermittent, work in Indigenous communities was a sustained focus of CPT over the years, and invitations to accompany certain communities often came from members who had heard of CPT's work with other Indigenous peoples. By 2008, all work in Indigenous communities was categorized under "Aboriginal Justice" on the CPT Web site, just as all work in Hebron, At-Tuwani and other West Bank locations was categorized under "Palestine."

a failed experiment, because one always learns something regardless of the outcome, also applies to the projects covered in this chapter. Some taught CPT that it was not equipped to do substantive nonviolence work in those locations, or that the needs of the local grassroots organizations did not quite fit into CPT's mandate. Others could have been considered a qualified success in that the need presented itself, CPT responded and the crisis ended.

After twenty years, with CPT knowing better what it can most effectively do in crisis locations, these short projects are worth reviewing—if only to evaluate why some projects, after they closed, became relegated to a few files in the Chicago office, rarely spoken of again, and others became classic illustrations for explaining CPT's history and mission.

GAZA 1993

Haiti was the first project staffed by CPTers who had gone through training, but it was not the first team-based project. As the brutality of the Israeli military in Gazan refugee camps during the first Intifada continued through the early 1990s without international intervention, CPT began exploring the idea of putting a team in the camps to serve as a violence-deterring presence.

Several of CPT's early founders such as Harry Huebner and Hedy Sawadsky had experience working in the Middle East and had hopes of CPT bringing a fresh approach to the Israeli-Palestinian conflict. This interest led CPT to organize two delegations in 1991 and 1992 to Israel and Palestine before sending a team to Gaza, the second of which committed civil disobedience by crossing the border (or Green Line) from Israel into the West Bank.[3]

During the second delegation, CPTers had discussions with Zoughbi Zoughbi—who would later be instrumental in helping CPT set up the Hebron project—Naim Ateek, and other Palestinian Christian leaders about the possibility of placing a team in one of Gaza's refugee camps. Stoltzfus noted in his proposal for the Gaza project that CPT received "significant encouragement," which continued after the delegation returned to North America, to start a project in one of these camps.

Stoltzfus wrote,

3. Gene Stoltzfus, e-mail, Aug 27, 2007.

In brief, our basic vision would be an initial project of two months with one month additional for a one or two person advance party. One person would be designated the group leader and the other four would rotate in and out of the camps, where they would stay with the families. The group leader would be designated the specific responsibility of explaining these peacemaking efforts to local or regional leadership as appropriate, Palestinian groups, Muslim groups, Christian groups, Israel Defense Force. If and when it is desirable, the group would report on events to the press or make their observations available through Gaza and Jerusalem-based human rights offices with which we are already in touch. The team will also report to the communications offices of our various sponsoring denominations in the hope that the effort might catch the imagination of the wider church community in North America, so that the project becomes a source of inspiration for the peacemaking there.

Peacemakers living in the camps would be primarily charged with a ministry of presence and observation. When violence threatens, they would be encouraged and trained to be present, and, if possible, to intervene. We are not assuming that the presences of this outside group would be respected by the authorities. The possibility exists that CPT people could be expelled at any time[;] however we believe that this would in itself be a witness in the long term [as] it's own teaching appeal for those whose ears can hear.[4]

On July 2, 1993, Duane Ediger and David Weaver flew into Tel Aviv to begin doing the necessary advance work for the Gaza team. Upon arrival, however, Ediger's arrest for crossing the Green Line during the 1992 CPT delegation came up on the immigration computer, and the Israeli authorities denied him entry. Weaver thus had to make the connections and set up housing by himself, while Ediger undertook project support from the Chicago office.

Weaver's work with the Palestine Human Rights Campaign in 1989 proved helpful in making the necessary connections, and he was able to arrange with the Gaza Center for Rights and Law to use its printer, telephone, and fax.[5]

4. Gene Stoltzfus, "Proposal to Place a Five Person Team in Gaza."

5. CPT, "Report of Forced Return of CPT Person from Israel"; David Weaver, faxes, July 6 and 11, 1993.

The three remaining team members, Phyllis Butt, Cliff Kindy, and Elayne King arrived on July 18, 1993, and moved the next day into refugee camps. For the next two months, the team members stayed with more than twenty families in five of the eight refugee camps in the Gaza Strip. Four times, they were present in homes when Israeli soldiers raided them.

In one instance, Cliff Kindy was staying at the home of a family in Rafah camp who had lost a son three days earlier when he blocked an Israeli military vehicle in pursuit of a wanted man. Shot eight times, the son was taken to Khan Younis hospital, but soldiers surrounded the building, refusing entry to doctors trying to treat him. He died the next day. Three times, the Israeli military governor of the area came to the family's home telling the mother, "Keep out your mourning clothes: We're going to kill your other son, too."

The night before the funeral, soldiers destroyed the plumbing in the family's home, trashed the furniture as they went room to room, and shot holes in the roof. One soldier ground his heel into the hand of a sleeping one-year-old.

Kindy was staying with the family the night after the funeral when soldiers returned to the house. He stood outside with the men of the family, whom the soldiers were forcing to take down the posters and whitewash over slogans on the walls of the house regarding the dead son. When asked what he thought could happen in Palestine and Israel, he said, "My faith provides a hope that people can live together peacefully in spite of differences, so I give my life to work for that goal." A soldier named Ariel, broke in, saying, "I have no faith. There is no hope. In our situation, only the strongest will survive and we're the strongest. You, Cliff, you go take down the posters."

As the soldiers began pushing against the men again, possibly to provoke a response, Kindy tried to stand between the two groups and was ordered by the soldiers to move away. At that moment, a white bird flew by. Kindy asked what it was and a soldier told him it was a Monkey-faced Owl. "We don't have them in Indiana," Kindy said. A mate joined the first owl and they circle over the yard, which seemed to "break the spirit of the raid," Kindy wrote.[6]

While the Gaza project was ending, the news of the Oslo negotiations burst onto the world scene. On September 13, 1993, the PLO and the

---

6. Cliff Kindy, "Indiana Peacemaker Softens Israeli Raid," Aug 2, 1993; Cliff Kindy, e-mail, Aug 23, 2007.

Israeli government signed the Oslo Declaration of Principles. As was noted in the chapter on CPT's Hebron project, these Accords ultimately did little to better the lives of average Palestinians and Israelis, but in September 1993, many Israelis, Palestinians, and the internationals who cared about them held out a skeptical hope that their situation might improve.

To Gazans, however, these negotiations in September 1993 did not signal a lessening of Israeli military brutality. "Israeli snipers shooting every day from rooftops in Khan Younis Refugee camp create a terrifying atmosphere," wrote David Weaver. "We are pleased that some common ground has been found in the talks, but peace is not right around the corner." Although the establishment of the Palestinian Authority to rule Gaza (and Jericho) would mean the withdrawal of Israeli troops, the people in the camps feared the desperate economic conditions brought on by border closures might lead to even greater conflict within Gaza.[7]

Three of the four people who had stayed in the camps wrote evaluations of the project. All agreed that the level of physical danger needing intervention was less than they had imagined, and expressed reservations about placing a longer-term team in the camps as a violence-deterring presence or symbolic expression of solidarity.

David Weaver wrote,

> At times in the past five weeks, I have had to ask myself what we are doing here. Are we, in fact, involved in symbolic nonviolent action at its worst? Repeatedly, we have heard from Palestinians, both those living in the camps and those with well-established professional positions, that groups like ours enthusiastically come and go, and nothing changes. In fact, life has gotten worse . . . ? What makes our work any different than the others? . . . I have felt at times like we are working for the headlines, a confrontation or drama, which will gain us some bold print. Then we can return home feeling like we were truly brave in the face of trial, like our presence somehow staved off the evil of violence one more time. However, this type of "flash in the pan" action does not provide the type of light that Palestinians need to keep hope alive. It may help us feel good, but what does it really do for them?
>
> Will we discover a way to integrate our symbolic nonviolent actions into a larger strategy that may bring real change, or will our symbolic nonviolent action become an end in itself?

---

7. David Weaver, "Gaza Team Applauds Peace Efforts."

Weaver recommended that CPT should shift its focus from living in the camps as a violence-deterring presence to sending people with the necessary skills to "augment work being done by Palestinians already." "If these persons were able to live in the camps and travel each day to their work," Weaver wrote, "thus experiencing the hassles and confrontations with soldiers like everyone else, CPT/CPC's integrity and effectiveness as an organization would have the possibility of affecting real change."[8]

However, the Oslo Accords seemed to call for a "wait and see" approach for CPT. The organization's focus was also taken up with the first training in 1993 and the preparation to set up a project in Haiti. CPTers serving on the Hebron Project would visit Gaza over the years, but the organization would never set up another project there.

Issues that Arose From the Gaza Project

Interpersonal Relationships

From the time that the four CPTers entered the Gaza Strip, personality conflicts within the group drained an enormous amount of energy. Indeed, during the first CPT training for full-timers, which began shortly after the Gaza project ended, the trainees heard frequent references to these fractious relationships that resulted in two of the group not being able to live in the same camp with each other.

As an organization with multiple projects, CPT would learn the danger of interpersonal dynamics, rather than the mission of the team, becoming the team's focus. The Gaza project affirmed the assertions of some within CPT that it needed to pay serious attention to relationship and team-building skills during training[9]

8. David Weaver, "CPT/CPC: What is our purpose in Gaza?"

9. In his August 27, 2007 e-mail regarding a draft of the Gaza section, Gene Stoltzfus wrote:

> I regarded working with team dynamics as part of the territory of human work. Over the twenty-three years since Techny I have experienced most of those breakdowns. Some were transformed into amazing healing experiences. Some were not. On the whole, I was enormously impressed by how little such troubling and painful moments there were rather than how many. . . . the world is human and we need to forgive ourselves for not being perfect. I always found pressure to make the training into much more of team building from selected individuals. I never felt that it should be de-emphasized and I think we got better with process suggestions over the years. But, I also felt that too much em-

Following lead of local partners

CPT has always attracted people with strong ideologies. For some people in the early years, what CPT should be looked like Ron Sider's vision of Christians interpositioning themselves between warring parties. For others, it looked like a violence-deterring presence, such as practiced by Witness for Peace and Peace Brigades International. Yet other CPTers had significant cross-cultural experience and never assumed Sider's model, or the models of other peace groups, would work in every location (see chapter 1).[10] The experience in Gaza confirmed that CPT could not expect people in another culture to rearrange their lives, religion, or philosophy to accommodate North American Christian models of peacemaking. For example, team members thought about addressing the issue of home demolitions in Gaza by a sort of confrontational rebuilding, with the assistance of Brethren and Mennonite Disaster programs or Habitat for Humanity. However, local partners informed them that doing so would be construed as giving material aid—particularly after the Oslo Accords were signed and Israel theoretically left the Gaza Strip. Another example involved team members's engagement with Israeli soldiers, which fit into the reconciling, enemy-loving theology of CPT, but was difficult to do without arousing the suspicions of Gazans who had been brutalized by the Israeli military for such a long time.

Although the Gaza project would never become something that the organization would point to as a stellar accomplishment, the time spent there was not wasted. Cliff Kindy would later become a founding member of the Hebron team, bringing with him his experiences living in Palestinian culture (although Hebronite and Gazan culture differed in some respects). The Gaza project also helped solidify contacts with Palestinian and international NGOs that Wendy Lehman and Kathleen Kern would find useful when undertaking the background research for the Hebron project.

---

phasis on what I considered unattainable goals of good team dynamics would set us up for failure. Organized bodies have to live through destructive periods and not allow them to dominate the organizational culture. In CPT, we dare never forget we are organized for a task.

10. In comparing CPT's work to that of Peace Brigades and Witness for Peace, Gene Stoltzfus wrote: "CPT was inherently more open-ended and guided by practical and open-ended notions of enemy loving [and] rootedness in the Christian message which actually gave more flexibility. This was not insignificant and inherently led to confusion for people seeking fast and easy formulas." E-mail, Aug 27, 2007.

And the stumbling of the Gaza team, if nothing else, validated the CPT Support Team's and Steering Committee's expectations that sending trained CPTers, rather than available volunteers, into crisis situations would make a difference.

CHECHNYA 1995–1996

In 1991, bitter factional infighting broke out in the Republic of Chechnya, between those Chechens who wanted independence and those who maintained an allegiance to Moscow. By October 1994, the "separatists" controlled most of the country. In November 1994, Russian forces, accompanying the pro-Moscow Chechen forces, attacked Grozny, the capital city of Chechnya. For the next months, tens of thousands of Russian troops, many of them poorly trained, poured into the country. The Russian air force relentlessly bombed Grozny as well as other areas of the country, displacing hundreds of thousands of civilians.

Although polls showed that most Russians opposed the war in Chechnya, President Boris Yeltsin and his followers seemed to demand the Chechens's total capitulation before he withdrew Russian troops. Desertion and disappearances of the Russian troops reached crisis proportions, which inspired the development of the "Committee of Soldiers' Mothers of Russia." In March 1995, these mothers organized a "March of Motherly Compassion, Moscow-Grozny" in which about two hundred people participated. Along with Buddhist organizations and other sympathizers, the mothers walked for two months to raise awareness of the atrocities in Chechnya, and express solidarity with victims of violence.[11]

Steve Hochstetler Shirk who, with his wife Cheryl, was serving as Mennonite Central Committee Country Representative for the Former Soviet Union, had some contact with the group that undertook the march. In his subsequent communications with CPT, it appears that the nonviolent witness started him thinking that Christian Peacemaker Teams might be able to contribute a violence-deterring presence to the conflict.

In the spring of 1995, Shirk sent a fax to Christian Peacemaker Teams, requesting that CPT make a "Christian Peacemaker Team Feasibility Study Trip" to the region. The welcoming local bodies would

11. Wallis, "Chechnya Peace Observers Feasibility Report"; Stoltzfus and Driedger, "Chechnya Report and Proposal."

be the Union of North Caucasian Women Omega and Soldiers' Mothers of St. Petersburg.

Under his "Rationale for CPT involvement," Shirk wrote,

> It is very important that Christians have a presence for peace in this region, where religious differences shadow the political conflict. Peace activists and Chechen women were astounded last week when Shirk spoke for the Christian Peacemaker Teams. They were glad to hear that groups in Japan and Western Europe were getting interested in some kind of action, but CPT aroused a different kind of response. They just could not believe that there are people who believe so strongly in peace that they maintain a standing organization and send groups into numerous conflicts, all on small-scale private financial support. . . .
>
> The Buddhist monks involved in anti-war activity wear their yellow robes and beat their drums, clearly not trying to soft-pedal the religious motivation behind their activity and have endeared themselves to many Chechens by their commitment to ending the bloodshed . . . [A]n explicitly Christian, faith-motivated witness for peace will have added significance.
>
> CPT is uniquely placed to carry out this ministry of presence and quiet witness of solidarity. This is an opportunity for a living witness to faith with peace and hope, in place of indifference of religious authorities and the faithlessness of so many.[12]

Accordingly, CPT director Gene Stoltzfus and Canadian social work professor Otto Driedger, accompanied by Shirk, who served as a translator, visited Chechnya from August 30 through September 4, 1995. They noted in their report about the trip that Grozny resembled Stalingrad, Berlin, and Dresden after the end of World War II. Under a section entitled "Experiences of Atrocities were Shared Ad Infinitum," Stoltzfus and Driedger listed stories, both confirmed and unconfirmed, they had heard. These included reports of grenades tossed into basements where Chechen women and children had sought refuge from the shelling, the Russian military dumping the bodies of their soldiers in a valley, so they could be reported missing rather than getting sent home in body bags, and the military using helicopters to pursue deserting Russian soldiers and shoot them. The CPT delegation spoke with a Chechen man who had been hung upside down from a helicopter in midair, and viewed a video

---

12. Steve and Cheryl Hochstetler-Shirk, "Christian Peacemaker Team Feasibility Study Trip."

showing Chechen men, women, and children being killed and burned. "Of particular horror" the report noted, "was a video picture of a woman, five months pregnant, with a block of firewood forced into her vagina."

At the end of the report, Driedger and Stoltzfus wrote that Steve Hochstetler Shirk and they had returned from the delegation "firmly convinced that CPT should envision a project in Chechnya." They recommended that a team of four people document human rights abuses and "explore and support opportunities for nonviolent action with Chechen and Russian partners." Because they would work with largely Russian-speaking human rights groups, some of the team members would have to be fluent in Russian. "All must be trained in human rights monitoring, spirituality for crisis, communications and nonviolent action," they wrote. They estimated that the cost of a one-year delegation would be $75,000 U.S., which would cover upkeep, travel, and the cost of maintaining a vehicle.[13]

Ray Hamm, a Canadian Mennonite pastor active in MCC-Canada and CPT reservist Jim Satterwhite joined a follow-up delegation in April 1996 that included representatives from War Resister's International; Peace Brigades International; a Buddhist order; Oxfam; Mothers of Russian Soldiers; the U.S. Chechen Congress; and two Japanese journalists. After talking to refugees, NGO representatives, leaders of the Chechen separatist movement and government representatives,[14] Satterwhite wrote in his trip summary that the Russian military was clearly waging war against the Chechen civilian population and that Boris Yeltsin's current "peace initiative" was reminiscent of Nixon's "peace with honor" strategy in Vietnam. "The clause in the peace initiative which states that actions against "terrorists" are still permitted seems to have been interpreted to mean that *any* action is permitted, since by their definition, all Chechens are classified as terrorists," Satterwhite wrote. He further noted that even if Yeltsin had proposed this peace in good faith, the Russian military seemed to be operating as though it had no need to clear its actions with Moscow.

13. Stoltzfus and Driedger, "Chechnya Report and Proposal."

14. In his report, "Report on Chechnya Delegation, April 1996," Satterwhite wrote, "Sunday we talked to a representative of the Zavgaev government—the Russian-installed government in Grozny. The man was an old Party Hack, without any imagination. The one thing he said of interest was that this government does not recognize the division of Chechnya and Ingushetia."

The report recommended that CPT consider placing one or two fluent Russian-speakers in neighboring Ingushetia, rather than Chechnya, due to the rampant criminal activity in Chechnya fostered by the war. Because of the Western governments's responsibility for helping to fund the war, and the fact that Bosnia seemed to be commanding the attention of international observers in a way that Chechnya had not, Satterwhite noted that Chechens felt they had been isolated and abandoned. "The representation of an alternative Christian viewpoint from N. America helps to dispel the sense of isolation, works against the polarization of Muslims and Christians, which has been a byproduct of the war, and helps to offset the Russian Orthodox church's re-emerging identification with the Russian state," Satterwhite wrote.[15]

As a professor at Bluffton College, Satterwhite was able to devote his 1996 summer break to an extended trip to the Caucasus region, during which he was able to meet with more local actors in the Chechen conflict. He initially based himself out of Ingushetia, because of safety concerns and the promise of a direct phone line to Moscow that never materialized. However, after several short trips to Grozny and surrounding villages, he finally got to the city for an extended two-week period before he was to return home—just before the Chechens retook Grozny from the Russians, effectively ending that phase of the Russian-Chechen war.

During his stay in Ingushetia and Chechnya, Satterwhite wrote more than a dozen reports, and translated depositions from Russian into English. These writings recorded a foul litany of human rights abuses:

- Russian soldiers shooting cattle herders, beating them until their bones broke, hanging them from a crane by the neck, burning them with cigarettes
- Soldiers shooting at civilian cars from helicopters and pushing live Chechens out of their helicopters
- Soldiers dragging living Chechens behind tanks
- Soldiers mutilating and burning corpses
- Soldiers attacking villages after Chechen fighters made a public departure to signal to the Russian army that only civilians remained

15. Ibid.

- Soldiers looting and bombing homes after villagers had clearly left and intentionally making these villages uninhabitable[16]

In his September 1996 report about his work in Chechnya, Satterwhite noted that the situation in Chechnya was "extremely fluid" since the Chechens had retaken Grozny, and that placing CPTers there would not be an effective use of resources. Instead, he suggested that CPT use funds earmarked for Chechnya to support the work of Quaker Peace Service volunteer Chris Hunter, who had been of great help to CPTers who visited Chechnya in 1995 and 1996. In the long term, he thought CPT might have a useful role in accompanying Ingush refugees back to North Ossetia.[17]

However, at that time, CPT had yet to reach its 1992 goal of twelve trained full-timers and was juggling projects in Haiti, Hebron, Washington DC, and Bosnia. It also had serious invitations for help from Chiapas and Puerto Rico, which CPT was better equipped to handle, given that Spanish speakers were easier to find than Russian speakers.[18] Because the organization was over-extended and Satterwhite was the only CPTer fluent in Russian, those involved with the Chechnya exploratory groups regretfully decided that CPT could not place a team there.

Issues Arising from the Chechnya Project

Tenuous U.S. Involvement

Satterwhite asserted in his reports that the U.S. and other Western governments bore a large share of responsibility for the continuation of the war in Chechnya. He wrote,

---

16. Satterwhite: "Chechnya: Peacemakers and Peace Agreements,"; "Chechnya Impressions"; "From Grozny to Moscow"; "Impressions from Ingushetia"; "Interplanetary Travel"; "Landscape after the Battle"; "Life in an Occupied City"; "Peace Rally in Grozny"; "Reflections on the War in Chechnya"; "Samashki Revisited"; "Sernovodsk Today"; "The war in Chechnya seen through the eyes of a child," Depositions of atrocities committed in the village of Katir-Yurt; "Document written by the Assembly of Independent Socio-Political Parties"; "Declaration from the Assembly of Independent Social-Political Parties." See also the CPTnet versions of some of these articles that were edited for length, available in the June–August 1996 CPTnet archives.

17. Satterwhite, "Chechnya Report." For Satterwhite's account of his visits with Ingush refugees, see "Refugees from the Other War."

18. Hull (CPT Steering Committee chair), e-mail to Gene Stoltzfus, Aug 24, 1995.

Because they regard Yeltsin as the candidate of "moderation," they tend to support him over all others. In addition, they have regarded the Chechen war as an internal affair of Russia, not subject to outside interference....

[The] war is no longer strictly an internal matter, since by joining the Council of Europe and entering into other international agreements, Russia has bound itself to respect human rights—an undertaking clearly violated by the indiscriminate targeting of civilians. By giving Russia money—either directly, or through international lending agencies, as with the recent IMF loan—the Western countries tacitly fund the very abuses they purport to condemn.[19]

However, most Americans regarded the war in Chechnya as remote, outside the realm of U.S. interest, unlike the Middle East and Latin America. U.S. President Bill Clinton's administration made it known that it regarded the Russian-Chechen conflict as an internal affair. However, the Clinton administration did so around the same time that the U.S. was preparing to invade Haiti and some believed that that the two invasions were connected. Yeltsin would not criticize the U.S. invasion of Haiti if the U.S. did not criticize Russia's invasion of Chechnya.[20]

In fact, Yeltsin appears to have believed that he could achieve popularity for invading Chechnya the way Clinton had in Haiti. Sergei Yushenkov, chairman of the Defense Committee of the lower house of the Russia parliament, was quoted as saying to Oleg Lobov, secretary of the Kremlin's security council:

On the telephone [Oleg] Lobov [said] 'It is not only a question of the integrity of Russia. We need a small victorious war to raise the President's ratings....' Clinton in Haiti could perform a successful operation and his ratings immediately jumped up. I was not able to convince Lobov that Chechnya was not Haiti.[21]

19. Satterwhite, "Christian Peacemaker Teams—Chechnya Fact-finding Trip." In his comments on a draft of this section, Satterwhite wrote that he and a Chechen man had met with the Political Officer at the U.S. Embassy in early August 1996 (after Satterwhite's time in Chechnya.) The Political Officer responded to their reports of the situation in Chechnya by saying, "'we know all that. You just have to understand that the United States interacts with Russia on many issues, and Chechnya is just one of them.' Thereby," Satterwhite wrote, "justifying the United States' unwillingness to condemn/censure the Russian war in Chechnya."

20. See, for example, Roazen, "U.S. Must Do More for Chechnya."

21. Cottrell, "Chechnya: How Russia Lost." In addition to the Haiti/Chechnya connection with CPT's work, there was a Hebron/Chechnya connection. See chapter 4, n. 37.

Regardless of what the Russian and American governments believed, however, Satterwhite noted that Chechens made the connection between their misery and U.S. policy. "The question most often directed to me as an American is: "why is America paying for this war?" he wrote. " How am I to answer, especially when I am standing amidst the rubble from a bomb made possible by our indifference?"[22]

Chechen Use of Violence

In most of the places CPT has worked, elements of the local population with whom CPT has stood in solidarity maintain the option of violent resistance to military occupiers. Part of CPT's job has involved documenting that the violence of the occupiers is far more lethal and comprehensive than, for example, the violence perpetrated by Palestinian militant groups or the Zapatistas, as well as explaining what the occupiers had done to provoke such resistance.

Chechnya was no exception. Chechens had been fighting Russian domination off and on for several decades. Satterwhite noted in one of his reports that the Fellowship of Reconciliation was reluctant to become involved in the conflict for that reason.[23]

Satterwhite took the opposite tack: Chechen resistance to Russian tyranny was in and of itself a noble venture. Therefore, those elements of the Chechen population who had strategically chosen nonviolent resistance needed ample international support. In two of his reports, written after the Chechen "separatists" took control of Grozny, he quoted a Chechen as saying, "The defeat of Moscow's forces [in Chechnya] is a miracle. It shows what can be achieved by men of steel who know how to bear and use arms, who are fired against tyranny by their faith, who fear nothing. The Chechen victory offers hope to oppressed peoples everywhere."

Satterwhite then wrote, "Would it not have been good if we could say that this peace shows what can be achieved by PEACEMAKERS who are fired against tyranny by their faith, who fear nothing?"[24]

22. Satterwhite, "Peace Groups in the Caucasus."

23. Ibid.

24. Satterwhite, "Chechnya: Peacemakers and Peace Agreements"; "Chechnya." A shorter, conflated version of these two pieces appeared on CPTnet on January 15, 1997 under the title, "Chechnya: Peacemakers and Peace Agreements." In the first piece, Satterwhite followed the quotation about the Russians' defeat in Ichkeria/Chechnya with, "Yet the defeat of Russian forces was not just through violent struggle; peacemakers also took risks to bring this miracle about."

BOSNIA 1996

As the hostilities raged in Chechnya, a better-publicized war was happening in the former Yugoslav republics—a war that introduced the term "ethnic cleansing" into common parlance. In the spring of 1992, Croatia and Slovenia had seceded from the Yugoslav Federation. Bosnians also voted in a referendum—which most Bosnian Serbs boycotted—to secede. With the assistance from the Serb-dominated remnant of the Yugoslav Federation, Bosnian Serbs began attacking Bosnian Croats and Muslims.[25]

While atrocities against Bosniak (Muslim), Serb, and Croat civilians in the shards of the former Yugoslavia continued to mount, the warring parties met in Dayton, Ohio to sign a U.S.-brokered peace accord. The Dayton Accords stipulated that all refugees had the right of return to their pre-war homes and named four towns—which had had ethnically diverse populations before the war broke out—to serve as pilot projects. Theoretically, these towns would each accept the return of two hundred families, out of two million refugees who had fled their homes.

Jajce (pronounced "yaitse") was one of the four towns. Formerly, it had had about forty thousand Serb, Bosniak, and Croat residents and had been occupied twice by two different armies. The vast majority of refugees from the town were Bosniak and Serb.

Randy Puljek-Shank, a reservist who had gone through the January 1995 CPT training, and his wife Amela were working with the International Mennonite Organization (IMO)[26] in August 1995 when they met with Jim Satterwhite in Split, Croatia, and then went to Konjic, Bosnia. They explored together a role for CPT in the former Yugoslav Republics that resulted in a January 1996 proposal for a CPT presence in Jajce.[27]

Regarding Chechen violence, Satterwhite also wrote, in his comments on a draft of this section, "The CPT presence here as elsewhere offered the chance for dialog about the use of violence (particularly in response to [a September 2004] Chechen hostage-taking in a school in an area neighboring Chechnya)."

25. "Timeline: Bosnia-Hercegovina," from *BBC News,* has noted under its entry for 1993, "The conflict is extremely complex. Muslims and Serbs form an alliance against Croats in Hercegovina, rival Muslim forces fight each other in north-west Bosnia, Croats and Serbs fight against Muslims in central Bosnia."

26. See Foth, "Internationale Mennonitische Organisation." German Mennonites had been working with refugees in Bosnia-Hercegovina under the auspices of IMO since 1992.

27. Satterwhite, e-mail, Sept 7, 2007.

Puljek-Shank noted in his proposal that parties involved in the conflict seemed to have "little political will" to resolve the situation of refugees and attendant issues of rights to previously owned housing, employment, political power-sharing, and security for minority populations.

He wrote,

> We believe there might be a place for a team of international monitors to accompany the return of refugees to one or more of these areas. Such a team would have as a goal to assist in the ethnic re-integration of Bosnia through the means of active nonviolence. ... They would accompany refugees when they return and also live themselves in the towns. ...
>
> The Croat-held areas have so far been the most intransigent for the return of refugees; therefore, I believe that the start must be there. ... Because we have more people in our teams from Jajce, this seems to be the best starting point.[28]

Amela Puljek-Shank was a native of the town—which also factored into the choice of that location. As the co-initiator of the Jajce project, she described its goals:

> Real peace is only possible in Bosnia if people live together, and hatred does not bring good to anybody. We can't believe and can't accept that people should be separate and should hate each other, because we remember how it was before and for us now it is time to show that people can live together and help those who want to. To love your neighbor as yourself, this is what the Bible tells us. ... We start this project in the name of friends which we had and love which we shared. In the name of old friendships and old life, in the name of what we had before.[29]

In response to this invitation, CPT—which was struggling to find people to serve on Haiti, Hebron, and Washington DC projects—sent Lena Siegers and reservist Suzanne O'Hatnick to Jajce for the summer of 1996. O'Hatnick, recording her first impressions as Amela Puljek-Shank gave her a tour of the town, noted the great natural beauty of the town's environs, the lakes, rivers, and old castle on a highest hill. However, when they got closer, she wrote, "I could see almost every house had been hit by

28. Randy Puljek-Shank, "Concept for a Refugee Return sponsorship program."
29. Amela Puljek-Shank, letter to supporters, n.d.

mortar shells, and many were completely gutted. As I gazed at the people in the street, I saw only guarded expressions, closed faces."[30]

As was the case with several other CPT projects, the initial goal—accompanying refugees back to Jajce—proved not to be feasible at the time O'Hatnick and Siegers arrived. Croats from decimated villages surrounding the town had moved into houses vacated by the Serbs and Bosniaks forced out of Jajce. Refugees coming to reclaim their homes would thus have to evict other people whom the war had also made homeless. Those of Jajce's inhabitants who had the financial resources had left the country during the war, which also angered impoverished squatters who had not had that opportunity.[31]

In the end, Siegers and O'Hatnick spent most of their time visiting with neighbors over coffee and hearing their stories, as well as hosting work groups that IMO sent to help repair or rehabilitate homes.[32]

The two major forms of accompaniment the team undertook that summer were escorting refugees to municipal offices so they could obtain the papers they needed to reclaim their homes and maintaining a presence at Muslim funerals.

Even though Muslim refugees from Jajce could not safely return to their homes, they could conduct funerals and bury their dead in the town. CPTers, other internationals, and NATO troops had usually monitored these funerals. For one funeral, however, Amela Puljek-Shank was the only person available to observe. She witnessed a Croat policeman running into the funeral grounds shouting at the Imam and other praying Muslims, "Hurry up! Finish your prayers and get out of here." He and his colleagues talked loudly and made crude jokes during the rest of the service. They then bullied the mourners as they returned to their bus, and followed the vehicle closely to make sure it got out of town. CPTers thus made a more concerted effort to attend other funerals that summer.

Although Siegers, O'Hatnick, and the Puljek-Shanks recommended that CPT consider placing a team in Jajce[33] or a long-term volunteer to facilitate the visits of work groups, CPT sent no further workers there after

30. O'Hatnick, *Journey to Bosnia, Return to Self,* 14.

31. Ibid., 40–41.

32. Ibid., 19–21. The IMO groups worked on equal numbers of Bosniak and Croat housing, giving preference to homes inhabited by women, children and elderly.

33. Lena Siegers, e-mail to Gene Stoltzfus, Sept 4, 1996; Suzanne O'Hatnick, e-mail to Gene Stoltzfus, Nov 26, 1996.

the summer of 1996. As was the case with Chechnya, language and lack of available workers were issues. Additionally, the aid and resettlement work of IMO was specifically outside CPT's mandate and the Puljek-Shanks were concluding their work with IMO in Jajce in December 1996.[34]

Nevertheless, the short presence CPT maintained in Jajce appeared to have some lasting impact. Randy Puljek-Shank wrote in 2007,

> The two CPT reserve members lived in a neighborhood where mostly Muslims had lived before and through their presence helped to change the atmosphere in that part of town. We believe that we helped contribute to the better organization of returnees, [and] pressure for increased return continued after our time in Jajce . . . Today Jajce is one of the most ethnically mixed towns in Bosnia, and signs commemorate Muslim holidays as well as Christian ones, something that was unthinkable during that time.[35]

Issues Arising from Bosnia Project

Partisanship

Given the role that ethnic divisions played in the conflict, CPT and the IMO workers had to proceed cautiously when interacting with the Bosniaks and Croats in Jajce. Bosniaks had suffered the brunt of the ethnic cleansing in the town, so the CPTers and Puljek-Shanks lived in the section of Jajce that had been predominantly Bosniak before the war, along with some elderly people who had not fled their homes.[36] The team's affiliations with Bosniaks made Croats reluctant to talk to them and former Croat friends of Amela Puljek-Shank now shunned her.

In the end, the volunteer groups that the team hosted provided a way for the team to make contact with Croats, given that these teams were helping rehabilitate both Croat and Muslim homes. The cheerful German banter the volunteers engaged in with the locals helped smooth

---

34. In his comments on a draft of this section, Randy Puljek-Shank wrote: "IMO saw its work in Jajce as also being a nonviolent presence. The aid and resettlement was a framework that made that possible given the reality at the time. Their presence in Jajce continued for some years including a period of violent demonstrations for and against refugee return."

35. E-mail, July 18, 2007.

36. In his comments on a draft of this section, Randy Puljek-Shank noted that almost all of Jajce's neighborhoods had been somewhat mixed before the war.

a path for the team to have more extended conversations. Nevertheless, Suzanne O'Hatnick wrote that she had difficulty visiting well-furnished Croat homes, knowing that furnishings that had once belonged to someone else.[37]

Role of the U.S. in the Bosnian Conflict

"I could laugh when President Clinton said that now there is peace in Bosnia," Amela Puljek-Shank wrote in a 1996 letter to her supporters. The Dayton Accords divided Bosnia-Hercegovina, a region where Serbs, Croats, and Muslims had lived together, into three small states in which ethnic minorities would have a great deal of trouble living. Furthermore, the fact that known war criminals, the men who had in fact started the nationalist violence, were negotiating the fate of her country in Dayton, Ohio, gave her very little faith in the process. She noted that the war could have been stopped in 1992, and Western nations had little interest in doing so, despite reports of atrocities. The atrocities only seemed relevant when used as support for policies four years later.

Randy Puljek-Shank wrote in his letter to supporters that the basic conditions the U.S.-brokered Dayton Accords set for democratic elections did not exist in Jajce. Only one party, the Croat Nationalist HDZ, had access to media for campaigning. Information about the HDZ played on the local stations for one hour every night. Other parties were not allowed or were afraid to organize assemblies. "The result was pretty predictable," he wrote. He also noted that the pullout of the American troops seemed timed to benefit U.S. President Bill Clinton's 1996 election campaign more than Bosnia's situation.[38]

Mixed Local and International Team

Six years before Colombian nationals became part of the Colombian team Amela Puljek-Shank worked with the Bosnia team—not only as a woman of mixed Bosniak and Croat heritage but as a native of Jajce. When asked

---

37. O'Hatnick, *Journey to Bosnia*, 21–22.

38. Ibid., 23–24; Randy Puljek-Shank, letter to supporters. Feeling helpless about the elections, and the US disinterest in brokering an actual just peace, O'Hatnick and the Puljek-Shanks began meeting nightly at 7:00 two weeks before the election to pray that it would be peaceful and that the refugees would return home. Although the second petition was not granted until much later, after the team disbanded, both Randy Puljek Shank and O'Hatnick wrote of these prayer sessions being a highlight of their time together.

to comment on the subsection entitled "Incorporation of Colombians into Team" under the "Issues" section of chapter 10, she wrote,

> If I would not have been married to Randy, I would not have been able to live in Jajce since I was not on the list of 200 people that could return. I was told very clearly that I can stay in Jajce only for the single fact that my husband is American; otherwise, the police would kick me out....
>
> On the other hand, my presence in the team definitely opened doors in the local community to internationals. The local people that we worked with knew me and my family many generations in the past and my presence with internationals created a trusting and open atmosphere. Also, I was able to "translate" cultural and social expectations as well as the political situation to internationals. Also, it was clear that the local Croat authorities could not hide the facts and cover up things since I knew very well what was happening and could on the spot correct certain facts that were not portraying truthfully what was happening in Jajce. My presence held them in check. [M]ore then once I thought that my marriage to Randy and relationship with Suzanne and Lena saved my life. So, having mixed teams is, from my perspective, the best solution since it protects both nationals and internationals. Both sides bring gifts to the teamwork and make things much more harder for the oppressor....[39]

Depression

In all of the major CPT projects, violence, political setbacks, and difficult human interactions have led to times of depression for CPTers and those with whom they worked most closely. But for the limited time CPT was in Jajce, the devastation wrought by the war—physical and emotional—seemed to weigh especially heavily on Siegers, O'Hatnick, and the Puljek-Shanks. Siegers wrote of a "fearsome evil that lurks over Jajce."

> The Muslims dream of atrocities done to them by the Serbs and worry about the Croats. The Croats fear that someone might see them talk to their Muslim friends and neighbours and report them to the Croat Police. The Croat police are afraid to wear nametags for fear that someone will accuse them carrying out their orders or not carrying out their orders. The few Serbs who dare venture into town are afraid of being accused of all the evil in town ... There is widespread depression. As people talk about the horrors of the last

39. E-mail, September 14, 2007.

four years of war, they break into tears. They tell the same stories over and over and lament the fact that their dreams have all been shattered. They are afraid to dream again.[40]

Jajce's situation was even more heart-rending for Amela Puljek-Shank, a native of the town. In a letter to her supporters, she wrote,

> Personally, I am disappointed with this world in which we are living. So much suffering, pain, and hatred. We are so far from God and we can see so little and we don't want to see and hear what God is telling us. For me personally, it is very hard to be in Jajce and watch how my town is falling apart . . . People don't want to open their hearts to God and they don't want for God to change them . . . they hate each other. Their souls are suffering. Sometimes I see that people are walking in a desert and trying to find water. Water is all the time in front of them, but they don't see it. The water is God and he is the source of life and love. But some people prefer to be thirsty. They are lost and their soul is dying slowly.

Nevertheless, in spite of all that Puljek-Shank and her family had suffered since 1992, she still held on to the scraps of human kindness she saw in Jajce. She wrote of people who maintained friendships in spite of the criticisms leveled at them by nationalists, saying, "These examples give me very much strength and power to continue." [41]

VIEQUES 2000–2003

For more than sixty years (beginning in the 1940s), the United States used the island of Vieques, part of the commonwealth of Puerto Rico, as a bombing range, dropping tons of live explosives and poisoning the environment with, among other contaminants, napalm and depleted uranium. Vieques's history chronicles displacement of civilians from lands the U.S. wanted for practice military operations, environmental catastrophes, and racism typical of colonial powers. The cancer rate on the island, at the time of CPT's involvement with the Viequense struggle against the Navy, was about 27 percent greater than the rate on the main island of Puerto Rico. The number of Viequenses living below the poverty line was

40. Siegers, "Report on Jajce."
41. Letter to supporters, n.d. (probably Autumn 1996).

72 percent, compared with approximately 48 percent of the entire population of Puerto Rico.[42]

Viequenses had spent several decades resisting the presence of the U.S. military and its callous disregard for their lives and environment. In 1993, Robert Rabin and Nilda Medina, building on years of small protests by the residents of Vieques, helped start the Committee for the Rescue and Development of Vieques (CRDV), which rapidly became a mass movement on the island, drawing in fishermen, labor unions, churches, and other branches of civil society. All of its participants, regardless of their political affiliation, had the same goals: to stop the bombings, force the U.S. Navy out of Vieques, and demand that the U.S. government clean up the toxic waste it left on the island.[43] When two five hundred pound bombs missed their target in April 1999, killing civilian guard David Sanes and injuring four other people, it touched off mass protests organized by CRDV. At the place he died, the CRDV established the first of fourteen protest camps, with the intention of conducting mass civil disobedience by occupying the bombing range when the U.S. Navy began bombing again.

Church of the Brethren pastor Juan Figueroa and Wanda Colon of the Caribbean project for Justice and Peace—both of whom had a relationship with CRDV—invited CPT to send a delegation to investigate the dispute between Puerto Ricans and the U.S. Navy over the bombing of Vieques. The first delegation arrived with an eye toward analyzing the feasibility of having a longer-term project on the island. While on Vieques, they had an opportunity on March 15, 2000, to join the Ecumenical Camp in the "restricted impact zone" of the bombing range after local people heard rumors that arrests would happen that night. The delegation wrote a proposal recommending that CPT send a two- to three-person team to Puerto Rico in order to facilitate visits of other delegations to the impact zone and the Peace and Justice Camp in Vieques.[44]

42. Marino, "Puerto Rico's New War on Poverty"; Todaro with Henjum, "The U.S. Navy's assault"; FOR, Task Force on Latin America and the Caribbean: "Puerto Rico Under the Gun"; FOR, "Puerto Rico Update: Disarming the U.S. Military Hub in Latin America"; FOR, "Environmental Impacts of Navy Training."

43. CRDV referred to "Four Ds": demilitarization, decontamination, devolution (return of all Navy land to Viequenses), and economic development. "The Vieques 4 D's—Our Historic Demands."

44 CPT Vieques Delegation, "Christian Peacemaker Teams Delegation to Vieques, Puerto Rico, March 11–17, 2000." CPT Vieques Delegation, "Report CPT Delegation to Puerto Rico March 11–18, 2000.

Due to the lack of personnel, CPT instead began sending "emergency delegations"—sometimes assembled by staff with less than two week's notice—to respond to calls from Puerto Ricans in the resistance camps.

Such a call went out at the end of April 2000, when two Navy warships left Virginia and stopped in North Carolina to pick up one thousand Marines and equipment, then headed for Puerto Rico to remove the protesters. CPT dispatched a nine-member delegation to arrive on Vieques May 1–2, 2000. Some of them joined Puerto Rican religious leaders and Pastors for Peace in the Ecumenical Camp[45] stationed at the High Impact Zone. Others went to the Peace and Justice Camp, situated just outside the gate of the Camp Garcia naval base.

At 6:00 a.m. on May 4, 2000, the Ecumenical encampment received word that arrests had started at the other camps. When the military trucks arrived at the delegates' encampment, they and their fellow protesters linked arms in a circle and began to sing Spanish hymns. U.S. Marshals searched the bags of the encampment participants, handcuffed them, and led them away to join more than one hundred arrestees from the other encampments. Marine helicopters flew them to the Roosevelt Roads Naval Base on the main island of Puerto Rico. After the delegates refused to sign or give any information without lawyers present, the authorities released everyone without charge.[46]

Just before the May 4 arrests, activists from the Mount David and Mapepe camps left them to go deeper into the live impact zone on the bombing range and serve as human shields to prevent the bombing.[47]

45. A photo of the encampment shows one of the tents bearing a sign reading, "Campamento Cristiano en Obediencia Evangelica," or, as Duane Ediger suggested in a September 11, 2007 e-mail, "Christian Encampment in Obedience to the Gospel." Ecumenical Encampment on Vieques, photo.

46. Burns, "Feds to Remove Vieques Protesters"; Villerrael, "Protesters Prepare in Puerto Rico"; Brown, e-mail to members of Vieques delegation, Apr 30, 2000; Ediger, "Emergency delegation"; John Buschert, "U.S. Navy should stop bombing"; CPT, "CPT Emergency Delegation Supports Resistance Camps"; CPT Vieques Delegation, "May 1–8, 2000," delegation log; CPT Vieques Delegation, "Report: CPT Emergency Delegation to Vieques."
CPTnet releases: "Puerto Rico Alert: U.S. Marshals Threaten," Apr 28, 2000; "Puerto Rico: CPT Sends Emergency Delegation, May 1, 2000; "Puerto Rico: CPTers and Peace Campers Detained," May 4, 2000.

47. Vieques Libre, "There Are Still Several People in the Live Impact Area in Vieques."

Given this ongoing resistance of the islanders, CPT sent another delegation from May 10 through 17, 2000 following on the heels of the previous one. JoAnne Lingle, Cliff Kindy, and Mary Anne Grady Flores remained from the first delegation. They were soon joined by Andy Baker and Dianne Roe and preceded to the Peace and Justice camp—one of the few camps the Navy had not destroyed.

Robert Rabin informed the CPTers that a vigil would be held at Monte Carmelo on Saturday night, May 13, 2000, so the delegation set up tents there. That evening after worship, fifty-six people divided into three groups went under the fence at Monte Carmelo onto the base. The treatment they received from the authorities was different from that received by activists arrested the previous week. A Mexican American officer called the mostly Puerto Rican arrestees on the bus, "lazy half-breeds." When one Puerto Rican arrestee referred to the officer as a "wetback," he was dragged out of the bus, beaten, and jumped on by several military personnel. When others protested this treatment, soldiers sprayed them with mace. A Navy officer told Baker when he was taken off the bus with other arrestees that he was going to sodomize him with his nightstick and make him "his bitch."

At the Guaynabo Federal Prison on Puerto Rico's main island, Baker, Ambrosia Brown, Mary Anne Grady Flores, and Cliff Kindy were issued numbers, strip-searched, and fingerprinted. The next day, May 15, a judge charged the fifty-six protesters with trespassing and released them on their own recognizance.[48]

JoAnne Lingle wrote, in her unpublished article, "Mother's Day March in Vieques," about meeting the mother of the two sons hiding on the bombing range:

> During World War II, mothers who had sons in the U.S. military put small gold banners edged with fringe in their window panes proclaiming they had a son in the war. These mothers were honored for their sons' sacrifice to their country. How different it seemed when I looked at Aleida and realized that her sons, Casimar and Pedro, had gone off to a bombing range willing to sacrifice their lives . . . completely unarmed.

48. CPT Vieques Delegation, "CPT Trip Report for Vieques May 10–17"; Griner, "Manchester protesters live out beliefs"; CPTnet, "Puerto Rico: CPTers arrested in Vieques," May 15, 2000; CPTnet, Cliff Kindy, "Vieques, Puerto Rico: CPTers arrested," May 18, 2000.

Regarding the overall behavior of the U.S. authorities on Vieques, Rich Williams wrote, in a September 18, 2007 e-mail:

> What is hard to communicate is the level of bullying and the extremes the Navy and Federal Marshals went to. Also it is hard to describe the creativity and enthusiasm of the Viequenses in finding ways to enable

CPT sent its next delegation to Vieques September 29 through October 9, 2000, in response to another call from CRDV to participate in a massive march and vigil at the Peace and Justice Camp outside the entrance to the Camp Garcia bombing range. This event was the first of several actions planned by local organizers to create obstacles to Navy bombing.[49] On October 1, Angela Freeman and Cliff Kindy entered the U.S. Naval Ammunition Storage Depot on the western end of Vieques and were arrested with fifty-three other people.[50] Since Kindy, referred to by the San Juan Star as "a self-described Christian peace activist," had violated the conditions of his May release by returning to Vieques, a judge revoked his bail and sent him to Guaynabo to await his trial. On October 10, Kindy pled guilty to the charges of trespassing for his participation in both the May and October witnesses "as a way," he said, "to tell the Puerto Rican people their voice is being heard." The court combined the charges, ordered him to pay a $300 fine and put no restrictions on his return to Vieques.[51]

With its January 25 through February 4, 2001, delegation, CPT attempted to summon a large scale CPT presence of up to forty delegates, broken up into affinity groups, to participate in Vieques actions. They eventually got twenty-seven delegates on board, divided into four affinity groups that did their worship and processing together.[52] However, organizers on Vieques had decided that they would wait to undertake further acts of civil disobedience until newly elected Governor Sila Calderon pulled out the riot police guarding the Naval base (as she had pledged

---

supporters in places of power to circumvent these acts of bullying. There was a real sense of David and Goliath—complete with the overblown hubris of the Navy and the precision and effectiveness of the challenges by the Viequenses.

49. CRDV, press release, Sept 27, 2000.

50. In "Recommendations to CPT/Delegation Coordinators," the CPT Vieques delegation noted, "If the coordinator is going to do CD, there must be a co-coordinator who has all the details of meetings scheduled, phone numbers of persons contacted, etc."

51. Irizarry, "Navy Detains protesters on Vieques.; Delfin, "Activist Jailed"; Kolster-Frye, "Ordeal Leading to Arrest"; CPT Vieques Delegation, "CPT Delegation to Vieques—Trip Report"; CPTnet, "Vieques, Puerto Rico: Christian Peacemakers Arrested," Oct 2, 2000; CPTnet, "Vieques, PR: CPTer arrested, detained," Oct 14, 2000; CPTnet, "Vieques, PR: In prison for peacemaking," Oct 27, 2000.

52. An affinity group is a small group of activists who work together on direct action, usually in confederation with other affinity groups.

to do) to avoid Puerto-Rican-on-Puerto-Rican violence.[53] The purpose of the large delegation was thus changed "engergizing" the grassroots resistance movement on Vieques, but Cliff Kindy also hoped to use the delegation to test CPT's ability to mobilize a large delegation for future events in which massive civil disobedience was needed.[54]

On February 1, at Roosevelt Roads Base on the main island, all twenty-seven delegates marched to the base gate in their red hats. Seven delegates—Jim Clune, Anne Herman, Brian Ladd, JoAnne Lingle, Lisa Martens, Steve Ratzlaff, and Brian Terrell—crossed into the base to deliver a letter signed by all the delegates to Navy Rear Admiral Kevin Green. The letter resembled in form the "ban and bar" letters that activists against the Navy presence on Vieques had received when courts found them guilty of trespassing. It concluded,

> Therefore, we, as people of faith and members of Christian Peacemaker Teams delegation from the United States, Canada, and Puerto Rico, after prayer and consulting with representatives of the affected parties, including the U.S. Navy, DEMAND THAT THE U.S. NAVY CEASE ALL OPERATIONS ON VIEQUES, CLEAN AND RECLAIM ALL TOXIC SITES AND LEAVE.
> Violations of this order may constitute violations of the laws of the United States, of international law and the sovereignty of God.

Navy personnel handcuffed the seven and took them to a holding area. A local police officer from the town of Ceiba then escorted them to town's police station and released them.[55]

53. After Calderon's November 2000 election, she sent a letter to President Clinton calling for the immediate withdrawal of the US Navy from Vieques, even though the previous governor had made a deal with the Clinton Administration that would have allowed the Navy to remain. That agreement had called for Puerto Ricans to vote in a referendum by February 2002, on whether the Navy should leave by May 1, 2003 or continue its war games on the island indefinitely, which would result in $50 million in aid. The referendum provided no option for ending the bombing immediately. Whitefield, "Vieques clash back on the front burner"; Damaso Lopez, "Letter from mayor-elect."

54. Evans, letter to College Peace Studies coordinators, Nov 13, 2000; Evans, e-mail to former Puerto Rico delegation members, Nov 10, 2000; Cliff Kindy, e-mail to Gene Stoltzfus, November 3, 2000.

55. CPT Vieques Delegation, letter to Rear Admiral Kevin Green, Feb 1, 2001; CPT Vieques Delegation, "Vieques Trip Report"; CPT Vieques Delegation, "Log for the CPT Delegation to Vieques"; Cliff Kindy, email to delegation affinity group leaders, Nov 29, 2000; Gonzales, "Protesters held by Navy"; Rutter, "Seeking sea change for Vieques"; CPTnet, "Puerto Rico: CPT delegation calls for End," Feb 2, 2001.

After a U.S. Navy ship left its port in Virginia for Vieques on April 27, 2001, the organization once again assembled an emergency delegation in response to the local activists's requests.[56] Four of the eight-member May 1 through 7, 2001 delegation committed civil disobedience within the first forty-eight hours after they landed in Vieques. Mark Byler, Brian Ladd, H. A. Penner, and Rich Williams—all of whom had participated in previous delegations to Vieques—entered the Naval Base through a hole in the fence with several dozen other protesters. They added their numbers to approximately 180 other activists who committed civil disobedience the last week of April 2001 in order to prevent the Navy's resumption of war games April 27 through May 1, 2001.[57] Included among this group were luminaries such as Reverend Al Sharpton, actor Edward James Olmos, Robert F. Kennedy Jr., 1199 Service Employees Union President Dennis Rivera (who would help arrange bail for the four CPTers), U.S. Representative Luis Gutierrez of Illinois, and other New York State and New York City legislators.

Dubbed the "Vieques 4" by the CPT support team, Ladd, Penner, Byler, and Williams were released on $450 bond and returned for a trial on June 28, 2001. A federal magistrate in San Juan convicted the four of trespassing after a seven-hour proceeding. Penner served a twenty-day sentence in the Guaynabo Metropolitan Detention Center—sharing a cell with New York State Assemblyman Adam Clayton Powell IV—and Williams served thirty days.[58] Byler and Ladd received a year's probation,

56. When the Navy announced its intention to resume bombing, Governor Calderon introduced legislation on April 18 to tighten noise restrictions in a way that would effectively prohibit the Navy from engaging in ship-to-shore gunfire. She also accused the Defense Department of violating an understanding to suspend training operations on Vieques pending the outcome of independent reviews of studies on the health-effects of the training. On April 24, 2001, Puerto Rico filed a federal lawsuit against the Navy and Defense Secretary Donald Rumsfeld to halt the Navy's exercise, arguing that the Navy's training activities would threaten public health and violate both the new noise-restriction law and the 1972 federal Noise Control Act. O'Rourke, "Vieques, Puerto Rico Naval Training Range."

57. The Human Rights Commission in San Juan estimated that between May 2000 and May 2001 more than 1500 people were arrested for civil disobedience. HRC, "Human Rights Violated in Vieques."

58. Williams wrote of the experience, in a September 15, 2007 e-mail, "Robert F. Kennedy, Jr. was with us for some of that time . . . During our stay, there was a malfunction in the automatic door locking system and the outside door of our prison unit was unlocked for an entire day. Like Peter in Acts 16:26–30 we remained in our cells."

were sentenced to community service, and had to spend nights in work-release facilities. Ladd had his wages garnished to pay lodging costs.[59]

Between the May 2001 and April 2 through April 9, 2002, delegations, a number of important political changes happened. In June 2001, President George Bush announced that Navy would stop bombing Vieques in 2003. The next month, 68 percent of Viequenses voted to call for an immediate end to the bombing and the cleanup and transfer of lands back to the island's residents.[60] Then came the September 11, 2001, Al Qaeda hijackings and attacks on the World Trade Center in New York and the Pentagon. The Committee for the Rescue and Development of Vieques put out a "Shout for Peace" on September 23, 2001, which read, in part,

> The presence and activities of the U.S. Navy in Vieques were immoral before the 11th of September and they continue to be immoral today. Our community in struggle has declared a moratorium on civil disobedience actions based upon our commitment to peace and as a show of solidarity with the victims and families affected by the tragic events of 11 September as well as concerns for the security of our people.
>
> However, we emphasize that our solidarity is directed toward the innocent victims of terrorist attacks and not toward the militaristic actions of the U.S. government. The pain brought on by these violent acts for thousands of families in the U.S., in Puerto Rico and around the world, is also our pain. And our struggle for peace

---

A book by Carlos Alá Santiago Rivera containing portraits and testimonies of the Vieques resisters was published in 2003: *El Rostro Oculto de la Desobediencia Civil: Testimonios desde la carcel* ("The Hidden Face of Civil Disobedience: Testimonies from Prison"). H. A. Penner appears on pages 213–14, and Williams is featured on 211–12.

59. "Navy officials arrest Boulder man in Vieques"; Langeland, "Boulder man released"; Rutter, "20-days in jail"; Clark, "Area prayer in Vieques now in 'jail.'"; Zuercher, "Mennonite begins work release sentence"; "Activist released after vote"; CPT Vieques Delegation, "CPT Delegation to Vieques, April–May 2001"; CPT Vieques Delegation, e-mail to Robert Rabin and Nilda Medina, May 8, 2001 (Rabin responded to Guynn in an e-mail the next day, "excelente lista de ideas. i think the uranium here stimulates thought process!!"); CPT, "CPT Vieques 4"; statements read by H. A. Penner and Rich Williams at their sentencing; Ladd, e-mails to Claire Evans, July 9 and 20, 2001; Byler, e-mail, June 12, 2001; Penner, letter to Claire Evans, July 7, 2001; Gibbel, letter to donors, July 31, 2001. See also CPTnet releases: "Puerto Rico: Peacemaker Delegation Arrives," May 1, 2001; "Vieques, PR: Four CPT delegates arrested," May 3, 2001; "Vieques, PR: Delegation ends," May 14, 2001; "Chicago/San Juan: Vieques 4 return to Puerto Rico," June 17 2001; "Puerto Rico: Four CPTers Sentenced," June 29, 2001.

60. FOR, Task Force on Latin America and the Caribbean, "Vieques Movement Faces Uncertain Future."

is also the struggle for peace for the U.S., for Puerto Rico and all the peoples of the world.[61]

In January 2002, the Navy unexpectedly moved its military exercises scheduled for Vieques to bases and bombing ranges in Florida and North Carolina, which instilled hope in the anti-navy activists that they were making an impact. The CRDV announced in February 2002 that it was preparing a series of actions to support imprisoned protesters and raise awareness in neighborhoods about the health effects of the military contamination of the island and the necessity of Viequenses in these neighborhoods to join the struggle. It also was planning a "multifaceted strategy of massive protests" in March or April 2002—depending on when the Navy resumed bombing.[62]

With all of these considerations, the April 2–9, 2002, delegation was a somewhat subdued, more education-oriented affair. However, the serious purpose of the post-September 11 delegation was articulated by delegate Chris Friedman, quoted in a CPTnet release announcing the arrival of the delegation: "By opposing the training on Vieques, we are also engaging directly in opposition to the war in Afghanistan and to the very real likelihood of expanded military strikes elsewhere in that region."[63]

On July 23, 2002, the CRDV put out a "Call to Action for Peace on Vieques," alerting supporters that the Navy was preparing for yet another round of bombing during the second half of August or September. As it happened, the four-person August 23 through September 3, 2002, delegation found out that the bombing was scheduled to begin on September 3, the day they left. Instead of doing the civil disobedience they had planned, they participated in a Relay for the Peace and Future of Vieques that took place on the delegation's first day and fasted in support of Robert Rabin and other incarcerated activists who were fasting until the bombing stopped. When Kindy called Puerto Rican contacts on September 5, 2002,

61. CRDV, statement in delegation orientation packet, Sept 31, 2001.

62. CRDV, press release, Sept 27, 2000.

63. Maney, "Being peacemaker not always popular"; Zimmer, "Area Mennonite travels to Puerto Rico"; Maney, "Pacifism a tough sell since Sept. 11"; HRC, "Human Rights Violated in Vieques"; "Puerto Rican Court orders Vieques vote readied"; CRDV, "Not one more Bomb! U.S. Navy Out Now!"; Friedman, "CPT delegation to Vieques"; Friedman, "Continuing the Struggle on Vieques"; CPT Vieques Delegation, "Christian Peacemaker Teams Delegation Log"; CPT Vieques delegation, "Report of Christian Peacemaker Teams emergency delegation"; CPTnet, "Vieques, Puerto Rico: CPT Delegation Joins Local Witness," April 2, 2002.

he learned that two hundred bombs had fallen in thirty hours, beginning on the afternoon of September 4, 2002.[64]

The U.S. Navy agreed to leave the island on May 1, 2003, and CPT sent a delegation to participate in the celebrations. Just before midnight, on April 30, 2003, Navy security left the entrance gate to Camp Garcia they had been guarding and the crowds waiting outside broke through it. People (not including the CPT delegation) then began tearing down the fence surrounding the base and knocking down the cement guard posts with sledgehammers. Several vehicles remaining on the base were burned. For the next four days, activists held commemoration ceremonies, basked on beaches previously unavailable to them, and renamed Navy sites. Camp Garcia became the "May 1 Free Zone."

In his report for the April 29–May 5, 2003, delegation, Mark Becker cited several concerns that would continue after the Navy left. The Navy had stopped bombing the Island but continued to operate a radar installation, and a communications outpost on Mount Pirata. Cleaning up toxic sites accumulated from sixty years of bombing would take an estimated $450 billion. The Navy had not actually turned the land over to the people of Vieques but instead gave it to the Department of the Interior's Fish and Wildlife service.

"Finally," Becker wrote,

> Local activists repeatedly emphasized that this was a nonviolent struggle for the peace of Vieques. It is important to recognize celebrate and embrace the end of the Navy's bombing as an example of the possibilities of nonviolent direct action. In contrast to this largely peaceful struggle, the press focused on the burning of vehicles in the early hours of May 1. . . . Most activists denounced the burning of the vehicles as an anomaly at odds with the movement's nonviolent struggle. . . . [But] many activists agreed that it was hypocritical to prosecute these relatively insignificant actions [which Governor Calderon pledged to do] while doing nothing about the much more abusive actions of the U.S. Navy over the past six decades.[65]

64. CRDV, "A Call to Action for Peace on Vieques"; CPT Vieques Delegation, "CPT Report—Delegation to Vieques"; "Christian Peacemaker Team delegation to Vieques"; CPTnet, Holmes, "Vieques, Puerto Rico: Passing on the Flame," Aug 25, 2002; CPTnet, "Puerto Rico: CPT Delegation participates in ongoing relay fast," Sept 6, 2002.

65. On June 20, the burning cars came back to haunt CRDV when Federal agents entered its offices and seized its property. Five days later, Nilda Medina and eleven other

When the final CPT delegation to Vieques asked Robert Rabin about the possibilities for further CPT intervention, he mentioned civil disobedience around the issues of cleaning up military waste and returning land in Vieques to its original owners. Asked what the future might hold for him and CRDV, he said, "Avoid speculation and create democracy."[66]

Issues Arising from the Vieques Project

Delegation Model

In 2000, CPT did not have the personnel to field a team in Vieques, and so chose to send delegations to arrive at the times that CRDV needed short-term international presences—usually when the U.S. military planned to commence operations. Rather than being "second best" to a full-time project, the delegation model—with its attendant concluding press conference—actually turned out to be more suitable for Vieques interventions. As Cliff Kindy noted in an e-mail to the author, "This model proved to be another way to do CPT, and this time in one of the very dramatic and successful nonviolent campaigns of the last century."[67]

---

activists were arrested for what appeared to be political motives, given that they had all served as leaders in the nonviolent campaign against the Navy. Indeed, witnesses reported that Medina had intervened publicly on the night of May 1, 2003, to calm the situation and bring order after the vehicles were set on fire. All but one of those arrested, Jose Perez Gonzalez, took plea bargains to avoid mandatory five to twenty year sentences. Jorge Armenteros, attorney for Perez Gonzalez, compared the toppling of the Berlin Wall and the statue of Saddam Hussein in Baghdad to the dismantling of the Camp Garcia base on May 1, 2003: "What happened in Iraq and Berlin, we applauded, and what happened here, we criminalize." FOR, Task Force on Latin America and the Caribbean, "Vieques Arrestees Set for Sentencing". See also Gene Stoltzfus, letter to Rep. Luis Gutierrez, July 11, 2003.

66. Becker, e-mail to the CPT Vieques Yahoo group, May 6, 2003; CPT Vieques Delegation, "Christian Peacemaker Teams April 29–May 5, 2003"; CPTnet, Erin Kindy, "Vieques, PR: Celebrate the struggle," May 7, 2003.

67. Sept 11, 2007. Gene Stoltzfus, in an October 2, 2007 e-mail, wrote regarding the press conferences:

> On several delegations our group was asked to do press conferences shortly after arrival in San Juan. Those gatherings and reports that went out were important for everyone and helped in the broader movement building. We could do that, because we always tried to have one or more good Spanish speakers and tried to prepare people for the unexpected.

Participation of Churches in Vieques Witness

In many ways, Vieques was the perfect project for Christian Peacemaker Team intervention. A core of local activists committed to nonviolent change had been organizing a sustained campaign against the Navy presence for years and knew what to do with a group of internationals. These activists had clear, articulated goals (The Four Ds—see n. 43). They used many of the skills to which CPT was most committed: public witness, taking risks, and civil disobedience.

However, Christian involvement in the Vieques resistance was especially meaningful to CPT as an organization and to those who participated in the Vieques delegations. Catholic, Mainline Protestant, Evangelical, and Pentecostal groups worked together on the island in the struggle against militarism—an anomaly in most of Latin America. A chapel was erected near the Catholic camp that a Protestant camper called, "The only chapel in Puerto Rico—and possibly Latin America—built specifically for ecumenical use."[68] The Puerto Rican Christians, in turn, drew energy from the CPT presence, since they saw the CPTers as representatives of the mainland churches coming to stand beside them.[69]

68. Ediger, fax to CPT Chicago Office during the May 1–9, 2000, delegation.

69. CPT's work in Vieques also had a major impact on the Mennonite Church U.S.A. It passed a resolution during its 2001 biennial conference in Nashville that committed the church to supporting Puerto Rican Mennonites in their call for an end to the bombing in Vieques, and sending a letter to President Bush asking him to comply with CRDV's demands. Significantly, the resolution also called for U.S. Mennonites, who hold a broad spectrum of political opinions, to "support the work of Christian Peacemaker Teams as they witness on Vieques."

Byler, Penner and Williams were all Mennonites, and Penner and Williams were incarcerated during the assembly. Their witness from prison had a powerful impact on the delegates, according to Stoltzfus (who, with the author, attended the assembly).

Perez, letter to Gene Stoltzfus, Apr 3, 2001; Stoltzfus, e-mail response, Apr 10, 2001; Penner, e-mail to Mark Byler, May 30, 2001 (in which he discussed travel arrangements that would get him to Nashville for the Mennonite convention, July 2–7, 2001, after his June 28 trial in San Juan); Stoltzfus, letter to Fermin Arraiza (lawyer for the "Vieques 4"), July 9, 2001; Thomas (General Minister and President of the Office of General Ministries of the United Church of Christ), letter to H. A. Penner, July 9, 2001; Penner, letter response, July 25, 2001; Bermudez (Executive Secretary of Puerto Rico Mennonite Convention), letters to Rich Williams and H. A. Penner in Guaynabo detention center, n.d.; Williams, letter response, July 15, 2001; Penner, letter response, July 25, 2001; MCUSA, "Vieques Resolution for Nashville 2001 Delegate Action," June 26, 2001; MCUSA, Nashville 2001 Delegate Actions Congregational Follow-up Resources, n.d.; MCUSA Executive Board, letter to Bush, July 20, 2001; Gene Stoltfuz, e-mail, Oct 2, 2007.

CPTers have worked on projects with Muslims, Jews, secular activists, and practitioners of indigenous religions, all of whom Christians persecuted at various points in history. On projects, they have struggled to maintain a balance between acting in solidarity with coworkers from these backgrounds and testifying to the nonviolent, transforming power of Jesus Christ in this world. In Vieques, CPTers could proclaim, without hesitation, that they were collaborating with other unabashed practitioners of the gospel and the churches were behind them.

AFGHANISTAN DECEMBER 2001–JANUARY 2002

The Al Qaeda hijackings and subsequent carnage at the World Trade Center and the Pentagon on September 11, 2001, happened at a particularly busy period in CPT history. Support team members in the Chicago office had received another request for an emergency delegation to Vieques and were planning the 2001 Peacemaker Congress in Indiana. The Chiapas team was in its final days, preparing to accompany the Abejas back to their home communities. In Hebron, the team was living through increasingly bloody months of the Al-Aqsa Intifada. Paramilitary killings were escalating in Barrancabermeja and its environs, and the Colombia team would soon experience its first episode of discovering bodies and body parts in the river. The Esgenoôpetitj team was attending trials of EFN fishers that arose from conflicts in the 2000 fishing season and dealing with mounting harassment of the EFN by non-native fishers.

Claire Evans, working in the Chicago office at the time, voiced the feelings of many CPTers when she wrote about her reaction, "My first thought was how everything we do is so, so small compared to that big event. How can what we do in CPT have any significance in the wake of that large catastrophe?"[70]

---

70. E-mail, Sept 27, 2007. The author was in Hebron at the time, where Palestinians, both friends and strangers, accosted team members on the street to express their sympathy. The team also fielded numerous phone calls from Palestinian friends who were weeping as they described what they were watching on their television.

William Payne wrote, in a September 28, 2007 e-mail:

I had only just arrived in Barrancabermeja a few days prior to 9/11. It was a surreal experience to have just entered one of the world's supposed hotspots and to watch the twin towers fall on the team's TV. What was also weird was having Colombian campesinos who have been displaced many times by extreme violence offering ME condolences, me in my confusion trying to explain that no, I'm not a US citizen, and then

As an immediate response, Doug Pritchard, who had been posting a weekly "Prayers for Peacemakers" on CPTnet since 1996, wrote,

PRAYERS FOR PEACEMAKERS, Wednesday, Sept 12, 2001

In light of the events of Sep 11, pray that we may walk in Jesus' way of nonviolence, both locally and globally, and that we may "get in the way" of comfortable analysis and unjust structures that lead to violence.

After four days of U.S. and British bombing of Taliban-related military and communications and suspected terrorist training camps October 7–11, 2001, CPT put out an organization-wide Statement of Conviction:

The act of terror that killed thousands of people in New York, Washington, DC and Pennsylvania on September 11, 2001 will not be set right by bombing Kabul or any other city. Bombings with the official authorization of western governments are also acts of terror.

As followers of Jesus Christ, we believe that we must choose the nonviolent way of the cross in these dangerous times. If we or our loved ones are attacked, injured or killed by acts of terror, we forbid our governments to retaliate in our names. We believe that our lives are no more important or valuable in God's eyes than the lives of Afghans, Arabs, Colombians, Sudanese, Mexicans, Angolans, East Timorese, Aboriginal peoples and others.

We maintain that those responsible for the September 11 attacks must be held accountable for their crimes through internationally recognized nonviolent means.

We also maintain that other leaders who have used their positions of power to design, order or commit acts of terror that have killed millions of civilians throughout the world must be held accountable for their crimes, including Henry Kissinger (Cambodia, Viet Nam), Israeli Prime Minister Ariel Sharon (Gaza, West Bank, Lebanon), former Indonesian President Suharto (East Timor), former U.S. Presidents Ronald Reagan (contra war against Nicaragua) and Bill Clinton (Iraq). The list goes on. . . .

We intend to continue resisting any foreign policy that results in the death or exploitation of human beings, whatever their na-

---

thinking even if I was would they need to offer me condolences for my citizenship when these are people directly affected by the violence of the way things are.

tionality. Again, we are putting our country on notice today that it does not have our permission to go to war in our names.[71]

But the enormity of the September 11 attacks and the imminent plans to attack Afghanistan—combined with CPT's working relationships with Arabs and Muslims likely to bear the brunt of a grief-stricken nation howling for revenge—compelled the organization to do more than make statements.

At the October 18–20, 2001, Steering Committee meeting in Harrisonburg, VA, SC members approved a statement saying that CPT should "actively explore the possibility of sending a couple persons on delegation to Afghanistan."[72] After extensive research by the CPT Support team, particularly Sara Reschly,[73] CPT Director Gene Stoltzfus, and CPT Canada coordinator Doug Pritchard took on this task and arrived in New York City on December 16, 2001, with the intention of traveling from Ground Zero (the site of the demolished World Trade Center) to the "new Ground Zero" in Afghanistan.[74]

At the "heap"—the term coined by rescue workers at the World Trade Center, Stoltzfus, Pritchard, Anne Montgomery, John Rempel of the Mennonite Central Committee United Nations office, and a few local supporters read a "Liturgy at the Twin Towers," written by CPTer Jane Pritchard. The liturgy included Scripture readings, passages from CPT's often-used "Litany of Resistance" (see chapter 7 on Chiapas) and prayers for the victims, perpetrators, and avengers of the Al Qaeda attacks.[75]

Over the next month, Pritchard and Stoltzfus spent most of their time in Peshawar, Pakistan trying to get permission to enter Afghanistan. The Home Secretary for Pakistan's NW Frontier Province grudgingly

---

71. CPTnet, Chicago/Toronto: CPT Statement of Conviction," Oct 12, 2001.

72. Pritchard, e-mail, Sept 28, 2007.

73. Reschly consulted heavily with NGOs who had worked in the region and Pakistanis and Afghans living in North America.

74. The original use of the term "ground zero" referred to the "the point on the earth's surface directly below an exploding nuclear bomb" (*Compact Oxford English Dictionary*). In a September 27, 2001 article entitled "Attack and Aftermath: A Glossary of Terms," journalist Derek Brown noted that the term became the "almost instantly coined nickname for the World Trade Centre site itself."

75. CPT, "Liturgy at the Twin Towers." Jane Pritchard's name does not appear on the manuscript, but her husband, Doug Pritchard, told the author that she had written it after reading a draft of this section.

gave them some of his time, because they were "elderly persons"[76] and told them that he could not allow them to pass through the tribal regions of Pakistan because they were not registered as journalists. They would have to go to Islamabad to get the necessary papers, and the process would take several months. The Afghan Development Association gave them sponsorship, saying Stoltzfus and Pritchard were employees, but the Home Secretariat still refused to let them exit Pakistan through the tribal areas. Other people at the office, including journalists, told them that September 11 had made entry difficult for everyone. Stoltzfus then tried to take a tourist trip to the Khyber Pass and talk the Pakistani guards at the border into letting him enter because he was a venerable old man. As he wheedled and cajoled, he heard someone say, "The Americans just poured bombs from B-52s into Afghanistan and now they want to look at it." The attempt failed.[77]

Although their inability to enter Afghanistan was frustrating, the two men put their time in Pakistan to good use. They visited dozens of NGOs who were undertaking peace and human rights efforts, working in aid and development, or assisting Afghan refugees, and asked them what sort of role they could see for CPT in Afghanistan. Pritchard and Stoltzfus were impressed with the depth of peacemaking skills present in exiled Afghan NGOs. One organization had already developed and implemented in the Afghan refugee camps a complete peacemaking curriculum from Kindergarten to Grade 12 in both of Afghanistan's official languages, Dari and Pushtu. Another had ideas for improving the traditional mediation vehicle of the village "jirga"—council of elders—by including women and youth.[78] Some of the suggestions for CPT work they received from the groups they consulted included,

- Tallying exact figures of Afghans who had died in the bombing, including the prison at Mazar al Sharif, the target of November

---

76. Respect for the elderly is an integral part of the culture in the tribal regions of Pakistan and Afghanistan. See CPTnet, "Peshawar, Pakistan: Listening to elders," Jan 1, 2002.

77. Pritchard and Stoltzfus, "Afghanistan/Pakistan trip log." See also CPTnet, "Chicago/Toronto: CPT staff to depart for Afghanistan," Dec 14, 2001; CPTnet, "Peshawar, Pakistan: Red Tape, Green Tape," Jan 13, 2002.

78. Doug Pritchard, comments on a draft of this section, e-mailed to author October 5, 2007.

25, 2001, air strikes after the prisoners inside—mostly Taliban and foreign fighters—revolted

- Documenting abuses in prisons run by the multinational forces
- Monitoring of multinational forces and assessing whether they were helping the Afghan people or the warlords
- Investigating whether UN and other humanitarian assistance was reaching the people who needed it
- Securing aid for human rights promotion
- Advocating for Afghan NGOs and Afghan refugees[79]

On January 4, 2002, Pritchard and Stoltzfus were finally able to get to Afghanistan on a UN flight carrying missionaries, journalists, and other NGO representatives. In the log, they noted that at Bagram Airport—a former Russian military base two hours from Kabul, the control tower was the only intact building. All other structures—hangars, barracks, and maintenance buildings—were destroyed. The scenery on the road to Kabul was similar: miles of destroyed homes, burnt-out vehicles, and bomb craters.[80]

As they had in Pakistan, Stoltzfus and Pritchard met with numerous NGO representatives in the Kabul area to learn about the current situation and field suggestions for what CPT might do in Afghanistan. These included collecting and verifying reports of human rights abuses from Afghan NGOs, advocating for human rights with local authorities and pressuring the current government to listen to ordinary Afghans. Several requests had significant education components. Afghan NGOs thought CPT could help Afghan grassroots communities understand the UN and how international organizations worked, talk about peace building, and conduct human rights trainings for local people.

As the two men were waiting at the Afghan Ministry for Foreign Affairs, where they were getting their exit visas and passports stamped on January 7, 2002, the First Secretary of the Afghan Embassy in Moscow ac-

79. See CPTnet, Pritchard, "Peshawar, Pakistan: The refugee business," January 10, 2002.

80. Pritchard wrote several CPTnet releases describing the extent of the devastation. See "Kabul, Afghanistan: Bombing the Red Cross," Jan 11, 2002; "Kabul, Afghanistan: Bombs by day and night," Jan 17, 2002; "Kabul, Afghanistan: The spoil of war," January 18, 2002.

costed the two men. He asked if they would consider a joint venture with one of the Afghan warlords to put the monies the Russians and warlords had to "work for something besides shooting." The trip log records,

> After a brief moment of silence, Doug and Gene enthusiastically moved the subject to something else after agreeing with great enthusiasm that it would be good to put soldiers to work doing something else. This is the most dramatic representation of a theme that we have been hearing, the fighters who only know shooting as a way to earn food must be put to work doing something productive."[81]

On January 13, 2002, Stoltzfus and Pritchard began the thirty-six hour journey home from Pakistan, stopping in New York for debriefings with UN personnel that John Rempel arranged.[82]

In their trip report, written as the two men were leaving the country, they proposed that CPT should "move as quickly as possible to develop a five-person peacemaker team to begin work in Afghanistan by June 1, 2002, with at least two persons going to Afghanistan before that date to begin language study." They noted the Afghan people to whom they spoke were "optimistic" that real change could occur after three decades of Russian, warlord, and Taliban misrule. However, the abundance of weapons, the generation of men who knew how to provide for themselves only with guns, and the presence of warlords within the interim government caused Afghans they had talked to say that if the security issue were not resolved in the next few months, Afghanistan would once again "slip into the pit."[83]

In its description of what life on a team in Afghanistan would look like, the report contained a daunting list of stipulations. Team members would have to commit themselves to remaining in Afghanistan for two to three years (instead of three to five months, as was the case on most other projects), taking breaks in Pakistan.[84] Team members would have

81. Pritchard and Stoltzfus, "Afghanistan/Pakistan trip log."

82. In a September 28, 2007 e-mail, Doug Pritchard wrote: "On arrival at JFK I was nervous about all the new Pakistan and Afghanistan stamps in my passport. So the immigration officer asked 'Where are you coming from?' 'Pakistan and Afghanistan.' 'What were you doing there?' 'It was a peacemaking mission.' 'Well, I guess we didn't do much to help that, did we?' Stamp, stamp, 'There you go.'"

83. See CPTnet, Pritchard, "Kabul, Afghanistan: Security," Jan 22, 2002.

84. At a staff retreat in Ontario, September 23–24, 2007, Pritchard told the author that his and Stoltzfus' own difficulties getting in and out of Afghanistan had prompted

to have confidence they could learn Dari (a dialect of Persian/Farsi), but Pushtu might be more useful in areas where the violence might persist longer. They would have to live in basic accommodations and get used to oily and monotonous food, cold weather, lack of entertainment, and inability to communicate with the outside. "And there is physical danger, at least as great as in Colombia," the report noted. Given the lack of an indigenous Christian presence in the country, team members would also have to develop spiritual support within the team. Getting money to Afghanistan would be difficult, because the country had no functioning banks, and registering CPT as an Afghan NGO would be long process needing "sensitivity and patience."

Aside from two CPTers (one of whom knew some Farsi and would have been able to pick up Dari), no other CPT fulltimers or reservists came forward to work in Afghanistan. Given the crises and transitions on other teams, CPT support team and Steering Committee ultimately concluded that a project in Afghanistan was not viable.

Issues Arising from Afghanistan Project

Because the "project" in Afghanistan never went beyond the exploratory delegation phase, it did not raise many issues for the organization as a whole. However, it provided CPT with a first-hand glimpse into a conflict that continues as of this writing in late 2007 and bears many similarities to the ongoing carnage in Iraq. It also introduced CPT to the wide variety of effective NGOs committed to peacemaking in the region.

Had a project developed, the name of the organization might have caused problems. Some advisors warned Stoltzfus and Pritchard that the name "would not open doors" in some areas of the country and might even make the work of the team more dangerous. However, most Afghans said, "We will watch what you do, not your name." The two men thought of some other possibilities like Afghan Peacemaker Project or Cooperative Peacemaker Teams, but in the end, they became more confident that they should stick with the name Christian Peacemaker Teams.[85]

---

this stricture. He said that travel became significantly easier for foreigners in subsequent months.

85. Pritchard, comments on draft of this section, Oct, 2007. In their January 2002 "Report from Afghanistan for Christian Peacemaker Teams," Stoltzfus and Pritchard noted that Afghans seemed to respect Norwegian Church Aid, which had its full name on its gate, and Christian Aid from the United Kingdom.

U.S.-MEXICO BORDERLANDS 2004–2006[86]

From 1998—the year that CPT began working in Chiapas, Mexico—to 2006 more than three thousand women, children, and men died as they attempted to cross the U.S. and Mexico border. Driven to the hazardous crossing because of the devastation that instruments of economic globalization, including NAFTA,[87] wrought on the Mexican economy and on small farmers in particular, the migrants perished from dehydration and injuries sustained along the way. Those who survived often had to contend with "coyotes" or desert guides who harassed or raped women and sometimes reneged on their agreement to get people across. But minimum-wage jobs in the U.S. taken by those who survived the journey still paid them twelve times more than similar jobs in Mexico.

As the economy began driving more people north, the U.S. began increasing the militarization of the border. Fences, sensors, cameras, and ever-increasing numbers of Border Patrol officers monitored all the most convenient entry points, which forced migrants to cross dangerous stretches of desert. This militarization actually served to keep migrants in the U.S. Many citizens of Latin American and Caribbean countries used to return home with their earnings every year. With the changes in U.S. immigration policy, frequent trips became too risky.[88]

In 2004, ten years after NAFTA went into effect, the organization No More Deaths (NMD), a coalition of humanitarian and human rights groups, invited CPT to place a team near Douglas, Arizona, to staff one its desert emergency assistance camps, where migrants could obtain water, food, and first aid during the perilous summer months. NMD also asked that CPT establish contacts in the area with churches, Border Patrol, ranchers, and vigilante groups. CPTers like Scott Kerr and Mark Frey who had witnessed the economic decline of small farmers when they worked

86. What to call this project in CPTnet releases was an issue. The team for most of its duration was based in Douglas, Arizona, but since it was also working with Mexicans just across the border, the releases initially referred to "Arizona/Mexico." Then, because Arizona was a state and Mexico a nation, "U.S./Mexico Borderlands" was also used—but given that the efforts of the team were fairly local and did not extend through Texas, that designation seemed too broad. Finally, CPTnet releases achieved parallelism by state-to-state pairing: "Arizona/Sonora."

87. For NAFTA's effect on the Mexicans living in poverty, see chap. 7.

88. CPT, "About CPT Borderlands"; CPTnet, Cliff Kindy, "Arizona/Sonora: Death and life," Apr 18, 2005.

on the Chiapas project (see chapter 7) were among the first people to work on the project.

From the start of CPT's presence in Douglas, Arizona, acts of public witness became a central part of its work. These included fasts, annual Migrant Trail Walks from the border town of Sasabe, in Sonora, Mexico to Tucson, and cross–border demonstrations at Mexican and U.S. towns, where participants could see and "pass the peace" to each other through the fence that divided them. Team members and CPT delegations also held vigils at Border Patrol stations and the Border wall that had forced migrants to cross dangerous parts of the desert.[89]

Most of the public witnesses in which CPT participated were memorials for migrants who had died in Cochise County, where Douglas is located. Along the Border Wall, they would paint white crosses and the names of the migrants and the dates of their deaths. When the Border Patrol would cover the crosses with black paint, the team would return and repaint the white crosses. The Borderlands team also committed itself in 2004 to conducting memorial services for every migrant who died in Cochise County, where Douglas is located. When possible, they held services in areas near where the bodies were found in the desert, fashioning cairns and crosses—on which they wrote the deceased migrant's name—from available stones and deadwood.[90]

89. See CPTnet releases: "Arizona/Mexico: CPT kicks off beginning of Sonoran desert project," June 3, 2004; Frey, "Arizona: CPTers aid migrants in need," June 4, 2004 (incorrectly dated 2002); "Arizona/Sonora Borderlands: Report from Cliff Kindy," June 8, 2004; "Arizona/Sonora Borderlands: CPTers fast to call attention," June 26, 2004; CPTnet, Rickard, "Arizona/Sonora Borderlands: Desert fast calls attention," July 3, 2004; "Arizona: Desert Fast Journal," July 15, 2004; "Arizona/Sonora: 'Tear Down This Wall,'" Sept 2, 2004; "Arizona/Sonora: CPTers walk the migrant trail," June 15, 2005; Durland, "Arizona/Sonora: Raising awareness on the Migrant Trail," June 22, 2005; "Arizona/Sonora: CPTers fast in the desert," Aug 31, 2005; "Chicago/Toronto: CPT announces Arizona Borderlands Migrant Trail Walk," Mar 29, 2006; Bryant, "Mexico/U.S. Borderlands: 'This Is Not a Welcome Mat!'" Apr 1 2006; Christman, "U.S./Mexico Borderlands: Walking the Migrant Trail," June 21, 2006.

90. See CPTnet releases: "Arizona/Sonora Borderlands: CPTers conduct first memorial prayer vigil," June 10, 2004; "Arizona/Sonora Borderlands: CPTers conduct second memorial prayer vigil," June 15, 2004; "Arizona/Sonora Borderlands: CPTers mark fourth migrant death," July 10, 2004 (incorrectly dated July 9); "Arizona/Sonora Borderlands: CPTers memorialize fifth desert death," July 11, 2004 (incorrectly dated July 9); "Douglas, Arizona: CPT Arizona paints crosses on wall," May 27, 2005; Chao, "Arizona/Sonora Poem: Desconocida," June 14, 2005; "Arizona/Sonora: As migrant death toll rises," July 8, 2005; "Arizona/Sonora: CPTers continue cross painting," Aug 3, 2005; Murphy, "Mexico/U.S. Borderlands Reflection: A Good Friday experience," Apr 27, 2006.

CPT reservist Haven Whiteside, who, with his wife Rose, had served on the Arizona team in the summer of 2005, wrote a reflection in 2006 about one migrant woman who died in the Douglas area without identification, comparing her death to that of Rose, who died in 2005.

> My wife, Rose, died of dehydration in November after a bout with cancer. Originally, she weighed 134 pounds. When I picked her up near the end, she was like a feather. After three weeks of taking in almost no food or water, the body functions shut down one by one: digestion, elimination, motion, memory, speaking, thinking, then seeing, and hearing, and finally breathing. Is it like that in the desert?
>
> Two weeks ago, we were at a vigil with a dozen other people, remembering those who died in the Cochise County desert over the last six years. We lay crosses beside the road, reading out the name of each victim, and responding, "Presente," to indicate that each is remembered and present in the spirit. Instead of a name, one cross has "Mujer no identificada" (Unidentified woman), and instead of a date it says 2/04 (only the month.) We will call her Desconocida (Unknown) because all we know is that she died unknown, she died alone, and she died in the desert.[91]

The public witnesses, intrinsic to CPT's mandate, often turned into opportunities to aid migrants. As the team drove Cliff Kindy to the Mexican border town of Sasabe to participate in the 2004 walk to Tucson, they found a group of six migrants with whom they left food and water. Before a dedication ceremony for an Ark of the Covenant—a donated trailer with carport tent that provided water and food to migrants—CPTer Elizabeth Garcia and a local partner found five Mexicans whose coyote had abandoned them because they were too slow. They had no provisions left, and thought that the lights of Douglas were the lights of Los Angeles. After receiving humanitarian assistance, the five participated in a dedication ceremony that approximately forty other people attended. During the Arizona team's "Desert Fast for Renewal" in July 2004, several groups of migrants approached them over the six days of the fast. The

---

Scott Kerr, in an October 3, 2007 e-mail, responded to the author's question about whether the desert memorial services for individual migrants continued after 2004. He said they had, but noted that after 2004 migrant traffic began to move east and west of Cochise county, so fewer deaths occurred there.

91. CPTnet, Whiteside, "Mexico Borderlands Reflection, Mujer No Identificada," May 1, 2006.

team and a CPT delegation had distributed all their supplies by the end of the first day and had to send for replenishments.

On their way to commemorate Alejandro Machada, who had died north of Douglas, the team picked up three migrants who had become lost and had decided to return to Agua Prieta, across the border from Douglas. After CPTers offered them a ride back following the memorial service, the men eagerly agreed to join the vigil for Machada and others who had lost their lives. Border Patrol officers pulled up at the beginning of the service and asked them what they were doing. One of the CPTers said, "We are having a vigil for a person who died at this spot." The same CPTer paused only a moment before responding to the Border Patrol's next question and affirmed that the three men were with them. Declining to join the service, the Border Patrol drove away. The release about the incident concluded, "Yes, sometimes it does feel like we are skating on thin ice, but that is always a cooling thought in the desert."[92]

The ice cracked on July 9, 2005, when the U.S. Border Patrol arrested Shanti Sellz and Daniel Strauss, two No More Deaths volunteers who were driving three migrants to get medical treatment in Tucson. They were part of a group of nine who had been lost in the desert for several days. After calling NMD medical personnel and a lawyer, Sellz and Strauss evacuated three who had reported vomiting, diarrhea, and blood in the stool—signs of a life-threatening stage of dehydration. The Border Patrol charged Sellz and Strauss with two felonies: "obstruction of justice" and "furtherance and abetting illegal entry."

Since CPT had worked closely with No More Deaths, and helped staff camps in both the U.S. and Mexican sides of the Sonoran desert,[93] the arrests had serious consequences for the work of the team. Sellz and Strauss rejected the plea agreement the government offered of less serious charges in exchange for an admission of guilt and No More Deaths called for concerned community members to "Flood the Desert" with volunteer patrols carrying food and water on designated roads the week of July

92 See CPTnet releases: Mark Frey, "Arizona: CPTers aid migrants in need," June 4, 2004; Rickard, "Arizona/Sonora Border Lands: Desert fast calls attention," July 3, 2004; "Arizona: Desert Fast Journal"; Lumley, "Arizona/Sonora Borderlands: Five migrants," July 28, 2004; Garcia, "Arizona/Sonora: CPTers rescue five strangers," Aug 10, 2004 (incorrectly dated 2003); "Arizona/Sonora: Skating on thin ice," May 21, 2005; "Arizona/Sonora: CPTers fast in the desert," Aug 31, 2005.

93. For an example of the latter, see "Arizona: Clang, Clang, Clang," May 5, 2005.

25, 2005, an effort CPT joined. While the case against Sellz and Strauss was pending, CPT continued its work assisting migrants, which included transporting them to places where they could get help.[94]

In September 2006, the Federal district Judge Raner C. Collins dropped all charges against the NMD volunteers, saying that the U.S. Attorney did not have a credible case against them. Collins based his decision on the fact that the NMD and other volunteers had been providing, with the Border Patrol's knowledge, humanitarian assistance for the previous three summers and the protocol for this assistance involved providing transportation in cases of medical danger. The ruling stopped short of declaring "Humanitarian aid is never a crime." "That assertion," Collins wrote in his opinion, "will have to be left for another day. There must be some way that both the government and the aid organizations can meet their obligations."[95]

Encounters with Anti-Immigration Vigilantes and Border Patrol

When members of a right-wing group referring to themselves as the Minutemen and later Civil Home Defense (CHD) called for hundreds of anti-immigrant activists to do "civilian border patrols," in the summer of 2005, CPT made monitoring these vigilantes part of its project.[96] In March 2005, on Easter morning, residents of Douglas—majorities of whom are Hispanic—found flyers distributed overnight on Eighth Street. They were distributed by a White supremacist group called the National Alliance that referred to immigration trends as a non-white "invasion" of the US.[97] Later in the summer, Scott Kerr would attend a counter-protest at the Arizona State Capitol building in Phoenix where Minutemen had gathered to protest immigration policy. Ten feet in front of Kerr, presumably attending the pro-Minutemen rally, was a man with his two children.

94. See CPTnet, "Mexico/U.S. Borderlands: A migrant's rescue," Apr 11, 2006; CPTnet, Small, "Mexico/U.S. Borderlands Reflection: 'Jesus get out of the truck,'" Apr 18, 2006.

95. CPTnet releases: "Arizona/Sonora: No More Deaths volunteers arrested," July 14, 2005; "Arizona/Sonora: CPTers respond," July 25, 2005; "Arizona: Charges against No More Deaths volunteers," Sept 11, 2006.

96. CPT and NMD were referred to as "invasion aides" on a Web site supporting these civilian border patrols. See "Eye on Reconquista Nuisances."

97. Local hate group monitors suggested that the National Alliance chose 8th street to honor Adolf Hitler—H is the 8th letter in the alphabet. CPTnet, Scott Kerr, "Phoenix, Arizona: Nationalism and border security," July 12, 2005.

One of them held a sign, saying "Stop the Invasion," bearing the same graphic that had appeared on the flyers in Douglas. Kerr wrote,

> Seeing the presence of this hate group at this rally was not surprising. What surprised me was seeing so many people casually greeting the man from the National Alliance, and talking about guns, ammo, and the increasing likelihood of using them. Before I left my shady place under the tree, I also observed the Master of Ceremonies of the event greet the same man as an old friend.
>
> Attending this Minutemen rally in Phoenix in some ways was as scary as [my work] in Colombia during a paramilitary invasion, or Baghdad during the bombings. Here in the middle of a large U.S. city are White Nationalist groups openly organizing and recruiting. Similar gatherings of people are planting and watering seeds of hate and violence around the country—people who will use "border security" as a code word for nationalism and/or racism.[98]

The Arizona team had two semi-scary encounters with the vigilantes in 2005. In one case, they shined a high wattage light in Scott Kerr's and Murray Lumley's eyes, saying they might get shot wandering around at night in the Coronado National Forest (where they were patrolling to keep migrants and the Minutemen from running into each other). In another incident, three trucks surrounded the team's vehicle, giving Scott Kerr, who was giving a tour to a group of media, the choice of stopping or driving into a ditch.[99]

However, for the most part in the spring and summer of 2005, the presence of the Minutemen generated more rumors and anxiety than they did actual incidents—and the rumors went both ways. In one incident, CPT had participated in a Border Barbecue and Cinema night held on the road between Douglas, Arizona, and Agua Prieta, Sonora. About halfway through a showing of *Hotel Rwanda*, a man from the Civil Homeland Defense who had been observing drove away. The next day, a reporter told the team, "CHD are saying that you folks had set 'diversionary fires' so that migrants could slip past CHD."[100]

98. CPTnet, "Arizona/Sonora: CPT Arizona Begins Violence Reduction Project," Apr 2, 2005; CPTnet, Scott Kerr, "Phoenix, Arizona: Nationalism and border security," July 12, 2005.

99. Scott Kerr, e-mail, Oct 9, 2007; CPTnet, "Arizona/Sonora: Confrontation and Hospitality," Apr 15, 2005.

100. CPTnet releases: "Arizona: Watching the Watchers," Apr 9, 2005; "Arizona/Sonora: The Rumor Mill," Apr 12, 2005; "Arizona/Sonora: Barbecue and cinema," April 20, 2005.

The Arizona team's relationship with the Border Patrol was more nuanced and ongoing. Documented cases of Border Patrol officers abusing migrants existed and CPTers encountered negative behaviors on the part of individual agents who appeared not to be considering the medical needs of migrants they were detaining. However, CPTers more often met Border Patrol personnel who genuinely cared about migrants dying in the desert.[101] The Borderlands team's releases from 2005 and 2006 thus showed a shift away from challenging the Border Patrol and its policies toward seeing the Border patrol as one facet of the increasing militarization of the border.[102] The team addressed this militarization with both public witness and legislative action.

As an example of the former, a spring 2006 delegation commenced "Operation Chalk and Awe" (a play on "Operation Shock and Awe" designation used by the U.S. military when it invaded Iraq). On Ash Wednesday 2006, delegates held a worship service at the border wall under the banner, "The Wall Kills/El Muro Mata." They then proceeded to the newly expanded patrol road and wrote on it "Operation Welcome mat!" "Welcome to Turtle Island," "Mi Casa Es Tu Casa" and other greet-

101. CPTnet, "Arizona: Desert Fast Journal, June 30–July 5, 2004," July 15, 2004. In a September 2005 report intended to document Border Patrol abuses, the team most often recorded the Border Patrol "speaking harshly" to local people. The three most serious cases of abuse in the report were a Border Patrol helicopter "dive-bombing" team and CPT delegation members, hearsay accounts of Border Patrol officers leaving one migrant to die in the desert, and Border Patrol officers throwing a woman to the ground and grinding her face in the dirt after she talked back to them. CPT Arizona, "Report: 'Under Siege.'"

102. In addition to increasing the number of Border Patrol agents the government also began sending National Guard and Army Corps of engineers units to oversee the expansion of the road used to patrol the border area—at a time when the lawmakers were theoretically still debating the issue of whether to send the National Guard. On Thanksgiving 2006 a colleague phoned CPTer Rick Ufford-Chase to tell him that she had had a run-in with security guards from Wackenhut—a company with a sinister history of human rights abuses—to whom the federal government had contracted out the provision of detention buses used in transporting migrants caught in the desert back to Mexico. See CPTnet releases: "CPT Arizona: Notes on Encounter," July 23, 2004; "Arizona, Sonora: Douglas is a boxing ring," Apr 29, 2005; "Douglas Arizona: CPT delegation holds prayer vigil," July 2, 2005; Van Drunen, "U.S./Mexico Borderlands: CPT delegation meets Massachusetts National Guard," Mar 15, 2006; Ufford-Chase, "US-Mexico Borderlands: Increasing militarization," Dec 8, 2006. See also Borowitz, "Wackenhut worries."

ings, finishing up just as the agent in charge bellowed, "THIS IS NOT A WELCOME MAT!"[103]

In September 2005, CPT participated in a delegation to Washington DC to advocate for immigration reform, along with the organizations No More Deaths, Frontera de Cristo, and Healing our Borders. People on the delegation met with more than seventy-five congressional staff and held a public briefing at the New York Avenue Presbyterian church.

In a follow-up "Open letter to U.S. Congressional staffers," Carol Rose noted that without exception, these aides seemed to accept the increased militarization of the border. "I find this position inconsistent with the intelligence and good-heartedness that I experienced among you," she wrote.

> One of you asked me what further enforcement border communities would choose in exchange for keeping provisions favorable to immigrants in the bill. I know you mean well. On the hill, it feels like you need to give in to further militarization. But it is a horrible question. It is a batterer asking his terrorized spouse, "Where shall I hit you this time? Where will the bruise not show?"
>
> The answer is, "Don't hit any more. Don't batter, ever again." Militarization needs to be rolled back so that communities can live unafraid. Border Patrol agents need to be accountable, to know that they cannot "do whatever they want" (a direct quote from an agent). Heavily armed vigilantes need to be restricted rather than encouraged as they impersonate law enforcement officials with hats that declare them "Border Patrol"—and hide the word "unofficial" on the brim.[104]

Issues Arising from Borderlands Project

Staffing

CPT's work in the Borderlands was primarily seasonal, designed to aid distressed migrants in the summer. However, having no CPTers on site during the intervening months caused a lack of continuity and difficulty

---

103. CPTnet, "Mexico/U.S. Borderlands: "This Is Not a Welcome Mat!" Apr 1, 2006.

104. See CPTnet releases: "Arizona/Sonora: CPT Leads delegation to Washington to advocate for immigration reform," September 22, 2005; Rose, "Arizona/Sonora: An open letter," Sept 29, 2005; and also "Arizona/Sonora Action Alert: Write to Support Immigration Reform," Oct 18, 2005; "Brownsville, TX: CPT Delegation responds to legislation," Feb 28, 2006.

in strategizing with local partners. To address these concerns, CPT authorized Scott Kerr to take on a year-round "Bridge position" that would maintain this continuity, help set up delegations, and possibly start a CPT regional group in the Tucson area. Kerr was supported by a "Reference Group," which participated in a conference call every other week, to discuss Kerr's work.[105]

In 2005 and 2006 evaluations of the Bridge model, those involved cited as positives that it was relatively cheap to maintain, "created space" for reservists to be involved, "kept CPT's foot in the waters of immigration issues, and provided moral and other types of support for other groups." As negatives, the evaluations noted that nothing substantive had occurred regarding the start of a regional group; coordinating delegations consumed most of Kerr's time; conference calls did not always work well; and the Reference Group sometimes felt disconnected from the work (the evaluations recommended an initial face-to-face meeting). Finally, the report noted, "a single person is not a team, and we work best as teams."[106]

The Bridge position ended in 2006 but CPT Reservist Rick Ufford-Chase, who lived in Tucson, Arizona, offered to facilitate CPT's future work in the area, maintaining and developing relationships with other groups and helping with delegations.[107]

"Fit" with CPT Mandate

When asked to describe how the Borderlands work fit within the CPT mandate, Scott Kerr—who was the linchpin of the Arizona project until he left for seminary in fall 2006—said, "Some days Arizona border work is a perfect fit with CPT and other days it might feel like a stretch."[108] Public witness, confronting the US government about its immigration policy, and involving the church constituency in the work of the team were all important parts of the CPT mandate. On the other hand, the violence affecting the migrants crossing the border was more abstract than, for ex-

105. Reference Group members included Wendy Lehman, Elizabeth Garcia, Murray Lumley, Mark Frey, Kim Lamberty, and Denis Murphy. Frey, e-mail, Oct 8, 2007.

106. CPT Arizona, "Evaluation of Model of Bridge Position"; CPT Arizona, "Summary of Seven-month CPT Borderlands."

107. Rick Ufford-Chase and his wife, Kitty, went through training in 2003. He was elected Moderator of the 216th General Assembly of the Presbyterian Church (U.S.A.), the church's highest elected office, from 2004–2006.

108. CPT Arizona, "CPT Arizona/Borderlands Report."

ample, Colombian civilians getting caught in the middle of paramilitary, guerrilla, and military violence. Providing food and water to migrants also gently buffeted against the CPT stricture forbidding CPTers giving material aid. Although one could argue that saving lives from economic and other systemic violence was indeed nonviolent direct action, one could also argue that Haitians were dying from lack of food and medical care while CPT was working in Jeremie, Haiti.

Yet despite the Borderland's imperfect "fit," CPT continued to participate in Borderlands work in 2006, sending an exploratory delegation to the Brownsville, Texas area in February 2006[109] and two delegations— one during Holy Week and one to participate in the 2006 Migrant Trail Walk.

In a CPT evaluation of the Arizona Project dated March 2007, Mark Frey, regarding the question "Why is a CPT presence still needed?" wrote,

> Immigration issues are at the forefront of the US national agenda. Anti-immigrant sentiment is growing as migration flows continue to increase. As Christians, we are called to welcome the stranger. CPT continues to struggle to find work that fits with our team-based model.[110]

OAXACA, MEXICO 2006

Ulises Ruiz Ortiz became the governor of the Mexican state of Oaxaca in January 2005, after what some claimed was a rigged 2004 election. Promising to "do away with social problems," the governor, a member of

---

109. See CPT Arizona, "Christian Peacemaker Teams Brownsville Report." The report concluded:

> Although Brownsville clearly has challenges of economic violence, narco and gang violence, and other issues of serious concern to undocumented migrants and others living in the community, it wasn't immediately obvious to the delegation—or to those we met with—how CPT's work would fit in at Brownsville, especially given CPT's immediate staffing and financial concerns. . . .

110. Whiteside, e-mail, Oct 6, 2007; CPT Arizona, "CPT semi-annual report." The CPT Support Team minutes for a September 11, 2007 meeting record, "No More Deaths would also like to see us back since we "push the boundaries." CPT, "Notes from Support Team call."

the PRI party (see chapter 7) ordered the arrest of more than 150 grass-roots activists and organizers during his first two weeks in office.

In May 2006, teachers in Oaxaca went on strike, demanding better pay and working conditions, improvements to the educational infra-structure, and an end to human rights violations. Ruiz sent hundreds of police into the central square of Oaxaca city on June 14, 2006, to drive out thousands of demonstrators who had gathered in support of the teachers. Despite the authorities' use of helicopters, tear gas, and beatings, the demonstrators remained. The following morning, three hundred thousand people marched through the city demanding Ruiz's resignation, and three days later the Oaxaca Popular People's assembly (APPO) established an alternative Oaxacan State government with two goals: removing Ruiz from office and building a grassroots political system that included civil society organizations.

One of these organizations was CACTUS (Centro de Apoyo Comunitario Trabajando Unidos),[111] a group that worked with alternative education projects, women's rights, farmers, and indigenous people in Oaxaca's Sierra Mountains. As CACTUS members left Oaxaca city after a November 25, 2006, demonstration, armed men pulled over their buses, burning one bus and detaining twenty-three members who ended up in Federal police custody. The Federal authorities sent most of the detainees to a prison in the state of Nayarit, hundreds of miles away, without informing their families.[112]

After the arrests, Sister Kathy Long, a friend of CPT training co-ordinator Kryss Chupp, put CPT in touch with the Lutheran Center in Mexico City, which, on behalf of civil society organizations in Oaxaca, asked the CPT to send an emergency team to Oaxaca.[113] Reservists Chris

111. Alternative translations in English are are "Center of Community Assistance Working Together," andor "Center of Community Support working together." The name has been shortened to "Center for Community support" and "Center for Communal support" by other organizations, including CPT. (The Spanish uses extra words to complete the acronym "CACTUS.")

112. CPT Oaxaca, "Final Report: Christian Peacemaker Teams accompaniment." CPTnet, "Oaxaca, MX Urgent Action: Ask Mexican authorities," Dec 4, 2006; CPTnet, "Oaxaca Urgent Action: Ask Mexican authorities to release political prisoners," Dec 13, 2006. See also Bacon, "Mexico Sportswriter at the Barricades" and "Oaxaca's Dangerous Teachers."

113. Nafziger, e-mails between Kryss Chupp and Kim Erno of the Lutheran Center, Nov 29–Dec 1, 2006.

Schweitzer and Matthew Wiens arrived in Mexico City on December 1, 2006, received a debriefing on the situation, and then traveled to Oaxaca on December 4.

Schweitzer and Wiens were accompanying two CACTUS leaders in Huajuapan, Oaxaca when the organization received word that four APPO members, including spokesperson Flavio Sosa, had been arrested in Mexico City. The CACTUS leaders had outstanding arrest warrants for their involvement in APPO and decided to go underground. Wiens and Schweitzer accompanied them to a safer temporary location and then to a place closer to Mexico City where they could check in on partners.[114]

After Wiens returned to Canada on December 9, 2006, Schweitzer traveled back to Oaxaca, where he observed a major APPO march in Oaxaca City. Although police were out in force, he saw little evident violence—which CACTUS members attributed to the large numbers of internationals present. He then finished his time in Oaxaca meeting with the families of CACTUS members who had been arrested, which gave him the idea to have the CPT church constituency send Christmas cards to encourage these families, some of whom were children now living without their parents.[115]

In a report compiled by CPT reservist Tim Nafziger, who served as volunteer Oaxaca project support coordinator, Wiens and Schweitzer recommended that CPT consider ongoing international accompaniment in Oaxaca. CACTUS suggested that CPT send delegations timed so that there was always an international presence in the state and so that human rights abuses suppressed in the Mexican media would be publicized regularly outside the country. The report concluded, "There is a need for support of nonviolent actions . . . to develop a deeper non-violent culture. The sense is that the movement is "peaceful" in order to avoid state repression, not that there is a commitment to non-violence and its effectiveness."[116]

114. Chupp, phone interview, Oct 9, 2007; CPT Oaxaca, "Final Report: Christian Peacemaker Teams accompaniment"; CPTnet, "Oaxaca, Mexico: "What's wrong with that?" Dec 18, 2006.

115. CPTnet, "Oaxaca Christmas Action: Send cards of encouragement and support," Dec 19, 2006.

116. CPT Oaxaca, "Final Report: Christian Peacemaker Teams accompaniment."

Despite these recommendations, no project proposal was forthcoming, and in February 2007, the support team concluded that they were not sure CPT had the people "to do it in an ongoing way."[117]

FUTURE DIRECTIONS

By 2006, the protocol for establishing a new CPT project had become somewhat standardized. The organization would usually send an initial delegation hosted by a key contact person who introduced the CPTers to members of local grassroots organizations. These resource people would present the broad outlines of the conflict and points of critical need with which they thought CPT could assist. CPTers, in turn, would tell them what CPT had done on other project locations and strategize next steps. Depending on information gleaned from the initial delegation, the organization would then send follow-up delegations—or exploratory teams who were in the country for longer periods—to assess how CPT could work most effectively in the local conflict. Sometimes the initial delegations concluded that CPT could not work effectively in the local context, or that limited resources should be allocated somewhere else. As of this writing in late 2007, the organization is still determining where 2005–2006 delegations to the Democratic Republic of Congo, Uganda, and the Philippines will lead.

In general, even when CPT decides through a process of consensus that a project is not workable, rarely do the people involved consider the resources and time invested in exploring project possibilities wasted. Relationships built and experiences shared in one context often prove useful in other contexts. Perhaps the Abejas' quotation cited in chapter 7 about their explorations into the ways nonviolence best expresses the CPT philosophy on project development, too:

"We look for the good path of peace without arms. . . . We do not know where this path will lead; we are creating it as we go."[118]

---

117. CPT, notes from Support Team phone call, Feb 13 2007.

118. Lehman, "Part of the Hope of God." For a longer quote, see O'Hatnick, "Las Abejas: Nonviolence on the Line."

14

Twenty Years and Counting

If these people were saints, they would not make us uneasy. They make us edgy because we know that what they have done, we could do. They have gone in peace where others move with armed guards. Where others speak of love, they risk living it. They have made the path by walking and would welcome us on the journey.

—Inscription on certificate acknowledging CPT's receipt of 40th annual Peace Award from the War Resister's League[1]

B Y 2000, CPT HAD grown large enough to staff all the projects (which included Hebron, Chiapas, and Esgenoôpetitj) with reservists, while bringing all the full-timers together for an August retreat to discuss the future of CPT.

The assembly, which also included CPT staff, reservists and Steering Committee members who were able to come, used the notes from the Steering Committee's "5 Year Visioning Process" to respond to the questions, "Should CPT grow, and if not, how CPT should draw boundaries so

---

1. CPTnet, "Chicago: War Resisters League honors Christian Peacemaker Teams," June 11, 2002. A partial list of other awards CPT has received includes:

- 1998 "Award for Social Courage" from the Consortium on Peace Research, Education, and Development (COPRED)

- 2003 Yoko Tada Human Rights Award from the Foundation of Human Rights in Japan (Although this recognition was specifically bestowed on Peggy Gish, she noted "I just happened to be the one interviewed (by Journalist Masakazu Honda) in Amman. It was the work he was excited about, what IPT and CPT were doing together. I'm accepting this award not just for myself, but for CPT's work in Iraq." CPTnet, "Japan: Peggy Gish to receive Yoko Tada award," Dec 11, 2003.

- German Mennonite Peace Committee (DMFK) Michael Sattler Peace Award, May 20, 2006.

that it did not become over-extended?" Given the composition of eighty-three people, many who were used to stubbornly asserting their opinions, the group came to consensus with surprisingly little effort at the end of the retreat.

All present wanted CPT to grow and drew up a plan that would result in CPT having, at the end of the five years, fifty full-timers, 250 reservists, and a budget of $1.2 million. The plan called for CPT to have six to ten projects distributed throughout the continents, one of which would be in a North American urban area and one with indigenous peoples.

In this vision, regional groups would develop all over the world. Priority for development would be given to those areas where people of color were the majority. These groups would address the violence in their own communities and provide support for the trained CPTers in their midst. Eventually, CPT would decentralize, with the Chicago and Toronto offices being two of several headquarters for CPT's work around the globe.[2]

By the end of 2006, CPT had forty-seven trained full-timers, 154 reservists, and fifteen support team members operating on a budget of $1,040,425. It had six projects in Arizona, Colombia, Hebron, Iraq, Kenora, and Tuwani and eight regional groups in Cleveland, Colorado, Washington DC, Manitoba, Northern Indiana, Ontario, the United Kingdom, and the Upper Midwest.

This data shows that the five-year plan was a partial success. Yet, as was the case for most CPT projects, and for the history of the organization as a whole, growth and change tended to happen more organically. Tightly scripted plans do not take into account surprising political developments, or the human idiosyncrasies and skills incoming CPTers bring to the organization or that outgoing CPTers take with them when they leave.[3]

What people in 1986 thought CPT would become bears some resemblance to CPT in 2006, but some emphases of the organization have

2. CPT, Steering Committee minutes; CPT, "Christian Peacemaker Teams: Getting in the Way for the Next Five Years," flier in Christian Peacemaker Teams 2000 annual report. (One version of the flier called for a budget of $2.2 million, and another for $1.2 million. Both are dated December 12, 2000.)

3. From experience in the field, CPT has learned that whenever one person comes onto a team or another leaves, the project has a whole new team, because the blends of skills and how people interact with each other change.

changed since its founding—changes based on experiences in the field. Following are some issues and emphases that have arisen in the last twenty years that have affected the course of CPT as an organization.

HUMAN RIGHTS DOCUMENTATION

CPT's founders and the participants in the 1993 training assumed that part of CPT's work would involve documenting human rights abuses, but they did not realize what a large part of the work it would become.[4] Since CPTers live in the locations where human rights abuses occur, and since they are "outsiders," more established human rights groups regard their reports as having more credibility than reports from the affected parties. This acceptance of CPT's documentation contains an undercurrent of racism—because it implies that, for example, Palestinians, campesinos, and indigenous peoples are not as credible as internationals. However, CPT's dissemination of information from the marginalized people with whom they work to organizations that otherwise might not have heard of these abuses has led to breakthroughs in media coverage of a conflict and the policies of various governments.

Yet, CPT differs from human rights groups in that it does not claim to be a group of neutral monitors and in that it testifies, through acts of public witness and lobbying, to the human rights abuses its workers witness. A Peace Brigades worker from the US told members of the 2000 exploratory delegation to Colombia that he could witness a massacre or its aftermath and go to his congressional representative and tell him about what he had witnessed, but because of Peace Brigades policy he could not tell him how to vote on bills affecting Colombia. CPTers, on the other hand, could visit their congressional or parliamentary representatives, urge them to vote for more humane policies, and inspire their church constituency to do likewise.[5]

---

4. Kern, when she needs to describe her job briefly to people who know nothing about CPT, says she works for a human rights organization.

5. The author was present for this conversation. The PBI people in Bogotá were excited by the prospect of CPT setting up a project in Colombia, because CPT could use their experiences and data from PBI projects to influence legislation.

ACCOMPANIMENT

As with human rights documentation, in the early years, those involved with CPT assumed that workers in the field might perform some accompaniment of threatened individuals and communities, in the style of Peace Brigades International. However, they thought CPTers would be doing far more Nonviolent Direct Action, more "Getting in the Way," than accompaniment. Accompaniment, however, has become a central feature of CPT's work on almost every project, and is often the effort for which local people express the most gratitude. In Iraq, Nonviolent Direct Action became too dangerous in the CPT project's later years, so accompaniment became the primary work of the team.

However, even if CPT has done more accompaniments than organizers thought it would, it has never let go of the Nonviolent Direct Action component, which organizations like Peace Brigades are not able to undertake because of their mandates. CPTers who do accompaniments often frame that work within the context of NVDA. For example, by accompanying shepherds and schoolchildren in the South Hebron Hills, CPTers are "Getting in the Way" of a system that seeks to rid the region of Palestinians and are supporting the creative and courageous acts of NVDA that the villagers in the area have developed themselves.[6]

COMMUNICATIONS

Those involved in the earliest years of CPT understood that communicating what its workers were witnessing and emphasizing a nonviolent perspective on the conflict was integral to CPT's work. However, that work has turned out to be even more vital and transforming than the founders thought—as witnessed to by the Iraq team's 2004 report on detainee abuses. Additionally, in 1986, few CPT founders anticipated how widely used the Internet would become in 2006, and how that would revolutionize not only CPT's human rights documentation but also that of the human rights community as a whole.

As mentioned in chapter 1, the newsletter *Signs of the Times* was CPT's first news organ. Now published quarterly, it profiles the work of the teams and contains suggestions for how its readership can take actions on issues raised by this work.

6. To examine how CPT has grappled with the racism that can underlie the principles of accompaniment, see chapter 10.

It also contains a lively "Dialogue" section that publishes comments from a variety of letters, emails, and discussion lists such as menno.org. cpt.d, and a "Letters" section that reports both kudos and scathing criticisms received. The following two notes came from the same newsletter:

> After much intellectual resistance, I finally read your "CPT Statement of Conviction Regarding the War on Terrorism." I had been told that your inflammatory rhetoric and theocratic political moralism rivaled the righteousness of Osama bin Laden and Al-Qaeda. The rumors were true. How strange that we now have in CPT our own Anabaptist Taliban.

> I commend your brave and ethical work in defense of human rights. CPT inspires all that is decent in our hearts.[7]

These letters serve to help CPT to monitor its constituency's and the public's reaction to its work and to understand both praise and criticism as transient.

CPTnet, CPT's Internet news service, began in 1993. Originally, CPTnet consisted of four to five releases a month. In the mid 1990s, Gene Stoltzfus told teams that CPTnet could not handle much more than three releases a week, or people would start unsubscribing. By 1999, however, the importance of communicating the realities on the ground where the teams were working trumped the fear of people unsubscribing. Indeed, during particularly busy periods over the next years, CPTnet sometimes ran two to three releases a day, six days a week. For people who found keeping up with all the information daunting, the subject heading of a posting always contained the location of the project. Thus, people who were only interested in CPT's Colombia work could easily delete postings from, say, Hebron or Esgenoôpetitj. Later, the subject headings would include the type of release as well, specifying whether a posting was a reflection piece or an update[8]—as opposed to a straight news release.

Hosting tour groups became another unanticipated communications strategy, particularly in Palestine and Israel. Although CPT had always included delegations as part of its program, the Hebron team from 1996 onward found itself hosting numerous groups from other organizations

7. "Letters."

8. The Hebron team invented updates in the spring of 1996 to give an account of events and interesting conversations team members had with soldiers, settlers, and Palestinians that did not merit full releases.

seeking to provide an alternative perspective on the conflict. Because the team had built relationships with Palestinians in a supposedly dangerous location, the Hebron team became a destination for Israeli peace and human rights groups, as well as church, academic, and political organizations that wanted to meet ordinary Palestinian families suffering from the Israeli occupation. By the time of the Al-Aqsa Intifada, giving tours was one of the major foci of the Hebron team.

These tours familiarized CPT with a wide variety of organizations—which would publicize their time with CPT in their own publications—and expanded its networking potential. They also inspired some individuals in these groups to go through CPT training.

LENGTH OF PROJECTS

The early founders of CPT envisioned that projects staffed by trained CPTers would have a definite exit strategy. Thus, in Haiti, the project was scheduled to end when Aristide returned, in Hebron when the settlers were removed, and in DC when a crack house closed. As time passed, however, people realized that they could not expect an obvious end date in regions such as the Middle East and Colombia where lethal violence was chronic. Often, when the situation a team had initially sought to address had become less problematic, other opportunities for CPT's skill set presented themselves: The Al-Aqsa intifada supplanted the threat of home demolitions, which had supplanted the settler violence on the streets the team came to address in 1995. Colombian mining and indigenous communities saw how CPT could assist them as lethal violence in the Opón communities diminished, freeing the team to move in new directions. The Iraq team had originally sought to address the violence of the US invasion and its attendant bombings, never knowing that working on behalf of detainees and their families would become the team's primary focus.

On the other hand, the prevailing philosophy that CPT ought to be an impermanent fixture within a conflict continues to undergird teams as they embark on new projects. Indigenous communities have been particularly effective in telling teams when their presence was no longer needed, or suggesting that they focus on a different issue, such as the Grassy Narrows people did when they told the team to consider setting up a project in Kenora.[9] What has changed at an organizational level is that people involved with the various projects understand that the decision to close a project takes time to process.

Length of Stay on Projects and Continuity

At the time that CPT held its first training, the general principle for the length of time that CPTers spent on a project was that its workers would spend two-thirds of their time in the field and one-third of their time in their home communities doing educational work. Eventually, the organization had to be more flexible, given visa restrictions and different levels of stress on the different projects. At the October 2000 full-timers's retreat, people who had served in both Chiapas and Hebron noted they could happily work in Chiapas for five months, but not in Hebron. Working on the Iraq team was also more draining than most of the other projects.[10]

Related to the coming and going of team members was the issue of continuity on projects. When a project has a complete turnover of workers in a short time, contacts and relationships get lost, as does the historic memory, which sometimes leads to teams reinventing the wheel. Gene Stoltzfus held that for a project to be successful, it needs at least five full-timers to provide the necessary continuity.

STRATEGIC PLANNING FOR EXPANSION

"Wide vs. Deep" characterizes a tension within CPT between those who want to see CPT undertake new projects in regions where CPT has not previously worked and those who want to see CPT build on the relationships and knowledge it has already accrued on one project and set up a similar project in the same region. The teams in Colombia and the Palestine have received numerous invitations to open projects in other

9. Lenore Keeshig-Tobias, a member of the Chippewas of Nawash First Nation (See chap. 8), when asked what CPT needed to do to work effectively in Indigenous communities, listed three objectives for the CPT Ontario training group in 1998: do the work well so it did not need to be repeated, be ready to step back when local people were ready to take leadership, and be ready to leave and be immediately forgotten. CPT, Steering Committee minutes. See Pritchard, e-mails, January 26 and 27, 2008.

10. An unanticipated upshot of the 2000 gathering was the realization that fulltime CPTers need to have retreats together periodically in order to share, in a relaxed atmosphere, experiences on the different projects. Two hours were set aside for this purpose at the Joyfield farm gathering, and participants found that the time was not nearly long enough. After the 2000 retreat, full timers began meeting biannually.

parts of those countries, and many CPTers believe that they could actually do more good if they expanded within a region, because they would avoid the stumbling and pitfalls that occur when learning to live in a new nation or culture. On the other hand, because CPT expanded into new territories over the years, it has brought wider constituency and media attention to these areas than might have occurred otherwise. In 2007, CPT has standing invitations to set up projects in Democratic Republic of Congo (DRC), Uganda, and the Philippines. Delegations to these regions in 2005 and 2006 have resulted in the exposure of situations about which the CPT constituency and the rest of the world were relatively ill informed.[11] However, these delegations were expensive and as of this writing might never lead to the establishment of projects in these locations, whereas new Palestinian and Colombian projects could probably be set up swiftly and relatively cheaply and might have more impact on the systems of domination in those regions.

Of all the teams, CPT's Colombia project has done the most work regarding strategic planning for expansion within a country. As the violence in the Opón region diminished, the team and CPT Project Support Coordinator Robin Buyers set aside time to look at possibilities of new work in a systematic way using the SWOT—Strengths, Weaknesses, Opportunities, Threats—methodology (see chapter 10). The example of the Colombia team may lead to other projects and CPT as an organization taking a more systematic approach to expansion, but the "Deep vs. Wide" debate will probably continue in the foreseeable future.

REGIONAL GROUPS

The first trained CPT regional groups—Colorado, Ontario, and Cleveland—developed around people who supported the work of CPT but could not travel to Chicago for a month-long training. Training was thus adapted to fit the schedules of the people involved. For example, the Cleveland group met for intensive sessions one weekend a month for six months.

Today, the regional groups are built around a core of trained CPTers and supporters that work to deter violence in their own communities and

11. When Kathleen Kern returned from the 2005 delegation to the DRC, she received several invitations to write about her experience there. See "Victims as Pariahs"; "Corporate Complicity in Congo's War"; "The Human Cost of Cheap Cellphones."

support wider CPT projects. (For an overview of Cleveland's work, see chapter 3.)

- CPT Manitoba chooses to focus primarily on First Nations issues and CPT's Colombia project.

- The Colorado group has regularly sent people to work on the various CPT projects and locally focuses on antiwar efforts, violent toys, and interpreting CPT to area churches and meetings.

- The Northern Indiana group (calling itself CPTNI: see-pee-tee-nee) had a core of about ten people who went through training in Chicago and, after the Ontario group, has supplied the most CPTers actively serving on projects. It was also the oldest regional group, even though Colorado was the first group to hold a regional training. Locally, CPTNI focuses on immigrants's rights issues, war taxes, and counter-recruitment. CPTNI also sponsors the Campaign to End Production of DU Weapons.

- CPT Ontario meets quarterly and practices, through role-play, nonviolent responses to incidents that CPTers have encountered in the field. They also participate in various antiwar actions and witnesses on behalf of environmental and indigenous rights. It has hosted three regional trainings—the most of any group.

- CPT Upper Midwest (CPT UP-MID) has members in Minnesota, Iowa, and Wisconsin and meets bimonthly, participates in local peace vigils, and provides support for CPTers recently returned from the field.

- CPT's regional group in Washington DC focuses on educating the public about CPT's work, provides a "comfortable and supportive space" for DC-area CPTers returning from projects, extends hospitality to other CPTers visiting the city, and cultivates relationships with members of Congress, supplying them with reports and eyewitness accounts from CPT project locations.

- The CPT United Kingdom (UK) group, launched in 2004, was the first regional group to start outside of North America. Currently the group holds informal meetings, since the trained UK CPTers and participants in CPT delegations are scattered around the country. As of this writing in 2007, CPT UK supports and nurtures groups of CPT "sympathizers" around the United Kingdom, helps set up speaking engagements for recently returned UK CPTers, and is hoping to conduct a regional training in the future.

Although regional groups have been an asset to the work of CPT, they have not, as was envisioned at Joyfield farm in 2000, resulted in more racially, culturally, or socially diverse corps of full-timers and reservists actively working in the field. CPT continues, however, to hold on to the vision of a decentralized organization, supported by many regionally based communities all over the world. How to implement that vision is still a question that the organization is exploring; it does not yet have a clear idea of *how* it needs to adapt in order to expand the base, but knows that it will need to adapt.

RELIGIOUS ISSUES

A high Christology permeated Ron Sider's 1984 address that sparked the formation of Christian Peacemaker Teams:

> Jesus' vicarious death for sinful enemies of God is the foundation of our commitment to nonviolence. The incarnate one knew that God was loving and merciful even toward sinful enemies. That's why he associated with sinners, forgave their sins, and completed his mission by dying for them on the cross. And it was precisely the same understanding of God that prompted him to command his followers to love their enemies. We as God's children are to imitate the loving characteristics of our heavenly God who rains mercifully on the just and the unjust. That's why we should love our enemies. The vicarious cross of Christ is the fullest expression of the character of God. At the cross, God suffered for sinners in the person of the incarnate Son.

Although the founders of CPT always thought that the organization would remain firmly rooted in Jesus' gospel message, as the organization evolved, it has in practice accepted workers over the last twenty years with high, low, and most-points-in-between Christologies. Some come to CPT because Jesus is central to their life and they feel him calling them to the field. Others have a minimal spiritual outlook, but respect the teachings of Jesus and want to do the work CPT is doing.

In general, CPT tends to attract relatively tolerant people, regardless of their level of spiritual grounding. Most have spent time working in coalitions with non-Christians. Most think they have something to learn from other faiths. Sometimes this openness does not sit well with the more conservative evangelical church constituency, which views proselytizing as an important part of the Christian walk.

Whether CPT should include non-Christians on its teams has also been at times a contentious issue. Some in CPT have argued that excluding non-Christians is a form of bigotry, akin to racism and sexism. In practice, non-Christian people of faith have participated in CPT trainings and interned on teams—often as a way to envision how CPT skills could be adapted to create peace teams in their own faith traditions. CPT has also had a few committed workers for whom Christianity does not resonate—but they respect the organization's spiritual roots and do not interfere with the religious life of the team. (One of these people once told Kathleen Kern that she appreciated times of spoken prayer because it helped her understand better the issues with which her fellow team members were struggling.)

However, most CPT workers understand and appreciate that CPT is a place where shared faith provides a "taproot of strength for gutsy nonviolence," according to CPT Co-Director, Carol Rose.[12] As of this writing in 2007, applicants to CPT must self-identify as Christians and sign off on the CPC "Basic Understandings."

Christian Peacemaker Corps and Reserve Corps participants will:

- respond to violent conflict out of the biblical teachings of nonviolence.

- understand that love is a central quality of the Christian faith and becomes the basis for our relationship with all people regardless of race, color, sex, religious views, sexual orientation, age or ability.

- possess the personal, emotional, spiritual and vocational resources needed for creative work in demanding and potentially life-threatening situations.

- identify with, and participate in, the life and activity of a local church and support community. . . .

- be responsible to members of the Christian Peacemaker Corps, Reserve Corps and CPT workers, accepting the disciplines of a working and worshipping community.[13]

12. E-mail, Oct 26, 2007.
13. CPT, Christian Peacemaker Corps application.

Move to a More Ecumenical Organization

The founders of CPT came from the Anabaptist tradition, which had rejection of violence as a central faith tenet.[14] However, from the beginning, including in Sider's speech, there was a vision that one day CPT would be an organization that thousands of Christians from many different denominations would join. In 2007, the largest percentage of Christians in both the office-based and field-based Christian Peacemaker Corps came from Anabaptist and Quaker backgrounds, and the organization still received most of its funding from those historic peace church circles.[15] However, Catholics were the second largest faith-bloc in CPT and mainline Protestants were gaining ground. In addition to groups of Anabaptist origin, official supporting denominations, agencies, and organizations included the Baptist Peace Fellowship of North America, the Congregation of St. Basil (Basilians), Every Church a Peace Church, Friends United Meeting, and the Presbyterian Peace Fellowship.

This move toward ecumenism has created tensions. Traditions such as *a capella* four-part singing are dear to CPTers from the Mennonite tradition and provide spiritual energy to sustain their work on projects.

---

14. See, for example, the Schleitheim Confession (Sattler, "Brotherly Union"): "Thereby shall also fall away from us the diabolical weapons of violence—such as sword, armor, and the like, and all of their use to protect friends or against enemies—by virtue of the word of Christ: "you shall not resist evil" (Matt 5:39).

Menno Simons, whose name somewhat accidentally attached itself to the disparate Anabaptist groups in Europe, wrote in the sixteenth century:

> Our weapons are not weapons with which cities and countries may be destroyed, walls and gates broken down, and human blood shed in torrents like water. But they are weapons with which the spiritual kingdom of the devil is destroyed . . . Christ is our fortress; patience our weapon of defense; the Word of God our sword . . . Iron and metal spears and swords we leave to those who, alas, regard human blood and swine's alike. ("Foundation of Christian Doctrine, 1539," 198)
>
> Peter was commanded to sheathe his sword. All Christians are commanded to love their enemies . . . Tell me, how can a Christian defend Scripturally retaliation, rebellion, war, striking, slaying, torturing, stealing, robbing, and plundering and burning cities, and conquering countries? ("Reply to False Accusations 1554," 555)

15. In her comments on a draft of this chapter, Claire Evans wrote: "In the Aug 16, 2007 directory I counted 6 Anabaptists and 8 Non-Anabaptist [staff]. Among the FT corps I counted 15 peace churchers (including Quaker) and 17 non-peace churchers." Carol Rose, in an October 26, 2007 e-mail, noted that the majority of CPT funding comes from individuals in these circles as opposed to congregations and denominations.

However, they can make those who did not grow up with such traditions feel left out.[16] Engrained cultural assumptions, for example regarding alcoholic drinks as a little sinister, do not cross over well to some Catholic CPTers, for whom wine and beer are an important aspect of Christian community.

Conversely, Mennonites and Brethren can feel a sense of loss when they see people no longer associating CPT with Anabaptism, something that occurred when the four hostages in Iraq—none of whom came from Anabaptist backgrounds—elevated the profile of the organization in the mainstream media. The successful NGO, Heifer Project, was originally an initiative of the Church of the Brethren, but few people, even members of the Church of the Brethren, know its origins, and some Mennonite CPT supporters worry that CPT will one day no longer be identified with the Mennonite Church. So far, CPT has kept both the Anabaptist roots and the growth toward ecumenism in tandem, but potential for further tensions as the organization grows is a reality.[17]

RELATIONSHIPS WITHIN TEAMS

As noted in the previous chapter's section on the Gaza project 13, those involved with CPT in the beginning knew that bad interpersonal dynamics could sink a movement, and so from the time of the first training in 1993 CPTers learned conflict resolutions skills and team-building activities. Nevertheless, even trained CPTers have brought a panoply of human defects to the teams they have worked on since 1993. Immaturity, intimate

---

16. When Presbyterian missionaries Marthame and Elizabeth Sanders were visiting the Hebron team in 2000 from Zababdeh, a village in the northern West Bank, they got into a deep conversation about Presbyterian affairs with CPT Reservist Gary Brooks, a Presbyterian pastor. Jamey Bouwmeester, from a Christian Reformed background, turned to the author and told her, "I think I've finally met a clique more annoying than the Mennonites."

17. Commenting on a draft of this section, Gene Stoltzfus wrote in an October 30, 2007 e-mail that the term "ecumenical" does not quite describe the expansion of CPT into multiple branches of the Christian church, because:

> such is the language of church councils. CPT works with and enjoys the support of those who read the Bible, take Jesus seriously, pray and believe that the Bible needs to be lived out. CPT has begun a very long task and conversation about this inherent part of the gospel and has done so in a time in history when the Western world of Christianity is fumbling for direction.

relationships that exclude others, an inability to empathize, arrogance, egotism, controlling and bullying behaviors, intentions to subvert the work of a team, poor communications skills, cliquishness, avoidance of conflict, psychological problems, burnout, and unhealthy responses to trauma have all, at one time or another, made the life of Christian Peacemaker Teams in the field difficult. In a few cases, they have brought teams to a state of real crisis. But given the vagaries of human nature, and the demise of so many peace and justice groups because of interpersonal squabbling in the leadership, perhaps the remarkable thing is that so few CPT team crises have occurred since 1993. Gene Stoltzfus, after reading a draft of this chapter wrote, "Some place in this history, someone has to say, 'teams work'... We are not perfect, but have learned something. Teams from this individualist world actually work."[18]

CPTers who have served with the organization for years have also learned to keep and eye out for bad team dynamics and thus avert crises. They have seen that the best teams tend to have a mix of ages and genders. This variety seems to help prevent teams forming into cliques along generational lines and enables teams to relate to wider cross-sections of the societies in which they have worked. They have learned that even if they are feeling tired from a long stint in the field, veteran CPTers need to be wary of dumping too much responsibility onto newer CPTers, even if the new people are eager to accept it. They have learned that regular meetings and times of worship help with team-building, and that one can dislike a teammate but still value the gifts he or she brings to the work.

The best-functioning teams often have significant spiritual undergirding and find fresh approaches to their work from times of prayer, worship, and Bible study. They also tend to have people with good senses of humor, which may be a spiritual discipline itself, in that it tends to acknowledge human frailty and shine light on the absurd actions and philosophies that powers and principalities have put in place.

More serious than the interpersonal dynamics on a team has been the presence of systemic oppressions, such as racism and sexism, within teams. Undoing racism has been part of the earliest CPT trainings, and yet people of color on the various teams have still felt marginalized by CPTers of European descent and by the Eurocentric history and composition of the organization as a whole. A workshop on Undoing Sexism

18. Gene Stoltzfus, e-mail, Oct 30, 2007.

was added to later trainings, and CPT has a policy of inclusion regardless of sexual orientation. Yet, women and queer CPTers, who are sometimes working in cultures that regard them as inferior or even abhorrent, have sometimes had to deal with more subtle devaluation of them and their abilities by team members.

As mentioned in chapter 10, CPT has initiated actions to change CPT into an anti-racist organization. In 2005, it established an Undoing Racism Working Group to give leadership to organization-wide work on dismantling racism. Between 2005 and 2007, both the Steering Committee and most of the Peacemaker Corps participated in continuing educational workshops to deepen the organization's commitment to undoing racism. In 2007, Sylvia Morrison joined the CPT Support Team as Undoing Racism Coordinator.

Most involved with CPT recognize that work needed to undo oppressions within the organization will be ongoing because CPTers are always arriving and leaving and because sins of oppression are rooted in the human cultures that shape them. The work can be emotionally difficult, but it is vital if "CPT wants to reflect Christ who breaks down all dividing walls, and become more diverse in ways that reflect the Reign of God," writes CPT Co-Director Carol Rose.[19]

***

Despite the foibles and sinfulness that have done their damage to CPT over the years—because it is an organization created and perpetuated by human beings—CPT's work has somehow transcended those human frailties. Through the years, most involved with CPT have maintained a unity of purpose—challenging violent structures by following Jesus' sacrificial example—even though they might disagree about the best method for doing so. Local partners on the various project locations have thanked CPT for saving lives, making invaluable organizing work possible, bringing their struggle to international attention, and fostering lasting friendships between people from different "enemy" factions. Sometimes, local activists have simply been grateful that CPTers recognized their cause was just and wanted to be with them as they took the necessary risks for which their struggle called. By putting their own lives on the line, sometimes with sad consequences, CPTers have also caused both Christians

---

19. Rose, e-mail, Oct 26, 2007.

and non-Christians to blink and take another look at the teachings of Jesus that have inspired CPT's work.

An acknowledgement of both the fault lines and transcendence in CPT's work appeared in a special "Beatitudes for the CPTer" read at the final worship session of the 2000 Joyfield Farm retreat:

> Blessed are those who recognize their spiritual inadequacies, for they will cut their co-workers some slack, and be respectful of the faith traditions of others.
>
> Blessed are those who mourn, for they will be able to enter into the lives of the oppressed and exploited.
>
> Blessed are the meek, for they will make room for their co-workers to express new ideas, move in new directions and make mistakes.
>
> Blessed are those who hunger and thirst for righteousness, for they will be able to put jealousies, quarrels and irritations aside to focus on challenging the violence of the domination system.
>
> Blessed are the merciful, for they will give their co-workers a second chance after dumb mistakes and hurtful words and behaviors. And maybe, just maybe, they will receive mercy.
>
> Blessed are the pure in heart—wherever they may be.
>
> Blessed are the peacemakers, for sometimes, through the grace of God and the prayers of the faithful, they actually manage to make peace.
>
> Blessed are those who are persecuted for righteousness' sake; who are interrupted, slighted and denigrated by their co-workers; who are called "Squalor on the Face of the Earth," and "Nazis"; who are spit on, attacked and slandered by agents of the status quo; who develop a variety of interesting tropical diseases; who are reviled for coming from a life of privilege; who bear scars from a life of deprivation; who are laughed at for saying stupid things; who are willing to continue working for peace after they have been humiliated; who choose to witness and participate in the pain caused by atrocities, massacres and systemic violence.
>
> Rejoice and be exceedingly glad, for you are a part of the cloud of witnesses who will bless the peacemakers coming after you; for you are the salt of the earth; you are the light of the world; and yours is the kingdom of Heaven.[20]

---

20. "Beatitudes for the CPTer."

Bibliography

Unless otherwise indicated, all unpublished documents are stored in the Christian Peacemaker Teams Collection, Mennonite Church USA Archives—Goshen, 1700 S Main St., Goshen, IN 46526. E-mails and other digital files cited in this manuscript are archived, but not necessarily retrievable, with the Mennonite Church USA Archives at http://www.mcusa-archives.org/.

Reports, evaluations, CPTnet releases, and other documents, in keeping with a tradition of viewing CPT's work as a collective effort, have often not been attributed to individuals over the course of CPT's history. The author has thus attributed documents that came out of the various teams to "CPT Haiti," "CPT Esgenoôpetitj," "CPT Iraq," etc. Documents coming out of CPT as an organization, or the exploratory work that led to the development of teams, are attributed to "CPT."

CPTNET

CPTnet releases 1998–2008. CPT Archives. http://www.cpt.org/news/archives.
CPTnet releases 1993–1997. CPT Chicago Office Digital Archives, and CPT Collection, Mennonite Church USA Archives—Goshen.

OTHER DOCUMENTS

"Abitibi cutting paper production in Ontario and Newfoundland." CBC News, December 14, 2005. http://www.cbc.ca/money/story/2005/07/27/abitibi-050727.html.
Abunimah, Ali. E-mail message to Kathleen Kern, December 5, 2005.
Abu-Sharif, Bassam, and Uzi Mahnaimi. *The Best of Enemies: The Memoirs of Bassam Abu-Sharif & Uzi Mahnaimi*. Boston: Little, Brown, 1995.
ACRI (Association for Civil Rights in Israel). "HCJ Orders State to Dismantle Concrete Wall in Southern Hebron Hills." December 25, 2006. http://www.acri.org.il/eng/story.aspx?id=346.
"Activist released after vote." *Boulder Daily Camera*, July 31, 2001.
AI (Amnesty International). "Canada: Why there must be a public inquiry into the police killing of Dudley George." Report, AMR 20/002/2003, September 4, 2003.

Available at http://www.amnesty.org/en/library/asset/AMR20/002/2003/en/dom-AMR200022003en.pdf.

———. "Israel/Occupied Territories: Demolition and dispossession: the destruction of Palestinian homes." By Coon Anthony. Amnesty International paper, MDE 15/059/1999, December 8, 1999. Available at http://www.amnesty.org/en/library/asset/MDE15/059/1999/en/dom-MDE150591999en.pdf.

AI Canada. "Colombia: Justice for the people of the Sinú River." May 31 2007, updated July 9, 2008. http://www.amnesty.ca/take_action/actions/colombia_justice_sinu_river.php.

———. "Mission to Grassy Narrows." http://www.amnesty.ca/grassy_narrows/main.php.

Al Aqsa Martyrs Brigade. "Statement by the Al Aqsa Martyrs Brigades Palestine on the CPT Hostages in Iraq." December 4, 2005. International Solidarity Movement. http://www.palsolidarity.org/main/2005/12/06/statement-by-the-al-aqsa-martyrs-brigades-palestine-on-the-cpt-hostages-in-iraq.

Alá Santiago Rivera, Carlos. *El Rostro Oculto de la Desobediencia Civil: Testimonios desde la cárcel* [The Hidden Face of Civil Disobedience: Testimonies from Prison]. Edited by Josean Ramos. San Juan, PR: Sociedad de Autores Libres, 2003.

Albrecht, Scott. E-mail message to Kathleen Kern, June 7, 2006.

Alexander, Justin. Comments on draft of chap. 12. E-mail message attachment to Kathleen Kern, August 3, 2007.

———. E-mail message to author, July 18, 2007.

Alfred, Taiaiake, and Lana Lowe. "Warrior Societies in Contemporary Indigenous Communities." Ipperwash Inquiry Paper, July 30, 2005. *Thunder Bay IMC.* http://thunderbay.indymedia.org/news/2005/07/20464.

AMMSA (Aboriginal Multi-Media Society). "Classroom Topic: Environment." http://www.ammsa.com/ammsa.html.

Anderson-Rosetti, Kristin. "Excerpts from Letters to Tom, Norman, Harmeet and Jim: Written from the Village of At-Tuwani, West Bank, Palestine." Chap. 5 in *118 Days: Christian Peacemaker Teams Held Hostage in Iraq,* edited by Tricia Gates Brown. Chicago: CPT, 2008. Earlier draft in Mennonite Church USA Archives.

Arendt (Hull), Cole. "D.C. Project moves in." *Signs of the Times* 5:4 (1995) 5.

———. E-mail message to CPT Chicago Office, October 10, 1994.

———. "Invisible Theatre Pieces." March 30, 1995. Mennonite Church USA Archives.

———. "Reflection on the Considerations for CPT/CPC Decision Making." January 5, 1994. Mennonite Church USA Archives.

———. Telephone interview with Kathleen Kern, June 20, 2003.

———. Telephone interview with Kathleen Kern, October 21, 2003.

———. "Urban Peacemaking: Neighbors work together to take back their streets." *Sojourners* 24:3 (1995). http://www.sojo.net/index.cfm?action=magazine.article&issue=soj9507&article=950744.

ARIJ (Applied Research Institute—Jerusalem). "The Segregation Wall . . . New map provided for the wall by the IOF." June 16, 2003. *Monitoring Israeli Colonization Activities in the Palestinian Territories.* http://www.poica.org/editor/case_studies/view.php?recordID=271.

Arraf, Huwaida. E-mail message to Kathleen Kern, May 23, 2004.

Ashrawi, Hannah, *This Side of Peace.* New York: Simon and Schuster, 1995

"At-Tuwani: Parting the Wall." *Signs of the Times* 16:3 (2006) 4.

Avissar, Oded. *Sefer Hevron.* Jerusalem: Keter, 1970.

Avnery, Uri. "Manufacturing Anti-Semites." *Counterpunch,* October 2, 2002. http://www
.counterpunch.org/avnery1002.html.
———. *My Friend, the Enemy.* Westport, CT: Lawrence Hill, 1986.
Backhouse, Constance, and Donald McCrae. "Report to the Canadian Human Rights
Commission on the Treatment of the Innu of Labrador by the Government of
Canada." March 26, 2002. Available at http://www.chrc-ccdp.ca/pdf/reports/
innureport2002.pdf.
Bacon, David. "Oaxaca's Dangerous Teachers: Cross-border organizing is part of the
background of the current crisis." *Dollars & Sense,* September–October 2006. http://
www.dollarsandsense.org/archives/2006/0906bacon.html.
———. "Sportswriter at the Barricades: An interview with Jaime Medina." *Z Magazine,*
January 2007. http://www.zmag.org/zmag/viewArticle/13551.
Bahnson, Fred. "'That all of them may be one': Radical ecumenism in a time of strife." *The
Mennonite,* August 22, 2000.
Bailey-Dick, Matthew. E-mail message to Kathleen Kern, March 15, 2005.
Ball, George W., and Douglas B. Ball. *The Passionate Attachment: America's Involvement
with Israel, 1947 to the Present.* New York: Norton, 1992.
Barak, Rafael. Letter to Kathleen Kern, May 5, 2003.
Barr, Cameron W. "'Aggressive pacifists' put their faith on the firing line." *Christian Science
Monitor,* February 13, 2002.
Bartel, Bob. E-mail message to Kathleen Kern, August 27, 2003.
"Beatitudes for the CPTer." *Signs of the Times* 10:4 (2000) 9.
Becker, Marc. E-mail message to CPT Vieques Yahoo group containing notes from Robert
Rabin's talk, May 6, 2003. Mennonite Church USA Archives.
"Before 60 Minutes II, before the Red Cross Warnings, before the Taguba Report, there
was the CPT Report, and it went to U.S. Ambassador L. Paul Bremer III and U.S. Lt.
General Richard Sanchez." *The Link* 37:3 (2004).
Ben, Aluf, and Gideon Alon. "PM demands 'quick' changes in Hebron for Jewish control."
Ha'aretz, November 18, 2002.
Benvenisti, Meron. *Conflicts and Contradictions.* New York: Random House, 1986.
———. *Intimate Enemies: Jews and Arabs in a Shared Land.* Berkeley: University of
California Press, 1995.
———. *Sacred Landscape: The Buried History of the Holy Land Since 1948.* Berkeley:
University of California Press, 2000.
Benvie, Jan. E-mail message to Kathleen Kern, June 27, 2007.
Benzimann, Uzi. *Sharon: An Israeli Caesar.* New York: Adama, 1985.
Bermudez, Ramon, Executive secretary of the Puerto Rico Mennonite Convention. Letters
to Rich Williams and H.A. Penner, n.d. Mennonite Church USA Archives.
"Blenheim, Ontario: CPT Keeps Watch With Caldwell Nation." *Signs of the Times* 9:2
(1999) 5.
Bookbinder, Hyman, and James G. Abourzek. *Through Different Eyes: Two Leading
Americans, A Jew and an Arab, Debate U.S. Policy in the Middle East.* Bethesda, MD:
Adler, 1987.
Borowitz, Adam. "Wackenhut worries: A company with a sketchy record has quietly taken
over deportation duties from the Border Patrol." *Tucson Weekly,* May 3, 2007. http://
www.tucsonweekly.com/gbase/Currents/Content?oid=95659.
Bouwmeester, Jamey. "In Sharm's Way." *Signs of the Times* 9:4 (1999) 1–2.

Breen, Cathy. "Azad's Story from Kurdistan." May 28, 2006. CPT. http://www.cpt.org/iraq/feature.htm.

Brown, Ambrosia. E-mail message to members of Vieques delegation with an alert from Vieques Libre, April 30, 2000. Mennonite Church USA Archives.

Brown, Chris. E-mail message to Kathleen Kern, July 8, 2004.

———. Untitled report on school accompaniment in Hebron 2002–2003. Mennonite Church USA Archives.

Brown, Derek. "Attack and Aftermath: A Glossary of Terms." *Guardian.co.uk,* September 27, 2001. http://www.guardian.co.uk/waronterror/story/0,1361,559312,00.html.

Brown, Tricia Gates. E-mail message to Kathleen Kern, September 1, 2005.

———, ed. *118 Days: Christian Peacemaker Teams Held Hostage in Iraq.* Chicago: CPT, 2008.

B'tselem, The Israeli Information Center for Human Rights in the Occupied Territories, "Border police Trial on Suspicion of Killing 'Imran'Imran Abu Hamdiya," B'tselem website, archived in Internet Archive Wayback Machine, http://web.archive.org/web/20030622104419/http://www.btselem.org/ (accessed September 18, 2008). See also "Hebron: Border Police officers beat 'Imran'Imran Abu Hamdia, age 17, to death, December 2002," Btselem testimonies, http://www.btselem.org/English/Testimonies/20021230_Beating_to_Death_of_Imran_Abu_Hamdiye_in_Hebron_Witness_Raed_a_Rajbi.asp (accessed September 18, 2008).

———. "Hebron, Area H-2: Settlements Cause Mass Departure of Palestinians." Status Report, August 2003. By Shlomi Swisa, edited by Yael Stein, translated by Zvi Shulman. Available at http://www.btselem.org/Download/200308_Hebron_Area_H2_Eng.pdf.

———. "Standing Idly By: Non-enforcement of the Law on Settlers, Hebron 26–28 July 2002." Case Study 15, August 2002. By Yael Stein, translated by Maya Johnston and Zvi Shulman. Available at http://www.btselem.org/Download/200208_Standing_Idly_By_Eng.pdf.

Bueckert, Dennis. "Mercury poisoning issue back: 30 years later, disease signs present in Indians, Health Canada funds new study in Grassy Narrows." *Toronto Star,* July 28, 2003.

Buhler, Christopher. E-mail message to Kathleen Kern, March 17, 2005.

Burns, E. Bradford. *Latin America: A Concise Interpretive History.* 3rd ed. Englewood Cliffs, NJ: Prentice-Hall, 1982.

Burns, Robert. "Feds to remove Vieques Protesters." Associated Press, April 24, 2000.

Buschert, John. "U.S. Navy should stop bombing at Vieques range." *Goshen News,* July 9, 2000.

Buscio, Mario. "Does History Really Teach Us Anything?" *The Conrad Grebel Review* 9 (1991) 169–170.

Buyers, Robin. E-mail message to Kathleen Kern, September 8, 2005.

Byler, Mark. E-mail message to Brian Ladd, H. A. Penner, Rich Williams and Claire Evans, June 12, 2001. Mennonite Church USA Archives.

Caldwell First Nation. "Caldwell Present Info." http://web.archive.org/web/20010205051500/www.caldwellfn.com/present.html.

———. "History of the Caldwell Band." http://web.archive.org/web/20010124073600/www.caldwellfn.com/history.html. Mennonite Church USA Archives.

Cameron, Barbara. "Letter by Barbara Cameron, community resident." *Signs of the Times* 5:2 (1995) 2.

Carr, Joe. "A Dove's Last Song." Lyrics. *Lovinrevolution.* http://lovinrevolution.org/beta/?q=olivebranch#dove.

———. Reflection and eyewitness account of Rachel Corrie's murder. March 17–20, 2003. *Lovinrevolution.* http://lovinrevolution.org/rachel_writings.htm.

CCR (Center for Constitutional Rights). "Shenandoah, et al. v. Halbritter." http://ccrjustice.org/ourcases/past-cases/shenandoah%2C-et-al.-v.-halbritter.

CESR (Center for Economic and Social Rights). "The Right to Water in Palestine: A Background." Fact Sheet 1. n.d. Available at http://cesr.org/filestore2/download/451/Fact%20Sheet%20#1.pdf.

———. "The Right to Water in Palestine: Crisis in Gaza." Fact Sheet 2. N.d. Available at http://cesr.org/filestore2/download/452/Factsheet2Gaza.pdf.

Chacour, Elias. *Blood Brothers.* Tarrytown, NY: Chosen Books, 1984.

Chernus, Ira. "Is Anyone Responsible for Iraq's Disaster?" October 24, 2005. *CommonDreams.org.* http://www.commondreams.org/views05/1024-26.htm.

"Chicago to Peoria Peace Walk." *Signs of the Times* 12:3 (2002) 12.

Chippewas of Nawash Unceded First Nation. http://www.nawash.ca/.

Chomsky, Noam. *The Fateful Triangle: The United States, Israel and the Palestinians.* Boston: South End, 1983.

———. "The New War Against Terror." Speech, October 18, 2001, MIT. Text available at *Chomsky.info.* http://www.chomsky.info/talks/20011018.htm.

———. "Unsustainable Non Development." Daily Commentaries, May 30, 2000. *ZMag.* http://zmag.org/ZSustainers/ZDaily/2000-05/30chomsky.htm (not retrievable).

———. *World Orders Old and New.* New York: Columbia University Press, 1994.

"Christian Peacemaker Teams: New wine in old wineskins? (From a report by Rudy Regehr)." *Mennonite Reporter* 18:5 (1988) 15.

CHRN (Colombia Human Rights Network). "An Overview of Recent Colombian History." http://colhrnet.igc.org/timeline.htm.

Chupp, Kryss. E-mail message to Kathleen Kern, June 5, 2003.

———. E-mail message to Kathleen Kern, October 26, 2003.

———. E-mail message to Kathleen Kern, March 4, 2005.

———. E-mail messages to Kim Erno of the Oaxaca Lutheran Center, November 29–December 1, 2006. Forwarded by Tim Nafziger to Kathleen Kern, October 9, 2007.

———. Telephone interview with Kathleen Kern, May 23, 2003.

———. Telephone interview with Kathleen Kern, October 9, 2007.

CIFAS (Comitas Institute for Anthropological Study). "Treaty of 1779: Treaty entered into with the Indians of Nova Scotia from Cape Tormentine to the Bay De Chaleurs, September 22nd, 1779." *Social Disparity.* http://www.tc.edu/centers/cifas/socialdisparity/background/1779.htm.

Clark, Olivia. "Area prayer in Vieques now in 'jail.'" *The Fort Wayne Journal-Gazette,* July 24, 2001.

CMEP (Churches for Middle East Peace). "Text of the Mitchell Report: Report of the Sharm El-Sheikh Fact-Finding Committee." May 20, 2001. http://www.cmep.org/documents/MitchellReport.htm.

Cohen, Aharon. *Israel and the Arab World.* New York: Funk and Wagnalls, 1970.

Coin, Glenn. "Families refuse to leave homes." *Syracuse Post-Standard,* May 9, 2005.

"Collective Punishment: Closures, Curfews and House Demolitions." *Signs of the Times* 6:2 (1996) 1–2.

Compact Oxford English Dictionary. "Ground zero." *AskOxford.com.* http://www.askoxford
.com/concise_oed/groundzero?view=uk.

"Concern grows for Iraq hostages." *BBC News,* December 10, 2005. http://news.bbc.
co.uk/1/hi/world/middle_east/4515814.stm.

"Confiscation Protest." *The Other Israel* 72 (1996) 14–15. Also available at http://
israelipalestinianpeace.org/issues/72toi.htm#Confiscation.

Contreras, Joseph. "Radicals in the ranks: A soldier's rampage undercuts Mideast
peacemaking." *Newsweek,* January 13, 1997, 40–42.

Cook, Jonathan. "'Democratic' racism." *Al-Ahram Weekly On-line,* July 8–14, 2004. http://
weekly.ahram.org.eg/2004/698/op11.htm.

Cottrell, Robert. "Chechnya: How Russia Lost." *The New York Review of Books,* September
24, 1998.

CPT. "About CPT Borderlands." http://www.cpt.org/work/borderlands/about/.

———. "A Brief History of CPT's Work." Flyer. December 12, 2000.

———. "Addenda to Statement." March 23, 2006. http://www.cpt.org/iraq/response/06-
23-03statement.htm.

———. "A Pledge by Christians to Our Jewish Neighbors." By Kathleen Kern (unattributed).
Brochure. N.d. Mennonite Church USA Archives.

———. "Arabic Materials - Links." http://www.cpt.org/iraq/response/arabicresources
.htm.

———. "Bear Butte, South Dakota." http://www.cpt.org/work/aboriginal_justice/bear_
butte.

———. Christian Peacemaker Corps application. Available at http://cpt.org/files/
CPCapplication.pdf.

———. "Christian Peacemaker Teams Activities 1984–2000." Prepared by Robert
Hull. March 22, 1991, updated December 2000. http://www.cpt.org/publications/
chronology.php.

———. Christian Peacemaker Teams annual report, 2000. Mennonite Church USA
Archives.

———. "Cleveland." http://www.cpt.org/participate/regional/cleveland.

———. "Considerations for CPT decision making [sic] entering into crisis situations."
October 10, 1993. Mennonite Church USA Archives.

———. "CPT Emergency Delegation Supports Resistance Camps on Vieques, Puerto
Rico." Press release, May 5, 2000. Mennonite Church USA Archives.

———. "CPTers Freed." March 23, 2006. http://www.cpt.org/iraq/response/06-23-
03statement.htm.

———. "CPT Sunday." Collection of worship materials. October 27, 1996. Mennonite
Church USA Archives.

———. "CPT Vieques 4." Contains short biographies of each man. N.d. Mennonite
Church USA Archives.

———. "Discussion Points for Middle East Peacemaking Hebron Ibrahimi Mosque
Massacre." March 1994. Mennonite Church USA Archives.

———. "Disney: Pass the Bread! Let's share with the Global Family." Flyer/church bulletin
insert. N.d. Mennonite Church USA Archives.

———. "George Weber Memorial." http://www.cpt.org/georgeweber.php.

———. "Liturgy at the Twin Towers for the CPT Delegation to Afghanistan." By Jane
Pritchard (unattributed). December 16, 2001. http://www.cpt.org/afghanistan/
afghantwintowersliturgy.php.

———. "Notes from December 1996 CPC/Reserves Gathering, Washington, D.C." N.d. Mennonite Church USA Archives.

———. Notes from Support Team telephone call, February 13, 2007. Sent as e-mail message by Doug Pritchard to GITW, February 21, 2007.

———. Notes from Support Team telephone call, September 11, 2007. Sent as e-mail message by Doug Pritchard to GITW, September 26, 2007.

———. "Proposal for a CPT project in Burnt Church, New Brunswick." February 7, 2000. Sent as e-mail message attachment by Doug Pritchard to Kathleen Kern, July 6, 2005. Mennonite Church USA Archives.

———. "Report of Forced Return of CPT Person from Israel." July 6, 1993. Mennonite Church USA Archives.

———. "Report on CPT Fact-Finding Mission to Asubpeeschoseewagong Netum Anisnabek (Grassy Narrows First Nation)." By Wes Hare, Cole Hull, and Doug Pritchard. June 16, 1999, updated January 19, 2001. http://www.cpt.org/canada/grassyffm.php.

———. "Report on Exploratory Trip by Christian Peacemaker Teams to British Columbia, March 17–26, 2002." CPT Chicago Office Digital Archives.

———. "Shine the Light Events: Daily and On-going Events and Vigils." http://www.cpt.org/iraq/shinelight/events.php.

———. "Some Evaluation/Reflections on the Fast for Rebuilding." By Gene Stoltzfus with a response from Mark Frey. April 16, 2007. Mennonite Church USA Archives.

———. Steering Committee minutes, April 6–8, 2000. Sent as e-mail message attachment by Mark Frey to Kathleen Kern, October 18, 2007. Mennonite Church USA Archives.

———. "The Innu Crisis and the Call of Christ." Brochure and attached program, statement and notes from Bob Hull. N.d. Mennonite Church USA Archives.

CPT Arizona. "Christian Peacemaker Teams Brownsville Report, February 12–17, 2006." N.d. Sent as e-mail message attachment by Mark Frey to Kathleen Kern, September 13, 2007. Mennonite Church USA Archives.

———. "CPT's Arizona Project: Summer 2005—Report and Evaluation." Prepared by Mark Frey, Arizona Project Support Coordinator. October 6, 2005. Sent as e-mail message attachment by Mark Frey to Kathleen Kern, September 13, 2007. Mennonite Church USA Archives.

———. "CPT Arizona/Borderlands Report." March 8, 2006. Sent as e-mail message attachment by Mark Frey to Kathleen Kern, September 13, 2007. Mennonite Church USA Archives.

———. "CPT semi-annual report; Project: Borderlands." Reported by Mark Frey to Steering Committee. March 7, 2007. Sent as e-mail message attachment by Mark Frey to Kathleen Kern, September 13, 2007. Mennonite Church USA Archives.

———. "Evaluation of Model of Bridge position." N.d. Sent as e-mail message attachment by Mark Frey to Kathleen Kern, September 13, 2007. Mennonite Church USA Archives.

———. "Proposal: Completion of CPT's Arizona Project—by the end of September 2004." Signed by Claire Evans, Mark Frey, Elizabeth Garcia, and Scott Kerr. N.d. Sent as e-mail message attachment by Mark Frey to Kathleen Kern, September 13, 2007. Mennonite Church USA Archives.

———. "Proposal for Continuation of CPT Borderlands/Arizona." N.d. Sent as e-mail message attachment by Mark Frey to Kathleen Kern, September 13, 2007. Mennonite Church USA Archives.

———. "Report: 'Under Siege' The Effects of Increased Militarization of the U.S.-Mexico Border." September 2005. Mennonite Church USA Archives.

———. Revised AZ proposal. September 29, 2005. Sent as e-mail message attachment by Mark Frey to Kathleen Kern, September 13, 2007. Mennonite Church USA Archives.

———. "Summary of Seven-month CPT Borderland Bridge Position and Reference Group Activities, November 2005–May 2006." Prepared by Mark Frey, CPT Arizona Project Coordinator. June 9, 2006. Sent as e-mail message attachment by Mark Frey to Kathleen Kern, September 13, 2007. Mennonite Church USA Archives.

CPT Asubpeeschoseewagong. "Evaluation of CPT's Role at the Asubpeeschoseewagong (Grassy Narrows) Blockades Nov. 2002–Aug. 2004." July 25, 2005. Mennonite Church USA Archives.

———. "Summary of Remembered History of Asubpeeschoseewagong." N.d. Mennonite Church USA Archives.

CPT At-Tuwani. "At-Tuwani Media Packet." http://www.cpt.org/hebron/documents/ Tuwani_media_packet (no longer retrievable).

——— and Operation Dove. "Immanent Peril: The Impact of the Proposed Security Wall along Route 317." February 7, 2006. http://www.cpt.org/palestine/at-tuwani/ documents/CPT_OD_317_security_wall_report.htm#proposed.

——— and Operation Dove. "Report on the Israeli Military and Police Escort of Palestinian Children from Tuba and Maghayir Al-Abeed to and from School in At-Tuwani for the 2005–2006 School Year." November 10, 2006. http://www.cpt.org/ palestine/at-tuwani/documents/CPT_OD_2005_2006_school_patrol_report.htm.

CPT Canada. "Judge Reserves Decision until May 18 in Trial of Christian Peacemakers Defending Mi'kmaq Fishing Rights." Press release, March 15, 2001. Sent as e-mail message attachment by Doug Pritchard to Kathleen Kern, July 6, 2005.

———. "Media Statement Re: Charges Laid in the Lobster Fishery." August 2, 2000. Sent as e-mail message attachment by Doug Pritchard to Kathleen Kern, July 6, 2005.

———. "Toronto Human Rights Workers and Mi'kmaq Fishers Charged in Lobster Conflict." Press release, August 1, 2000. Sent as e-mail message attachment by Doug Pritchard to Kathleen Kern, July 6, 2005.

———. "Toronto Human Rights Workers Call for an End to the Federal Harassment of Mi'kmaq Fishers." Press release, August 2, 2000. Sent as e-mail message attachment by Doug Pritchard to Kathleen Kern, July 6, 2005.

CPT Chiapas. "Chiapas Update: July 31–August 15, 1998." CPT Chiapas e-mail newslist message, n.d. Mennonite Church USA Archives.

———. "CPT Log and Debrief—Guadalupe Tepeyac Action, January 4–8, 2001." Report from Carl Meyer's files sent to Kathleen Kern, n.d. Mennonite Church USA Archives.

CPT Colombia. Dear Colleague letter, April 2, 2003. Kathleen Kern's files.

———. "Up from the Ashes—A Lenten Liturgy." http://www.cpt.org/publications/ltg_ ashes.html.

"CPTers imprisoned, released and resuming work in Hebron." *Signs of the Times* 6:3 (1996) 1–3.

CPT Esgenoôpetitj. "A Summary of Responses from the Burnt Church Listening Project." October 12, 2000. Sent as e-mail message attachment by Doug Pritchard to Kathleen Kern, n.d. Mennonite Church USA Archives.

———. "Gunboat Diplomacy: Canada's Abuse of Human Rights at Esgenoôpetitj (Burnt Church, New Brunswick)." February 2001. http://www.cpt.org/canada/enreport .htm.

———. Report describing events of August 13, 2000. By Matthew Bailey-Dick. N.d. Sent as e-mail message attachment by Doug Pritchard to Kathleen Kern, n.d. Mennonite Church USA Archives.

CPT Haiti. "Closing Week of CPT's long term presence in Jérémie, Haiti." By Ari Nicola, translated by Carla Bluntschli. February 6, 1995. Mennonite Church USA Archives.

———. "Evaluation of Mobile Teams in Haiti Project, August 27–December 24, 1996." January 22, 1997. Mennonite Church USA Archives.

———. "Jérémie Final Report: October 2 to December 15, 1993, Cry for Justice." N.d. Mennonite Church USA Archives.

———. "Proposal for Mobile Teams in Haiti: April 1, 1996–January 1, 1997." N.d. Mennonite Church USA Archives.

———. "Proposal for presence in Latibonit, Haiti." December 15, 1996. Mennonite Church USA Archives.

———. "Report on Activities February 26–June 27 [1997]." By Pierre Shantz and Joshua Yoder (unattributed). June 24, 1997. Mennonite Church USA Archives.

CPT Hebron. "Atta Jaber Family." Report for Campaign for Secure Dwellings. N.d. CPT Hebron Office.

———. "Chronology, 1995–2003." http://www.cpt.org/work/palestine/hebron/chronol-ogy.

———. "CSD—Sample Urgent Action appeal." http://www.cpt.org/csd/csdsampleua.php.

———. Direct e-mail newslist message, January 2, 2001. Mennonite Church USA Archives.

———. "Dividing Walls." Bulletin insert. N.d. CPT Chicago Office Digital Archives.

———. Draft of e-mail message to Sen. Joseph Lieberman's office in response to "CPT—Squalor on the Face of the Earth," by David Wilder. N.d. Mennonite Church USA Archives.

———. E-mail message to Kathleen Kern, November 18, 2007.

———. "General Background on the Beqa'a Valley and the Story of Atta Jaber (in his words)." N.d. Mennonite Church USA Archives.

———. "Getting in the Way of Guns." Report on January 10, 1999 intervention. March 1, 1999. Mennonite Church USA Archives.

———. "Urgent Action Appeal." E-mail message printout, November 9, 1995. Extended version of "Hebron Action Alert." CPTnet press release, November 13, 1995. Mennonite Church USA Archives.

CPT Iraq. "Report and Recommendations on Iraqi Detainees." January 2004. http://www .cpt.org/iraq/detainee_summary_report.htm.

CPT Kenora. "Evaluation of CPT's presence in Kenora June 2005–August 2006." Compiled by William Payne. March 13, 2007. Sent as e-mail message attachment by Doug Pritchard to Kathleen Kern, November 15, 2007.

CPT Oaxaca. "Final Report: Christian Peacemaker Teams accompaniment to Oaxaca, Mexico in December 2006." Compiled by Tim Nafziger. N.d. Sent as e-mail message attachment by Mark Frey to Kathleen Kern, September 13, 2007. Mennonite Church USA Archives.

CPT Oceti Sakowin Encampment. "Celebrating Sovereignty: East Indians and Christian Peacemaker Teams Welcomed to Great Sioux Nation." Press release, n.d. Mennonite Church USA Archives.

———. "CPT, Pierre, South Dakota: A six-month observer presence with the Sioux People on La Framboise Island." Report by Joanne Kaufman, Cliff Kindy, and Rick Polhamus. N.d. Mennonite Church USA Archives.

———. Letter to local law enforcement agencies regarding "Oceti Sakowin Camp; Report on recent events," from "Christian Peacemaker Teams, observers." Mennonite Church USA archives.

———. "Memorandum re: events of Tuesday afternoon, June 22, to South Dakota Highway Patrol, Pierre Police Department, Hughes County Sheriff's Department, Federal Bureau of Investigation, U.S. Department of Justice." Mennonite Church USA Archives.

———. "Report on harassment and arrest, Tuesday, June 22, 1999." Mennonite Church USA Archives.

———. "Taking Treaty Land by an Act of Congress: The 'Wildlife Mitigation' or 'Wildlife Restoration Act.'" Bulletin insert. N.d.

———. "Update from Pierre last week: Not for distribution." May 24, 1999. Mennonite Church USA Archives.

CPT Oneida. "Oneida Report." February 21, 2002. http://www.cpt.org/usa/oneida.php.

CPT PUP (Project in Urban Peacemaking). "Christian Peacemaker Teams—Community Listening Project: Columbia Heights Neighborhood, Washington, D.C., Fall 1995." N.d. Mennonite Church USA Archives.

———. "CPT Listening Project: Project in Urban Peacemaking, September–November 1994." N.d. Mennonite Church USA Archives.

———. "Evaluation and Reflection on CPT Washington Work." Coordinated by Val Liveoak. June 1996. Mennonite Church USA Archives.

———. "Period Report: Project in Urban Peacemaking, Washington, DC, September–December 1994." N.d. CPT Chicago Office Archives.

———. "Project in Urban Peacemaking, Washington, DC." By Cole Arendt, sent as email message to CPT Chicago Office, October 10, 1996. Mennonite Church USA Archives.

———. "Proposal for Overcoming Violence-Investigation into Washington DC." By Cole Arendt, John Reuwer, and Kathleen Kern (mistakenly attributed to Kathy Kelly). May 3, 1997. Mennonite Church USA Archives.

———. Untitled report on Washington DC Project, August–October 1995. Name withheld by request. November 1, 1995. Mennonite Church USA Archives.

———. "Urban Violence Reduction Report." By Cole Arendt. August 11, 1994. CPT Chicago Office Archives.

"CPT rallies neighborhood for Halloween safety and fun." *Signs of the Times* 4:11 (1994) 3

CPT Richmond PUP. "Extending the RichPUP through 1998." By Wes Hare. October 9, 1997. Mennonite Church USA Archives.

———. "Proposal: A Richmond VA Project on Urban Peacemaking (RichPUP) (a team of three persons working during the months of May–December 1997)." By Wes Hare. March 31, 1997. Mennonite Church USA Archives.

CPT Vieques Delegation (assorted delegations between 2000 and 2003). "Christian Peacemaker Teams Delegation Log: April 2–9, 2002." Mennonite Church USA Archives.

———. "Christian Peacemaker Teams Delegation to Vieques, Puerto Rico, March 11–17, 2000. David Jehnsen and Cliff Kindy. N.d. Mennonite Church USA Archives.

———. "CPT delegation to Vieques, April 2002." Chris Friedman, April 22, 2002. Mennonite Church USA Archives.

———, "CPT delegation to Vieques," April 22, 2002. Mennonite Church USA Archives.

———. "Christian Peacemaker Team Delegation to Vieques, Puerto Rico, August 23–September 3, 2002—Daily Log." Mennonite Church USA Archives.

———. "Christian Peacemaker Teams April 29–May 5, 2003 Delegation to Vieques, Puerto Rico." Marc Becker. N.d. Mennonite Church USA Archives.

———. "CPT Delegation to Vieques, April–May 2001: Verbal evaluation, May 6, 2001 in San Juan Puerto Rico." Mennonite Church USA Archives.

———. "CPT Delegation to Vieques—Trip Report—September 29–October 9, 2000." N.d. Mennonite Church USA Archives.

———. "CPT Report—Delegation to Vieques, Puerto Rico, August 23–September 3, 2002." N.d. Mennonite Church USA Archives.

———. "CPT Trip Report for Vieques: May 10–17 extension of previous delegation May 1–9, 2000." Andy Baker. May 23, 2000. Mennonite Church USA Archives.

———. "Continuing the Struggle on Vieques," Chris Friedman, April 22, 2002.

———. E-mail message to Robert Rabin and Nilda Medina (subject heading: "Ideas for Escalating the Nonviolence in Vieques"). Sent by Matt Guynn, May 8, 2001.

———. Letter to Rear Admiral Kevin Green, February 1, 2001. Mennonite Church USA Archives.

———. "Log for the CPT Delegation to Vieques, Jan. 25–Feb. 4, 2001: Schedule and highlights." Mennonite Church USA Archives.

———. "May 1–8, 2000" Delegation log. Mennonite Church USA Archives.

———. "Recommendations to CPT/Delegation Coordinators: From CPT Delegation to Vieques, October, 2000." N.d. Mennonite Church USA Archives.

———. "Report: CPT Emergency Delegation to Vieques, Puerto Rico, May 1–9, 2000." N.d.

———. "Report of Christian Peacemaker Teams emergency delegation to Vieques, Puerto Rico, April 2–April 9, 2002." By Rebecca Yoder Neufeld. N.d. Mennonite Church USA Archives.

———. "Report CPT Delegation to Puerto Rico March 11–18, 2000" N.d. Mennonite Church USA Archives.

———. "Vieques Trip Report." Covering the January 25–February 4, 2001 delegation. N.d. Mennonite Church USA Archives.

CRDV (Committee for the Rescue and Development of Vieques). "A Call to Action for Peace on Vieques." Press release, July 23, 2002. Mennonite Church USA Archives.

———. Press release. Translation of "Actividades especiales en Vieques anticipan marcha-concentración y desobediencia civil el 1 de Octubre." Sent as e-mail message, September 27, 2000. Mennonite Church USA Archives.

———. "Not One more Bomb! U.S. Navy Out Now!" Pamphlet, n.d. Mennonite Church USA Archives.

——— "Shout for Peace." Statement in delegation orientation packet, September 23, 2001. Also available at http://www.geocities.com/notowars/views/vieques.html.

————. "The Vieques 4 D's—Our Historic Demands." In Not One more Bomb! U.S. Navy Out Now!" Mennonite Church USA Archives.

————. "Vieques committee works non-stop for peace." Press release, February 2, 2002. Mennonite Church USA Archives.

Crossman, Richard. "Field Report: The Truth about Haiti." *The Resister: The Official Publication of the Special Forces Underground* 1:3 (1995). Available at http://www .totse.com/en/politics/right_to_keep_and_bear_arms/resist11.html.

Cuevas, Jesús Ramirez. "Queremos de las Armas que Matan Mucha Gente" [We want the guns that kill a lot of people]. *La Jornada, Weekend Supplement, Masiosare,* January 4, 1998. Translated by Duane Ediger. Available at http://www.eco.utexas.edu/~archive/ chiapas95/1998.01/msg00694.html.

Curling, Rusty. E-mail message to Kathleen Kern, August 31, 2005.

Danner, Mark. "Beyond the Mountains II." *The New Yorker,* December 4, 1989.

David, Anita. E-mail message to Kathleen Kern, June 30, 2007.

"DC Landlord fails to Win Cut in Sentence." *Washington Post,* September 21, 1995.

"Delegation to Chiapas." *Signs of the Times* 5:3 (1995) 5.

Delfin, Marty Gerard. "Activist Jailed for Re-entering Camp Garcia." *The San Juan Star,* October 6, 2000.

"Demolition Season Reopened." *The Other Israel* 91 (1999) 14. http://www.Israeli palestinianpeace.org/issues/91toi.htm.

d'Errico, Peter. "Jeffrey Amherst and Smallpox Blankets: Lord Jeffrey Amherst's letters discussing germ warfare against American Indians." *NativeWeb.* http://www .nativeweb.org/pages/legal/amherst/lord_jeff.html#1.

Dobbs, Kevin. "Visions of a new future." *Argus Leader,* May 4, 2003.

Drake, Laura. "A Netanyahu Primer." *Journal of Palestine Studies* 26:1 (1996) 58–69.

Ecumenical Encampment on Vieques. Photograph, chap. 13. Mennonite Church USA Archives.

Ediger, Duane. E-mail message to Kathleen Kern, August 30, 2006.

————. E-mail message to Kathleen Kern, November 27, 2006.

————. E-mail message to Kathleen Kern, September 11, 2007.

————. "Emergency delegation stands with Puerto Ricans on Vieques." Fax message, n.d. Mennonite Church USA Archives.

————. Fax message to CPT Chicago Office, sent during May 1–9, 2000 delegation to Vieques. Mennonite Church USA Archives.

————. "Letter from Duane Ediger." *Signs of the Times* 5:3 (1995) 7.

Electronic Intifada. "Sign the Urgent Appeal: Please Release Our Friends in Iraq." Nigel Parry News e-mail newslist message, December 2, 2008. Available at http://lists.electronicintifada.net/mail.cgi?flavor=archive;list=nigelparrynews;i d=20051202133506.

Electronic Intifada representative. E-mail correspondence with Rich Meyer, March–April 2006. Forwarded by Rich Meyer to Kathleen Kern, August 8, 2007.

Elon, Amos. *A Blood-Dimmed Tide: Dispatches from the Middle East.* New York: Columbia University Press, 1997.

Elvidge, Suzanne. "Captive of Conscience." Interview with Norman Kember, Greenbelt festival, August 2006. *Surefish.* Christian Aid. Transcript available at http://www .surefish.co.uk/greenbelt/greenbelt06/010906_norman_kember.htm.

E-mail message to CPT Chicago Office via Cole Arendt, November 6, 1995. Name withheld by request.

————. E-mail message to Kathleen Kern, April 7, 2008.

Emke, Ivan, and Nancy Gautsche. "Consultation Sets Agenda for Helping Innu." *Mennonite Reporter* 20:5 (1990) 1–2.

————. "CPT participants agree to walk with Innu in their struggle." Unpublished article sent to *Mennonite Reporter*. Mennonite Church USA Archives.

Enders, David. "Amid Hostage Vigils, Peace Work Endures." *The Nation*, December 10, 2005. http://www.thenation.com/doc/20051226/enders/.

Engle, John. Circles of Change blog. See especially posts from February 28–March 16, 2004. http://johnengle.blogspot.com.

Esquivia Ballestas, Ricardo, and Peter Stucky. "A Call from the Colombian Churches to the Churches in the North in Response to Bill Clinton's Visit to Colombia." September 10, 2000. Mennonite Church USA Historical Committee. http://www.mcusa-archives.org/library/resolutions/colombia.html.

Evans, Claire. Comments on draft of chap. 14. E-mail message attachment to Kathleen Kern, October 24, 2007.

————. E-mail message to former Puerto Rico delegation members and CPT Regional groups, November 10, 2000. Mennonite Church USA Archives.

————. E-mail message to Kathleen Kern, March 4, 2005.

————. E-mail message to Kathleen Kern, July 24, 2007.

————. E-mail message to Kathleen Kern, September 27, 2007.

————. Letter to College Peace Studies coordinators, November 13, 2000.

"Eye on Reconquista Nuisances . . . Aiding and Abetting Invaders Under the Guise of Religion." Glenn Spencer's American Patrol Report. http://www.americanpatrol|.com/REFERENCE/NoMoreDeathsRecons.html.

Filkins, Dexter. "The Fall of the Warrior King." *New York Times Magazine*, October 23, 2005.

Findley, Paul. *Deliberate Deceptions: Facing the Facts about the US-Israeli Relationship.* New York: Lawrence Hill, 1993.

Finkelstein, Norman G. *Image and Reality of the Israel-Palestine Conflict.* New York: Verso, 1995.

Flapan, Simha. *The Birth of Israel: Myths and Realities.* New York: Pantheon, 1987.

FOR (Fellowship of Reconciliation), Task Force on Latin America and the Caribbean. "Environmental Impacts of Navy Training." *Vieques Issue Brief,* Fall 2001. Mennonite Church USA Archives.

————. "Puerto Rico Under the Gun: A Nation in Struggle." Report from International Delegation to Puerto Rico. Pamphlet. August 21–29, 1999. Mennonite Church USA Archives.

————. "Puerto Rico Update: Disarming the U.S. Military Hub in Latin America, no. 33." Summer 2001. Mennonite Church USA Archives.

————. "Puerto Rico Update: Disarming the U.S. Military Hub in Latin America, no. 43." November 2001. Mennonite Church USA Archives.

————. "Puerto Rico Update: Vieques Arrestees Set for Sentencing." December 2003. http://www.forusa.org/programs/puertorico/pr-update-1203-3.html.

Forero, Juan. "Paramilitary Scandal Takes Colombian Elite by Surprise." *Washington Post*, February 22, 2007.

Foth, Peter J. "Internationale Mennonitische Organisation." 1987. *Global Anabaptist Mennonite Encyclopedia Online.*. http://www.gameo.org/encyclopedia/contents/i5876.html.

Fox, Tom. "Fight or Flight?" Waiting in the Light blog, October 22, 2004. http://waitinginthelight.blogspot.com/2004/10/fight-or-flight.html.

———. "Remembering Margaret Hassan." Waiting in the Light blog, November 15, 2004. http://waitinginthelight.blogspot.com/2004/11/remembering-margaret-hassan.html.

———. "Snapshots from the Syrian Border." Waiting in the Light blog, October 26, 2005. http://waitinginthelight.blogspot.com/2005/10/snapshots-from-syrian-border.html.

Fransen, David. "Facing the Oka Crisis: A Response." *The Conrad Grebel Review* 9 (1991) 133–138.

Frey, Mark. E-mail message to Kathleen Kern, April 2, 2005.

———. E-mail message to Kathleen Kern, November 23, 2004.

———. E-mail message to Kathleen Kern, October 8, 2007.

Friedman, Chris. "Continuing the Struggle on Vieques." April 22, 2002.

———. "CPT delegation to Vieques." April 22, 2002. Mennonite Church USA Archives.

Friedman, Robert I. *Zealots for Zion: Inside Israel's West Bank Settlement Movement.* New York: Random House, 1992.

Friesen, Lorne. E-mail message to Kathleen Kern, August 1, 2004.

Fulk (Fulcher) of Chartres. "Gesta Francorum Jerusalem Expugnantium" [The Deeds of the Franks Who Attacked Jerusalem]. In *Parallel Source Problems in Medieval History,* edited by Frederick Duncan and August C. Krey, 109–115. New York: Harper & Brothers, 1912.

Galeano, Eduardo. *Open Veins of Latin America: Five Centuries of Pillage of a Continent.* New York: Monthly Review Press, 1973.

Garza, Anna Maria, R. Aida Hernandez, Marta Figueroa, and Mercedes Olivera. "En Acteal Micaela oyo que gritaban: 'Hay que acabar con la semilla'" [In Acteal, Micaela heard them shout, "We need to finish off the seed"]. *La Jornada,* January 23, 1998. Translation by Duane Ediger. Available at http://www.eco.utexas.edu/~archive/chiapas95/1998.01/msg00893.html. Mennonite Church USA Archives.

George-Kanentiio, Doug. "History of the Onyota'a:ka Oneida: A Historical Journey." Oneidas for Democracy. http://www.oneidasfordemocracy.org/history.php. Mennonite Church USA Archives.

Gibbel, Jim. Letter to donors who contributed money for Vieques 4 travel and fines. July 31, 2001. Mennonite Church USA Archives.

Gilmore, Gerry J. "Rumsfeld: Colombia Is Doing 'An Excellent Job' Fighting Narcoterrorists." American Forces Press Service, August 19, 2003. http://www.defenselink.mil/news/newsarticle.aspx?id=28587.

Gish, Art. E-mail message to Kathleen Kern, August 9, 2004.

———. E-mail message to Kathleen Kern, August 23, 2004.

———. *Hebron Journal.* Scottdale, PA: Herald, 2001.

———. "Hebron: Opening Gates to Freedom." *Signs of the Times* 6:1 (1996) 1–2.

———. "Love Overcomes Fear in Hebron." *Signs of the Times* 10:1 (2000) 4–5.

Gish, Peggy. "Continuing the Work in Iraq: The Work of CPT and the Iraq Team." Chap. 2 in *118 Days: Christian Peacemaker Teams Held Hostage in Iraq,* edited by Tricia Gates Brown. Chicago: CPT, 2008. Earlier draft in Mennonite Church USA Archives.

———. E-mail message to Kathleen Kern, July 16, 2007.

GITW (Getting in the Way, internal CPT discussion group). "A Letter to fellow CPTers." Posting by Peggy Gish, February 23, 2007.

———. Posting by Kathleen Kern, October 8, 2004. CPT Chicago Office Archives.

————. Posting by James Loney, June 27, 2005. CPT Chicago Office Archives.

————. Posting by Matt Schaaf, May 25, 2005.

————. Posting by Sara Reschly, October 12, 2004. CPT Chicago Office Archives.

————. Posting by William Payne, October 8, 2004. CPT Chicago Office Archives.

————. Postings, April–June 2005.

Glatthaar, Joseph T., and James Kirby Martin. *Forgotten Allies: The Oneida Indians and the American Revolution.* New York: Hill and Wang, 2006.

Goldenberg, Suzanne. "Israel turns its fire on Arafat." *The Guardian,* March 30, 2002. http://www.guardian.co.uk/world/2002/mar/30/israel5.

Gonzales, Clarisel. "Protesters held by Navy as they try to get letter to Green." *The San Juan Star,* February 3, 2001.

Goodman, Amy. Interview of Seymour Hersh and Greg Rollins. *Democracy Now,* November 30, 2005. Transcript available at http://www.democracynow.org/article.pl?sid=05/11/30/153252.

Grand Council of Treaty No. 3. "Paypom Treaty—Terms of the treaty held at North West Angle Oct. 3, 1873." http://www.gct3.net/grand-chiefs-office/gct3-info-and-history/paypom-treaty/.

Grassy Narrows Chief and Council, Environmental Committee, Blockaders, Trappers, Clan Mothers, Elders, Youth. "Re: Moratorium on industry in our Traditional Territory, and Opposition to MNR tender process." Open letter, January 17, 2007. Available at http://freegrassy.org/fileadmin/materials/old_growth/free_grassy/2007_Moratorium_Call/GrassyMoratorium070.pdf.

Green, Stephen. *Living by the Sword: America and Israel in the Middle East 1968–87.* Brattleboro, VT: Amana, 1988.

Greenbelt Festival. "Norman Kember tells his story to the Festival he has attended for years." August 28, 2006. http://www.greenbelt.org.uk/?p=705.

Griner, David. "Manchester protesters live out beliefs." *Fort Wayne Journal Gazette,* May 28, 2000.

Gush Shalom. "Barak's Generous Offers." http://www.gush-shalom.org/generous/generous.html.

————. "Who's violating Oslo?" *PS: The Intelligent Guide to Jewish Affairs,* May 13, 1998.

————. "Who is violating the Agreements?" Gush Shalom research paper. January 28, 1998. http://gush-shalom.org/archives/oslo.html.

Gutiérrez Castaño, Julian. E-mail message to Kathleen Kern, November 28, 2006.

Guynn, Matt. E-mail message from CPT Vieques delegation to Robert Rabin and Nilda Medina, May 8, 2001. Mennonite Church USA Archives.

Haggerty, Richard A., ed. *Haiti: A Country Study.* Washington, DC: GPO, 1989. Available at http://countrystudies.us/haiti/21.htm.

Halifax Initiative. "Simiti Gold Mine." http://www.halifaxinitiative.org/index.php/miningmap/861.

Halper, Jeff (under the auspices of ICAHD). ICAHD e-mail newslist message to British Ambassador to Israel David Manning, March 23, 1998.

Hare, Wes. E-mail message to Kathleen Kern, February 23, 2005.

————. "Extending the RichPUP through 1998." E-mail message to CPT Steering Committee, October 9, 1997.

————. Telephone interview with Kathleen Kern, October 22, 2003.

————. Telephone interview with Kathleen Kern, September 16, 2003.

Harel, Amos, and Jonathan Lis. "Minister's aide calls Hebron riots a 'pogrom.'" *Ha'aretz*, July 31, 2002.

Harlan, Bill. "Land transfer gets OK: Missouri shoreline deal has drawn fire." *Rapid City Journal*, August 21, 1999.

————. "WRDA not an appropriation." *Rapid City Journal*, August 21, 1999.

Hass, Amira. "The mirror doesn't lie." *Ha'aretz*, November 1, 2000.

"Haudenosaunee tradition and culture." *Degiya'göh Resources*. http://www.degiyagoh .net/.

Hauser, Christine. "U.S. nun plays witness to Israeli-Palestinian strife." *USA Today*, December 7, 2000.

"Hebron hooligans." *Ha'aretz*, January 16, 2006.

Herman, Anne. E-mail message to Kathleen Kern, March 18, 2005.

————. E-mail message to Kathleen Kern, August 29, 2005.

————. E-mail message to Kathleen Kern, August 31, 2005.

Hersh, Seymour. "Chain of Command: How the Department of Defense Mishandled the Disaster at Abu Ghraib." *The New Yorker*, May 17, 2004.

————. *Chain of Command: The Road from 9/11 to Abu Ghraib*. New York: HarperCollins, 2004.

————. Interview with Amy Goodman. *Democracy Now*, November 30, 2005. Transcript available at http://www.democracynow.org/article.pl?sid=05/11/30/153252.

Hicks, Donna. E-mail message to Kathleen Kern while serving on the Hebron Team, November 27, 2007.

————. E-mail message to Kathleen Kern while serving on the Hebron Team, November 29, 2007.

Hochstetler-Shirk, Steve and Cheryl. "Christian Peacemaker Team Feasibility Study Trip to Chechnya and Ingushetia." Fax message to CPT Chicago Office via Florence Driedger, n.d. Mennonite Church USA Archives.

Holmes, Bob. E-mail message to Kathleen Kern, February 8, 2004

————. E-mail message to Kathleen Kern, June 15, 2004.

————. "Standing Firm." Eulogy for Tom Fox, April 2, 2006, Toronto. Text available at http://cpt.org/memorial/tomfox/eulogies.htm.

Horst, Benjamin. E-mail message to Kathleen Kern, August 15, 2006.

————. E-mail message to Kathleen Kern, August 17, 2006.

HRC (Human Rights Commission). "Human Rights Violated in Vieques." Pamphlet. N.d. Mennonite Church USA Archives.

HRW (Human Rights Watch). "Israel/Palestine: Armed Attacks on Civilians Condemned." February 21, 2001. http://www.hrw.org/press/2001/02/isr-pa-0221.htm.

————. "Second Class: Discrimination against Palestinian Arab Children in Israel's Schools." September 2001. Available at http://www.hrw.org/reports/2001/israel2/ ISRAEL0901.pdf.

HSC (Hebron Solidarity Committee). *Apartheid in Hebron: The True Face of Oslo*. Booklet. Jerusalem, 1995. Mennonite Church USA Archives.

————. "Second Anniversary of Oslo: Hebron Settlers Incite Riots at Palestinian Girls' School." E-mail newslist message, September 13, 1995. Mennonite Church USA Archives.

Huber, Tim. "Former Iraq hostage reflects on captivity." *Mennonite Weekly Review*, July 9, 2007.

Hull (Arendt), Cole. "Signs of the Times in Hebron." *Signs of the Times* 6:1 (1996) 3.

————. "Weed and Seed." Sermon, July 21, 1996, Seattle Mennonite Church. Mennonite Church USA Archives.

Hull, Robert. E-mail message to Gene Stoltzfus, August 24, 1995. Mennonite Church USA Archives.

————. "Kanienkehaka Chronology: The Mohawk Crisis in Quebec and Its Aftermath, July to December 1990." *The Conrad Grebel Review* 9 (1991) 103–113.

"Hundreds of settlers rampage in Hebron." *New York Times*, October 1, 1995.

Hunt, Dan. "Taken Twice." Chap. 10 in *118 Days: Christian Peacemaker Teams Held Hostage in Iraq*. Edited by Tricia Gates Brown. Chicago: CPT, 2008. Earlier draft in Mennonite Church USA Archives.

ICAHD (Israeli Committee Against House Demolitions). "Frequently Asked Questions." http://www.icahd.org/eng/faq.asp?menu=9&submenu=1.

INAC (Indian and Northern Affairs Canada). "Backgrounder: Caldwell Claim and Additions to Reserve Policy." February 2000. http://www.ainc-inac.gc.ca/nr/prs/j-a2000/00110bk_e.html.

————. "Facts on File: Treaty Land Entitlement (TLE) in Manitoba." http://www.ainc-inac.gc.ca/nr/prs/m-a2005/02693bk_e.html.

————. "Negotiations on the Caldwell First Nation's Specific Claim - January 2007." http://www.ainc-inac.gc.ca/ps/clm/cfn_e.html.

————. "The Administration of Treaty No. 3." http://www.ainc-inac.gc.ca/pr/trts/hti/t3/adm_e.html.

————. "Treaty 3 between Her Majesty the Queen and the Saulteaux Tribe of the Ojibbeway Indians at the Northwest Angle of the Lake of the Woods with Adhesions." 1871–1874. http://www.ainc-inac.gc.ca/pr/trts/trty3_e.html.

"In Depth: Inquiry testimony—a timeline." CBC News, May 24, 2005. http://www.cbc.ca/news/background/ipperwash/timeline.html.

"In Depth: The Ipperwash inquiry." CBC News, updated May 31, 2007. http://www.cbc.ca/news/background/ipperwash/.

Irizarry, Lilliam. "Navy Detains Protesters on Vieques." Associated Press, October 1, 2000.

Ismi, Asad. "Profiting from Repression: Canadian Investment in and Trade with Colombia." *Americas Update*, November 2000. Available at http://security.tao.ca/colombiareport.html.

Israeli-Palestinian Interim Agreement on the West Bank and the Gaza Strip ("Oslo 2"). Signed September 28, 1995, Washington, DC. Available at http://www.jewishvirtuallibrary.org/jsource/Peace/interim.html.

"It could have been worse." Sidebar. *Signs of the Times* 6:3 (1996) 3.

Jack, Maureen. E-mail message to Kathleen Kern, August 4, 2007.

James, Peter. "Kenora paper mill closed." *Kenora Daily Miner and News*, December 15, 2005.

Janzen, Diane. Comments on draft of chap. 6. E-mail message attachment to Kathleen Kern, October 25, 2007.

————. E-mail message to Kathleen Kern, November 28, 2007.

Japanese Ministry of the Environment. "Minamata Disease: The History and Measures." 2002. http://www.env.go.jp/en/chemi/hs/minamata2002.

Jaradat, Ahmad. "Hebron: Another Apartheid Wall in the Making." June 21st, 2004, The Alternative Information Center website, archived in Internet Archive Wayback Machine, http://web.archive.org/web/20040624085030/http://www.alternativenews.org.

Jewish Community of Hebron. "The Jewish Community of Hebron condemns the murder of Prime Minister Yitzhak Rabin." E-mail newslist message, n.d. *Hebron Today,* November 5, 1995. Mennonite Church USA Archives.

Jiménez Pérez, José Alfredo. E-mail message (in Spanish) to Kathleen Kern, April 21, 2005.

Jones, Colman. "Claws of power: Bureaucrats use lobster war to maintain fishery control." *Now* 20:1 (2000). http://www.nowtoronto.com/issues/2000-09-07/newsfront.html.

Judd, Terry. "Abu Qatada appeals for release of the hostages." *The Independent,* December 8, 2005. http://www.independent.co.uk/news/world/middle-east/abu-qatada-appeals-for-release-of-hostages-518582.html.ece.

Juhnke, James C. "The Original Peacemakers: Native America." *Mennonite Life* 56:4 (2001). Available at http://www.bethelks.edu/mennonitelife/2001dec/juhnke.php.

Kairos: Canadian Ecumenical Justice Initiatives. "Kimy Pernia Domicó was assassinated, admits Colombian paramilitary leader." January 19, 2007. http://www.kairoscanada.org/e/countries/colombia/kimyUpdate070119.asp.

Kaufman, Joanne. Comments on draft of chap. 2. E-mail message attachment to Kathleen Kern, September 11, 2003.

———. Comments on draft of Oceti Sakowin section of chapter 8. Mennonite Church USA Archives.

———. E-mail message to Kathleen Kern, June 23, 2005.

———. E-mail message to Kathleen Kern, June 27, 2005.

———. E-mail message to Kathleen Kern, October 4, 2004.

———. "From the 'Violence of the Stick,' to the 'Violence of the Stomach': CPT Haiti 1996–97." Chap. 7 in *Getting in the Way: Stories from Christian Peacemaker Teams.* Edited by Tricia Gates Brown. Scottdale, PA: Herald, 2005.

———. "Haiti: Oh Lord, We Are Just by Ourselves." Unattributed. *Signs of the Times* 6:4 (1996) 2. (Pre-published version with slightly different wording in Mennonite Church USA archives.)

Kelly, Kathy. E-mail message to Kathleen Kern, January 6, 2007.

Kember, Norman. "Christianity Is a Radical Call to Peacemaking." *Daily Telegraph,* December 12, 2007.

Kern, Kathleen. ""A clash of views at the Canadian border." *The Buffalo News,* April 6, 2003.

———. "Christian Peacemaker Teams." Chap. 9 in *Nonviolent Intervention Across Borders: A Recurrent Vision,* edited by Yeshua Moser-Puangsuan and Thomas Weber. Honolulu: University of Hawaii Press, 2000.

———. Ambassadors for the End Times: The International Christian Embassy Jerusalem." *The Door* 142 (1995) 23–24.

———. "Corporate Complicity in Congo's War." *Tikkun,* March–April 2006, 38–40, 67.

———. "Crossing the Weirdness Threshold: Christian Zionism in Jerusalem." *Mennonot* 6 (1995) 11–12.

———. "From Haiti to Hebron with a Brief Stop in Washington, D.C.: The CPT Experiment." Chap. 12 in *From the Ground Up: Mennonite Contributions to International Peacebuilding,* edited by John Paul Lederach and Cynthia Sampson. New York: Oxford University Press, 2000.

———. "Hebron's Theater of the Absurd." *The Link* 29:1 (1996).

———. "Interventions of Truth in Hebron." *Signs of the Times* 5:4 (1995) 3.

———. "Hebron—H-2: The Necklace of Umm Yusef." *Challenge Magazine* 65 (2001).

———. "Rage Rocks Hebron." *Signs of the Times* 10:4 (2000) 1–2.

———. Response to Rabbi Moshe Yehudai-Rimmer. Email message, n.d. Appears in *Signs of the Times* 11:1 (2001) 8.

———. "Settler Violence and September 11: A Report from the Mean Streets of Hebron." *Tikkun* 16:6 (2001) 29–30.

———. "Sobbing on the Stairs." *Buffalo News,* April 8, 2001.

———. "The Bees Set Nonviolent Example." *Mennonite Weekly Review,* April 13, 1998.

———. "The Human Cost of Cheap Cellphones." Chap. 5 in *A Game as Old as Empire: The Secret World of Economic Hit Men and the Web of Global Corruption.* Edited by Steven Hiatt. Berkeley: Berrett-Koehler, 2007.

———. "The rest of the story." *The Mennonite,* February 17, 2004, 16–17.

———. "Under-cover with Christian Zionists at Kiryat Arba." *Bridge: A Forum on Christian-Muslim Relations,* January 1998, 9–11. Also in the CPT discussion group menno.org.cpt.d@mennolink.org, November 4, 1997. CPT Chicago Office Digital Archives.

———. "Victims as Pariahs." *The Christian Century* 124:3 (2007) 9.

———. *Where Such Unmaking Reigns.* Philadelphia, PA: Xlibris, 2003.

———. and Wendy Lehman. "Teaching Nonviolence in Hebron: Christian Peacemaker Team's Experiences with Palestinian High School and University Students." *The Acorn: Journal of the Gandhi-King Society* 9:1 (1997) 37–43.

Kerr, Scott. E-mail message to Kathleen Kern, August 7, 2006.

———. E-mail message to Kathleen Kern, August 25, 2006.

———. E-mail message to Kathleen Kern, February 16, 2007.

———. E-mail message to Kathleen Kern, July 14, 2007.

———. E-mail message to Kathleen Kern, March 4, 2005.

———. E-mail message to Kathleen Kern, March 10, 2005.

———. E-mail message to Kathleen Kern, March 15, 2005.

———. E-mail message to Kathleen Kern, October 3, 2007.

———. E-mail message to Kathleen Kern, October 9, 2007.

Khalidi, Rashid. *Palestinian Identity: The Construction of Modern Nation Consciousness.* New York: Columbia University Press, 1997.

Kifner, John. "The Zeal of Rabin's Assassin Springs from Rabbis of Religious Right." *New York Times, International Edition,* November 12, 1995.

Kinane, Ed. "Cry for Justice in Haiti, Fall 1993." Chap. 11 in *Nonviolent Intervention Across Borders: A Recurrent Vision,* edited by Yeshua Moser-Puangsuan and Thomas Weber. Honolulu: University of Hawaii Press, 2000.

———. "Project Evaluation: Cry for Justice, Jérémie." December 31, 1993. Mennonite Church USA Archives.

Kindy, Cliff. E-mail message to delegation affinity group leaders, November 29, 2000. Mennonite Church USA Archives.

———. E-mail message to Gene Stoltzfus, November 3, 2000. Mennonite Church USA Archives.

———. E-mail message to Kathleen Kern, January 8, 2007.

———. E-mail message to Kathleen Kern, January 29, 2007.

———. E-mail message to Kathleen Kern, February 17, 2007.

———. E-mail message to Kathleen Kern, August 23, 2007.

———. E-mail message to Kathleen Kern, September 11, 2007.

————. "Indiana Peacemaker Softens Israeli Raid on Palestinian Home." August 2, 1993. Mennonite Church USA Archives.

Kindy, Erin. E-mail message to Kathleen Kern, April 1, 2005.

————. E-mail message to Kathleen Kern, August 14, 2005.

————. E-mail message to Kathleen Kern, August 19, 2006.

————. E-mail message to Kathleen Kern, August 22, 2006.

————. E-mail message to Kathleen Kern, March 15, 2005.

————. E-mail message to Kathleen Kern, October 18, 2006.

————. E-mail message to Kathleen Kern, September 4, 2006.

————. E-mail message to Kathleen Kern, September 6, 2006.

————. E-mail message to Kathleen Kern, September 16, 2006.

————. E-mail message to Kathleen Kern (subject heading: "Re: Change in Accompaniment guidelines"), August 12, 2006.

————. E-mail message to Kathleen Kern (subject heading: "Re: Some early Colombia project questions"), August 12, 2006.

Klassen, Joel. E-mail message to Kathleen Kern, February 7, 2000.

————. E-mail message to Kathleen Kern, June 9, 2006.

————. E-mail message to Kathleen Kern, November 27, 2004.

————. E-mail message to Kathleen Kern, September 4, 2006.

————. "Grief and Hope in Haiti." April 23, 1994. Mennonite Church USA Archives.

————. "Haiti as viewed from Sent Elen." Email message printout, October 21, 2003. Mennonite Church USA Archives.

————. Telephone interview with Kathleen Kern, July 21, 2003.

Klassen, Nicholas. E-mail message to Kathleen Kern (with attached photo of sign at Grassy Narrows blockade), August 7, 2005.

Knockwood, Noel, B.A. Elder. "Mohawk History, Thoughts and Wisdom . . ." 1996. JaVaMaN's Web site. http://home.comcast.net/~jerzyguy39/NAwords.html.

Kolster-Frye, Christa. "Ordeal Leading to Arrest Is Over for Kindy." *The News-Journal* (North Manchester, IN), October 17, 2000.

Kostner, Jeanne. "South Dakota Invitation to CPT to be neutral observers of FBI at Oglala peaceful Tent-in." March 26, 1999, rev. April 1, 1999. Mennonite Church USA Archives.

Krause, Tammy. "Murders up in D.C." *Signs of the Times* 6:3 (1996) 6.

————. Telephone interview with Kathleen Kern, November 15, 1994.

————. Telephone interview with Kathleen Kern, November 16, 1994.

Lacharite, Gretchen. "City eliminates problem house; neighbors hit street to celebrate." *Washington Times*, December 8, 1994.

Ladd, Brian. E-mail message to Claire Evans, July 9, 2001. Mennonite Church USA Archives.

————. E-mail message to Claire Evans, July 20, 2001. Mennonite Church USA Archives.

LaDuke, Winona. "Innu Women and Nato: The Occupation of Nitassinan." *Cultural Survival Quarterly* 14:2 (1990). http://www.cs.org/publications/csq/csq-article.cfm?id=388.

Lamberty, Kim, comments on draft of Chapter 6. E-mail attachment to Kathleen Kern, November 28, 2007.

————. E-mail message to Kathleen Kern, October 11, 2004.

————. E-mail message to Kathleen Kern, November 7, 2007.

———. E-mail message to Kathleen Kern, November 13, 2007.

———. E-mail message to Kathleen Kern, November 18, 2007.

———. E-mail message to Kathleen Kern, November 27, 2007.

———. E-mail message to Kathleen Kern, November 28, 2007.

———. E-mail message to Kathleen Kern, December 1, 2007.

———. E-mail message to Kathleen Kern, December 7, 2007.

———. E-mail message to Kathleen Kern, December 21, 2007.

LaMotte, Greg. "Iraq/Kidnappings." *Voice of America,* 2-314995, April 13, 2004. Transcript available at http://www.globalsecurity.org/military/library/news/2004/04/mil-040413-22e8668b.htm.

Lancaster, John. "Hebron Daunting for Ex-DC Activist: Advocate's Efforts Result in Israeli Detention." *Washington Post,* July 15, 1995.

Landau, Saul. "Five Years After Mayan Uprising: Time to Review US-Mexico Policy." December 25, 1998. Transnationional Institute. http://www.tni.org/detail_page.phtml?page=archives_landau_chiapas2.

Langeland, Terje. "Boulder man released: Protesters out on bail following trespass on Vieques Navy Base." *Boulder Daily Camera,* May 4–6, 2001.

Las Abejas of Chenalhó. "History of the birth of 'Las Abejas' (The Bees) of Chenalhó." March 1998. Chiapas95 e-mail newslist message, June 27, 1998. Available at http://www.eco.utexas.edu/~archive/chiapas95/1998.06/msg00532.html.

———. "Our word to the UN: The massacre that could have been avoided." March 1998. Chiapas95 e-mail newslist message, June 27, 1998. Available at http://www.eco.utexas.edu/~archive/chiapas95/1998.06/msg00532.html.

Lederach, John Paul. E-mail message to Kathleen Kern, August 25, 2005.

———. E-mail message to Kathleen Kern, August 26, 2005.

———. "Facing the Oka Crisis: A Conflict Resolution Perspective." *The Conrad Grebel Review* 9 (1991) 115–132.

Lehman, Wendy. "Arrest Report." July 25, 1995. Mennonite Church USA Archives.

———. "Christian Peacemaker Team Lays Foundation in Hebron." June 27, 1995. Mennonite Church USA Archives.

———. "Christian Peacemaker Team Report by Wendy Lehman and Duane Ediger, following their exploratory visit to Chiapas August 21–September 3, 1997." N.d. Mennonite Church USA Archives.

———. E-mail message to Kathleen Kern, March 2, 2005.

———. E-mail message to Kathleen Kern, November 12, 1995.

———. "Hebron Team Confronts Violence." *Signs of the Times* 5:3 (1995) 1.

———. "Israeli settler and soldiers assault Palestinians, one killed." July 1, 1995. Mennonite Church USA Archives.

———. "Israeli Settlers Assault CPTers." *Signs of the Times* 5:4 (1995) 1–2.

———. "Israeli Soldier Opens Fire on Palestinian Marketplace." *Signs of the Times* 7:1 (1997) 3.

———. "Military Detains Two American Members of Christian Peacemaker Teams." July 12, 1995. Mennonite Church USA Archives.

———. "One of God's Mouthpieces of Liberation." N.d. Mennonite Church USA Archives.

———. "Part of the Hope of God." *The Other Side* 35:6 (1999) 20–22.

———. "Prepared to die, but not to kill." *Signs of the Times* 8:1 (1998) 5.

———. "Uncle of slain Palestinian teenager talks about attack." July 3, 1995. Mennonite Church USA Archives.

———. "Unmasking Injustice: State Terrorism, Paramilitary Groups and Nonviolent Civilian Resistance in Chiapas." Paper, International Political Violence course, Notre Dame University, November 19, 1998.

Leis, Vernon. Letter to Pastors Peace and Justice Coordinators, June 19, 1990. Mennonite Church USA Archives.

"Letters." *Signs of the Times* 12:1 (2002) 14–15.

Levin, Sis. *Beirut Diary: A Husband Held Hostage and a Wife Determined to Set Him Free* Downer's Grove: InterVarsity, 1989.

Levy, Gideon. "The cement mixer is in our hands." *Ha'aretz,* March 27, 1998, 3

Lingle, JoAnne. "Mother's Day March in Vieques." Unpublished article from Vieques delegation. May 14, 2000. Mennonite Church USA Archives.

Lis, Jonathan, and Ofra Edelman. "Border policeman convicted in brutal killing of Hebron teen jailed for 6 years." *Ha'aretz,* April 29, 2008.

Liveoak, Val. "Low Intensity Civil War in Chiapas." *Signs of the Times* 6:4 (1996) 5.

Loewen, James. *Lies My Teachers Told Me.* New York: Touchstone, 1995.

Loney, Jim. "Confronting the Violence of 'Normal,'" *Signs of the Times* 15:1 (2005) 11.

———. E-mail message to Kathleen Kern, August 20, 2007.

———. E-mail message to Kathleen Kern, July 3, 2007.

———. "From the Tomb." *Toronto Star,* April 15, 2006.

———. "'I won't testify against my abductors.'" *Toronto Star,* May 23, 2007.

———. "Litany of Resistance." CPT. http://www.cpt.org/publications/litanyofresistance .php.

———. "No Greater Love." Chap. 22 in *118 Days: Christian Peacemaker Teams Held Hostage in Iraq,* edited by Tricia Gates Brown. Chicago: CTP, 2008. Earlier draft in Mennonite Church USA Archives.

Lopez, Damaso Serrano. "Letter from mayor-elect of Vieques to President Clinton." November 10, 2000. Mennonite Church USA Archives.

Lopez, Reynaldo. E-mail message to Kathleen Kern, October 29, 2003.

Lurie, John. "A Life or Death Last Stand: The Story of the Laframboise Island Occupation." 1999. CPT. http://www.cpt.org/usa/southd.php.

Lynes, John. E-mail message to Kathleen Kern, November 22, 2004.

Lynfield, Ben. "In Mideast, crossfire more careless." *Christian Science Monitor,* May 22, 2001.

MachsomWatch: Women against the Occupation and for Human Rights. http://www .machsomwatch.org/en.

Mahoney, Liam, and Luis Enrique Eguren. *Unarmed Bodyguards: International Accompaniment for the Protection of Human Rights.* West Hartford, CT: Kumarian, 1997.

Maiese, Michelle. ""What is Neutrality?" *Beyond Intractability.* June 2005. http://www .beyondintractability.org/essay/neutrality/?nid=6713

Malthaner, Tom. "The night I was mugged." *Signs of the Times* 5:4 (1995) 5.

Maney, Bob. "Being peacemaker not always popular." *Paxton Record* (IL), April 17, 2002.

———. "Pacifism a tough sell since Sept. 11." *Bloomington Pantagraph* (IL), April 20, 2002.

Marino, John. "Puerto Rico's New War on Poverty: Critics Fault $1 Billion Proposal as Paternalistic and No Substitute for Statehood." *Washington Post,* September 22, 2002.

Martens, Lisa. E-mail message to author, August 4, 2005.

Matthiesen, Peter. *In the Spirit of Crazy Horse.* New York: Penguin, 1992.

MCC (Mennonite Central Committee). "Christian Peacemaker Teams: A Study Document." Booklet. February 1986. Mennonite Historical Library and Mennonite Church USA Archives.

———. *MCC Peace Section Newsletter,* July–August 1987.

———. "Techny Call." *Mennonite Central Committee Peace Section Newsletter,* July–August 1987.

MCC CMS (Council of Moderators and Secretaries). "Christian Peacemaker Teams: Presented for discussion by Council of Moderators and Secretaries." Flyer. January 1986. Mennonite Church USA Archives.

McKenna, Lee. E-mail message to Kathleen Kern, February 24, 2005.

MCUSA (Mennonite Church USA). "Nashville 2001 Delegate Actions Congregational Follow-up Resources for Vieques Resolution." N.d. Available at http://peace .mennolink.org/resources/deathpenaltyf.pdf. Mennonite Church USA Archives.

———. "Resolution on Colombia, 2001." July 7, 2001. Mennonite Church USA Historical Committee. http://www.mcusa-archives.org/library/resolutions/colombia.html.

———. "Vieques Resolution for Nashville 2001 Delegate Action." Draft. June 26, 2001. Mennonite Church USA Archives.

MCUSA Executive Board. Letter to President George W. Bush, July 20, 2001. Mennonite Church USA Archives.

Melillo, Wendy. "D.C. Landlord Given Nearly 6 Years in Jail; Judge Ignores Plea Deal in Imposing Harsher Term." *Washington Post,* September 20, 1995.

———. "D.C. Landlord Pleads Guilty to 1,318 Violations; Criminal Charges Brought against Hyattsville Man Involve 11 Dilapidated Rooming Houses." *Washington Post,* August 9, 1995.

Mencimer, Stephanie. E-mail message to themail@DCWatch.com (subject heading: "Attorney General"), February 25, 1998. Posted on "Your Electronic Backfence." *DCWatch.* http://www.DCwatch.com/themail/1998/98-02-25.htm.

MENCOLDES (Columbia Commission of Jurists, Colombian Mennonite Foundation for Development). "Follow Up to Recommendations of the Representative of the Secretary-General of the United Nations on Internally Displaced Persons 1999–2002." Translated by Edward Helbein. November 15, 2002. Available at http://www.internal-displacement.org/8025708F004CE90B/(httpDocuments)/08D725EA585124608025 70B700590383/$file/CCJ+Mencoldes.pdf.

Metzler, Edgar. Letter attached to draft of chapter with comments to Kathleen Kern, August 5, 2004 (incorrectly dated 2003). Mennonite Church USA Archives.

Meyer, Carl. E-mail message to Kathleen Kern, March 6, 2005.

———. E-mail message to Kathleen Kern, June 25, 2005.

Meyer, Rich. "Bulldozers and Steamrollers." *Signs of the Times* 9:4 (1999) 2.

———. E-mail message to Kathleen Kern (subject heading: "Correspondence with [N] from EI"), August 8, 2008.

———. E-mail message to Kathleen Kern (subject heading: " Re: [GITW] Role of Electronic Intifada during hostage crisis"), August 8, 2008.

———. Telephone interview with Kathleen Kern, February 5, 2008.

———. Telephone interview with Kathleen Kern, January 18, 2005.

———. Telephone interview with Kathleen Kern, March 25, 2007.

———. "With a Lot of Help from Our Friends: The Call from Palestine for Release of Peacemakers." Chap. 6 in *118 Days: Christian Peacemaker Teams Held Hostage in Iraq*, edited by Tricia Gates Brown. Chicago: CPT, 2008. Earlier draft in Mennonite Church USA Archives.

Mi'kmaq timeline. Excerpt from "Mi'kmaw Resource Guide 2007." *Mi'kmaq Resource Centre.* http://mrc.uccb.ns.ca/timeline.html.

Milne, David. E-mail message to Kathleen Kern, July 16, 2007.

Montgomery, Anne. E-mail message to Kathleen Kern, July 14, 2007.

———. E-mail message to Kathleen Kern, June 20, 2004.

Morey, Melyssa. "A Tale of Two Killings: Observations of Media Bias in Reports of Palestinian and Israeli Deaths." Cited in "The Media War We Are Losing But Can Win." June 17, 2001. Washington Watch, Arab American Institute. http://www.aaiusa.org/washington-watch/1561/w061801.

Morris, Benny. *1948 and After: Israel and the Palestinians.* Oxford: Clarendon, 1994.

———. *The Birth of the Palestinian Refugee Problem, 1947–49.* Cambridge: Cambridge University Press, 1989.

Mortellito, Nicole. "West Bank: Under Fire in Beit Jala." *Signs of the Times* 11:4 (2001) 11–12.

Mustus, Ruth. "500 Missing Indigenous Women: They Don't Seem to Matter." *Institute of American Indian Arts Chronicle* 6:4 (2007). http://www.iaiachronicle.org/archives/MISSINGINDIGENOUSWOMEN.htm.

Naar-Obed, Michele. "The Baghdad Morgue." Chap. 8 in *118 Days: Christian Peacemaker Teams Held Hostage in Iraq*, edited by Tricia Gates Brown. Chicago: CPT, 2008. Earlier draft in Mennonite Church USA Archives.

Nafziger, Tim. E-mail messages between Kryss Chupp and Kim Erno of the Lutheran Center, November 29–December 1, 2006. Forwarded by Nafziger to Kathleen Kern, October 9, 2007.

———. E-mail message to Kathleen Kern, July 24, 2007.

———. and Simon Barrows. "Writing Peace out of the Script." Chap. 15 in *118 Days: Christian Peacemaker Teams Held Hostage in Iraq*, edited by Tricia Gates Brown. Chicago: CPT, 2008. Earlier draft in Mennonite Church USA Archives.

NAHO (National Aboriginal Health Organization). "Terminology Guide." 2003. Available at www.naho.ca/english/pdf/terminology_guidelines.pdf.

Natshe, Mustafa. Fax message to Mennonite Church USA Chicago Office, April 3, 1995. Mennonite Church USA Archives.

"Navy officials arrest Boulder man in Vieques: Son of Boulder couple also held in connection with protests of bombing exercises." *Boulder Daily Camera*, May 3, 2001.

Neihardt, John Gneisenau. *Black Elk Speaks.* Lincoln: University of Nebraska Press, 2004.

Nicola, Ari. "Let the People Come." *Signs of the Times* 3:2 (1993) 1.

Nijim, Germana. "The Saga of Greg Rollins and the Christian Peace Teams (CPT): A series of reports from Germana Nijim on a CPT volunteer from Canada, Greg Rollins, and how CPT members are treated by the Israeli government." May 18–May 21, 2003. *American Perspectives on the Middle East.* http://www.apomie.com/greg.htm.

Nir, Ori. "Anti-Arab policy bias worsens." *Ha'aretz*, June 24, 2002.

"Notes from December 1996 CPC/Reserves Gathering, Washington, D.C." N.d. Mennonite Church USA Archives.

Novick, Peter. *The Holocaust in American Life*. Boston: Houghton Mifflin, 1999.

OAS (Organization of American States). "Hazard Mitigation & Vulnerability Reduction Plan, Jérémie, Haiti: A Programme to Mitigate the Impacts of Natural Hazards; Appendices." CDMP (Caribbean Disaster Mitigation Project) report. http://www .oas.org/CDMP/document/jeremie/appen.htm.

OCHA (UN Office for the Coordination of Humanitarian Affairs). "Special Focus, the Closure of Hebron's Old City." Includes map of Hebron closures. *Humanitarian Update*, July 2005. Available at http://www.humanitarianinfo.org/opt/docs/UN/ OCHA/ochaHU0705_En.pdf.

O'Hatnick, Suzanne Hubbard. E-mail message to Gene Stoltzfus, November 26, 1996. Mennonite Church USA Archives.

———. E-mail message to Kathleen Kern, June 13, 2007.

———. *Journey to Bosnia, Return to Self*. Pendle Hill pamphlet 348. Wallingford, PA: Pendle Hill, 2000.

———. "Las Abejas: Nonviolence on the Line." *Peace Team News* 3:2 (1998). http://fptp .quaker.org/32bees.html.

Olsen, Kaaren. E-mail message to Kathleen Kern, June 12, 2007.

Oneida Action Newsletter 1:1 (2002). Mennonite Church USA Archives.

Oneida Indian Nation. "A Brief History of the Oneida Nation." http://www.oneida-nation .net/BRHISTORY.HTML (no longer accessible).

Operation Dove: Nonviolent Peace Corps. http://www.operationdove.org.

Orme, William J. "Jerusalem Christians Now Back Palestinian Sovereignty." *New York Times*, December 24, 2000.

O'Rourke, Ronald. "Vieques, Puerto Rico Naval Training Range: Background and Issues for Congress." Congressional Research Service report. Updated December 17, 2001. *Navy Department Library*. http://www.history.navy.mil/library/online/vieques.htm.

Payne, William. E-mail message to Kathleen Kern, August 11, 2006.

———. E-mail message to Kathleen Kern, August 16, 2006.

———. E-mail message to Kathleen Kern, August 22, 2006.

———. E-mail message to Kathleen Kern, August 25, 2006.

———. E-mail message to Kathleen Kern, March 12, 2005.

———. E-mail message to Kathleen Kern, March 15, 2005.

———. E-mail message to Kathleen Kern, March 16, 2005.

———. E-mail message to Kathleen Kern, October 16, 2006.

———. E-mail message to Kathleen Kern, September 28, 2007.

———. "Gunboat Diplomacy in Canada." *Toronto Star*, September 12, 2000.

———. "Media Statement Re: Charges Laid in the Lobster Fishery." Press release, August 2, 2000. Sent as e-mail message attachment by Doug Pritchard to Kathleen Kern, n.d.

———. "On Silence, Closets and Liberation." Chap. 14 in *118 Days: Christian Peacemaker Teams Held Hostage in Iraq*, edited by Tricia Gates Brown. Chicago: CPT, 2008. Earlier draft in Mennonite Church USA Archives.

PBI (Peace Brigades International). " Justice and Healing in Sheshatshit and Davis Inlet." By Anne Harrison, Muriel Meric, and Alan Dixon. November 1995. http://www .peacebrigades.org/archive/nap/nap95-02.html.

PBS Frontline. "Ralph Nader on Free Trade & Immigration." *The Choice 2000.* http://www
.issues2000.org/Frontline/issues/Ralph_Nader_Free_Trade_&_Immigration.htm.

PCHR (Palestinian Centre for Human Rights). "Uprooting Palestinian Trees and Leveling
Agricultural Land: The Nigh Report on Israeli Land Sweeping and Demolition
of Palestinian Buildings and Facilities in the Gaza Strip, 1 July, 2002–31 March,
2003." August 2003. Available at http://www.reliefweb.int/rw/RWFiles2003.nsf/
FilesByRWDocUNIDFileName/OCHA-64BSU5-pchr-opt-31mar.pdf/$File/pchr-
opt-31mar.pdf.

"Peace Factory Tour Booklet: Ideas and Inspiration." Coordinated by Susan Mark Landis.
March 5, 1996. Mennonite Church USA Archives.

"Peacemakers fast for 700 hours." *Signs of the Times* 7:2 (1997) 1–2.

"Peace Reserve." *Signs of the Times,* November 1992, 1–2.

Penner, H. A. Draft of statement to U.S. Federal Judge on June 28, 2001. Sent as e-mail
message to CPT Chicago Office and other defendants and fellow delegation members,
June 23 2001. Printout in Mennonite Church USA Archives.

———. E-mail message to Mark Byler, May 30, 2001. Mennonite Church USA Archives.

———. Letter to Claire Evans (while H. A. Penner was incarcerated in the Guaynabo
Detention Center), July 7, 2001. Mennonite Church USA Archives.

———. Letter to John H. Thomas, July 25, 2001. Mennonite Church USA Archives.

———. Letter to Puerto Rican Mennonite Convention, July 25, 2001. Mennonite Church
USA Archives.

Perez, Gilberto. Letter to Gene Stoltzfus, April 3, 2001. Mennonite Church USA Archives.

Perle, Richard. "Building inspector with a bullet-proof vest." *Washington Post Magazine,*
June 27, 1999.

Phillips, Jessica. E-mail message to Kathleen Kern, August 5, 2005.

———. E-mail message to Kathleen Kern, August 31, 2005.

———. Telephone interview with Kathleen Kern, August 5, 2005.

PHRMG (Palestinian Human Rights Monitoring Group). "Settler Violence Hotline: One-
year Report." *Palestinian Human Rights Monitor* 6:5 (2002). http://www.phrmg.org/
monitor2002/Dec2002-4.htm.

PNA (Palestinian National Authority). "A Plea to the Iraqi People." Press release, November
20, 2005. Available with translation at http://www.palsolidarity.org/main/2005/12/06/
statement-by-the-national-committee-to-resist-settlement-and-the-wall-on-the-
cpt-hostages-in-iraq/.

Polhamus, Rick. E-mail message to Kathleen Kern, May 11, 2004.

———. E-mail message to Kathleen Kern, June 10, 2004.

———. E-mail message to Kathleen Kern, June 28 2005.

"Police launch 'zero tolerance' policy for Hebron rioters." *Ha'aretz,* January 16, 2006.

Pritchard, Doug. Comments on draft of Afghanistan section of chap. 13. E-mail message
attachment to Kathleen Kern, October 5, 2007.

———. Comments on draft of chap. 8 (formerly 9). E-mail message attachment to
Kathleen Kern, October 8, 2005.

———. Comments on draft of chap. 9 (formerly 10). E-mail message attachment to
Kathleen Kern, October 8, 2005.

———. Comments on draft of chap. 11. E-mail message attachment to Kathleen Kern,
July 27, 2007.

———. Comments on draft of chap. 12. E-mail message attachment to Kathleen Kern,
July 27, 2007.

———. E-mail message to CPTers working at Oneida, September 10, 2002.

———. E-mail message to CPT Ontario regional group, January 15, 2001, Forwarded by Janet Shoemaker to Kathleen Kern, July 13, 2005.

———. E-mail message to CPT Ontario regional group, March 26, 2001. Forwarded by Janet Shoemaker to Kathleen Kern, July 13, 2005.

———. E-mail message to Kathleen Kern, August 8, 2007.

———. E-mail message to Kathleen Kern, August 31, 2005.

———. E-mail message to Kathleen Kern, January 26, 2008.

———. E-mail message to Kathleen Kern, January 27, 2008.

———. E-mail message to Kathleen Kern, June 10, 2007.

———. E-mail message to Kathleen Kern, July 1, 2007.

———. E-mail message to Kathleen Kern, July 4, 2007.

———. E-mail message to Kathleen Kern, July 26, 2007.

———. E-mail message to Kathleen Kern, July 23, 2007.

———. E-mail message to Kathleen Kern, July 27, 2007.

———. E-mail message to Kathleen Kern, October 8, 2005.

———. E-mail message to Kathleen Kern, November 21, 2007.

———. E-mail message to Kathleen Kern, September 12, 2005.

———. E-mail message to Kathleen Kern, September 28, 2007.

———. "Evaluation of CPT's presence in Kenora June 2005—August 2006." E-mail message attachment to Kathleen Kern, November 15, 2007.

———. Interview with Kathleen Kern, June 18, 2007.

———. "Notes from a Trip to Esgenoôpetitj First Nation (EFN) April 15–17, 2003." Sent as E-mail message attachment to Kathleen Kern, July 6, 2005.

———. and Carol Rose. "Unless a Grain of Wheat Falls: A View from the CPT Crisis Team." Chap. 1 in *118 Days: Christian Peacemaker Teams Held Hostage in Iraq*, edited by Tricia Gates Brown. Chicago: CPT, 2008. Earlier draft in Mennonite Church USA Archives.

———. and Carol Rose. "Update on Hostages: Response to Torture Rumors." March 24, 2006. CPT. http://www.cpt.org/iraq/response/06-23-03statement.htm.

———. and Gene Stoltzfus. Afghanistan/Pakistan trip log covering December 16, 2001–January 13, 2002. Mennonite Church USA Archives.

———. and Gene Stoltzfus. "Report from Afghanistan for Christian Peacemaker Teams." January 2002. Mennonite Church USA Archives.

Project Censored. Top 25 Censored Stories for 2006. http://www.projectcensored.org/top-stories/category/y-2006/

Provencher, Sheila. E-mail message to Kathleen Kern, January 25, 2007.

———. E-mail message to Kathleen Kern, January 26, 2007.

———. E-mail message to Kathleen Kern, July 18, 2007.

———. E-mail message to Kathleen Kern, June 25, 2007.

———. E-mail message to Kathleen Kern, February 12, 2007.

———. "One Family: From Syria to Jordan, Stories of Compassion." Chap. 4 in *118 Days: Christian Peacemaker Teams Held Hostage in Iraq*, edited by Tricia Gates Brown. Chicago: CPT, 2008.

———. "Our Refugee Family: Al Hol, Syria." Draft of chap. 4 in *118 Days: Christian Peacemaker Teams Held Hostage in Iraq*, edited by Tricia Gates Brown. Chicago: CPT, 2008. Mennonite Church USA Archives.

————. "Responsibility and healing in Iraq." *America: The National Catholic Weekly,* October 4, 2004. https://www.americamagazine.org/content/article.cfm?article_ id=3785.

"Puerto Rican court orders Vieques vote readied." Reuters, October 17, 2001.

Puleo, Mev. "A Bishop Who Hears the Cry of Haiti's Poor." *St. Anthony Messenger,* May 1993, 36–41.

Puljek-Shank, Amela. E-mail message to CPT Chicago Office, n.d. (Spring 1996, probably before May 15). Mennonite Church USA Archives.

————. E-mail message to Kathleen Kern, September 14, 2007.

————. Letter to supporters. E-mail message, n.d. (probably Autumn 1996). Mennonite Church USA Archives.

Puljek-Shank, Randy. Comments on draft of Bosnia section of chap. 13. E-mail message attachment to Kathleen Kern, September 14, 2007.

————. E-mail message to Kathleen Kern, July 18, 2007.

————. Letter to supporters. E-mail message, n.d. (probably Autumn 1996). Mennonite Church USA Archives.

————. (representing International Mennonite Organization). "Concept for a Refugee Return sponsorship program." Sent as e-mail message to CPT Chicago Office, January 12, 1996. Mennonite Church USA Archives.

Pyles, Elizabeth. Comments on draft of chap. 12. E-mail message to Kathleen Kern, August 1, 2008.

————. E-mail message to Kathleen Kern, July 16, 2007.

————. Further comments on draft of chap. 12. E-mail message attachment to Kathleen Kern, August 8, 2007.

————. "Practicing Peace." Chap. 21 in *118 Days: Christian Peacemaker Teams Held Hostage in Iraq,* edited by Tricia Gates Brown. Chicago: CPT, 2008. Earlier draft in Mennonite Church USA Archives.

Quandt, William B. *Peace Process: American Diplomacy and the Arab-Israeli Conflict since 1967.* Washington, DC: Brookings Institute, 1993.

Rabin, Robert. E-mail message to Matt Guynn, May 9, 2001. Mennonite Church USA Archives.

"Rachel Corrie Memorial, 1979–2003." *Critical Concern.* http://www.criticalconcern.com/ rachelcorrie.html.

Rempel, Terry. "Redeployment and division of Hebron." *Signs of the Times* 7:1 (1997) 1–2.

"Report of Peacemaker Delegation to Haiti, May 5–15, 1993." *Signs for Our Times* [sic]: *Haiti,* N.d.

"Report of the CPT Delegation to Haiti, June 8–19, 1996." By Pierre Gingerich and John Sherman (unattributed). N.d. Mennonite Church USA Archives.

"Report reveals humiliation of Iraqis at the hands of U.S. soldiers." *Toronto Globe and Mail,* January 19, 2004.

Reschly, Sara. Comments on draft of chap. 4. E-mail message attachment to Kathleen Kern, May 4, 2004.

————. E-mail messages to and from NGOs in Afghanistan, and Pakistanis and Afghans living in North America, n.d. Mennonite Church USA Archive.

————. E-mail message to Kathleen Kern, July 9, 2007.

————. E-mail message to Kathleen Kern, March 3, 2005.

————. E-mail message to Kathleen Kern, March 14, 2005.

————. E-mail message to Kathleen Kern, March 15, 2005.

———. E-mail message to Kathleen Kern, October 12, 2004.

Rhodes, Robert. "Hostage struggled with desire to escape, but remained nonviolent during ordeal." *Mennonite Weekly Review*, April 27, 2006.

Rich, Adrienne. *Dream of a Common Language: Poems, 1974–77*. New York: Norton, 1978.

Rincón, Sandra Milena. E-mail message to Kathleen Kern, October 11, 2006.

———. E-mail message to Kathleen Kern, October 14, 2006.

———. "The Road Traveled in Colombia." Chap. 7 in *118 Days: Christian Peacemaker Teams Held Hostage in Iraq*, edited by Tricia Gates Brown. Chicago: CPT, 2008. Earlier draft in Mennonite Church USA Archives.

Roazen, Diane. "U.S. Must Do More for Chechnya." *Amina: Chechen Republic Online*. http://www.amina.com/article/usmust_more.html.

Roe, Dianne. E-mail message to Kathleen Kern, August 7, 2004.

———. E-mail message to Kathleen Kern, June 17, 2004.

———. E-mail message to Kathleen Kern, November 22, 2003.

Rokach, Livia. *Israel's Sacred Terrorism: A Study based on Moshe Sharett's Personal Diary and Other Documents*. Belmont, MA: Association of Arab-American University Graduates, 1986.

Rollins, Greg. E-mail message to Kathleen Kern, August 16, 2004.

———. E-mail message to Kathleen Kern, June 2, 2004.

———. E-mail message to Kathleen Kern, June 3, 2004.

———. E-mail message to Kathleen Kern, June 18, 2004.

———. E-mail message to Kathleen Kern, May 29, 2007.

———. E-mail message to Kathleen Kern, October 27, 2005.

———. "The Response from Baghdad." Chap. 3 in *118 Days: Christian Peacemaker Teams Held Hostage in Iraq*, edited by Tricia Gates Brown. Chicago: CPT, 2008. Earlier draft in Mennonite Church USA Archives.

Rose, Carol. "A Day in the Life." N.d. Mennonite Church USA Archives.

———. E-mail message to Kathleen Kern, October 26, 2007.

———. E-mail message to Kathleen Kern, September 1, 2006

Ross, Matt. "Disappeared aboriginal women not forgotten." *Wotanging Ikche* 13:48 (2005). http://www.nanews.org/archive/2005/nanews13.048.

Rubenberg, Cheryl A. *Israel and the American National Interest: A Critical Examination*. Urbana: University of Illinois Press, 1986.

Rubinstein, Danny. "Slouching toward Jerusalem." *Ha'aretz*, February 28, 2001.

———. "Things fall apart." *Ha'aretz*, January 30, 2004.

Ruether, Rosemary Radford, and Herman J. Reuther. *The Wrath of Jonah: Crisis of Religious Nationalism in the Israeli Palestinian Conflict*. New York: Harper & Row, 1989.

Rutter, Jon. "Seeking sea change for Vieques: area residents work with Puerto Rican islanders who want to stop Navy training." *Lancaster Sunday News*, February 18, 2001.

———. "20-days in jail wasn't vacation for this activist." *Lancaster Sunday News*, July 22, 2001.

Said, Edward. *The Politics of Dispossession: The Struggle for Palestinian Self Determination 1969–1994*. New York: Pantheon, 1994.

———. *The Question of Palestine*, New York: Random House, 1980.

———. and Christopher Hitchens, eds. *Blaming the Victims: Spurious Scholarship and the Palestinian Question*. London: Verso, 1988.

Salinas, Oscar. Homily, December 28, 1997 (Feast of the Holy Innocents). Translated by Duane Ediger. Text available at http://www.eco.utexas.edu/~archive/chiapas95/1998.01/msg00080.html.

"San Andres accords." Translated by Rosalva Bermudez-Ballin. January 18, 1996. *The Struggle Site*. http://struggle.ws/mexico/ezln/san_andres.html.

Satterwhite, Jim. "Chechnya." N.d. Mennonite Church USA Archives.

———. "Chechnya: Peacemakers and Peace Agreements." N.d. Mennonite Church USA Archives.

———. "Chechnya Report." September 1996. Mennonite Church USA Archives.

———. "Christian Peacemaker Teams—Chechnya Fact-finding Trip, April 2–10, 1996." Mennonite Church USA Archives.

———. Comments on draft of Chechnya section of chap. 13. E-mail message attachment to Kathleen Kern on August 30, 2007.

———. "Declaration from the Assembly of Independent Social-Political Parties and Movements of the Chechen Republic of Ichkeria on the Occasion of the Mass Killings of the of the Peaceful Civilian Population on July 15–16, 1996." Translation. N.d. Mennonite Church USA Archives.

———. "Document written by the Assembly of Independent Socio-Political Parties and Movements, regarding atrocities in Katir-Yurt." Translation. N.d. Mennonite Church USA Archives.

———. E-mail message to Kathleen Kern, June 8, 2004.

———. E-mail message to Kathleen Kern, September 7, 2007.

———. "From Grozny to Moscow or Through the Looking Glass." Mennonite Church USA Archives.

———. "Impressions from Ingushetia." N.d. Mennonite Church USA Archives.

———. "Interplanetary Travel." N.d. Mennonite Church USA Archives.

———. "Landscape after the Battle." N.d. Mennonite Church USA Archives.

———. "Life in an Occupied City—Impressions from Grozny." N.d. Mennonite Church USA Archives.

———. "Peace Groups in the Caucasus." N.d. Mennonite Church USA Archives.

———. "Peace Rally in Grozny." N.d. Mennonite Church USA Archives.

———. "Reflections on the War in Chechnya." N.d. Mennonite Church USA Archives.

———. "Refugees from the Other War." N.d. Mennonite Church USA Archives.

———. "Report on Chechnya Delegation, April 1996." N.d. Mennonite Church USA Archives.

———. "Samashki Revisited." N.d. Mennonite Church USA Archives.

———. "Sernovodsk Today." N.d. Mennonite Church USA Archives.

———. "The war in Chechnya seen through the eyes of a child." N.d. Mennonite Church USA Archives.

Sattler, Michael. "Brotherly Union of a number of children of God concerning Seven Articles (The Schleitheim Confession)." Translated and edited by John Howard Yoder. *Anabaptist Vision*. http://www.anabaptistvision.org/Confessions/schleitheim/index.htm. Reprinted from *The Legacy of Michael Sattler* (Scottdale, PA: Herald, 1973).

Savir, Uri. *The Process: 1,100 Days that Changed the Middle East*. New York: Random House, 1998.

Sawadsky, Hedy. Comments on draft of chap. 1, June 24, 2003. Mennonite Church USA Archives.

———. Telephone interview with Kathleen Kern, June 24, 2003.

Schaaf, Matt. E-mail message to Kathleen Kern, August 24, 2005.

Schiller, Eric. E-mail message to Kathleen Kern, August 17, 2004.

Schirch-Elias, Lisa. "Land Claims and the Oka Crisis." *The Conrad Grebel Review* 9 (1991) 139–151.

———. Letter to June Schwartzentruber Fund Committee, October 30, 1990. Mennonite Church USA Archives.

School of the Americas Watch. "SOA Graduate Database." http://soaw.org/grads/.

Segev, Tom. *1949: One Palestine, Complete: Jews and Arabs Under the British Mandate.* 2nd ed. New York: Owl Books, 2001.

———. *The First Israelis.* New York: Free Press, 1986.

———. *The Seventh Million: Israel and the Holocaust.* New York: Hill and Wang, 1993.

"Settlers complete Hebron wholesale market eviction." *Ha'aretz,* January 31, 2006.

Shacochis, Bob. *The Immaculate Invasion.* New York: Viking, 1999.

Shantz, Pierre. E-mail message to Kathleen Kern, April 19, 2005.

———. E-mail message to Kathleen Kern, August 22, 2006.

———. E-mail message to Kathleen Kern, August 25, 2006.

———. E-mail message to Kathleen Kern, October 12, 2006.

———. E-mail message to Kathleen Kern, September 6, 2006.

———. E-mail message to supporters, June 7, 2001.

———. "Tent for Lent: Return to the path of God." *The Mennonite,* August 23, 2000.

Shlaim, Avi,. *The Iron Wall: Israel and the Arab World.* New York: Norton, 2000.

Shoemaker, Janet. E-mail message to Kathleen Kern, August 31, 2005.

———. E-mail message to Kathleen Kern, July 20, 2005.

———. E-mail message to Kathleen Kern, July 28, 2005.

Sidebar. *Signs of the Times* 4:11(1994) 1.

Sider, Ronald J. "God's People Reconciling." Speech, Summer 1984, Strasbourg. Text available at http://www.cpt.org/resources/writings/sider.

———. *Nonviolence: The Invincible Weapon?* Dallas: Word, 1989.

———. *Rich Christians in an Age of Hunger.* Downer's Grove: InterVarsity, 1977. See also reprinted and expanded edition, *Rich Christians in an Age of Hunger: Moving from Affluence to Generosity* (Nashville: Thomas Nelson, 2005).

Siegers, Lena. E-mail message to Gene Stoltzfus, September 14, 1996. Mennonite Church USA Archives.

———. Letter to supporters, August 27, 1995. Mennonite Church USA Archives.

———. Letter to supporters, June 19, 1995. Mennonite Church USA Archives.

———. Letter to supporters, July 23, 1995. Mennonite Church USA Archives.

———. Letter to supporters, October 18, 1996. Mennonite Church USA Archives.

———. "Report on Bosnia, Jajce June 15–August 15, 1996," June 15, 1996. Mennonite Church USA Archives.

Simons, Menno. "Foundation of Christian Doctrine, 1539." In *The Complete Writings of Menno Simons: c. 1496–1561,* edited by J. C. Wenger, translated by Leonard Verduin. Scottdale, PA: Herald, 1956.

———. "Reply to False Accusations, 1554." In *The Complete Writings of Menno Simons: c. 1496–1561,* edited by J. C. Wenger, translated by Leonard Verduin. Scottdale, PA: Herald, 1956.

Sipaz (International Service for Peace). "Brief history of the conflict in Chiapas, 1994–2003." http://www.sipaz.org/crono/proceng.htm.

————. "Las Abejas (the Bees) Continue to Fly: Promoting Peace in Times of War." *Sipaz Report* 3:2 (1998). http://www.sipaz.org/informes/vol3no2/vol3no2e.htm.

————. "Summary: The Uncertainty of Peace." *Sipaz Report* 3:2 (1998). http://www.sipaz.org/informes/vol3no2/vol3no2e.htm.

Slater, Allan. E-mail message to Kathleen Kern, January 23, 2007

————. E-mail message to Kathleen Kern, January 24, 2007.

————. E-mail message to Kathleen Kern, June 11, 2007.

Smith, Mary Lynn. "Charlotte Taylor's Time Line (pre-1800)." *Charlotte Taylor: Her Life and Times.* http://www3.bc.sympatico.ca/charlotte_taylor/Folder1/Charlotte%27s%20Time%20Line%20%20Pre-1800.htm.

Snyder-Penner, Russel. "A Select Bibliography on Indigenous Peoples in Canada." *The Conrad Grebel Review* 9 (1991) 171–178.

"Soldier's question puts Rumsfeld on spot." *All Things Considered*, NPR, December 8, 2004. Audio stream available at http://www.npr.org/templates/dmg/dmg.php?prgCode=ATC&showDate=08-Dec-2004&segNum=15&NPRMediaPref=WM.

Spring, Carol Foltz. E-mail message to Kathleen Kern, August 23, 2006.

————. E-mail message to Kathleen Kern, August 25, 2006.

————. E-mail message to Kathleen Kern, August 31, 2006.

————. E-mail message to Kathleen Kern, September 13, 2006.

————. "Journal entries, 2002-2003." Mennonite Church USA Archives.

Spring, Charles Bunche. E-mail message to Kathleen Kern. August 23, 2006.

Stein, Janice Gross. *The Widening Gyre of Negotiation: From Management to Resolution in the Arab-Israeli Conflict.* Jerusalem: Hebrew University of Jerusalem, 1999.

Stein, Jerry. E-mail message to Kathleen Kern, August 5, 2007.

————. E-mail message to Kathleen Kern, March 4, 2005.

Stoesz, Donald B. "The Conquest of Canaan as an Oppressive Event." *The Conrad Grebel Review* 9 (1991) 153–168.

Stoltzfus, Gene. E-mail message to Cliff Kindy, November 3, 2000. Mennonite Church USA Archives.

————. E-mail message to CPT Steering Committee, October 7, 1996. Mennonite Church USA Archives

————. E-mail message to Kathleen Kern, October 2, 2007.

————. E-mail message to Kathleen Kern, October 30, 2007.

————. E-mail message to Kathleen Kern, September 11, 2007.

————. E-mail message to Kathleen Kern (subject heading: "More on Gaza piece," August 27, 2007.

————. E-mail message to Kathleen Kern (subject heading: "some thoughts ref. Gaza"), August 27, 2007.

————. "Iraq Peacemaker Team Activity Report and Recommendations." December 2, 1990. Mennonite Church USA Archives.

————. Letter to Fermin Arraiza, July 9, 2001. Mennonite Church USA Archives.

————. Letter to Gilberto Perez, April 10, 2001. Mennonite Church USA Archives.

————. Letter to Rep. Luis Gutierrez regarding the arrest of Nilda Medina, July 11, 2003. Mennonite Church USA Archives.

————. "Memo to CPT co-workers." December 25, 1996. Mennonite Church USA Archives.

————. "Memo to Program Committee and interested persons." January 6, 1995. Mennonite Church USA Archives.

————. "Proposal to Place a Five-Person Team in Gaza for the Period of Two Months." April 30, 1993. MennoniteChurch USA Archives.

————. "Report to Steering Committee." October 6, 1996. Sent as e-mail message, October 7, 1996. Mennonite Church USA Archives.

————. Telephone interview with Kathleen Kern, February 13, 2004.

————. Telephone interview with Kathleen Kern, June 11, 2003.

————. Telephone interview with Kathleen Kern, May 1, 2003.

————. Telephone interview with Kathleen Kern, May 23, 2003.

————. "Warrior Strategies." Peace Talk blog, July 25, 2007. http://gstoltzfus.blogspot.com/2007/07/warrior-strategies.html.

————. and Otto Driedger. "Chechnya Report and Proposal." September 15, 1995. Mennonite Church USA Archives.

Stoltzfus, Lynn. E-mail message to Kathleen Kern, March 30, 2005.

————. E-mail message to Kathleen Kern (subject heading: "Other things non-Chiapas CPTers might not know"), March 22, 2005.

————. E-mail message to Kathleen Kern (subject heading: "Re: FW: [GITW] Chiapas routine"), March 22, 2005.

————. E-mail message to Kathleen Kern (subject heading: "Re: FW: [GITW] Looking for Chiapas material"), March 22, 2005.

Stoltzfus Jost, Ruth. E-mail message (in Spanish)to Kathleen Kern, April 23, 2005.

————. E-mail message to Kathleen Kern, August 28, 2003.

————. E-mail message to Kathleen Kern, September 2, 2003.

————. E-mail message to Kathleen Kern, September 28, 2004.

————. E-mail message to Kathleen Kern, September 29, 2004.

————. E-mail message to Kathleen Kern, September 30, 2004.

————. Telephone interview with Kathleen Kern, October 28, 2004.

————. Telephone interview with Kathleen Kern, September 29, 2004.

Sultzman, Lee. "Micmac History." *First Nations: Issues of Consequence.* http://www.dickshovel.com/mic.html.

————. "Ojibwe History." First Nations Histories Web site. http://www.tolatsga.org/ojib.html.

Tanner, Adrian, "Innu History." 1999. *Newfoundland and Labrador Heritage.* http://www.heritage.nf.ca/aboriginal/innu_history.html.

TARR (Treaty and Aboriginal Rights Research). "'We have kept our part of the treaty': The Anishinaabe understanding of treaty no. 3." Flyer. November 2001. Mennonite Church USA Archives.

Tasnaheca. "History of the Sioux." *Lakhota.com.* http://web.archive.org/web/19971222022439/lakhota.com/default.htm.

"The handicam revolution." *Seeingisbelieving.ca.* http://www.seeingisbelieving.ca/handicam/timeline/ (not retrievable).

"The Loosing of the Hounds." *The Other Israel* 72 (1996) 1–4. Available at http://israelipalestinianpeace.org/issues/72toi.htm#THE.

The Tom Hurndall Foundation Archive. http://web.archive.org/web/20030524044939/http://www.tomhurndall.co.uk.

Thomas, John H., General Ministries of the United Church of Christ. Letter to H. A. Penner in Guaynabo detention center, July 9, 2001. Mennonite Church USA Archives.

Thompson, Cheryl. "D.C. Police Often Close Cases without Arrests." *Washington Post,* December 4, 2000.

"Timeline: Bosnia-Hercegovina." *BBC News,* updated July 22, 2008. http://news.bbc .co.uk/2/hi/europe/country_profiles/1066981.stm.

Tivnan, Edward. *The Lobby: Jewish Political Power and American Foreign Policy.* New York: Simon and Schuster, 1987.

Todaro, Lenora, with Michelle Henjum. "The U.S. Navy's Assault on the Puerto Rican Island of Vieques: One-stop bombing." *The Village Voice,* May 9–15, 2001.

Tolan, Sandy. "Mideast Water Series: Collision in Gaza." *Living on Earth,* March 6, 1998. Transcript available at http://www.loe.org/shows/segments.htm?programID=98-P13-00010&segmentID=6.

———. "Mideast Water Series: The Politics of Mideast Water." *Living on Earth,* March 13, 1998. Transcript available at http://www.loe.org/shows/segments .htm?programID=98-P13-00011&segmentID=5.

"Treaty with the Six Nations, 1784." In *Indian Affairs: Laws and Treaties,* compiled and edited by Charles J. Kappler. Vol. 2. Washington: GPO, 1904. Available at http:// digital.library.okstate.edu/KAPPLER/Vol2/treaties/nat0005.htm.

Turki, Fawaz. *The Disinherited.* New York: Monthly Review Press, 1972.

Unicef. "Iraq surveys show 'humanitarian emergency.'" August 12, 1999. http://www .unicef.org/newsline/99pr29.htm.

Upstate Citizens for Equality. http://www.upstate-citizens.org.

U.S. Census Bureau. "Statistical Abstract of the United States: 2006." N.d. Available at http://www.census.gov/prod/2005pubs/06statab/pop.pdf.

U.S. Congress. House. Committee on Conference. *Making Appropriations for Energy and Water Development for the Fiscal Year Ending September 30, 2000, and for Other Purposes.* 106th Cong., 1st sess., 1999. Committee print 106-336. Available at http:// thomas.loc.gov/cgi-bin/cpquery/T?&report=hr336&dbname=cp106&.

Valtierra, Pedro. Photo of Abejas girl pushing back Mexican soldier. *Zapatista Block.* http:// www.geocities.com/zapatistablock/index12.gif.

Van der Werf, Maarten. "CPT Update (from Europe)." January–February 1990. Mennonite Church USA Archives.

———. Letter to Gene Stoltzfus, January 26, 1990. Mennonite Church USA Archives.

Vieques Libre. "There Are Still Several People in the Live Impact Area in Vieques." Press release sent as e-mail message, May 5, 2000. Mennonite Church USA Archives.

Villerrael, Sandra. "Protesters Prepare in Puerto Rico." Associated Press, April 25, 2000.

Walch, Tad. "Kidnapped BYU grad home safe from Iraq Captors held the peace worker for more than week." *Deseret Morning News,* February 15, 2007.

Walking Thunder, Michael (Hawk). "Hawk's Letter." *Oneida Action News Center.* http:// www.angelfire.com/indie/oneidas/Hawklet.html.

Wallis, Tim. "Chechnya Peace Observers Feasibility Report." Sponsored by War Resisters International, International Fellowship of Reconciliation, International Peace Bureau. October 1995. Mennonite Church USA Archives.

Ward, James, and Lloyd Augustine. "Draft for the Esgenoopotitj First Nation Fishery (EFN) Fishery Act (Fisheries Policy)." May 11, 2000. *Social Disparity.* CIFAS. http:// www.tc.edu/centers/cifas/socialdisparity/background/EFNfa.htm.

WCC (World Council of Churches). "Ecumenical efforts towards peace in the Israeli-Palestinian conflict." Press release, PU-02-02, February 11, 2002. http://www2.wcc-coe.org/pressreleasesen.nsf/index/pu-02-02.html.

————. "Ecumenical solidarity and action promised in Palestinian-Israeli conflict." Press release, PR-02-06, February 11, 2002. http://www2.wcc-coe.org/pressreleasesen.nsf/index/pr-02-06.html.

————. "First group of ecumenical accompaniers begin work in Palestine and Israel." Press release, PU-02-25, August 26, 2002. http://www2.wcc-coe.org/PressReleases_ge.nsf/index/pu-02-25.html.

Weaver, David. "CPT/CPC: What is our purpose in Gaza?" August 14, 1993. Mennonite Church USA Archives.

————. Fax message to CPT Chicago Office, July 6, 1993. Mennonite Church USA Archives.

————. Fax message to CPT Chicago Office, July 11, 1993. Mennonite Church USA Archives.

————. "Gaza Team Applauds Peace Efforts, Reports Deep Suspicions." September 1, 1993. Mennonite Church USA Archives.

Weaver, Paul Neufeld. E-mail message to Kathleen Kern, February 24, 2005.

————. "Restoring the Balance: Peace Teams and Violence Reduction in Chiapas Mexico—Contrasting Approaches to Critical Transformation through International Nonviolent Solidarity with Indigenous Struggle, Christian Peacemaker Teams, SIPAZ and Las Abejas." Ph.D. diss., University of St. Thomas, 2002.

Weiner, Tim. "Haitian Ex-Paramilitary Leader Confirms CIA Relationship." *New York Times*, December 3, 1995.

Wetter-Smith, Brooks de, and Michael Brown. "Photostory: Injured ISM activist Brian Avery returns home." *The Electronic Intifada*, June 16, 2003. http://electronicintifada.net/v2/article1607.shtml.

Whiteface, Charmaine. "Sacred Ceremony Held at the Spiritual Camp on LaFramboise Island." April 23, 1999. *The People's Paths*. http://www.thepeoplespaths.net/News99/0499/990423ceremony.htm.

————. "We have another chance to learn 'mitakuye oyasin.'" September 21, 2001. *Indian Country Today*. http://www.indiancountry.com/content.cfm?id=515.

Whitefield, Mimi. "Vieques clash back on front burner: Puerto Rico's new leader talks tough." *Miami Herald*, December 4, 2000,

Whiteside, Haven. E-mail message to Kathleen Kern, October 6, 2007.

Wilder, David. "CPT—Squalor on the Face of the Earth." E-mail newslist message, May 3, 1998. Hebron-Past, Present and Forever. Available at http://davidwilder.blogspot.com/1998_07_01_archive.html. Mennonite Church USA Archives.

Williams, Rich. E-mail message to Kathleen Kern, September 15, 2007.

————. E-mail message to Kathleen Kern, September 18, 2007.

————. Letter to Puerto Rican Mennonite Convention, July 15, 2001. Mennonite Church USA Archives.

————. Statement delivered to U.S. Federal Judge, June 28, 2001. Mennonite Church USA Archives.

Willson, S. Brian. "Section IV: Militarization and Repression in Mexico." In *The Slippery Slope: U.S. Military Moves into Mexico*. Rev. ed. Santa Cruz, CA: Bill Motto Veterans of Foreign Wars Post 5888, April 1998. Available at http://www.globalexchange.org/countries/americas/mexico/slope/section4.html.

Wilson, James. *The Earth Shall Weep: A History of Native America*. New York: Grove, 2000.

Wilson, Joe. "What I Didn't Find in Africa." *New York Times*, July 6, 2003.

Wilson, Scott. "Colombian Right's 'Cleaning' Campaign: Takeover in Major City Illustrates Political Side of Drug War." *Washington Post,* April 17, 2001.

Womack, John. *Rebellion in Chiapas: An Historical Reader.* New York: New Press, 1999.

"World Refugee Day highlights worsening crisis." *Canada AM,* CTV, June 20, 2007. http://www.ctv.ca/servlet/ArticleNews/story/CTVNews/20070620/refugee_day_070620/20070620?hub=CanadaAM.

Worrell, John. "Iraq: Why Don't They Hate Us?" *Signs of the Times* 12:4 (2002) 10–11.

Yehudai-Rimmer, Moshe. E-mail message to CPT. In *Signs of the Times* 11:1 (2001) 8.

Yoder, Mary. E-mail message to Kathleen Kern, August 17, 2004.

"Ziisbaakdoke-Giizis" (Sugar Making Moon). *The Stoney Point Nishnaabeg Newsletter,* March 16, 1996. Web page printout. Mennonite Church USA Archives.

Zimmer, Lynda. "Area Mennonite travels to Puerto Rico for demonstration." *Champaign/Urbana News-Gazette,* April 17, 2002.

Zuercher, Melanie. "Mennonite begins work release sentence for protest action in Puerto Rico." Mennonite Church USA press release, July 27, 2001. Mennonite Church USA Archives.

About the Author

Kathleen Kern has worked with Christian Peacemaker Teams since 1993, serving on assignments in Haiti; Washington, DC; Palestine; Chiapas, Mexico; South Dakota; Colombia; and the Democratic Republic of Congo.

Kern has published two books: *When It Hurts to Live: Devotions for Difficult Times* (Faith and Life Press, 1994) and *We Are the Pharisees* (Herald Press, 1995.) She has had essays appear in *Tikkun* magazine and *The Baltimore Sun*. Her article, "Against the System: Civil Disobedience and the Biblical Record" (*The Mennonite*, April 20, 1999) won the "Theological Reflection" category of the 1999 Associated Church Press awards. In 2002, Kern's satirical novel, *Where Such Unmaking Reigns* (based on her experiences working in Hebron) was selected as a finalist in Barbara Kingsolver's Bellwether Prize. Her chapter on the war in the Democratic Republic of Congo, "The Human Cost of Cheap Cellphones," appeared in *A Game As Old As Empire: The Secret World of Economic Hit Men and the Web of Global Corruption* (Berrett-Koehler Publishers, 2007).

Kern currently lives in the Rochester, NY, area with her husband, Michael, and his children Beth Melissa and David Mark.

About CPT

Christian Peacemaker Teams (CPT) arose from a call in 1984 for Christians to devote the same discipline and self-sacrifice to nonviolent peacemaking that armies devote to war. Enlisting the whole church in an organized, nonviolent alternative to war, today CPT places violence-reduction teams in crisis situations and militarized areas around the world at the invitation of local peace and human rights workers. CPT embraces the vision of unarmed intervention waged by committed peacemakers ready to risk injury and death in bold attempts to transform lethal conflict through the nonviolent power of God's truth and love.

Initiated by Mennonites, Brethren, and Quakers with broad ecumenical participation, CPT's ministry of biblically-based and spiritually-centered peacemaking emphasizes creative public witness, nonviolent direct action, and protection of human rights.

A strategy developed thoughtfully over the years has taught us that:

- trained, skilled, international teams can work effectively to support local efforts toward nonviolent peacemaking;

- "getting in the way" of injustice through direct nonviolent intervention, public witness and reporting to the larger world community can make a difference;

- peace team work engages congregations, meetings and support groups at home to play a key advocacy role with policy makers.

CPT understands violence to be rooted in systemic structures of oppression. CPT is committed to undoing oppressions as part of our violence reduction work, starting within our own organization.

UNITED STATES
Box 6508
Chicago, IL 60680-6508
Tel. 773-277-0253
Fax. 773-277-0291
E-mail: peacemakers@cpt.org

CANADA
25 Cecil St, Unit 307
Toronto ON M5T 1N1
Tel. 416-423-5525
Fax. 416-423-7140
E-mail: canada@cpt.org

CPSIA information can be obtained at www.ICGtesting.com
Printed in the USA
BVOW04s0456230714

360164BV00002B/26/P

9 781556 351341